THINKING ABOUT PUNISHMENT

PIONEERS IN CONTEMPORARY CRIMINOLOGY

Series Editor: David Nelken

The titles in this series bring together the best published and unpublished work by the leading authorities in contemporary criminological theory. By drawing together articles from a wide range of journals, conference proceedings and books, each title makes readily available the authors' most important writings on specific themes. Each volume in this series includes a lengthy introduction, written by the editor and a significant piece of scholarship in its own right, which outlines the context of the work and comments on its significance and potential. The collected essays complement each other to give a retrospective view of the authors' achievements and a picture of the development of criminology as a whole.

Titles in the series

Working Out of Crime
David Downes

Criminological Forays and Skirmishes
David Greenberg

Crime, Victimisation and Criminological Theory
Paul Rock

Essays on Transnational Crime and Policing
James Sheptycki

Thinking about Punishment
Michael Tonry

Thinking about Punishment

Penal Policy Across Space, Time and Discipline

MICHAEL TONRY
University of Minnesota, USA

PIONEERS IN CONTEMPORARY CRIMINOLOGY SERIES

ASHGATE

Published by
Ashgate Publishing Limited
Wey Court East
Union Road
Farnham
Surrey GU9 7PT
England

Ashgate Publishing Company
Suite 420
101 Cherry Street
Burlington, VT 05401-4405
USA

Ashgate website: http://www.ashgate.com

ISBN 978-0-7546-2905-4

British Library Cataloguing in Publication Data
Tonry, Michael H.
Thinking about punishment : penal policy across space, time and discipline. – (Pioneers in contemporary criminology)
1. Criminal justice, Administration of. 2. Punishment.
3. Punishment–Cross-cultural studies.
I. Title II. Series
364.6–dc22

US Library of Congress Control Number: 2009930406

Printed and bound in Great Britain by
TJ International Ltd, Padstow, Cornwall

Contents

Part III American Penal Policy

Part IV Sentencing Policy

Part V Punishment Theory

Acknowledgements

The chapters in this volume are taken from the sources listed below. The editor and publishers wish to thank the authors, original publishers or other copyright holders for permission to use their material as follows:

Chapter 1: 'Malign Neglect', in Michael Tonry, *Malign Neglect—Race, Crime, and Punishment in America*, New York: Oxford University Press, 1995, pp. 3–47.

Chapter 2: 'Ethnicity, Crime, and Immigration', in Michael Tonry (ed.), *Ethnicity, Crime, and Immigration Comparative and Cross-National Perspectives*, *Crime and Justice: A Review of Research*, 21, Chicago: University of Chicago Press, 1997, pp. 1–30.

Chapter 3: 'The Malign Effects of Drugs and Crime Control Policies on Black Americans', in Michael Tonry and Matthew Melewski, *Crime and Justice: A Review of Research*, 37, Chicago: University of Chicago Press, 2008, pp. 1–44. Copyright © 2008 The University of Chicago. All rights reserved.

Chapter 4: 'Symbol, Substance, and Severity in Western Penal Policies', *Punishment and Society*, 3, 2001, pp. 517–36. Copyright © SAGE Publications.

Chapter 5: 'Punishment Policies and Patterns in Western Countries', in Michael Tonry and Richard S. Frase (eds), *Sentencing and Sanctions in Western Countries*, New York: Oxford University Press, 2001, pp. 3–28.

Chapter 6: 'Determinants of Penal Policies', in Michael Tonry (ed.), *Crime, Punishment, and Politics in Comparative Perspective, Crime and Justice: A Review of Research*, vol. 36, Chicago: University of Chicago Press, 2007, pp. 1–48. Copyright © 2007 The University of Chicago. All rights reserved.

Chapter 7: 'Sense and Sensibility in American Penal Culture', in Michael Tonry, *Thinking about Crime: Sense and Sensibility in American Penal Culture*, New York: Oxford University Press, 2004, pp. 3–20.

Chapter 8: 'Cycles and Sensibilities', in Michael Tonry, *Thinking about Crime: Sense and Sensibility in American Penal Culture*, New York: Oxford University Press, 2004, pp. 63–84.

Chapter 9: 'Emerging Explanations of American Punishment Policies', *Punishment and Society*, 11, 2009, pp. 374–99.

Chapter 10: 'Sentencing Reform in America', Michael Tonry and Norval Morris in P.R. Glazebrook (ed.), *Reshaping the Criminal Law: Essays in Honor of Glanville Williams,* London: Stevens and Sons, 1978, pp. 434–48.

Chapter 11: 'Mandatory Penalties', in Michael Tonry (ed.), *Crime and Justice: A Review of Research*, vol. 16, Chicago: University of Chicago Press, 1992, pp. 243–73.

Chapter 12: 'Sentencing Matters', in Michael Tonry, *Sentencing Matters*, New York: Oxford University Press, 1996, pp. 3–24.

Chapter 13: 'Purposes and Functions of Sentencing', in Michael Tonry (ed.), *Crime and Justice: A Review of Research*, vol. 34, Chicago: University of Chicago Press, 2006, pp. 1–53.

Chapter 14: 'Interchangeability of Punishments in Principle', in Michael Tonry and Norval Morris, *Between Prison and Probation: Intermediate Punishments in a Rational Sentencing System*, New York: Oxford University Press, 1990, pp. 82–108.

Chapter 15: 'Proportionality, Parsimony, and Interchangeability of Punishments', in Antony Duff, Sandra Marshall, Rebecca Emerson Dobash and Russell P. Dobash (eds), *Penal Theory and Penal Practice*, Manchester: Manchester University Press, 1994, pp. 60–83.

Chapter 16: 'Obsolescence and Immanence in Penal Theory and Policy', *Columbia Law Review*, 105, 2005, pp. 1233–75.

Every effort has been made to trace all the copyright holders, but if any have been inadvertently overlooked the publishers will be pleased to make the necessary arrangement at the first opportunity.

Michael Tonry

Introduction

A book such as this one is conceivably useful to the academic whose writings are memorialized, but it is not obvious to whom else. I delayed for a considerable time replying to series editor David Nelken's invitation to collect some of the things I have written into what I self-consciously referred to as a 'Greatest Hits' book. That is an ironic and self-mocking description, signalling my suspicion that little of what academics write attracts much attention or lingers long in readers' memories, and that the rest might best be allowed to slumber in the obscurity it deserves.

No matter. The die is cast. In this brief essay – meant, I suppose, to frame the writings reprinted and thereby conceivably to spike the interest of anyone so intellectually peripatetic as to be reading these words – I do two things. I explain how it happened that I've written what I have, and I speculate on the possibility that I learned some things along the way.

How It Happened

My involvement with criminology and the criminal law is serendipitous. I had no training in the first and took only a routine first-year law school course in the latter. Nearly 40 years ago I stumbled into a job at the University of Chicago Law School's Center for Studies in Criminal Justice, headed by the late Norval Morris. I had no particular interest, probably no interest at all, in the criminal justice system. What I had was a deep abhorrence for commercial law practice, which I was desperate to leave, and a willingness to do most anything else. In the law school's basement library stacks, I happened upon the wife of a casual friend. On hearing that I wanted to do something, almost anything, other than practice law, she told me that a friend of hers was moving to New York and his law school job, she guessed, might not yet have been filled. I went upstairs, knocked on doors, got myself interviewed, and miraculously got hired as a research associate in a criminal justice programme.

I worked with Morris off and on until his death in 2004. He believed that the prison is a microcosm of society and that how those inside are treated tells much about a society's values.[1] Winston Churchill, who observed that the ways a society deals with crime and the criminal are symbols which 'mark and measure the stored-up strength of a nation, and are

[1] Morris was the founding director of the criminology programme at the University of Melbourne, the first in an English-speaking country. His peripatetic career took him to the law school deanship at the University of Adelaide, the founding directorship of the first United Nations criminal justice institute (the United Nations Asia and Far East Institute for the Prevention of Crime and the Treatment of Offenders, in Tokyo) and the deanship of the University of Chicago Law School. Along the way he became one of the world's pre-eminent scholars of prisons and punishment (see, for example, Morris, 1974; Morris and Tonry, 1990).

the sign and proof of the living virtue within it', seems to have believed much the same thing (quoted in Gilbert, 1992).

Turned round that is a bleak view. It implies that little can be done to make prisons better, less-destructive places. They are as they are precisely because they reflect and result from predominant social values. On this account, Scandinavian, German and Swiss prisons are relatively decent places because they reflect strong social welfare and human rights values, and American and English prisons are pretty awful places because they reflect punitive Anglo-Saxon political values. Those values must change before the prison will, and the prison itself is an unlikely fulcrum on which to leverage that change. Americans early in the twenty-first century have a remarkable capacity for tolerating the suffering of others, whether they be poor or handicapped or drug-dependent or maladjusted, and that tolerance must change before the prison will, much.

I do not know whether Morris or Churchill saw their views as counsels of despair. Perhaps they did. Both chose in their actions, and Morris in his writing, however, to act as if they did not and as if meaningful changes can be effected in the humanity and decency with which crime and criminals are handled. Churchill's much-quoted words were uttered during House of Commons debates in 1910 when as Home Secretary he proposed liberalizing changes in British punishment policies. Reform of the prison, and the justice system institutions linked with it, was the focus of Morris's work for more than a half century (see, for example, Morris, 1974).

Norval Morris was interested in sentencing, and sanctions, and punishment theory. The first deals with who is sent to prison and for how long, the second with how prisons and other punishments are operated and used, the third with normative frameworks relative to thinking about the first two. Not surprisingly, especially given my lack of prior contact with the criminal justice system, I also became interested in sentencing, and sanctions, and punishment theory. Decades passed.

Looking back, I can see that the interests I inherited from Morris provided a framework for much that I have done. Inevitably, especially in the past 20 years, my interests diverged from his. The core subject, punishment of offenders, remains the same, but in my case seen through the prisms of race and ethnicity, crime control policy and circumstances in countries other than the United States.

Those prisms are products of time and place. I came of age in the United States in the 1960s, when the Civil Rights Movement was in its heyday, and began to write on criminal justice subjects about the time American politics turned to the right and the 'wars' on crime and drugs began. Although the sentencing reform movement of the 1970s was concerned to reduce racial disparities in sentencing and racial disproportion in imprisonment (see, for example, American Friends Service Committee, 1971), the wars on crime and drugs were fought mostly against poor inner-city blacks and resulted in many more being sent to prison (see, for example, Tonry, 1995 and Chapter 1, this volume).

That realization led to my continuing preoccupation with documenting and explaining the ways American crime control and drug policies disproportionately affect poor blacks. Part of the explanation, expressed non-tendentiously, is that the wars on drugs and crime targeted behaviours in which blacks are more likely than whites to be involved (for example trafficking in crack rather than in cocaine, heroin or marijuana; street violence rather than domestic violence or white-collar crime). Another part is that American policy-makers enacted laws of unprecedented severity relative to other developed countries in our time or to the United States in earlier times. Since the early 1980s, black imprisonment rates have been seven to eight times those of whites. They result from historically severe punishments mandated for offences for which blacks are disproportionately likely to be arrested, prosecuted, convicted and imprisoned.

That in turn led to a second continuing preoccupation – to understand why American drug and crime control policies (usually outside the US referred to as penal policies) have taken the forms they have, and in particular why they have been so severe. The only way to answer those questions is to see whether other countries have adopted the same kinds of policies and produced the same kinds of racial and ethnic disparities the United States has experienced, and why or why not.

Racial Disparities

The irony of racial disparities in the United States is that they are morally unjustifiable, and yet little different from disparities affecting other minority groups in many other countries. Go figure. Here is that story.

Although reduction in racial disparities was a primary motivator of the sentencing reform movement in the United States (American Friends Service Committee, 1971), relatively little was written about the sources of disparity until the mid-1980s. A primary reason for this was a concern that academic attention to the causes of disparity would lead to a political focus on disproportionate involvement by blacks in violent crime. This was widely seen as undesirable because it would feed stereotypes of black criminality (which then presidential candidate George H. Bush's Willie Horton adverts famously exploited in 1988) and because it in effect 'blamed the victims' for the miserable life chances a history of racism had given many young black people, some of whom became offenders.

The subject was deemed by most academics too hot to touch (see, for example, Wilson, 1987, p. vii) until Alfred Blumstein published a controversial article on racial disparities in imprisonment. In an analysis that was seminal in its time and looks crude in retrospect, he compared percentages of blacks among prisoners sentenced for particular crimes with percentages of blacks among people arrested for those crimes. He concluded that 80 per cent of black/white racial disparities in imprisonment could be explained by reference to black/white differences in involvement in crime (Blumstein, 1982). His broad conclusion, hedged with methodological and measurement qualifications, was that racial differences in behaviour, and not racially biased actions of officials, were the primary drivers of disparities in imprisonment.

Lots of objections, besides accusations of blaming victims and perpetuating unhealthy stereotypes, could have been made to Blumstein's analysis, and were. He used arrest data as an indicator of crime involvement; racial patterns of arrest may be the result of biased policing practices. He used national data on imprisonment; patterns of racial bias might vary widely between states and use of national data might obscure extreme bias in some places. He compared arrest rates with prison population data; prison admission data might be better.

At day's end, Blumstein's broad conclusion held. Many other scholars, often using data and methods that addressed potential weaknesses in Blumstein's analysis, reached substantially the same conclusion. A new consensus emerged: it is better to face up to the problem of disproportionate black involvement in serious crime so that its causes can be addressed, its sources in policy and practice revealed, and its consequences ameliorated, than to ignore the subject.

In due course I wrote a book, *Malign Neglect: Race, Crime, and Punishment in America* (1995), which pulled together what was then known about racial disparities and their causes, and discussed ways the criminal justice system might do less harm to black Americans. The book contained some new analyses, for example comparing racial patterns in victims' identifications of their assailants for particular offences over time with racial patterns in arrests for the same offences (the patterns were the same and consistent over time) and comparing black/white drug use patterns with black/white drug arrest patterns (for most drugs, fewer blacks than whites used or had used them, but over 30 years black arrest rates varied between three and six times those of whites).

Malign Neglect reached three main conclusions. Blumstein was right: racial patterns of crime involvement are primary drivers of prison disparities. Newly enacted drug and crime control policies calling for penalties that were exceedingly severe by historical standards, however, had substantially worsened racial disparities in prison because they targeted offences for which blacks are disproportionately convicted. The racial effects of new drug and punishment policies were foreseeable (and by some people were foreseen), which justified an indictment that policy-makers had knowingly increased racial disparities, an action no different morally from having adopted policies with that purpose. A recent essay with Matthew Melewski (Chapter 3, this volume) tells the same story using data through 2007 and 2008 and reaches the same conclusions. Policies adopted in the 1980s and 1990s – for example a federal '100-to-1' policy that punishes crack offences, for which mostly blacks are convicted, as severely as powder cocaine offences (for which whites are commonly convicted) 100 times larger – continue to afflict blacks much more acutely than they do whites. If the 1995 indictment was valid, it remained valid in 2008.

Makers of American drug and crime control policies acted immorally in adopting policies that they knew or should have known would disproportionately affect black Americans (at least for disadvantaged blacks, the 'blaming the victim' concern remains valid). Under the *mens rea* (guilty mind) doctrines of the criminal law, doing something with the purpose of causing harm (for example destroying an airplane to kill a passenger) is often as bad as doing something with knowledge that it will cause harm (for example destroying an airplane to collect insurance on its cargo, knowing the people on board will almost certainly be killed).

The only possible justification for knowingly causing such harm to black Americans is that even greater harm could thereby have been avoided. The evidence was clear in the 1980s, however, as it is now, that wars on drugs do not reduce drug use or sales, or increase drug prices by making them scarcer, as James Q. Wilson (1990), the leading conservative crime control policy expert of the last 30 years, has acknowledged (along with most leading drug policy scholars). And no credible case could be made on the basis of systematic research findings in the 1980s that morally justifiable incremental changes in penalties reduce crime rates (Blumstein, Cohen and Nagin, 1978). Nor could that case credibly be made early in the twenty-first century (Doob and Webster, 2003; Tonry, 2008). So there was no credible case that could be made to justify policies that did so much damage to black Americans.

In the aftermath of *Malign Neglect*, I became curious about racial disparities in other English-speaking countries. In the early 1990s I compared racial disparities in England and Wales (Afro-Caribbeans compared with whites), Canada (native Canadians, non-native Canadians) and Australia (aborigines, non-aborigines). I learned that disparities were least pronounced in the United States (6.44:1 in the US, 7:1 in England, 12:1 in Australia, 16:1 in Canada) (Tonry, 1994). Research on the causes of disparities in all four countries reached Blumstein's conclusion: behavioural differences, not biased officials, were primarily responsible for racial and ethnic disparities (see Chapter 2, this volume).

That finding was a mite dismaying. Those other countries had not experienced recent histories of slavery. Nor had they experienced anything like the Republicans' 'southern strategy', beginning in the mid-1960s, which manipulated racial anxieties and stereotypes in order to appeal to white and working-class voters (Edsall and Edsall, 1991; Phillips, 1991). Nor, at least through the early 1990s, had law and order become a primary theme in partisan politics or had any of them adopted unprecedentedly severe crime control policies. Racial disparities in imprisonment were at least as extreme in each of those countries as in the United States, and only in the United States could the smoking gun of racialized politics and policies be found to explain them. Something else was going on. One possibility was that something in the Anglo-Saxon political culture the United States, Canada and Australia shared with their colonial mother country produced patterns of race relations that kept whites on top and non-whites in prison.

I created a project to test that hypothesis. I asked well-informed people in Australia, Canada, France, Germany, the Netherlands, Sweden and Switzerland to do what I had done for the United States in *Malign Neglect* – document patterns of differential treatment of members of minority groups, and review the literatures that tried to explain those patterns. The result was a book called *Ethnicity, Crime, and Immigration* (Tonry, 1997). Same result. In every country, members of some disadvantaged ethnic group or nationality were much more likely than others to be arrested, prosecuted, convicted and imprisoned. The research literatures mostly concluded that group differences in crime involvement were the primary explanations for the disparities. Strikingly, however, the minority groups affected were not all blacks and native populations as in the English-speaking countries. In France and the Netherlands, they were North Africans from the Maghreb countries of Algeria, Morocco and Tunisia. In Germany, they were Turks and people from western Asia. In Sweden, they were Finns and people from a wide range of countries. In Switzerland, they came from many countries. In England, until recently, they were Irish, though in recent decades they have been Afro-Caribbean.

So the hypothesis that racial disparities result from historical patterns of race relations uniquely found in the United States, or in the English-speaking countries, was wrong, or at best only part of the story. Something is going on in developed countries that results in some disadvantaged groups living lives that make them disproportionately likely to be involved in crime and disproportionately likely to be imprisoned. Recent national experiences of slavery cannot be the answer, nor can racialized contemporary politics in most countries, although the latter explanation partly explains the increase in imprisonment of blacks in the United States since 1980.

Second and third generation members of economic migrant groups often face assimilation problems that produce high crime rates. That analysis might explain contemporary European disparities and they may as a result be transitory. If so, they will disappear in time as did similar disparities affecting European economic migrants to the United States in the eighteenth, nineteenth and early twentieth centuries. My guess, though, is that that analysis is wrong.

Group disparities in the English-speaking countries have endured for many generations. I suspect that something in human social organization produces in every society disadvantaged subgroups who will play the criminal justice roles that Moroccans now do in the Netherlands, Turks do in Germany, Finns do in Sweden, and blacks do in America. Durkheimian ideas about the law provide reasons why crime will exist everywhere and at all times, and why someone will commit it, but not why those people will disproportionately come from particular ethnic or national-origin groups.

Recognition that some disadvantaged minority group in every country is likely to be heavily over-represented among arrestees, defendants and prisoners does not, however, get the United States off the moral hook. American policy-makers knowingly chose policies that foreseeably worsened black–white disparities, something that happened nowhere else. In addition, there is a radical difference between countries that confine 50-to-100 per 100,000 of their residents and the only one that confines nearly 800 per 100,000. High American imprisonment rates mean that racial disparities bite much more deeply into the American black population than happens to any other minority group in any other country. In a country in which minority imprisonment rates are seven times those of majority residents, locking up 40 majority citizens per 100,000 means locking up 280 minority citizens. A country that locks up 400 majority citizens per 100,000 will lock up 2,800 minority citizens. Imprisonment is not evenly distributed within a population. That's why nearly a third of black male American babies born in 2001 are expected to spend parts of their lives in state or federal prisons, compared with 5.9 per cent of white baby boys (Bonczar, 2003), and why nearly a third of young black men in their twenties are in prison or jail or on probation or parole (Sabol, Minton and Harrison, 2007).

Relatively speaking, imprisonment disparities affecting blacks in America are comparable to disparities affecting other groups in other places. In absolute terms, the experiences of black Americans are incomparably worse, and the damage done to black prisoners' families and children (Murray and Farrington, 2008) and communities (Clear, 2007) is enormously greater. The extraordinary severity of American crime control and punishment policies is the explanation, and historic patterns of race relations may explain the severity. I take that up in the next section.

Determinants of Penal Policy

Race is at the beginning and the end of the search for what causes American punishment policies to be so severe. That they are extraordinarily severe cannot be denied. American imprisonment rates are five to ten times higher than those in other developed countries. Among Western countries, only the United States executes convicted offenders, commits large numbers of people (45,000 at last estimate) to prison under sentences of life without the possibility of parole (commonly called LWOPs), routinely sentences people to sentences measured in decades and routinely punishes children as if they were adults.

So why are American punishments so harsh? Why has the imprisonment rate risen by a factor of five since 1973? Lots of answers have been offered. Most of them are wrong. Rising crime rates are not the answer. Nor is a fearful or vindictive public. Every developed country experienced rising crime rates from the 1970s through the 1990s, and shifts towards more punitive public attitudes, but in most neither punishment policies nor punishment practices became markedly more severe (see Chapter 6, this volume). Only in the United States were 'wars' on drugs and crime launched, executions allowed to continue and three-strikes, LWOP and Megan's laws enacted. In most countries imprisonment rates have increased somewhat in the past 30 years, but comparatively little (except in the Netherlands where they increased fivefold from 18 per 100,000 in 1973 to 100 in 2004) (Tonry and Bijleveld, 2007).

If not crime rates or fear of crime or a vindictive public, then what is the answer? The most elegant explanation was offered by sociologist David Garland (2001), who identified a number of conditions of 'late modernity' said to explain what happened – a greater prevalence of victimization, governments that felt obliged to adopt punitive 'expressive' policies, a public increasingly worried about all manner of risks, more diverse populations. He focused mostly on the United States and England, but the analysis if right should apply to every developed country. All experienced the same conditions. Only the US, the Netherlands and since 1993 England and Wales, and New Zealand (Pratt, 2006) became conspicuously more punitive. Garland's answer, if correct, is correct in two or possibly three countries.

At about the same time as Garland's magisterial book appeared, I wrote a series of short articles about explanations of penal policy changes in the US and elsewhere. Looking at developments in a number of countries, it became clear that the explanations for toughening policy changes, or their absence, were invariably local (see, for example, Chapter 4, this volume). In a 2004 book, *Thinking about Crime* (Tonry, 2004b), I pulled together the literature that then existed on penal policy changes in the United States and other Western countries (I also wrote a parallel book, *Punishment and Politics* (2004a), on English crime control policies). That book examined all the then prevalent explanations for what some called 'penal populism' or 'populist punitiveness' and the harsh attitudes and policies said to accompany them. I concluded that none of the ideas in use – conditions of late modernity, rising crime rates, harsher public attitudes, cynical politicians, the 'risk society' – offered convincing generalizable explanations. The best explanation for US developments is a combination of the history of American race relations, constitutional arrangements that make policy decisions highly vulnerable to short-term public emotion, long-term cycles of intolerance of crime and criminals (at their peaks in the early 1990s), and a series of moral panics about violent and sexual offences (see Chapters 7 and 8, this volume).

To look further for explanations of American policy trends, by contrasting them with policy trends elsewhere, I asked well-informed people in Belgium, Canada, England and Wales, France, Japan, the Netherlands and Scandinavia to do what I had tried to do for the United States in *Thinking about Crime* – document and explain policy changes over the preceding 30 years. *Crime, Punishment, and Politics in Comparative Perspective* (Tonry, 2007) is the result. Its essays make it clear that the causes of penal policy patterns and changes are local, not global. Finnish policies became steadily less punitive over a 30-year period, despite rising crime rates indistinguishable from those in other Western (and Scandinavian) countries. In most Western European countries – Germany, Belgium, Switzerland, France, the other Scandinavian countries – imprisonment rates changed comparatively little over 30 years and policies did not become conspicuously harsher. In a handful of countries – Portugal, Spain, Italy, New Zealand – imprisonment rates grew, though not uninterruptedly, after the mid-1990s, and those in Portugal and Italy later plummeted. New Zealand's began to fall after 2006. Dutch imprisonment rates grew continuously after 1973 and English rates doubled after 1993. The explanations for the patterns were distinctively local and included the nature of the media, political consensuses about preferred policies, deference to experts in policy matters and the political insulation of justice system officials, especially prosecutors and judges.

Since then, there has been a proliferation of books on the determinants of penal policy. A few still focus on global or general explanations (for example the influence of neoliberal political views (Cavadino and Dignan, 2005; Lacey, 2008) or of world-encompassing 'penal populism' (Pratt, 2007)). Most look for explanations in distinctive national cultures (Gottschalk, 2006; Simon, 2007; Green, 2008; Cusac, 2009) or combinations of governmental structure and local long-term political culture (Miller, 2008; Barker, 2009).

My own view is that America's miserable history of race relations offers the key to explaining American crime control policies since 1970 (Tonry and Melewski, Chapter 3, this volume; and Chapter 9, this volume). The strong version of the argument is that American whites have managed for 300 years to maintain a pattern of racial hierarchy with whites on top, and that recent crime control policies and mass incarceration are merely the latest manifestation of that pattern following slavery, nineteenth-century laws and social conventions that sustained overt racial discrimination until the 1960s, and the urban ghetto of the mid and late twentieth century (see, for example, Wacquant, 2002a, 2002b; Loury, 2007; Massey, 2007). The weak version is that rising crime rates, rising public anxieties and the Republican 'southern strategy' created pressures for harsh policies that were in effect 'free goods' to whites because their implementation heavily disproportionately affected blacks. Either way, race mattered.

Sentencing Policy

If I am well known in any academic field, it is in relation to American and comparative sentencing policies. So it may be a surprise to the few people who know my work (and the fewer of them who read this introduction) that this section on sentencing policy is listed last and is shortest of the three subjects I've chosen to emphasize.

My first substantial efforts to understand something complex concerned sentencing. Few people wrote systematically about sentencing policy before the 1990s. I started in the mid-1970s, when Norval Morris and I wrote one of the earliest overviews of the American sentencing reform movement (Morris and Tonry, Chapter 10, this volume). It was not astonishing at a time when no other academic specialized in sentencing that I was consulted by most of the sentencing commissions that started work in the late 1970s and early 1980s. I worked for the first five – in Minnesota, Washington, Oregon, Pennsylvania and the federal system – and others, and for a while was the only American academic who closely followed policy developments, impact evaluations and sentencing research generally. As a result I wrote most of the early surveys of what was happening and with what results (for example Cohen and Tonry, 1983; Tonry, 1986; Tonry, 1993; Tonry, 1996, chaps 2 and 3). In a nutshell, during those years we learned that voluntary sentencing guidelines and statutory determinate sentencing had few discernible effects, that presumptive sentencing guidelines created by sentencing commissions sometimes reduced sentencing disparities generally and in relation to race and gender, and that mandatory minimum sentences seldom achieved their ostensible objectives.[2]

I wrote on most subjects relating to sentencing including community punishments (Morris and Tonry, 1990; Tonry and Lynch, 1995; Tonry, 1998), mandatory penalties (Chapter 11, this volume) and normative issues (Chapter 15, this volume). Most of this got pulled together and updated once in *Sentencing Matters* (1996) and a second time ten years later (Chapter 13, this volume). Along the way I wrote about English sentencing policy (for example Tonry, 2004a) and a series of articles on comparative sentencing subjects (Chapters 4, 5, 6 and 9, this volume). Following the patterns of my work on race and ethnicity, and determinants of penal policy, I asked well-informed people in a number of countries to do what I had tried to do for the United States in *Sentencing Matters* in respect to adult and juvenile justice systems. *Sentencing and Sanctions in Western Countries* (Tonry and Frase, 2001) and *Youth Crime and Youth Justice: Comparative and Cross-national Perspectives* (Tonry and Doob, 2004) are the result. In retrospect, the distinctively different stories they told about many countries paved the way for subsequent work on the determinants of penal policy.

Sentencing policy encompasses both practical and normative issues (Morris and Tonry, 1990; Chapters 10 and 14, this volume; Chapters 12, 15 and 16, this volume). My writing on normative issues builds on Norval Morris's *The Future of Imprisonment* (1974), the classic work on 'limiting retributivism' as a theory of punishment and a framework for sentencing. There are two core elements. First is the Benthamite (utilitarian) moral claim that pain is inherently a bad thing and accordingly that no more pain should ever be imposed on an offender than is minimally required to achieve valid social purposes. Second is the observation that people agree much more readily that some punishments are unjustly severe (and sometimes unjustly light) than on the precise amount of punishment deserved in an individual case. From these two premises comes a framework for sentencing: for every offence there is an upper limit of deserved punishment that should never be exceeded, and occasionally a lower limit; within those limits, the least severe 'not undeserved' feasible punishment should be imposed; a strong presumption runs in favour of the least severe punishment within the allowable range, and a judge must have strong, empirically grounded reasons to impose a more severe

[2] 'Voluntary' guidelines have no legal authority but are meant to provide a general starting point for judicial consideration. 'Presumptive' guidelines have legal authority; judges are expected to sentence in accordance with them unless they give reasons for imposing some other sentence. The adequacy of those reasons can be appealed to a higher court. 'Statutory determinate sentencing' systems abolished parole release and set out nominally applicable penalties in the criminal code. 'Mandatory minimum sentence laws' require judges to impose prison sentences of at least a specified minimum length on everyone convicted of a particular offence (for example ten years for trafficking in 10 grams of crack cocaine). Details of the evaluations can be found in Tonry (1996), chaps 2 and 3.

sentence. Morris and I worked out the implications of that framework for the American sentencing reform movement in a 1978 article. We developed the analysis in considerable detail in a 1990 book (Morris and Tonry, 1990). I developed its implications for punishments other than imprisonment in a 1994 article and ten years later (Chapter 16, this volume) began the work of adapting it to a new century.

What, if Anything, I've Learned

Alas, I cannot claim to have learned anything very profound. Four themes stand out. The first is the importance of mentors. Most of my early work was influenced by Norval Morris and the example he set. On various important occasions he opened doors, or prevented doors from closing. That was my good luck and so far as I can tell has little to do with desert or talent or anything other than friendship and affectionate concern. Morris often said that his greatest satisfactions came from helping people he cared about make their way. I understand what he meant and feel the same way.

The second is that the ankle bone is connected to the shin bone and the shin bone is connected to … . I would not have guessed in the 1970s that my interest in sentencing reform as a means to reduce racial injustice would eventually lead me to ponder the plights of Moroccans in the Netherlands and Turks in Germany, or to understand that the history of race relations is at least a major part of the explanation of draconic American punishment policies. However, one step followed another and those are places I arrived at, seemingly inexorably.

The third is that the world is a complicated place. To attempt to understand and explain it we need to know it. That requires one or both of extensive involvement in empirical work and extensive experience working in and with the institutions and processes of the criminal justice system. Much of what I have learned was unexpected and sometimes defied conventional wisdom. As a result, and as I've gotten older, I've become increasingly disenchanted with data-free armchair theorizing about the operation of the criminal justice system.[3] In its setting, armchair theorizing does little harm, even though it is often academic in the bad sense – arcana for the sake of the arcane. Outside its setting, however, it is irrelevant rather than dangerous. So long as armchair theory is mostly consumed by the small set of people who produce it, like a balanced aquarium it produces nothing outside itself, but does no harm. Unhappily, however, because armchair theorizing often is fashionable, though the fashions typically have short half-lives, it sometimes has unhappy influence on young minds. People who might try to understand the world and attempt to change it get diverted into dead ends from which sometimes they do not emerge. That is a pity because many people who choose to study or change the criminal justice system do so from a sense of idealism. Life in a dead end must often be unsatisfying. Great social theorists from Marx, Durkheim and Weber through Foucault attempted to understand the world, and limited though their sources of information may have been, built their theories on what they thought they knew. David Garland in our time, and in fields cognate to mine, has done the same thing, usefully and provocatively. There are few David Garlands.

---

[3] Normative analyses, of course, are a different matter. Armchair theorizing is what philosophers do.

The fourth – actually, I've known this all along but I repeat it because it is important – is that knowledge does sometimes influence policy and practice. This happens much less than any rational person should want, and sometimes does not happen at all, but it does happen. Over the last 30 years, and much more in the United States than elsewhere, knowledge and policy concerning the criminal justice system have generally marched in different directions. If policy-making were rational, we would have no Drug Abuse Resistance Education (DARE), Neighborhood Watch programmes or mandatory minimum sentencing laws; for decades credible research has consistently documented their ineffectiveness. Similarly, there would have been no American war on drugs, and drug policies would have focused on drug use rather than on drug distribution. And on and on.

For research evidence to influence policy, windows through which the news can pass must be open (Tonry and Green, 2003). They remain closed in the United States in relation to gun control policy, drug control policy, sex offender policy and policies towards violent offenders. However, they have been open for at least a decade to evidence about effective early life interventions aimed at enhancing children's life chances and lessening their likelihood of falling prey to crime, drug abuse and too-early parenthood. They have recently opened to decades of previously unheeded evidence on the ineffectiveness of juvenile boot camps – boot camps are being closed and radically reorganized throughout the United States – and appear to be opening to evidence on overuse of capital punishment and its irrelevance to the deterrence of homicide.

This excursus began with Norval Morris and Winston Churchill and the question of how rigidly prevailing values constrain efforts to bring humanity and decency into the criminal justice system. The constraints, I'd say, are real and formidable. The bounds of possible improvement are probably pretty narrow. Problems that can be cast as failures to respect prevailing values – for example sexual abuse in institutions for young offenders, racial profiling – are the most amenable to amelioration. Other problems and policies – capital punishment, drug prohibition, treating violent children as adults, prison sentences so long they deny prisoners the possibility of hope for the future – probably will not much improve, no matter how compelling the evidence about their ineffectiveness or cruelty, until prevailing values change.

I don't know for myself any better than I do for Morris and Churchill whether the bleak picture I just painted is true. It seems to be true. I've lived most of a lifetime in a country in which commitments towards human rights are weak and in which respect for them, even setting aside the Bush administration and the 'war against terror', has long been declining. Steadily more repressive laws were enacted from the mid-1970s through the mid-1990s, and few have been repealed or substantially changed. The prison population has grown continuously and will continue to do so for at last several more years despite more than 18 years of declining crime rates. The election of Barack Obama as president of the United States is a wonderful thing but it has occurred in a country in which a third of black baby boys are bound for prison.

Research and researchers have, however, in the last 30 years illuminated many dark places in criminal justice systems and social systems related to them. They have sometimes produced evidence that has led to changes in policies and practices, and have accumulated other evidence that will be available when more windows of opportunity open. Research and researchers also, and maybe more importantly, have expressed and acted upon belief in a world that is rational, humane and generous.

In Kurt Vonnegut's novel *Mother Night*, a German-speaking American in Berlin in the 1930s is persuaded by American authorities to become a Nazi radio commentator. His mission is to support the American war effort by broadcasting coded messages disguised in anti-Semitic vituperation. He is eventually prosecuted by the Israelis for crimes against humanity and, rather than accept exculpation, kills himself. The moral is sometimes said to be, in respect to pretences to villainy, that we must be careful who we pretend to be because we tend to become that person.

Perhaps the reverse is true. If we act as if we believe that humane change is possible, that policy-makers sometimes will recognize that there but for God's grace go they, and more often accept that rationality rather than emotion should govern human affairs, perhaps those things will happen more often. In any case, we are likely to be better people if we act as if we believe those things to be true.

References

American Friends Service Committee (1971), *Struggle for Justice: A Report on Crime and Punishment in America*, New York: Hill & Wang.

Barker, Vanessa (2009), *The Politics of Punishment: How the Democratic Process Shapes the Way America Punishes Offenders*, New York: Oxford University Press.

Blumstein, Alfred (1982), 'On Racial Disproportionality of the United States' Prison Populations', *Journal of Criminal Law and Criminology*, **73**, pp. 1259–81.

Blumstein, Alfred, Cohen, Jacqueline and Nagin, Daniel (eds) (1978), *Deterrence and Incapacitation: Estimating the Effects of Criminal Sanctions on Crime Rates*, Washington, DC: National Academy Press.

Bonczar, Thomas P. (2003), *Prevalence of Imprisonment in the U.S. Population, 1974–2001*, Washington, DC: US Department of Justice, Bureau of Justice Statistics.

Cavadino, Michael and Dignan, James (2005), *Penal Systems: A Comparative Approach*, London: Sage.

Clear, Todd (2007), *Imprisoning Communities: How Mass Incarceration Makes Disadvantaged Neighborhoods Worse*, New York: Oxford University Press.

Cohen, Jacqueline and Tonry, Michael (1983), 'A Critical Review of Impact Evaluations of Sentencing Innovations', in Alfred Blumstein, Jacqueline Cohen, Susan Martin and Michael Tonry (eds), *Research on Sentencing: The Search for Reform*, vol. II, Washington, DC: National Academy Press.

Cusac, Anne-Marie (2009), *Cruel and Unusual: The Culture of Punishment in America*, New Haven: Yale University Press.

Doob, Anthony and Webster, Cheryl (2003), 'Sentence Severity and Crime: Accepting the Null Hypothesis', in Michael Tonry (ed.), *Crime and Justice: A Review of Research*, vol. 30, Chicago: University of Chicago Press.

Edsall, Thomas and Edsall, Mary (1991), *Chain Reaction: The Impact of Race, Rights, and Taxes on American Politics*, New York: Norton.

Garland, David (2001), *The Culture of Control: Crime and Social Order in Contemporary Society*, Chicago: University of Chicago Press.

Gilbert, Martin (1992), *Churchill: A Life*, New York: Henry Holt.

Gottschalk, Marie (2006), *The Prison and the Gallows: The Politics of Mass Incarceration in America*, Cambridge: Cambridge University Press.

Green, David A. (2008), *When Children Kill Children: Penal Populism and Political Culture*, Oxford: Oxford University Press.

Lacey, Nicola (2008), *The Prisoner's Dilemma: Political Economy and Punishment in Contemporary Democracies*, Cambridge: Cambridge University Press.

Loury, Glenn C. (2007), 'Racial Stigma, Mass Incarceration and American Values', The Tanner Lectures in Human Values delivered at Stanford University on 4 and 5 April 2007. Available at: http://www.econ.brown.edu/fac/Glenn_Loury/louryhomepage/

Massey, Douglas S. (2007), *Categorically Unequal*, New York: Russell Sage Foundation.

Miller, Lisa L. (2008), *The Perils of Federalism: Race, Poverty, and the Politics of Crime Control*, New York: Oxford University Press.

Morris, Norval (1974), *The Future of Imprisonment*, Chicago: University of Chicago Press.

Morris, Norval and Tonry, Michael (1990), *Between Prison and Probation: Intermediate Punishments in a Rational Sentencing System*, New York: Oxford University Press.

Murray, Joseph, and Farrington, David P. (2008), 'Effects of Parental Imprisonment on Children', in Michael Tonry (ed.), *Crime and Justice: A Review of Research*, vol. 37, Chicago: University of Chicago Press.

Phillips, Kevin P. (1991), *The Politics of Rich and Poor: Wealth and the American Electorate in the Reagan Aftermath*, New York: HarperCollins.

Pratt, John (2006), 'The Dark Side of Paradise: Explaining New Zealand's History of High Imprisonment', *British Journal of Criminology*, **46**(4), pp. 541–60.

Pratt, John (2007), *Penal Populism*, London: Routledge.

Sabol, William J., Minton, Todd D. and Harrison, Paige M. (2007), *Prison and Jail Inmates at Midyear 2006*, Washington, DC: US Department of Justice, Bureau of Justice Statistics.

Simon, Jonathan (2007), *Governing Through Crime: How the War on Crime Transformed American Democracy and Created a Culture of Fear*, New York: Oxford University Press.

Tonry, Michael (1986), *Sentencing Reform Impacts*, Washington, DC: US Government Printing Office.

Tonry, Michael (1993), 'Sentencing Commissions and their Guidelines', in Michael Tonry (ed.), *Crime and Justice: A Review of Research*, vol. 17, Chicago: University of Chicago Press.

Tonry, Michael (1994), 'Racial Disproportion in U.S. Prisons', *British Journal of Criminology*, **34** (Special Issue), pp. 97–116.

Tonry, Michael (1995), *Malign Neglect: Race, Crime, and Punishment in America*, New York: Oxford University Press.

Tonry, Michael (1996), *Sentencing Matters*, New York: Oxford University Press.

Tonry, Michael (ed.) (1997), *Ethnicity, Crime, and Immigration: Comparative and Cross-national Perspectives*, *Crime and Justice: A Review of Research*, vol. 21, Chicago: University of Chicago Press.

Tonry, Michael (1998), 'Intermediate Sanctions in Sentencing Guidelines', in Michael Tonry (ed.), *Crime and Justice: A Review of Research*, vol. 23, Chicago: University of Chicago Press.

Tonry, Michael (2004a), *Punishment and Politics: Evidence and Emulation in the Making of English Crime Control Policy*, Cullompton, Devon: Willan.

Tonry, Michael (2004b), *Thinking about Crime: Sense and Sensibility in American Penal Culture*, New York: Oxford University Press.

Tonry, Michael (ed.) (2007), *Crime, Punishment, and Politics in Comparative Perspective*, *Crime and Justice: A Review of Research*, vol. 36, Chicago: University of Chicago Press.

Tonry, Michael (2008), 'Learning from the Limitations of Deterrence Research', in Michael Tonry (ed.), *Crime and Justice: A Review of Research*, vol. 37, Chicago: University of Chicago Press.

Tonry, Michael and Bijleveld, Catrien (2007), 'Crime, Criminal Justice, and Criminology in the Netherlands', in Michael Tonry and Catrien Bijleveld (eds), *Crime and Justice in the Netherlands*, *Crime and Justice: A Review of Research*, vol. 35, Chicago: University of Chicago Press.

Tonry, Michael and Doob, Anthony N. (eds) (2004), *Youth Crime and Youth Justice: Comparative and Cross-national Perspectives*, *Crime and Justice: A Review of Research*, vol. 31, Chicago: University of Chicago Press.

Tonry, Michael and Frase, Richard (eds) (2001), *Sentencing and Sanctions in Western Countries*, New York: Oxford University Press.

Tonry, Michael and Green, David (2003), 'Criminology and Public Policy in the US and UK', in Andrew Ashworth and Lucia Zedner (eds), *The Criminological Foundations of Penal Policy*, Oxford: Oxford University Press.

Tonry, Michael and Lynch, Mary (1995), 'Intermediate Sanctions', in Michael Tonry (ed.), *Crime and Justice: A Review of Research*, vol. 20, Chicago: University of Chicago Press.

Wacquant, Loïc (2002a), 'Deadly Symbiosis: Rethinking Race and Imprisonment in Twenty-first Century America', *Boston Review* (April/May).

Wacquant, Loïc (2002b), 'From Slavery to Mass Incarceration', *New Left Review*, **13**(January–February), pp. 41–60 (http://bostonreview.net/BR27.2/wacquant.html).

Wilson, James Q. (1990), 'Drugs and Crime', in Michael Tonry and James Q. Wilson (eds), *Drugs and Crime*, *Crime and Justice: A Review of Research*, vol. 13, Chicago: University of Chicago Press.

Wilson, William Julius (1987), *The Truly Disadvantaged: The Inner City, the Underclass, and Public Policy*, Chicago: University of Chicago Press.

Published Writings

Books

The Oxford Handbook of Crime and Criminal Justice (Oxford University Press, forthcoming 2010); editor.
The Oxford Handbook of Crime and Public Policy (Oxford University Press, 2009); editor.
Crime and Justice in the Netherlands (University of Chicago Press, 2007, paperback 2008); editor with Catrien Bijleveld.
Crime, Punishment, and Politics in Comparative Perspective (University of Chicago Press, 2007, paperback 2008); editor.
Crime and Punishment in Western Countries, 1980–99 (University of Chicago Press, 2005, paperback 2006); editor with David P. Farrington.
Cross-national Studies of Crime and Justice (US Bureau of Justice Statistics, 2004); editor with David P. Farrington and Patrick Langan.
The Future of Imprisonment (Oxford University Press, 2004, paperback 2006); editor.
Punishment and Politics: Evidence and Emulation in the Making of English Crime Control Policy (Willan, 2004, paperback 2004).
Thinking about Crime: Sense and Sensibility in American Penal Culture (Oxford University Press, 2004, paperback 2006).
Youth Crime and Youth Justice: Comparative and Cross-national Perspectives (University of Chicago Press, 2004, paperback 2005); editor with Anthony Doob.
Confronting Crime: Crime Control under New Labour (Willan, 2003); editor.
Ideology, Crime and Criminal Justice: A Symposium in Honour of Sir Leon Radzinowicz (Willan, 2002); editor with Anthony E. Bottoms.
Reform and Punishment: The Future of Sentencing (Willan, 2002); editor with Susan A. Rex.
Penal Reform in Overcrowded Times (Oxford University Press, 2001, paperback 2001); editor.
Sentencing and Sanctions in Western Countries (Oxford University Press, 2001, paperback 2001); editor with Richard S. Frase.
Prisons (University of Chicago Press, 1999, paperback 2000); editor with Joan Petersilia.
The Handbook of Crime and Punishment (Oxford University Press, 1998, paperback 2000); editor.
Youth Violence (University of Chicago Press, 1998, paperback 1999); editor with Mark H. Moore.
Ethnicity, Crime, and Immigration: Comparative and Cross-national Perspectives (University of Chicago Press, 1997, paperback 1997); editor.
Intermediate Sanctions in Sentencing Guidelines (US Government Printing Office, 1997).

Sentencing Reform in Overcrowded Time: A Comparative Perspective (Oxford University Press, 1997, paperback 1997); editor with Kathleen Hatlestad.

Sentencing Matters (Oxford University Press, 1996, paperback 1997); chapter four reprinted in Joan Petersilia (ed.), *Community Corrections: Probation, Parole, and Intermediate Sanctions* (Oxford University Press, 1997); reprinted in part in C.M.V. Clarkson and H.M. Keating (eds), *Criminal Law: Cases and Materials* (Sweet and Maxwell, 2003).

Building a Safer Society (University of Chicago Press 1995, paperback 1995); co-editor with David P. Farrington.

Intermediate Sanctions in Overcrowded Times (Northeastern University Press, 1995); editor with Kate Hamilton.

Malign Neglect: Race, Crime, and Punishment in America (Oxford University Press, 1995, paperback 1996); reprinted in part in Marc L. Miller and Ronald F. Wright (eds), *Criminal Procedures: Cases, Statutes, and Executive Materials*(Aspen, 1998); in Leo Katz, Michael S. Moore and Stephen J. Morse (eds), *Foundations of Criminal Law* (Oxford University Press, 1999); in part in Nora Demleitner, Douglas Berman, Ronald Wright and Marc Miller (eds), *Sentencing Law and Policy* (Aspen, 2003); in part in John Monahan and Laurens Walker (eds), *Social Science and the Law* (6th edn) (Foundation, 2006); and in part in Kate E. Bloch and Kevin C. McGunigal (eds), *Criminal Law: A Contemporary Approach* (Aspen, 2005); and chapter 3 reprinted in part in John Kaplan, Robert Weisberg and Guyora Binder (eds), *Criminal Law Cases and Materials* (Aspen, 2000).

Beyond the Law: Crime in Complex Organizations (University of Chicago Press, 1993, paperback 1994); editor with Albert J. Reiss, Jr.

Modern Policing (University of Chicago Press, 1992, paperback 1993); editor with Norval Morris (Portuguese version published in 2003 by Editora da Universidade de Saõ Paolo as *Policiamento Moderno* (Brazil)).

Human Development and Criminal Behavior (Springer-Verlag, 1991); with Lloyd Ohlin and David P. Farrington.

Between Prison and Probation: Intermediate Punishments in a Rational Sentencing System (Oxford University Press, 1990, paperback 1991), with Norval Morris; chapter 2 reprinted in James M. Marquart and Jonathan R. Sorensen (eds), *Corrections Contexts* (Roxbury, 1997); in George F. Cole and Marc G. Gertz (eds), *The Criminal Justice System: Politics and Policies* (7th edn) (Wadsworth, 1998); and in George F. Cole. Marc G. Gertz and Amy Burger (eds), *The Criminal Justice System: Politics and Policies* (8th edn) (Wadsworth, 2001).

Drugs and Crime (University of Chicago Press, 1990, paperback 1991); editor with James Q. Wilson.

Family Violence (University of Chicago Press, 1989, paperback 1990); editor with Lloyd Ohlin.

Managing Appeals in Federal Courts (US Government Printing Office, 1988); with Robert A. Katzmann.

Prediction and Classification (University of Chicago Press, 1987, paperback 1989); editor with Don M. Gottfredson.

The Sentencing Commission: Guidelines for Criminal Sanctions (Northeastern University Press, 1987); with Kay Knapp and Andrew von Hirsch.

Sentencing Reform Impacts (US Government Printing Office, 1987).

Communities and Crime (University of Chicago Press, 1986, paperback 1988); co-editor with Albert J. Reiss, Jr. (Japanese version published in two volumes in 1994 and 1995 by Joshi Bohan Kenkyu of Tokyo).

Hypnotically Refreshed Testimony: Enhanced Memory or Tampering with the Evidence? (US Government Printing Office, 1985); with Martin T. Orne *et al.*

Reform and Punishment: Essays on Criminal Sentencing (University of Chicago Press, 1983); editor with Franklin E. Zimring.

Research on Sentencing: The Search for Reform, report of the National Academy of Sciences Panel on Sentencing Research (National Academy Press, 1983); co-editor with others (and principal author of Chapters 1, 3 and 4).

Crime and Justice: A Review of Research, volumes 1–38 (University of Chicago Press 1979–2009); editor.

Transfer between Courts, Juvenile Justice Standards Project (American Bar Association and Institute for Judicial Administration, 1977), special editor (and ghost-writer).

Articles

'Antisocial Behavior' (with Harriet Bildsten), in Michael Tonry (ed.), *The Oxford Handbook of Crime and Public Policy* (Oxford University Press, 2009).

'Crime and Public Policy', in Michael Tonry (ed.), *The Oxford Handbook of Crime and Public Policy* (Oxford University Press, 2009).

'Emerging Explanations of American Punishment Policies', *Punishment & Society*, **11**, 2009, pp. 377–94.

'Foreword', in Richard D. Wright (ed.), *Sex Offender Laws: Failed Policies, New Directions* (Springer, 2009).

'The Mostly Unintended Effects of Mandatory Penalties: Two Centuries of Consistent Findings', in Michael Tonry (ed.), *Crime and Justice: A Review of Research*, vol. 38 (University of Chicago Press, 2009).

'Rebalancing the Criminal Justice System in Favour of the Victim: Victims' Programmes, Policies, and Politics in England and Wales', in Anthony E. Bottoms and Julian Roberts (eds), *Punishment, Restoration, and Victims* (Willan, forthcoming 2009).

'The Untold Story of America's First Sentencing Commission', *Federal Sentencing Reporter*, **21**(4), 2009, pp. 265–70.

'Why are American Penal Policies so Harsh?' *Japanese Journal of Sociological Criminology*, **33**, 2008, pp. 11–28; reprinted in Koichi Hamai (ed.), *Globalized Penal Populism and Its Countermeasures* (Ryukoku University Press, 2009).

'Crime and Human Rights: How Political Paranoia, Protestant Fundamentalism, and Constitutional Obsolescence Combined to Devastate Black America', *Criminology*, **46**, 2008, pp. 1–33.

'Learning from the Limitations of Deterrence Research', in Michael Tonry (ed.), *Crime and Justice: A Review of Research*, vol. 37 (University of Chicago Press, 2008).

'The Malign Effects of Drugs and Crime Control Policies on Black Americans' (with Matthew Melewski), in Michael Tonry (ed.), *Crime and Justice: A Review of Research*, vol. 37 (University of Chicago Press, 2008).

'Onderzoek naar afschrikking: de noodzaak om klein te denken als we iets nieuws willen leren', in *Justitiële Verkenningen*, **34**(2), 2008, pp. 98–117.

'Why Have Dutch Penal Policies and Practices become More Punitive?' in Y. Buruma, J. Fleuren, P.H. van Kempen, F. Kusters and T. Mertens (eds), *Op het rechte pad: Peter J. P. Tak bundel* (Wolf Legal Publishers, 2008).

'Crime, Criminal Justice, and Criminology in the Netherlands' (with Catrien Bijleveld), in Michael Tonry and Catrien Bijleveld (eds), *Crime and Justice in the Netherlands* (University of Chicago Press, 2007).

'Crime Does Not Cause Punishment: The Impact of Sentencing Policy on Levels of Crime', *South African Crime Quarterly*, **20**, June 2007, pp. 13–20.

'Determinants of Penal Policies', in Michael Tonry (ed.), *Crime, Punishment, and Politics in Comparative Perspective* (University of Chicago Press, 2007).

'Foreword' to David A. Green (ed.), *When Children Kill: Penal Populism and Political Culture* (Oxford University Press, 2007).

'Looking Back to See the Future of Punishment in America', *Social Research*, **74**(2), 2007, pp. 353–78.

'Penal Policy, Political Culture, and Constitutional Obsolescence', in Kauko Aromaa (ed.), *Penal Policy: Justice Reform and Social Exclusion* (European Institute for Crime Prevention and Control, Helsinki, 2007).

'Polityka Karna, Kultura Polityczna, A Zasady Konstytcyyjnet' (Penal Policy, Political Culture, and Constitutional Obsolescence), *Archiwum Kriminologii (Polish Archives of Criminology)*, **27**, 2007, pp. 95–110.

'Preface', in Tom R. Tyler (ed.), *Legitimacy and Criminal Justice: International Perspectives* (Russell Sage Foundation, 2007).

'Sentencing in South Africa', in *Sentencing in South Africa* (Open Society Foundation of South Africa, 2007).

'Treating Juveniles as Adult Criminals: An Iatrogenic Violence Prevention Strategy if Ever There Was One', *American Journal of Preventive Medicine* (2007).

'Criminology, Mandatory Minimums, and Public Policy', *Criminology and Public Policy*, **5**(1), 2006, pp. 45–56.

'¿Debe México armonizar su sistema punitivo de Derecho Penal?' in Instituto Nacional de Ciencias Penales and Instituto Max Planck para el Derecho Penal Extranjero e Internacional. Logros y deafíos de la armonización y homologación en México y en el mundo, *Hacia la unificación del Derecho Penal* (Mexico City: INACIPE, 2006).

'The Prospects for Institutionalization of Restorative Justice Initiatives in Western Countries', in Ivo Aertsen, Tom Daems and Luc Robert (eds), *Institutionalizing Restorative Justice* (Willan, 2006).

'Purposes and Functions of Sentencing', in Michael Tonry (ed.), *Crime and Justice: A Review of Research*, vol. 34 (University of Chicago Press, 2006).

'Successful Transition and Reentry for Safer Communities: A Call to Action for Parole', with Peggy Burke (Council of State Governments, 2006).

'Cross-national Measures of Punitiveness' (with Alfred Blumstein and Asheley van Ness), in Michael Tonry and David P. Farrington (eds), *Crime and Punishment in Western Countries, 1980–1999* (Chicago 2005).

'The Functions of Sentencing and Sentencing Reform', *Stanford Law Review*, **58**, 2005, pp. 37–66.

'Obsolescence and Immanence in Penal Theory and Policy', *Columbia Law Review*, **105**, 2005, pp. 1233–75.

'Punishment and Crime Across Space and Time' (with David P. Farrington), in Michael Tonry and David P. Farrington (eds), *Crime and Punishment in Western Countries, 1980–1999* (Chicago 2005).

'Why are Europe's Crime Rates Falling?' *Criminology in Europe*, **5**(1), 2005, pp. 8–11.

'Cambridge Institute of Criminology', *Criminology in Europe*, **3**(1), 2004, pp. 20–22.

'Crime', in George Ritzer (ed.), *Handbook of Social Problems* (Sage, 2004).

'Criminology and Criminal Justice Research in Europe', in Gerben Bruinsma, Henk Elffers and Jan de Keijser (eds), *Developments in Criminology and Criminal Justice Research* (Willan, 2004).

'Has the Prison a Future?' in Michael Tonry (ed.), *The Future of Imprisonment* (Oxford University Press, 2004).

'Varieties of Youth Justice' (with Anthony Doob), in Michael Tonry and Anthony Doob (eds), *Youth Crime and Youth Justice* (Chicago University Press, 2004).

'Why aren't German Penal Policies Harsher and Imprisonment Rates Higher?' *German Law Review*, **5**, 2004, pp. 1187–206.

'Criminology and Public Policy in the US and UK' (with David A. Green), in Andrew Ashworth and Lucia Zedner (eds), *The Criminological Foundations of Penal Policy* (Oxford University Press, 2003).

'Evidence, Elections and Ideology in the Making of Criminal Justice Policy', in Michael Tonry (ed.), *Confronting Crime: Crime Control under New Labour* (Willan, 2003).

'Is Sentencing in England and Wales Institutionally Racist?' (with Amanda Matravers), in Michael Tonry (ed.), *Confronting Crime: Crime Control under New Labour* (Willan, 2003).

'Reducing the Prison Population', in Michael Tonry (ed.), *Confronting Crime: Crime Control under New Labour* (Willan, 2003).

'Community Penalties in the United States', in Hans-Jörg Albrecht and Anton van Kalmthout (eds), *Community Sanctions and Measures in Europe and North America* (Freiburg, Germany: Max-Planck Institute, 2002).

'The Death Penalty in the United States', in Volker Dittmar, André Kuhn, Renie Maag and Hans Wiprächtiger (eds), *Zwischen Mediation und Lebenslang – Neue Wege in der Kriminalitätsbekämpfurg* (Chur/Zurich: Verlag Rüegger, 2002).

'Foreword' to Neil Hutton and Cyrus Tata (eds), *Sentencing and Society: International Perspectives* (Ashgate, 2002).

'Reconsidering Sentencing and Punishment in England and Wales' (with Sue A. Rex), in Sue A. Rex and Michael Tonry (eds), *Reform and Punishment: The Future of Sentencing*, (Willan, 2002).

'Setting Sentencing Policy through Guidelines', in Sue A. Rex and Michael Tonry (eds), *Reform and Punishment: The Future of Sentencing* (Willan, 2002).

'Transnational' 'Organized' 'Crime', in Hans-Jörg Albrecht and Cyrille Fijnault (eds), *The Containment of Transnational Organized Crime* (Freiburg: Max-Planck Institute, 2002).

'Interactions between Immigration and Crime Control Policies in the United States' (with Leena Kurki), in Anton von Kalmthout and Hans-Jörg Albrecht (eds), *Detention of Illegal Aliens* (Freiburg: Max-Planck Institute, 2001).

'Penal Policy at the Beginning of the 21st Century', in Michael Tonry (ed.), *Penal Reform in Overcrowded Times* (Oxford University Press, 2001).

'Prisons and Imprisonment', in Neil J. Smelser and Paul B. Baltes (eds), *International Encyclopedia of the Social Sciences* (Elsevier Science, 2001).

'Punishment Policies and Patterns in Western Countries', in Michael Tonry and Richard S. Frase (eds), *Sentencing and Sanctions in Western Countries* (Oxford University Press, 2001).

'Punishment Policies and Politics in America', in Clemens Bartollas, *Invitation to Corrections* (Allyn and Bacon, 2001).

'Symbol, Substance, and Severity in Western Penal Policies', *Punishment and Society*, **3**(4), 2001, pp. 517–36.

'Unthought Thoughts – the Influences of Changing Sensibilities on Penal Policies', *Punishment and Society*, **3**(1), 2001, pp. 167–81; reprinted in David Garland (ed.), *Mass Imprisonment in the United States: Social Causes and Consequences* (Sage, 2001).

'Prison', *World Book Year Book – 2000* (World Book Publications, 2000).

'American Prisons at the Beginning of the Twenty-First Century' (with Joan Petersilia), in Michael Tonry and Joan Petersilia (eds), *Prisons* (University of Chicago Press, 1999).

'Community Penalties in the United States', *European Journal on Criminal Policy and Research*, **7**(1), 1999, pp. 5–22.

'Federal Sentencing can be made More Just, if the Sentencing Commission wants to make it so', *Federal Sentencing Reporter*, September–October 1999.

'Foreword' to J.C.J. Boutellier, *Crime and Morality: The Significance of Criminal Justice in a Post-Modern Culture* (Kluwer, 1999).

'Fragmentation of Sentencing and Corrections in America', *Sentencing & Corrections: Issues for the 21st Century* (US Department of Justice, National Institute of Justice, 1999); reprinted in *Overcrowded Times* (1999); and in Michael Tonry (ed.), *Penal Reform in Overcrowded Times* (Oxford University Press, 2001).

'Parochialism in American Sentencing Policy', *Crime and Delinquency*, **45,** January 1999, pp. 48–65.

'Prison', *World Book Year Book – 1999* (World Book Publications, 1999).

'Reconsidering Indeterminate and Structured Sentencing', *Sentencing & Corrections: Issues for the 21st Century* (US. Department of Justice, National Institute of Justice, 1999).

'Rethinking Unthinkable Punishment Policies in America', *UCLA Law Review*, **46**, 1999, pp. 1751–91.

'Why are U.S. Incarceration Rates So High?' *Crime and Delinquency*, **45**, October 1999, pp. 419–37; reprinted in *Overcrowded Times*, **10**(3), 1999, pp. 1, 8–16; in *The Angolite*, **25**(1), pp. 26–33; in Michael Tonry (ed.), *Penal Reform in Overcrowded Times* (Oxford

University Press, 2001); in Robert C. Culbertson and Ralph A. Weisheit (eds), *Order Under Law* (6th edn) (Waveland, 2001); and in William T. Lyons, Jr. (ed.), *Crime and Criminal Justice* (Ashgate, 2006).

'Building Better Policies on Better Knowledge', in President's Commission on Law Enforcement, *The Challenge of Crime in a Free Society: Looking Back, Looking Forward* (US Government Printing Office, 1998).

'A Comparative Perspective on Minority Groups, Crime, and Criminal Justice', *European Journal on Crime, Criminal Law, and Criminal Justice*, **6**(1), 1998, pp. 60–73.

'Crime and Punishment in America', in Michael Tonry (ed.), *The Handbook of Crime and Punishment* (Oxford University Press, 1998).

'Interchangeability, Desert Limits, and Equivalence of Function', in Andrew von Hirsch and Andrew Ashworth (eds), *Principled Sentencing: Readings in Theory and Practice* (2nd edn) (Hart Publishing, 1998).

'Intermediate Sanctions', in Michael Tonry (ed.), *The Handbook of Crime and Punishment* (Oxford University Press, 1998).

'Intermediate Sanctions in Sentencing Guidelines', in Michael Tonry (ed.), *Crime and Justice: A Review of Research*, vol. 23 (University of Chicago Press, 1998); reprinted in Chris W. Eskridge (ed.), *Criminal Justice: Concepts and Issues* (3rd edn) (Roxbury 1999) (4th edn, 2004).

'Prison', *World Book Year Book – 1998* (World Book Publications, 1998).

'Transfer of Criminal Justice Policies Across National Boundaries', in Hans-Jörg Albrecht *et al.* (eds), *Internationale Perspektiven in Kriminologie und Strafrecht* (Duncker & Humblot, 1998).

'Youth Violence in America' (with Mark H. Moore), in Michael Tonry and Mark H. Moore (eds), *Youth Violence* (University of Chicago Press, 1998).

'Building Safer Societies: Crime Prevention in Developed Countries', *European Journal on Criminal Policy and Research*, **5**(3), 1997, pp. 49–60.

'Ethnicity, Crime, and Immigration', in Michael Tonry (ed.), *Ethnicity, Crime, and Immigration: Comparative and Cross-national Perspectives*, *Crime and Justice: A Review of Research*, vol. 21 (University of Chicago Press, 1997); reprinted in part in Dan Kahan, Neal Katzal and Tracey Meares (eds), *Criminal Law: Cases and Materials* (Foundation, 2007).

'Forfeiture Laws, Practices, and Controversies in the U.S.', *European Journal on Crime, Criminal Law, and Criminal Justice* (1997), **5**(3), pp. 294–307.

'Gender, Race, and Sentencing' (with Kathleen Daly), in Michael Tonry (ed.), *Crime and Justice: A Review of Research*, vol. 22 (University of Chicago Press, 1997).

'Gewinnabschöpfung in den USA', in Michael Kilchling (ed.), *Möglichkeiten der Gewinnabschöpfung zur Bekämpfung der Organisierten Kriminalität* (Freiburg: Max-Planck Institute, 1997).

'President Clinton, Mandatory Minimums, and Disaffirmative Action', *Tikkun*, **12**(6), 1997, pp. 32, 71–73.

'Prison', *World Book Year Book – 1997* (World Book Publications, 1997).

'Controlling Prison Population Size', *European Journal on Criminal Policy and Research*, **4**(3), 1996, pp. 26–45.

'The Effects of the American War on Drugs on Black Americans, 1980–96', *European Journal on Criminal Policy and Research*, **4**(2), 1996, pp. 36–62.

'Intermediate Sanctions' (with Mary Lynch), in Michael Tonry (ed.), *Crime and Justice: A Review of Research*, vol. 20 (University of Chicago Press, 1996).

'Prison', *World Book Year Book – 1996* (World Book Publications, 1996).

'Between Prison and Probation: The Development of Intermediate Sanctions in Western Countries or Be Careful What You Ask for in Community Corrections Programmes Because You May Get It', The Sixth Eva Saville Memorial Lecture (London: Institute for the Study and Treatment of Delinquency, June 1995).

'Intermediate Sanctions in Sentencing Reform', *University of Chicago Law School Roundtable*, **2**, 1995, pp. 391–411.

'Law and Crime Prevention', in Per-Olof Wikström (ed.), *Integrating Crime Prevention Strategies: Propensity and Opportunity* (Stockholm: BROD, 1995).

'The Rockefeller Drug Laws' and 'Mandatory Sentencing', in Gerald Jaffe (ed.), *Encyclopedia of Drugs and Alcohol* (Macmillan, 1995).

'Sentencing Reform Across National Boundaries', in Chris Clarkson and Rod Morgan (eds), *The Politics of Sentencing Reform* (Oxford University Press, 1995).

'Special Report on New Proposals for Fighting Crime in America', 'Prison' and 'Crime', *World Book Year Book – 1995* (World Book Publications, 1995).

'Strategic Approaches to Crime Prevention' (with David P. Farrington), in Michael Tonry and David P. Farrington (eds), *Building a Safer Society* (University of Chicago Press, 1995).

'Twenty Years of Sentencing Reform', *Judicature*, **78**, January 1995, pp. 169–72; reprinted in *University of Minnesota Law School Alumni Journal* (1996); in Marilyn McShane and Frank P. Williams (eds), *Essays on Criminal Justice* (Garland, 1997); in Jodi S. Lane and Joan Petersilia (eds), *Criminal Justice Policy* (Edward Elgar, 1998); in Elliot Slotnick (ed.), *Judicial Politics: Readings from Judicature* (2nd edn) (American Judicature Society, 1999); and in Elliot Slotnick (ed.), *Judicial Politics: Readings from Judicature* (3rd edn) (CQ Press, 2005).

'Wrong Place, Wrong Time', *Times Literary Supplement*, 18 April 1995, pp. 25–26.

'Prison', *World Book Year Book – 1994* (World Book Publications, 1994).

'Proportionality, Parsimony, and Interchangeability of Punishments', in R.A. Duff, S.E. Marshall, R.E. Dobash and R.P. Dobash (eds), *Penal Theory and Penal Practice* (Manchester University Press, 1994); reprinted in R.A. Duff and D. Garland (eds), *The Philosophy of Punishment* (Oxford University Press, 1994) and in part in Andrew von Hirsch and Andrew Ashworth (eds), *Principled Sentencing: Readings in Theory and Practice* (2nd edn) (Hart Publishing, 1998); in Allan Manson, Patrick Healy and Gary Trotter (eds), *Sentencing and Penal Policy in Canada* (Edmond Montgomery Publications, 2000); and in Allan Manson, Patrick Healy, Gary Trotter, Julian Roberts and Dale Ives (eds), *Sentencing and Penal Policy in Canada* (2nd edn) (Edmond Montgomery Publications, 2008).

'Race and the War on Drugs', *University of Chicago Legal Forum*, 1994, pp. 25–81.

'Racial Disparities in Courts and Prisons', *Criminal Behaviour and Mental Health*, October 1994.

'Racial Disproportion in U.S. Prisons', *British Journal of Criminology* **34** (Special Issue), 1994, pp. 97–116; reprinted in Roy King and Mike Maguire (eds), *Prisons in Context*

(Oxford University Press, 1994); in Timothy J. Flanagan, James W. Marquart and Kenneth Adams (eds), *Incarcerating Criminals: Prisons and Jails in Social and Environmental Context* (Oxford University Press, 1998); in Jodi S. Lane and Joan Petersilia (eds), *Criminal Justice Policy* (Edward Elgar, 1998); and in Roger Matthews (ed.) *Imprisonment* (Dartmouth, 1999).

'Racial Politics, Racial Disparities, and the War on Crime', *Crime and Delinquency*, **40**, October 1994, pp. 475–94; reprinted in John E. Conklin (ed.), *New Perspectives in Criminology* (Allyn & Bacon, 1995); in Barbara Hudson (ed.), *Race and Criminal Justice* (Dartmouth, 1996); in James Inciardi (ed.), *Examining the Justice Process: A Reader* (Wadsworth, 1996); in Stuart A. Scheingold (ed.), *Politics, Crime Control, and Culture* (Dartmouth, 1997); in Christopher G. Ellison and W. Allen Martin (eds), *Race and Ethnic Relations in the United States: Readings for the 21st Century* (Roxbury, 1998); in Frank R. Scarpitti and Amie L. Nielsen (eds), *Criminology: A Reader*, (Roxbury 1998); in George F. Cole and Marc G. Gertz (eds), *The Criminal Justice System: Politics and Policies* (7th edn) (Wadsworth, 1998); in Frank R. Scarpitti and Amie L. Nielsen (eds), *Crime and Criminals: Contemporary and Classic Readings* (Roxbury, 1999); in Robert L. Bing III and Alejandro del Carmen (eds), *Perspectives: Race and Crime* (Courselinks, 2000); in George F. Cole, Marc G. Gertz, and Amy Burger (eds), *The Criminal Justice System: Politics and Policies* (8th edn) (Wadsworth, 2002); in Charles E. Reasons, Darlene J. Conley, and Julius Debro (eds), *Race, Class, Gender and Justice in the United States* (Allyn & Bacon, 2002); and in Bradley R.E. Wright, Jr. and Ralph B. McNeal, Jr. (eds), *Boundaries: Readings in Deviance, Crime, and Justice* (Prentice Hall, 2002).

'Sentencing Guidelines, Disadvantaged Offenders, and Racial Disparities', *Philosophy and Public Policy*, Fall 1994, pp. 7–13.

'Sentencing Reforms and Racial Disparities', *Judicature*, **78**, November–December 1994, pp. 118–19, 159–60.

'The Failure of the U.S. Sentencing Commission's Guidelines', *Crime and Delinquency*, **39**, April 1993, pp. 131–49; reprinted in G. Larry Mays and Peter R. Gregware (eds), *Crime and Justice: A Reader* (Waveland, 1995); in part in John Kaplan, Robert Weisberg and Guyora Binder (eds), *Criminal Law: Cases and Materials* (3rd edn) (Little, Brown, 1996); in Stan Stojkovic, John Klofas and David Kalinich (eds), *The Administration and Management of Criminal Justice Institutions* (3rd edn) (Waveland, 1999); and in John Kaplan, Robert Weisberg and Guyora Binder (eds), *Criminal Law: Cases and Material* (4th edn) (Aspen, 2000).

'Foreword' to Lloyd Ohlin and Frank Remington (eds), *Discretion in Criminal Justice* (SUNY-Albany Press, 1993).

'Organizational Crime' (with Albert J. Reiss, Jr.), in Michael Tonry and Albert J. Reiss, Jr. (eds), *Beyond the Law* (University of Chicago Press, 1993); reprinted in part in Neal Shover and John Paul Wright (eds), *Crimes of Privilege* (Oxford University Press, 2001).

'Sentencing Commissions and Their Guidelines', in Michael Tonry (ed.), *Crime and Justice: A Review of Research*, vol. 17 (University of Chicago Press, 1993).

'Special Report on the Growing U.S. Prison Population', *World Book Yearbook – 1993* (World Book Publications, 1993).

'The Success of Judge Frankel's Sentencing Commission', *Colorado Law Review*, **64**, 1993, pp. 713–22.

'GAO Report Confirms Failure of U.S. Sentencing Commission's Guidelines', *Federal Sentencing Reporter*, **5**, 1992, p. 144.

'Judges and Sentencing Policy', in Colin Munro and Martin Wasik (eds), *Sentencing, Judicial Training, and Discretion* (Butterworths, 1992).

'Mandatory Penalties', in Michael Tonry (ed.), *Crime and Justice: A Review of the Research*, vol. 16 (University of Chicago Press, 1992); reprinted in Mary Vogel (ed.), *Crime, Inequality, and the State* (Routledge, 2006).

'Salvaging the Sentencing Guidelines in Seven Easy Steps', *Federal Sentencing Reporter*, **4**, 1992, p. 355; reprinted in Norman Abrams and Sara Sun Beale (eds), *Federal Criminal Law and Its Enforcement* (2nd edn) (West Publishing Company, 1993); in *Federal Sentencing Reporter*, **10**, 1997, pp. 51–55; and in Sara Sun Beale *et al.* (eds), *Federal Criminal Law and its Enforcement* (3rd edn) (West, 2000).

'Tribute to Sheldon L. Messinger' (with Norval Morris), *California Law Review*, **80**, 1992, p. 307.

'Mandatory Penalties and the U.S. Sentencing Commission's "Mandatory" Guidelines', *Federal Sentencing Reporter*, **4**, 1991, p. 129.

'The Politics and Processes of Sentencing Commissions', *Crime and Delinquency*, **37**, July 1991, pp. 307–29.

'Public Prosecution and Hydro Engineering', *Minnesota Law Review*, **75**, 1991, p. 971.

'Between Prison and Probation: Intermediate Punishments in a Rational Sentencing System' (with Norval Morris), *NIJ Reports*, January 1990; reprinted in Andrew von Hirsch and Andrew Ashworth (eds), *Principled Sentencing* (Northeastern University Press, 1992).

'Research on Drugs and Crime', in Michael Tonry and James Q. Wilson (eds), *Drugs and Crime* (University of Chicago Press, 1990).

'Stated and Latent Functions of Intensive Supervision Probation', *Crime and Delinquency*, **36**, January 1990, pp. 174–91; reprinted in David L. Bender (ed.), *Opposing Viewpoints* (5th and later edns) (Greenhaven Press, 1991); and in Thomas Ellsworth (ed.), *Contemporary Community Corrections* (2nd edn) (Waveland, 2000).

'Are the U.S. Sentencing Commission's Guidelines "Working Well"?' *Federal Sentencing Reporter*, **2**, 1989, p. 122.

'Family Violence in Perspective' (with Lloyd Ohlin), in Lloyd Ohlin and Michael Tonry (eds), *Family Violence* (University of Chicago Press, 1989).

'Presiding in Criminal Court' (with Norval Morris), *Judicature* (1988), pp. 7–11.

'Sentencing Guidelines and the Model Penal Code', *Rutgers Law Review*, **19**, 1988, p. 823.

'Structuring Sentencing', in Michael Tonry and Norval Morris (eds), *Crime and Justice: A Review of the Research*, vol. 10 (University of Chicago Press, 1988).

'Enforcing Sentencing Guidelines: Plea Bargaining and Review Mechanisms' (with John C. Coffee, Jr.), in Andrew von Hirsch, Kay Knapp and Michael Tonry, *The Sentencing Commission* (Northeastern University Press, 1987).

'Prediction and Classification: Legal and Ethical Issues', in Don M. Gottfredson and Michael Tonry (eds), *Prediction and Classification* (University of Chicago Press 1987); reprinted in part in Andrew von Hirsch and Andrew Ashworth (eds), *Principled Sentencing*

(Northeastern University Press, 1992); and in Andrew von Hirsch and Andrew Ashworth (eds), *Principled Sentencing: Readings in Theory and Practice* (2nd edn) (Hart Publishing, 1998).

'Sentencing Commissions and Sentencing Guidelines – The Second Generation', in Ken Pease and Martin Wasik (eds), *Sentencing Reform in England: Guidance or Guidelines* (Manchester University Press, 1987).

'A Survey of Sentencing Guidelines and their Effects', in Andrew von Hirsch, Kay Knapp and Michael Tonry, *The Sentencing Commission* (Northeastern University Press, 1987); reprinted in part in Marc L. Miller and Ronald F. Wright (eds), *Criminal Procedures: Cases, Statutes, and Executive Materials* (Aspen, 1998).

'Blacks, Crime Rates, and Prisons' (with Norval Morris), in Gordon Hawkins and Franklin E. Zimring (eds), *The Pursuit of Criminal Justice* (University of Chicago Press, 1984).

'The Allocation of Sentencing Authority in the United States', 'Jury Sentencing' and 'Sentencing Councils', *Encyclopedia of Crime and Justice*, ed. Sanford H. Kadish (3 vols, Macmillan, 1983).

'A Critical Review of Impact Evaluations of Sentencing Innovations' (with Jacqueline Cohen), in Alfred Blumstein, Jacqueline Cohen, Susan E. Martin and Michael H. Tonry (eds), *Research on Sentencing: The Search for Reform*, vol. II (National Academy Press, 1983).

'Hard Choices' (with John C. Coffee, Jr.), in Michael Tonry and Franklin E. Zimring (eds), *Reform and Punishment* (University of Chicago Press, 1983).

'Comparative Criminal Procedure – Symposium', *Maryland Law Review*, 1982.

'Criminal Law – the Missing Element in Sentencing Reform', *Vanderbilt Law Review*, **35**, 1982, p. 607; also in *Waseda Law Review*, **60**, 1985, p. 671 (Japanese translation by Tadashi Morijama); reprinted in Martin Wasik (ed.), *The Sentencing Process* (Dartmouth, 1996).

'More Sentencing Reform in America', *Criminal Law Review*, March 1982, pp. 157–67.

'Professional Mediation Services for Prisoners' Complaints' (with William Reynolds), *American Bar Association Journal*, **67**, 1981, p. 294.

'Real Offense Sentencing – The Model Sentencing and Corrections Act', *Journal of Criminal Law and Criminology*, **72**, 1981, p. 1550.

'The Sentencing Commission in Sentencing Reform', *Hofstra Law Review*, **7**, 1979, p. 315.

'Sentencing Reform in America' (with Norval Morris), in Peter Glazebrook (ed.), *Reshaping the Criminal Law: A Festschrift in Honor of Glanville Williams* (Stevens, 1978); reprinted in Gordon Hawkins and Franklin E. Zimring (eds), *The Pursuit of Criminal Justice* (University of Chicago Press, 1984).

'Juvenile Justice and the National Crime Commissions', in Margaret Rosenheim (ed.), *Pursuing Justice for the Child* (University of Chicago Press, 1976).

Review essay on *Cannabis*, Canadian Commission of Inquiry into the Non-medical Use of Drugs, and *Marihuana – A Signal of Misunderstanding*, US National Commission on Marihuana and Drug Abuse, *Yale Law Journal*, **82**, 1973, p. 1736.

Part I
Race and Ethnicity

[1]
Malign Neglect

Throughout this century, black Americans, especially men but increasingly also women, have been more likely than whites to commit violent and property crimes. They have also been more likely to be in jail or prison, on probation or parole. People of goodwill, from W. E. B. Du Bois at the turn of the century through Gunnar Myrdal in the 1940s, to most contemporary scholars of crime, agree that disproportionate black criminality is the product of social and economic disadvantage, much of it traceable to racial bias and discrimination, more overt in earlier times than today.

For at least seventy years, scholars have differed on how much more involved in crime blacks are than whites. Bias in police arrest and crime-recording practices, insufficient sympathy for black victims, exaggerated sympathy for white victims, and official practices adverse to blacks are often said to distort official statistics. The disagreements, however, have principally concerned the extent, not the existence, of higher levels of black crime.

Racial disparities in prisons, jails, and other corrections programs trigger larger and harsher disagreement. Some argue that the disparities result from racial bias operating at every criminal justice stage from arrest to parole release. However, although no one denies that there is bias in the system, many scholars and most officials believe that racial disproportions result largely from different racial patterns of criminality and that bias is a relatively small, though immensely important, part of the problem.

So summarized, it might appear that these are chronic problems about which broadly shared understandings have emerged. That appearance would be deceptive. Crimes and punishments of blacks are acute social problems; their ramifications dig deeply into the fabric of American life; and there is no agreement on their solution.

Crime by blacks is not getting worse. The proportions of serious violent crimes committed by blacks have been level for more than a decade. Since the mid-1970s, approximately 45 percent of those arrested for murder, rape, robbery, and aggravated assault have been black (the trend is slightly downward). Disproportionate punishments of blacks, however, have been getting worse, especially since Ronald Reagan became president. Since 1980, the number of blacks in prison has tripled. Between 1979 and 1992 the percentage of blacks among those admitted to state and federal prisons grew from 39 to 54 percent. Incarceration rates for blacks in 1991 (1,895 per 100,000) were nearly seven times higher than those for whites (293 per 100,000). Widely publicized studies in 1990 showed that 23 percent of black males aged 20 to 29 in the United States were under criminal justice system control (as were 23 percent in New York and 33 percent in California). Studies by the National Center on Institutions and Alternatives showed that in 1991 in Washington D.C., and Baltimore, 42 and 56 percent, respectively, of black males aged 18 to 35 were under justice system control.

Those numbers are, or ought to be, shocking to every American. It is not hard to understand why many interpret them as *prima facie* evidence of a racist criminal justice system. Disturbing though the numbers are on the surface, what lies below is even more disturbing, for three reasons. First, the rising levels of black incarceration did not just happen; they were the foreseeable effects of deliberate policies spearheaded by the Reagan and Bush administrations and implemented by many states. Anyone with knowledge of drug-trafficking patterns and of police arrest policies and incentives could have foreseen that the enemy troops in the War on Drugs would consist largely of young, inner-city minority males. Blacks in particular are arrested and imprisoned for drug crimes in numbers far out of line with their proportions of the general population, of drug users, and of drug traffickers.

Although damaging the lives of countless young blacks was probably not their primary aim, the architects of the War on Drugs no doubt foresaw the result. Any conventional ethical analysis would hold them accountable for the consequences of their policies. For most purposes, an action taken to achieve a result is ethically indistinguishable from an action taken with knowledge that a result will almost certainly occur. In the criminal law, for example, if death results, setting fire to a house for the purpose of killing the sleeping occupants is first-degree murder, as is setting fire to a house for the purpose of defrauding an insurance company, but with knowledge that the occupants will most likely die. In equal employment opportunity law, use of screening criteria for job applicants with knowledge that they will exclude proportionately more minority than white applicants is as objectionable as use of a device intended to achieve that result, and is allowable only if exacting tests can be met to show that the screening criteria validly measure qualities related to successful job performance.

Sometimes, of course, undesirable side effects are an inevitable consequence of socially desirable policies. Using automobiles predictably results in traffic fatalities, and building skyscrapers predictably results in the deaths of construction workers, so knowledge of undesired side effects is not always a basis for ethical indictments. Undesired side effects like these can be distinguished from the racial disparities caused by recent crime control policies. Although automotive engineers and architects try to minimize the collateral harms their activities cause, crime controllers made no effort to minimize foreseeable racial disparities. Although automakers and builders are involved in self-evidently useful activities, the effectiveness of recent crime control policies is far from self-evident. Finally, foreseeable racial disparities in human suffering are, in the late twentieth century, a uniquely undesirable side effect.

Race Matters (1993), the title of Cornel West's recent book reminds us. Howell Raines, a *New York Times* editor, writes of the shame that he and his family felt on meeting a former, much loved family maid thirty-four years after she left them. Her life had been hard, and her opportunities for developing talents and improving material conditions had been few. The family, however, could easily have paid to send her to college, and if they had, her life would have been very different.

Raines writes:

> Mother said at dinner last night, "If we had just known, we could have done something." Mary Jo said: "Well, how could we not have known?"
>
> Yes, precisely, how could we not have known—and how can we not know of the carnage of lives and minds and souls that is going on among young black people in this country today?

In the 1950s, Raines's family may well have been blind to the interests of blacks around them. Government officials in the 1980s cannot credibly claim to have been similarly blind.

Second, and worse, support for repressive crime control policies, with their foreseeable disproportionate impact on blacks, has been national Republican policy at least since the presidential campaigns of Richard Nixon, part of what Thomas Edsall calls "a conservative politics that had the effect of polarizing the electorate along racial lines." The text may be crime. The subtext is race. The infamous Willie Horton ads run to support George Bush's presidential election campaign in 1988, ostensibly a critique of Michael Dukakis's criminal justice policies, again quoting Edsall, "tapped these concerns through a particularly threatening and dangerous archetype: of the black man as the rapist of a white woman."

Third, and perhaps worst of all, the crime control policies of recent years have undermined achievement of the overriding national goal of full unbiased incorporation of black Americans into the nation's social, political, and economic life. No modern social policy subject has received more attention than the black urban underclass, living in pockets of concentrated poverty, unemployment, and disadvantage, in which illegitimacy, teenage pregnancy, single-parent households, and welfare dependency are at record and growing levels. As one indicator of the problems of the black underclass, William Julius Wilson developed an index that shows changes over time in the number of employed males per 100 females for whites and nonwhites. Among whites, the number of employed men per 100 women has been stable or increasing for every age group. Among nonwhites, the number of employed men per 100 women has been declining since 1960 for every age group, with the sharpest declines among those under twenty-five. There is disagreement, especially from radical feminists, about the normative relevance of Wilson's index (after all, it implies that marriage is a good thing), but it captures a commonsense reality. Men who have no jobs, no prospects, and few skills are not attractive candidates for marriage or a long-term relationship.

Particularly since 1980, the effects of crime control policies have been a major contributor to declining levels of lawful employment by young black males. The extraordinary levels of black male involvement with the justice system—far, far higher than twenty years ago—are a serious impediment to the achievement of welfare policy goals. Many disadvantaged black males start out with bleak life chances, and disadvantaged young men ensnared in the criminal justice system have even bleaker prospects. No solution to problems of the urban underclass or, more broadly, of black poverty can succeed if young men are not part of it. The crime problem is no longer simply a criminal justice system concern. Unless America can devise ways to make its crime control policies less destructive of poor black males and poor black communities, there can be no solution to the problems of the black underclass.

The traditional left/right disagreement over whether crime control efforts should concentrate on root causes or on the preventative effects of punishment, exemplified by then Attorney General Richard Thornburgh's acerbic remark at a 1991 "Crime Summit," "We are not here to search for the roots of crime or to discuss sociological theory," is obsolete. The issue is no longer whether social disorganization and economic disadvantage predispose the people affected by them to crime; it is whether crime control policies and justice system practices can be made less socially destructive.

This introduction has three aims: first, to demonstrate that crime control and social welfare policies are inextricably connected; second, to show that blacks disproportionately bear the burdens of the crime control policies of the Reagan and Bush administrations; and third, to sketch the elements of a crime policy that would reduce conflicts with social welfare policies and begin to undo the damage caused by twelve years of indifference.

Social welfare is an elastic term that could encompass virtually any domestic social policy from economic development to prenatal health care. Here I use it more narrowly to refer generally to social programs aimed at improving the living conditions and incomes of disadvantaged people and specifically to programs like Aid to Families with Dependent Children that provide cash payments to enable recipients to cover their basic living costs.

Crime and Social Welfare

Intellectual dishonesty and political cynicism have long characterized both crime control and social welfare policies in the United States. We are unlikely to improve either until we become less cynical and more honest. Both crime and social welfare are conundra, because they provoke conflicting emotions. We are at once afraid and resentful of criminals and yet troubled by our understanding of the miseries that shaped them. We are at once disdainful and resentful of welfare recipients and yet troubled by our understanding of the miseries of their lives, especially the lives of the children.

Welfare dependence elicits different reactions from the stony puritannical side of our national pysche and from the sunny optimistic side. We sympathize with people whose work cannot support them and their children, and yet wonder whether they ought not to have gotten more education or delayed having children until they could afford them. We want to help those in need, without patronizing those who are struggling barely to get by. We want to boost the incomes of those whose work cannot support them, without giving them incentives to work less. We empathize with mothers and children in disadvantaged, single-parent households, but do not want to encourage the births of more such children or the formation of more such households.

Crime likewise elicits contradictory reactions. Crime and fear of crime corrode our collective sense of well-being. We want our streets safe, our homes secure, our children protected. We want government to devise ways to prevent crime, the police to come when we call, the courts to convict wrongdoers, and punishments to work. However, we also know that experiences of physical and sexual abuse, poverty, and single-parent homes as a child are strongly associated with offending as an adult. We wish that children could be spared those experiences, and we wish that erring adults could be helped to become self-supporting, law-abiding citizens.

These all are hard problems without easy answers. That is why, as anyone who has spent time around criminal courts knows, many trial judges' ideological preconceptions disappear soon after they begin hearing cases. Whether newly selected judges are liberal Democrats or conservative Republicans, they are soon disabused of simplistic stereotypes by the suffering of victims, the sadness of the lives of most victims and offenders, and the limited ability of the legal system to rebuild broken lives or make a safer society. (Appellate judges are a different matter; they see lawyers and paper, not defendants; it is far easier to believe in stereotypes when you never see the people they purportedly describe.)

And so it is with the American public. Notwithstanding the sensationalism of media coverage of crime and the simplicities of pandering politicians, the public has the same conflicted reactions to crime and criminals that practitioners do: Crime is inexcusable and should be punished; if we can rehabilitate offenders and make them less likely to offend again, we should, for our sake and theirs.

Most people believe that a deprived background is the primary cause of criminality. According to Julian Roberts of the University of Ottawa, the leading North American authority on research on public opinion about crime, "Gross economic factors predominate in public explanations of crime." A 1989 Gallup survey found that when asked to choose between improving law enforcement and "attacking social and economic problems that lead to crime," 61 percent of a representative national sample of adults would rather attack social problems. Thirty-two percent preferred law enforcement measures. Similarly, the Public Agenda Foundation, a nonprofit research organization that uses focus groups in order to get richer, fuller views of public opinion, found the same thing in Delaware. When asked to identify the most important or major causes of crime, 94 percent cited drug use, followed by a breakdown in family structure (71 percent) and lack of education (67 percent). By contrast, half or fewer cited "the belief that crime pays," "bad or greedy people," or "not enough emphasis on basic law and order."

Similarly, although National Opinion Research Center surveys for many years have shown that large majorities of respondents say they believe that sentences are insufficiently harsh, large majorities of Americans also want prisons to rehabilitate offenders. When the Gallup survey just mentioned asked respondents to choose between punishment and rehabilitation as the primary goal of imprisonment, by 48 percent to 38 percent they chose rehabilitation. When the Public Agenda Foundation asked Delawareans whether the state should "build more prisons and pay for them by raising taxes," only 32 percent answered yes. Yet when the same Delawareans were asked whether taxes should be increased to pay for drug treatment for every drug addict, 67 percent answered yes.

Crime and poverty are part of the human condition and likely always will be. In most Western countries, public safety is not a partisan political issue on which electoral campaigns are based, but is one of the unglamorous continuing responsibilities of government, like public health or public transportation. Public officials, with such expert assistance as is available, work to prevent crime and to manage decent, efficient justice system institutions. In the United States, by contrast, especially in the last twenty years, both criminal justice and social welfare have been converted by conservative politicians from subjects of policy to objects of politics.

Americans have negative feelings and resentments about both subjects, and conservative politicians have exploited them. In doing so, they have relied on racial stereotypes that have fanned the embers of racial enmity. In the politics of racial division, Willie Horton is to crime control as the Welfare Queen is to welfare policy. Willie Horton is known to anyone who lived through the 1988 presidential campaign. The person caricatured by Ronald Reagan in his 1976 campaign for the Republican nomination and in the 1980 general election was Linda Taylor, a Chicago woman who reportedly collected welfare benefits under several aliases and, as mythology has it, traveled to the welfare office in a rented limousine to pick up her checks. Both Willie Horton and Linda Taylor were black.

These two black people were used as metonyms to caricature in their blackness and in their behavior entire areas of government policy. Their blackness reminded voters that in 1991 there were slightly more non-Hispanic black (38.8 percent) than non-Hispanic white (38.1) families among AFDC recipients and that slightly more than half of those admitted to prison that year were black.

Willie Horton and the Welfare Queen communicate to voters that the foreseeable failures of criminal justice and welfare policies are the most important things about them, rather than unhappy but inevitable aspects of human institutions. No program that distributes things of value—export subsidies, public works contracts, subsidized loans to disaster victims, or welfare benefits—can avoid fraud. If men were angels, none would be tempted to take more than is their due, but men are not angels. When the subject is defense contracts or compliance with environmental laws or securities regulations, conservative politicians tend to regard fraud as a predictable but regrettable side effect of otherwise worthy programs. Of course, we should work to prevent, discover, and punish fraud, the argument goes, but we should not let it obscure the value of important programs or policies. Equally foreseeable and regrettable welfare cheating, however, is used to symbolize both the nature and the problems of income maintenance programs for the nonelderly.

Similarly, no program that relies on predictions of human behavior can avoid making bad predictions. To the rue of bankers and merchants, predictions of creditworthiness are often wrong. So are predictions from the Educational Testing Service and college admissions offices about prospective students' academic performance. So are doctors' prognoses about their patients' future health and psychiatrists' predictions about their patients' likely dangerousness to themselves or others. Inevitably, decisions by criminal justice officials are sometimes wrong.

Willie Horton's is a terrible story, but it shows the cynicism of racial politics. Horton, who in 1975 had been convicted of the 1974 murder of a seventeen-year-old boy, failed to return from a June 12, 1986 furlough. In April of the following year, he broke into an Oxon Hill, Maryland, home where he raped a woman and stabbed her companion.

Lee Atwater, George Bush's campaign strategist, decided in 1988 to make Willie Horton a "wedge" issue for the Republicans. Atwater reportedly told a group of party activists that Bush would win the election "if I can make Willie Horton a household name." He reportedly told a Republican gathering in Atlanta, "There's a story about a fellow named Willie Horton who, for all I know, may end up being Dukakis's running mate." For a time, Atwater denied making both widely reported remarks. In 1991, however, when he was dying of cancer, he apologized for the "naked cruelty" of the attacks on Dukakis: "In 1988, fighting Dukakis, I said that I would 'strip the bark off the little bastard' and 'make Willie Horton his running mate.' I am sorry for both statements."

The sad reality is that tragedies like the crimes of Willie Horton are inevitable. So are airplane crashes, 40,000 to 50,000 traffic deaths a year, and Defense Department cost overruns. Every person convicted of a violent crime cannot be held forever. Furloughs are used in most corrections systems as a way to ease offenders back into the community and to test their suitability for eventual release on parole or by commutation. (Another politically awkward truth: The sentences of most prisoners serving life sentences are eventually commuted or otherwise shortened.) While Horton had been granted nine previous furloughs, from each of which he had returned without incident, under a Massachusetts program established in 1972 under a Republican governor, Francis Sargent. The tenth was a disaster, but it should not have been used to exacerbate racial tensions and caricature corrections policies.

Public discourse about crime and social welfare has been debased by the cynicism that made Willie Horton and the Welfare Queen major participants in presidential campaigns. That cynicism has made it difficult to develop sensible public policies.

Policy and Mendacity

Crime control and welfare policies of recent years have been based on false premises. Welfare policies have been based on the premise that benefit levels will allow a modest living standard of safety and decency. They won't, as even a cursory look at benefit levels and policy research shows and as every honest politician knows. Crime control policies have been based on the premise that harsh penalties and escalating prison populations will make Americans safe. They won't, as the accumulated research in this and other countries shows and as every honest politician knows.

Social Welfare

Conservative critiques of social welfare programs focus mainly on Aid to Families with Dependent Children, commonly known as AFDC, and on the claim that experience with AFDC shows that social welfare programs foster dependence, sap character, and provide perverse incentives to recipients to have illegitimate children and to form single-parent households.

Focusing on AFDC is itself a distortion, since AFDC is a tiny part of federal social welfare spending. In 1992, the federal share of AFDC benefits was a little over $12 billion. In 1990, AFDC spending for children totaled $7 billion, and Social Security spending for the elderly exceeded $193 billion. Social Security spending for children totaled $9 billion.

American social welfare policies, notably Medicare and Social Security, have greatly improved the lives of older Americans, who vote. The story concerning children, who do not vote, is not so encouraging. If there is one point on which conservatives and liberals agree, it is that expansion of Social Security coverage and annual cost-of-living–indexed increases in benefits have greatly diminished poverty among the elderly. The percentage among those over sixty-five living in poverty fell from 29.5 percent in 1967 to 12.4 percent in 1991, according to the Census Bureau. Among children, the shift was in the opposite direction: 16.6 percent lived in poverty in 1967, a level that rose to 21.8 percent in 1991.

Most of the details of conservative critiques even of AFDC, such as those in Charles Murray's *Losing Ground* (1984) and Lawrence Mead's *The New Politics of Poverty* (1992), are wrong or misleading, as important recent books by Andrew Hacker and Christopher Jencks show. High rates of illegitimacy among recipients, for example, are often blamed on AFDC. Illegitimacy rates, however, have been rising for twenty-five years, for a variety of reasons, in every racial group and income class. During much of that period, fertility rates (live births per 1,000 women) were declining, but an increasing proportion of births were out of wedlock. The same pattern held for poor women, including AFDC recipients: By 1991, the average AFDC household contained 2.9 people; 42 percent consisted of a woman and one child, and another 30 percent consisted of a woman and two children. For comparison, among all households with children in 1992, 41 percent had one child and 38 percent had two, numbers not much different from those for AFDC families.

The largest percentage increase in illegitimate births between 1980 and 1990 was not among teenage women but among women aged 35 to 39, with the next largest increases among those 40 and over and those aged 30 to 34. In all age groups, the percentage increases in illegitimacy were higher among white women than among blacks. So in the end, the honest conclusion is yes, increasing percentages of children born to AFDC recipients were illegitimate, but they were having fewer children overall, and the patterns mirrored those occurring throughout American society.

Many of the detailed conservative critiques are similarly misleading. But this is a book about crime control policy, not social welfare, and so I do not discuss other examples. Interested readers should consult Andrew Hacker's *Two Nations* (1992) and Christopher Jencks's *Rethinking Social Policy* (1992).

Those arguments, however, obscure the more important point that AFDC is a fundamentally dishonest program premised on the notion that benefits provide an adequate subsistence income. Failure to report additional income is a crime and is the basis of many allegations of cheating by AFDC recipients. The reality, however, is that women cannot raise children in minimum standards of comfort and security on AFDC benefits. This can be seen by contrasting benefit levels with the federal poverty level and by considering a recent study by Kathryn Edin and Christopher Jencks of the household economies of AFDC recipients in Chicago.

In January 1993, not one state provided AFDC benefits for a single-parent household of three people that reached the Bureau of the Census's 1992 poverty threshold of $11,187 ($932 per month) for a household of that size. The median monthly benefit level nationally was $367, ranging from $120 and $164 in Mississippi and Alabama to $703 in Suffolk County, New York, and $923 in Alaska (where living costs are the nation's highest). In Mississippi, AFDC benefits equal 13 percent of the federal poverty level. In only fourteen states did benefits reach even half the federal poverty level.

The inadequacy of AFDC to provide even a poverty-level income should be no surprise. Unlike Social Security, AFDC payments are not adjusted to take account of changes in the Consumer Price Index. As a result, adjusting for inflation, the average monthly benefit per family fell from $644 in 1970 to $388 in 1992, a 40 percent decline.

A critic might argue that focusing on AFDC benefit levels understates recipients' incomes because other federal programs provide support. Some, like Medicaid and Head Start, do provide valuable services but do not put food in children's stomachs, roofs over their heads, or shoes on their feet. The exception is the federal food stamp program, which provides certificates that can be exchanged for food. When food stamps and AFDC benefits are combined, recipients' incomes in Alaska and Hawaii reach the federal poverty level, and those in a few other states exceed 90 percent. But even taking food stamps into account, only in nineteen states do recipients' incomes reach 75 percent of the poverty line. The national median is 70 percent. Thus, the picture changes slightly, but the final conclusion is unchanged: AFDC, augmented by food stamps, does not provide enough money for people to live on.

In 1988 and 1990, Kathryn Edin interviewed fifty women living in Chicago and Cook County about their incomes and expenses. It was not a representative sample. Many women would understandably be reluctant to discuss possibly felonious behavior with a stranger and would be unlikely to cooperate, thereby ruining the representativeness of a scientifically selected sample. Instead, Edin asked people she knew to refer her to AFDC recipients and then moved through networks of acquaintances. Fifty of fifty-nine women contacted were willing to talk to her. As the findings indicate, they were apparently willing to trust her.

Four crucial findings stand out. First, each of the fifty women had outside sources of support, ranging from unreported jobs to support from families to illegal income from prostitution and drug dealing. Second, not one reported all her additional income and support to the welfare authorities, and only four reported any of it. Third, adding together AFDC benefits, food stamps, housing subsidies that a few received, and unreported income, most nonetheless had below-poverty-line incomes, and living standards that few Americans would willingly endure. Fourth, they felt morally entitled to ignore the income-reporting rules because otherwise there was no way they could support their children or improve their and their children's lives through working.

Edin and Jencks concluded that without cheating, an AFDC-dependent big-city mother "will almost inevitably end up in a public shelter." Legal income and outgo just do not match. To reach this conclusion, they looked in detail at the women's finances. Some of the women were slightly better off because they lived in subsidized housing. Of twenty-eight who did not, Edin found that their AFDC checks averaged $327 monthly and their combined rent, heat, and electricity averaged $364. For all fifty mothers, food costs exceeded food stamp allowances by $50 per month. Thus before paying for clothing, laundry, cleaning supplies, school supplies, telephone, transportation, and all the other things besides housing and food that families need, a typical AFDC mother was $90 in the hole each month. These other expenses averaged $351 per month, meaning that the household ran a monthly deficit of $440. Almost all this money came from unreported income.

The fruits of the women's welfare crimes did not include lavish living. Six families escaped absolute deprivation because of earnings from drug dealing and theft, undisclosed support from family or boyfriends, an unreported $8.00-an-hour job, or a $7,000 award in an auto accident. The other forty-four families

> did without things that almost everyone regards as essential. Half lived in very bad neighborhoods. Half lived in badly run-down apartments, where the heat and hot water were frequently out of order, the roof leaked, plaster was falling off the walls, or windows fitted so badly that the wind blew through the apartment in the winter. One in four did without a telephone. . . . Most said their food budgets were too tight for fresh fruit or vegetables.

Edin and Jencks's most powerful finding, however, is that the welfare mothers operated on the same moral principles as do other Americans. They believed they were obligated to feed, dress, house, and love their children. When following welfare rules would make that impossible, they felt entitled to ignore the rules. Many wanted to improve their circumstances by working. When welfare rules denied them any benefit from working, by reducing their benefits dollar-for-dollar, they felt entitled to ignore the income-reporting rule.

The genius of the Edin and Jencks study is its systematic demonstration that AFDC benefits and food stamps do not provide enough money for recipients to live on, a conclusion that should be numerically evident from comparing benefit levels with the poverty level. Edin and Jencks, however, converted numbers into people. Anyone who has struggled to provide for a child or who has been unable to pay for a child's eyeglasses or school trip or videogames or whatever clothes "everyone else" is wearing can empathize with a mother who, month after month, can do few or none of those things.

The scandal of American welfare policy is that policymakers know this. Whether they be cabinet secretaries, Department of

Health and Human Services bureaucrats, legislators, or staffers to congressional subcommittees, and whether they be liberals or conservatives, anyone who has worked with welfare policy knows that benefit levels do not support people in decency and that as a result many or most recipients must cheat to survive. When, therefore, conservative politicians try to define welfare cheating as the central welfare problem and the Welfare Queen as the typical welfare recipient, they are indulging in a particularly cruel form of intellectual dishonesty, and one that disproportionately injures black Americans.

Crime Control Policy

Crime control policy has similarly been debased. For at least twenty-five years, researchers have shown and honest politicians have known that manipulations of penalties have relatively little or no effect on crime rates. In 1993, for example, a National Academy of Sciences report commissioned and paid for by the Reagan administration's Department of Justice, noting that the average prison time per violent crime had *tripled* between 1975 and 1989, asked, "What effect has increasing the prison population had on levels of violent crime?" The answer, "Apparently, very little."

No one doubts that society is safer having some penalties for crime rather than none at all, but that choice is not in issue. On the real-world question of whether increases in penalties significantly reduce the incidence of serious crimes to which they attach, the answer is maybe, a little, at best, but usually not. Minor misconduct is a different matter. Parking patterns do change, for example, when ticketing becomes more common, towing is more often used, or "boots" immobilize illegally parked vehicles. Financial crimes involving extensive planning and calculation likewise are susceptible to influence through penalties. This is why the Internal Revenue Service initiates tax evasion prosecutions each spring, shortly before income tax returns are due, and it is why great prominence is given to securities law and antitrust prosecutions.

The evidence concerning the limited influence of penalties on ordinary crimes against people and property comes from research in many countries on the deterrent and incapacitative effects of penalties, from evaluations of mandatory penalty laws in the

United States, and from governmental surveys in the United States, Canada, Australia, and England of knowledge concerning the effects of penalties.

That the question is not even close is shown by official statements of conservative national governments in other English-speaking democracies. In Margaret Thatcher's England, for example, a 1990 White Paper (an official policy statement of the government), based on three years' study, called for a major overhaul of sentencing laws to emphasize the reduction of sentencing disparities as a primary objective. The government expressed its skepticism about the preventive effects of penalties:

> Deterrence is a principle with much immediate appeal. . . . But much crime is committed on impulse, given the opportunity presented by an open window or unlocked door, and it is committed by offenders who live from moment to moment; their crimes are as impulsive as the rest of their feckless, sad, or pathetic lives. It is unrealistic to construct sentencing arrangements on the assumption that most offenders will weigh up the possibilities in advance and base their conduct on rational calculation.

Canada is the other English-speaking democracy that recently had a conservative government. In Brian Mulroney's Canada, the Committee on Justice and the Solicitor General of the Canadian House of Commons, chaired by a member of Mulroney's party, proposed in February 1993 that Canada shift from an American-style law enforcement approach to crime to a European-style preventative approach. The report observed that "the United States affords a glaring example of the limited impact that criminal justice responses may have on crime. . . . If locking up those who violate the law contributed to safer societies then the United States should be the safest country in the world." Six years earlier, the Canadian Sentencing Commission had premised its recommendations on similar conclusions: "Evidence does not support the notion that variations in sanctions (within a range that could reasonably be contemplated) affect the deterrent value of sentences. In other words, deterrence cannot be used, with empirical justification, to guide the imposition of sentences."

American governments have not always been outside the mainstream of knowledge about the effects and limits of criminal penalties. In 1967, the President's Commission on Law Enforcement and Administration of Justice concluded that measures directed expressly at crime and criminals could have little effect without much larger simultaneous efforts being directed at crime's underlying social and economic causes. "The Commission . . . has no doubt whatever that the most significant action that can be taken against crime is action designed to eliminate slums and ghettos, to improve education, to provide jobs. . . . We will not have dealt effectively with crime until we have alleviated the conditions that stimulate it." In 1978, the National Academy of Sciences Panel on Research on Deterrent and Incapacitative Effects concluded more narrowly, "In summary . . . we cannot assert that the evidence warrants an affirmative conclusion regarding deterrence." The panel's principal consultant on the subject, Daniel Nagin of Carnegie–Mellon University, was more categorical: "The evidence is woefully inadequate for providing a good estimate of the magnitude of whatever effect may exist. . . . Policymakers in the criminal justice system are done a disservice if they are left with the impression that the empirical evidence . . . strongly supports the deterrence hypothesis."

Nonetheless, from 1981 onward, the Reagan and Bush administrations repeatedly called for tougher penalties, mandatory penalties, death penalties, more prisons, and reduced habeas corpus rights—as if those policies would make a safer America. And in arguing for those proposals, they repeatedly made claims that defied well-established knowledge. Three warrant discussion: that the greater use of imprisonment reduces crime rates, that 95 percent of those in prison are violent or other dangerous offenders, and that building prisons saves, not costs, money.

REDUCING CRIME RATES

The clear weight of the evidence in every Western country indicates that tough penalties have little effect on crime rates. In addition, in 1993, after the most exhaustive and ambitious analysis of the subject ever undertaken, the National Academy of Sciences Panel on the Understanding and Control of Violent Behavior concluded that greatly increased use of imprisonment has had little effect on violent crime rates. Recent national administrations, however, on the basis of deceptive and distorted presentations of data, have claimed the contrary. The baldest claims came from Steven D. Dillingham, director during the Bush administration of the Department of Justice's Bureau of Justice Statistics, an agency that should be a nonpartisan source of statistical knowledge concerning criminal justice in America, and from William Barr, attorney general during the Bush administration's final months. At the Attorney General's 1991 Crime Summit, Dillingham claimed that "statisticians and criminal justice researchers have consistently found that falling crime rates are associated with rising imprisonment rates, and rising crime rates are associated with falling imprisonment rates." For authority, he cited the 1978 report of the National Academy of Sciences Panel on Research on Deterrent and Incapacitative Effects which, as I demonstrated a few paragraphs ago, found no such thing. Barr, in a tract entitled "The Case for More Incarceration" that was released late in his administration, made the same claim in much the same language. Because Barr's claims purport to be well documented, I discuss them in some detail.

Before presenting Barr's evidence, a look at data on crime trends provides a necessary backdrop, because Barr's claims refer to it. Figure 1-1 shows police data from the FBI's *Uniform Crime Reports* on aggravated assaults, robberies, burglaries, thefts, and total index crimes from 1970 to 1992. Rates for burglary, theft, and total index crimes have been divided by 10 in order to show trends for all these offenses in a single figure. The broad pattern is of an increase in rates for most crimes until the early 1980s, followed by declines until the mid-1980s and increases thereafter. Among important offenses not shown in Figure 1-1, the homicide rate in 1980 was 10.2 per 100,000 population, falling to 7.9 in 1984 and 1985 and returning to 9.3 in 1992. The rape rate in 1980 was 36.8 per 100,000 and in 1992 was 42.8. Because public attitudes have rightly become less tolerant of assaults and sex offenses, in recent decades most analysts believe that significant parts of the apparent increases for rape and aggravated assault result from the greater likelihood that incidents will be reported to the police and that the police will record them as crimes. That this is so for assaults can be seen by comparing the steadily growing rates for assault with the mild decline for homicide. A homicide is a lethally successful assault. Given the greater availability of ever-more-lethal firearms, the proportion of assaults proving fatal (that is, the ratio of homi-

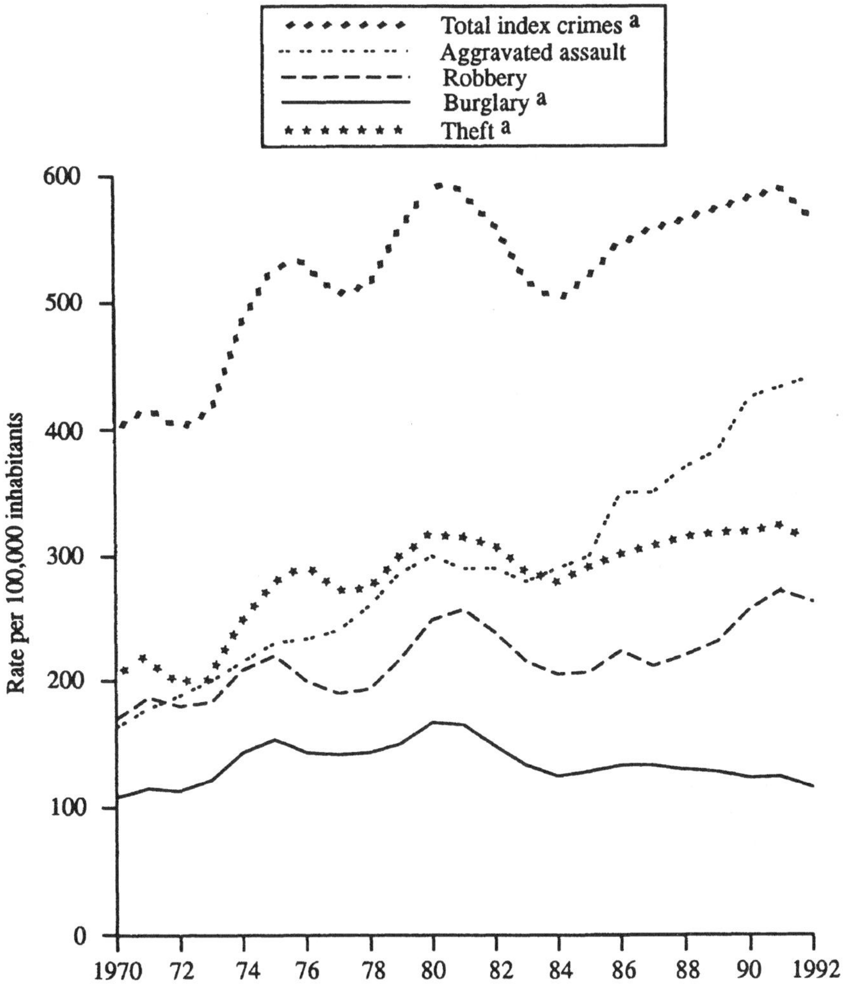

Figure 1-1. U.S. Rates of Aggravated Assault, Robbery, Burglary, Theft, and Total Index Crimes and Offenses Known to Police, 1970–92

[a]Rates for these offenses have been divided by 10 to fit to scale. "Total index crimes" include homicide, rape, robbery, aggravated assault, burglary, theft, and auto theft.

Sources: Maguire, Kathleen, Ann L. Pastore, and Timothy J. Flanagan, *Sourcebook of Criminal Justice Statistics—1992* (Washington, D.C.: U.S. Government Printing Office, 1993); Federal Bureau of Investigation, *Uniform Crime Reports for the United States—1992* (Washington, D.C.: U.S. Government Printing Office, 1993), Table 1, p. 58.

cides to assaults) should be increasing. To the contrary, it has steadily fallen. This suggests that much of the apparent rise in assault rates reflects higher reporting and recording rather than a higher incidence of assault.

Barr's "Case for More Incarceration" came from deceptive presentation of some of the data shown in Table 1-1. Barr explained that Table 1-1 shows a declining incarceration rate in state and federal prisons in the 1960s, when crime rates increased, and sharply increased incarceration rates in the 1970s and 1980s, when violent crime rates also rose but at lower percentage rates; the rates for "all crimes" fell slightly during the 1980s. From this comparison, Barr claimed that reduced use of incarceration led to the substantial increase in rates for "all crimes" between 1960 and 1970 and that the 112 percent increase in incarceration between 1980 and 1990 led to a 2 percent decline in crime rates.

The problems with Barr's analysis can be seen in Table 1-2, which repeats Table 1-1 but in highlighted form fills in missing data so that differences are shown at five- rather than ten-year intervals. It becomes apparent that the years Barr compared were chosen deceptively. For example, had he compared the crime rates in 1985 with those in 1990, a five-year period when the percentage and absolute increases in prison populations were the largest in the nation's history, he would have found it difficult to claim a cause-and-effect relation between incarceration and crime rates. Crime

Table 1-1. Crime and Incarceration Rates, State and Federal Prisons, 1960–90 (per 100,000 population)

	1960	1970	% Change 1960–70	1980	% Change 1970–80	1990	% Change 1980–90
"All crimes"	1,887	3,985	+111	5,950	+49	5,820	−2
Violent crimes	161	364	+126	597	+64	732	+23
Incarceration	117	96	−18	138	+44	292	+112

Sources: William P. Barr, "The Case for More Incarceration" (Washington D.C.: U.S. Department of Justice, Office of Policy Development, 1992), table 2.; Bureau of Justice Statistics, *Prisoners in America,* various years.

Table 1-2. Crime and Incarceration Rates, State and Federal Prisons; 1960–90 (per 100,000 population)

	1960	1965	% Change 1960–65	1970	% Change 1965–70	1975	% Change 1970–75	1980	% Change 1975–80	1985	% Change 1980–85	1990	% Change 1985–90
"All crimes"	1,887	**2,449**	**+30**	3,985	**+63**	**5,282**	**+33**	5,950	**+13**	**5,206**	**−13**	5,820	**+12**
Violent crimes	161	**200**	**+24**	364	**+82**	**482**	**+32**	597	**+24**	**556**	**−7**	732	**+32**
Incarceration	117	**108**	**−8**	96	**−11**	**111**	**+16**	138	**+24**	**200**	**+45**	292	**+46**

Note: **Bold** data not provided in "The Case for More Incarceration."

Sources: William P. Barr, "The Case for More Incarceration." (Washington, D.C.: U.S. Department of Justice, Office of Policy Development, 1992),table 2; FBI, *Uniform Crime Reports,* various years; Bureau of Justice Statistics, *Prisoners in America,* various years.

rates overall rose 12 percent, and violent crime rates climbed more than 32 percent. There is little to celebrate in a one-third increase in violent crime.

Barr also deceptively selected the crime rates to be compared: "From 1960 to 1970, the crime index rate [for all crimes] more than doubled, increasing by 111 percent; from 1970 to 1980, it rose by 49 percent; but from 1980 to 1990, it actually *declined* by 2 percent" (emphasis in original). By focusing on 1980 and 1990 rates for "all crimes," Barr could claim that a decade's more-than-doubling of incarceration rates had produced a slight decrease in crime rates (from 5,950 per 100,000 population to 5,820). Had he focused on changes in violent crime rates during the same years, he would have had to acknowledge (and explain away) a 23 percent increase.

A critic might suggest that it is unfair to subject a politician's numbers to close scrutiny. In this case, however, "The Case for More Incarceration" was more than an unstudied speech by a politician. It was, after all, a formal public statement by the attorney general of the United States. Moreover, it was an official, widely disseminated publication of the U.S. Department of Justice, and as an accompanying press release made clear, it was prepared under the direction of Stephen R. Schlesinger, for many years director of the department's Bureau of Justice Statistics. Between them, Schlesinger and Steven Dillingham, whose Barr-like claims were quoted earlier, were directors of the bureau through most of the Reagan and Bush presidencies. They are the most sophisticated conservative students of criminal justice statistics in America, and Barr's claims are theirs. Thus, the "Case" is probably the best statement of their position that can be made. It does not provide a very strong basis for explaining why, alone among the governments of the major English-speaking countries, the United States government long claimed that harsh law-and-order policies would decrease crime rates.

WHO IS IN PRISON?

A second defense of law-and-order imprisonment policies is the claim that any sympathy with prisoners is misplaced because the vast majority of those sent to prison are dangerous people who have committed very serious crimes. In speeches, the claim is usually made that only 5 percent of offenders are nonviolent first offenders. In writing, the statements are slightly more careful. Thus Steven Dillingham at the Attorney General's 1991 Crime Summit: "National statistics reveal that 95 percent of state prisoners have been convicted of violent crimes, or are recidivists." This suggests that prisons are used parsimoniously and are reserved for violent and other serious offenders. That impression is false, for two reasons.

First, the combination of violent offenders and "recidivists" in one category suggests that both are equally threatening. They are not. Numerous minor nonviolent offenders have been convicted before of theft, shoplifting, passing bad checks, selling small amounts of marijuana or other drugs, or other trifling crimes. This makes them recidivists, but neither very important nor very scary ones, and certainly not ones who need to be held in expensive prisons.

So what proportion of the 95 percent are violent offenders, most of whom presumably deserve to be in prison, and what proportion are recidivists who may or may not deserve to be in prison? We know the answer for 1991, the latest year for which sufficiently detailed national data have been published. In that year, 46.6 percent of those in state prisons on a census date had been convicted of violent crimes (another 25 percent had been convicted of property crimes, 21 percent of drug crimes, and 7 percent of "public-order" crimes). And of those in prison in 1991, 38 percent had not been incarcerated before. In other words, well over half of state prisoners had been convicted of crimes not involving violence, and two-fifths had never before been sentenced to jail or prison. The claim that only 5 percent of prisoners are nonviolent first offenders begins to take on a different, less threatening, hue.

Second and more important, the 95 percent claim confuses prison populations with prison admissions. Because people convicted of violent crimes deservedly receive longer sentences than do people convicted of most property crimes, they remain in prison longer. On any day, the proportion of violent prisoners among those in prison is larger than the proportion of violent offenders among those admitted to prison. The proportion of those admitted to prison for violent crimes has been declining steadily (down from 42 percent in 1977 to 35 percent in 1985 to 27 percent in 1990).

Perhaps the most extreme claims about the threatening nature of modern prisoners were made by John DiIulio of Princeton University, who ought to know better. In a January 26, 1994, column in the *Wall Street Journal,* DiIulio wrote, "More than 95 percent of state prisoners are violent criminals, repeat criminals (with two or more felony convictions), or violent repeat criminals." Pretty scary, if true, but it is not true. Here is what the U.S. Department of Justice had to say in its report on the 1991 survey of state prisoners: "About 38% of all inmates had not been incarcerated before: 19% were sentenced for the first time [hence this was a first conviction]; 19% had [previously been sentenced] to probation." DiIulio's numbers do not add up.

In thinking rationally about imprisonment policies, what we should want to know is who goes to prison, not what percentage of those in prison are "nonviolent first offenders." We know the answer for 1990. Twenty-seven percent were violent offenders; 32 percent each were property and drug offenders; 8 percent were "public-order" offenders, and 1 percent were "other." There is lots of room for debate about the wisdom of contemporary patterns of prison use.

THE COST-EFFECTIVENESS OF IMPRISONMENT

The final disingenuous explanation for why more imprisonment is appropriate is that incarcerating offenders saves money and that building more prisons will save more money. As former Attorney General Barr put it in the 1992 "Case for More Incarceration", "inadequate prison space *costs* money" (emphasis in original). This implausible proposition is based on a series of discredited cost-benefit analyses of prison use. The first, by Edwin Zedlewski of the Justice Department's National Institute of Justice, claimed that locking up one additional prisoner, net of criminal justice system and prison costs, would save $430,000. His estimate was based on the assumption that each confined offender would otherwise have committed 187 offenses and thus that each offense avoided would save $2,300. His use of the number 187, taken from a RAND Corporation survey in the late 1970s in which prisoners were asked about their past criminality, involved, however, a number of confusions. It was an average, for example, and half the inmates surveyed admitted to offending at less than one-tenth the average rate. More important, because only a small percentage of offenders are highly active, as more people are sent to prison, their average criminal activity declines. The RAND survey was done in the 1970s when the average state prisoner was a much more serious offender than today.

Franklin Zimring and Gordon Hawkins of the University of California at Berkeley soon published a rejoinder to Zedlewski's analysis, pointing out his mistakes. They also reran his analysis by applying it to 1977 FBI data on reported crime and showed that, given Zedlewski's assumptions, the 237,000 increase in the American prison population between 1977 and 1986 should have "reduce[d] crime to zero on incapacitation effects alone . . . On this account, crime disappeared some years ago." Zedlewski's analysis lost all credibility, except in the eyes of the U.S. Department of Justice.

A series of later, similar analyses were made by John DiIulio of Princeton University and Mark A. R. Kleiman and David Cavanagh of Harvard's Kennedy School of Government. These studies used methods and assumptions similar to Zedlewski's and reached similarly implausible conclusions. The Kleiman and Cavanagh anaysis, though never published, was cited by Barr as demonstrating "benefits of incarcerating that *one inmate* for a year at between $172,000 and $2,364,000" (emphasis in original).

The Kleiman–Cavanagh findings in turn were premised on a farfetched cost–benefit analysis of imprisonment by economist Mark Cohen of Vanderbilt University. Cohen attempted to calculate the "true" cost of crimes by taking account of the economic value of victims' "pain and suffering." To do this, he obtained data from jury awards in accident cases and applied the resulting dollar estimates to crime. There were, however, two fundamental problems in doing this, and they paralleled Zedlewski's mistakes. First, contested tort actions that are resolved by jury trials are that small percentage of cases in which the liability is so clear, the plaintiff so sympathetic, or the damages sought so large as to make worthwhile the time and expense of years-long civil litigation. In other words, such cases are far from representative of run-of-the-mill accident claims or, by implication, of ordinary crimes. Second, civil damage awards are inflated to take account of enormous transactions costs, including attorneys' fees and expenses that frequently equal one-third to one-half of any award.

On the basis of Cohen's estimates, raised to take account of inflation since the time of Cohen's analysis, Barr claimed that the total cost in 1990 to victims of ordinary crimes (that is, excluding white-collar crimes, environmental crimes, and so forth) was $140 billion. That this is somewhat exaggerated may be seen by comparing it with an estimate prepared by Barr's own Bureau of Justice Statistics—direct economic losses to victims in 1992 of $17.6 billion.

None of these financial or empirical claims about the need for or benefits of harsh crime control policies withstands scrutiny. Even Princeton's DiIulio eventually backed away from the most exaggerated claims:

> A debate has raged over the cost-effectiveness of imprisonment. This debate has been waged as a numbers game, with conservatives citing figures to show that "prison pays," and liberals citing figures to insist that it doesn't. The truth, we find, lies in between, though arguably closer to the liberal than to the conservative view.

Reasonable people disagree over what penalties should attach to what crimes and over the general directions that crime control efforts should follow. There are, however, important costs to alternative choices, and one of the most important is the effects of policies of historically unprecedented harshness on members of minority groups. The claims of the Reagan and Bush administrations notwithstanding, these are and should be hard choices, not easy ones.

The Burden on Black Americans

American crime policies since 1980 have had disastrous consequences for black Americans. On any given day, blacks are six to seven times more likely than whites to be in jail or prison. Astonishingly high percentages of young black males are under the control of the criminal justice system. These patterns, all of which have worsened steadily since 1980, do not result from increases in the proportions of serious crimes committed by blacks.

Black Americans are far more likely than whites to be in prison or jail. Although blacks make up less than 13 percent of the U.S. population, they comprise nearly half of the populations of U.S. prisons and jails and, in recent years, more than half of those sent to jails and prisons. Most people's first reaction is to compare 13 percent of the general population with 50 percent of the prison population and to be surprised that black imprisonment rates are four times higher than they ought to be. Although the surprise is warranted, the calculation is misleading because it understates racial disparities.

What should be compared is the likelihood, relative to their numbers, that black and white Americans will be locked up. In 1991, the black rate was 6.47 times higher than the white rate. Among black Americans, 1,895 per 100,000 were in prison or jail on the counting dates. Among white Americans, 293 per 100,000 were in prison or jail. Between December 1991 and December 1993, the number of jail and prison inmates grew by more than 150,000. Both the incarceration rates by race and the black–white differentials have also grown.

Another, even more remarkable pattern of black–white disparities has been revealed by a series of studies attempting to determine the proportions of blacks under the control of the criminal justice system on a given day. Of all the people in prison or jail, on probation or parole, or released on bail or recognizance pending trial, what percentage are black? The first such analysis, in 1990 by Marc Mauer of The Sentencing Project, showed that nationally 23 percent of black males aged 20 to 29 were under justice system control. Table 1-3 shows the findings of five such recent studies.

Two studies done at the state level have been widely reported. The Correctional Association of New York found that 23 percent of black males aged 20 to 29 were under justice system control in 1990. California's Center on Juvenile and Criminal Justice found in 1990 that 33 percent of black males aged 20 to 29 were under justice system control.

Two studies at the city level were carried out by Jerome Miller of the National Center on Institutions and Alternatives. In Washington, D.C., Miller found that 42 percent of black males aged 18 to 35 were under justice system control in 1991. In Baltimore in

Table 1-3. Percentages of Young Black Males Under Justice System Control

Source	Area	Coverage	Year	Ages	Percent
Correctional Association of New York (1990)	New York State	JPPP	1990	20–29	23
Mauer (1990, The Sentencing Project)	United States	JPPP	1990	20–29	23
Center on Juvenile and Criminal Justice (1990)	California	JPPP	1988/89	20–29	33
Miller (1992a, National Center on Institutions and Alternatives)	Washington, D.C.	JPPP, PTAW	1991	18–35	42
Miller (1992b, National Center on Institutions and Alternatives)	Baltimore	JPPP, PTAW	1991	18–35	56

JPPP = Jail, prison, probation, parole.
PTAW = Pretrial release or sought on arrest warrant.

1991, the corresponding figure for 18- to 35-year old black males was 56 percent.

All of these estimates are based on readily available statistical data. Some of them may be slightly exaggerated because of the double counting of people who are simultaneously in two corrections populations. Louis W. Jankowski, a senior career statistician at the Bureau of Justice Statistics, however, estimates the effects of double counting at between 3 and 10 percent and probably nearer the lower estimate: "The number of inmates double counted may be small relative to the total population under correctional control." This is because there is little chance of double counting between people in prison and jail or between people in jail and released before trial. There is some chance of overlap between offenders in confinement and those in parole and probation caseloads. People committing new offenses may be in jail and, until news of the arrest reaches a probation or parole officer, may continue to be counted in a supervision population. However, because new arrests typically result in revocation proceedings and because justice system records in most jurisdictions have been computerized, the likely overlap is small.

In addition, there is a special problem with the city analyses. If the justice system control percentage—56 percent in Baltimore—is thought of as a fraction—56/100 of young blacks—the numerator and denominator will not match up. First, the Census Bureau is known to undercount mobile, inner-city young people, which means that the denominator is too small. There are more young blacks in Baltimore than the Census Bureau knows about. Second and more important, the numerator is too large because it includes all young blacks under justice system control, whether they are residents of Baltimore City, Baltimore County, the District of Columbia, or anywhere else.

The problems of double counting and, in the city studies, with identifying the relevant populations to be compared do not in any significant way deprive these studies of their force. Even if the correct national level of justice system control of black 20 to 29 year olds is *only* 21 percent or the Baltimore 18 to 35-year-old figure is *only* 46 percent, they still are astonishing figures that should disturb anyone who thinks about them.

The punishment patterns underlying those different rates are explained in Chapters 2 and 3. Since 1980, the black incarceration rate has been rising much faster than the white rate; the proportions of blacks among those admitted to prisons and jails have been climbing to historic highs; and the proportions of blacks among those held in prisons and jails have been growing also to historic highs.

Justifying the Unjustifiable

It seems a bit odd in the 1990s to have to explain why the adoption of policies with foreseeable racially disparate impacts is a bad thing. Avoiding undesirable side effects and rejecting iatrogenic policy options seem obviously right. Consider, for example, the questions of registering of persons who are HIV positive and of notifying family members and other inmates of the infection. Homosexuals have consistently opposed registration laws and notification policies because of fears that they would be stigmatizing and would adversely affect them as a group. Public health officials' views have changed over time. In the mid-1980s, many supported registration policies and contact tracing. More recently, because registration might deter people from being tested for HIV, most public health officials have been opposed, and few such policies have been adopted, in part from respect for homosexuals' concerns about their disparate impact.

Other examples are available of policy realms in which the desirability of avoiding disparate impacts is generally seen as self-evident. In employment discrimination law, proof of a disparate impact on women or members of minority groups is enough to create inferences of discriminatory intent and to shift burdens of proof. Likewise, on constitutional grounds, statistical evidence that jury-selection criteria or processes create racial disparities is enough to create an inference of bias and, often, to win a jury-composition lawsuit.

As a matter of policy, de facto discrimination on racial or ethnic grounds is as damaging to the people affected as is de jure discrimination; the law's failure to treat them identically results not from a judgment that one form of discrimination is less harmful than another but from practical concerns. Whether or not remediable by the courts, many claims of innocent de facto discrimination meet with skeptical reactions from bystanders.

There are a number of other ways to think about the ethical justification of law-and-order crime policies' disparate impact on blacks. The criminal law's mens rea analyses, for example, offer the law's most highly developed schema for analyzing culpability and moral responsibility. In the criminal law, purpose and knowledge are equally culpable states of mind. An action taken with a purpose to kill is no more culpable than an action taken with some other purpose in mind but with knowledge that a death will probably result. Blowing up an airplane to kill a passenger is equivalent to blowing up an airplane to destroy a fake painting and thereby to defraud an insurance company, knowing that the passenger will be killed. Both are murder. Most people would find the latter killing more despicable. By analogy with the criminal law, the responsibility of the architects of contemporary crime control policies is the same as if their primary goal had been to lock up disproportionate numbers of young blacks.

The architects do no better under criminal law actus reus analysis. Although the common law imposed no criminal responsibility for harms caused by omissions, unless the actor put the victim at risk or had some duty regarding that person's care, this is almost universally seen as a retrograde doctrine. If with no significant risk to himself a person can save a child from drowning in a shallow pool, why should he not be expected to do so? In any case, whatever the criminal law provides, most people would hold the bystander morally responsible. If the crime control architects could have adopted policies that would not have damaged the lives of so many young black Americans, as of course they could have done, why should they not have done so? Are they not morally responsible for having omitted to do so?

One last argument using a criminal-law analogy involves the defense of necessity. In most American legal systems, an action that produces harm can be justified if a greater harm is thereby avoided. A classic example is of people who open a swollen dam and divert its flow into a valley, thereby destroying a farm and perhaps killing its inhabitants, in order to prevent the dam's breaking and jeopardizing an entire town and its inhabitants. Whether the defense of necessity applies depends on balancing the harms caused and avoided. Given the absence of credible evidence for believing that harsh crime and drug policies would significantly reduce crime rates, the harms that those policies have caused to black Americans cannot be justified.

There are thus a number of modes of analysis that condemn the conscious adoption of policies foreseeably detrimental to blacks. One final step, however, is to examine three defenses that have been or could be put forward by conservative crime controllers.

The "Don't blame us" defense is that in a democracy, public officials respond to the fears and preferences of the electorate and, in the 1980s, the "public" was concerned about crime and drug abuse. The public wanted harsh penalties and a drug war, and the federal government (and those state governments that followed the federal lead) were simply, and rightly, giving the public what it wanted. In his *No Escape* (1991), Princeton's DiIulio argued that "the sensitivity of politicians to the will of a persistent majority of their constituents should be a cause for celebration, not lamentation."

The defect of "Don't blame us" is that it gets the causal chain backward. Throughout the 1980s and earlier, conservative politicans used "law and order" (remember Willie Horton?) as an emotional issue to curry favor with voters, in effect heightening their fears and then promising to assauge them. Common-law and street criminals do not vote very much and do not attract much sympathy from those who do vote. It is easy to provoke voters' fears, and, as both Michael Dukakis's fumbling of the crime issue in the 1988 presidential campaign and the immobilizing fears of many elected officials to be portrayed as "soft on crime" attest, it is difficult for others to dampen them.

Almost all the premises underlying the "Don't blame us" defense were wrong. First, as explained above, there is no basis for claiming a good-faith belief that harsh crime control policies can achieve their ostensible objectives.

Second, although politicians' harping on rising crime rates made the public believe that crime was increasing, all of the evidence points the other way. FBI data on reported crimes showed that reported rates of most serious crimes fell from 1980 through 1986 and slowly rose thereafter (during the height of toughened crime control initiatives) to levels that in 1993 for most offenses remained below those in 1980. The other source of national data on crime trends—data on victimization published by the Bureau of Justice Statistics of the U.S. Department of Justice—showed that victimization rates for all serious crimes, except murder, fell throughout the 1980s. (Murder rates did decline during the 1980s, but murder victims do not participate in victimization surveys.) Most crime statistics experts consider the victimization data a more dependable indicator of crime trends because they are not affected by changes in victims' willingness to report crimes to the police or in police willingness to record reported incidents as crimes. Although the data sources have different strengths, weaknesses, and uses, the critical finding for present purposes is that neither shows a significant overall increase in crime since 1980.

Third, politicians' claims that the public "wanted" tougher crime policies were disingenuously based on misleading poll results. It is true that, when asked simplistic questions like "Are the sentences that judges impose too harsh, too lenient, or about right?" most people answer "too lenient," and they have done so for as long as such questions have been asked. Relying on such results as the basis for policy is no more warranted than relying on similar, uninformed, off-the-cuff answers to pollsters' questions about foreign policy or support for DNA research. The problem is not that people answering pollsters do not know what they think. It is that people's uninformed first reactions often change once they give informed consideration to a problem.

A huge body of public opinion data is available that shows that Americans have complicated opinions about crime and punishment, just as most practitioners do. Most people want to see offenders punished, for example, but they also want to see them rehabilitated. Americans believe that many offenders should be sentenced to meaningful community-based penalties rather than to prison. Americans believe that a disadvantaged upbringing is the primary cause of crime and want to see efforts made to rehabilitate offenders. Surveys show that people who do not want their taxes increased to pay for more prisons do support tax increases to pay for drug treatment and other rehabilitative programs. Americans are not alone in harboring ambivalent feelings about offenders. Similar results were found in Australia, England and Wales, Canada, Germany, Scotland, and the Scandinavian countries. Complicated problems elicit complicated reactions.

The point is not that Americans lack punitive instincts. They have them. But they also have other more generous instincts that policymakers can encourage or ignore. The architects of recent crime control policies chose to ignore them.

A second defense, "It's not unconstitutional," is that despite their foreseeable disparate impact on blacks, punitive crime control strategies were not wrong, in the sense that they were not unconstitutional. This is a non sequitur. It is true that since *Washington v. Davis,* 426 U.S. 229 (1976), an intent to discriminate must be shown to establish a civil rights claim under the Constitution. Since courts will not look behind the ostensible crime- and drug-use reduction goals claimed for the anticrime and antidrug policies, the unconstitutionality claim can be set aside. However, that a policy is not unconstitutional does not make it right, or even not wrong. One need only look at the U.S. Supreme Court's death penalty jurisprudence to see that law and morality sometimes march in different directions.

Last, there is the "We are concerned about black victims and black communities" defense. As Attorney General Barr put it in his *Case for More Incarceration,* perhaps in ill-chosen words, "The benefits of increased incarceration would be enjoyed disproportionately by black Americans." Fleshed out, the argument is that most crime is intraracial, that drug trafficking is associated with guns, gangs, and violence, that drug markets ruin neighborhoods and make it nearly impossible for law-abiding people to enjoy the peace and stability that should be every person's right, and that wars on crime and drugs were launched to vindicate that right. All the empirical statements that precede the last comma are true. What is false is the final clause. The cure does not follow from the diagnosis, as previous parts of this chapter demonstrate.

A variation on the concern-for-black-victims defense is the assertion that black inner-city residents want the police to close down street drug markets and to arrest drug dealers and that failing to do these things would be a form of bias against blacks. This also is a half-true argument. No one wants to live in a neighborhood in which drug dealing is common, in which gangs are active, in which children cannot be allowed to go outdoors, in which ordinary citizens feel at risk. Minority citizens want help from the police in dealing with acute problems, even if the young men and women who will be arrested are their neighbors' sons and daughters, nieces and nephews. In a crisis, people need help and ask for it, and the police are often the only source of available help. There is little reason to doubt that minority citizens want order brought to their communities.

Requesting help in a crisis and supporting harsh crime and drug control strategies with racially disparate impacts, however, are not the same thing. The relevant distinction is between acute and chronic problems. Recent crime control policies treat crime and drug trafficking as if they were only acute problems: Apply a deterrence and incapacitation poultice and the problem will be solved. But inner-city crime and drug abuse and related social pathologies are not acute problems amenable to easy solutions. Rather, they are symptoms of chronic social and economic conditions shaping disadvantaged inner-city communities and the life chances of the people in them.

Law-abiding minority citizens would much prefer policy solutions that preponderantly treated crime and drug abuse as chronic rather than as acute conditions. This may explain, for example, why the Congressional Black and Hispanic Caucuses opposed the harsh crime bills under consideration in the winter of 1993/94 and why they have consistently favored more spending on drug treatment, early childhood programs, and crime prevention initiatives. A recent *New York Times* story reports on a January 1994 meeting of black politicians, academics, ministers, and civil rights leaders to consider solutions to crime problems affecting black communities: "While they agreed that the problem was spinning out of control, they condemned the solution most often offered to deal with it: stiffer prison sentences and more jail cells." Representative John Conyers, Jr., observed that "we've got to take the initiative . . . to move government and the country away from this simplistic approach to the crime problem."

That people in frustration and desperation want to see their neighbors' children and their children's friends locked up (virtually no one wants to see his or her own children incarcerated) does not mean that they would not prefer policies that made the locking up less likely. Given the choice, minority citizens would greatly prefer social policies that made it much less likely that so many minority young people would wind up living lives in which crime and drugs are common. Most parents I know want good lives and rich opportunities for their children and for other people's children. People who live in disadvantaged minority communities do not hope for less for their children. "Hello Brother—What a Wonderful World," a staple in Louis Armstrong's repertory, gets it right:

> You can travel all around the world and back.
> You can fly or sail or ride a railroad track.
> But no matter where you go—
> You're gonna find that people have the same things on their mind.
>
> A man wants to work for his pay.
> A man wants a place in the sun.
> A man wants a gal proud to say that she'll become his loving wife.
> He wants the chance to give his kids a better life.

There is some evidence to support the preceding speculations. First, there are chilling reports that large percentages of black Americans see contemporary crime and drug policies as a near-genocidal effort by whites to control blacks. University of Chicago law professor Norval Morris describes a seminar with black maximum security inmates in Stateville Prison in Illinois in which patterns of race, crime, and punishment were discussed. Of twenty-six prisoners present, only three doubted that American drug and crime policies were a genocidal (their word) assault on blacks by whites. In their 1991 book *Chain Reaction: The Impact of Race, Rights, and Taxes on American Politics,* Thomas and Mary Edsall describe focus groups held in the late 1980s under both Democratic and Republican party auspices; in every session with black participants, the view was expressed that crime and drug control policies were a deliberate effort to destabilize black communities. A Democratic pollster, Ed Reilly, reported a belief among northern, urban blacks "that there is an organized approach to keep them [blacks] isolated from mainstream America, that the government system is rigged to keep them in poverty." A *New York Times*/WCBS-TV poll in 1990 found that 29 percent of blacks (only 5 percent of whites) thought it was true or might be true that the HIV virus was "deliberately created in a laboratory to infect black people," that 60 percent (16 percent of whites) believed it was true or might be true that government makes drugs available "in poor black neighborhoods in order to harm black people," and that 77 percent of blacks believed the government "singles out and investigates black officials in order to discredit them." (The poll results were reported in an October 29, 1990 *Times* article by Jason DeParle.)

Second, evidence from public opinion surveys over many years shows that much larger percentages of blacks than whites believe that the government has social welfare responsibilities to its citizens. In 1986 in surveys conducted as part of the University of Michigan's National Election Studies, blacks by 64 to 36 percent said they believed the federal government had a responsibility to guarantee every adult a job and a good standard of living (whites came out the other way, by 66 to 34 percent). During most of the 1980s, whites split evenly on whether the government should increase spending for improved services; blacks were in favor by margins as high as 77 to 23 percent (These data are reported in

Warren E. Miller and Santa A. Traugott's *American National Election Studies* [1989]). According to National Opinion Research Center surveys conducted from 1975 to 1989 and summarized in a book by Floris Wood, among blacks, 53 to 70 percent believed that the government has a "special obligation to help blacks improve their living standards." Only 12 to 20 percent of whites agreed, and 60 percent of whites disagreed. With similar and sometimes sharper racial contrasts, blacks supported and whites opposed more spending on welfare, on income redistribution, and on improving conditions in cities.

Crime and drug abuse do disproportionately affect disadvantaged minority communities. Amelioration of their effects should be a paramount policy priority. So much is clear. Racially sensitive policies would, however, take account of foreseeable racially disparate impacts as well as the policies' likely instrumental effects.

All that is left is politics. The War on Drugs and the set of harsh crime control policies in which it was enmeshed were undertaken to achieve political, not policy, objectives. It is the adoption for political purposes of policies with foreseeable disparate impacts, the use of disadvantaged black Americans as means to achieving politicians' electoral ends, that must in the end be justified. It cannot.

Doing Less Harm

Basic changes in the social and economic conditions that shape the lives of disadvantaged black Americans and cause their disproportionate involvement in crime are beyond the power of the criminal justice system. However, although we do not know much about using the criminal justice system to do good, we do know how to change its policies so that they do less harm. Such a harm-reduction strategy would have six elements.

First, be honest. Admit that no war against crime will ever be won, that criminal sanctions have at most a modest influence on short-term crime rates, and that locking up many more people is not likely to produce a demonstrably safer America. Crime is part of all human societies and is shaped by the ways in which societies organize themselves. If crime rates in America are to decline in the long term, the causes will lie in major changes in social policies toward job creation, income maintenance, medical care, housing, education, drugs, and firearms.

If the insight that crime rates are the product of fundamental social and economic forces were to be ignored, it would be easy to blame the Reagan and Bush administrations for increasing crime rates. Here is how the argument would go. Both administrations openly and successfully fought to reduce federal funding for social, educational, and housing programs and for aid to cities. Authorized federal spending on low-income housing programs, for example, fell by 75 percent between 1981 and 1989. Presidents Reagan and Bush promoted a strategy of federal disinvestment in the inner cities, which accelerated their deterioration and diminished the scope and quality of urban public services. The Reagan and Bush administrations thereby increased criminogenic pressures in the cities.

The only reason that this Republican crime-causing process is not widely recognized is that Republican crime control strategies simultaneously raised the number of people in jail or prison from under 500,000 in 1980 to nearly 1.5 million in 1994. Crime rates in 1993 were at about the same level as in 1980. There are two plausible explanations for the contrast between stable crime rates and soaring incarceration rates. The first is a proposition that Reagan and Bush administration spokesmen would reject, that increased incarceration has had little effect on crime rates. Second, crime rates would have risen to unprecedented levels between 1980 and 1993, but increased incarceration prevented this, in effect soaking it up. But why would crime rates have climbed to unprecedented levels? Something must have happened during the 1980s that would have caused more crimes to take place. Disinvestment in the cities and in social services for poor people are the most probable answers. Increased violence surrounding drug trafficking, a result of the punitive policies of the War on Drugs, no doubt would be part of the explanation, as would the refusal, for political reasons, to adopt serious gun control measures. Thus, if the second explanation is the right one, increased incarceration has prevented the rise in crime that the social and drug policies of the Reagan and Bush administrations would otherwise have caused.

There is probably some truth to this Reagan-and-Bush-policies-cause-crime argument. Crime rates are highest in the most disadvantaged neighborhoods and policies that create more disadvantaged neighborhoods and make the existing ones worse are likely to be criminogenic. The problems of poverty, social disadvantage, and the black underclass existed, however, when Ronald Reagan took office, and they would exist had he never taken office. There are no quick or easy solutions to crime, and we debase policy discussions when we pretend there are.

As long as politicians continue to make cynical and disingenuous appeals to the deepest fears and basest instincts of the American people, and to make crime-preventive promises that police, courts, and prisons cannot keep, the prospects of reducing racial disparities in the criminal justice system will remain small. There is considerable evidence in this country and others that most people are deeply ambivalent about crime, fearful and wanting wrongdoers to be punished and yet sympathetic and wanting wrongdoers to be rehabilitated. Appeals to only one side of that ambivalence with allusions to Willie Horton and similarly visceral and powerful stereotypes make honest policymaking impossible.

Second, think about the foreseeable effects of crime control policies on members of minority groups. When policies are likely to burden members of minority groups disproportionately and, through them, their families and communities, reconsider the policies. One extreme example is the 100-to-1 distinction made between crack and powder cocaine in federal law and the federal sentencing guidelines. Presumptive sentences vary directly with the amount of illicit substance involved, and the guidelines direct judges to multiply quantities of crack by 100 in order to determine the amount on which the sentence will be based. The problem is that crack, though it is pharmacologically indistinguishable from powder, tends to be used and distributed by blacks, and powder by whites. One federal court of appeals reported that 95 percent of federal crack defendants are black and 40 percent of powder defendants are white. As could have been expected, blacks convicted of crack offenses receive much harsher sentences in federal courts than do whites convicted of powder offenses.

Another extreme example is the War on Drugs. All sources of relevant knowledge, ranging from experienced police narcotics squad members to ethnographers studying inner-city street life, supported predictions that the enemy troops would consist mostly of young minority males. Any experienced police official could have predicted that policies of wholesale arrests of dealers would sweep up mostly young minority user-dealers in the cities. This is not necessarily because more members of minorities use or sell drugs, but because arrests are easier to make in disorganized inner-city areas where many minority dealers operate than they are in middle- and working-class neighborhoods where white dealers operate. As could have been expected, the number of blacks in prison for drug crimes has risen sharply. In 1986, among white non-Hispanic state prisoners, 8 percent had been convicted of drug crimes, compared with 7 percent of black non-Hispanic prisoners. By 1991, the white percentage had increased by half to 12 percent, and the black percentage had increased by three and one-half times to 25 percent.

The examples of policies with foreseeable racially disparate effects could go on and on and include the effects of refusing to make drug abuse treatment available on demand, underinvestment in other treatment programs, greater use of capital punishment, and sharp increases in penalties for crimes for which blacks are disproportionately likely to be arrested. Asking whether contemplated policies will adversely affect blacks and other members of minority groups will seldom provide easy answers, because the problems that crime poses are difficult. Much serious crime, for example, is intraracial, and the interests of black victims, especially of violent crimes, need to be considered. Nonetheless, routinely asking the race-effects question should provide some easy answers: The 100-to-1 crack/powder cocaine punishment differential is hard to defend once challenged. So is the death penalty: Death rows are nearly as disproportionately black as are prisons generally. At least in Georgia, research whose validity even the death penalty–promoting U.S. Supreme Court in *McCleskey v. Georgia,* 107 S. Ct. 1756 (1987) accepts, shows that blacks who killed whites were, in that state, twenty-two times more likely to be sentenced to death than were blacks who killed blacks.

Third, establish sentencing guidelines with strong presumptive upper limits on punishment severity. Experience with guidelines in the United States has been mixed. Some guidelines are broad and flexible and place few constraints on judges' discretion. Others are narrow and rigid and greatly constrain judges' options. Most have reduced sentencing disparities and racial differences in sentencing. Some are followed most of the time; others are often ignored. In every system on which data are available, we know that judges much more often impose sentences less severe than the guidelines direct than more severe, and that sentences more severe than the guidelines direct are everywhere uncommon.

The worst injuries that biased sentencing can produce are cases in which racial bias or judicial idiosyncrasy results in the imposition of aberrantly severe penalties. In American systems of indeterminate sentencing that existed in every state before 1976, maximum lawful penalties were often extremely long. Twenty-year, thirty-year, and life maximums were not uncommon. The rationale was that the maximum had to cover the worst imaginable instance of any crime and had to allow for sentence reductions for good behavior (often one-third to one-half the maximum) and for release on parole (eligibility often ripened after serving one-third the sentence). Thus a thirty-year sentence meant ten to twenty years served, and sometimes less if good-behavior time reduced both maximum and minimum terms. In many modern determinate sentencing systems, good-behavior time has been reduced and parole release eliminated. In the federal system, for example, a nominal twenty-year sentence means at least seventeen years in prison. In both indeterminate and determinate sentencing systems, a willfully biased judge can easily impose an exceedingly harsh sentence, but the risk is greater under determinate sentencing.

There are two solutions. First, cut the statutory maximums. The difficulty is that a move to cut a twenty-five year maximum for burglary to a more realistic five years will open legislators to accusations of reducing sentences and being soft on crime. The second solution is to establish sentencing guidelines that, if past experience is repeated, will reduce sentencing disparities in general to some degree and will greatly lower the risk of aberrantly long, racially motivated sentences. Even if the guidelines are exceptionally harsh, like the current federal guidelines, they will lessen the risks of even longer extraordinary sentences.

Fourth, abolish all mandatory penalties. The evidence is overwhelming that mandatory penalties for serious crimes have few if any deterrent effects (which, if they exist, soon waste away), are frequently circumvented by judges and lawyers, and sometimes result in imposition of penalties that everyone involved believes are too severe. Moreover, they are often applied to drug and other crimes with which blacks are disproportionately likely to be charged and accordingly have a disproportionate impact on blacks.

Mandatory penalties are an especially pernicious part of contemporary punishment policies. Their principal purposes are political and short term—to allow officials at a time of heightened concern about crime to show that they are "tough on crime." Such laws, however, once passed, are seldom repealed and continue to affect the lives of offenders long after the concern that produced them has dissipated. For at least two centuries, the failures of mandatory penalties to achieve their ostensible purposes have been well documented and well known. There are no bases other than cynical politics to justify their retention.

Fifth, empower and encourage judges to mitigate sentences to take account of individual circumstances. Minority offenders would especially benefit from broadened judicial discretion. The movement in the last twenty years toward systems of rigid sentencing standards based solely on offenders' crimes and criminal records, and premised on just-deserts theories, was a mistake. Ethically and humanly relevant differences among offenders extend well beyond their crimes, and most judges and many prosecutors want to take account of some of those differences. Examples include distinctions between user and nonuser drug dealers, between offenders from distressed and privileged backgrounds, between offenders with and without dependent spouses and children, between offenders motivated by want and motivated by greed, and between stranger and nonstranger assailants.

Part of the rationale in many jurisdictions for limiting judges' powers to mitigate sentences was the just-deserts argument that crimes, not criminals, should be punished and that basing punishments only on crimes and criminal histories will ensure equality in sentencing, that "like cases are treated alike." The second half of the equality maxim, "and treat different cases differently," highlights the problem. Criteria must be prescribed by which cases are deemed alike and unlike, and crimes and criminal histories offer only an impoverished set of criteria. As Nigel Walker, the English criminologist, pointed out, a system of punishment truly premised on notions of moral culpability and morally deserved punishments would take account of all the particulars of an offender's life, just as the Recording Angel would for purposes of grander judgments.

A second rationale for limiting judges' powers to mitigate punishments was that the resulting discretion would be exercised for the benefit of middle-class defendants. This is why many sentencing guidelines systems expressly forbid judges to take into account employment prospects, education, and family status as mitigating considerations. The problems are that there are very few "middle-class" defendants in most felony courts and that the offenders who might benefit from mitigating consideration of personal circumstances are mostly disadvantaged people who to some degree have overcome the odds against their establishing a conventional pattern of life. Thus the people most likely to benefit from increased powers of mitigation are mostly disadvantaged, and many are from minority backgrounds.

Sixth, greatly limit the use of imprisonment, and use part of the money saved to support enhanced community corrections and treatment programs. The rest can be applied to putting state and federal budgets back in balance. If the combined prison and jail population was lowered to 1980 levels, adjusted for population increase and a bit more, $10 billion to $20 billion a year could be saved on institutional corrections budgets, and additional billions could be saved (or reallocated) on police, prosecutorial, and court operations. Crime rates in 1993 were about the same as in 1980 when the prison and jail population was under 500,000, which makes 600,000 a reasonable target to set for 1999. Between 1980 and 1993, the resident population of the United States rose by less than 12 percent. Thus 600,000 inmates would allow for population growth and still permit some increase over 1980 levels. It would also generate a national incarceration rate of 225 per 100,000 population, which is somewhat higher than the 1980 rate and would still be two to five times higher than that of any other country with which the United States ordinarily wants to be compared. Many would still find these levels unacceptably high in light of recent evidence that American crime rates, except for gun crimes, are about the same as those of most Western nations.

Several questions arise. How could inmate populations be cut so sharply? If my first two proposals, be honest and worry about race effects, were taken seriously by policymakers, the answers would be easy. Stop imprisoning most user-dealers and most property offenders. Revise sentencing standards and guidelines to prescribe prison sentences for violent offenses at 1980 levels. Rescind all mandatory penalty laws retroactively. Create special parole boards with the power to consider the release of every prisoner who is over age fifty and has served at least five years and every prisoner who has served ten years or more. The only valid general criterion for denying release would be that, on actuarial grounds, the offender presents an unacceptable risk of future violent criminality. Denying release might also be justified for especially notorious offenders like political assassins and serial murderers.

How much money would be saved? At a modest estimate of $25,000 in annual operating costs per inmate, the gross savings from 900,000 fewer inmates would be $22.5 billion. The net would be less; experience with deinstitutionalization of mental health programs demonstrates that governments have difficulty terminating employees and closing facilities that are no longer needed. However, many new jobs would open up in community corrections and in treatment programs for which current corrections workers would be qualified. There would also be one-time charges as outmoded facilities were closed forever, offset to some extent by gains from converting some prisons and jails to other uses. Whatever the details, in the end the annual net savings would permit a massive rise in funding for community corrections and treatment programs and still lower government spending by many billions.

What would be done with the diverted offenders? For some, nothing. Most former prisoners over age thirty-five present little threat of violence or other serious offending. The best thing to do is to let many of those released early get on with their lives. For current offenders, depending on the gravity of their crimes, confinement or community penalties are the answer. Those confined should receive sentences scaled down at least by half from current levels of time served to 1980 levels and never more than is commensurate with the relative severity of their offenses. Most, however—again depending on the gravity of their crimes—should be sentenced to community penalties like intensive supervision probation, community service, house arrest, daytime or nighttime confinement, and financial penalties coupled when appropriate with compulsory participation in treatment programs. When it is feasible, restitution or community service should routinely be ordered. Conditions of community penalties should be vigorously enforced, with prompt but graduated consequences attaching to violations.

From a public safety perspective, a combination of community penalties and greatly expanded treatment programs for offenders is more effective than the current program of excessive incarceration and insufficiently supported community punishments and treatment programs. Community penalties do no worse than prisons in regard to recidivism, and sometimes better. Well-managed drug treatment programs have repeatedly been shown to be capable of reducing both drug use and offending by drug-dependent offenders. Sex offender programs likewise have been shown to lessen later offending when the programs are well run and appropriately targeted. A number of types of programs for young offenders have been shown to lower reoffending. Educational and vocational training programs must enhance peoples' employment prospects, or millions of people would not pay to participate in them. Even public-sector programs like manpower training and the Jobs Corps, although often badly managed and insufficiently funded, have modest positive effects.

My first two proposals, be honest and think about the foreseeable race effects of policy decisions, are odd in a way, because they should go without saying. If they were widely accepted, the rest of my proposals would be uncontroversial. There are no sound, knowledge-based justifications for current crime control policies, and they create disastrous racial disparities, with all the accompanying negative consequences. Only the proposal to roll back prison and jail populations to slightly above 1980 levels is likely to be startling, but that need not even be a separate goal. It would happen as the other proposals were implemented.

So there are things that could be done to make current criminal justice policies less destructive of the lives and life chances of disadvantaged black Americans and their children. Of course, disadvantaged Americans of all races would benefit, but that is a happy product of nondiscriminatory public policies. All Americans would benefit from saving the tens of billions of unnecessary dollars now spent on crime control policies that are cruel and destructive and that do not make America a safer place. All Americans would also benefit from living in a kinder, gentler country.

References

Barr, William P. 1992. "The Case for More Incarceration." Washington, D.C.: U.S. Department of Justice, Office of Policy Development.

Blumstein, Alfred, Jacqueline Cohen, and Daniel Nagin. 1978. *Deterrence and Incapacitation*. Report of the National Academy of Sciences Panel on Research on Deterrent and Incapacitative Effects. Washington, D.C.: National Academy Press.

Bureau of Justice Statistics. Various years. *Sourcebook of Criminal Justice Statistics—[1992 and various years]*. Washington, D.C.: U.S. Government Printing Office.

Center on Juvenile and Criminal Justice. 1990. *Young African American Men and the Criminal Justice System in California*. San Francisco: Center on Juvenile and Criminal Justice.

Cohen, Mark. 1988. "Pain, Suffering and Jury Awards: A Study of the Cost of Crime to Victims." *Law and Society Review* 22:537–55.

Committee on Justice and the Solicitor General. 1993. *Crime Prevention in Canada: Toward A National Strategy*. Ottawa: Canada Communication Group.

Correctional Association of New York. 1990. *Imprisoned Generation: Young Men Under Criminal Justice Custody in New York State*. New York: Correctional Association of New York.

DeParle, Jason. 1990. "Talk of Government Being out to Get Blacks Falls on More Attentive Ears." *New York Times*, October 29, p. B7.

DiIulio, John J. 1991. *No Escape: The Future of American Corrections*. New York: Basic Books.

———. 1994. "Let 'Em Rot." *Wall Street Journal*, January 26, ed. page.

Edin, Kathryn, and Christopher Jencks. 1992. "Reforming Welfare." Chap. 5 in *Rethinking Social Policy* by Christopher Jencks. Cambridge, Mass.: Harvard University Press.

Edsall, Thomas, and Mary Edsall. 1991. *Chain Reaction: The Impact of Race, Rights, and Taxes on American Politics*. New York: Norton.

Federal Bureau of Investigation. Various Years. *Uniform Crime Reports for the United States—[1993 and various years]*. Washington, D.C.: U.S. Government Printing Office.

Hacker, Andrew. 1992. *Two Nations: Black and White, Separate, Hostile, Unequal.* New York: Scribner.

Holmes, Steven A. 1994. "Prominent Blacks Meet to Search for an Answer to Mounting Crime." *New York Times,* January 8, p. A1.

Home Office. 1990. *Crime, Justice, and Protecting the Public.* London: H. M. Stationery Office.

Jankowski, Louis W. 1992. *Correctional Populations in the United States, 1990.* Washington, D.C.: U.S. Department of Justice, Bureau of Justice Statistics.

Jencks, Christopher. 1992. *Rethinking Social Policy.* Cambridge, Mass.: Harvard University Press.

Kleiman, Mark A. R., and David Cavanagh. 1990. "A Cost–Benefit Analysis of Prison Cell Construction and Alternative Sanctions." Working Paper 90-06-03, prepared for the National Institute of Justice. Guggenheim Program in Criminal Justice Policy and Management. Cambridge, Mass.: Harvard University, Kennedy School of Government.

Mauer, Marc. 1990. *Young Black Men and the Criminal Justice System: A Growing National Problem.* Washington, D.C.: The Sentencing Project.

Miller, Jerome G. 1992a. "42% of Black D.C. Males, 18 to 35, Under Criminal Justice System Control." *Overcrowded Times* 3(3):1, 11.

———. 1992b. "56 Percent of Young Black Males in Baltimore Under Justice System Control." *Overcrowded Times* 3(6):1, 10, 16.

Miller, Warren E., and Santa A. Traugott. 1989. *American National Election Studies Data Sourcebook, 1952–1986.* Cambridge: Harvard University Press.

Murray, Charles. 1984. *Losing Ground—American Social Policy, 1950–1980.* New York: Basic Books.

National Academy of Sciences Panel on Research on Deterrent and Incapacitative Effects. See Blumstein, Cohen, and Nagin 1978.

National Academy of Sciences Panel on The Understanding and Control of Violence. See Reiss and Roth 1993.

President's Commission on Law Enforcement and Administration of Justice. 1967. *The Challenge of Crime in a Free Society.* Washington, D.C.: U.S. Government Printing Office.

Raines, Howell. 1991. "Grady's Gift." *New York Times Magazine,* December 1, p. 50.

Reiss, Albert J., Jr., and Jeffrey Roth. 1993. *Understanding and Controlling Violence.* Report of the National Academy of Sciences Panel on the Understanding and Control of Violence. Washington, D.C.: National Academy Press.

47c *References*

Roberts, Julian V. 1992. "Public Opinion, Crime, and Criminal Justice." In *Crime and Justice: A Review of Research,* vol. 16, edited by Michael Tonry. Chicago: University of Chicago Press.

U.S. Department of Justice. 1991. "Attorney General's Summit on Law Enforcement Responses to Violent Crime: Public Safety in the Nineties." Conference Summary. Washington, D.C.: Bureau of Justice Statistics.

Walker, Nigel. 1991. *Why Punish?* Oxford: Oxford University Press.

West, Cornel. 1993. *Race Matters.* Boston: Beacon Press.

Wood, Floris W. 1990. *An American Profile: Opinions and Behavior, 1972–1989.* New York: Gale Research.

Zedlewski, Edwin. 1987. "Making Confinement Decisions." Research in Brief Series. Washington, D.C.: National Institute of Justice.

Zimring, Franklin E., and Gordon Hawkins. 1991. *The Scale of Imprisonment.* Chicago: University of Chicago Press.

———. 1992. *The Search for Rational Drug Control.* Cambridge: Cambridge University Press.

[2]
Ethnicity, Crime, and Immigration

Members of *some* disadvantaged minority groups in every Western country are disproportionately likely to be arrested, convicted, and imprisoned for violent, property, and drug crimes. This is true whether the minority groups are members of different "racial" groups from the majority population, for example, blacks or Afro-Caribbeans in Canada, England, or the United States, or of different ethnic backgrounds, for example, North African Arabs in France or the Netherlands, or—irrespective of race or ethnicity—are recent migrants from other countries, for example, Yugoslavs or Eastern Europeans in Germany and Finns in Sweden. Important social policy dilemmas that are seen in individual countries to be uniquely their own, such as race relations in the United States or assimilation of Maghreb-derived guest workers in France or the experience of Aborigines in Australia, are not unique at all but are instead variations on common themes of social structure that characterize many countries.

It is important, however, not to be reductionist. The different offending patterns and justice system experiences of members of different groups in a country are not simply the result of group differences in wealth, social status, or political power. That is why the word "some" is emphasized in the phrase "some disadvantaged minority groups" in the first sentence of this essay. Not all economically and socially disadvantaged groups are disproportionately involved in crime.

In England and Wales, for example, Afro-Caribbeans and migrants from the Indian subcontinent began to arrive in large numbers at about the same time—the 1950s and 1960s—and experienced comparable forms and levels of invidious discrimination. In the 1990s, Bangladeshis in particular are on average poorer and more disadvantaged than Afro-Caribbeans. Yet Afro-Caribbeans in England are as disproportionately involved in crime and the justice system compared with whites, as are blacks in the United States compared with whites. Indians, Pakistanis, and Bangladeshis in England, however, are less involved in crime and the justice system than are whites. (It is possible that crime rates for some Asian groups will rise. Bangladeshis arrived in England later than other groups and are on average younger and poorer. One might also hypothesize that anti-Muslim feelings are rising in England and that this will produce greater alienation and higher crime rates. No evidence to sustain either theory has as yet been reported.)

Similarly, Moroccans and Turks came to the Netherlands as guest workers in the 1950s and 1960s. Many stayed and were later joined by family members after the doors closed to new labor migrants in the early 1970s. By the 1990s, both groups were comparably disadvantaged economically and socially compared with the majority population, but crime and incarceration rates for Turks were not much higher than those of the Dutch, while those for Moroccans were much higher.

The English and Dutch experiences capture all of the themes which the phrases "race and crime," "ethnicity and crime," and "immigration and crime" encompass. The criminal justice system experience of Afro-Caribbeans in England is often seen as a problem of race and crime. The experience of Moroccans in the Netherlands is often seen as a problem of ethnicity and crime. The experiences of minority groups in both countries are often seen as problems of immigration and crime. In all the countries examined in this book, disproportionate crime involvement all too often fosters negative stereotypes of minority groups and both discrimination and xenophobia directed at them and, conversely, provokes passionate arguments and accusations about racial, ethnic, or anti-immigrant bias as a or the primary cause of justice system disparities.

These are not small problems. Race relations and political controversies about immigrants are high on the political and policy agendas of many countries. In an era of rapid social and economic changes in many countries, persistent high unemployment in Europe, and declining real wages in North America, many people feel threatened and insecure and nativist politicians have been quick to blame minority and immigrant groups for much of what seems wrong. Hate crimes are increasingly common and publicized in many countries, and violent attacks against minority groups are more evident in Europe. Members of victimized minority groups in turn are likely to become more alienated from majority populations.

This book, no book, can realistically aspire to affect those powerful social forces, but it can and does aspire to shed light on the narrower question of what is now known about crime and justice system involvement of members of minority groups in nine countries and about the reasons for the differences that exist. Public policy does not always take account of systematic knowledge about the subjects it addresses, but in civilized countries it should. The aim of this book therefore is to establish what is now known about racial and ethnic patterns of crime and justice system involvement in nine Western countries. They were selected because they are among the relatively few countries, Western or otherwise, that have empirical research traditions that have generated research findings or well-maintained official statistics on which credible assertions can be based. The writers of the essays in this book have examined evidence concerning both "minority groups and crime" and "immigration and crime," two subjects that are seldom brought together which, once brought together, can teach more than can either alone.

This introduction, most readers will be relieved to learn, does not summarize and comment on the contents of each of the essays. I have never understood why introductions so often do that; the essays are after all but a few pages away, and if they do not stand on their own and say what they mean should not have been published. Instead, these introductory pages explain why the volume was conceived and suggest some of the things that a look across national boundaries can teach us about "race, ethnicity, and crime" and "immigration and crime." The essays are vertical or longitudinal looks at the experiences of individual countries. This introduction attempts to look horizontally across national boundaries to indicate common findings and ways in which cross-national inquiry on this subject can modify or enrich current knowledge based on the experiences of individual countries.

There are four sections. The first describes some of the difficulties that confront efforts to investigate these issues. Most human beings, including this one, are captives of their own experiences and both more parochial and more ethnocentric than they know. The seemingly straightforward questions that this volume examines are not easy to answer cross-nationally, not only because of differences in criminal codes and legal processes but also because of important cultural differences in views about things as seemingly mundane as compilation of official statistics. The second section discusses racial and ethnic differences in offending, victimization, and system processing, relative to majority populations, and shows that similar patterns occur in every country, whatever the race, ethnicity, or nationality of the overrepresented minorities. The third discusses "immigration and crime" and shows that the widespread conventional wisdom that first-generation immigrants typically are more law-abiding than the resident population, while their children and grandchildren typically have higher crime rates, is true, but for a much smaller proportion of immigrants than is commonly recognized. Very different patterns characterize other groups of immigrants. The fourth, finally, offers suggestions for how genuinely comparative and cross-national research might advance current understanding and provide knowledge that can help policy makers predict conditions and circumstances associated with high rates of offending by minority and immigrant groups and devise measures to ameliorate those otherwise foreseeable results.

I. Impediments to Looking across National Boundaries

Although none of the essays in this volume attempts to compare sentencing severity for particular crimes in different countries, the problems involved in trying to make that comparison provide a good starting point. If the goal were to compare average severity of sentences for burglary of a dwelling, street robbery, and rape in Germany, Sweden, and the United States, a number of important contextual differences would have to be taken into account. Definitions of offenses vary between countries, as do traditions about reporting crimes to the authorities, so it would be necessary to look beyond the formal definitions to make sure that similar criminal behaviors were being compared. In principle, this could be done by use of statistical controls, if sufficiently rich data were available in each country on "actual offense behavior." A second problem, however, is that criminal processes vary substantially between countries. In Germany (Weigend 1993) and the Netherlands (Tak 1994), for example, large percentages of cases are disposed of by means of conditional dismissals in which the defendant acknowledges guilt and agrees to pay a penalty, often a fine, comparable to that which might have been imposed following conviction, in exchange for conditional dismissal of the charges (and thus no criminal conviction). Comparisons of average prison sentences between countries in which conditional dismissals are common and countries in which they are not will suffer from selection bias: all other things being equal, in the former countries the average seriousness of the crimes for which convictions are entered will likely be greater. Comparisons of prison sentences for robbery, for example, would be biased since the comparison would be between a smaller proportion of more serious robberies in one country and a larger proportion of both more and less serious robberies in another. Similar problems are presented by national differences in the use of suspended prison sentences, whether a discretionary parole release system exists and how it is used, and whether nominal sentences include a period, often one-third of the total, of automatic remission of sentence ("good time" in the United States).

Comparisons of sentencing patterns in different countries must, accordingly, be made with caution and evaluated with skepticism. None of the essays in this volume make cross-national comparisons. All of the comparisons between groups are made within countries, and the formal legal context is in effect controlled for. That does not mean that there may not be selection biases within a jurisdiction's legal system that occur when members of some groups are more likely to be arrested or prosecuted or convicted and, conversely, less likely to benefit from informal diversions or gentler sentences. Those selection biases within countries, however, have often been studied and many of the essays in this volume report the results. Nonetheless, the warnings above about the need to be skeptical of cross-national comparisons also apply, if with weaker force, to assessment of writings on countries about which the reader lacks detailed knowledge.

A number of other impediments exist to national and cross-national studies of racial and ethnic disparities. They are described below, and illustrated, but not discussed at length.

A. Measuring Racial Disparities

It is not possible with existing data to make even crude cross-national comparisons of racial disparities in the justice systems of Western countries other than the major English-speaking countries. Partly this is because the social construct "race" has played a larger role in the history of the English-speaking countries, and partly it is because in many countries maintenance of official data on race is forbidden for ethical reasons.

When Americans think about racial bias and racial disparities, they tend to think first about the experience of black Americans. Given America's race relations history and that blacks, at 12 percent of the population, are the largest nonwhite minority group, this is not surprising. Thus, if the subject is disparities in imprisonment, a natural question is whether and to what extent blacks compared with whites are locked up. The answer on an average day in 1990 was that 1,860 per 100,000 American blacks were in jail or prison, compared with 289 per 100,000 whites. That is a difference of 6.44 to 1 (Tonry 1995, table 2-1). Stated differently, the chance that a black American was in prison or jail in 1990 was six-and-a-half times higher than for a white American. Racial disparities in prison have worsened since 1990. According to the U.S. Bureau of Justice Statistics, 2,316 per 100,000 blacks were confined in federal or state prisons on December 1994, compared with 291 whites per 100,000 (Bureau of Justice Statistics 1995). That is an 8 to 1 difference (and ignores jail populations which would make the absolute confinement rates half again higher, but probably not significantly affect the ratio).

The first and easiest international comparison is to look at equivalent data in other English-speaking common-law countries. At least for 1990, when that comparison is made, racial disparities in the United States can be seen to be not unique. In that year the 6.44 racial difference in total incarceration rates in the United States was lower than the corresponding disparities in England (a 7:1 Afro-Caribbean/white difference). Disparities in countries with sizable aboriginal populations are worse: Canada (a 16:1 native/nonnative difference in 1986), and Australia (a 12:1 Aborigine/non-Aborigine difference in 1993) (Tonry 1994).

That, however, is where the international comparisons must stop. No other country retains data in official records on defendants' or offenders' race. Only the United States routinely records and publishes such data in its justice system records; England records and publishes racial data in its prison statistics. Canada, Australia, and New Zealand retain data that permit native/nonnative, Aborigine/non-Aborigine, Maori-Pacific Islander/other comparisons. None of the last three countries, however, records data that permits black/white comparisons.

There are two reasons why black/white racial identification data are not recorded in official records in most countries. First, on ethical grounds, lawmakers in many countries have decided that such data should not be recorded. One rationale is that race is not a morally relevant difference between individuals and that recording such data is to treat it as if it were a relevant difference and thereby to tend to reify it into a relevant difference. Another is that recording such data, especially when minorities are overrepresented among offenders, may create or support stereotypes that are stigmatizing or otherwise damaging to members of minority groups. Still another is that recording such data might make it easier for biased officials to discriminate against minority offenders. Outside the United States, this is an intensely controversial subject. In Canada, for example, in the early 1990s the use of racial identifiers in official records was widely discussed in the editorial columns of national newspapers among other places (e.g., Doob 1991). The conclusion at that time was that racial identifiers should remain forbidden. More recently, Ontario's Commission on Systemic Racism proposed a five-year data collection pilot project using racial identifiers (1995, p. 405), with the caveat that the pilot project follow "guidelines . . . established in collaboration with racialized communities." England's Royal Commission on Criminal Justice (1993) likewise concluded that efforts to reduce racial disparities could not be assessed unless data on racial disparities were collected.

The second reason in most countries for not recording racial identifiers is that the data would be overaggregated and lack social validity. In most countries "blacks" are as heterogeneous a grouping as "whites." In Ontario, for example, where recent allegations of racial bias, especially on the part of police, have been vigorous, many black Canadians have protested that "black" is overinclusive (Commission on Systemic Racism in the Ontario Criminal Justice System 1995). Until thirty years ago, most black Toronto residents were members of families that had migrated from the United States generations earlier. Since then there have been successive waves of immigrants from the West Indies, especially Jamaica, and Africa, especially Ethiopia and Somalia. At least in public stereotype, high crime rates have been most characteristic of West Indian immigrants, and both long-time residents and African immigrants have resented being victims of guilt by stereotyped racial association. (And members of Ethiopian immigrant groups often insist that Tigreans and Amharic-speakers be distinguished.)

In most countries, there is little reason to lump dark-skinned people into one "racial" group. In Germany, as Hans-Jörg Albrecht shows in this volume, at different times in recent years people from Gambia, Nigeria, and Senegal have been active in drug trafficking. In England, the black population includes both a sizable proportion who derive from the West Indies and another sizable group who derive from various African countries. In much of his discussion of racial disparities in England's justice system, David Smith (in this volume) is careful to note that heterogeneity even though English official records do not.

Disaggregation below the category "black" is seldom attempted or discussed in the United States. A large percentage of black Americans are descendants or members of families that have lived in the United States for many generations, so that may not be surprising. Nonetheless, it must obscure important differences between groups such as Puerto Ricans, Haitians, black Cubans, West Indians, recent migrants from many African countries, and descendants of long-time residents. There is, for example, substantial evidence that West Indian migrants to the United States in the middle third of this century assimilated more successfully both economically and socially into the American mainstream than have other groups (Sowell 1983).

B. Measuring Ethnicity Disparities

Cross-national comparisons of ethnic disparities cannot be made. With only a few anomalous exceptions in individual countries, ethnic identifiers are not recorded in justice system data. In Europe especially, widespread aversion to ethnicity classifications by government is one legacy of the horrors of Nazi Germany. If the subject were open to reconsideration, presumably the concerns about stigmatization, reification, and potential invidious use that lead most countries to reject racial identifiers would be among the concerns opponents would urge, but the subject is nowhere open for reconsideration.

As the next subsection notes, some countries record data on "nationality" which sometimes may be a proxy for ethnicity, but only sometimes. Concerning relatively homogeneous countries like Denmark and Norway in which nationality and ethnicity are largely congruent, the categories "Danish" and "Norwegian" might efficiently characterize people who speak the national language as a first tongue and share cultural traditions and customs and, in those respects, share a common ethnicity. For many nationalities, however, that would not be so. In the Netherlands, for example, "Surinamese" include subgroups commonly distinguished by others and themselves as "Creoles," "Hindustanis," and "Asians"; while "Antilleans" may be disaggregated further by particular islands. "Turks" make up sizable minority groups in many European countries, but the category includes both ethnic Turks and ethnic Kurds, two subgroups that in some places differ substantially (and sometimes violently). "Yugoslavs," the world will not soon forget, include Croats, Serbs, Bosnians, Albanians, and Slovenians, among others. And so forth. In the same way that "black" is an overaggregated category in Ontario, nationality is an overaggregated category in many places and for many nationalities.

There are major exceptions to the general aversion to use of ethnic identifiers. Some countries with sizable aboriginal populations, for example, Australia and New Zealand, routinely use Aborigine/non-Aborigine identifiers. Perhaps surprisingly, given the Canadian reluctance to use black/white racial identifiers, Canadian official records have long, and with little controversy, distinguished natives from nonnatives (Roberts and Doob, in this volume). Perhaps most surprisingly, although German laws prohibit use of ethnicity identifiers, including "Gypsy," German police have long recorded other euphemistic data that allow them to identify Gypsies (Albrecht, in this volume).

The anomalies, however, are anomalies and are not useful for making cross-national ethnicity comparisons except, possibly, between the experiences of Aborigines in Australia and New Zealand. Anyone who wanted to compare the criminal justice system experiences in different countries of Kurds or (before the breakup of Yugoslavia) Croats would have to look somewhere other than official records.

C. Measuring Nationality Disparities

Some countries do use nationality identifiers, but as many do not. In Germany, many statistical systems record nationality data. For most purposes, French data distinguish only between French nationals (*citoyens*) and foreigners (*étrangers*). Similarly, although nationality is commonly recorded in official records in Switzerland, published Swiss crime statistics distinguish among Swiss nationals, resident foreigners, and nonresident foreigners. Swedish official statistics also commonly distinguish among Swedish nationals, resident foreigners, and nonresident foreigners, and for some purposes report data for geographical regions (e.g., Africa, Nordic countries, South America). In the Netherlands, neither ethnicity nor nationality data is recorded in police or court records, but some use of national origin data is permitted in prison records.

Data systems in the English-speaking countries are even less informative about nationality. At state and national levels, American data typically distinguish only among black, white, Native American, "other," and Hispanic individuals. Australian official data contain only the Aborigine/non-Aborigine distinction (although some systems routinely collect "country of birth" data), and most Canadian data identify only natives and nonnatives. Through the 1930s, U.S. and Canadian data often recorded nationality, but as "crime and the foreign born" declined as a controversial political issue after large-scale immigration stopped in the mid-1920s, use of nationality identifiers stopped.

The prospects for cross-national studies are not as bleak as this summary may suggest. Germany has the richest nationality data and, as the essay by Albrecht (in this volume) shows, permits highly discriminant and informative analyses. In some countries, for example, Sweden, special studies are done that link official justice system records to other records that contain nationality identifiers. In the Netherlands and Sweden, self-report and victimization studies validated against official records provide much useful information.

This is not the place to explore measurement problems in detail, but a few general problems concerning measurement of nationality should be mentioned. They relate to comparisons within countries both between the experiences of nationals and foreigners and between different nationality groups. A major problem is that countries differ in their naturalization policies and in how naturalized citizens are classified. Naturalization has traditionally been readily available to immigrants in Sweden, France, and the Netherlands, which means that comparisons between citizens and noncitizens are weakened; "citizens" include many people who are recent immigrants, and their children, and thus both sides of the comparison include recent immigrants. If individuals sharing a particular national origin have higher crime rates than ethnic Swedes, the comparison will understate the difference. Germany and Switzerland, by contrast, have traditionally been less open to naturalization, and the citizen/foreigner distinction is sharper.

A second complication is that many countries' records do not distinguish between resident and nonresident foreigners (Sweden and Switzerland do). In a country like Switzerland, where annual border crossings exceed the resident population by a factor of thirty (Killias, in this volume), tourists and illegal entrants may commit a large proportion of crimes by foreigners, making it difficult to compare the behaviors of resident citizens and resident foreigners. As Europe continues its movement toward political and economic unification, and as drug and economic crimes become increasingly transnational, this problem will become more important.

This litany of complications is intended only to show that complexity faces efforts to make cross-national comparisons and not that they are impossible. The complications can be overcome by creative analytic techniques and by collection of original data. And, more important, notwithstanding all these problems, as the essays in this volume show, a great deal has been learned within each country which reveals strong similarities in every included countries' experiences with ethnicity, crime, and immigration, which offers hypotheses for understanding other countries' experiences, and which provides a rich foundation on which later research can build.

II. Racial and Ethnic Disparities

Many readers of this volume, I suspect, will be surprised to learn that racial disparities in America's justice system are paralleled by comparable minority group disparities in other countries. Similarly, in most countries in which researchers have attempted to learn whether disparities occur primarily because of group differences in offending or because of bias, the general conclusion, as in the United States, has been that most of the measured disparity appears to be attributable to offending differences. Finally, in every country in which case processing studies have been carried out, similar patterns of systematic adverse effects for minority groups appear as a result of "neutral" policies and practices.

Two prefatory points need making. First, as mentioned earlier, most comparisons of offending or system processing are based on such overaggregated categories as race, aboriginality, and nationality. Substantial behavioral and experiential differences often distinguish subgroups.

Second, countries have distinct research traditions, and the kinds of research findings and official data available to investigate specific questions vary a great deal. On the question of whether invidious bias is a major cause of racial and ethnic disproportions, although large between-group disparities occur in every country, only in a few has there been much research on the subject. There is a vast American empirical literature on justice system bias. There is a smaller English literature. In Australia and Canada, there have been a few studies concerning aboriginal and native disparities; the findings from the first major Canadian study on black/white disparities are reported in the essay by Roberts and Doob in this volume. No studies of this type appear to have been done in France or Sweden and but a few each in Germany and the Netherlands.

Victimization studies offer another example. Victimization studies can be used to compare group patterns in arrests with victims' reports of the identities of their assailants or to investigate the extent to which offending is intragroup. Comparisons of arrest and victim-identification patterns for particular crimes may suggest the presence or absence of police bias. If offending typically occurs within groups, if, for example, black offenders in the United States typically victimize black victims, epithets of racism are less likely to be used to explain high rates of prosecution of black offenders; not doing so would in effect undervalue crimes against blacks, a form of discrimination and insensitivity which is difficult to justify. Here, too, countries vary widely. Long-term national victimization studies exist in the United States and England, and to a lesser extent in Canada and the Netherlands. Occasional surveys with large samples have been conducted in Switzerland (Killias, in this volume). The Swiss and English surveys, like the American ones, find that assailants' ethnic or national background has little influence on victims' decisions to report to the police.

Still and all, for all the differences in data availability and research tradition in various countries, on some subjects the findings are so robust and so consistent across national boundaries that meaningful generalizations can be offered. The essays that follow discuss the evidence in detail.

1. *In Every Country, Crime and Incarceration Rates for Members of Some Minority Groups Greatly Exceed Those for the Majority Population.* Perhaps most important, comparable disparities exist both for racial and ethnic minorities and for national origin minorities who are not visible racial minorities. In England and Wales, and the United States, black residents are seven-to-eight times more likely than whites to be confined in prisons, and the black/white imprisonment disparities in the Canadian province of Ontario are greater (Roberts and Doob, in this volume). In Australia and Canada, arrest and imprisonment disparities affecting Aborigines and natives are even greater than black/white disparities in the other English-speaking countries. In the Netherlands, however, the greatest disparities affect people from Morocco and Surinam (Junger-Tas, in this volume). In Sweden, Finns have higher rates than Swedes, and the highest disproportions in arrests affect immigrants from Arab countries, South America (notably Chileans, of whom those in Sweden are mostly of European descent), and Eastern Europe (Martens, in this volume). In the German state of North Rhine–Westphalia in 1993, Romanians experienced by far the highest arrest rates (nearly 740 per year per 1,000 people, 44 times the German arrest rate) and the most disproportionate imprisonment rate (1608 per 100,000 population, 21 times the German rate) (Albrecht, in this volume). In France, the highest imprisonment rates characterize people from the Maghreb countries of Algeria, Morocco, and Tunisia (Tournier, in this volume).

Too much should not be made of numbers like those in the preceding paragraph. They tell us something important—that stark disparities in arrests and imprisonment exist in many countries, not simply those in which blacks or Aborigines are the most politically and socially salient minority—but they do not tell much more. Most important, they do not indicate what kinds of offenses are being disproportionately committed and sanctioned and why. Albrecht's essay in this volume, for example, graphically shows that the kinds of offenses different groups commit in different countries vary greatly. Romanians have by far the highest arrest rates in the state of Hessen in Germany, but their offenses are mostly minor property and immigration offenses; their arrests rates for violent and drug crimes are lower than those for many other much less often arrested groups. The essays on Sweden and Germany describe relatively high crime rates for people from Eastern Europe, but both describe their crimes as being principally theft and shoplifting, crimes that are arguably explicable in terms of the exposure of materially deprived people moving into wealthy societies to consumer goods that are readily accessible by illicit means. And in many countries, some groups may be recent migrants who are temporarily in assimilation or acculturation phases often afflicted by high crime rates. Finally, at any time groups may differ from others in age and gender composition, wealth and social status, and other social and economic characteristics that are strongly correlated with criminality; apparent differences in behavior between groups may on closer examination reflect nothing more than composition differences between groups.

2. *Minority Groups Characterized by High Crime and Imprisonment Rates Are Also Characterized by Various Indicators of Social and Economic Disadvantage.* This should be no surprise. For as long as social reformers and researchers have studied criminality, the correlation between criminality and disadvantage has been clear. Those correlations were as clear in nineteenth-century England (Mayhew 1861) and early twentieth-century America (Shaw 1929), when the high-crime groups were white, as today in those countries when some of the high-crime groups are black. The essays in this volume on Switzerland (Killias), Sweden (Martens), and the Netherlands (Junger-Tas) discuss the links between disadvantage and crime most fully and all make the relationship clear.

However, and it is a big however, not all disadvantaged groups exhibit high crime rates. In England, as already noted, migrants from the Indian subcontinent were as disadvantaged and as discriminated against as migrants from the Caribbean and Africa; Afro-Caribbeans have crime and imprisonment rates far higher than those for whites, while rates for Indian subcontinent migrants are lower. While, in the United States, it remains unclear whether recent Southeast Asian immigrants will have high crime rates, it is clear that the typically impoverished Chinese and Japanese migrants of the nineteenth century did not. In the Netherlands, Turks and Moroccans first arrived in large numbers as guest workers in the 1950s and 1960s; although labor migrant entry ceased in the early 1970s, the two groups have increased both naturally and as a result of family reunification policies under the immigration laws. In the 1990s both groups are comparably less well-off economically, educationally, and vocationally than the Dutch. Yet the Turks have crime and imprisonment rates much like those for the Dutch while Moroccans have rates that are far higher.

3. *In Countries in Which Research Has Been Conducted on the Causes of Racial and Ethnic Disparities in Imprisonment, Group Differences in Offending, Not Invidious Bias, Appear to Be the Principal Cause.* I have phrased that conclusion in as nontendentious a way as I can. It could be phrased differently. If the critical aim were to demonstrate that racial and ethnic stereotypes and animus influence disparities, the conclusion would be that, all other things being equal, members of racial minorities receive harsher sentences. The hypothesis to be tested is that race and ethnicity matter, and research findings support the conclusion that they do. If the apologetic aim were to demonstrate that stereotypes and animus have little influence, the conclusion would be that, controlling for offense circumstances and criminal histories, race and ethnicity explain little of the variation in sentencing outcomes. The hypothesis is that neutral or legally relevant factors are the principal determinants of sentences, and the data support the conclusion that they are. Put another way, neither proponents of the claim that bias is the sole or primary cause of disparities nor proponents of the claim that bias has no influence on disparities will find empirical evidence to prove their claims.

Whether bias or behavior was the primary cause of racial disparities in arrests and imprisonment was for two decades a highly controversial question in English-speaking countries, and, as a result, much of the relevant research has been in those countries. However, a significant body of German research has also investigated the causes of disparities from police stops through sentencing (Albrecht, in this volume), as has a smaller body of Dutch research (Junger-Tas, in this volume). Relatively little research on the causes of disparities has been done in the other three countries. The writers of the essays in this volume on France (Tournier) and Sweden (Martens) offer informed speculation. The essay on Switzerland (Killias) compares proportions of foreigners among arrestees to those among prison admissions and populations and finds reasonable consistency, but neither detailed case studies on system processing nor sophisticated statistical analyses have been done to buttress that observation.

Much the largest volume of work has been in the United States and has several times been summarized (e.g., Wilbanks 1987; Mann 1993; Tonry 1995; Sampson and Lauritsen, in this volume). There have been case processing studies, both qualitative and quantitative, at every stage of the justice system from police stops to parole release, aggregate statistical analyses of the relations between national crime data and national imprisonment data, and statistical comparisons of victimization data on victims' identifications of assailants with police data on the racial characteristics of arrestees. With only minor exceptions, the evidence, while certainly not showing that bias has no role, indicates that criminality past and present is the major determinant of officials' decisions.

The next largest literature is in England and Wales and, as summarized by Smith in this volume, supports much the same conclusions as in the United States. Work in Australia and Canada is not inconsistent with the American and English findings, but so little work has been done that no strong conclusions can be offered.

Curiously, although much work has been done in Australia in recent years to document Aborigine/non-Aborigine disparities at every stage of the adult and juvenile systems (Royal Commission into Aboriginal Deaths in Custody 1991; Harding et al. 1995; Broadhurst, in this volume), there have been only a few case processing studies to test bias hypotheses, and although one rigorous study found significantly higher arrest risks after controlling for key factors, this was not conclusively or solely attributed to racial prejudice (e.g., Gale and Wundersitz 1987; Gale, Bailey-Harris, and Wundersitz 1990; Duguid 1992).

The first major statistical analyses in Canada to test antiblack bias hypotheses were completed in 1995 under the auspices of the Ontario Commission on Systemic Racism and are reported in the Roberts and Doob essay in this volume. The findings, depending on the starting point, either show that most of existing sentencing disparities are attributable to legally relevant differences or that, after all legally relevant differences are controlled for, some disparities remain that may be evidence of racial bias. In other words, the findings are broadly consistent with American and English findings. Some work has been done on the causes of native/nonnative disparities, and there too differential behavior patterns seem to be the primary explanation (Laprairie 1990).

4. *Seemingly Neutral Case Processing Practices, Especially Pretrial Confinement Decisions and Sentence Reductions for Guilty Pleas, Operate to the Systematic Disadvantage of Members of Minority Groups.* This is a perplexing problem because practices that are justifiable in their own terms, such as detaining those people who seem least likely to remain in the jurisdiction and appear for trial, produce outcomes, greater proportions of minority offenders in confinement, that are widely seen as regrettable.

The pretrial detention problem appears in many countries. The essays on the Netherlands (Junger-Tas), Germany (Albrecht), Switzerland (Killias), England (Smith), Canada (Roberts and Doob), and the United States (Sampson and Lauritsen) discuss the relevant research in each country. The difficulty is that the rational and humane policy of restricting pretrial confinement to those least likely to appear for trial means that those who live the least settled lives—those without permanent residences, or stable family lives, or jobs—will be held. Those traits more commonly characterize disadvantaged people, and many minority groups are disadvantaged. The resulting disparities are especially unfortunate because, at least in England (Hood 1992) and the United States (Blumstein et al. 1983, chap. 2; Petersilia and Turner 1986; Klein et al. 1991), all else being equal, being detained before trial increases the likelihood that a prison sentence will be imposed after trial.

A second, similar problem—rewarding prisoners who plead guilty with sentencing concessions—may be more troubling. There is convincing evidence in the United States (Petersilia and Turner 1986; Klein et al. 1991), England (Hood 1992), and the Netherlands (Maas and Stuyling de Lange 1989; Junger-Tas, in this volume) that members of some minority groups are less likely than other defendants to plead guilty. From a management perspective, it makes sense to encourage defendants to plead guilty, and thereby conserve resources, by providing a sentence reduction. From a sentencer's perspective, it will often seem appropriate to acknowledge a defendant's contrition and acceptance of responsibility, evidenced by a guilty plea, by reducing the sentence that would otherwise be imposed. These phenomena are particularly explicit in England where appellate courts have elaborated a doctrine of "progressive loss of mitigation" under which defendants who plead guilty are entitled to a lesser sentence than if they were convicted after trial, the amount of the discount depending on when the plea is made; the later the plea, the smaller the discount. Hood's landmark study (1992) of sentencing disparities in the English Midlands found that Afro-Caribbean defendants were less likely than white defendants to plead guilty and, when they pled guilty, often did so later in the process than did whites. Thus Afro-Caribbeans lost sentence mitigation under both branches of the progressive mitigation doctrine.

This to many people is more troubling than the pretrial detention disparities because the guilty plea pattern may be shaped by many minority defendants' alienation from the justice system and beliefs that the system is biased against them. Research in many countries, including the Netherlands (Junger-Tas, in this volume), Germany (Albrecht, in this volume), Australia (Broadhurst, in this volume), England (Smith, in this volume), and the United States (Sampson and Lauritsen, in this volume), shows that members of minority groups are more likely to be stopped by police than majority citizens (albeit in most countries there is little evidence of bias in arrest decisions) and to believe that the police are biased against them. If minority defendants are hostile and distrustful toward the justice system because they believe (with some basis) they are treated unfairly, and as a result are less likely to cooperate, including by pleading guilty early or at all, progressive loss of mitigation penalizes them for their (to many people, understandable) alienation.

In both these instances, pretrial confinement based on legitimate criteria that disproportionately characterize minority defendants and sentencing policies that reward defendants who plead guilty, facially neutral policies disadvantage minority defendants for reasons that have nothing to do with their alleged crimes. To detain more minority offenders, or punish them more severely, as a matter of conscious policy would be seen as wrong in all Western countries. To maintain policies which foreseeably have that effect is not exactly the same thing but deserves more hard ethical scrutiny than typically it receives (Tonry 1995, chaps. 1, 8). There is no easy way to resolve this dilemma, but at the very least policy makers should consider whether seemingly neutral, disparity-causing policies can be revised to achieve their express goals in ways that produce fewer disparities.

5. *Subcultural Behaviors and Stereotypes Sometimes Associated with Mi-*

nority Group Members Often Work to Their Disadvantage in Contacts with the Justice System. Two behavioral patterns interact to create special problems for members of some minority groups. First, disproportionately large numbers of members of some groups, including blacks in the United States, Surinamese and Moroccans in the Netherlands, and Aborigines in Australia, commit crimes. Many offenders in particular subcultures share characteristics such as distinctive patterns of dress and speech, places of recreation and residence, and social and economic backgrounds. As a result, justice system officials and many ordinary citizens often assume that individuals who possess those characteristics are likely to be offenders. Social welfare scholars call this statistical discrimination. Psychologists call it attribution. Sociologists call it stereotyping. Whatever it is called, it makes people suspicious of entire groups of individuals. In the United States, young black men are particular victims, as is illustrated by a much-quoted statement by civil rights leader Jesse Jackson: "There is nothing more painful to me at this stage of my life than to walk down the street and hear footsteps and start thinking about robbery—then look around and see somebody white and feel relieved" (Cohen 1993). Stereotyping of this sort is one reason why, as noted earlier, members of minority groups in many countries are especially likely to be stopped by the police.

The second pattern compounds the first. For many reasons, including self-esteem, self-assertion, and peer group expectations, some members of some disadvantaged minority groups behave and act in ways that other people find strange and threatening. Novelist Tom Wolfe in *Bonfire of the Vanities* (1987), a novel that describes the workings of high-volume urban American felony courts as well as any political scientist's case study, describes the "pimp roll," the rolling, loose-jointed walk, which, combined with an off-the-shoulder black leather jacket, blue jeans, gold chains, and untied hightop basketball shoes, were then the fashion for young underclass black men in New York City. In the novel, a black juvenile defendant lost the benefit of a favorable plea bargain when, rather than dress for success in middle-class style as his attorney instructed, he pimp-rolled into the courtroom with two similarly attired friends. To the judge his appearance was that of an incorrigible, antisocial offender, and nothing like the redeemable minor participant in a crime, entitled to another chance and the benefit of the doubt, whom his lawyer had described.

Put together, these two phenomena, widely held stereotypes of minority offenders and distinctive dress and behaviors that evoke the stereotypes, probably explain the consistent finding in many countries that young minority men are especially likely to be stopped by police and, when stopped, to react defiantly and hostilely. Hostility and defiance toward the police are likely to elicit hostility and authoritarian responses from the police. And, in turn again, police aggressiveness is likely often to confirm minority offenders' belief that they are being treated discriminatorily and unfairly. Evidence of this vicious spiral is discussed in the essays on Australia (Broadhurst), Canada (Roberts and Doob), England (Smith), Germany (Albrecht), the Netherlands (Junger-Tas), and the United States (Sampson and Lauritsen). Small wonder then that many minority defendants are not more cooperative when they get to court.

What is most striking about the five findings discussed in this section is that they come from so many countries. They apply to many groups and many countries, suggesting that bias, disparities, and disparate impact policy dilemmas are not uniquely the characteristics and problems of any particular minority groups or countries but are endemic to heterogeneous developed countries in which some groups are substantially less successful economically and socially than the majority population.

III. Immigration and Crime

Although nonimmigrants often attribute many social problems to the presence of immigrants in their midst, especially in periods of high population movement, for at least sixty years there has been a widely shared different understanding among researchers. The popular perception is not surprising; as the essays in this volume show, in each of the European countries examined, "foreigners," who are preponderantly recent immigrants or their descendants, are disproportionately involved in crime. Nonetheless, on the basis of research on the experiences of Western European immigrants to Canada and the United States early in this century, it has often been asserted that first-generation immigrants are typically more law-abiding than the resident population, that their children and grandchildren suffer assimilation problems that produce higher-than-normal offending and imprisonment rates higher than those of either their parents or the resident population, and that subsequent generations have crime experiences indistinguishable from those of the general population.

The first American national crime commission, the National Commission on Law Observance and Enforcement, popularly known as the

Wickersham Commission after its chairman, former Attorney General George W. Wickersham, devoted an entire volume to "Crime and the Foreign Born." Noting that public opinion attributed high crime rates to immigrants throughout most of American history, the commission devoted substantial energies and impressively extensive data collection and analysis to determining whether public opinion was justified. Among other things, the commission assembled data from many jurisdictions (e.g., arrest and crime statistics from fifty-two cities) on recorded crime, arrests, convictions, and prison commitments.

The commission's conclusions were signaled by use of the phrase "foreign born" in the immigration volume's title. The commission observed that there was substantial evidence that foreign born persons committed fewer major offenses, in proportion to their numbers, of the same sex and age, than did native-born persons, concluding that available data "seem to disagree radically with the popular belief that a high percentage [of contemporary crime] may be ascribed to the 'alien'" (National Commission on Law Observance and Enforcement 1931).

Thus the "foreign born" were not the problem, leaving the possibility that their American-born children were extensively involved in crime. Unfortunately, although many official records indicated (however accurately) foreign-born defendants' countries of origin, records for American-born defendants did not, making it impossible for the commission to array much data on the subject and leading it to recommend "a continuing study of a scientific character over a period of at least five years and on a national scale of the subject." (This difficulty in identifying children of immigrants in justice system records exists today in most countries.)

However, there were other sources of evidence. The commission's staff conducted extensive interviews with justice system officials and the commission received formal testimony. Every police officer, prosecutor, probation officer, and judge interviewed on the subject expressed the belief that there was an immigrant crime problem but that it was attributable not to immigrants but to their sons.

This "not the foreign born but their children" conclusion, though contrary to public opinion, probably did not surprise informed people who had previously taken an interest in the subject. Two earlier federal commissions had reached the same conclusions although on the basis of less evidence. The Industrial Commission of 1901 issued a "Special Report on General Statistics of Immigration and the Foreign Born" which discussed crime. That commission observed that foreign-born whites were less criminal than native whites but also that the large proportion of native-born prisoners having foreign parents was "just as strong an argument as to the injurious effect of immigration as would be a high proportion among the foreign born themselves" (Industrial Commission 1901).

A few years later, in 1911, the Immigration Commission, which existed from 1907 to 1911, issued a report on "immigration and crime." Although expressed cautiously in recognition of the limited evidence on which its conclusions were based, this commission reached the same conclusions: "No satisfactory evidence has yet been produced to show that immigration has resulted in an increase in crime disproportionate to the increase in adult population. . . . Such figures as are presented . . . indicate that immigration has not increased the volume of crime to a distinguishable extent, if at all. . . . In fact, the figures seem to show a contrary result" (Immigration Commission 1911). And, although the evidence was spotty, the immigration commission found that for some offenses American-born children of immigrants had higher crime rates than did American-born children of American-born parents.

From the 1920s through the 1940s, crime and immigration was a central interest of American criminologists who continued to observe, and then tried to explain, the broad patterns of findings of the three commissions (e.g., Reckless and Smith 1932; Sutherland 1934). The explanations for the relatively low crime rates of the foreign born are straightforward: self-selected economic migrants who braved an ocean voyage and left their home countries and families thousands of miles away came to America for economic opportunity and to improve their and their children's lives. Most were hard-working, ready to defer gratification in the interest of longer-term advancement, and therefore likely to be conformist and to behave themselves.

Their children, however, were caught between two worlds. Even if life were better in America than in the place their parents came from, the children often were unable to make or find solace in that comparison. What they knew was that their families often were poor, that others were much better off, and that opportunities for legitimate economic advancement were less available to them than to many nonimmigrant young people. Various theories have been offered to explain why the second generations' crime rates were higher than those of their parents or those of children of native-born parents: alienation, blocked opportunities, lack of role models, deviant subcultural values of youth gangs which young people joined as a source of self-identification and self-esteem. Whatever the reasons, the immigration and crime model that distinguishes the experiences of the generations settled into the conventional wisdom of criminology.

Large-scale immigration into the United States stopped after 1924, and, as time passed, the descendants of immigrants assimilated into the American mainstream. "Immigration and crime" attracted less attention as a political issue and other issues attracted American criminologists' attention. Interest first revived not in the United States but in Europe as the result of the migration of guest workers from southern Europe and North Africa into many European countries in the 1950s and 1960s.

Contemporary research in Germany (Kaiser 1974; Albrecht 1988, 1993), France, Switzerland (Killias 1977; Queloz 1986; Kunz 1989), and Sweden (Sveri 1987; Martens 1990; Ahlberg 1996) has attempted to test that model and has to some extent validated it. Killias (1989) has surveyed the German and French research. Earlier Swiss research showed that Italian labor migrants in the 1950s and 1960s had lower crime (conviction) rates than native Swiss males of comparable ages (Neumann 1963; Pradervand and Cardia 1966; Gillioz 1967).

However, from the essays on European research in this volume, we now know that the multigeneration immigration and crime model based on American experience is simplistic and is only partly true even for the self-selected economic migrants whose experience it describes.

1. *Self-Selected Economic Migrants from Many Asian Cultures Have Lower Crime Rates than the Resident Population in the First and in Subsequent Generations.* The traditional model does not take account of Asians: immigrant groups deriving directly (Chinese, Japanese, and Koreans to the United States, Indian subcontinent migrants to England) and sometimes indirectly (e.g., "Hindustanis" from Surinam to the Netherlands, "African Asians" from East Africa to England) from South and East Asia typically have low crime rates in the first and in subsequent generations.

In England, where comparisons have been made between the experiences of Asian immigrants from the Indian subcontinent and black immigrants from the Caribbean and Africa, Asian immigrants typically have lower crime and imprisonment rates than whites' and Afro-Caribbeans' higher ones. The contrast is particularly marked for Bangladeshi immigrants who are as, if not more, economically and socially disadvantaged as Afro-Caribbeans (also though, as noted earlier, Bangladeshis are relatively recent immigrants and their crime rates could rise over time). David Smith's essay in this volume summarizes research that shows that Asians were no less the victims of bias and stereotyping in England than were Afro-Caribbeans but from the outset adapted differently. Most notably, many expected to be discriminated against and organized their lives in ways that depended less on fair treatment than on self-help and ethnic-group networks (as, for example, seeking economic opportunities primarily within their own ethnic communities).

2. *Cultural Differences between Structurally Similarly Situated Immigrants Can Result in Sharply Different Crime Patterns.* The traditional model insufficiently takes account of cultural differences between groups that differentially affect their adaptation: the model would predict that Moroccans and Turks should have similar experiences in the Netherlands, both being economically and socially disadvantaged migrant groups who arrived as self-selected guest workers between 1950 and 1973, augmented by natural increase and by family unification policies; yet Turks have markedly lower self-reported and official crime rates than Moroccans (Junger-Tas, in this volume), and similar contrasts distinguish the two guest-worker groups in other countries (e.g., in Germany: Albrecht, in this volume). The essays in this volume on Sweden (Martens) and Germany (Albrecht) document other stark contrasts between the experiences of different nationality groups. Some of the contrasts may reflect age or class composition differences between groups, or the influence of the behavior of transients (illegals and tourists), but those considerations cannot explain all of the differences.

3. *There Are Grounds for Hypothesizing That, All Else Being Equal, Some Countries' Policies for Aiding Immigrants' Assimilation Can Reduce Crime Rates, Including Those of Their Second- and Third-Generation Descendants.* The traditional model insufficiently takes account of differences in receiving countries' social welfare (and settlement) policies. Martens (in this volume) provides plausible evidence that Swedish social welfare policies have reduced the "second-generation effect" even among economic intra-European migrants. Data covering many national origin groups, developed by Ahlberg (1996), indicate that crime rates for most groups are lower in the second than in the first generation, but that relative crime rate differences between groups remain the same. Overall, however, the second generation's crime rates were higher than those for nonimmigrant Swedes. These findings are striking because they simultaneously suggest that settlement policies can

suppress crime rates and confirm the observation in the preceding paragraph that cultural or other differences between groups are independently predictive of criminality.

4. *The Reasons Groups Migrate Powerfully Shape Criminality and Other Indications of Successful Adaptation.* The traditional model insufficiently takes account of the reasons why groups migrate: Swedish research shows that the adaptation experiences of guest-worker migrants in the fifties and sixties from Croatia and Serbia have been very different from those of demographically comparable war refugees from Serbia and Croatia in the eighties and nineties. The experience of the first wave roughly followed the North American pattern. In the second wave, first-generation migrants had high crime and victimization (and unemployment, welfare dependence, family breakup, and mental health problem) rates (Martens 1995).

A remarkable essay by Peter Martens (1995) gives insight into the special problems refugees face. It has been estimated that between 20 and 25 percent of recent refugees who immigrated to Sweden had earlier experienced physical torture. Many suffer from post-traumatic stress disorder. Angel and Hjern (1992, p. 36) observe that "seeing a close relative being ill-treated, killed or arrested or personally being subject to injustice are examples of mentally traumatic experiences that are common in refugees." Human beings suffer many kinds of traumatic experiences, and sizable psychological and psychiatric literatures document their effects. These include alienation, apathy, lack of trust in personal relationships, reduced ability to plan for the future, irritability, and exaggerated reactions to emotionally charged situations. Martens (1995, p. 287) observes, "Reduced self-esteem and alienation are expressed both in reduced self-control and in social isolation, which increase the individual tendency to commit crime."

Martens's work, and that of other Swedish researchers, forces attention on the reasons why people immigrate. Once the question is recast from "What do we know about the adaptation and criminality of economic migrants?" to "What do we know about the ways people respond to traumatic experiences?" the observation that the reasons why people immigrate are important predictors of their subsequent behavior becomes unexceptionable. It is, however, an observation that is seldom made concerning "immigration and crime."

5. *Many Categories of Immigrants Do Not Fall within Any of the Preceding Generalizations.* The traditional model does not describe the experiences of many immigrant groups that for one or another reason have

economic or social characteristics that fundamentally shape predicted criminality. Large numbers of Hong Kong Chinese have in the 1980s and 1990s either moved to Pacific Canada or purchased homes and made investments that will make it possible to make such a move after the transfer of governance of Hong Kong from Great Britain to China. As a group, expatriate Hong Kong Chinese are likely to be affluent and well-educated, characteristics that are seldom associated with high crime rates. Similarly, thousands of Americans migrated to Canada in protest against the Vietnam War. As a group the American expatriates were by definition politically conscious and are likely disproportionately to have been middle-class and relatively well-educated. For these two groups and for many others, their economic, social, and cultural characteristics are likely to be much better behavioral predictors than is any broadly phrased immigration and crime hypothesis.

IV. Learning More

Unanswered questions leap from the pages of this book. Why do some Asian groups adjust more readily to immigration than other groups? Are there lessons that can be drawn from such groups' experiences and then incorporated into settlement policies to help other groups adapt as successfully? Is it true that Swedish settlement policies have suppressed the second-generation effect and, if so, how? Can a taxonomy of settlement policies be developed that will permit matching of optimal policies to address the distinctive special needs of different migrant groups? Why do some seemingly similarly situated groups, like the Turks and Moroccans in the Netherlands, have such different crime patterns? Are there ways that legal practices and rules can be altered to lessen the adverse effects of some "neutral" policies on disadvantaged minority groups? Does the traditional immigration and crime model provide grounds for optimism that Afro-Caribbeans in England, who until the mid-1970s were not seen as a high-crime-rate group (Smith, in this volume), are simply passing through the second- and third-generation phases, amplified by an age distribution skewed toward young adults? If so, as with many other economic migrant groups in many countries, the problem of race and crime in England is likely gradually to disappear. Less optimistically, are the aboriginal populations of Canada and Australia in effect chronically traumatized peoples whose overinvolvement in crime is not likely to abate until the underlying causes abate, something that has not happened over several hundred years of exposure to colonization?

This book focuses primarily on crime and the justice system, but the focus could be made broader. There are a number of important related, but little studied, phenomena. First, minority group involvement in organized and transnational crime receives much media and policy attention in Europe. Second, similarly, minority groups are at least as likely as majority groups (probably more likely) to participate in black markets and the underground economy. Third, in Europe, at least, members of many migrant groups retain active ties to their home countries and yet intend to remain in their new countries; the effects of these multiple bonds on economic, social, and psychological integration (and crime) remain unstudied. Fourth is the increasing social segmentation of many European countries; members of many migrant groups fall into blue-collar and low-wage strata, which makes them highly vulnerable as semi-skilled and low-paid jobs become less available and economic pressures to survive make both work in the underground economy and crime more tempting.

A great deal can be learned about "race and crime" and "immigration and crime" by looking at the issues comparatively and cross-nationally. What needs to be done now is to move beyond single-country analyses to work that integrates those analyses: comprehensive efforts to combine learning in different countries, comprehensive efforts to establish what data are needed and available in each country to answer the questions that should be asked, development of a comprehensive research agenda that can begin to provide policy makers with the information they need to anticipate and work to prevent or ameliorate the kinds of problems that particular kinds of migrant groups are likely to experience. The political and ethical sensitivities that cause many countries to omit race and ethnicity data from their official records no doubt present a formidable challenge to the kind of projects described here. Unless that challenge can be overcome, however, little more will be learned and governments will have great difficulty improving the justice system experiences of members of minority groups.

Every Western country faces and will continue for many years to face political and policy issues related to race, ethnicity, population migration, and crime. Work like that discussed in this volume promises to provide crucial knowledge for addressing those issues.

The next step is to create a community of researchers and policy makers in many countries who will attempt to establish what is known, what is knowable, and how current knowledge might be advanced through comparative inquiry.

REFERENCES

Ahlberg, Jan. 1996. *Criminality among Immigrants and Their Children. A Statistical Analysis.* (In Swedish.) BRÅ-report. Stockholm: Fritzes.

Albrecht, Hans-Jörg. 1988. "Ausländerkriminalität." In *Fälle zum Wahlfach Kriminologie, Jugendstrafrecht, Strafvollzug,* 2d ed., edited by Heike Jung. München: Beck Verlag.

———. 1993. "Ethnic Minorities: Crime and Criminal Justice in Europe." In *Crime in Europe,* edited by Francis Heidensohn and Michael Farrell. London and New York: Routledge.

———. In this volume. "Ethnic Minorities, Crime, and Criminal Justice in Germany."

Angel, B., and A. Hjern. 1992. *To Meet Children of Refugees and Their Families.* (In Swedish.) Lund: Studentlitteratur.

Blumstein, Alfred, Jacqueline Cohen, Susan E. Martin, and Michael Tonry, eds. 1983. *Research on Sentencing: The Search for Reform.* 2 vols. Report of the National Academy of Sciences Panel on Sentencing Research. Washington, D.C.: National Academy Press.

Broadhurst, Roderic. 1996. In this volume. "Aborigines and Crime in Australia."

Bureau of Justice Statistics. 1995. "State and Federal Prisons Report Record Growth during Last 12 Months." Advance for release, December 3. Washington, D.C.: U.S. Department of Justice, Bureau of Justice Statistics.

Cohen, Richard. 1993. "Common Ground on Crime." *Washington Post* (December 21), p. A23.

Commission on Systemic Racism in the Ontario Criminal Justice System. 1995. *Report of the Commission on Systemic Racism in the Ontario Criminal Justice System.* Toronto: Queen's Printer for Ontario.

Doob, Anthony. 1991. *Workshop on Collection of Racial and Ethnic Statistics in the Criminal Justice System.* Toronto: University of Toronto, Centre of Criminology.

Duguid, A. M. 1992. "Police and Aboriginal Youth—Arrest or Report? Are Aboriginal Youth Treated Differently?" Paper presented to the conference on Measurement and Research in Criminal Justice, Griffith University, Mt. Gravatt, August.

Gale, F., R. Bailey-Harris, and J. Wundersitz. 1990. *Aboriginal Youth and the Criminal Justice System: The Injustice of Justice?* Melbourne: Cambridge University Press.

Gale, F., and J. Wundersitz. 1987. "Police and Black Minorities: The Case of Aboriginal Youth in South Australia." *Australian and New Zealand Journal of Criminology* 20:78–94.

Gillioz, E. 1967. "La criminalité des étrangers en Suisse." *Revue pénale suisse* 83(2):178–91.

Harding, R., R. Broadhurst, A. Ferrante, and N. Loh. 1995. *Aboriginal Contact with the Criminal Justice System and the Impact of the Recommendations of the Royal Commission into Aboriginal Deaths in Custody.* Sydney: Federation Press.

Hood, R. 1992. *Race and Sentencing.* Oxford: Clarendon Press.

Immigration Commission. 1911. *Report of the Immigration Commission.* U.S. Congress, Senate, 61st Congress, S. Doc. 750, Vol. 36. Washington, D.C.: U.S. Government Printing Office.

Industrial Commission. 1901. *Special Report on General Statistics of Immigration and the Foreign Born Population.* Washington, D.C.: U.S. Government Printing Office.

Junger-Tas, Josine. In this volume. "Ethnic Minorities and Criminal Justice in the Netherlands."

Kaiser, Günther. 1974. "Gastarbeiterkriminalität und ihre Erklärung als Kulturkonflikt." In *Gastarbeiter in Gesellschaft und Recht,* edited by Tugrul Ansay and Volkmar Gessner. München: Beck.

Killias, M. 1977. "Kriminelle Fremdarbeiter-Kinder? Strukturelle Determinanten der Delinquenz bei Fremdarbeitern unter besonderer Berücksichtigung der zweiten Generation." *Revue suisse de sociologie* 3(2):3–33.

———. 1989. "Criminality among Second-Generation Immigrants in Western Europe. A Review of the Evidence." *Criminal Justice Review* 14:13–42.

———. In this volume. "Immigrants, Crime, and Criminal Justice in Switzerland."

Klein, Stephen, Patricia Ebener, Allan Abrahamse, and Nora Fitzgerald. 1991. *Predicting Criminal Justice Outcomes: What Matters?* Santa Monica, Calif.: RAND.

Kunz, K.-L. 1989. "Ausländerkriminalität in der Schweiz—Umfang, Struktur und Erklärungsversuch." *Revue pénale suisse* 106(4):373–92.

Laprairie, C. 1990. "The Role of Sentencing in the Over-representation of Aboriginal People in Correctional Institutions." *Canadian Journal of Criminology* 32:429–40.

Maas, C. J., and J. Stuyling de Lange. 1989. "Selectiviteit in de rechtsgang van buitenlandse verdachten en verdachten behorende tot etnische groepen." *Tijdschrift voor Criminologie* no. 1:1–14.

Mann, Coramae Richey. 1993. *Unequal Justice—a Question of Color.* Bloomington: Indiana University Press.

Martens, P. L. 1990. "Criminal Behaviour among Young People with Immigrant Background." In *Crime and Measures against Crime in the City,* edited by P.-O. H. Wikström. BRÅ-Report 1990:5. Stockholm: National Council for Crime Prevention/Allmanna Förlaget.

———. 1995. "Immigrants and Crime Prevention." In *Integrating Crime Prevention Strategies: Propensity and Opportunity,* edited by Per-Olof H. Wikström, Ronald V. Clarke, and Joan McCord. Stockholm: Fritzes.

———. In this volume. "Immigrants, Crime, and Criminal Justice in Sweden."

Mayhew, H. 1861. *London Labour and London Poor.* London: Griffin, Bohn.

National Commission on Law Observance and Enforcement. 1931. *Crime and the Foreign Born.* Washington, D.C.: U.S. Government Printing Office.

Neumann, J. 1963. "Die Kriminalität der italienischen Arbeitskräfte im Kanton Zürich." Law faculty doctoral dissertation, University of Zurich.

Petersilia, Joan, and Susan Turner. 1986. *Prison versus Probation in California.* Santa Monica, Calif.: RAND.

Pradervand, P., and L. Cardia. 1966. "Quelques aspects de la délinquance italienne à Genève; Une enquête sociologique." *Revue international de criminologie et de police technique* 20:43–58.

Queloz, N. 1986. *La réaction institutionnelle à la délinquance juvénile*. Neuchâtel: EDES.

Reckless, W., and H. Smith. 1932. *Juvenile Delinquency*. New York: McGraw-Hill.

Roberts, Julian V., and Anthony N. Doob. In this volume. "Race, Ethnicity, and Criminal Justice in Canada."

Royal Commission into Aboriginal Deaths in Custody. 1991. *Report*. Canberra: Australian Government Printing Service.

Royal Commission on Criminal Justice. 1993. *Report*. London: H.M. Stationery Office.

Sampson, Robert J., and Janet L. Lauritsen. In this volume. "Racial and Ethnic Disparities in Crime and Criminal Justice in the United States."

Shaw, Clifford R. 1929. *Delinquency Areas*. Chicago: University of Chicago Press.

Smith, David. In this volume. "Ethnic Origins, Crime, and Criminal Justice in England and Wales."

Sowell, Thomas. 1983. *The Economics and Politics of Race*. New York: William Morrow.

Sutherland, E. 1934. *Principles of Criminology*. Philadelphia: Lippincott.

Sveri, B. 1987. *Recidivism in Crime among Foreign Citizens*. (In Swedish.) Stockholm: Stockholm University.

Tak, Peter J. P. 1994. "Sentencing and Punishment in the Netherlands." *Overcrowded Times* 5(5):5–8.

Tonry, Michael. 1994. "Racial Disproportion in U.S. Prisons." *British Journal of Criminology* 34(special issue):97–115.

———. 1995. *Malign Neglect: Race, Crime, and Punishment in America*. New York: Oxford University Press.

Tournier, Pierre. In this volume. "Nationality, Crime, and Criminal Justice in France."

Weigend, Thomas. 1993. "In Germany, Fines Often Imposed in Lieu of Prosecution." *Overcrowded Times* 4(1):1, 15–16.

Wilbanks, William. 1987. *The Myth of a Racist Criminal Justice System*. Monterey, Calif.: Brooks/Cole.

[3]
The Malign Effects of Drugs and Crime Control Policies on Black Americans

ABSTRACT

The disproportionate presence of blacks in American prisons, jails, and Death Rows, and the principal reasons for it—higher rates of commission of violent crimes and racially disparate effects of drug policies and sentencing laws governing violent and drug crimes—are well known. Since the late 1980s, black involvement in violent crime has declined substantially, but racial disproportions have not. Blacks are six to seven times more likely than whites to be in prison. Nearly a third of young black men are under criminal justice system control. A third of black boys born in 2001 are predicted to spend some time in prison. The simplest explanation for these patterns is that drug and sentencing policies that contribute to disparities have not been significantly changed in decades. The question then is, why not? The answer is that the white majority does not empathize with poor black people who wind up in prison. That in turn is because recent punishment policies have replaced the urban ghetto, Jim Crow laws, and slavery as a mechanism for maintaining white dominance over blacks in the United States.

Seen from outside the United States, and, we expect, as it will be seen by future generations of Americans, four aspects of contemporary crime control policies stand out: the world's highest imprisonment rate, the Western world's only use of capital punishment, the Western world's most severe punishments short of death, and the effects of those policies on black Americans. Gross racial disparities in impris-

Michael Tonry is Sonosky Professor of Law and Public Policy, University of Minnesota Law School, and senior fellow, Netherlands Institute for the Study of Crime and Law Enforcement. Matthew Melewski is a 2008 graduate of the University of Minnesota Law School. They are grateful to Alfred Blumstein, Richard Frase, Marc Mauer, Myron Orfield, and Kevin Reitz for helpful comments on earlier drafts.

onment and entanglement in the criminal justice system result partly from racial differences in offending, but preponderantly from adoption and continuation of drug and crime control policies that affect black Americans much more severely than whites. Much of the harm being done to disadvantaged black Americans and their loved ones in the name of crime control was, and is, avoidable.

The litany of ways crime control policies disproportionately affect black Americans by now is so familiar as to be unsurprising. Blacks constituted 12.8 percent of the general population in 2005 but nearly half of prison inmates and 42 percent of Death Row residents. Imprisonment rates for black men were nearly seven times higher than for white men. About a third of young black men aged 20–29 were in prison or jail or on probation or parole on an average day in 2005. The Bureau of Justice Statistics (BJS) estimated in 2003 that 32 percent of black men born in 2001 will spend some part of their lives in a state or federal prison. That is a substantial underestimate of the likelihood that black men will spend time behind bars; it does not take account of jail confinement, which is much more common than time in prison (Bonczar 2003; BJS 2007, tables 6.33.2005, 6.17.2006, 6.80.2007).

What is surprising is not that these things are true, but that they are well known, have long been well known, and have changed little in recent decades. Few people except academics and liberal law reformers—seemingly almost no policy makers—much notice or care. The racial disparities caused by the federal 100-to-one law that punishes crack cocaine offenses much more severely than powder cocaine offenses were foreseeable when the law was passed (Tonry 1995, pp. 4–6) and were irrefutably documented long ago (McDonald and Carlson 1993). The law remains in effect, successively endorsed by the Reagan, Bush I, Clinton, and Bush II administrations.[1]

To take another example, the Congressional Black Caucus, during consideration of federal crime legislation in 1994, fought hard for a Racial Justice Act that would allow statistics on racial disparities in

[1] The U.S. Sentencing Commission repeatedly urged the Congress to repeal or diminish the crack/powder sentencing differential (e.g., U.S. Sentencing Commission 1995). Attorney General Janet Reno initially endorsed the commission's 1995 proposal to eliminate the 100-to-one differential, and, backtracking, she and "drug czar" General Barry McCaffrey later called for it to be reduced to 10-to-one, but to no avail (Tonry 2004, chap. 1). In 2007, the commission proposed amendment of guideline provisions that made federal sentencing even tougher than the mandatory minimum law required. The Congress through inaction allowed the amendments to take effect. The statute itself, which does the main damage, continued in effect early in 2008, unchanged.

capital punishment to be introduced in death penalty cases. David Baldus and his colleagues, using Georgia data on 2,000 cases from the 1970s, had convincingly shown that the racial characteristics of murder defendants and victims were powerfully associated with whether capital punishment is imposed (Baldus, Woodworth, and Pulaski 1990). Twenty-two percent of black killers of white victims were sentenced to death compared with 3 percent of white killers of blacks (prosecutors sought death in 70 percent of black-on-white killings and 19 percent of white-on-black). The U.S. Supreme Court in *McCleskey v. Kemp* (481 U.S. 279 [1987]) decided that such evidence was irrelevant in deciding claims about racial discrimination. Even though the court "assumed the study is statistically valid" (n. 8), it ruled that a defendant alleging discrimination had to prove that the prosecutor in that particular case had acted in a biased way. This is almost impossible to do; bigoted officials seldom admit to acting in bigoted ways.

For a time, it appeared likely that President Clinton would support the caucus. In the end, he did not. Instead he signed the Violent Crime Control and Law Enforcement Act of 1994, which created more than 50 new federal capital offenses; the caucus's proposed provision had been dropped (Gest 2001, pp. 230–35). For a few years in the 1990s, the caucus continued to support federal legislation attempting to reduce racial disparities in death penalty cases, but the issue gradually died down. The proportion of blacks on Death Row was about the same in 2007 as it had been in 1994.

A third example: Daniel Patrick Moynihan in 1965 urged a controversial welfare policy of benign neglect toward poor black Americans, arguing that they needed mostly to be let alone to get on with their lives. American crime control policies in the early twenty-first century do the opposite of that. They diminish the life chances of black men (Western 2006; Provine 2007) and undermine the social fabric of many poor black communities (Clear 2007).

Since at least 1980, American crime control policies have undermined achievement of full unbiased participation of black Americans in the nation's social, economic, and political life. Modern wars on crime and drugs, which date from the early 1970s, shortly after the first serious federal antidiscrimination laws were enacted, could not more effectively have kept black Americans "in their place" had they been designed with that aim in mind.

The following list of social, vocational, educational, and economic differences between blacks and whites is drawn from the 2007 *Statistical Abstract of the United States*:

- 33.3 percent of black children lived in households below the poverty line in 2004, compared with 14.2 percent of white children;
- the mortality rate for black infants in 2003 was 14 per 1,000 live births, compared with 5.7 per 1,000 for whites;
- per capita income for black Americans was $16,035 in 2004, compared with $25,203 for whites;
- 10 percent of adult blacks were unemployed and 35.8 percent were not in the labor force in 2005, compared with 4.4 and 33.7 percent of whites;
- 17.6 percent of blacks 25 and older had college degrees in 2005, compared with 28 percent of whites; and
- 48.1 percent of blacks owned their own homes in 2005, compared with 72.7 percent of whites (U.S. Department of Commerce 2006, tables 107, 214, 575, 685, 693, 954).

Those differences have been at least exacerbated by, and are probably substantially attributable to, the nearly seven-to-one racial difference in imprisonment rates that has been typical for the past quarter century, the staggering difference in black and white men's lifetime chances of going to prison, and the entanglement of a large minority of young black men in their 20s in the justice system at a time of life when other young men are building careers and conventional lives (Western 2006). Accumulating bodies of research show that going to prison reduces employment prospects and average and lifetime earnings (Fagan and Freeman 1999; Raphael, Holzer, and Stoll 2006) and reduces the later well-being of prisoners' children (Murray and Farrington, in this volume). A different literature shows that disadvantaged communities are damaged, not helped, when large numbers of their residents are sent to prison. Low levels of imprisonment at least arguably may prevent crime through deterrence, incapacitation, and removal of antisocial role models; high levels cause crime rates to increase and neighborhoods to deteriorate (Clear 2007; in this volume).

If incarceration rates for jail and prison together had remained at 1970 levels (around 130 per 100,000) or at 1980 levels (around 200), American crime control policies would have bitten much less deeply into black American communities. American crime rates reached their all-time high in 1981, so the 1980 comparison is probably the better one. Less than a third of black Americans in prison in 2008 would be there had 1980 rates continued. Many fewer black men would have suffered the pains of imprisonment, resulting stigma, and reduced employment prospects. There would have been many fewer broken black families, fewer negative role models for black boys, and more marriageable black men. There would have been less deterioration in poor black communities because tipping points would not have been reached. At a time when civil rights and welfare policies aimed at improving opportunities and living standards for black Americans, drug and crime policies worsened them.

Scholars have long paid attention to interactions among race, crime, and criminal justice (e.g., Du Bois [1899] 1988; Myrdal 1944). The modern literature dates from Alfred Blumstein's at the time courageous 1982 article showing that a principal reason why so many more blacks than whites were in prison was that they were much more often arrested for the kinds of crimes that typically resulted in prison sentences.[2] The more serious the crime, the more fully offending patterns appeared to explain racial disparities in imprisonment.[3] That conclusion was tested in lots of ways—for example, by comparing racial patterns in victims' identifications of assailants with racial patterns in arrests and by comparing arrests and victims' reports to prison admissions—but held up at least through the mid-1990s (Langan 1985; Tonry 1995, chaps. 2, 3).

Substantial literatures have continued to accumulate on racial pat-

[2] "Courageous" because at the time racial issues were so sensitive that few scholars, black or white, could write about racial differences in offending without being accused of racism, blaming the victims of racial discrimination, or perpetuating racially harmful stereotypes. William Julius Wilson, a black American who is among the most distinguished and influential sociologists of his generation, wrote a landmark book, *The Declining Significance of Race*, in which he argued that poor blacks' main problem was not racism and discrimination per se but the deindustrialization of the American economy and the loss of semi- and unskilled industrial jobs in American cities (Wilson 1978). In the preface to his next major book, *The Truly Disadvantaged*, he observed that critics "either labeled me a neoconservative or directly or indirectly tried to associate *The Declining Significance of Race* with the neoconservative movement. . . . I am a social democrat and probably to the left politically of the overwhelming majority of these critics" (1987, p. viii).

[3] Conversely, the less serious the offense, the less offending differences appeared to explain disparities. For drug offenses, arrests are simply artifacts of police tactics and cannot sensibly be used as behavioral measures. Blumstein's article was controversial at the time but in retrospect is easily consonant with research on sentencing outcomes, which generally shows few racial differences in the probability of imprisonment for the most serious offenses. The space for bias, unconscious stereotyping and attribution, and other nonoffense factors to affect outcomes increases as prison sentences become less likely (Spohn 2000).

terns in arrests (with particular emphasis on profiling) and on racial differences in sentencing. The arrest literature shows that blacks in most places are more likely than whites to be stopped by the police, regardless of whether rates for pedestrian stops are calculated according to neighborhood population or according to transient population, and for traffic stops regardless of whether rates are calculated according to general population or to drivers of automobiles vulnerable to being stopped. Once stopped, blacks (and Hispanics) are more likely than whites to be searched, to be arrested, and to have force used against them. Percentages of stops resulting in seizures of contraband, however, tend to be lower for blacks than for whites, suggesting that police are likelier to stop blacks for less valid, often pretextual, reasons (e.g., Engel and Calnon 2004, pp. 77–81).[4]

The sentencing literature documents relatively small racial differences. Black defendants, all else being equal, are slightly more likely than whites to be sentenced to confinement but, among those incarcerated, not to receive longer sentences (Spohn 2000, 2002). Blacks are less likely than whites to be diverted to nonincarcerative punishments and more likely in guidelines states to receive sentences at the tops rather than the bottoms of sentencing guidelines ranges (Tonry 1996, chap. 2). Individual studies present divergent findings, often showing disparities by race and ethnicity for men but not for women (or to different extents), for Hispanics but not for blacks, and for young offenders but not for older ones (or in each case vice versa) (e.g., Walker, Spohn, and DeLone 2006; Harrington and Spohn 2007, pp. 40–45).

In this essay we examine the empirical issues that Michael canvassed nearly 15 years ago in *Malign Neglect* (Tonry 1995) to see to what extent black/white differences in victimization, offending, drug use, arrest, sentencing, imprisonment, and capital punishment have changed. They have changed very little.

Section I surveys case processing data on arrest through capital punishment and discusses recent survey data on racial differences in drug use and trafficking. Although conscious bias and stereotyping probably explain some portion of racial disparities, and unconscious stereotyping surely does, the principal drivers of disparities in imprisonment continue to be racial differences in commission of "imprisonable" offenses

[4] Table 1 in Engel and Calnon (2004) summarizes data from 16 studies, of which 10 report higher hit rates for whites. Engel and Calnon's own study, based on National Crime Victimization Survey (NCVS) data, finds substantially higher white hit rates.

and the foreseeable disparate effects on blacks and whites of police tactics in the war on drugs and sentencing policies for violent and drug offenses.

Section II explains the patterns the preceding sections document. Because much racial disparity is attributable to the effects of policies that could have been foreseen to affect black offenders disproportionately severely and are now widely recognized to have that effect, the fundamental questions are how that could have happened and why it has been allowed to continue to happen. The answer is that political and ideological exigencies of the last quarter century have conduced to the adoption of crime control policies of unprecedented severity, the primary burdens of which have been borne by disadvantaged blacks (and, increasingly, Hispanics). The history of American race relations has produced political and social sensibilities that made white majorities comparatively insensitive to the suffering of disadvantaged blacks.

Section III proposes ways that avoidable disparities can be reduced.

I. Racial Differences in Criminal Justice System Case Processing

Here is what was known in the mid-1990s about racial disparities in the criminal justice system (Tonry 1995, chap. 2). For a century before the 1960s black people had been more likely to be held in prison than whites. Racial disparities began to rise in the 1960s and then shot up to all-time highs in the 1980s: blacks by then were half of American prisoners, though only 12 percent of the U.S. population, and had an imprisonment rate seven times higher than the white rate. Part of the reason for this was that blacks were sometimes treated more harshly than whites for reasons of bias or unconscious stereotyping. A larger part of the explanation, however, was that blacks were more likely than whites to be arrested for the "imprisonable" offenses of robbery, rape, aggravated assault, and homicide. Victimization data on victims' descriptions of assailants and police data on victim and offender characteristics in homicide cases suggested that the racial offending patterns shown in arrest data for serious crimes were not far off from reality. Critically, however, there had been no significant shifts in racial patterns in arrests for a quarter century, and involvement in serious violent crime could not explain why black imprisonment rates had risen so rapidly since the late 1960s. A principal driver of the increase was imprisonment for drug crimes (Blumstein and Beck 1999), and policy makers knew or should have known that the enemy foot soldiers in the war on drugs would be young, disadvantaged, inner-city members of minority groups (Tonry 1995).

Little in that paragraph would need to be changed to describe conditions in 2007 rather than in 1993–94. Racial differences in commission of serious violent crimes continue to be an important contributor to imprisonment disparities, but the absolute overrepresentation of blacks among arrestees has declined significantly. Imprisonment rates, however, were much higher in 2007 than in 1993, and with their increase the lifetime probability of imprisonment for black men and the percentage of young black men under justice system control both increased substantially. The black fractions of the prison, jail, and Death Row populations have changed little. Nor has the difference in black imprisonment rates compared to white rates changed significantly. Policies authorizing or requiring harsh punishments for drug offenses continue to be one major contributor to racial disparities. Another is staggering increases in severity of sentences for violent crime: if 40–50 percent of people arrested for violent crimes are black, then black Americans are foreseeably bearing the burdens of increased harshness.

A. Incarceration Rates

Figure 1 shows black and white percentages of state and federal prisoners from 1950 to 2006. Blacks were about a third of prisoners in 1960 and under 40 percent in 1970. The black percentage rose continuously to the mid-40s around 1980, rising slowly thereafter until the early 1990s and plateauing at about 50. For most years between 1991 and 2002, in absolute numbers there were more black than white prisoners. The black percentage has since declined slightly.

Calculation of trend data has been complicated by a BJS decision beginning in the late 1990s to report separate figures for blacks, whites, and Hispanics. In earlier years, Hispanics were included within racial categories and sometimes also reported separately. The BJS change had the effect of reducing "black" imprisonment rates. In our view, skin color and "racial" identity have been more salient social characteristics in recent decades in the United States than the Hispanic/non-Hispanic difference has been. Insofar as racial bias, stereotypes, and attributions have influenced officials' decisions, appearance is much more likely than a Hispanic surname or ancestry to have influenced decisions. Ac-

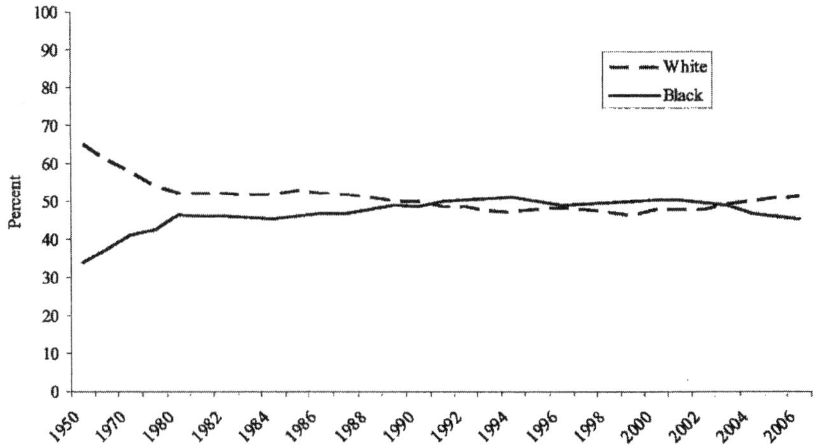

FIG. 1.—Percentage of state and federal prisoners, by race, 1950–2006. Sources: For 1950–80: Cahalan (1986); for 1980–2006: BJS, "Prisoners," various years. Until the late 1990s, race was broken down into three categories for all statistics: white, black, and other. In recent years, BJS added Hispanic as a racial category to various statistics, thus complicating linear representations of the data. In 1999, BJS added Hispanic as a racial category to combined state and federal prison statistics (skipping 1998 in the process). BJS also revised some data in later years, occasionally creating three different data points for a single year. In 2004, BJS added the category of "two or more races," further complicating the data. We have adopted the approach taken in Tonry (2005). The Hispanic category has been removed and redistributed for every year since 1999. This redistribution was made by examining the years 1990 and 1995, for which BJS has supplied data both with and without a separate Hispanic category. Approximately one-fourth of Hispanics were formerly counted as black in those years, and three-quarters were counted as white. For all years, the most recent published BJS data were used, except for 1990 and 1995. For those years, the older data without the Hispanic separation were used. The category of "two or more races" has been redistributed evenly between blacks and whites.

cordingly, in figure 1 (and other figures) we adjusted BJS prison population data to take account of the estimated black/white fractions among Hispanics.[5]

The jail story is much the same, as figure 2 shows. About a third of

[5] The method for redistributing Hispanics was determined by examining 1990 and 1995 data in which the BJS reported black/white figures including Hispanics and also reported Hispanics separately. For 1995, e.g., 17.6 percent of prisoners were classified as Hispanic. Excluding Hispanics, 45.7 percent of prisoners were black and 33.5 percent were white. Including Hispanics, 49.9 percent were black and 47.7 percent were white. Simple math shows that approximately one-fourth of Hispanics were counted as black and three-fourths as white (Tonry 2005, p. 1255, n. 99).

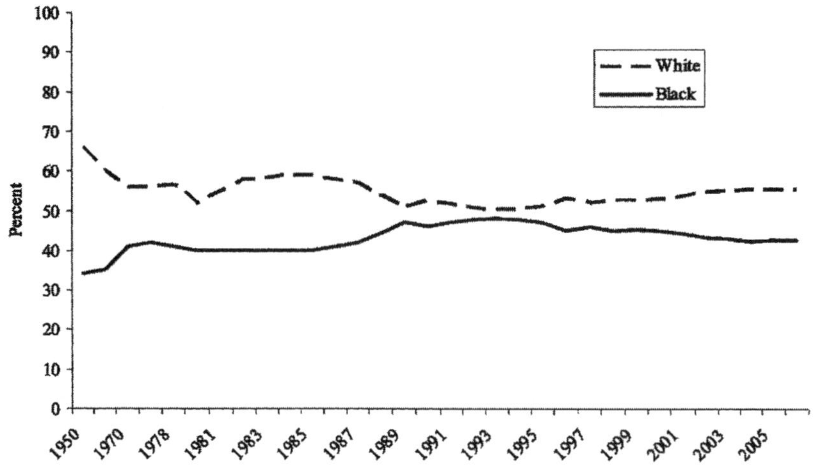

FIG. 2.—Percentage of local jail inmates, by race, 1950–2006. Sources: For 1950–83: Cahalan (1986); BJS (1984, 1990); for 1983–89: BJS, "Jail Inmates," various years; for 1990–95: Gilliard and Beck (1996); for 1996–2006: BJS, "Prison and Jail Inmates at Midyear," various years. BJS began using a separate Hispanics category much earlier in reporting jail data than in reporting prisoner data. For every year starting in 1990 the Hispanic category has been removed and redistributed, estimating that one-fourth of Hispanics were previously counted as black and three-quarters were counted as white.

jail inmates were black in 1950 and about 40 percent in 1970, a level around which the black percentage oscillated until the late 1980s. For a decade after that, coinciding with the most aggressive years of the war on drugs, blacks were 45–48 percent of inmates, after which the percentage declined somewhat. BJS data for the years 1990–2006 have been adjusted to distribute Hispanics between blacks and whites.

Because the preceding two figures are expressed in black/white percentages, they do not reflect the true magnitude of racial differences in imprisonment rates. It would be natural for someone new to the subject to compare the black percentage of the general population (12–13 percent) to the black percentages of the combined jail and prison populations (48–50 percent) and conclude that blacks are four times more likely to be confined than should be expected. The true difference in recent years has typically been about seven times. The reason is that whites are underrepresented in prison compared with their presence in the population and blacks are overrepresented. In 2006, for example, the total imprisonment rate for black men for jail

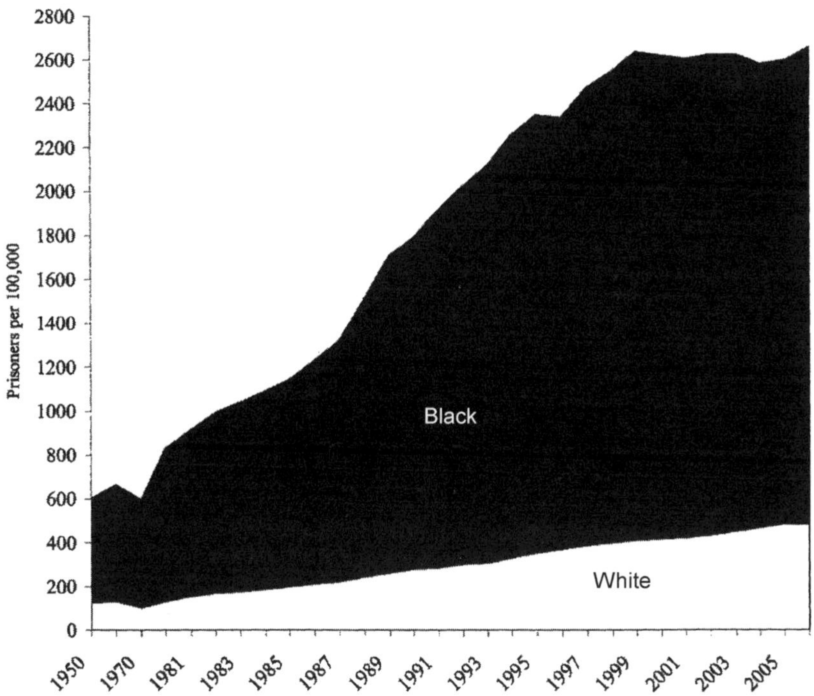

FIG. 3.—Incarceration in state and federal prisons and local jails per 100,000, by race, 1950–2006. Sources: BJS (1984, 1990; "Jail Inmates," various years; "Prisoners," various years; "Prison and Jail Inmates at Midyear," various years); Cahalan (1986); Gilliard and Beck (1996). The BJS occasionally publishes the number of prisoners in state and federal prisons and local jails, by race, as a ratio of the races' respective general populations (what we might call the total imprisonment rate). The publications are sporadic and interspersed with the ratio only for state prisons, only for state and federal prisons, only for local jails, or (most commonly) only for males. This graph is based on data used in figs. 1 and 2, then compared with population statistics provided by the Census Bureau.

and prison combined was 4,789 per 100,000 residents and the white rate was 737 per 100,000 (the corresponding rates for black and white women were 358 and 94) (Sabol, Minton, and Harrison 2007, table 14).[6]

Figure 3 shows aggregate black/white incarceration rates for jails and federal and state prisons from 1950 to 2006. Black rates dwarf those of whites. The increase in the black rate between 1980 and 2006 (1,834

[6] These numbers understate the rates since, per current BJS practice, Hispanic blacks and whites are excluded.

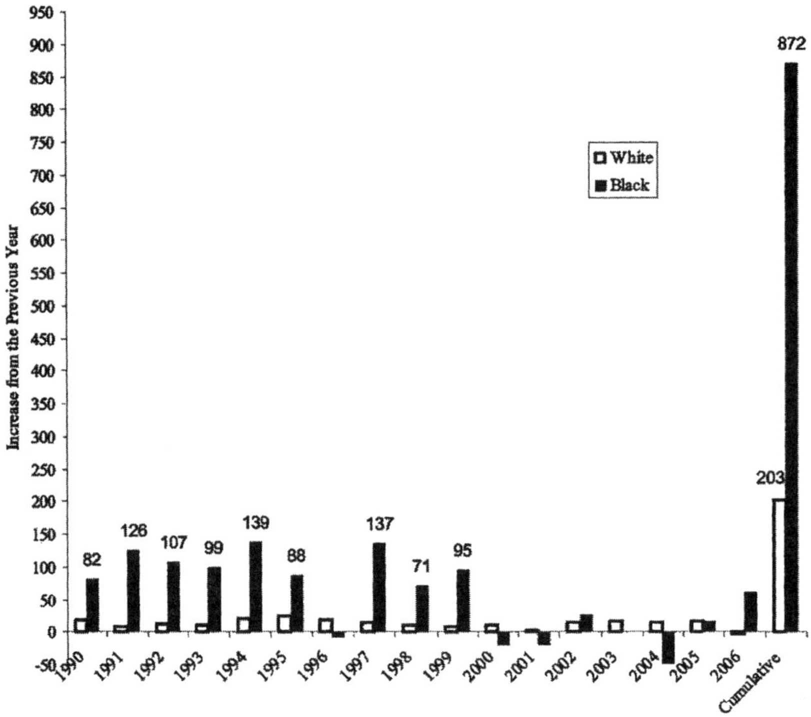

FIG. 4.—Increases in the total imprisonment rate per 100,000, by race, 1990–2006. Sources: Same as fig. 3.

per 100,000) was 3.8 times the total white rate (483 per 100,000) in 2006. The magnitude of racial differences in combined incarceration rates can be illustrated in another way. By 2006, the white rate (483), after 33 years of increases beginning in 1973, failed to reach the black rate in 1950 (598).

The racial difference in aggregate imprisonment rates is huge, as figure 3 shows. The extent to which increased imprisonment over recent decades has destabilized America's black population can be shown in another way. The nearly seven-to-one difference in imprisonment rates continued nearly unchanged for a quarter century. That means that the incremental increase for blacks each year, on average, has been seven times higher than the increase for whites. Figure 4 shows this. It depicts year-to-year increases in total imprisonment rates for blacks and whites from 1990 to 2006 and, following 2006, the cumulative

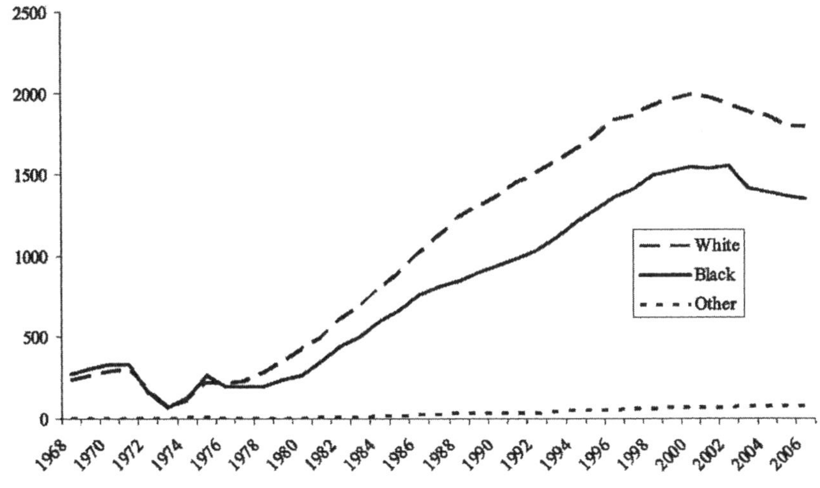

FIG. 5.—Prisoners under sentence of death, by race, 1968–2006. Source: Snell (2007)

increases. In 9 of the 17 years shown, the increase in black imprisonment rates exceeded 70 per 100,000. In four of those years, the increase exceeded 100 per 100,000. Those 1-year increases exceed the total imprisonment rates of Canada and most European countries.[7] Over 17 years, the black rate increased by 872 per 100,000 and the white rate by 203, a difference approaching 500 percent.

Racial disparities on Death Row parallel those for imprisonment generally. Figure 5 shows absolute numbers of blacks and whites on Death Row. The black fraction has not changed significantly for 25 years, despite a steep decline in homicide rates and despite, as we show below, a significant decline in the percentages of blacks arrested for homicide.

The disproportionate presence of blacks in American prisons and jails has not changed substantially since 1980. The important question is why.

[7] In 2005, the imprisonment rates for the Scandinavian countries ranged between 70 and 85 per 100,000 population. The rates for France, Germany, Belgium, and Austria were under 100 per 100,000. The Canadian rate was just above 100 per 100,000 (Walmsley 2007).

B. Racial Differences in Criminality as Explanations for Imprisonment Rates

Twenty-five years ago possible explanations for why the prison population was nearly half black were contentious and hotly disputed. Suspicions that criminal justice officials were racially biased and labored under the influence of racial stereotypes detrimental to blacks were widespread (e.g., American Friends Service Committee 1971). Within a decade, however, a consensus view emerged that, though bias and stereotyping existed, they were not the primary drivers of racial disparities in imprisonment. For serious violent crimes, a primary driver was racial differences in offending. Blacks committed homicides, rapes, robberies, and serious assaults at much higher rates than whites did. Much violent offending is intraracial. Failure to take black offenders' violent crimes seriously in effect would constitute indifference to black victims' violent victimization, and few people would want to do that. Racial disparities preponderantly based on offending differences were difficult to challenge on normative grounds.

There were two important caveats to the explanation that differences in racial offending explain differences in imprisonment. First, it applied mostly to serious violent offenses; for less serious offenses, offending explained much less of imprisonment disparities. For the most serious crimes, the crime itself appeared to be the primary factor explaining sentencing decisions, leaving comparatively little room for bias or stereotyping to operate. Less serious crimes allowed more room for discretionary decision making and the crime explained less. Second, for some crimes, arrest differences have no necessary link to offending differences; drug arrests are the most important example. Police can arrest street-level inner-city drug dealers almost at will, meaning that arrests are more a measure of police than of criminal activity. Disparities in arrests for drug offenses are the result of police policy choices.

The preceding paragraphs summarize analyses catalyzed by a landmark article by Alfred Blumstein (1982) that compared racial differences in arrests to racial differences in imprisonment, by offense and overall. It prompted additional more refined analyses by others (e.g., Langan 1985; Tonry 1995). The basic conclusion held up and was broadly confirmed by research on sentencing disparities that generally concluded that there are few racial differences in sentence lengths for offenders sent to prison (presumably mostly for more serious offenses and more chronic offenders); disparities are much more likely concerning the in/out decision (typically often concerning less serious offenses and offenders) (Blumstein et al. 1983; Spohn 2000; Harrington and Spohn 2007).

In this subsection, we summarize Blumstein's analysis, replicate the analysis for the year 2004, and consider other sources of data that might confirm or refute conclusions reached.

1. *Blumstein's Original Analysis.* Blumstein compared racial percentages among arrestees for particular offense categories to racial percentages among state prisoners sentenced following convictions for those offenses. Lots of questions can be raised as to whether arrests are a valid measure of offending (e.g., they might be systematically biased or erratically incomplete), whether jail inmates should have been taken into account, and whether they should be compared with racial patterns in prison admissions rather than in prison populations.[8] We return to some of those questions below. First we present Blumstein's analysis.

Table 1 sets out Blumstein's original analysis and adds one additional column of information. Columns 1 and 2 show black/white percentages among people serving prison sentences in 1979 for 11 offense categories and overall. Columns 3 and 4 show black/white percentages of people aged 18 and up arrested in 1979 for those offense categories and overall. Column 6, which was not in Blumstein's analysis, compares the black percentages in the preceding columns and shows, for example, that black arrests for homicide account for all but 1.3 percent of the black percentage among people imprisoned for homicide. The unexplained variations among people imprisoned for robbery and aggravated assault are larger, but still small. For lesser assaults, auto theft, and burglary, the unexplained variation ranges from 16.6 to 29.8 percent, with the largest unexplained variation being for drug crime (36.7 percent).

Blumstein used a different analysis. Results are shown in column 5. He compared black imprisonment relative to arrests to white imprisonment relative to arrests. Whites were relatively underrepresented in prison compared with their presence among arrestees (e.g., 47.7 percent of homicide prisoners but 48.5 percent of homicide arrestees; 57.7

[8] Blumstein (1982) identifies others. Use of aggregate national data, e.g., could camouflage stark differences between states (some of which might be very discriminatory, but this would pass unrecognized) and overlook offsetting racial biases (e.g., punishing blacks with white victims very harshly while punishing crimes involving black victims leniently or not at all).

TABLE 1

Comparison of Crime-Specific Percentage of Blacks in State Prison and in Arrests, 1979

Crime	Prisoners		Arrests		% Black Prisoners Unexplained by Arrest	
	White (1)	Black (2)	White (3)	Black (4)	Between Races (5)	Within Race (6)
Murder and nonnegligent manslaughter	47.7	52.3	48.4	51.6	2.8	1.3
Forcible rape	43.7	56.3	51.3	48.7	26.3	13.5
Robbery	38.8	61.2	42.9	57.1	15.6	6.7
Aggravated assault	57.7	42.3	59.0	41.0	5.2	3.1
Other violent	53.1	46.9	60.9	39.1	27.3	16.6
Burglary	57.7	42.3	67.1	32.9	33.1	22.2
Larceny/auto theft	50.7	49.3	65.4	34.6	45.6	29.8
Other property	64.4	35.6	65.4	34.6	4.3	2.8
Drugs	60.5	39.5	75.0	25.0	48.9	36.7
Public order	61.4	38.6	69.3	30.7	29.5	20.5
Other	71.7	28.3	66.3	33.7	−28.7	−19.1
Total	50.9	49.14	56.6	43.45	20.5	11.6

SOURCE.—Blumstein (1982).

percent of burglary prisoners but 67.1 percent of burglary arrestees). He thus compared blacks' presence in prison given an arrest for a particular offense to whites' presence. Between-race calculations (col. 5) produce higher rates of unexplained variation than do within-race calculations (col. 6) (20.5 percent overall compared with 11.6), but the results using either calculation were inconsistent with the hypothesis that racial bias and stereotyping explained the largest part of disparities in imprisonment rates for serious crimes.

Two primary objections to Blumstein's analysis are that arrests may themselves be a biased basis for comparison and that prison population data reflect a combination of prison admission rates with sentence lengths. Patrick Langan (1985) explored these objections. His aim was to get behind arrests by looking at data on assailants identified by victims and, to avoid the confounding interaction effects of prison admission rates and average sentence lengths, by looking at prison admission rates alone. He compared data from the NCVS for 1973, 1979, and 1982 on victims' characterizations of their assailants' race with racially disaggregated data on prison admissions. Because victimization

TABLE 2

Comparison of Crime-Specific Percentage of Blacks in State Prison and in Arrests, 2004

	Prisoners		Arrests		% Black Prisoners Unexplained by Arrest	
Crime	White (1)	Black (2)	White (3)	Black (4)	Between Races (5)	Within Race (6)
Murder and nonnegligent manslaughter	48.9	51.1	52.0	48.0	11.6	6.0
Forcible rape	61.7	38.3	67.7	32.3	23.2	15.7
Robbery	37.6	62.4	49.0	51.0	37.2	18.2
Assault	53.3	46.7	73.5	26.5	58.8	43.2
Burglary	59.1	40.9	72.6	27.4	45.5	33.0
Larceny/theft	58.8	42.2	71.1	28.9	44.3	31.5
Motor vehicle theft	63.3	36.7	67.4	32.6	16.7	11.2
Drugs	45.5	54.5	66.2	33.8	57.4	38.0
Violent crime	52.1	47.9	63.9	36.1	38.4	24.6
Property crime	60.3	39.7	71.1	28.9	38.3	27.3
Total	53.2	46.8	65.0	35.0	38.9	25.3

SOURCES.—Federal Bureau of Investigation (2005); BJS (2006).

NOTE.—Changes in BJS and FBI offense classifications since 1979 required that we estimate some numbers. We believe that we have closely approximated Blumstein's original calculations.

data do not include homicide and rape numbers in victimization data are too small to permit meaningful analyses, he looked at robbery, aggravated assault, and three property crimes. For robbery, his findings paralleled Blumstein's: victims' reports on offenders' race and prison admission data by race were nearly identical. Like Blumstein, Langan concluded that about 80 percent of racial disparity was explainable by reference to offending patterns and, overall, that "test results generally support the differential involvement [in crime] hypothesis" (p. 678).

2. *Replication Using 2004 Data.* We replicated Blumstein's analysis using arrest and prison population data for 2004. Table 2 shows the results. A much smaller part of racial disparities in imprisonment can be explained by arrest patterns in 2004 than Blumstein found for 1979. In Blumstein's between-race comparisons, arrests explained all but 2.8 percent of imprisonment disparities in homicide imprisonment; 11.6 percent remained unexplained in 2004. For robbery in 1979, 15.6 percent of imprisonment disparities went unexplained; in 2004, 37.2 per-

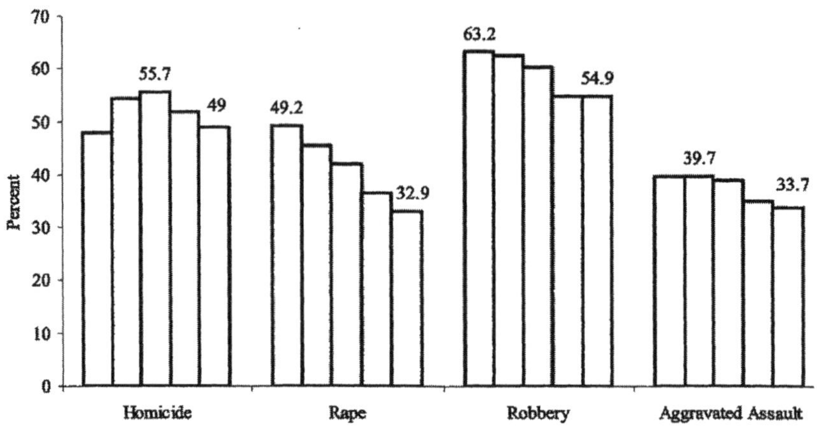

FIG. 6.—Black percentages among Uniform Crime Report violent index arrestees, 1982–2006 (5-year averages). Source: Federal Bureau of Investigation, *Crime in the United States*, various years.

cent. Overall, Blumstein's 1979 analysis left 20.5 percent of imprisonment disparities unexplained. He replicated the analysis using 1991 data and concluded that unexplained disparities had increased to 25 percent (Blumstein 1993). Our 2004 analysis left 38.9 percent unexplained. Had Blumstein in his 1982 article found unexplained disparities as large as we find for 2004, surely his conclusion would have been the opposite of what it was: such large unexplained variation creates a strong presumption of racial bias.

In trying to understand why the results are so different for 2004, we looked at racial trends in arrest patterns. Perhaps black percentages among arrestees for serious crimes rose rapidly after 1979, with black percentages in 2004 being anomalously low. As figure 6 shows, however, the opposite is true. Black Americans' involvement in violence is declining. The figure shows black percentages, averaged over 5-year periods, among people arrested for homicide, forcible rape, robbery, and aggravated assault. Although black Americans continue to be overrepresented among arrestees, the degree of overrepresentation has been falling for a quarter century. Fifty-six percent of homicide arrestees in 1992–96 were black; 49 percent were in 2002–6. In 1982–86, 49 percent of rape arrestees were black; 33 percent were in 2002–6. The declines are almost as steep for robbery and aggravated assault. That's

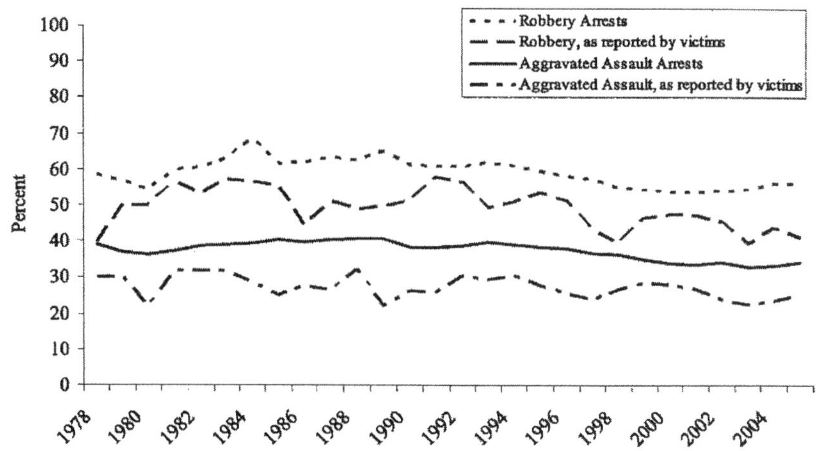

FIG. 7.—Percentage of blacks among lone offenders as perceived by victims and percentage of black arrests, 1978–2005. Sources: BJS, *Sourcebook of Criminal Justice Statistics* (http://www.albany.edu/sourcebook/), various years; Federal Bureau of Investigation, *Crime in the United States*, various years.

good news: black involvement in serious violent crime has been declining.

Perhaps, we thought, the explanation is to be found in changes in arrest data that operated to underreport black violence. To check this, using NCVS data we compared arrest percentages with robbery and aggravated assault victims' characterizations of the racial characteristics of their assailants. Figure 7 shows the result: no significant change in a quarter century. Black percentages among arrestees for both offenses have consistently tracked victims' characterizations but been higher. The reason is at least in part that many robberies and assaults involve more than one assailant, and the NCVS data pertain to crimes involving lone offenders.

So why are so many blacks in prison compared with whites? That question can be answered at (at least) two levels. The first, which we discuss in the remaining portion of this section, is mechanical: what are the mechanisms that put more blacks in prison than their population or crime participation percentages appear to justify? The second, which we discuss in Section II, is more difficult: what is it about American society and cultural norms that allowed those mechanisms to exist and allows them to persist?

C. What Are the Direct Causes of Racial Disparities in Imprisonment?

There are four plausible explanations for why there are so many more black prisoners than offending patterns suggest there should be. First, invidious bias and conscious stereotypes ("Many young black men are dangerous, so I must treat this young black man harshly") may cause police, prosecutors, and judges to treat black defendants more severely than they treat whites. Second, subtler forms of subconscious stereotyping and attribution may be operating. Third, disparities may be worsened by police practices that disproportionately affect blacks. Fourth, disparities may be worsened by sentencing policies relating to violent and drug crimes.

1. *Bias and Conscious Stereotyping.* We have the least to say about this hypothesis. No doubt some Americans, including some public officials, are racists and are biased against blacks. Larger numbers are no doubt affected by conscious stereotypes about blacks. Still more engage in "statistical discrimination," the attribution of traits that characterize groups to individual members of groups. This is one central issue in analyses of racial profiling. If many young black men in particular neighborhoods, who adopt particular styles of dress, are involved in gang activities or drug dealing, police seeing a young man in that neighborhood who fits that pattern may believe it likely that he is a gang member or drug dealer and stop him, even if the individualized basis for a stop that the law requires does not exist. To a police officer, this may seem an obvious and sensible thing to do. To a civil libertarian, such a stop is an obvious and intolerable instance of crude racial stereotyping. Efforts to establish from police stop data whether "yields" or "hit rates" for blacks and whites stopped by the police are higher or lower effectively assume that this form of statistical stereotyping could be acceptable: if blacks are stopped at twice the rate of whites but contraband is found in the same or a higher percentage of cases, that implicitly demonstrates that police are not acting in an invidious way but have valid reasons more often to be suspicious of blacks.

The effects of bias and stereotyping are likely to be different at police and sentencing stages. Research on profiling generally concludes that police do stop blacks disproportionately often on the streets and on the highway, generally do not achieve higher hit rates for blacks than for whites (e.g., Engel and Calnon 2004), but usually make more arrests. Inevitably this means that police practices lead to higher levels of black arrests, and therefore convictions and prisoners, than would otherwise exist. These practices are particularly likely to worsen racial disparities for drug and firearms offenses since those are the two kinds of illegal contraband police stops are most likely to yield. We discuss this further below in relation to drug policy.

On the basis of personal interactions over decades with judges in many American jurisdictions, we do not believe that invidious racial bias and gross stereotypes are likely substantially to affect sentencing decisions. This is a subject judges worry about and discuss often among themselves and with others. Sentencing research showing that there are few racial differences in sentence lengths is consistent with our belief (e.g., Spohn 2000, 2002). Sentencing research showing that there are often in/out differences is not necessarily strongly inconsistent with it. Black defendants, especially young ones, often have more extensive criminal records than whites, and judges take criminal records into account when deciding which defendants "deserve another chance." Similarly, black defendants on average have less stable home lives, less conventional employment records, and fewer educational attainments than whites, and judges take such things into account in deciding which defendants are more likely to succeed in community sentences and programs and which are more likely to reoffend.[9]

2. *Unconscious Stereotyping and Attribution.* In some ways it is surprising that the literature on sentencing disparities shows comparatively few differences in outcomes on the basis of race. Recent research on "colorism" and the significance of Afrocentric features in stereotyping offenders shows that stereotypes are deeply embedded in American culture and affect both white and black people (the fullest examination of this literature can be found in Blank, Dabaddy, and Citro [2004]). Analysts of "Afrocentric feature bias" posit that certain stereotypically African American facial features influence decision makers' (and research subjects') judgments about individual offenders. Although the number of studies is small, their implications are disturbing. One study found that people with more Afrocentric features appeared more "criminal" to observers and that the more Afrocentric features

[9] Our point in the text is not that the practices described in this and the preceding sentence are necessarily unobjectionable, but that many judges engage in them in good faith. Argument can be made that black defendants acquire more extensive criminal records at younger ages than whites because police are more likely to arrest them, and accordingly that the criminal record at least in part is more a product of police than of criminal activity, and in fairness should not be held against black defendants. Similarly, objections have long been made to taking account of social factors (household stability, employment, education) in sentencing, precisely because they are correlated with race.

an individual possessed, the more "criminal" he appeared (Eberhardt et al. 2004). In other studies, Afrocentric features were associated with longer prison sentences and increased frequency of capital sentencing (Blair, Judd, and Fallman 2004; Eberhardt et al. 2006).[10]

The study of Afrocentric feature bias emerged from research on "colorism," discrimination within racial groups on the basis of gradations in skin color (Jones 2000). Many studies have shown that people associate lighter skin tones among blacks with positive characteristics and darker skin tones with negative characteristics (e.g., Maddox and Gray 2002), but no published work has investigated colorism in criminal justice settings.

Several recent studies have tried to assess the significance of Afrocentric feature bias. Blair et al. (2002) found that individuals with more Afrocentric features were judged by college undergraduates to have stereotypical African American traits. Blair, Chapleau, and Judd (2005) showed that research subjects believed that individuals with more Afrocentric features were likely more often than others to behave aggressively.

Eberhardt et al. (2004) asked 182 police officers to examine photographs of male students and employees at Stanford University. Half were shown white faces and half were shown black faces. One-third of the officers were asked to rate the stereotypicality of each face on a scale, that is, how stereotypical each face was of members of the person's race. Another third, told that some of the faces might be of criminals, were asked to indicate whether the person "looked criminal." The last third were asked to rate attractiveness on a scale. Each officer completed only one of the three measures.

More black than white faces were thought to look criminal. Black faces rated above the median for stereotypicality were judged as criminal significantly more than were black faces rated below the median. The opposite was found for white faces. The authors concluded that the police officers thought that black faces looked more criminal and that "the more black, the more criminal" (Eberhardt et al. 2004, p. 889).

Blair, Judd, and Chapleau (2004) analyzed the Afrocentric features

[10] Another explanation is that many biases people harbor are not consciously accessible. The Implicit Association Test, which has been used to assess implicit attitudes toward different groups, has shown a significant implicit preference for whites among all races and ethnicities (Greenwald and Krieger 2006).

of inmates in the Florida Department of Corrections database. They asked undergraduates to rate the faces of a randomly selected sample of 216 inmates, 100 black and 116 white, in terms of the "degree to which each face had features that are typical of African Americans" (p. 676). After they controlled for race and criminal history, Afrocentric features were a significant predictor of sentence length. Within each race, more Afrocentric features were associated with longer sentences.[11]

Pizzi, Blair, and Judd (2005, p. 351) argued that judges and prosecutors have adapted to differences between racial groups but have not been sensitized to sentencing differences on the basis of Afrocentric features: "Racial stereotyping in sentencing decisions still persists. But it is not a function of the racial category of the individual; instead, there seems to be an equally pernicious and less controllable process at work. Racial stereotyping in sentencing still occurs based on the facial appearance of the offender. Be they White or African American, those offenders who possess stronger Afrocentric features receive harsher sentences for the same crimes."

Eberhardt et al. (2006, p. 383), using a database of death-eligible cases in Philadelphia, "examined the extent to which perceived stereotypicality of Black defendants influenced jurors' death-sentencing decisions in cases with both White and Black victims." Stanford undergraduates were shown pictures of 44 defendants, presented randomly and edited for uniformity, and asked to rate the stereotypicality of each black defendant's appearance. With stereotypicality as the only independent variable, 24.4 percent of black defendants rated below the median for stereotypicality received a death sentence, compared with 57.5 percent of black defendants rated above the median.

3. *Drug Policy.* American drug policies are a primary aggravator of racial disparities in imprisonment. Blumstein's 1982 analysis of 1979 prison population showed that arrest patterns for drug offenses explained the smallest percentage of racial disproportionality in imprisonment (48.9 percent unexplained) of any offense category at a time when 5.7 percent of prisoners (about 16,000 total) had been convicted of drug crimes (see table 1). Our analysis of 2004 data again showed

[11] Blair, Judd, and Fallman (2004, p. 677) note, however, that this does not necessarily imply explicit bias: "this form of stereotyping appears to occur without people's awareness and outside their immediate control."

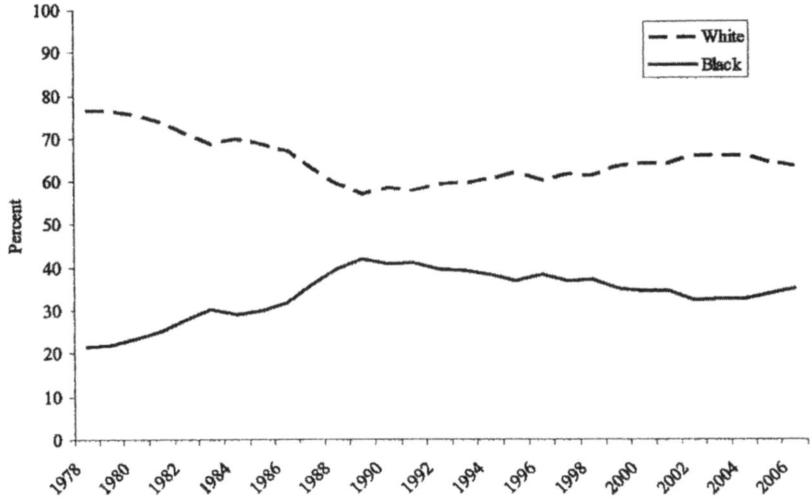

FIG. 8.—Total arrests for drug offenses, by race, 1978–2006. Sources: BJS, *Sourcebook of Criminal Justice Statistics* (http://www.albany.edu/sourcebook/), various years; Federal Bureau of Investigation, *Crime in the United States*, various years.

that drug arrests explained the smallest percentages of prison disproportionality (57.4 percent unexplained; see table 2).[12]

Figures 8 and 9 show why the black imprisonment rate for drug crimes is so high. Figure 8 shows black and white percentages among people arrested for drug crimes between 1978 and 2006. As recently as 1978, approximately 80 percent of adult drug arrestees were white. By 1989, the black share among all arrestees exceeded 40 percent, and in the years since it has fluctuated between 32 and 40 percent. How does it happen that 13 percent of the population make up 40 percent of drug arrestees?

The answer is that blacks are much more likely than whites to be arrested for drug crimes. Figure 9 shows total arrest rates of blacks and whites from 1978 to 2006. The white rate since 1978 has been approximately one-fourth the black one. Why are blacks so much more often arrested for drug crimes?

The answer is not, as table 3 shows, that blacks use drugs at much

[12] For assaults, 58.8 percent of disproportionality went unexplained, no doubt partly because assaults in 2004 were not limited to aggravated assaults as in Blumstein's (1982) data but included a substantial preponderance of less serious events.

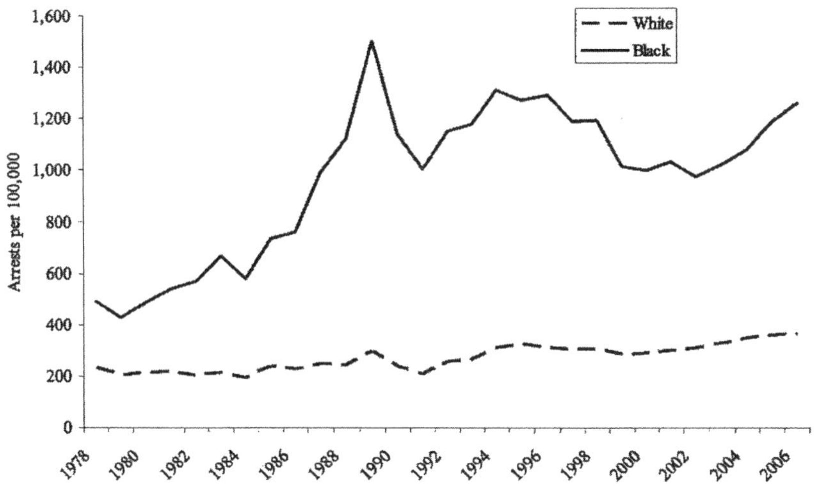

FIG. 9.—Total arrest rate for drug offenses, by race, 1978–2006. Sources: BJS, *Sourcebook of Criminal Justice Statistics* (http://www.albany.edu/sourcebook/), various years.

higher rates than whites do. National Institute of Drug Abuse surveys have tracked self-reported drug use since the 1970s. The table shows percentages of blacks and whites who reported using alcohol, any other drugs, and four categories of illicit substances ever, in the last year, and in the last month. In 2005 and 2006, larger percentages of whites reported using alcohol, cocaine (including crack), and hallucinogens, and the differences are large. Larger percentages of whites than blacks report having ever used marijuana, and slightly higher percentages of blacks report using marijuana recently. Only for crack (considered alone) do blacks report significantly higher use levels than whites, but the absolute levels are low. One conclusion is clear: the reason so many more blacks than whites are arrested or imprisoned for drug crimes is not that they use drugs much more extensively than whites do.

Another plausible reason why blacks might more often be arrested for drug crimes than are whites is that they are much more extensively involved in drug trafficking. National Institute of Drug Abuse (NIDA) surveys based on representative samples of the U.S. population indicate that this is not true.[13] Figure 10 shows self-reported drug selling by

[13] In recent years, reports of the National Survey on Drug Use and Health have identified the author as the Office of Applied Studies, Substance Abuse and Mental Health

TABLE 3

Percentage of Drug Use, by Race, 2005–6

	2005		2006	
Drug	White	Black	White	Black
Alcohol:				
Ever used	86.9	75.2	86.9	75.4
Within last year	70.5	55.5	70.4	55.1
Within last month	56.5	40.8	55.8	40.0
All illicit drugs:*				
Ever used	48.9	44.7	49.0	42.9
Within last year	14.5	16.0	14.8	16.4
Within last month	8.1	9.7	8.5	9.8
Marijuana:				
Ever used	43.7	39.0	43.9	37.6
Within last year	10.6	12.3	10.7	12.4
Within last month	6.1	7.6	6.4	7.4
Cocaine:†				
Ever used	15.5	9.8	16.3	9.1
Within last year	2.4	2.0	2.5	2.1
Within last month	1.0	1.1	.9	1.3
Crack:				
Ever used	3.2	4.9	3.3	5.3
Within last year	.5	1.2	.5	1.3
Within last month	.2	.8	.2	.8
Hallucinogens:				
Ever used	16.3	6.5	17.0	6.6
Within last year	1.8	.8	1.7	1.4
Within last month	.5	.2	.4	.5

SOURCE.—Office of Applied Studies, *National Survey on Drug Use and Health*, various years.

* Illicit drugs include marijuana/hashish, cocaine (including crack), heroin, hallucinogens, inhalants, or prescription-type psychotherapeutics used nonmedically.

† Includes crack cocaine.

12–17-year-old blacks and whites for the years 2001–6. Three to four percent of both groups reported selling drugs at least once in the preceding year, and 1 percent reported selling drugs at least 10 or more times during the preceding year. The black and white rates for most measures are nearly identical; on average for the entire period and for most years, white rates are slightly higher than black rates.

Representative national surveys undercount transient and homeless

Services Administration, which is how we refer to data from the survey in source notes. Predecessor surveys were published by the NIDA. Because most readers will be more familiar with that attribution, we refer to NIDA when discussing survey data in the text.

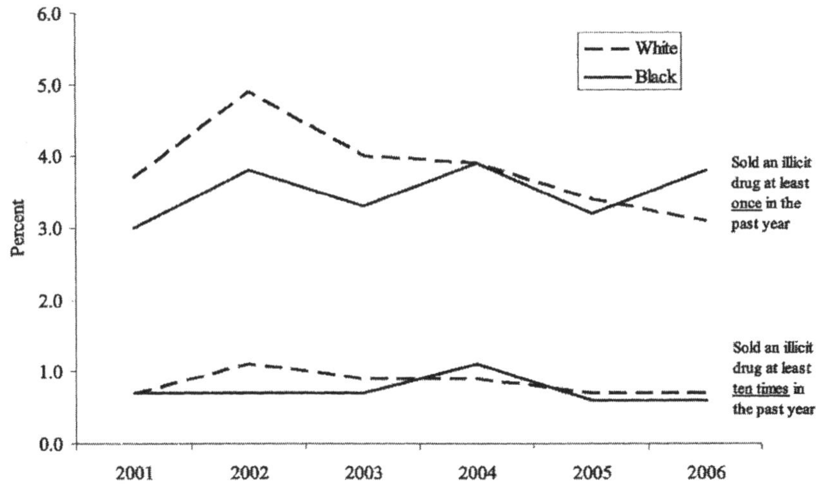

FIG. 10.—Illicit drug sales among youths aged 12–17, by race, 2001–6. Source: Office of Applied Studies, *National Survey on Drug Use and Health*, various years.

populations and do not count institutionalized populations (in prisons, jails, or mental institutions) at all. The effect is that measures that distinguish black and white rates may undercount black rates because relatively more blacks than whites have no permanent address and are confined in institutions. These problems, however, are much less significant for 12–17-year-olds, most of whom live with a parent or caretaker and few of whom are confined in institutions. However, even if these sampling problems to some degree affect the data in figure 10, they are unlikely to change significantly the drug trafficking patterns shown; for example, increasing black rates by 25 percent would not materially alter the black/white comparisons. It would make the black rates slightly higher than the white rates rather than slightly lower.

The reason why so many more blacks than whites are arrested and imprisoned for drug crimes is well known and long recognized. They are much easier to arrest. Much white drug dealing occurs behind closed doors and in private. Much black drug dealing occurs in public or semipublic, on the streets and in open-air drug markets. And much black drug dealing occurs between strangers. Figures 11 and 12 present NIDA self-report data for the total population for 2001–6 on locations and sources of subjects' most recent marijuana purchases. As figure 12 shows, in each year, 87–88 percent of whites made their purchases from

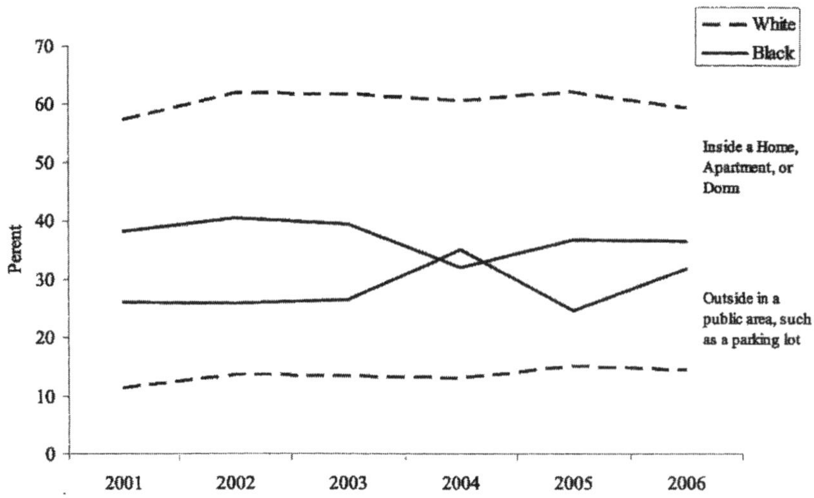

FIG. 11.—Location of last purchase of marijuana, by race, 2001–6. Source: Office of Applied Studies, *National Survey on Drug Use and Health*, various years. Categories do not account for 100 percent of purchases because the following response categories were excluded: inside a public building, such as a store or restaurant; inside a school building; outside on school property; and some other place.

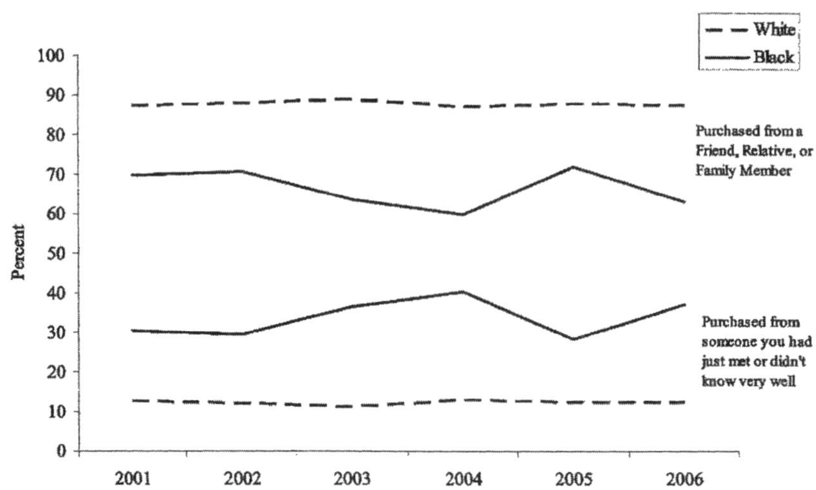

FIG. 12.—Source of last purchase of marijuana, by race, 2001–6. Source: Office of Applied Studies, *National Survey on Drug Use and Health*, various years.

friends, relatives, and family members. By contrast, blacks purchased marijuana from people they had just met or did not know well 30–40 percent of the time.

Figure 11 presents data on where marijuana is purchased. Depending on the year, 57–62 percent of purchases by whites occurred inside a home, apartment, or dorm, and only 11–14 percent outdoors in public spaces such as parking lots. For black purchasers, the pattern was starkly different. Forty percent or less of purchases occurred in private indoor spaces; 26–35 percent were made outdoors in public spaces.

Undercover drug agents can penetrate black urban drug markets relatively easily and make arrests almost at will. Most white drug dealing, by contrast, occurs within existing social networks in which people know one another, and in private. Undercover agents have to invest much more time in establishing their bona fides; the arrest yield from a fixed amount of time or effort is much lower when pursuing white than when pursuing black sellers.

In other words, black arrest rates are so much higher than white rates because police choose as a strategic matter to invest more energy and effort in arresting blacks. So many more blacks than whites are in prison because police officials have adopted practices, and policy makers have enacted laws, that foreseeably treat black offenders much more harshly than white ones.

4. *Sentencing Policies for Violent and Drug Crimes.* Sentencing policies for drug crimes and violent crimes have been a major driver of racial disparities in imprisonment since the mid-1970s. Until the early 1980s, the tougher laws mainly established mandatory minimum sentences for violent and gun crimes, but the minimums were usually 1 or 2 years or at most 5 (Shane-DuBow, Brown, and Olsen 1985). Beginning in the mid-1980s and continuing through the mid-1990s, epitomized by the federal 100-to-one law governing cocaine sentencing and California's three-strikes law that required sentences ranging from 25 years to life for third felonies, sentences for drugs, guns, and violence were made incomparably harsher.

Black Americans have borne the brunt of this tougher sentencing. For drug crimes, as we have already shown, police arrest policies produce arrest rates for blacks that are far out of proportion to blacks' drug use or involvement in drug trafficking. For understandable reasons of social disadvantage and limited life chances, blacks engage more

TABLE 4

New Commitments to State Prisons, by Race, 2003

	All	Black*	White*	Hispanic†
Violence, of which	28.2%	27.7%	26.1%	34.9%
Homicide	2.9	2.9	2.5	3.5
Robbery	7.6	**10.4**	**4.7**	**8.3**
Property	27.9	24.2	32.8	22.2
Drugs	30.7	**37.5**	**25.5**	**30.6**
Public order, of which	12.7	10.2	15	11.8
Guns	3.3	**4.2**	**2.1**	**3.7**
All	100	100	100	100

SOURCE.—BJS, National Corrections Reporting Program—2003 (fi6ncrp0304.csv), table 4.

* Includes persons of Hispanic origin.

† Includes persons of all races.

often in gun crimes and serious violent crimes. Laws that increase sentences for such crimes inevitably exacerbate racial disparities.

Table 4, for example, shows new state prison commitments by conviction offense and race for 2003, the most recent year for which data are available from the BJS National Corrections Reporting Program. Among whites, 53.7 percent were committed for violent, drug, or gun crimes, compared with 69.4 percent of black offenders (in both cases including Hispanic same-race offenders). The racial skew is even greater when the focus is narrowed to robbery, drugs, and guns (52.1 percent of black prisoners, 32.3 percent of whites). Among black prisoners, 37.5 percent were committed for drug crimes; among white prisoners, 25.5 percent were.

There have long been good reasons to believe that longer sentences for drug crimes have no effect on levels of drug use, drug prices, or drug trafficking (e.g., Wilson 1990; Dills, Miron, and Summers 2008; MacCoun and Martin, forthcoming). And there are good reasons to doubt that increasing penalties for particular violent or drug crimes from 3 years to 5, 5 years to 10, or 10 years to 20 has any discernible effects on crime rates (e.g., Doob and Webster 2003; Dills, Miron, and Summers 2008; Tonry, in this volume). Those things being true, to increase penalties for crimes with which blacks are charged, for whatever reason, is to increase racial disparities in prison for no good reason or for a not well-justified one.

5. *In Sum.* Black Americans suffer from imprisonment rates six to seven times higher than those of whites primarily for two reasons.

Police arrest policies for drugs target a type of drug trafficking (street-level transactions in inner-city areas) in which blacks are disproportionately involved. American sentencing laws and policies specify punishments that are both absolutely and relatively severe for violent, drug, and gun crimes for which blacks are more likely than whites to be arrested and prosecuted. Conscious bias and stereotyping, and unconscious stereotyping and attribution, no doubt play some roles in causing disparities, but smaller ones.

II. Making Sense of Racial Disparities

A primary aim of this essay was to see how patterns of racial disparity have changed since the mid-1990s. We learned three important things that provided one bit of good news and two of terrible news. The good news is that patterns of racial involvement in serious crime as shown in arrest data have changed. The percentages of people arrested for aggravated assault, robbery, rape, and homicide who are black have been declining and in 2006 were much lower than in 1985. One might hope, and expect, that racial disparities in imprisonment would have fallen commensurately.

The two bits of terrible news: The first is that blacks continue to make up about half of the prison population[14] and about the same percentage of Death Row inmates as in the 1980s. The chance that a black American is in prison in 2007 remains six to seven times higher than the chance that a white American is in prison. The declining involvement of blacks in serious violent crime has had no effect on racial disparities in prison.

The second is that insensitivity to the interests of black Americans continues to characterize American crime policies. Racial disparities in imprisonment continue to be generated by policy choices that were known, or should have been known, disproportionately to affect disadvantaged black Americans. In no significant respect have American drug policies changed since the 1980s—the federal 100-to-one rule is

[14] BJS (2007) data for midyear 2006 show that black men constituted 41 percent of male jail and prison inmates. The true figure in a country in which skin color matters much more than ethnicity is 46–48 percent (because a few years ago the BJS stopped counting black Hispanics as black and thereby reduced the black percentage by 10–12 percent; a quarter to a third of imprisoned Hispanics, who made up 21 percent of male inmates, are dark skinned). Forty-seven percent is to be sure less than 50 and is the result of the rapid increase in imprisonment of Hispanic people in recent years. There were more non-Hispanic blacks than non-Hispanic whites imprisoned in 2007.

the symbol of that—and they continue grossly disproportionately to ensnare young blacks and, increasingly, young Hispanics.[15] And American policies toughening penalties for violent crime have had the same effect. If the conditions of life faced by disadvantaged minority youths make them disproportionately likely to be involved in violent crime, then policies making punishments for violent crime enormously harsher will disproportionately affect them, and they have.

Loïc Wacquant's work provides insight into how that happened.[16] For a decade now, he has been writing articles on race and crime control policy. His basic argument is that American cultural practices and legal institutions have operated to maintain patterns of racial dominance and hierarchy for two centuries. Until the Civil War, slavery assured white domination. Within 30 years after the war, the practices and legal forms of discrimination known as "Jim Crow" laws restored white domination of blacks. In the "Great Migration" in the 1910s and 1920s, millions of blacks moved from the South to the North to escape Jim Crow; the big city ghettos, housing discrimination, and other forms of discrimination kept blacks in their subordinate place (Lieberson 1980). And when deindustrialization and the flight of jobs to the suburbs left disadvantaged blacks marooned in the urban ghettos, the modern wars on drugs and crime took over (Wacquant 2002*a*, 2002*b*).

Wacquant's writing is passionate and controversial, but it is time more people paid attention to it. The civil rights movement has borne fruit in the forms of increased economic and social integration of blacks in American society. The progress made is remarkable in light of the justice system experiences of black Americans.

Wacquant's argument is a functionalist one, about what criminal justice policies and practices do, rather than a political one about what

[15] The U.S. Sentencing Commission (2007) revisions to its crack and cocaine guidelines merely nibble at the edges of the disparities caused by the 100-to-one statute: "The sentencing commission's striking move on Tuesday, meant to address the wildly disproportionate punishments for crack and powder cocaine, will have only a minor impact. Unless Congress acts, many thousands of defendants will continue to face vastly different sentences for possessing and selling different types of the same thing" (Liptak 2007, p. A21).

[16] We do not here discuss features of American politics that made racial insensitivity more explicable in the last 30 years: the political ascendancy of the right wing of the Republican Party, embodying the contemporary resurgence of what Richard Hofstadter (1965) called the "paranoid streak in American politics," and the influence on it of fundamentalist Protestants. If crime and drugs are matters of good and evil, and criminals and drug users are evil, then there is little reason to expect sympathy or empathy toward them from the holders of those views (especially if the criminals and drug users are black and different). See Tonry (2008).

those practices and policies are intended to do. Thought of that way, thinking of what the machinery of the criminal justice system produces, it is hard not to see that it produces devastatingly reduced life chances for black Americans. If its aims were to reduce disadvantaged black men's chances of earning a decent living, or being successfully married and a good father, or being socialized into prosocial values, it is hard to see how the criminal justice system could do those things better (Western 2006). There has to be a reason why the criminal justice system treats American blacks so badly, why its foreseeable disparate impacts on blacks and whites are disregarded, and Wacquant's analysis provides a better explanation than any other that has been offered.

Wacquant's passion sometimes makes it easy for critics to dismiss his arguments as polemics. He is, however, no longer alone in suggesting that American criminal justice practices operate to keep poor blacks in their places. Here is what Douglas Massey, author (with Nancy Denton) of *American Apartheid* (1993), a widely praised and decidedly nonpolemical account of housing discrimination, had to say in *Categorically Unequal*, his 2007 book on social stratification:

> Whether whites care to admit it or not, they have a selfish interest in maintaining the categorical mechanisms that perpetuate racial stratification. As a result, when pushed by the federal government to end overt discriminatory practices, they are likely to innovate new and more subtle ways to maintain their privileged position in society. If one discriminatory mechanism proves impossible to sustain, whites have an incentive to develop alternatives that may be associated only indirectly with race and are therefore not in obvious violation of civil rights law. The specific mechanisms by which racial stratification occurs can thus be expected to evolve over time. (P. 54)

> [The] new emphasis on retribution and punishment was achieved . . . through the deliberate racialization of crime and violence in public consciousness by political entrepreneurs. (P. 94)

> As discrimination moved underground, new mechanisms for exclusion were built into the criminal justice system for Afro Americans. (P. 251)

And, to complete this span of the political spectrum, here is what Glenn C. Loury, a conservative black economist and the author of *The*

Anatomy of Racial Inequality (2002), had to say in introducing his 2007 Tanner Lectures at Stanford:

> We have embraced what criminologist Michael Tonry calls a policy of "malign neglect," and in doing so we, as a society, have stumbled more or less wittingly into a God-awful cul de sac. I will claim that the connection of this apparatus to the history of racial degradation and subordination in our country (lynching, minstrelsy, segregation, ghetto-ization) is virtually self-evident, and that the racial subtext of our law and order political discourse over the last three decades has been palpable. (Loury 2007, p. 9; references omitted)

There are also psychological explanations for racial disparities' persistence. System justification theory posits "a general human tendency to support and defend the social status quo, broadly defined" (Blasi and Jost 2006, p. 1123). People, regardless of their situation, try to rationalize the injustices and inequities they see (Chen and Tyler 2002). Stereotypes (such as that the rich are smart and the poor are lazy) are often employed to demonstrate that all members of the system deserve their status. Concerning the criminal justice system, about which concern about racial disparities in imprisonment might be expected, comfort can be found in racial stereotypes, such as that black Americans are especially criminal, so of course many of them are in prison.

The incentive to rationalize is clear. People who believe in a just system experience, by and large, more positive emotions than people who blame the system. For example, poor people who blame themselves for their own poverty are happier and more satisfied with life in general (Blasi and Jost 2006, p. 1141). By rationalizing the inequities one sees in American sentencing, one finds mental comfort.

A considerable literature on racial differences in attitudes toward and opinions about crime control policy shows that whites have substantially harsher attitudes concerning punishment and greater confidence in the justice system and its practitioners than do blacks (e.g., Unnever, Cullen, and Lero-Jonson, in this volume). Lawrence Bobo and Devon Johnson, concluding an extensive analysis of black/white differences in attitudes toward capital punishment and laws punishing crack cocaine traffickers (mostly black) much more harshly than powder cocaine traffickers (mostly white), observe that

> The most consistent predictor of criminal justice policy attitudes

> is, in fact, a form of racial prejudice. While white racial resentment does not ever explain a large share of the variation in any of the attitudes we have measured, it is the most consistently influential of the variables outside of race classification itself. This pattern has at least two implications. It further buttresses the concern that some of the major elements of public support for punitive criminal justice policies are heavily tinged with racial animus and thus quite likely to be resistant to change based on suasion and information-based appeals. What is more, this pattern reinforces the claim . . . that one major function of the criminal justice system is the regulation and control of marginalized social groups such as African Americans. (2004, pp. 171–72)

There are no easy paths out of the racial dead end in which American crime policy finds itself. The damage has been done to living black Americans: lives have been blighted, life chances have been reduced, and communities have been undermined. Even radical changes in American crime policies can change none of that.

III. How Can We Do Better?

Nonetheless, things can be done. One approach, radical decarceration, is corrective. Three others, elimination of bias and stereotyping, abandonment of policies and laws that do unnecessary damage, and creation of devices making their later replication of such policies and laws less likely, are preventative.

A. Radical Decarceration

Efforts to eliminate bias and stereotyping in official decision making are being made throughout the United States and should continue to be made. Unfortunately, such efforts, even if completely successful, can have only modest effects. The primary drivers of racial disparities are drug and sentencing policies. Table 5 illustrates why elimination of bias and disparities will not significantly lessen the damage racial disparities do. The top row shows black and white imprisonment rates in 2006.[17] The second row shows what would happen if black rates were decreased by 10 percent, which is a high estimate of the degree to which

[17] The black/white ratio is not higher than 5.5 : 1 because the table uses BJS data that exclude Hispanics of either race and because it contains combined data on men and women. The disparity ratio for women in 2006 (3.8 : 1) was significantly lower than that for men (6.3 : 1) (Sabol, Minton, and Harrison 2007, table 14).

TABLE 5

Disparity in Incarceration Rates, by Race

	Black	White	Ratio
	A. Disparity Reduced 10%		
Imprisonment rate, 2006	2,661	483	5.5 : 1
10% less disparity	2,395	483	5.0 : 1
Reduction in prison per 100,000	266	0	
	B. Use of Imprisonment Halved		
Imprisonment rate, 2006	2,661	483	5.5 : 1
Imprisonment halved	1,330	241	5.5 : 1
Reduction in prison per 100,000	1,330	241	
	C. Return to 1980 Imprisonment Rates		
Imprisonment rate, 1980	827	134	6.2 : 1
Reduction in prison per 100,000	1,834	349	

SOURCE.—Office of Applied Studies, *National Survey on Drug Use and Health*, various years.

bias and stereotyping enhance disparities, while white rates were left unchanged. The black imprisonment rate would fall from approximately 2,661 per 100,000 to 2,395 and the ratio of black-to-white imprisonment rates would fall from 5.5 : 1 to 5.0 : 1.

If instead, as the fifth row shows, the prison population were cut by half across the board, the ratio of imprisonment rates would remain the same but the black imprisonment rate would fall from 2,661 to 1,330. Or if, as the penultimate row shows, imprisonment rates were cut to 1980 levels, the black imprisonment rate would be 827 per 100,000.

The differing implications of these different approaches are enormous. The U.S. Census estimates that 38.34 million U.S. residents in 2006 were black. If the imprisonment rate were halved, the black rate would fall from 26,613 per million to 13,306. That means that over 500,000 fewer black Americans would be in prison or jail. Returning to the 1980s imprisonment rate would mean 702,400 fewer black Americans behind bars. By contrast, eliminating all effects of bias and stereotyping would free at most 101,900 black Americans.

Of course, every effort should be made to eliminate bias and stereotyping. Their diminution will reduce racial disparities and the absolute size of the bite prisons take out of the black population. In absolute terms, though, that will only nibble at the problem. Only radical decarceration can make a big difference. To attempt to limit damage done to people now entangled in the arms of the criminal justice system, devices need to be created for reducing the lengths of current prison sentences and releasing hundreds of thousands of people from prison. New systems of parole, pardon, and commutation will need to be developed, as well as programs of social welfare and support to ease peoples' transitions back into the free community.

B. Abandonment of Disparity-Causing Policies

To limit damage to disadvantaged young people not yet ensnared, legislatures will need to repeal laws authorizing capital punishment and creating mandatory minimum sentences, sentences of life without the possibility of parole, and truth-in-sentencing laws. Most such laws were adopted primarily for symbolic or expressive purposes rather than with any basis for believing that they would significantly affect crime rates and patterns, and they do great and disproportionate harm to black Americans.

American jurisdictions will need to establish principled new systems of sentencing guidelines coupled with mechanisms for shortening unduly, disparately, or disproportionately long prison sentences. New guidelines will need to call for proportionate sentences for most crimes measured mostly in weeks and months, as in most other Western countries, and in years only for the most serious crimes.

These may seem millenarian proposals. They are not. They would do little more than return American crime control and punishment policies to the mainstream of Western developed countries. Every other Western country manages to get by without capital punishment, life without the possibility of parole, and prison sentences measured primarily in years and decades.

Alfred Blumstein (1993) years ago showed that American practitioners and policy makers can respond quickly to racial disparity problems. He observed that from 1965 to 1969, white and nonwhite arrest rates for young offenders were indistinguishable; that from 1970 to 1980 white rates exceeded nonwhite rates; and that thereafter by 1989 nonwhite rates nearly tripled and white rates halved, leaving nonwhite rates nearly four times higher. Figure 13 tells the story. Here is what Blumstein surmises happened:

> The decline [in white arrest rates] after the 1974 peak was undoubtedly a consequence of the general trend toward decriminali-

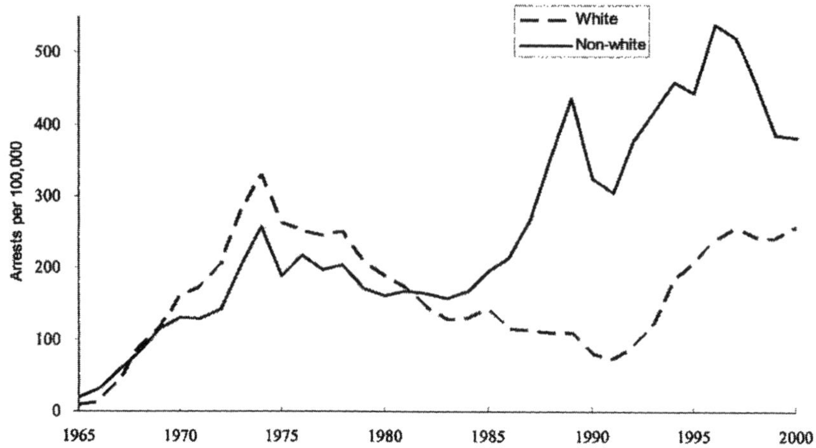

FIG. 13.—Juvenile arrest rate for drug offenses, by race, 1965–2000. Sources: Blumstein (1993); Blumstein and Wallman (2006).

zation of marijuana in the United States. A major factor contributing to that decriminalization was probably a realization that the arrestees were much too often the children of individuals, usually white, in positions of power and influence. These parents certainly did not want the consequences of a drug arrest to be visited on their children, and so they used their leverage to achieve a significant degree of decriminalization. Following the peak, arrest rates for both racial groups declined, and continued to decline for whites. On the other hand, for non-whites, the decline leveled out in the early 1980s and then began to accelerate at a rate of between twenty and twenty-five percent per year, until the peak in 1989. This clearly reflects the fact that drug enforcement is a result of policy choices. (P. 758)

It is not completely cynical to wonder why soaring arrest rates for nonwhite kids in the 1980s did not provoke the kinds of reactions that Blumstein attributes to soaring arrest rates of white kids in the 1970s, and a comparable policy adjustment. Racially differentiated effects of American drug and sentencing policies have been starkly evident for a quarter century.

C. Race and Ethnicity Impact Statements

American governments have long used prophylactic measures to guard against unwanted effects of governmental decisions. To protect the public purse, legislatures in many states require that legislative proposals be accompanied by or trigger fiscal impact statements. Federal and state laws routinely require the preparation of environmental impact statements before building and other permits may be issued. It is a small step to require that proposals for policy and statutory changes relating to drug and crime control policies carry with them or trigger race and ethnicity impact statements. Projected new laws or policies likely disproportionately to affect members of minority groups adversely should be made subject to strong presumptions against their adoption.

If racially disparate effects of public policies are a problem, and in most policy realms that proposition is self-evident, policy makers in this realm also should be required to declare and justify disparate effects. The second edition of the *Model Penal Code* (American Law Institute 2007) provides that such statements be required, and a literature on the subject is beginning to develop (Tonry 2004, pp. 221–26; Mauer 2007).

D. Are Meaningful Changes Possible?

We realize that our proposals for radical reduction in America's prison population, repeal of repressive legislation, and requirement of race and ethnicity impact statements may strike some readers as fanciful. If racial disparities and the damage they have unarguably done to millions of individual black Americans and their families, and to black Americans as a group, are pressing social problems, then radical measures are called for.

There are pessimistic and optimistic ways to contemplate the future. The pessimistic one is to recall Loïc Wacquant's functionalist analysis of racial hierarchy in American history and the succession of mechanisms by which white domination has been maintained. If slavery was succeeded by Jim Crow, which was succeeded by the racially segregated northern ghettoes, which was succeeded by mass imprisonment, it is hard not to wonder what will substitute for mass imprisonment, or whether mass imprisonment will endure for the reasons Wacquant sketched.

The optimistic one focuses on the good things the civil rights movement accomplished. Sixty years ago, nearly all black Americans were second-class citizens; nearly all were victims of discriminatory practices, norms, and laws. That is no longer true. Today it is primarily disadvantaged black Americans who suffer, seemingly for the accident of their births. Perhaps as the normative developments that underlay the civil rights movement wrestle with the functionalist developments that Wacquant described, a time will come when our proposals do not look fanciful. They are simple proposals that aim to redress profound social injustices. Seen that way, they are not radical at all.

REFERENCES

American Friends Service Committee. 1971. *Struggle for Justice*. New York: Hill and Wang.

American Law Institute. 2007. *Model Penal Code: Sentencing*. 2nd ed. Tentative draft no. 1 (April 9). Philadelphia: American Law Institute.

Baldus, David C., George G. Woodworth, and Charles A. Pulaski Jr. 1990. *Equal Justice and the Death Penalty: A Legal and Empirical Analysis*. Boston: Northeastern University Press.

BJS (Bureau of Justice Statistics). 1984. "The 1983 Jail Census." Washington, DC: U.S. Department of Justice, Bureau of Justice Statistics.

———. 1990. "Profile of Jail inmates 1978." Washington, DC: U.S. Department of Justice, Bureau of Justice Statistics.

———. 2006. "Prisoners in 2004." Washington, DC: U.S. Department of Justice, Bureau of Justice Statistics.

———. 2007. "Prison and Jail Inmates at Midyear 2006." Washington, DC: U.S. Department of Justice, Bureau of Justice Statistics.

Blair, Irene V., Kristine M. Chapleau, and Charles M. Judd. 2005. "The Use of Afrocentric Features as Cues for Judgment in the Presence of Diagnostic Information." *European Journal of Social Psychology* 35:59–68.

Blair, Irene V., Charles M. Judd, and Kristine M. Chapleau. 2004. "The Influence of Afrocentric Facial Features in Criminal Sentencing." *Psychological Science* 15(10):674–79.

Blair, Irene V., Charles M. Judd, and Jennifer L. Fallman. 2004. "The Automaticity of Race and Afrocentric Facial Features in Social Judgments." *Journal of Personality and Social Psychology* 87(6):763–78.

Blair, Irene V., Charles M. Judd, Melody S. Sadler, and Christopher Jenkins. 2002. "The Role of Afrocentric Features in Person Perception: Judging by Features and Categories." *Journal of Personality and Social Psychology* 83(1): 5–25.

Blank, Rebecca M., Marilyn Dabaddy, and Constance F. Citro, eds. 2004. *Measuring Racial Discrimination*. Washington, DC: National Academy Press.

Blasi, Gary, and John T. Jost. 2006. "System Justification Theory and Research: Implications for Law, Legal Advocacy, and Social Justice." *California Law Review* 94:1119–68.

Blumstein, Alfred. 1982. "On Racial Disproportionality of the United States' Prison Populations." *Journal of Criminal Law and Criminology* 73:1259–81.

———. 1993. "Racial Disproportionality of U.S. Prison Populations Revisited." *University of Colorado Law Review* 64:743–60.

Blumstein, Alfred, and Allen Beck. 1999. "Population Growth in U.S. Prisons, 1980–1996." In *Prisons*, edited by Michael Tonry and Joan Petersilia. Vol. 26 of *Crime and Justice: A Review of Research*, edited by Michael Tonry. Chicago: University of Chicago Press.

Blumstein, Alfred, Jacqueline Cohen, Susan Martin, and Michael Tonry, eds. 1983. *Research on Sentencing: The Search for Reform*. Washington, DC: National Academy Press.

Blumstein, Alfred, and Joel Wallman. 2006. "The Crime Drop and Beyond." *Annual Review of Laws and Social Sciences* 2:125–46.

Bobo, Lawrence, and Devon Johnson. 2004. "A Taste for Punishment: Black and White Americans' Views on the Death Penalty and the War on Drugs." *Du Bois Review* 1:151–80

Bonczar, Thomas P. 2003. "Prevalence of Imprisonment in the U.S. Population, 1974–2001." Washington, DC: U.S. Department of Justice, Bureau of Justice Statistics.

Cahalan, Margaret W. 1986. *Historical Correction Statistics in the United States, 1850–1984*. Washington, DC: U.S. Department of Justice, Bureau of Justice Statistics.

Chen, Emmeline S., and Tom R. Tyler. 2002. "Cloaking Power: Legitimizing Myths and the Psychology of the Advantaged." In *The Use and Abuse of Power: Multiple Perspectives on the Causes of Corruption*, edited by Annette Y. Lee-Chai and John A. Bargh. New York: Psychology Press, Taylor and Francis.

Clear, Todd. 2007. *Imprisoning Communities: How Mass Incarceration Makes Disadvantaged Neighborhoods Worse*. New York: Oxford University Press.

———. In this volume. "Communities with High Incarceration Rates."

Dills, Angela K., Jeffrey A. Miron, and Garrett Summers. 2008. "What Do Economists Know about Crime?" Working Paper no. 13759. Cambridge, MA: National Bureau of Economic Research.

Doob, Anthony, and Cheryl Webster. 2003. "Sentence Severity and Crime: Accepting the Null Hypothesis." In *Crime and Justice: A Review of Research*, vol. 30, edited by Michael Tonry. Chicago: University of Chicago Press.

Du Bois, W. E. B. 1988. "The Negro Criminal." In *The Economics of Race and Crime*, edited by Samuel L. Myers and Margaret C. Simms. New Brunswick, NJ: Transaction Books. (Originally published 1899.)

Eberhardt, Jennifer L., Paul G. Davies, Valerie J. Purdie-Vaughns, and Sheri Lynn Johnson. 2006. "Looking Deathworthy: Perceived Stereotypicality of Black Defendants Predicts Capital-Sentencing Outcomes." *Psychological Science* 17(5):383–86.

Eberhardt, Jennifer L., Phillip Atiba Goff, Valerie J. Purdie, and Paul G. Davies. 2004. "Seeing Black: Race, Crime and Visual Processing." *Journal of Personality and Social Psychology* 87(6):876–93.

Engel, Robin Shepard, and Jennifer M. Calnon. 2004. "Examining the Influence of Drivers' Characteristics during Traffic Stops with Police: Results from a National Survey." *Justice Quarterly* 21(1):49–90.

Fagan, Jeffrey, and Richard B. Freeman. 1999. "Crime and Work." In *Crime and Justice: A Review of Research*, vol. 25, edited by Michael Tonry. Chicago: University of Chicago Press.

Federal Bureau of Investigation. 2005. *Crime in the United States, 2004*. Washington, DC: U.S. Department of Justice.

Gest, Ted. 2001. *Crime and Politics: Big Government's Erratic Campaign for Law and Order.* New York: Oxford University Press.

Gilliard, Darrell K., and Allen J. Beck. 1996. *Prison and Jail Inmates, 1995*. Washington, DC: U.S. Department of Justice, Bureau of Justice Statistics.

Greenwald, Anthony, and Linda Hamilton Krieger. 2006. "Implicit Bias: Scientific Foundations." *California Law Review* 94:945–67.

Harrington, Michael P., and Cassia Spohn. 2007. "Defining Sentence Type: Further Evidence against Use of the Total Incarceration Variable." *Journal of Research in Crime and Delinquency* 44(1):36–63.

Hofstadter, Richard. 1965. *The Paranoid Style in American Politics and Other Essays*. Chicago: University of Chicago Press.

Jones, Trina. 2000. "Shades of Brown: The Law of Skin Color." *Duke Law Journal* 49:1487–1557.

Langan, Patrick. 1985. "Racism on Trial: New Evidence to Explain the Racial Composition of Prisons in the United States." *Journal of Criminal Law and Criminology* 76:666–83.

Lieberson, Stanley. 1980. *A Piece of the Pie—Blacks and White Immigrants since 1980*. Berkeley and Los Angeles: University of California Press.

Liptak, Adam. 2007. "Whittling Away, but Leaving a Gap." *New York Times* (November 17), p. A21.

Loury, Glenn C. 2002. *The Anatomy of Racial Inequality*. Cambridge, MA: Harvard University Press.

———. 2007. "Racial Stigma, Mass Incarceration and American Values." Tanner Lectures in Human Values delivered at Stanford University, April 4 and 5. http://www.econ.brown.edu/fac/Glenn_Loury/louryhomepage/.

MacCoun, Robert, and Karin D. Martin. Forthcoming. "Drug Abuse." In *Handbook on Crime and Punishment*, edited by Michael Tonry. New York: Oxford University Press.

Maddox, Keith B., and Stephanie A. Gray. 2002. "Cognitive Representations of Black Americans: Reexploring the Role of Skin Tone." *Personality and Social Psychology Bulletin* 28:250–59.

Massey, Douglas S. 2007. *Categorically Unequal*. New York: Russell Sage Foundation.

Massey, Douglas S., and Nancy Denton. 1993. *American Apartheid: Segregation and the Making of the Underclass*. Cambridge, MA: Harvard University Press.

Mauer, Marc. 2007. "Racial Impact Statements as a Means of Reducing Unwarranted Sentencing Disparities." *Ohio State Journal of Criminal Law* 5: 19–46.

McDonald, Douglas C., and Kenneth C. Carlson. 1993. *Sentencing in the Federal Courts: Does Race Matter?* Washington DC: U.S. Department of Justice, Bureau of Justice Statistics.

Moynihan, Daniel Patrick. 1965. *The Negro Family: The Case for National Action.* Washington, DC: U.S. Department of Labor, Office of Policy Planning and Research.

Murray, Joseph, and David P. Farrington. In this volume. "Effects of Parental Imprisonment in Children."

Myrdal, Gunnar. 1944. *An American Dilemma—the Negro Problem and Modern Democracy.* New York: Harper and Row.

Pizzi, William T., Irene V. Blair, and Charles M. Judd. 2005. "Discrimination in Sentencing on the Basis of Afrocentric Features." *Michigan Journal of Race and Law* 10:327–53.

Provine, Doris Marie. 2007. *Unequal under Law: Race in the War on Drugs.* Chicago: University of Chicago Press.

Raphael, Steven, Harry Holzer, and Michael Stoll. 2006. "How Do Crime and Incarceration Affect the Employment Prospects of Less Educated Black Men?" In *Black Males Left Behind*, edited by Ronald Mincy. Washington, DC: Urban Institute.

Sabol, William J., Todd D. Minton, and Paige M. Harrison. 2007. "Prison and Jail Inmates at Midyear 2006." Washington, DC: U.S. Department of Justice, Bureau of Justice Statistics.

Shane-Dubow, Sandra, Alice P. Brown, and Erik P. Olsen. 1985. *Sentencing Reform in the United States: History, Content and Effect.* Washington, DC: U.S. Government Printing Office.

Snell, Tracy L. 2007. "Capital Punishment, 2006." Washington, DC: U.S. Department of Justice, Bureau of Justice Statistics.

Spohn, Cassia. 2000. "Thirty Years of Sentencing Reform: The Quest for a Racially Neutral Sentencing Process." In *Criminal Justice 2000*, vol. 3, edited by the U.S. National Institute of Justice. Washington, DC: U.S. Department of Justice, National Institute of Justice.

———. 2002. *How Do Judges Decide? The Search for Fairness and Justice in Punishment.* Thousand Oaks, CA: Sage.

Tonry, Michael. 1995. *Malign Neglect: Race, Crime, and Punishment in America.* New York: Oxford University Press.

———. 1996. *Sentencing Matters.* New York: Oxford University Press.

———. 2004. *Thinking about Crime: Sense and Sensibility in American Penal Culture.* New York: Oxford University Press.

———. 2005. "Obsolescence and Immanence in Penal Theory and Policy." *Columbia Law Review* 105:1233–75.

———. 2008. "Crime and Human Rights—How Political Paranoia, Religious Fundamentalism, and Constitutional Obsolescence Combined to Devastate Black America." *Criminology* 46(1):1–34.

———. In this volume. "Learning from the Limits of Deterrence Research."

Unnever, James D., Francis T. Cullen, and Cheryl N. Lero-Jonson. In this volume. "Race, Racism, and Support for Capital Punishment."

U.S. Department of Commerce. 2006. *Statistical Abstract of the United States: 2007*. Washington, DC: U.S. Government Printing Office.

U.S. Sentencing Commission. 1995. *1995 Special Report to the Congress: Cocaine and Federal Sentencing Policy*. Washington, DC: U.S. Sentencing Commission.

———. 2007. *Cocaine and Federal Sentencing Policy*. Washington, DC: U.S. Sentencing Commission.

Wacquant, Loïc. 2002*a*. "Deadly Symbiosis: Rethinking Race and Imprisonment in Twenty-first-Century America." *Boston Review* (April/May).

———. 2002*b*. "From Slavery to Mass Incarceration." *New Left Review* 13(January–February):41–60.

Walker, Samuel, Cassia Spohn, and Miriam DeLone. 2006. *The Color of Justice: Race, Ethnicity, and Crime in America*. 4th ed. Belmont, CA: Wadsworth.

Walmsley, Roy. 2007. *World Prison Population List*. 7th ed. London: International Centre for Prison Studies.

Western, Bruce. 2006. *Punishment and Inequality in America*. New York: Russell Sage Foundation.

Wilson, James Q. 1990. "Drugs and Crime." In *Drugs and Crime*, edited by Michael Tonry and James Q. Wilson. Vol. 13 of *Crime and Justice: A Review of Research*, edited by Michael Tonry and Norval Morris. Chicago: University of Chicago Press.

Wilson, William Julius. 1978. *The Declining Significance of Race: Blacks and American Institutions*. Chicago: University of Chicago Press.

———. 1987. *The Truly Disadvantaged: The Inner City, the Underclass, and Public Policy*. Chicago: University of Chicago Press.

Part II
Comparative Penal Policy

[4]
Symbol, Substance, and Severity in Western Penal Policies

Abstract
Similar economic transformations, public opinion patterns, social developments and crime trends have affected most western countries over the past few decades. Punishment trends, however, whether measured in terms of imprisonment rates, average sentence lengths, preferences for or against short or long prison sentences and adoption of various forms of new community penalties vary widely. Why similar economic, social, crime and public opinion trends have such different effects on penal policy is not known. Many explanations for penal policy trends have some explanatory weight for particular countries but few are broadly generalizable.

Key Words
imprisonment • normative cycles • populist punitivism • punishment • sensibilities • tolerance

Penal reform is or recently has been on the policy agenda of every western country. The details vary, but everywhere change is underway or under consideration. Scandinavian countries have recast their sentencing laws and created new sanctions. Western European countries have adopted new systems of prosecutorial guidelines, plea bargaining, day fines, electronic monitoring and community service. Most US jurisdictions have comprehensively overhauled their sentencing laws and policies, usually to reduce officials' discretion and make penalties harsher. England and several Australian states have followed the American lead and adopted similar policies in diluted forms. Sometimes, in some countries, notably Sweden (Jareborg, 1995, 2001) and Finland (Lappi-Seppälä, 2001), changes have been premised on human rights considerations. In a number of countries changes have been influenced by political and popular pressures that Anthony Bottoms famously called 'populist punitivism' (Bottoms, 1995).

And these are overcrowded times in the prisons of many countries. The more than 2 million people behind bars in American jails and prisons constitute 700 of every 100,000 residents. If children and those over 65 are dropped from the denominator, nearly one in 50 adult Americans is locked up. Those rates are five times higher than at any time this century prior to 1973 when they began their unprecedented climb (Bureau of Justice Statistics, 2000).

But the USA is not alone. Imprisonment rates have increased and sentences become harsher in many countries. In Holland (Junger-Tas, 2001; Tak, 2001), England (Ashworth, 2001), Italy (Kuhn, 2001), Portugal (Kuhn, 2001) and some Australian states (Freiberg, 2001), imprisonment rates are higher than at any time in the preceding century. In France, the numbers of people sentenced to imprisonment and average sentence lengths have increased, and American-style population increases have been avoided largely by periodic use of broad-based amnesties, pardons and commutations (Kensey and Tournier, 2001; Kuhn, 2001). Elsewhere, for example, in Germany (Weigend, 2001), Canada (Sprott and Doob, 2001), Norway (Larsson, 2001), Denmark (Kysgaard, 2001), and Sweden (Jareborg, 2001) imprisonment use and rates have increased moderately or fluctuated. Only in a few countries, most notably Japan (Hamai, 2001) and Finland (Lappi-Seppälä, 2001), have incarceration rates declined substantially in recent decades.

This article examines efforts to explain recent trends in the severity of punishment and in penal policy innovation in western countries. It concludes that the best explanations remain parochially national and cultural. The world increasingly may be a global community, have a global economy and be moving towards adoption of English as a global language, but explanations of penal policy remain curiously local or, as Zimring and Hawkins (1991) called them, 'contingent'.[1]

People increasingly commonly argue that punishment must be understood in expressive rather than instrumental terms (e.g. Kennedy, 2000). By this it is meant, in vaguely neo-Durkheimian terms, that enunciation and implementation of penal policies should be understood primarily as symbolic statements about good and bad values, and accordingly that instrumental claims about effectiveness and normative claims about injustice miss the point. Both the latter are concerned with the substantive operation of the penal system, either in how it produces measurable good or bad consequences, or in how well or poorly it apportions punishments to offenders' culpability or the harm they cause. Durkheimian (or Marxist or Foucauldian) accounts, by contrast, are functionalist explanations of how social institutions operate. They are not normative theories about how institutions ought to operate and, unlike most consequentialist and all retributivist theories, they do not take individuals seriously. In most of this article, I try to make sense of current knowledge about differences in penal policy across time and space, and assume that penal policies should take individuals seriously. In the conclusion, I return to arguments about expressive and instrumental accounts and suggest how they might be enriched.

This article contains four sections. The first discusses the central role of penal policy in democratic societies and the various ways that countries reconcile crime control and due process values. It concludes that, compared with other western countries, the United States has got the balance seriously wrong.

The second section then reviews a range of general explanations for recent US penal policy trends and concludes that none of them explains enough. So far, at least, none of those in wide use can explain why countries subject to similar crime trends and social changes varied so much in their reactions. The prevalent US explanations make some sense of US developments, but not other countries'.

The third section examines recent experience in the import and export of penal policies. The substantive effectiveness of policy innovations has little influence on whether they are adopted elsewhere. The USA in particular is neither a successful importer nor an influential exporter.[2] More generally, countries in Western Europe actively emulate seemingly successful innovations from elsewhere in Europe but seem largely impervious to US influence. Common law countries, particularly England and Australia, have nibbled at replication of some, principally symbolic,[3] US policies, but half-heartedly, and seem to pay little heed to what happens in Europe.

The fourth section pulls together the conclusions of the preceding three, and considers why there are pronounced national differences in penal policy, in the relative importance of symbolic and substantive policy making, and in receptivity to ideas first developed elsewhere, and how we might improve our understanding of such matters.

THE IMPORTANCE OF PENAL POLICY

Penal policy encompasses the fundamental values of freedom from fear and harm, and the right to be let alone. Whether directly through deterrence, incapacitation and rehabilitation, indirectly through community, developmental and situational crime prevention, or diffusely through norm-reinforcement, socialization and moral-educative effects, criminal justice systems influence levels and patterns of crime. And the state's authority to take power over citizens in the name of law enforcement or crime prevention impinges on and often diminishes the autonomy and liberty of citizens.

It is not easy to get the balance right. Too little security, and the state fails to satisfy an irreducible core obligation. Too much, and it intrudes unduly and unjustly on citizens' liberty. Herbert Packer (1968) encapsulated these competing interests in the terms 'the crime control model' and 'the due process model' The first gives primacy to protecting citizens from disorder and insecurity, the second to protecting citizens from unwarranted intrusions. Neither can be realized without sacrifice, and pursuing one single-mindedly necessarily incurs sacrifices to the other. Neither of Packer's models necessarily implies anything about the severity of punishment: as Grant Gilmore observed:

> The values of a reasonably just society will reflect themselves in a reasonably just law. The better the society, the less law there will be. In Heaven there will be no law, and the lion will lie down with the lamb. The values of an unjust society will reflect themselves in an unjust law. The worse the society, the more law there will be. In Hell there will be nothing but law, and due process will be meticulously observed. (Grant Gilmore, 1977: 110–11)

Packer's distinction is all the same important and likely to support penal policy predictions. Countries in which due process values are predominant are less likely than others to be willing to sacrifice individual citizens' interests to achieve public goods. Countries in which crime control values are predominant are more likely than others to be prepared to sacrifice individuals' interests. In this article, then, I use Packer's terms somewhat differently than he did, coupling due process with its underlying normative premise of fair treatment of individuals' interests, and coupling crime control with its implicit greater willingness to disregard individuals' interests in pursuit of public safety. That is why I refer to due process and crime control 'values' rather than 'models'.

How societies balance these competing values varies over time. I use the contemporary United States as a frame of reference because I know it best and because in penal policy terms it is on most issues the extreme case. American courts and legislators gave relatively greater weight to due process values in the 1960s, and less to crime control values, than they have since. In 2001, policy makers and, implicitly, citizens, in a state like California that enacted broadly defined three-strikes and sexual psychopath laws give less weight to due process values than do policy makers and citizens in a state like Washington which enacted such laws narrowly, or in Maine, which did not enact such laws at all.

The balance also varies across space. While it was conventional to argue that American law in the 1950s through the 1970s gave greater weight to due process values than did the inquisitorial processes of Western Europe, at the beginning of the 21st century that is no longer true. As American enthusiasm has waned, European enthusiasm, under the influence of the European Human Rights Convention (Kurki, 2001; Morgan, 2001), has waxed. Professor Hans-Heinrich Jeschek, founding and long-time director of the Max Planck Institute for International and Comparative Penal Law in Freiburg, Germany, has told me of his dismay that American courts and law makers in the 1980s and 1990s so extensively repudiated values that post-World War II German policy makers and scholars greatly admired, and successfully sought to emulate and entrench in the German constitution and legal system.

Examples can be given of changes and differences in the balance of influence of crime control and due process values. These include capital punishment, incarceration, defendants' procedural protections and acceptance of international human rights standards. By all those criteria, the United States is a country more committed to crime control and less to due process values in 2001 than any Western European or other major English-speaking country, or than it itself was in 1970.

Concerning capital punishment, for example, there was a de facto moratorium in 1970 and a widespread belief that the Supreme Court would soon declare the death penalty unconstitutional. In 1999, capital punishment was authorized in 38 states and the federal system, 98 people were executed and at year's end 3625 were on death row (Death Penalty Information Center, 2000). No Western European country, or Australia, Canada, England or New Zealand, allows capital punishment. Courts in South Africa and Hungary declared their countries' capital punishment laws unconstitutional, and the dozens of Eastern and Southern European countries joining the Council of Europe agreed to forgo capital punishment as a condition of membership.

Concerning incarceration, the US rate per 100,000 population of 700 per 100,000 in 1999 was five times the 1970 US rate of 135 (Maguire and Pastore, 1999). It was also five times the rates in 2000 of Portugal, New Zealand and England, the western countries that, at rates around 150 per 100,000, confine the next largest fractions of their residents. Similarly, in 1970, US mandatory minimum sentences were modest in scope and severity, there were no meaningful three-strikes or sexual-psychopath laws and few prisoners were sentenced to terms of life-without-possibility-of-parole or to non-parolable terms measured in decades. All of those sentences, including lengthy mandatory minimums, are commonplace in the USA in 2001 and rare or non-existent elsewhere.

Concerning defendants' procedural protections, the names of the Warren Court compared with the Burger and Rehnquist Courts have come in the United States to symbolize courts that are and are not deeply concerned with assuring that defendants are fairly treated. By contrast, in Europe, the influences of the European Human Rights Court and Convention have steadily increased and constitutional courts of individual countries have become more protective of defendants' interests. Even in England, committed for centuries to the constitutional principle of Parliamentary Supremacy and the related idea that there can be no entrenched written constitution, the provisions of the European Convention of Human Rights became enforceable in the courts in autumn 2000. Thus the European Convention's more protective approach to criminal procedure became part of English law.

Finally, concerning international human rights norms, the United States is notorious in the international community for its unwillingness to subject itself to the jurisdiction of international human rights treaties or institutions. When it appears to do so, it does so only sophistically by adopting ratification qualifications that provisions are adopted only insofar as they are consistent with the holdings of US courts construing parallel provisions of the US Constitution (Albrecht, 2001; Kurki, 2001). The USA was alone among western countries, but in company with China, when it refused to sign the treaties creating an International Criminal Court with power to try alleged crimes against humanity and war crimes.

My guess is that most informed western observers outside the United States (e.g. Pfeiffer, 1996; Windlesham, 1998) would say that contemporary American penal policies get the balance between crime control and due process values wrong. An extreme example is the retention of capital punishment generally and particularly recent placement of Supreme Court imprimaturs on execution of mentally retarded people and people who were 16- and 17-years-old when they committed their crimes. Another is real offence sentencing in the federal court. This is the practice of sentencing offenders for all crimes the judge by a civil law standard of proof finds they committed, regardless of whether charges were never filed, were dismissed or resulted in a jury acquittal (Tonry, 1999a). A third is the California three-strikes statute requiring a mandatory 25-year or sometimes life-without-possibility-of-parole sentence for some offenders sentenced for a third felony, no matter how trivial. Notorious examples include such third felonies as taking of two pieces of pizza and sale of a few grams of marijuana (Zimring et al., 2001).

Much more important than characterization of contemporary US practices is recognition that penal policy raises issues at the core of democratic values. The USA may or may not have got the balance between security and liberty grievously wrong but setting that balance is a centrally important issue for democratic countries. For the past quarter century in the USA and the past decade in England, governments in power have treated penal policy as if it were not a centrally important subject but something subsidiary to electoral politics and as if only crime control values need be acknowledged. This is the adoption of what Snacken et al. (1995) call expansionist policies, which predict both greater penal severity and rising prison populations. Although all western countries have felt the pressures of populist punitivism, most have continued to give substantial weight to due process values and human rights concerns.

THE DETERMINANTS OF PENAL POLICY

The extraordinary increase in the severity of US sentencing laws and in the number of prison inmates, and the lesser but recently rapid increases in England, have precipitated a revived literature on the determinants of penal policy (e.g. Zimring and Hawkins 1991; Young and Brown, 1993; Bottoms, 1995; Caplow and Simon, 1999; Tonry, 1999b; Garland, 2001). This builds on earlier works in Durkheimian (1893; Garland, 1990) and political economy (Rusche and Kircheimer, 1939) traditions that offered functionalist explanations in terms, respectively, of normative change and labour discipline. The Durkheimian perspective remains vital, and underlies much of the newer literature. The political economy perspective, though offering insights, by itself, has repeatedly been shown to have relatively little explanatory force (e.g. Young and Brown, 1993; D'Alessio and Stolzenberg, 1995; Myers, 1998).

Many of the central arguments in the last decade's literature on explanations for penal policy and prison population changes are plausible enough, but they raise more and deeper questions than they answer. Not surprisingly, perhaps, since the prison population increase is greatest in the United States, and the harshest policies have been adopted there and in England, most of the writers are from and the writing is about those countries (but not all: e.g. Snacken et al., 1995; HEUNI, 1997; Wacquant, 2001). Hans-Jörg Albrecht has pointed out that the English-language literature is a bit ethnocentric in its tendency to assume the developments it explains occurred in England, the USA 'and elsewhere', when often elsewhere they have not (Albrecht, 2001: 294).

Most explanations for harsher public policies in England and the USA are curiously parochial and invoke causal explanations that, if valid, should apply to many countries. For example, if the four forces of rising crime rates, economic and social disruption, post-modernist angst and populist punitivism caused modern shifts in American and English penal policies (and in Australia: Freiberg, 2001), why did they not have the same effects in other western countries that experienced the same things? Finnish policies have become less harsh and imprisonment rates have declined since the early 1970s, and those in Sweden, Norway and Denmark remained broadly stable, and yet the four forces were not absent. Nor were they absent from Germany where policies became milder and imprisonment rates fell in the 1970s and have fluctuated within a narrow band since, from France where imprisonment rates seesawed for two decades or from Canada which retains in 2001 penal and sentencing policies not greatly different from those it had in 1965.

The destabilizing four forces affected all western countries (but not Japan which avoided at least rising crime rates). In most countries both official crime data and, where available, victim survey findings showed substantial crime-rate increases from the early 1970s through the early-to-mid 1990s. It is not implausible to hypothesize that increased victimization would anger and frighten citizens, that they would demand harsher policies, and that punishments would become severer and prison populations rise as a result. The evidence, however, does not support the hypothesis. In only two countries, the Netherlands and the United States, did incarceration rates rise more or less continuously after 1975, and in Holland the rise was not attributable primarily to enactment of harsher laws.

Nor, relatedly, is it implausible to assume that crime and punishment trends would move in parallel: increased crime rates would produce more arrests, convictions, and sentences, and prison use would increase accordingly. Something like this seems to have happened in Holland (Junger-Tas, 2001), where rising prison admissions and harsher sentences imposed by judges primarily explain rising prison populations, but crime rates increased in most western countries and no other except the United States experienced continuous rising prison populations.

The other three destabilizing forces – economic and social disruption, post-modernist angst and populist punitivism – I discuss together for the same reason that they were ubiquitous. What we see is as affected by when we look as by where we stand, and so it is hard to know whether the past quarter century has experienced more and more profound disruption than any other. Whether or not recent decades have been more disrupted than others, no one can disagree that there have been major social, political and technological changes. These include the economic restructuring and destabilization of work associated with the global economy; changes in social norms and institutions associated with the civil, gay and women's rights movements; global population movements and the increasing heterogeneity of most countries; the end of the Cold War and the collapse of the Soviet Union; and massive technological change.

These three forces can be linked: massive social and economic changes have disrupted most people's lives, often traumatically and repeatedly. There is widespread resulting insecurity, unease and what might be called post-modernist angst. Because people are unhappy they look for scapegoats, and criminals, immigrants and welfare recipients are easy and vulnerable targets. Crime rates have risen, and mass media have amplified people's awareness of crime. Ergo, populist punitivism, a mass phenomenon superficially about crime and criminals but really a displacement onto vulnerable targets of angers and fears associated with larger, incomprehensible and seemingly invulnerable social forces.

Lack of convincing answers to two questions seriously undermines this composite disruption/angst/punitivism argument. First, if it explains US and English crime politics and policies, why have not the same forces produced similar politics and policies in Scandinavia, Germany and Canada? Relatedly, why did they produce such policies in England only in the 1990s, at the end of two decades' crime-rate increases and in a decade when crime rates for at least several years fell?

Second, more fundamentally, are there valid bases for believing that the disruptions and insecurities of the past quarter century are worse or more important than those of any other period? Explanations built on post-modernist platforms take it as given that recent decades have witnessed social changes of unprecedented disruption, but is that true? The past century experienced, before 1975, numerous garden-variety economic recessions, Prohibition, the Great Depression, the 'Roaring 20s', decolonization of much of Asia and Africa, World Wars I and II, numerous colonial wars for independence, many civil wars, the Korean War, the Vietnam War and the Cold War, not to mention technological advances from the automobile to the computer and nuclear weapons. The direct and indirect effects of these things on individuals' lives and social norms, practices and institutions were not small. In every era, I suspect, people attribute much that they dislike or disapprove to the seemingly unprecedented changes of their times, and, with the benefit of imperfect memory and good-old-days nostalgia, believe the changes in their lives are more consequential than those of other times.

For these reasons, I do not believe that explanations of the centrality of crime as a contentious public issue based on the four destabilizing forces are persuasive.

There are, however, at least three plausible causal explanations for American crime policy developments, but they suffer the limitation that they do not seem generalizable to other countries. First, Ted Caplow and Jonathan Simon have argued that elected US officials have adopted a 'governing through crime' strategy for winning elections (Caplow and Simon, 1999). They argue that the breakdown of broad-based political parties and geographical political stabilities (e.g. Democrats in the South, Republicans in the West), the rise of single-issue interest groups and Americans' lack of confidence in government have made it difficult for politicians to win elections based on broad positive appeals. Issues must be found that do not alienate important single-issue interest groups – which may each constitute only a few percent of voters but can easily be the margin of victory or loss in a close election – and that have comparatively broad appeal. Such issues tend to be negative: no important constituency is offended when campaigns are launched against welfare recipients, immigrants or criminals, and criminals least of all (or formerly, communism or the Soviet Union, but that negative appeal is no longer galvanizing). As a result, in order to win elections and thereby to govern, politicians have addressed crime issues in polemical and stereotyped ways. Because it is difficult to oppose polemical claims about emotional subjects with reasoned arguments, American politicians compete to show who is tougher.

President Clinton is often said to have taken the crime issue away from the Republicans by deciding never to let the Republicans get to his right. Similar claims are made in England about Tony Blair and his Home Secretary, Jack Straw, in relation to the Tories (Downes and Morgan, 1998). Crime and punishment have received less attention in US elections since 1992, because the parties are now stalemated on the issue. Unfortunately, that means there can be no significant changes in US penal (including drug) policy until elected officials are willing to risk being accused of softness. Most politicians' risk-aversion makes that unlikely any time soon.

The governing-through-crime argument is coherent and plausible. However, the US background story does not apply to England where a similar crime policy stalemate is in place. England still has two dominant political parties with strong traditions of party discipline. Single-issue interest groups are not electorally crucial, and cynicism about government is less pronounced than in the USA. The need to appeal to a fractured electorate seems less urgent in England than in the USA. Yet political risk-aversion concerning crime policy seems as present in England.

Conversely, the governing-through-crime analysis prima facie might be more applicable to European countries like Holland, Belgium, Germany and Italy that have many well-established political parties and a tradition of coalition governments. Right-wing, nativist parties exist in most continental countries, and have focused attention on crime, often in association with anti-immigrant rhetoric. However, mainstream political parties in no continental European country have as yet adopted US-style rhetoric or policy and none but Holland has had a dramatic, long-term run-up in incarceration rates.

The second plausible US account concerns race. Southern Republicans, and conservatives more generally, it is said (Edsall and Edsall, 1992), appealed to the anxieties and biases of working-class whites by focusing on welfare and crime, two issues that are in the abstract racially neutral but in media imagery have black faces. Voting for candidates who were tough on crime or welfare was a respectable way for whites to express latent or unexpressed racist sentiments. No one can credibly deny that blacks in the 1970s and 1980s were over-represented among recipients of Aid to Families with Dependent Children, the principal US income support programme for the poor, or among people arrested for serious crimes (Tonry, 1995: 1). This supported the political stereotypes. Nor can anyone credibly deny that crime and drug policies from 1985 to 2000 greatly worsened the disproportionate presence of blacks in jails, prisons and death rows. Whether this was because conservatives cynically adopted policies that they foresaw would simultaneously elicit white support and damage black interests, or because they adopted crime and drug policies in good faith that turned out to disadvantage blacks, is a matter on which no uncontroversial judgement is ever likely to be possible. Nor is there any way to prove or disprove Löic Wacquant's functional hypothesis that modern imprisonment policies serve to retain whites' dominance over blacks that slavery and Jim Crow formerly but no longer provided (Wacquant, 2001). It is at very least not unlikely that such policies would have been changed had their disproportionate effects burdened middle-class whites rather than poor blacks and Hispanics (Blumstein, 1993).

The racial politics arguments have considerable weight in explaining American policies in the late-20th century. Conservatives did play the race card, many were motivated by or at least indifferent to the disparate effects of crime control policies on blacks, and many were less impelled to change policies that exacerbated racial disparities affecting blacks than if they had affected whites (Tonry, 1995). However, the racial politics argument does not seem to have much weight elsewhere.

In England, for example, racial disparities in imprisonment affecting Afro-Caribbeans are worse than in the USA (Tonry, 1994), but Afro-Caribbeans have never been a potent political group or made up more than 2 percent of the population. Moreover, no one argues that any British party has played the race card for short-term political advantage as it was played in the USA, or that stereotyped racial politics have had or could have the mobilizing effects they had in the USA.[4]

That racial disparities affecting blacks in England are worse than those in the USA seriously undermines any claim that racial or ethnic politics have motivated penal policy changes and prison population increases in western countries generally. Ethnic and national minorities, their identities varying widely with time and place, are as over-represented in the prisons of every western country as are blacks in the USA (Tonry, 1997). The population fractions represented by members of minority groups are increasing in many countries. In some, such as Germany (Albrecht, 1997), recent increases in the prison population are attributable solely to rising incarceration rates for non-citizens. The time may come when ethnic tensions are as salient in other countries to formulation and understanding of penal policy as black/white tensions have been in the United States, but so far as least that does not appear to be so.

The third explanation is that contemporary US crime and drug policies are the product of an interaction between long-term patterns of tolerance and intolerance of deviance, a series of late-20th-century moral panics and the ubiquity and sensationalism of mass-media crime coverage (Tonry, 1999a). The argument is based on historical works showing how long-term cycles of tolerance and intolerance concerning drug use (Musto, 1987), religious belief (Johnson, 1976), sexual practices (Boswell, 1980) and artistic expression (Gilmore, 1974) predict popular beliefs and public policies. At times of declining drug use, for example, popular attitudes towards drugs become more rigid and moralistic, laws harsher and law enforcement more zealous. During moral panics, people tend to exaggerate the dangers and scale of things they fear, to overreact and to adopt policies and do things they often will later regret. The argument, by analogy to drug tolerance cycles, is that American crime rates have fallen since the early 1980s, attitudes have hardened, voices that would have been raised against draconian policies in earlier times were stilled and severe policies and overcrowded prisons resulted. Moral panics about crack cocaine, youth violence and street gangs made it worse.

Zimring et al.'s (2001) analysis of the origins and operation of California's three-strikes law, which is broader in scope and ampler in consequences than any other, relates policy changes to interactions between declining crime rates and broadening policy consensus. Though they attribute the California law's scope and severity in part to partisan politics,[5] their analysis also relates harsh policies to declining crime rates. Noting the absence of consensus on crime policies in the 1960s and 1970s, a time of sharply rising crime rates, they suggest that a time lag may have been necessary to achieve consensus on harsh modern policies:

> Political action on crime may be more likely in periods of decline . . . than in periods of increase . . . This sort of hypothesis might help to explain the gap that sometimes exists between periods of high public anxiety and periods of extensive political and governmental change. (Zimring et al., 2001: 165)

This third explanation is loosely Durkheimian. Periods of increasing drug use, overt homosexuality, or religious heterodoxy are periods of normative flux and dissensus, when relative tolerance might be expected. Periods of decline may reflect shifts towards greater social consensus in favour of abstinence from drugs, heterosexuality and religious orthodoxy, and that predicts per Durkheim that law and its institutions would shift to favour the stronger normative consensus.

There is a ring of truth in this concerning the USA, but it does not offer much for other countries besides England. English crime rates steadily rose through the mid-1990s, but imprisonment rates did not. Since then, imprisonment rates have increased by 50 percent and punishment, laws, policies and rhetoric have become steadily harsher. Most other western countries' crime rates rose steadily through the 1970s and 1980s and their incarceration rates varied widely (Kuhn, 2001). Crime rates in many countries began to fall in the early or mid-1990s but there was no converse general pattern of an increase in incarceration or harshening in punishment policies.

No single factor, or several, can possibly explain why countries' punishment policies and practices differ or why they change over time. Most of the developments and arguments canvassed above contain at least grains of truth about the USA. Crime rates rose and then fell, public attitudes became tougher, politicians exploited public fears for partisan advantage and massive social changes occurred. All of these things happened and in various ways influenced penal sensibilities and through them punishment policies and practices (Tonry, 2001a).

Populist punitivism is a recognizable phenomenon in many western countries. However, its origins are unclear and its effects widely diverse. Most systematic efforts to explain national differences in penal policies or punitiveness offer a few tentative hypotheses (e.g. Zimring and Hawkins, 1991; Young and Brown, 1993), as I have, and conclude that the explanations are most likely to be found in distinctive differences in national history and culture, as I do.

Prison populations and trends towards greater punitiveness are broad outcomes of changing social and political processes. The next section shifts to a narrower focus. Just as there are distinct differences between countries in how they respond to rising crime rates, there are distinct differences in their receptiveness to new penal measures.

THE TRANSFERABILITY OF PENAL POLICY

Countries and their subdivisions can learn from other jurisdictions' penal policy experiences, and ought to be better able to do so in our time than in earlier times. The widespread use of English and the speed of modern communication assure that little goes on that can not be learned about elsewhere. Processes of adoption and adaptation, however, are not easy or straightforward, and any hope that the simple attractiveness or effectiveness of an innovation in one place will lead to its emulation elsewhere is Pollyannaish. Human resistance to change, even concerning seemingly objective scientific developments (Kuhn, 1996), often requires that there be shifts in paradigms before new ways seem imaginable. Mundanely, for example, parole and sentencing guidelines were nearly unimaginable in the USA until the indeterminate sentencing paradigm began to break down. Similarly, the political science literature on innovation instructs that policy making is often serendipitous and that better knowledge seldom leads directly to better policies (e.g. Lynn, 1978; Lindblom, 1990). That transfers of policies and practices are not simple does not mean that they do not happen. At least three different kinds of stories can be told.

First are dispersion stories about innovations that seem to satisfy important needs better than previous practices. The gradual spread of day fines, community service and prosecutorial fines offers examples (Albrecht, 2001). Day fines can be scaled to offenders' means (prototypically, a day's net income) and the seriousness of crimes (the number of day fines rising with the seriousness of the offence). Thus they provide a punitive sentencing option that can plausibly substitute for imprisonment, and be calibrated to assure proportionality of punishment. They can spare offenders the pains and the state the costs of imprisonment. Day fines began in Scandinavia, spread to Germany in the 1970s and to Portugal and Austria a little later and were adopted for some crimes in other European countries (Albrecht, 2001). In the USA, where there were federally funded pilot projects in the 1980s and 1990s, and in England, where they were authorized by statute but abandoned less than a year after taking effect, they failed. In Australia, Canada and New Zealand, they were not attempted. The day fine thus appears to be a sanction that appeals to the sensibilities of Western European Civil Law countries but not to those of English-speaking Common Law countries.

Community service – performing a specified number of hours of unpaid work for public benefit – began as an institutionalized sanction in California in the 1960s, spread to England in the 1970s, Scotland in the early 1980s, the Netherlands in the late 1980s and Finland in the 1990s (Tonry, 1999c). In the last four instances, community service was conceived as an alternative to incarceration and the early evaluations suggested it was used that way half or more of the time. In the Netherlands, particularly, its use grew rapidly in the 1990s (Tak, 2001). Community service has now been adopted in some form in most western countries. It is seldom used as a confinement alternative or as a punishment in its own right in the United States. Instead it is generally ordered as one among many conditions to probation sentences.

Prosecutorial fines, also called conditional dismissals, began in the 1970s with German efforts to reduce case-processing costs and find alternatives for short prison sentences. The German innovation began with authority for prosecutors to offer a charge dismissal to offenders charged with designated offences if they would agree to accept the penalty, nearly always a fine, that would be imposed if they were convicted (Weigend, 2001). The dismissal was conditioned on not committing other crimes. Over the years conditional dismissal's scope in Germany has expanded and in 2001 it encompasses serious offences and large penalties. Austria and Portugal soon emulated the German practice. So did the Netherlands, where the transaction, as it is called, constitutes a large fraction of case dispositions (Tak, 2001). Belgium soon adopted the Dutch practice and transactions there too make up a large share of dispositions. Conditional dismissal, like the day fine, has not been widely adopted in Common Law countries.

The second kind of story concerns innovations that serve important purposes but appeal to policy makers only in particular regions or countries. The day-fine and conditional-dismissal stories could be told this way as examples of sanctions that seem to hold great appeal only to Western European policy makers. From an American perspective, numerical sentencing guidelines are the pre-eminent example. Their demonstrated ability to reduce sentencing disparities, implement changes in sentencing policy, and tie sentencing policy to correctional resources led to their serious consideration or adoption in many states – initially in bellwether Minnesota, Pennsylvania and Washington, then in a handful of other states, but eventually in more than half (Reitz, 2001). No other country has followed, though English academics have flirted with the idea and law reform commissions in Canada and Australia have proposed its adoption (Morris and Tonry, 1990: ch. 2). Holland in 1999 adopted numerical prosecution guidelines but they are successors to earlier Dutch guidelines and were not much influenced by US developments (Schurer and van Loon, 2001).

The third kind of story concerns symbolic innovations that serve primarily ideological ends. Some might call such policies expressive (though this seems to me slightly simplistic since in a functionalist sense all policies are expressive). Most of these originate in the United States and elicit significant interest only in other English-speaking countries. 'Boot camps', institutions patterned on military basic training, are an example. Whatever the good faith may have been of officials in Georgia and other pioneering states which established the first boot camps, evaluations soon showed that they were seldom used as prison alternatives, that they cost not saved public monies and that they had no effects on recidivism rates or offenders' post-release self-esteem (Tonry, 1996: ch. 4). Nonetheless, for a decade after these findings became well known, American politicians from President Clinton down found the image of vigorous physical discipline appealing and actively promoted their creation and use for juvenile 'non-violent first offenders'. This last shows the hypocrisy of the promotion of boot camps since most members of that group are not likely to be sent to prison; that made prison diversion and related cost savings rationales not credible. Many are likely to age out of offending in any case but be at increased risk of socialization into deviant values if placed in any correctional institution. Thus the research evidence by 1992 fundamentally undermined the instrumental case for boot camps. Nonetheless, they were eventually established in more than two-thirds of the states, primarily to demonstrate their proponents' toughness.

The only countries that I have been able to learn about that created boot camps are England, Australia and Canada, and all quickly abandoned them. In England, the Conservative Home Secretary Michael Howard, generally characterized as the political figure who more than any other brought American-style law and order politics to England, saw the symbolic value of boot camps and sought their establishment. Prison Service and other Home Office civil servants were doubtful and the institutions when established reflected some learning from the US evaluation literature. Entry was controlled by prison officials, not judges, thereby avoiding the net-widening problem, and the institutions were enriched by various treatment programmes (US research had shown that the only boot camps that showed glimmers of positive treatment effects were those that were treatment-resource rich). The English boot camps were abandoned soon after the Labour government of Tony Blair took office. Canada also for a short time operated but then abandoned a boot camp in the federal system. Western Australia established and for a short time operated a boot camp but it soon closed amid bad publicity (Freiberg, 2001: 47).

American-style sentencing changes like three-strikes rules, lengthy mandatory minimum sentences and 'truth in sentencing' (elimination of good time/remission, parole release or both) are another instance of American innovations that seem to have appeal only in Common Law jurisdictions. There are sizeable evaluation literatures on all of them (Tonry, 1996: ch. 5). For three-strikes and mandatory minimum laws the weight of the evidence is clear: they cause injustices in individual cases of people sentenced unduly harshly, they foster circumvention and nullification by practitioners wanting to avoid injustice and they produce stark disparities in sentences of like-situated offenders. The evidence on truth in sentencing is more ambiguous but at very least, since neither parole nor prison officials can influence release dates, they increase the dangers of judicial idiosyncrasies.

Despite evidence of the instrumental failings of these US laws, they swept the United States and milder versions have been adopted in England (Ashworth, 2001) and some Australian states (Freiberg, 2001). Parole release elimination also occurred in Holland but the rationale was a civil liberties concern about disparities that led to automatic parole release of all prisoners at the first eligibility date, which thereby retained the name but ended the practice (Tak, 2001).

CONCLUSIONS

Notwithstanding the variability in countries' interest in developments elsewhere, it is inevitable that legal systems will converge and that countries will change institutions or practices to incorporate what look like good ideas. New technologies spread across the developed world in months or years and technology transfers are in principle no different in the justice system than elsewhere. For hardware like electronic monitoring equipment, prison security equipment and credit/debit/smart card technology, or for systems for delivering core services like correctional privatization, the markets are already global. Legal institutions and processes are slower to change, but the pressures of international human rights standards, common information sources and internationalized professional communities will provide unceasing pressures in particular directions.

There is as yet no meaningfully comparative literature on penal reform. An internationally accessible literature on developments in individual jurisdictions is accumulating, however, and we can look across national boundaries in search of generalizations. The USA is no longer the only country in which politicians' short-term self-interest and punitive popular attitudes regularly trump human rights, effectiveness or cost-effectiveness considerations. No one could expect that legal institutions or practices would be immune from popular attitudes or changes in prevailing norms and values, but in most countries elites at least long believed that legal decisions affecting individuals' liberty and property interests should be insulated from short-term popular passions and public opinion. That began changing in the United States in the 1970s. As such examples as boot camps, three-strikes rules, overbroad sexual psychopath laws and mandatory minimum laws demonstrate, American policy making on penal subjects has for a quarter century been more symbolic than substantive. This has meant that evidence about dangers of individual injustices or about the instrumental effectiveness of particular programmes has often been ignored. Until the 1990s, the USA was the only western country in which penal policies had been heavily politicized, but England and Australia have started down that path. So far, most continental European countries have not, but the growing influence of nativist and xenophobic social movements and political parties is likely to create pressures for the politicization of crime. Criminals are even easier to scapegoat than foreigners.

Continental Europe appears more receptive to rationalistic technology transfers than do the English-speaking countries. The acceptance of European Human Rights Convention obligations and the rapid dispersion of day fines, conditional dismissal policies and community service are examples. The English have only grudgingly after decades of foot-dragging accepted the Convention into English law and the USA has refused to accept the application of any external human rights standards. Day fines and conditional dismissal have not been accepted.

Why Civil Law countries are more receptive to outside influence is unclear. Perhaps it is a by-product of the movement embodied in the EU and many treaties towards a federal Europe. Perhaps European étatist political traditions compared with Common Law egalitarian traditions have left European countries more comfortable with the idea that elites and experts, not public opinion, should decide penal policy issues (Savelsberg, 1994; Lappi-Seppälä, 2001). Perhaps the typically stronger and more extensive social welfare systems of Europe have fostered value systems in which crime raises more complex social issues than many politicians in moralistic America believe or will admit.

There remain strong cultural differences between countries that affect penal policy. Populist punitivism may exist everywhere, but its influences are widely divergent. The Swedes and the Finns continue to subscribe to a combination of humane and moralistic ideas that relate punishment to the moral culpability expressed by the crime but involve modest penalties. The Americans and lately the English subscribe to moralistic ideas of a different sort – offenders as offenders deserve to suffer but as citizens warrant little solicitude – and accept the legitimacy of political expediency as a determinant of penal policy. This shapes the limits of the politically feasible and the practically possible.

Penal values no doubt vary among Western European countries. Some, for example, Holland and Germany, still seem to incorporate strong social welfare values. Prevailing penal values, whatever they are, necessarily shape and constrain penal reform.

The editor of this journal asked me to conclude with some research suggestions. Here are five. First, we need genuinely cross-national research on crime and punishment levels and trends. Most of the existing literature consists of larger or smaller accounts of experience in individual countries (e.g. articles in Clarkson and Morgan, 1995; Tonry, 2001b; Tonry and Frase, 2001) or of efforts to collect data on a subject from many countries (e.g. Kuhn, 2001 on imprisonment rates). Speculative articles such as this one are about all that can be written on the basis of such evidence. Prospective cross-national studies of punishment patterns and practices, using standardized instruments and measures, would tell us much more. So would efforts to devise models for describing case dispositions in a country from arrest (or reported victimization) through final release from custody, followed by research using such models to compare countries in order to identify differences that require explanation.[6] The International Crime Victimization Survey (van Kesteren et al., 2001) and the *European Sourcebook of Crime and Criminal Justice Statistics* (European Committee on Crime Problems, 1999) are steps in that direction.

Second, we need more, fuller, and more nuanced policy histories for individual countries and their component sub-jurisdictions.[7] Most of the evidence on which efforts to generalize or theorize about determinants of penal policy or practice is anecdotal. Few academics have professional incentives to write policy histories but such as we have often provide information that is nowhere else available (e.g. Zimring et al.'s (2001) California three-strikes analysis).

Third, though so far macrosociological and econometric and other modelling efforts to characterize or explain penal policies have shed little useful light, more such studies are needed to test and disprove hypotheses and to establish patterns that need explaining. Martha Myers's recent (1998) effort to test political economy, Durkheimian and racial conflict hypotheses against 70 years of data on Georgia prison sentences is exemplary in that respect.

Fourth, theoretical work needs to disentangle functional and normative analyses of punishment. They operate at different levels of abstraction and explanation and are not, as some American writers suggest (e.g. Kahan, 1998a, 1998b), irreconcilable. To observe or conclude that a policy or practice performs expressive functions does not inexorably mean that normative analyses about just or effective punishments are irrelevant. The Finnish ethos that couples moral-educative, and general preventive ideas about how socialization operates with retributive ideas about the distribution of punishment, is illustrative (Lappi-Seppälä, 2001). Multi-level theories are common in many realms and more are needed concerning punishment.

Fifth, more people need to devote their energies and minds to this topic. Punishment and crime control are becoming steadily more central to western societies, and surprisingly little has been written about that trend, its causes, its effects and its dangers. Bob Newhart may or may not have been right when he hypothesized that an infinite number of monkeys working at an infinite number of typewriters would eventually write every great work of literature. It must be right, though, that we would learn more about this poorly understood subject if more people worked at it.

Acknowledgement

I am grateful to David Garland and several anonymous reviewers for helpful comments on an earlier draft. This article is based on the introduction to *Penal reform in overcrowded times*, edited by Michael Tonry and published by Oxford University Press in 2001.

Notes

1 I invoke Zimring and Hawkins's (1991) distinction between contingent and mechanical explanations of changes in penal severity. By mechanical explanations, Zimring and Hawkins refer to the simplistic view that changes in severity are the inexorable and mechanistic product of changes in policy. Life is more complicated than that and the effects of policy changes are necessarily dependent on a wide array of influences that vary with time, place and human idiosyncrasy. Any plausible explanation of changes in penal severity is thus about contingency.

2 I offer this observation on the basis of experience with alternative penalties and diversions (community service, day fines, conditional dismissals, boot camps) and with laws meant to structure sentencing discretion (guidelines, mandatory penalties, three-strikes laws). A reader suggested that electronic monitoring and prison privatization are examples of successful US exports. I disagree. Electronic monitoring is a surveillance technology, not a sanction, and privatization is a mechanism for implementing penal policy, but not a penal policy in itself.

3 'Symbolic' has long been used in the sentencing policy literature to refer to policies or postures adopted by officials with the aim of communicating their concern about an issue but without necessarily believing that the policy will be instrumentally effective or even be implemented (e.g. Zimring et al., 2001: ch. 11). Mandatory minimum sentence laws adopted in the 1950s and 1960s were symbolic in this sense; both policy makers and practitioners assumed they would usually meet with adaptive, nullifying responses from practitioners (e.g. Newman, 1966: 179–82). Symbolic in this sense resembles, but is not wholly synonymous with 'expressive' as in 'expressive theories of punishment' (e.g. Kennedy, 2000).

4 I refer to anti-black appeals as parts of electoral strategies; racial stereotyping occurs in England, as it does everywhere else, and many observers accuse both major parties of xenophobic politics in relation to immigrants generally.

5

> Public attitudes are both a cause and an effect of the politics of criminal justice . . . We suspect that much of the transformation in public opinion was caused by the way in which political actors talked about crime in the intervening years. The different opinions of the 1990s were as likely to be an effect of political rhetoric as its cause . . . Those who wish to undermine faith in government find that cultivating fear of crime is a promising means of doing so. (Zimring et al., 2001: 161, 231–2)

6 David P. Farrington and I, together with collaborators from eight countries, are doing this for a thematic volume of *Crime and Justice* on crime and punishment trends.

7 The use of national data in making international comparisons increasingly looks nonsensical. In federal countries like Australia, Canada, Germany and the United States, there are often stark differences in practice and policy between states/provinces. State

imprisonment rates in the United States, for example, in 1999 varied between Minnesota (125 per 100,000), Maine (133) and North Dakota (137), and Texas (762), Oklahoma (776) and the District of Columbia (1314). By this measure, the first three US states have more in common with Ontario (Sprott and Doob, 2001), New South Wales (Freiberg, 2001), Germany (Albrecht, 2001) and France (Kensey and Tournier, 2001) than they do with Texas, Oklahoma and the District of Columbia.

References

Albrecht, Hans-Jörg (1997) 'Ethnic minorities, crime, and criminal justice in Germany', in Michael Tonry (ed.), *Ethnicity, crime, and immigration – comparative and cross-national perspectives.* Chicago, IL: University of Chicago Press.

Albrecht, Hans-Jörg (2001) 'Post-adjudication dispositions in comparative perspective', in Michael Tonry and Richard S. Frase (eds), *Sentencing and sanctions in western countries.* New York: Oxford University Press.

Ashworth, Andrew (2001) 'The decline of English sentencing and other stories', in Michael Tonry and Richard S. Frase (eds) *Sentencing and sanctions in western countries.* New York: Oxford University Press.

Blumstein, Alfred (1993) 'Making rationality relevant – the American Society of Criminology 1992 presidential address', *Criminology* 31(1): 1–16.

Boswell, John (1980) *Christianity, social tolerance, and homosexuality.* Chicago, IL: University of Chicago Press.

Bottoms, Anthony E. (1995) 'The philosophy and politics of punishment and sentencing', in C.M.V. Clarkson and R. Morgan (eds), *The politics of sentencing reform.* Oxford: Clarendon.

Bureau of Justice Statistics (2000) *Prisoners in 1999.* Washington, DC: Bureau of Justice Statistics, US Department of Justice.

Caplow, Theodore and Jonathan Simon (1999) 'Understanding prison policy and population trends', in Michael Tonry and Joan Petersilia (eds) *Prisons.* Chicago, IL: University of Chicago Press.

Clarkson, Chris and Rod Morgan (1995) *The politics of sentencing reform.* Oxford: Oxford University Press.

D'Alessio, Stewart J. and Lis Stolzenberg (1995) 'Unemployment and the incarceration of pretrial defendants', *American Sociological Review* 60: 350–9.

Death Penalty Information Center (2000) Available at www.deathpenaltyinfo.org/index.html (click on 'Information Topics' and 'General').

Downes, David, and Rod Morgan (1998) 'Dumping the "hostages to fortune"? The politics of law and order in post-war Britain', in Mike Maguire, Rod Morgan and Robert Reiner (eds), *The Oxford handbook of criminology,* 2nd edn. Oxford: Oxford University Press.

Durkheim, Emile (1893) *The division of labor in society.* Paris: Alcan (translation by G. Simpson published in the United States in 1938 by The Free Press, New York).

Edsall, Thomas B. and Mary D. Edsall (1992) *Chain reaction: The influence of race, rights, and taxes on American politics.* New York: Norton.

European Committee on Crime Problems (1999) *The European sourcebook of crime and criminal justice statistics.* Strasbourg: Council of Europe.

Freiberg, Arie (2001) 'Three strikes and you're out – it's not cricket', in Michael Tonry and Richard S. Frase (eds), *Sentencing and sanctions in western countries*. New York: Oxford University Press.

Garland, David (1990) *Punishment and modern society: A study in social theory*. Oxford: Oxford University Press.

Garland, David, ed. (2001) *Mass imprisonment in the United States: Social causes and consequences*. London: Sage.

Gilmore, Grant (1974) *The death of contract*. Columbus, OH: Ohio State University Press.

Gilmore, Grant (1977) *The ages of American law*. New Haven, CT and London: Yale University Press.

Hamai, Koichi (2001) 'Prison population stable in Japan for thirty years', in Michael Tonry (ed.), *Penal reform in overcrowded times*. New York: Oxford University Press.

HEUNI (European Institute for Crime Prevention and Control) (1997) *Prison population and control in Europe and in North America – problems and prospects*. Helsinki: Ministry of Justice, Finland.

Jareborg, Nils (1995) 'The Swedish sentencing reform', in C.M.V. Clarkson and R. Morgan (eds), *The politics of sentencing reform*. Oxford: Clarendon.

Jareborg, Nils (2001) 'Sentencing law, patterns, and policies in Sweden', in Michael Tonry (ed.), *Penal reform in overcrowded times*. New York: Oxford University Press.

Johnson, Paul (1976) *A history of Christianity*. New York: Atheneum.

Junger-Tas, Josine (2001) 'Dutch penal policies changing direction', in Michael Tonry (ed.), *Penal reform in overcrowded times*. New York: Oxford University Press.

Kahan, Dan (1998a) 'Punishment and incommensurability', *Buffalo Law Review* 1: 691–708.

Kahan, Dan (1998b) 'The anatomy of disgust in criminal law', *Michigan Law Review* 96: 1621–43.

Kennedy, Joseph E. (2000) 'Monstrous offenders and the search for solidarity through modern punishment', *Hastings Law Journal* 51: 829–908.

Kensey, Annie and Pierre Tournier (2001) 'French prison numbers stable since 1988, but populations changing', in Michael Tonry (ed.), *Penal reform in overcrowded times*. New York: Oxford University Press.

Kuhn, André (2001) 'Incarceration rates across the world', in Michael Tonry (ed.), *Penal reform in overcrowded times*. New York: Oxford University Press.

Kuhn, Thomas (1996) *The structure of scientific revolutions*, 3rd edn. Chicago, IL: University of Chicago Press.

Kurki, Leena (2001) 'International standards and limits on sentencing and punishment', in Michael Tonry and Richard S. Frase (eds), *Sentencing and sanctions in western countries*. New York: Oxford University Press.

Kysgaard, Britta (2001) 'Penal sanctions and the use of imprisonment in Denmark', in Michael Tonry (ed.), *Penal reform in overcrowded times*. New York: Oxford University Press.

Lappi-Seppälä, Tapio (2001) 'Sentencing and punishment in Finland', in Michael Tonry and Richard S. Frase (eds), *Sentencing and sanctions in western countries*. New York: Oxford University Press.

Larsson, Paul (2001) 'Norway prison use up slightly, community penalties lots', in Michael Tonry (ed.), *Penal reform in overcrowded times*. New York: Oxford University Press.

Lindblom, Charles E. (1990) *Inquiry and change: The troubled attempt to understand and shape society*. New Haven, CT: Yale University Press.

Lynn, L.E. (1978) *Knowledge and policy: The uncertain connections*. Washington, DC: National Academy of Sciences.

Maguire, Kathleen and Ann L. Pastore, eds (1999) *Sourcebook of criminal justice statistics [online]*, table 6.36. Available at http://www.albany.edu/sourcebook [2000].

Morgan, Rod (2001) 'International standards and controls on sentencing and incarceration use', in Michael Tonry and Richard S. Frase (eds), *Sentencing and sanctions in western countries*. New York: Oxford University Press.

Morris, Norval and Michael Tonry (1990) *Between prison and probation: Intermediate punishments in a rational sentencing system*. New York: Oxford University Press.

Musto, David (1987) *The American disease: Origins of narcotic control*, rev. edn. New York: Oxford University Press.

Myers, Martha A. (1998) *Race, labor and punishment in the new south*. Columbus, OH: Ohio University Press.

Newman, Donald (1966) *Conviction*. Boston, MA: Little, Brown.

Packer, Herbert L. (1968) *The limits of the criminal sanction*. Palo Alto, CA: Stanford University Press.

Pfeiffer, Christian (1996) 'Crisis in American criminal policy? Questions and comments. A letter to Mrs J. Reno, Attorney General of the United States of America', *European Journal of Criminal Policy and Research* 4(2): 119–39.

Reitz, Kevin (2001) 'The disassembly and reassembly of U.S. sentencing practices', in Michael Tonry and Richard S. Frase (eds), *Sentencing and sanctions in western countries*. New York: Oxford University Press.

Rusche, Georg and Otto Kircheimer (1939) *Punishment and social structure*. New York: Columbia University Press.

Savelsberg, Joachim J. (1994) 'Knowledge, domination, and criminal punishment', *American Journal of Sociology* 99: 911–43.

Schurer, Gerrit and Reinier van Loon (2001) 'The Netherlands adopts numerical prosecution guidelines', in Michael Tonry (ed.), *Penal reform in overcrowded times*. New York: Oxford University Press.

Snacken, Sonja, Kristel Beyens and Hilde Tubex (1995) 'Changing prison populations in western countries: Fate or policy?', *European Journal of Crime, Criminal Law, and Criminal Justice* 1: 18–53.

Sprott, Jane B. and Anthony N. Doob (2001) 'Imprisonment rates in Canada: One law, ten outcomes', in Michael Tonry (ed.), *Penal reform in overcrowded times*. New York: Oxford University Press.

Tak, Peter (2001) 'Sentencing and punishment in the Netherlands', in Michael Tonry and Richard S. Frase (eds), *Sentencing and sanctions in western countries*. New York: Oxford University Press.

Tonry, Michael (1994) 'Racial disproportion in U.S. Prisons', *British Journal of Criminology* 34 (Special Issue): 97–115.

Tonry, Michael (1995) *Malign neglect – race, crime, and punishment in America*. New York: Oxford University Press.

Tonry, Michael (1996) *Sentencing matters*. New York: Oxford University Press.

Tonry, Michael, ed. (1997) *Ethnicity, crime, and immigration – comparative and cross-national perspectives*. Chicago, IL: University of Chicago Press.

Tonry, Michael (1999a) 'Rethinking unthinkable punishment policies in America', *UCLA Law Review* 46: 1751–91.

Tonry, Michael (1999b) 'Why are U.S. incarceration rates so high?', *Crime and Delinquency* 45(4): 419–37.

Tonry, Michael (1999c) 'Parochialism in U.S. sentencing policy', *Crime and Delinquency* 45(1): 48–65.

Tonry, Michael (2001a) 'Unthought thoughts: The influence of changing sensibilities on penal policies', *Punishment and Society* 3: 167–82.

Tonry, Michael, ed. (2001b) *Penal reform in overcrowded times*. New York: Oxford University Press.

Tonry, Michael and Richard S. Frase, eds (2001) *Sentencing and sanctions in western countries*. New York: Oxford University Press.

Van Kesteren, John, Pat Mayhew and Paul Nieuwbeerta (2001) *Criminal victimisation in seventeen industrialised countries*. The Hague: Ministry of Justice, the Netherlands.

Wacquant, Loïc (2001) 'Deadly symbiosis: When ghetto and prison meet and merge', *Punishment and Society* 3: 95–133.

Weigend, Thomas (2001) 'Sentencing policy in Germany', in Michael Tonry and Richard S. Frase (eds), *Sentencing and sanctions in western countries*. New York: Oxford University Press.

Windlesham, Lord (1998) *Politics, punishment, and populism*. New York: Oxford University Press.

Young, Warren and Mark Brown (1993) 'Cross-national comparisons of imprisonment', in Michael Tonry (ed.), *Crime and justice – a review of research*, vol. 17. Chicago, IL: University of Chicago Press.

Zimring, Franklin E. and Gordin Hawkins (1991) *The scale of imprisonment*. Chicago, IL: University of Chicago Press.

Zimring, Franklin E., Gordon Hawkins and Sam Kamin (2001) *Punishment and democracy: Three strikes and you're out in California*. New York: Oxford University Press.

MICHAEL TONRY is director of the Institute of Criminology and professor of law and public policy, University of Cambridge, and Sonosky Professor of Law and Public Policy, University of Minnesota.

[5]
Punishment Policies and Patterns in Western Countries

We can learn things about crime and punishment by looking across national boundaries. For despite many important similarities in how Western nations respond to crime, and in the values that underlie those responses, sentencing and punishment policies vary greatly. U.S. Supreme Court Justice Louis Brandeis observed, in *New State Ice Co. v. Liebmann*, 285 U.S. 262, 311 (1932), that "it is one of the happy incidents of the federal system that a single, courageous state may, if its citizens choose, serve as a laboratory and try social and economic experiments without risk to the rest of the country." Countries likewise can learn from one another's experiments if they will.

The formal similarities are great. Among the Western countries, at least, there is widespread commitment to democratic values and Enlightenment ideals, and the institutions of criminal justice are everywhere much the same. These include professional police, public prosecutors' offices, an independent judiciary, and reliance on imprisonment as the primary sanction for very serious crimes and chronic criminals and on various community penalties for others. There is much more similarity than difference in the content of criminal law doctrine, rules of evidence, and procedural safeguards.

Nonetheless, and despite broad similarity in most countries in crime trends over the past thirty years, sentencing and punishment policies and patterns vary enormously. In the United States, England, and the Netherlands and many other western European countries, crime rates rose rapidly from the mid-1960s until the late 1980s or early 1990s and have been declining since (see, e.g., Downes and Morgan 1997; van Dijk 1997; Mirrlees-Black et al. 1998; Pfeiffer 1998; Bureau of Justice Statistics 1999b). Similarity in crime trends, however, has not been paralleled by similarity in policy or institutional responses. At least four areas for comparison stand out.

First, prevailing beliefs vary greatly among policymakers about the causes of crime and the capacity of criminal justice policy changes to affect crime rates. In the United States and more recently in England and some Australian states, many policymakers believe that crime is primarily the result of bad or irresponsible people, not criminogenic conditions and inadequate socialization, and that harsher and more restrictive punishments will reduce crime rates through deterrent and incapacitative processes. As a result, as U.S. crime rates went up for two decades and penalties steadily became harsher, little thought was given to the possibility that crime rates may not be much affected by punishment policies. More recently, as crime rates have fallen in many countries, newly adopted harsh polices have been retained in the United States, England, and Australia, possibly because of a belief that declining crime rates are attributable to them. By contrast, the absence of steadily increasing imprisonment rates in many western European countries suggests that crime rates and patterns are not regarded as something easily controlled or necessarily much affected by punishment policies. The polar case is the widespread Finnish view that sentencing and punishment play an important backup role in norm-reinforcement, but that primary institutions, such as the family, the church, and the school, play the primary roles in socializing people into law-abiding habits. Accordingly, though punishment should be certain, it need not be harsh. Such premises, Patrik Törnudd observes, do not imply that "changes in policy, such as increases in the severity of punishment, would be widely seen as an appropriate or cost-effective means of controlling the level of crime" (Törnudd 1997, p. 190).

Second, relationships between crime and imprisonment patterns vary greatly. Against the backdrop of similar crime trends, imprisonment rates and prisoner numbers increased continuously in the United States after 1973 and in the Netherlands after 1975, decreased continuously in Finland after 1976, fluctuated widely in France and Italy, fluctuated slightly in Germany, Sweden, and Denmark, and followed other patterns elsewhere. In the 1990s, imprisonment rates have increased in many but not all countries. Whatever else these data show, they refute the existence of any inexorable or even general relationship between crime rates and imprisonment, directly, or, through intermediate effects on public fears, opinions, or policies, indirectly.

Third, policies governing types and amounts of punishment vary greatly. The most dramatic difference is between the United States, which continues to use the death penalty and life sentences without possibility of parole and where prison sentences exceeding ten years are common, and the rest of the Western world, which has renounced the death penalty and where prison sentences longer than a few years are uncommon. But there are many more differences than this. In some countries, for example, Germany and Austria, prison sentences shorter than six months are regarded as destructive and serving no valid penal purpose and are therefore strongly discouraged. In others, including Sweden and Finland, certainty of punishment is seen as important, but not severity, and as a result many sentences to days or weeks of imprisonment are imposed. And there are wide divergences in the use of community punishments. Community service is a commonly used prison alternative in England, Scotland, and the Netherlands, but is seldom used as a primary punishment in many other countries. Day fines are an oft-imposed punishment in Germany and much of Scandinavia but are used not at all in the

English-speaking countries and many others (e.g., the Netherlands) and only sparingly in still others (e.g., France). Electronic monitoring has been common in the United States for a decade but has only recently begun to catch on in most other countries (chap. 8, this volume).

Fourth, though nearly all Western countries attempt to insure use of fair procedures for determining guilt or innocence at and before adjudication of guilt (see, e.g., Weissbrodt and Wolfrum 1997), they vary greatly in whether, how, and how seriously they try to achieve just outcomes at the sentencing stage. Put differently, countries vary greatly in what they do to minimize unwarranted disparities in sentencing and to insure horizontal and vertical equity among sentences imposed. The approaches range from use of numerical guidelines for sentencing in many U.S. jurisdictions (and for prosecutors' sentence recommendations in the Netherlands), guideline judgments in England issued by the Court of Appeal, sentencing information systems in Scotland and New South Wales (and earlier in several Canadian provinces), and statutory sentencing principles enunciated in the Finnish and Swedish criminal codes to the approach of most European countries, Canada, Australia, New Zealand, and large parts of the United States that leaves the matter in the hands of sentencing judges.

Most of the chapters in this volume concern sentencing policies and practices in individual countries, and a few concern more general cross-cutting issues that arise in all countries. The chapters speak for themselves and I see no point in summarizing them or in commenting on them except in passing. Instead, I approach the subject from the back, from punishment policies and patterns, and suggest some of their implications for thinking about sentencing policies in individual countries and comparatively.

Some might think this gets things backwards, since punishment is the outcome of sentencing, and the populations and flows of offenders in prisons and subject to other criminal penalties are merely the outcome of sentencing in the aggregate. Many judges and prosecutors firmly assert the irrelevance to them of such things as prison capacity and correctional resources. Their jobs, they say, are to see that just punishments are imposed and public safety interests are advanced; handling sentenced offenders is someone else's business. In a small minority of jurisdictions in the United States, legislators and corrections officials believe that correctional resources and capacities should influence sentencing policies, and a few jurisdictions have incorporated "prison capacity constraints" into their sentencing policies and required that sentencing commissions develop guidelines whose application is not projected to produce larger numbers of inmates than can be housed within the jurisdiction's existing prison capacity. That is important and has helped shape the details of sentencing policy in those jurisdictions (chap. 6, this volume), but it reflects the wholesale views of people with systemic interests and not the retail views of front-line practitioners.

Several lessons for comparative understanding of sentencing stand out if one thinks from punishment to sentencing rather than from sentencing to punishment. First, the punishment backdrop has important implications for assessing the merits of proposed innovations in particular places. In countries, such as Finland and Sweden, with relatively low incarceration rates and a tradition of imposing sentences measured in days or months, strong sentencing standards are less desirable than in countries, such as the United States, eastern Europe, and increasingly England and Australia, with higher incarceration rates and a tradition of imposing sentences measured in years and decades. Sentencing standards must try to reconcile both parts of the equality principle. That is, they must be concerned to treat like cases alike and to treat different cases differently. U.S. federal guidelines, three-strikes laws, and mandatory sentences, for example, prescribe sentences for offenders who are like situated in terms of their crimes, but at the cost of ignoring differences in their lives and circumstances that many judges (and others) believe ethically relevant to thinking about just punishments. Indeterminate sentencing, as in Australia and Canada and some U.S. states, by contrast, allows ample latitude to differentiate sentences to take account of offenders' biographies, but critics argue that they often produce unwarranted disparities in relation to offense severity. No system of sentencing standards can perfectly reconcile the two parts of the equality principle, but approaches can make one or the other kind of injustice more likely. Concerns about unwarranted disparities, for example, may be less important in Scandinavia, and hence the case for detailed sentencing standards less strong, than in the United States. When judges' human idiosyncrasies result in disparate two-, three-, and four-month sentences for like-situated offenders in Sweden, the stakes are much lower than in the United States, where the same idiosyncrasies might yield one-, three-, and five-year prison sentences. Many U.S. sentencing policies, in Arie Freiberg's terms (chap. 1, this volume), risk unwarranted parities in the interest of treating formally like cases alike, and Sweden may risk unwarranted disparities in the interest of treating factually different cases differently. Against their different punishment backdrops, both those acceptances of risk may make sense, and the cases for Swedish adoption of numerical guidelines or U.S. adoption of Swedish-style statutory sentencing principles be correspondingly weak. Thus one major implication for sentencing policy of comparisons of punishment polices and patterns is diagnostic: one size does not fit all. Sentencing reforms need to be sensitive to the problems to which they can serve as (partial) solutions.

Second, comparative assessment of punishment policies and patterns supports a strong case for development of international and cross-national human rights conventions concerning sentencing and punishment. The enormous differences in punishment patterns in Western countries cannot be justified in human rights terms. International human rights conventions have long enunciated minimum standards concerning defendants' pretrial and trial rights but not concerning sentencing and punishment. In Europe, the European Convention on Human Rights increasingly is being used to override national laws and practices in trial and pretrial settings (Weissbrodt and Wolfrum 1997) but so far only at the furthest margins of sentencing and punishment (chap. 9, this volume). The European Torture Convention is increasingly effective as an extra-legal device (i.e., acting through moral suasion and publicity rather than court orders) for improving conditions in prisons, jails, and police lockups (chap. 10, this volume). There is, of course, a chicken-and-egg problem that the cultural and political forces that produce inhumanely harsh practices also prevent countries from subscribing to international conventions that ban or repudiate such practices (e.g., the U.S. and Chinese refusals to ratify without qualification international conventions against the death penalty [see chap. 8, this volume] and the same two countries' opposition to creation of an International Criminal Court to handle war crimes, genocide, and crimes against humanity). However, moral example and suasion often matter. Many eastern European countries have abolished the death penalty in order to join the Council of Europe, and the United States continues to try to influence the development of the International Criminal Court. Widely endorsed international human rights standards, even if they are solely precatory, can in the long term influence the evolution of sensibilities, policies, and practices in all countries, including those that initially reject them.

This introduction consists of three main sections. The first looks at crime and punishment trends in many countries to ask and answer the question whether differences in crime rates and patterns explain punishment differences between countries. Because imprisonment is the punishment everywhere mostly used for serious crimes, the focus is on imprisonment. Somewhat parochially, the issue is approached by using claims about U.S. experience as an example, and using data from other countries to test those claims. The evidence is clear; national differences in imprisonment rates and patterns result not from differences in crime but from differences in policy.

The second section accordingly looks at national differences in policies about crime. The major differences relate to whether crime policy has become a major contested issue in partisan and ideological politics, whether moral notions about the need to punish wrongdoers are dominantly influential, and whether policy makers appear to believe that punishment policies and practices are likely importantly to influence crime rates. The answers to these questions provide explanations for punishment trends and also set the conditions that determine what sentencing injustices—unwarranted disparities or parities, "undue leniency," racial, class, or gender-bias—are perceived as important problems. Here, too, the evidence is clear: there are stark differences in the political salience of crime and punishment issues in various countries and those differences fundamentally shape sentencing policies and punishment practices.

The third section then surveys approaches taken in various countries to achieve consistency in sentences imposed. Discussions are short since many of the chapters in this volume discuss developments in particular countries in detail. Approaches vary, but their value and significance also vary greatly depending on punishment politics and conventions. The overriding lesson to be learned is that the feasibility and desirability of a system of sentencing standards depends crucially on the environment in which it is introduced. U.S.-style numerical guidelines, for example, may be the best among several undesirable choices in a punitive country like the United States but would likely do more harm than good in a northern European country in which crime policy has not been heavily politicized and in which punishment severity is restrained.

8 SENTENCING AND SANCTIONS IN WESTERN COUNTRIES

I. Comparative Imprisonment Trends

The relations between crime and imprisonment are complex and diverse. Stunning dissimilarity in imprisonment trends between countries becomes apparent when longitudinal data are examined. This dissimilarity is not as widely recognized as it might be because longitudinal data are generally well known only within countries and international comparisons are typically based on cross-sectional data on prisoners per 100,000 population in a given year. Thus, in the United States, it is well known that imprisonment rates have been increasing for twenty-five years, (see figure I.1) and that the United States has imprisonment rates four to twelve times those of other countries with which it is ordinarily compared (see table I.1). From these comparisons come arguments over whether the U.S. rates are too high, whether rising crime rates justified the initial increased use of imprisonment, and whether subsequently declining crime rates justify continued increased use of imprisonment. These, however, are at best oversimplified arguments, and at most naive, as quickly becomes evident when better international comparisons are made.

Looking only at one country's trend data misleads because it invites parochial reactions either that local experience is "normal" and need not be examined closely or critically, or that unique local crime problems and trends explain local differences (e.g., Wilson and Herrnstein 1986; Bennett, DiIulio, and Walters 1996). Both of these claims are made in explanation of why U.S. imprisonment

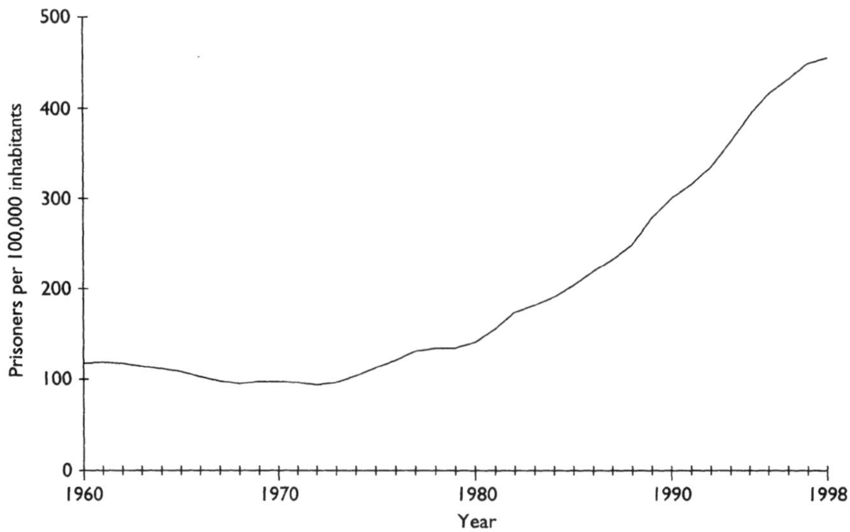

Figure I.1. Combined federal and state prisoners in the United States, 1960 to mid-year 1998 (per 100,000 population). *Sources*: Maguire and Pastore (1998); Bureau of Justice Statistics (1999c).

Table I.1: Various Western Countries Ranked by Incarceration Rate per 100,000, 1997–1998

	Total in Penal Institutions (Including Pretrial Detainees)	Date	Prison Population per 100,000 National Population
United States	1,725,842	6/30/97	645
New Zealand	5,236	1997	145
Portugal	14,336	3/15/98	145
England and Wales	65,906	9/30/98	125
Canada	34,166	1997–98	115
Spain	42,827	9/1/97	110
Australia	17,661	1997	95
France	53,259	10/1/98	90
Germany	74,317	9/1/97	90
Austria	6,946	9/1/97	85
Italy	49,477	9/1/97	85
Netherlands	13,618	9/1/97	85
Belgium	8,342	9/1/97	80
Denmark	3,508	11/6/98	65
Sweden	5,221	9/1/97	60
Greece	5,577	9/1/97	55
Finland	2,798	9/1/97	55
Norway	2,318	9/1/97	55

Source: Walmsley (1999).

rates are so much higher than in other countries: U.S. crime rates are higher and long rose more sharply than other countries' and higher imprisonment rates are the result; or U.S. crime is more serious than elsewhere and that explains the difference. Both of those assertions could be true. However, the first is completely untrue and the second is mostly untrue but with an important qualification.

A. Do Imprisonment Rate Changes Track Crime Rate Changes?

There is nothing inherently implausible in claims that rising crime rates drive rising imprisonment rates and that crime rates in the 1970s and 1980s rose faster in the United States than elsewhere and imprisonment rose with them. Without international comparisons, there is no way to assess those claims. But international comparisons can be made that shed some light on both crime rate trends and absolute levels. The available data, of course, are not perfect but they are good enough to undermine the crime-driven explanations for U.S. imprisonment patterns.

Because countries define and record crimes differently, statements about absolute differences in rates based only on official crime data inevitably are suspect. In figures I.2, I.3, and I.4 for example, U.S. homicide data include completed murders and non-negligent homicides, while the Finnish data also include at-

10 SENTENCING AND SANCTIONS IN WESTERN COUNTRIES

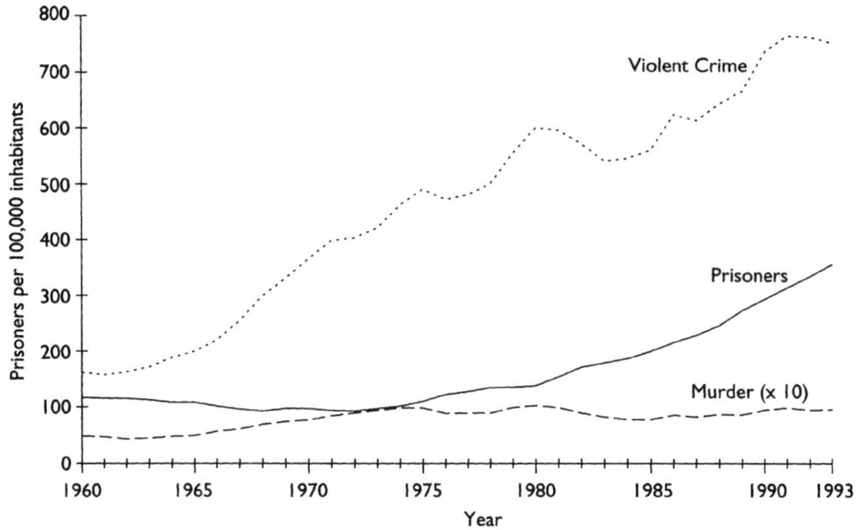

Figure I.2. Imprisonment, violent crime, and murder rates in the United States, 1960–1993 (per 100,000 population). *Note*: Crime rates are somewhat differently calculated in the United States than in Finland and Germany; U.S. incarceration rates do not include jail inmates. *Sources*: Bureau of Justice Statistics, Prisoners, various years (Washington, D.C.: U.S. Department of Justice, Bureau of Justice Statistics); Federal Bureau of Investigation, *Crime in the United States*, various years (Washington, D.C.: U.S. Government Printing Office).

tempts. Definitional differences should not matter, however, because the comparison is not between absolute crime rates but between trends in each country in events that country counts as violent felonies and homicides. The trend is what is important.

Two things stand out. First, in all three countries, violent crime and homicide rates increased a great deal and nearly continuously through the early 1990s. (The ending date was chosen because it precedes recent declines in crime rates.) The upward curves are comparably steep in each country. Second, the imprisonment rate patterns in the three countries are very different. In the United States, imprisonment rates increased steeply and continuously after 1972, tripling in the following twenty years. In Finland, imprisonment rates fell significantly and continuously after 1975, declining 38.2 percent in the following fourteen years (Törnudd 1993). In Germany, imprisonment rates fell from 1968 to the mid-1970s, rose for a few years, fell again in the early 1980s, and then roughly stabilized (Weigend 1997).

There is no necessary relationship between crime rates and imprisonment rates. The three figures refute both the notion that crime rate increases directly cause imprisonment to rise (more people to lock up) and the notion that rising crime rates necessarily indirectly cause imprisonment to rise (increased public fear, anx-

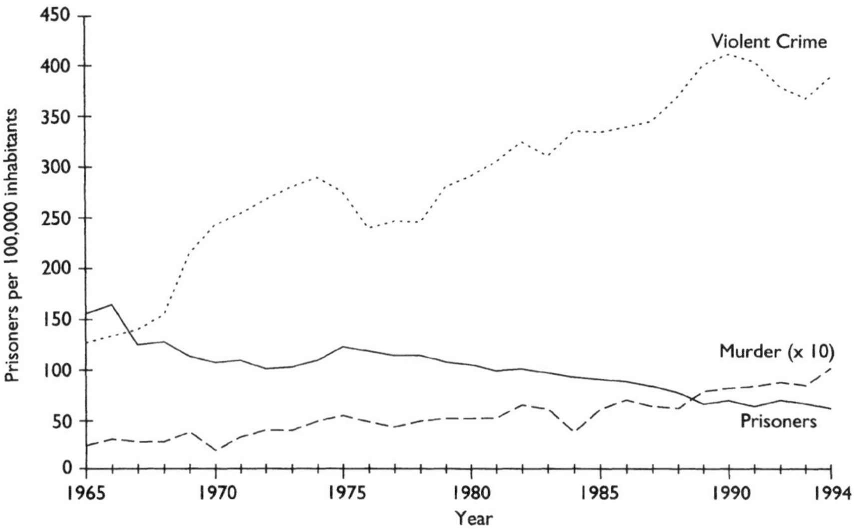

Figure I.3. Imprisonment, violent crime, and murder rates in Finland, 1965–1994 (per 100,000 population). *Note*: Violent crime and murder rates are somewhat differently calculated in Finland than in the United States; the Finnish imprisonment rate includes pretrial detainees. *Source*: Finnish Ministry of Justice (unpublished data provided to author).

iety, and anger compel harsher policies). Imprisonment patterns are not immune to influence from changes in crime rates and patterns, but they are at least as much and often more the consequences of conscious policy choices made by public officials. In the United States, many elected officials wanted punishments made harsher and more people to be sent to prison and to be held there longer (during periods of both rising and falling crime rates), and they were (Tonry 1998; chap. 6, this volume). In Finland, officials and others wanted imprisonment rates to decline, and they did, despite very large crime rate increases (Törnudd 1993, 1997; chap. 3, this volume). In Germany, officials wanted fewer people sentenced to prison and especially wanted the use of prison sentences under six months drastically curtailed, and they were, and imprisonment rates fell, despite rising violent crime rates (Weigend 1997; chap. 5, this volume).

B. Higher Imprisonment Rates Result from Higher Crime Rates

If crime rate trends do not drive imprisonment rates, it would be surprising if absolute levels of crime did. Comparisons between Finland in 1960, 1970, 1980, and 1990 provide a strong counterexample; if those data were thought of as if they were cross-sectional data from different countries at the same time rather than from the same country at different times, the absence of a causal relationship

12 SENTENCING AND SANCTIONS IN WESTERN COUNTRIES

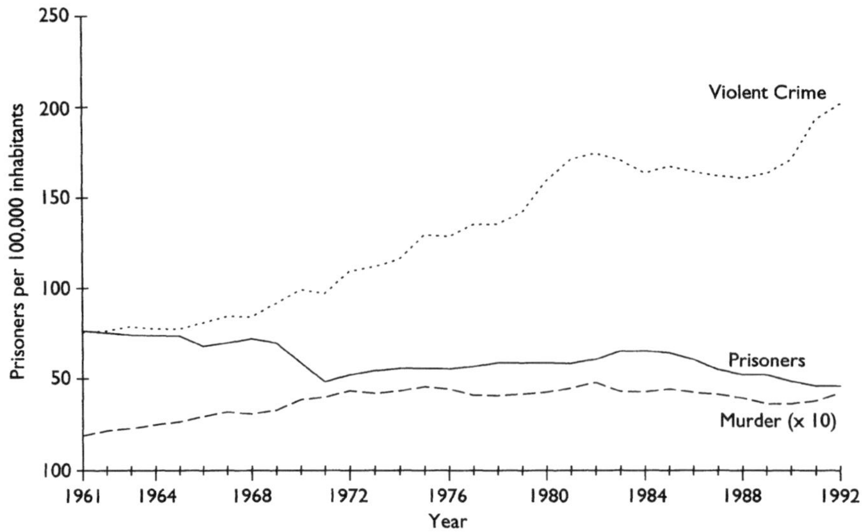

Figure I.4. Imprisonment, violent crime, and murder rates in Germany, 1961–1992 (per 100,000 population). *Note*: Violent crime and murder rates are somewhat differently calculated in Germany than in the United States; the German imprisonment rate excludes pretrial detainees. *Source*: German Ministry of Justice (unpublished data provided to author).

would be clear. Nonetheless, it is commonly said in the United States that U.S. crime rates are much higher than those elsewhere and that is why so relatively many more people are in prison and jail (e.g., Wilson and Herrnstein 1986; Bennett, DiIulio, and Walters 1996). The corollary would be that places with lower or low crime rates would have low levels of imprisonment. Because of the near impossibility of making comparative statements about crime trends based on official data (Lynch 1995), it is not easy to offer strong conclusions about this based on reliable data, but findings from the International Crime Victimization Survey (Mayhew and van Dijk 1997) suggest that U.S. imprisonment rates cannot be explained in this way.

The International Crime Victimization Survey (ICVS) has been carried out in Western countries three times since 1989. Designed to avoid the problems involved in trying to compare official data, the ICVS uses standard questionnaires employing common definitions of crimes to collect data from randomly selected residents of various countries. Table I.2 summarizes findings from the latest survey on self-reported victimizations per 1,000 residents aged 16 and over in eleven countries. For no offense are U.S. rates the highest, though they are among the highest for some violent offenses, and for some property crimes U.S. rates are among the lowest. As with any survey, methodological issues can be raised concerning the ICVS, particularly sample sizes, variable nonresponse rates, and cul-

Table I.2: Victimization Rates per 1,000, by Country and Offense, 1995

Country	Burglary	Robbery	Car Theft	Personal Theft[1]	Sexual Incidents	Assaults and Threats	Eleven Specific Crimes[2]
England and Wales	3.0	1.4	2.5	5.0	2.0	5.9	30.9
Scotland	1.5	0.8	1.7	4.5	1.3	4.2	25.6
Northern Ireland	1.5	0.5	1.6	2.5	1.2	1.7	16.8
Netherlands	2.6	0.6	0.4	6.8	3.6	4.0	31.5
Switzerland	1.3	0.9	0.1	5.7	4.6	3.1	26.7
France	2.4	1.0	1.6	4.0	0.9	3.9	25.3
Finland	0.6	0.5	0.4	3.2	2.6	4.1	18.9
Sweden	1.3	0.5	1.2	4.6	2.9	4.5	24.0
Austria	0.9	0.2	0.2	5.1	3.8	2.1	18.9
United States	2.6	1.3	1.9	3.9	2.5	5.7	24.2
Canada	3.4	1.2	1.5	5.7	2.7	4.0	25.2

Source: Kurki (1997).

[1]Thefts of personal property.

[2]Based on eleven crimes standard across sweeps, omitting thefts from garages.

tural differences in willingness to discuss embarrassing subjects, that caution against unqualified acceptance of findings, but there are several indications that the findings are broadly reliable. First, the patterns of between-country comparisons in the latest survey in 1997 replicate those in the two earlier rounds. That is, the relative rank ordering of countries by reported victimization rates for various crimes is fairly stable. Second, more important and persuasive, for individual countries the victimization trends shown in the three surveys parallel those shown in official data and victim surveys in the same countries (van Dijk 1997). For the United States, for example, the ICVS shows a rise in victimization rates between 1988 and 1992 and a fall between 1992 and 1995, which is the same pattern shown by official data from the FBI's Uniform Crime Reports (Federal Bureau of Investigation 1999) and by victimization data from the Department of Justice's National Crime Victimization Survey (Bureau of Justice Statistics 1999a).

An important qualification needs to be made. The ICVS does not and could not measure homicide rates, and U.S. violence rates involving firearms are higher than elsewhere. Even after recent declines, the 1998 U.S. homicide rate of 6.3 per 100,000 residents is two to four times higher than those of most Western countries. Franklin Zimring and Gordon Hawkins in *Crime Is Not the Problem* (1997) show that violence rates are considerably higher in U.S. cities than in comparable cities elsewhere. To a considerable extent both these patterns are entangled in U.S. cultural attitudes about guns and gun control. Assaults, robberies, and attempts to kill people are substantially more likely to result in death when guns are involved than otherwise (Zimring 1972), so to some extent the higher U.S. homicide rates are a product of higher rates of gun use in crime and, compared with most other countries, higher levels of gun availability and ownership. Nonetheless, U.S. homicide rates remain higher than those in other developed countries even when only data on nongun homicides are compared (but not so much higher; the 1998 nongun homicide rate in the U.S. was 4.1 per 100,000 and that in England was well under 1 per 100,000), and violent crime, though probably no more common in the United States, is more violent.

This contradictory pattern within a pattern—lower violent crime rates overall than in some other developed countries, but a higher fraction (and absolute rates) of those involving death, guns, and serious violence—no doubt is a partial explanation for high U.S. imprisonment rates. Two trends, however, cut in the opposite direction. The percentage of people sentenced to U.S. prisons for violent crimes is low (29.5 percent in 1996) (Bureau of Justice Statistics 1999b, table 1.23) and has not increased since 1991, so it is hard to attribute rising prison populations to violent offenders. Moreover, much the largest component of recent prison population growth has been a vast increase in admissions of people convicted of drug crimes (Blumstein and Beck 1999).

Prison population levels and trends, accordingly, do not happen automatically or as the result of simple relations between crime and punishment. They happen because people will them to happen or because people decide not to take action to control them when they begin to increase. As the chapters in this volume on Australia (chap. 1), England (chap. 2), the Netherlands (chap. 4), and the United States (chap. 6) show, recent increases in prison populations in Australia, England, and the Netherlands, and the longer-term increases in the United States, happened because politicians willed it.

II. Comparative Crime Policy Trends

In every country and at every time there is a range of views about punishments for crime that range from classic Kantian arguments that wrongdoers must be punished because they deserve it to classic Benthamite views that wrongdoers must be punished only so much and in such ways as will maximize net public benefit. Likewise in every country and at every time there are individuals who see some punishments of some offenders as unduly lenient and coddling and individuals who see some punishments as unduly severe and cruel. Over time the balances of such views change and both general policies and particular policies change with them.

Prevailing attitudes about punishment set limits on sentencing policy. Where attitudes are harsh and moralistic, the bounds for development of principled, humane policies are narrow, but the stakes are high. Where attitudes are less stereotyped and moralistic, the potential for innovation may be greater but the need less. As in the preceding section, I explore this subject by using the United States as an example and use data and experience from other countries to demonstrate that the United States is atypical and that the prospects for humane policy innovations elsewhere may therefore be greater.

For the past twenty-five years, many people in the United States have called for harsher punishments. In the 1970s at the beginning of the modern "sentencing reform movement," many proponents of change were conservatives and law enforcement officials who urged adoption of determinate and fixed sentencing laws in order to prevent lenient judges from coddling criminals (Messinger and Johnson 1978). In the early 1990s, one Republican gubernatorial candidate in Virginia, George Allen, campaigned primarily on a platform to toughen sentences by abolishing parole and when elected oversaw changes that make Virginia's among the harshest sentencing laws in the United States. In many states, conservatives launched campaigns for "truth in sentencing," by which they meant abolition or restriction of parole release and remission or time off for good behavior. By 1994, those campaigns had become so effective that the U.S. Congress authorized $8 billion in subsidies for prison building to states that would enact truth-in-sentencing laws requiring designated violent, drug, and other offenders to serve at least 85 percent of the announced sentence in prison. By 1999, more than thirty states had changed their laws to qualify for the federal money.

Thus there seems in the United States to be a widespread vicarious interest in ensuring that offenders are severely punished or, at least, that they experience all the punishment ordered. Many proponents of harsh sentencing policies appear to worry that offenders may not be punished enough, but not to worry that they may be punished too much. Put differently, certainty and severity are seen as governing values, with proportionality and parsimony being given much less weight. Such sentiments impose significant limits on efforts to reduce the prison population, repeal or amend harsh laws, or in other ways reduce sentencing severity. Some three-strikes laws, for example, most infamously California's, require minimum twenty-five-year sentences, and sometimes life sentences without possibility of parole, for third-time felons convicted of minor property offenses or trafficking in marijuana (Dickey and Hollenhorst 1998). One recurring criticism of the federal sentencing guidelines is that they often result in imposition of harsh mandatory minimum five-, ten-, and twenty-year sentences on low-level drug traffickers or on drug couriers while other provisions of the guidelines allow for imposition of much slighter sentences on large-scale traffickers and importers (Stith and Cabranes 1998). Andrew von Hirsch (chap. 11, this volume) tries to account for the development of such policies, now common in many U.S. jurisdictions, and the principled justifications, assuming there are some, for removing considerations of fairness to offenders from among the important values to be served by sentencing policies.

Are U.S. punishment policies harsher than those of other countries? The answer is yes, though reaching it is not simple. That then raises the question why (the answer is that U.S. officials want punishments to be severe, and with the passage of time have wanted them made more severe). In at least some other Western countries, the popular and political cultures seem less resolute in their determination that offenders be punished in full measure, as can be shown in a number of ways. This difference between U.S. moralism and other countries' lesser commitment to seeing that offenders suffer their full desert provides an important backdrop to sentencing policy formulation.

In terms of conventional categories, the United States has the most punitive crime policies in the Western world and various Scandinavian countries probably have the least punitive. There are several bases for such a claim. First, U.S. incarceration rates per 100,000 residents, as presented in table I.1, are four to twelve times higher than those of other Western countries. This comparison is not decisive, of course, as various people have shown (Young and Brown 1993; Pease 1994; Kommer 1994), because it assumes that prisoners per population is the right way to compare punitivism. Other possibilities include prisoners per crime, arrest, or conviction. Warren Young and Mark Brown (1993), using United Nations and Council of Europe data, show that punitiveness rankings change significantly when the denominator used in the calculation changes. Or, as table I.3, adapted from Kommer 1994, shows, punitiveness rankings change substantially when annual admissions to prison per 100,000 population are compared, rather than prison population on an average or given day per 100,000. Although from the perspective of an individual offender, a U.S.-style ten- or fifteen-year sentence must be more punitive than a Dutch- or Swedish-style one- or two-year sentence for the same offense, reasonable people could differ over whether a society like Sweden with a high rate of prison admissions but short sentences is more punitive than a society with a much lower admissions rate but longer sentences. Nonetheless, the imprisonment rate is vastly higher in the United States than in any other country and cannot be attributed to commensurately higher crime rates.

Second, some penalties in the United States are harsher than the harshest in other Western countries. The most striking evidence is that the United States is the only major Western country that retains the death penalty. But also striking are the mandatory minimum ten-, twenty-, and thirty-year sentences required by federal and some state laws; three-strikes laws in states such as California, which requires life sentences without possibility of parole for some felons and lengthy minimums for others; and the proliferation of life-without-possibility-of-parole laws in many states. Some other countries allow unqualified life sentences, though they are seldom imposed (the European Human Rights Convention does not forbid such sentences; chap. 9, this volume). However, many European countries have established ten to fifteen years as the maximum prison sentence that can be imposed (Kyvsgaard 1998; Larsson 1999; chap. 3, this volume), and the German Constitutional Court has set fifteen years as the longest sentence that may be imposed without eligibility for release consideration (chap. 8, this volume).

Third, although lack of careful comparative analyses makes this a more tentative assertion, it appears that the average severity of sentences in the United States is greater than elsewhere (e.g., Tonry 1996, table 7.1). Probably the most honest way to explore this question is to provide reasons for believing U.S. practice is more severe than elsewhere and then summarize the objections that can be made to such a claim. The clear weight of the evidence supports the conclusion of greater U.S. severity.

One argument is that greater severity can be inferred from the vastly higher U.S. incarceration rates. A response, however, is that we lack data for making such a claim since it would have to be based on a comparison disaggregated by offense type and taking account of differences in average offense severity. Substantially higher U.S. homicide rates combined with substantially greater use of guns in U.S. violent crime probably makes the average violent U.S. crime a more serious crime than are crimes of the same generic type in other developed countries.

Table I.3: Prison Statistics for Various European Countries, 1990

	Imprisonment Rate per 100,000	Convicted Prisoner Rate	Admission Rate per 100,000	Average Duration of Detention
Netherlands	44.4 (1)	27.2 (1)	137.8 (2)	3.9 (3)
Norway	56.5 (2)	44.9 (4)	237.1 (6)	2.7 (1)
Italy	56.6 (3)	33.6 (2)	—	—
Sweden	58.0 (4)	58.8 (9)	591.5 (8)	3.0 (2)
Denmark	63.0 (5)	46.3 (5)	—	—
Belgium	66.1 (6)	35.2 (3)	184.4 (4)	4.5 (5)
Switzerland	76.9 (7)	47.0 (6)	—	—
FRG	77.8 (8)	57.3 (8)	149.6 (3)	6.7 (7)
France	82.2 (9)	48.7 (7)	135.3 (1)	6.9 (8)
England and Wales	90.3 (10)	70.3 (10)	226.7 (5)	5.1 (6)
Northern Ireland	109.5 (11)	84.4 (11)	314.4 (7)	4.3 (4)

Source: Adapted from Kommer (1994), table 1.

Note: Figures in parentheses = rank number.

However, as noted above, well under one-third of prison admissions are for violent crimes.

Another argument is that comparisons of data on lengths of sentences imposed typically show that only a few percent of prison sentences in most countries are for terms longer than one year (e.g., Sweden: Jareborg 1995; Finland: chap. 3, this volume; Germany: chap. 5, this volume; Netherlands: chap. 4, this volume; Australia: chap. 1, this volume), while, by contrast, in 1994, the most recent year for which U.S. data are available, the mean average maximum sentence of persons committed to U.S. state prisons was seventy-one months (Bureau of Justice Statistics 1997, table 7). An important response here, however, is that the U.S. federal system makes such cross-national comparisons impossible. Data on federal and state prisoners include only prisoners receiving sentences of one year or longer, so sentence-length averages exclude nearly all sentences under one year. Such sentences are typically served in local jails, about which national aggregate data on sentence lengths are not readily available. However, data are available on sentences imposed. In 1994, combining state and federal data, of persons convicted of murder or manslaughter, rape, robbery, and aggravated assault, the percentages sentenced to state or federal prisons were 95, 71, 78, and 48 percent, respectively, and jail sentences represented an additional 2, 11, 17, and 27 percent of cases (Bureau of Justice Statistics 1997, table 5.52). Thus while the U.S. distinction between prison and jail exaggerates severity of prison sentence lengths in comparative analyses, because other countries' data on mean average sentence lengths are "diluted" by inclusion of data for less serious offenses that might receive jail sentences in the United States, the effect is not likely to be large since nearly all of the sentences for serious violent crimes are to prisons.

18 SENTENCING AND SANCTIONS IN WESTERN COUNTRIES

A final argument is that average sentences of people in U.S. prisons at any one time are vastly longer than those elsewhere. In 1991, the average length of sentence being served by a state prisoner was 108 months (Beck et al. 1993) and, as just noted, the mean average sentence of people admitted to state prisons in 1994 was 71 months (Bureau of Justice Statistics 1998). As the chapters on particular European countries in this volume (and table I.3) show, the averages in European countries are much shorter. There are several qualifications to be considered in addition to the inflation that results from excluding jail sentences. They are also inflated by long sentences. People serving lengthy sentences accumulate, whereas those serving short sentences cycle in and out. Thus the average sentence of prisoners as calculated on a given day will contain an overrepresentation of long sentences and thus exaggerate average sentence length. Finally, though this is less true than in earlier times, nominal sentence lengths can be misleading since parole release eligibility was broader in the United States than elsewhere and the important comparison would be between sentences actually served rather than between nominal sentence lengths.

Overall, despite the qualifications, there is little reason to doubt that sentence lengths in the United States are longer than elsewhere, at least for more serious crimes. Why might that be so? The answers probably include some combination of American moralism, distinctive features of the U.S. historical experience, and peculiarities of modern America that have caused crime and punishment to become major issues in partisan and ideological politics (Caplow and Simon 1999; Tonry 1999a, 1999b; Garland 2000).

Punitive sentiments exist in all countries. An influential article by Anthony Bottoms (1995) discusses the causes and consequences of "populist punitivism" in England and Wales and elsewhere, and most writers on punishment policy now cite Bottoms's analysis in reference to their own countries. There is evidence in many countries that ordinary people, when asked whether criminal punishments are too harsh, too lenient, or just about right, by large majorities answer, "too lenient" (Hough and Roberts 1997; Roberts and Stalans 1997). In many countries, crime is receiving increasing attention in political discussion (Kyvsgaard 1998; Larsson 1999; chaps. 1 and 4, this volume). Incarceration rates in the Netherlands, long renowned for its progressive penal policies, have been increasing since the mid-1970s and between 1988 and 1998 increased by two and one-half times (as rapidly as in the United States) (Junger-Tas 1998).

Nonetheless, the force of punitivist populism seems nowhere else to be as powerful and monolithic as in the United States. This can be shown in several ways. In England and Australia, for example, crime control politics have most resembled those in the United States (especially in England where Tony Blair, like Bill Clinton, apparently resolved always to be to the right of conservatives on crime issues) (Downes and Morgan 1997). Yet, as is shown in this volume by Ashworth on England (chap. 2) and Freiberg on Australia (chap. 1), the relevant legislation in those countries is typically much less severe than in the United States and often contains escape clauses that provide flexibility. England's controversial, recently enacted "mandatory life sentences for murder," for example, do not affect an offender's eligibility for parole or pardon. U.S. sentences of "life without possibility of parole" mean exactly that. Similarly, recently enacted English mandatory minimum sentence laws, for selected drug crimes and burglaries, contain provisions allowing judges in unusual circumstances to impose some other sentence. U.S. mandatory minimum laws seldom include such provisions.

Widespread opposition to softening, weakening, or shortening sentences, which underlay U.S. truth in sentencing, does not appear to be as prevalent or as powerful in most other countries. Unlike incarceration rates for Finland, Germany, and the United States, shown in figures I.2, I.3, and I.4, the French incarceration rate, shown in figure I.5, varies erratically. The explanation for this variation is the many large-scale pardons and amnesties granted by every government of the past thirty years, combined with enactments of legislation designed to reduce prison numbers by creation of alternatives to incarceration. If there were important political prices to be paid in France for releasing large numbers of people from prison early, or if it were deeply unpopular with a large fraction of the population, such practices could not be put into effect. Similar patterns have occurred in Spain and Italy in recent decades (Kuhn 1999).

A similar limited influence of popular punitivism can be seen in a Dutch (chap. 4, this volume), Danish (Kyvsgaard 1998), and Norwegian (Larsson 1999) method for dealing with prison crowding. When in the 1980s and 1990s a combination of rising crime rates and harsher sentences overburdened prison capacity, officials in those countries dealt with the problem by creating prison entrance queues. Convicted, sentenced prisoners for whom space was unavailable would be told as much and would be informed when and where they should appear to begin serv-

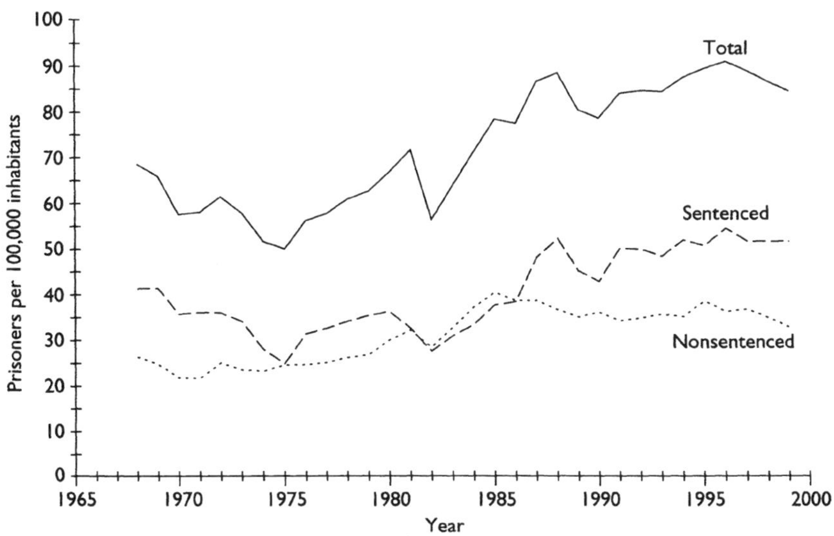

Figure I.5. Incarceration rate in France, 1969–1999 (per 100,000 population). *Source:* Kuhn (1999).

ing their sentences. The Dutch also developed detailed policies for determining, on the basis of offense seriousness, which categories of convicted offenders should be immediately admitted to prison and which categories of current prisoners should be released early to open up space (chap. 4, this volume). Sometimes in the United States, courts have created population caps for unconstitutionally overcrowded prisons, thereby effectively requiring prisons to offset front-door entries with back-door releases. Such orders have been deeply unpopular and resented by state officials and have resulted in massive prison building and in pressure for truth-in-sentencing laws designed to prevent such ad hoc releases in the future.

Thus, there do seem to be fundamental differences between countries in attitudes toward punishment and offenders. These attitudes create political and cultural pressures for greater or lesser harshness in general and in individual cases. They also set a context for thinking about alternate sentencing policy choices.

III. Comparative Sentencing Policies

Most judges, and most thoughtful people who have closely considered the subject, believe that justice in sentencing depends on ever-provisional resolutions between the injunctions to treat like cases alike and different cases differently. Few people disagree fundamentally with the proportionality ideas at the core of Andrew von Hirsch's influential works (e.g., 1976, 1985, 1993): more serious crimes, all else equal, should be more severely punished than less serious crimes, and comparably serious crimes, all else equal, should be comparably severely punished. At the same time, though more people may disagree, at least most judges believe that sentences to be just must be individualized to the particular circumstances of the crime and the convicted offender before the court. It is easy to tease judges about the rhetoric in which they express that belief, for example, the Australian appellate courts' celebration of the "intuitive synthesis" by which judges should fashion sentences or the Austrian "existential conversation" (Tonry 1996, chap. 7, pp. 178–79), but it is hard not to admire the conviction that justice must be decided not in general but in relation to the individual human being whose liberty and well-being are in the court's hands.

The like-cases-alike intuition gives rise to various attempts to reduce or eliminate sentencing disparities. The different-cases-differently intuition gives rise to calls for individualized and indeterminate sentencing. Both intuitions have caused excesses and injustice. U.S. federal guidelines or mandatory minimum laws may require that all persons convicted of a particular crime receive the same lengthy prison sentence and thereby treat like cases alike in terms of current crimes and past criminal records, but they are often decried for prohibiting judges from taking account of ethically important differences between offenders (e.g., Stith and Cabranes 1998). Indeterminate U.S. sentencing laws of the 1960s and earlier permitted judges and parole authorities to tailor every sentence to the offender's circumstances and thereby treat different cases differently, but they were decried for giving little if any weight to proportionality concerns (American Friends Service Committee 1971; von Hirsch 1976).

Efforts have been made in many countries to reconcile the equality and difference principles in sentencing. Various of the chapters in this book discuss some of the better known such efforts. All are premised on the equality principle's goal of reducing unwarranted sentencing disparities. They can be arrayed in a continuum of concerns from avoidance of unwarranted disparities to avoidance of unwarranted parities. In the following paragraphs, I canvass them briefly, leaving detailed discussion and exploration of relevant literatures to other chapters. I review most of the literature on which these assertions are based elsewhere (Tonry 1996, chap. 5), and do not repeat references here.

A. Mandatory Standards

Only in the United States have large numbers of mandatory sentencing laws been enacted. All are premised on notions that legislation should precisely prescribe the sentence, or the minimum sentence, to be imposed for designated crimes (typically homicide, designated violent or sexual crimes, firearms offenses, and many drug trafficking offenses) or on types of offenders (typically, second- or third-time felons). Such laws include habitual-offender laws first enacted in the 1920s and 1930s (though seldom applied between ca. 1970 and 1990), mandatory minimum sentencing laws (mostly enacted between 1975 and 1985 though often subsequently amended and toughened), three-strikes laws (mandatory lengthy or life sentences for qualifying third-felony convictions), and life-without-possibility-of-parole laws (variously for homicide, other designated violent crimes, some drug trafficking, and some repeat felons).

The three mandatory minimum sentencing laws that recently took effect in England (chap. 2, this volume), in various ways allow for discretionary exceptions to how they are applied.

Because such laws, especially in their U.S. forms, do not allow for different cases to be treated differently openly, often they are treated differently surreptitiously. Techniques include plea bargaining practices that enable the defendant to be convicted of an offense different from one governed by the mandatory law, various forms of "swallowing the gun" in which counsel stipulate to facts other than those that actually happened, and willful disregard of a literally applicable sentencing standard by tacit or overt agreement of the judge and counsel. However, patterns of circumvention are generally ad hoc and idiosyncratic with the result that sentencing disparities are often extreme: among like situated offenders, some will be sentenced to the ten- or twenty-year minimum sentence and others, benefiting from circumventions, will receive much less severe sentences.

B. Presumptive Numerical Judicial Guidelines

Presumptive sentencing guidelines typically specify types (prison or not; occasionally a specific community penalty) and amounts (e.g., twenty-four months) or ranges (e.g., twenty-four to thirty months) of presumptively applicable sentences for designated cases. The presumption can be rebutted but judges must provide reasons for believing the presumptively applicable sentence inappropriate. The persuasiveness of those reasons may be appealed, typically by the defendant or the state, to a higher court.

Guidelines of this sort exist only in the United States. They are in effect in approximately fifteen jurisdictions (chap. 6, this volume), and they vary substantially in format (matrices, narrative statements, offense-specific scoring sheets), in scope (all felonies and misdemeanors, all felonies, only some felonies), in specificity (e.g., narrow ranges, such as twelve to fifteen months, to broad ranges, such as three to six years), and in the degree to which appellate courts carefully scrutinize sentence appeals (from nearly not at all as in Pennsylvania to excruciatingly closely as in the federal system).

A modest evaluation literature shows that, compared with predecessor indeterminate sentencing systems, well-designed presumptive guidelines systems backed up by meaningful appellate sentence review, as in Minnesota, Oregon, and Washington, can reduce sentencing disparities in general and in relation to race, gender, and geography in particular and, by making sentencing more predictable, can be used to tie sentencing and corrections policies more closely together than theretofore.

Few presumptive guidelines systems, however, are well-designed and reviewed and as a result few realize the goals just described. At one extreme, the federal guidelines, by statute "presumptive" but in the U.S. Sentencing Commission's publications "mandatory," are detailed and rigid and suffer all the problems of mandatory sentencing generally. At the opposite extreme, Florida's presumptive guidelines were so little respected and so little backed up by appellate courts that they were little more than voluntary and thus achieved none of their aims.

C. Presumptive Numerical Administrative Guidelines

Numerical sentencing guidelines have been used by parole agencies in the United States since the mid-1970s (e.g., Gottfredson, Wilkins, and Hoffman 1978) and by the Netherlands Public Prosecution Service since 1999 (Schurer and van Loon 1999). Evaluation research in the 1970s and 1980s in the United States showed that guidelines in an administrative parole agency could successfully reduce disparities in prison sentences and execute policies governing criteria to be used in setting release dates and conditions (Blumstein et al. 1983, chap. 3). Probably a majority of surviving U.S. parole systems now use parole guidelines, but they are not glamorous and receive relatively little attention from researchers or lawmakers. As systems of sentencing standards, their great drawback in the United States is that they apply only to offenders sentenced to state prisons and therefore can have no effect on disparities in type of sentence (community penalty, local jail, state prison) or lengths of jail sentences.

Dutch numerical prosecution guidelines for sentence recommendations are of much broader scope because they can potentially apply to all offenders and offenses. Because they are used within an administrative agency, they are potentially subject to the kinds of internal administrative controls, to insure reasonable consistency of application, that helped some parole guidelines systems succeed. Because, however, they concern sentence recommendations rather than sentences, their effects are subject to the independent discretion of judges, so risks of overly rigid application are reduced. Pilot studies conducted for the Dutch Prosecution Service showed significant reduction of disparities compared with earlier periods. The current guidelines, however, which replaced previous guidelines adopted in the 1970s and generally adjudged ineffective, took effect only on April 1, 1999, and it is much too early to say how they are working.

D. Voluntary and Informative Sentencing Guidelines

Two separate developments—voluntary sentencing guidelines systems in the United States (Wilkins et al. 1978; Kress 1980) and sentencing information systems in Canada, Australia, and Scotland—derive from the same hypothesis (Doob and Park 1987; Hogarth 1988; Tata and Hutton 1997). That is that knowledge of a court's past sentencing patterns, its going rates, will influence the sentences judges impose. One rationale is that courts have going rates, often vaguely understood and loosely recognized, and that empirical research on sentencing patterns will bring the going rates to light. A second rationale is that conscientious judges will want to sentence even-handedly and to minimize the chances that their own idiosyncrasies will produce sentences significantly different from those of other judges, and that knowledge of the going rates will help them do that. A third, minimalist, rationale is that descriptive data on sentencing patterns will identify anomalous outliers and reduce the incidence of aberrantly severe sentences.

The difference between voluntary guidelines and information systems is primarily semantic. They involve the same kind of underlying empirical efforts to document a court's past or ongoing sentencing decisions. Voluntary guidelines present the resulting data in grid format that sets out the ranges of sentence within which the middle 80 or 90 percent of sentences fall for various crime and criminal record combinations. Sentencing information systems have evolved gradually but essentially provide the raw data in aggregate and case-by-case formats from which guidelines would be developed.

Unfortunately, the evidence on their effectiveness so far is not promising. Most of the early U.S. voluntary guidelines systems were abandoned in the face of evaluation research findings showing that they had few or no discernible effects on sentencing patterns (Blumstein et al. 1983, chap. 3). The earliest information systems in Canada in the 1980s (Doob and Park 1987; Hogarth 1988) atrophied and fell into disuse. A system developed in New South Wales in the mid-1980s continued operating well into the 1990s, but no evaluations or scholarly writings document its operation. The newest system, in Scotland, has been in operation for several years and benefits from technological advances that make it much easier to use than earlier systems, but no impact evaluations have been published (Tata and Hutton 1997).

E. Appellate Guideline Judgments

The English Court of Appeal has been issuing decisions on sentencing appeals since early in the twentieth century and since the early 1980s has been issuing guideline judgments that set out starting points for consideration of sentence for generic categories of cases. So far as I am aware, there is no credible evaluation literature that demonstrates that adoption and elaboration of guideline judgments has reduced sentencing disparities in general or that patterns of sentences for particular kinds of cases change after issuance of a pertinent new judgment. However, many English judges and some informed observers believe that guideline judgments do influence sentencing patterns. The most formidable criticism is that they are narrow in scope and deal only with the relatively small numbers of serious violent cases, while providing no guidance for high-volume offenses, such as shoplifting, simple assault, and unaggravated burglary, or for the mine-run of minor offenses (e.g., chap. 2, this volume). The verdict appears to resemble that for well-designed parole guidelines—useful as far as they go, but they do not go nearly far enough.

F. Statutory Sentencing Principles

Finland in 1975 (chap. 3, this volume) and Sweden in 1988 (Jareborg 1995) adopted systems of statutory sentencing principles that provide detailed guidance about the considerations that should guide sentencing in general (proportionality notions) and in particular (the relevance of prior record, various personal characteristics, etc.). In a system like the American in which sentences are typically long and judges and prosecutors are politically selected, there would be grounds for skepticism that the effects of statutory sentencing principles would be any greater than those achieved by voluntary guidelines. In Scandinavian systems characterized by professional, career judges and prosecutors and relatively short sentences, the prospects are much rosier.

IV. Conclusion

The preceding litanies of differences could overwhelm, but they are provided to make two main points. First, the desirability and prospects of various approaches for bringing consistency and predictability to sentencing depend on the sentencing traditions and politics of a jurisdiction. Dangers of unwarranted disparities and unwarranted parities vary greatly and proponents of rational, humane sentencing policy changes should be clear about which is the greater danger and choose their weapons accordingly.

Second, in Western countries that share a common history, values, and commitments to human rights, there should not be such great differences in punishment practices and policies as now exist. Existing international covenants, conventions, and declarations contain few enforceable provisions that relate to the nature and amount of criminal punishments (the most notable exception being the European Convention on Human Rights' prohibition of capital punishment), but they should and some day they will.

The stock objection is that such proposals ignore important cultural differences that are made manifest in national policy through democratic processes, and that such normative differences should be respected. But this misleads. There is already broad agreement among Western countries about values and principles that just sentencing should respect, and there is growing congruence in policy. At least three examples can be offered as demonstration. Within countries and some regional groups, human rights standards forbid particular policy choices (the death penalty in member states of the Council of Europe, whipping and other corporal punishments throughout the United States and most other Western countries). In some countries, particularly in northern Europe, human rights ideas have led to enactment of laws creating upper limits on prison sentences that may be imposed; with very few exceptions, ten to fifteen years is the longest prison sentence that may be imposed in Norway, Finland, Denmark, and Germany for the most serious offenses. Finally, the vertical proportionality proposition that more serious crimes should, all else equal, be punished more severely than less serious crimes, and the horizontal equity proposition that comparably serious crimes, all else equal, should be punished comparably severely, are increasingly influential in sentencing systems as diverse as U.S. guidelines, English guideline judgments, and Scandinavian sentencing principles. Formal concerns for respecting national sovereignty have so far prevented adoption of many enforceable international standards concerning sentencing and the imposition of punishment, but their creation is inevitable.

That human rights concerns will eventually trump national sovereignty interests (and claims about respect for cultural differences) is suggested by sentencing policy trends in the United States, a country among the most zealous in protecting its autonomy. Every time a U.S. sentencing commission, including in the federal system, has discovered substantial differences in sentencing practice in different areas or regions of the jurisdiction, the uncontroversial policy decision has been made that such differences are unjust and that an offender's loss of liberty or property should not depend greatly on where within a state he is sentenced. No one doubts that there may be significant regional and cultural differences in assessments of the gravity of offenses, but few disagree that equal treatment values require that sentencing policies be uniform throughout a jurisdiction. Though at present there are no applicable authoritative international standards, it is difficult to understand why human rights values should not require compliance with substantive standards (e.g., proportionality requirements and absolute limits on punishments in general and for particular crimes) whenever a person is sentenced, wherever a person is sentenced. The important question is the frame of reference, and for human rights questions, the answer should be the international community of (at least) developed Western states.

REFERENCES

American Friends Service Committee. 1971. *Struggle for Justice*. New York: Hill & Wang.

Beck, Allen, Darrell Gilliard, Lawrence Greenfeld, Caroline Harlow, Thomas Hester, Louis Jankowski, Tracy Snell, James Stephan, and Danielle Morton. 1993. *Survey of State Prison Inmates, 1991*. Washington, D.C.: U.S. Department of Justice, Bureau of Justice Statistics.

Bennett, William J., John J. DiIulio, and John P. Walters. 1996. *Body Count: Moral Poverty and How to Win America's War against Crime and Drugs*. New York: Simon & Schuster.

26 SENTENCING AND SANCTIONS IN WESTERN COUNTRIES

Blumstein, Alfred, and Allen Beck. 1999. "Population Growth in U.S. Prisons, 1980–1996." In *Prisons*, edited by Michael Tonry and Joan Petersilia. Vol. 26 of *Crime and Justice: A Review of Research*, edited by Michael Tonry Chicago: University of Chicago Press.

Blumstein, Alfred, Jacqueline Cohen, Susan E. Martin, and Michael Tonry, eds. 1983. *Research on Sentencing: The Search for Reform*. 2 vols. Washington, D.C.: National Academy Press.

Bottoms, Anthony. 1995. "The Philosophy and Politics of Punishment and Sentencing." In *The Politics of Sentencing Reform*, edited by C. M. V. Clarkson and Rod Morgan. Oxford: Clarendon Press.

Bureau of Justice Statistics. 1997. *Felony Sentences in the United States, 1994*. Washington, D.C.: U.S. Department of Justice, Bureau of Justice Statistics.

———. 1998. *Prisoners in 1997*. Washington, D.C.: U.S. Department of Justice, Bureau of Justice Statistics.

———. 1999a. *Criminal Victimization 1998*. Washington, D.C.: U.S. Department of Justice, Bureau of Justice Statistics.

———. 1999b. *Correctional Populations in the United States, 1996*. Washington, D.C.: U.S. Department of Justice, Bureau of Justice Statistics.

———. 1999c. *Prison and Jail Inmates at Midyear 1998*. Washington, D.C.: U.S. Department of Justice, Bureau of Justice Statistics.

Caplow, Theodore, and Jonathan Simon. 1999. "Understanding Prison Policy and Population Trends." In *Prisons*, edited by Michael Tonry and Joan Petersilia. Vol. 26 of *Crime and Justice: A Review of Research*, edited by Michael Tonry. Chicago: University of Chicago Press.

Dickey, Walter, and Pam Stiebs Hollenhorst. 1998. "Three-Strikes Laws: Massive Impact in California and Georgia, Little Elsewhere." *Overcrowded Times* 9(6):2–8.

Doob, A., and N. Park. 1987. "Computerised Sentencing Information for Judges: An Aid to the Sentencing Process." *Criminal Law Quarterly* 30:54.

Downes, David, and Rod Morgan. 1997. "Dumping the 'Hostages to Fortune': The Politics of Law and Order in Post-War Britain." In *The Oxford Handbook of Criminology*, 2d ed., edited by Mike Maguire, Rod Morgan, and Robert Reiner. Oxford: Oxford University Press.

Federal Bureau of Investigation. 1999. *Crime in the United States: Uniform Crime Reports 1998*. Washington, D.C.: U.S. Government Printing Office.

Garland, David. 2000. "The Culture of High Crime Societies: The Social Precondition of the New Politics of Crime Control." *British Journal of Criminology* 40 (forthcoming).

Gottfredson, Don M., Leslie T. Wilkins, and Peter B. Hoffman. 1978. *Guidelines for Parole and Sentencing*. Lexington, Mass.: Lexington Books.

Hogarth, J. 1988. *Sentencing Database System: User's Guide 4th Draft*. Vancouver: University of British Columbia.

Hough, Michael, and Julian Roberts. 1997. *Attitudes to Punishment: Findings from the British Crime Survey*. Home Office Research Study no. 179. London: Home Office.

Jareborg, Nils. 1995. "The Swedish Sentencing Reform." In *The Politics of Sentencing Reform*, edited by C. M. V. Clarkson and Rod Morgan. Oxford: Clarendon Press.

Junger-Tas, Josine. 1998. "Dutch Penal Policies Changing Direction." *Overcrowded Times* 9(5):1, 14–20.

Kommer, Max. 1994. "Punitiveness in Europe: A Comparison." *European Journal on Criminal Policy and Research* 2:29–43.

Kress, Jack M. 1980. *Prescription for Justice: The Theory and Practice of Sentencing Guidelines*. Cambridge, Mass.: Ballinger.

Kuhn, André. 1999. "Incarceration Rates across the World." *Overcrowded Times* 10(2):1, 12–20.

Kurki, Leena. 1997. "International Crime Survey: American Rates about Average." *Overcrowded Times* 8(5):1, 4–7.

Kyvsgaard, Britta. 1998. "Penal Sanctions and the Use of Imprisonment in Denmark." *Overcrowded Times* 9(6):1, 9–10.

Larsson, Paul. 1999. "Norway Prison Use Up Slightly, Community Penalties Lots." *Overcrowded Times* 10(1):1, 11–13.

Lynch, James. 1995. "Crime in International Perspective." In *Crime*, edited by James Wilson and Joan Petersilia. San Francisco, Calif.: Institute for Contemporary Studies.

Maguire, Kathleen, and Ann L. Pastore, eds. *Sourcebook of Criminal Justice Statistics, 1997*. Washington, D.C.: U.S. Department of Justice, Bureau of Justice Statistics.

Mayhew, Pat, and Jan van Dijk. 1997. *Criminal Victimisation in Eleven Industrialized Countries*. The Hague: Dutch Ministry of Justice.

Messinger, Sheldon, and Phillip Johnson. 1978. "California's Determinate Sentencing Laws." In *Determinate Sentencing: Reform or Regression?* Washington, D.C.: U.S. Government Printing Office.

Mirrlees-Black, Catriona, Tracey Budd, Sarah Partridge, and Pat Mayhew. 1998. *The 1998 British Crime Survey, England and Wales*: London: Her Majesty's Stationery Office.

Pease, Ken. 1994. "Cross-National Imprisonment Rates: Limitations of Method and Possible Conclusions." *British Journal of Criminology* 34 (special issue):116–30.

Pfeiffer, Christian. 1998. "Juvenile Crime and Violence in Europe." In *Crime and Justice: A Review of Research*, vol. 23, edited by Michael Tonry. Chicago: University of Chicago Press.

Roberts, J. V., and L. J. Stalans. 1997. *Public Opinion, Crime, and Criminal Justice*. Boulder, Colo.: Westview.

Schurer, Gerrit, and Reinier van Loon. 1999. "The Netherlands Adopts Numerical Prosecution Guidelines." *Overcrowded Times* 10(3):1, 4–7.

Stith, Kate, and José A. Cabranes. 1998. *Fear of Judging: Sentencing Guidelines in the Federal Courts*. Chicago: University of Chicago Press.

Tata, Cyrus, and Neil Hutton. 1997. "Scottish High Court Develops Sentencing Information System." *Overcrowded Times* 8(6):1, 14–20.

Tonry, Michael. 1996. *Sentencing Matters*. New York: Oxford University Press.

———. 1998. "Introduction: Crime and Punishment in America." In *The Handbook of Crime and Punishment*, edited by Michael Tonry. New York: Oxford University Press.

———. 1999a. "Rethinking Unthinkable Punishment Policies in America." *UCLA Law Review* 46:1751–91

———. 1999b. "Why Are U.S. Incarceration Rates So High?" *Crime and Delinquency* 45(4): 419–37.

Törnudd, Patrik. 1993. *Fifteen Years of Declining Prisoner Rates*. Research Communication no. 8. Helsinki: National Research Institute of Legal Policy.

———. 1997. "Sentencing and Punishment in Finland." In *Sentencing Reform in Overcrowded Times: A Comparative Perspective*, edited by Michael Tonry and Kathleen Hatlestad. New York: Oxford University Press.

van Dijk, Jan J. M. 1997. "Towards a Research-Based Crime Reduction Policy." *European Journal on Criminal Policy and Research* 5(3):13–26.

von Hirsch, Andrew. 1976. *Doing Justice: The Choice of Punishments*. New York: Hill & Wang.

———. 1985. *Past or Future Crimes?* New Brunswick, N.J.: Rutgers University Press.

———. 1993. *Censure and Sanctions*. Oxford: Clarendon Press.

28 SENTENCING AND SANCTIONS IN WESTERN COUNTRIES

Walmsley, R. 1999. *World Prison Population List*. Research Findings no. 88. London: Home Office Research, Development and Statistics Directorate.

Weigend, Thomas. 1997. "Germany Reduces Use of Prison Sentences." In *Sentencing Reform in Overcrowded Times: A Comparative Perspective*, edited by Michael Tonry and Kathleen Hatlestad. New York: Oxford University Press.

Weissbrodt, David, and Rüdiger Wolfrum. 1997. *The Right to a Fair Trial*. Berlin: Springer.

Wilkins, Leslie T., Jack M. Kress, Don M. Gottfredson, Joseph C. Calpin, and Arthur M. Gelman. 1978. *Sentencing Guidelines: Structuring Judicial Discretion—Report on the Feasibility Study*. Washington, D.C.: U.S. Department of Justice.

Wilson, James Q., and Richard J. Herrnstein. 1986. *Crime and Human Nature: The Definitive Study of the Causes of Crime*. New York: Simon & Schuster.

Young, Warren, and Mark Brown. 1993. "Cross-National Comparisons of Imprisonment." In *Crime and Justice: A Review of Research*, vol. 17, edited by Michael Tonry. Chicago: University of Chicago Press.

Zimring, Franklin E. 1972. "The Medium Is the Message: Firearms Caliber as a Determinant of Death from Assault." *Journal of Legal Studies* 1:97–123.

Zimring, Franklin E., and Gordon Hawkins. 1997. *Crime Is Not the Problem*. New York: Oxford University Press.

[6]
Determinants of Penal Policies

Many of the generalizations bandied about in discussions of penal policy in Western countries are not true. If penal populism (Pratt 2007) or populist punitiveness (Bottoms 1995) exists at all, it is mostly as reifications in academics' minds of other academics' ideas. Imprisonment rates have not risen substantially everywhere in the last fifteen years. Penal policies are not becoming harsher everywhere. Some policies in some places have become harsher, but in most places this is offset by changes in practice that moderate and sometimes nullify the policy changes, and by other policy changes that move in the opposite direction. If a few governments are moving in illiberal directions in relation to the procedural rights of defendants, most are moving to strengthen their procedural rights and protections (Snacken 2005). If with things such as antisocial behavior orders (Morgan 2006) in England and three-strikes laws in America (Zimring, Hawkins, and Kamin 2001), some governments are adopting primarily "expressive" policies without concern for their iatrogenic effects, most governments are not. In countries in which most or some penal policies have become more severe, the reasons are not rising crime rates, increased awareness of risk, globalization, or the conditions of late modernity, but rather distinctive cultural, historical, constitutional, and political conditions. Tip O'Neill, for many years speaker of the U.S. House of Representatives, famously observed that "all politics are local." So are penal cultures and policies.

All Western countries in recent decades experienced rising then fall-

Errors of analysis or fact in this introduction are alas my own, but I am grateful to the following people who kindly read an earlier draft and helped me avoid some errors and tried to save me from others: Jean-Paul Brodeur, Anthony Doob, David Downes, Richard Frase, David Green, René Lévy, Sebastian Roché, and René van Swaaningen.

ing crime rates, major economic and social dislocations, and the congeries of anxieties and attitudes some associate with "late modernity" and postmodernist angst. Everywhere some political parties raised crime control as a campaign issue, and public attitudes toward crime and criminals at times hardened. Despite all those similarities, the determinants and characteristics of penal policies remain curiously local.

In the United States, crime rates rose from the late 1960s through the early 1990s. Then they fell substantially, and almost continuously, to levels not seen for a third of a century. Imprisonment rates began to rise in 1973 and have risen ever since. To many people, it probably appears obvious that those trends are connected. During the first period in which both crime and imprisonment rose, more crimes might be expected mechanically to have produced more arrests, prosecutions, convictions, prison sentences, and prisoners. It probably seems inevitable that policy makers toughened up by enacting mandatory minimum, truth-in-sentencing, and three-strikes laws in order to deter and incapacitate offenders and respond to heightened public anxiety.

After American crime rates began their steady decline in the early 1990s, to many it may have seemed self-evident that larger prison populations and tougher punishments caused crime rates to fall, that imprisonment use should remain high as insurance against a future upturn, and that policy makers, entirely sensibly, have kept in place the policies that drove crime down and filled the prisons. When comparisons are made between the experiences of the United States and those of other countries, however, it becomes obvious that what appears self-evident in recent American experience is not self-evident elsewhere.

Crime rates in the other English-speaking countries and most European countries also rose from the 1960s through the early to mid 1990s and after that fell, or stabilized, or alternated between decline and stability (van Kesteren, Mayhew, and Nieuwbeerta 2001; Tonry 2004*b*; Aebi et al. 2006; van Dijk et al. 2007). If the American conventional wisdom about relations between crime and imprisonment were true, the seemingly inexorable increase in imprisonment that the United States experienced should have occurred everywhere.

It didn't. Only in the Netherlands did imprisonment rates continuously increase after 1973, albeit from such a lower base (18 per 100,000 compared with 150–160) that a sevenfold increase produced a rate around 134 per 100,000 in 2004, well below the American starting point and less than a fifth of the then-American rate of nearly 725 per

100,000 (Downes and van Swaaningen 2007). England and New Zealand have followed the U.S. and Dutch pattern of continuous increase, but only since the mid-1990s (Newburn, in this volume; Pratt 2007).

In other countries, imprisonment rate trends varied widely. In Finland, rates fell by two-thirds between 1965 and the early 1990s and then stabilized; elsewhere in Scandinavia they fluctuated between 60 and 80 per 100,000 (Lappi-Seppälä, in this volume). In Japan, they fell steadily for decades but in more recent years have turned upward (Johnson, in this volume). In Germany, Canada, and Belgium, imprisonment rates were basically flat in the final quarter of the twentieth century (Weigend 2001; Snacken, in this volume; Webster and Doob, in this volume). In France they fluctuated between peaks and troughs caused by frequent use of pardons and amnesties (Lévy, in this volume; Roché, in this volume).

Any assumption or hypothesis, therefore, that there is a simple, common, or invariant relationship between the crime patterns that befall a country and the number of people it confines is wrong. Faced with similar crime trends, different countries react in different ways.

Even so capacious a scholar as David Garland in 1996 described developments in crime control policy in contemporary Britain "and elsewhere," implicitly assuming that the crime trends, social forces, and political pressures afflicting England and the United States were affecting other developed countries in similar ways. Hans-Jörg Albrecht, the distinguished director of Germany's Max Planck Institute on International and Comparative Penal Law, noted the "and elsewhere" and sardonically observed of such generalizations that they derived their strength solely from "forgetting about the 'and elsewhere'" (2001, p. 294).

Garland pulled back in his magisterial *The Culture of Control* (2001) and observed that similar stressors need not produce the same results in different countries.[1] It was not, however, unreasonable in the mid-

[1] Not everyone has learned this: "Toward the end of the twentieth century, a clear pattern seemed to be emerging in crime control policy in modern society. On the one hand, the state had been prepared to respond to concerns about monstrous criminals and demonic others with increasingly severe penalties; on the other there was a strategy of 'defining deviance down' . . . . [More recently,] the punishment of the monstrous . . . has become significantly more severe as liberal restraints . . . have been pushed aside. At the same time, 'minor deviations' are no longer 'defined down'" (Pratt 2007, pp. 94–95). That is not the picture most of the essays in this volume paint of particular countries other than the United States and the United Kingdom (and, per Pratt, New Zealand). See, e.g., the essays by Green, Lappi-Seppälä, Roché, Snacken, and Webster and Doob in this volume.

1990s for Garland to have assumed that many or most developed countries would follow America's policy lead, as England as early as 1993 appeared to be doing and by 2004 transparently had done (Tonry 2004*a*; Newburn 2006; Morgan and Downes 2007). In the mid-1990s there was next to no comparative literature on crime control or penal policy. There were only two important works in criminology. David Downes's *Contrasts in Tolerance* (1988) compared Dutch and English postwar policies through the mid-1980s, arguing that Holland's more humane policies and practices resulted from differences in the views of national policy elites. Joachim Savelsberg (1994) compared German and American crime policies and politics and stressed the importance of German practitioners' greater insulation from public attitudes and emotions compared with their elected or politically appointed counterparts in the United States. Outside criminology, political scientists studying comparative political cultures occasionally mentioned crime in passing, but their principal interests were elsewhere (e.g., Lijphart 1984, 1999), and few criminologists were familiar with their work.[2]

Since the mid-1990s, however, a literature has begun to emerge. Garland gets part of the credit for this; his 2001 book attracted enormous attention and provoked many to try to refute, qualify, and amplify his analyses. Credit also goes to an increasingly international scholarly world in which more people are motivated to look across national boundaries in order to see more clearly what is happening within their own. The results include lengthening lists of comparative books (e.g., Whitman 2003; Tonry 2004*b*; Cavadino and Dignan 2005; Pratt 2007; Green, forthcoming), comparative collections (e.g., Clarkson and Morgan 1995; Tonry and Frase 2001; Tonry and Doob 2004; Pratt et al. 2005; Armstrong and McAra 2006; Newburn and Rock 2006) and numerous articles (many published in *Punishment and Society*). There are also a few books tracing policy developments in one or two countries (Windlesham 1987–96 [England and Wales]; Windlesham 1998 [United States]; Dunbar and Langdon 1998 [England and Wales]; Garland 2001 [England and Wales, the United States]; Faulkner 2002 [England and Wales]; Ryan 2003 [England and Wales]; Tonry 2004*b* [United States]; Tonry 2004*a* [England and Wales]; Boutellier 2005 [Netherlands]; Buruma 2005 [Netherlands]; Gottschalk 2006 [United States]; Jones and Newburn 2006 [England and Wales]; Roché 2006

[2] Green (in this volume, forthcoming) is a notable exception.

[France]; Simon 2007 [United States]). Others no doubt are on the way.

This essay takes stock of the literature as it now stands. The aims are to search for generalizations—there are some—that help explain national differences in penal policies and practices and to suggest ways to build on what we now (tentatively) know. Section I does some ground clearing, focusing on the dependent variable, the thing to be explained. Imprisonment rates per 100,000 population provide the usual metric. Whether such rates by themselves, however, are the only, the best, or even plausible measures of penal policy differences is doubtful.

Use of any single measure of punitiveness is incomplete and often misleading. A mix of policies, practices, procedures, and outcomes needs to be considered before generalizations about particular countries can sensibly be offered. Among important indicators are the promotion, enactment, and effectuation of harsher policies, whether harsher policies are broadly or narrowly focused, whether and in what ways practices change in response to new policies, and whether harsher policies and practices characterize both the juvenile and adult systems or only one of them. When multiple criteria are used, it becomes apparent that the United States and England are in a class by themselves in moving toward harsher penal systems across the board. Although many countries have recently adopted policies that are on their faces harsher than those they supplant, most have made comparatively fewer and much more tightly focused changes. In many countries, practices have not become conspicuously more severe.

Section II sets out a framework for thinking about the determinants of penal policies, stealing from developmental psychology the concepts of risk and protective factors. Few people disagree that some behaviors, such as childhood pregnancy, drug dependence, and serious antisocial behavior, are undesirable. Knowing what factors make their occurrence more likely and what factors protect against them may make it possible more often to prevent them. That something is a risk factor does not mean that the unwanted outcome is inevitable, but that the likelihood is greater than were the factor not present. The comparative literature on penal policy identifies characteristics of countries that make them more or less likely to adopt punitive policies or to adopt more or less punitive policies. It also identifies nonfactors, things that by themselves do not explain anything about penal policy.

The assumption underlying use of the risk and protective factors framework is that increases in punitiveness are generally undesirable. That may not always be true or widely agreed on. Reasonable people can, of course, disagree about the desirability of particular forms of punishment and whether punishments should be made severer in particular times and places for particular crimes and categories of offenders. Many American criminal justice professionals and scholars, however, believe that modern American imprisonment rates are highly undesirable, and that many punishment policies including capital punishment, life sentences without possibility of parole, three-strikes laws, and lengthy mandatory minimum sentence laws are unjust and unwise (e.g., Gottschalk 2006; Simon 2007). Many English criminal justice professionals and scholars feel the same way about English imprisonment rates and punishment policies (e.g., Morgan and Downes 2007). Situations elsewhere vary from country to country, as the essays in this volume demonstrate. Almost everywhere, however, many professionals and scholars believe that the use of imprisonment should be avoided to the extent possible and that punishments should be moderate, restrained, proportionate, and respectful of offenders' human rights.

The main section, Section III, distills a series of generalizations about national characteristics that increase risks of adopting (unnecessarily) punitive policies or protect against them and about characteristics that lack explanatory power. Prominent risk factors include "conflict" political systems, elected judges and prosecutors, sensationalist journalism, Anglo-Saxon political cultures, and a populist view that criminal justice policy should be strongly influenced by public sentiment and partisan politics. Other comparative risk factors are relatively greater income inequality, relatively weaker social welfare systems, lower levels of trust in fellow citizens and government, and relatively lower levels of perceived legitimacy of legal institutions.

Prominent protective factors include consensus political systems, nonpartisan judges and prosecutors, Francophonic political cultures, and a predominant view that criminal justice policy falls appropriately within the province of expert knowledge and professional experience. Among the characteristics that lack explanatory power are crime rates and trends, population heterogeneity, globalization, and existentialist angst.

Section IV suggests ways we might test what we think we know and ways we might learn more. What is needed now is a combination of genuinely comparative studies, in place of the single-country descriptions and analyses that constitute nearly all the existing literature, and studies that examine and try to explain a much wider range of penal characteristics than simply imprisonment rates.

I. Measuring Punitiveness

A modest but growing literature examines the determinants of penal policy or attempts to explain why punishment policies, practices, and outcomes have become harsher in recent decades or years in some countries, particularly the United States and England. The preceding sentence uses two phrases—"penal policy" and "punishment policies, practices, and outcomes"—to describe the phenomena to be explained. The second, which unpacks the first, is better, but in the interest of conciseness I mostly refer to penal policy.

Much current writing attempts to explain national differences in penal policy, generally taken to be represented by differences in imprisonment rates, or in "penality," "punitiveness," "punitivism," or "punitivity." These are all ugly words.[3] Usually the thing being described is left vague; what is usually meant is an unspecified mix of attitudes, enactments, motivations, policies, practices, and ways of thinking that taken together express greater intolerance of deviance and deviants, and greater support for harsher policies and severer punishments. The imprisonment rate, the number of people held in prison on an average day or an annual census count day per 100,000 population, is often used as a primary measure of punitiveness.

There are plausible reasons to use the imprisonment rate, though it is but one possible measure. Its advantages are that it is readily available,[4] is calculated more or less consistently over time and space, and is a measure of diverse practices and policies that collectively result in a state imposing greater or lesser aggregate suffering on its residents in the names of deserved punishment and crime prevention.

[3] Calling to mind C. S. Lewis's quip in "The Humanitarian Theory of Punishment" about "the 'expert penologist' (let barbarous things have barbarous names)" (reprinted in Lewis [1970]).

[4] The Home Office for some years annually published rates for many countries; the series has been taken over by the International Centre for Prison Studies (ICPS) (e.g., Walmsley 2007). The ICPS publishes latest rates on its Web site (http://www.prisonstudies.org). The Council of Europe produces annual reports on prison use for countries belonging to the council. Forty-four of forty-six member states participated in the 2005 survey (Aebi and Stadnic 2007).

Despite this, care needs to be taken in comparing imprisonment rates. What look to be comparable rates often are not. Many countries, for example, include only imprisoned adults in their calculations. In Finland and Sweden, however, which have no separate juvenile justice systems, prison population totals include fifteen- to seventeen-year-olds. That does not distort their rates much because few young people are sent to prison. In the United States, where some states lowered the maximum age of juvenile court jurisdiction to fifteen, sixteen, or seventeen, and many juveniles in other states are transferred to adult courts to be tried, the adult prisons contain many thousands of juveniles. The Netherlands for some reason includes juveniles confined under both civil and criminal laws in the prison population it reports to the Council of Europe. As a result the "official" imprisonment rate in 2004 was 134 per 100,000; when juveniles and a few other nontypical categories are excluded, the 2004 rate was fewer than 100 per 100,000, which makes the increase in imprisonment in that country considerably less than is commonly recognized (Tonry and Bijleveld 2007). Whether immigrants confined for illegal entry (in most European countries not a criminal offense) are included can distort comparisons in similar ways.[5]

There are also things to be said against using the imprisonment rate. It combines figures for pretrial detainees[6] and convicted, sentenced offenders. It obscures relations among convictions, prison admissions, and sentence lengths. An increasing imprisonment rate can reflect increasing numbers of people convicted, rising chances that convicted offenders are sentenced to imprisonment, lengthening prison terms, changes in release policies, or combinations of some or all of these. The overall imprisonment rate also obscures changes in sentencing patterns for different offenses: rape sentences might be becoming more severe and shoplifting less so, for example, a bifurcation some people

[5] And at least at the margins, national imprisonment rates vary in their inclusion of particular categories of confined people: illegal aliens and others confined for noncriminal violations of immigration laws, mentally ill offenders, young offenders convicted in adult courts, and young offenders beneath the age of majority. Comparisons involving the United States are bedeviled by America's multiple levels of government. American and non-American scholars alike often compare the oranges of aggregate European imprisonment rates with the apples of American imprisonment rates for sentenced prisoners serving terms of one year or more in state and federal prisons, thereby disregarding the additional 30–35 percent of prisoners in pretrial detention or serving sentences shorter than one year.

[6] Typically called "remand prisoners" outside the United States.

would celebrate. Data in most national statistical systems can be disaggregated in these ways, as many of the essays in this volume demonstrate.

A different critique of using the imprisonment rate as the primary measure of punitiveness is that gross imprisonment may be a misleading or even perverse measure. This critique takes two forms. The older one is that, especially in a time of rising crime rates, imprisonment rates per se may be importantly misleading (Pease 1991; Young and Brown 1993; Kommer 1994, 2004). A slightly rising imprisonment rate during a period of rapidly rising crime rates might indicate not harsher but softer average punishments. Other, better, measures might include the probability of imprisonment and average days of imprisonment served, in the aggregate or disaggregated by types of offense, relative to victimizations, recorded crimes, arrests, prosecutions, convictions, or (for sentence length) prison sentences.[7] Were some of these indicators used, especially relative to victimizations and recorded crimes, especially in 1975–95, time series would show that many criminal justice systems became less punitive, not more (e.g., Young and Brown 1993).

International punitiveness rankings vary substantially depending on the indicator used. If annual prison admission rates per capita are the basis of comparison, for example, rather than imprisonment rates, rankings change radically. Max Kommer (1994) and Warren Young and Mark Brown (1993) some time ago showed that some European countries, which impose many short prison sentences, rather than fewer but longer ones as in the United States, top the international punitiveness league tables when annual admissions per capita are the measure, even though they are near the bottom when imprisonment rates per capita are the measure.[8] Table 1 shows rankings by imprisonment (1990) and admission (1987) rates per 100,000 population calculated for seven Western countries by Young and Brown (1993). The Netherlands and Sweden had the lowest and second-lowest imprisonment rates in 1990 but in 1987 had the second- and third-highest rates per 100,000 of prison admissions for sentenced offenders. By a wide margin Sweden had the highest total prison admission rates of all seven countries

[7] The essays in Tonry and Farrington (2005) report changes in many of these measures over twenty years for eight countries.

[8] Among Western and developed countries, Scandinavian imprisonment rates, typically 60–80 per 100,000 in recent years, are high compared with the rates of 30–40 per 100,000 that characterize many Asian countries (Walmsley 2007).

TABLE 1

Imprisonment Rates, Sentenced, Remand, and Total Admission Rates per 100,000 in Seven Countries

Country Rankings	Imprisonment (1990)	Sentenced Admissions (1987)	Remand Admissions (1987)	Total Admissions (1987)
1	New Zealand (106)	New Zealand (190)	Sweden (405)	Sweden (583)
2	England and Wales (93)	Sweden (178)	Scotland (335)	Scotland (434)
3	Scotland (95)	Netherlands (137)	New Zealand (203)	New Zealand (393)
		England and Wales (137)		
4	France (82)		England and Wales (169)	England and Wales (306)
5	West Germany (78)	Scotland (99)	France (104)	France (168)
6	Sweden (58)	West Germany (84)	West Germany (78)	West Germany (162)
7	Netherlands (44)	France (64)	Netherlands (NA)	Netherlands (NA)

SOURCE.—Young and Brown (1993), tables 1, 3.

(Dutch remand admission rates were not available). Kommer's analysis (1994, table 1) also included Denmark, which then had an imprisonment rate lower than Sweden's, the second-lowest among eleven countries, but the third-highest total rate for prison admissions (after Sweden and Northern Ireland).

A newer critique is that imprisonment rates narrowly, or punishment policies and practices more broadly, are by themselves incomplete and often misleading. Sonja Snacken (2005) pointed out that, whatever their divergent recent imprisonment patterns, all European countries having the death penalty abolished it in recent decades and strengthened human rights protections of suspects and convicted offenders, suggesting that analyses of punitiveness that consider only imprisonment miss much that is important.

Sebastian Roché (in this volume) offers a similar critique of the imprisonment rate, demonstrating that French imprisonment rates have increased somewhat in the past twenty-five years and would have increased substantially more save for frequent large-scale amnesties and pardons. During the same period, however, France abolished the death penalty, established a wide array of diversion programs and alternative sentences, insulated juvenile offenders from increases in punishment severity, enacted no mandatory penalty laws, and held to a cross-party consensus view that imprisonment is an undesirable thing to be avoided to the extent possible.

In the Netherlands, the only country that increased its imprisonment rates as much as or more than the United States in recent decades, sentencing policies per se were not made harsher. Policies for dealing with young offenders, however, were toughened in the 1990s and waivers to the adult court were made easier. In practice, fewer young offenders were transferred to adult courts, and fewer young offenders were sent to prison (Junger-Tas 2004). Canada, likewise, made transfers of juveniles to adult courts easier during the 1990s only to see the incidence of transfers decline (Doob and Sprott 2004). Go figure.

Use of multiple measures gives a better basis for comparing national differences in punitiveness, or changes in punitiveness over time in a single country, than any single indicator does. The resulting comparisons, however, are more complex and conclusions harder to draw. In both France and the United States during the period 1990–99, prison admissions stabilized or fell, but average sentence lengths increased overall and when controlling for offense (Blumstein and Beck 1999;

Roché, in this volume). Reasonable people might disagree as to which approach is more punitive: sending more people to prison for shorter periods or fewer for longer.

So far I have described differences in policies (e.g., capital punishment, mandatory minimums, juvenile waivers, alternatives to imprisonment), practices (e.g., use of waivers, changes in prison admissions), and outcomes (e.g., prison population and admission rates, sentence lengths). Procedures also matter. In much of western Europe, under the influence of the European Convention and Court of Human Rights (Kurki 2001; Snacken 2005) and the Torture Convention (Morgan 2001), countries have been strengthening procedural protections afforded criminal defendants. In England, the Labour government has recently systematically weakened defendants' procedural protections, including abolishing the double jeopardy rule, weakening prophylactic evidentiary rules, and narrowing jury trial rights (Tonry 2004*a*, chap. 1). Likewise in the United States, the U.S. Congress and Supreme Court over the past thirty years have systematically reduced procedural protections (e.g., weakening controls over police searches and seizures, limiting or eliminating habeas corpus protections, weakening jury trial rights, greatly narrowing prisoners' ability to challenge prison conditions).

Finally, comparisons of changes in penal policy need to differentiate among their enactment, their implementation, and their practical use. Sometimes policies are enacted to send messages, to make expressive or symbolic statements with no clear expectation that they will be implemented. Conservative Republican Senator Alfonse D'Amato (NY), for example, in 1991 proposed changes to federal mandatory minimum sentence laws that professional prosecutors said were unenforceable. According to *New York Times* reporter Gwen Ifill, "Mr. D'Amato conceded that his two successful amendments, which Justice Department officials said would have little practical effect on prosecution of crimes, might not solve the problem. 'But,' he said, 'it does bring about a sense that we are serious'" (Ifill 1991, p. A6). David Garland (2001) has brought increased attention to expressive policy making. Sometimes, nothing more than expression is meant. This may be why waivers to adult courts of young offenders in Canada declined after the Canadian Parliament enacted laws making waiver easier (Doob and Sprott 2004). This may also explain the English practice in which new criminal laws often do not take effect automatically; they take effect only if and when the Home Secretary of the day elects to put them into force.[9]

Even when new laws are implemented, sometimes they are not applied, or they are applied only occasionally. The history of mandatory sentencing laws in England and America is full of examples from the eighteenth century to the present of laws that practitioners declined to apply (e.g., Tonry 1996, chap. 5). Sometimes prosecutors exercise discretion not to file charges under new laws or to insist on the penalties they prescribe. Other times, lawyers, judges, and juries adapt their ways of doing business to avoid applying laws they believe to be unjust. Sometimes enactment and implementation of new laws, even laws policy makers want applied, make no practical difference in how the justice system operates.

There are thus numerous ways in which a legal system can be said to be more or less punitive compared with other systems or with itself at other times.[10] Informative comparative analyses would take account of them all. Table 2 lists a range of measures of increased (or decreased) punitiveness that a rich account of the evolution of penal policy in an individual country would at minimum incorporate.

II. Risk and Protective Factors

The development of problem behaviors and delinquency over the life course is often described as a function of interactions between risk and protective factors. Truancy and school failure, adolescent pregnancy and paternity, drug and alcohol abuse, and delinquency are things that nearly everyone considers unfortunate. Some characteristics of children (e.g., impulsivity, aggressiveness, low IQ) and their environments (e.g., criminal or abusive parents, inconsistent discipline, delinquent peers) make unfortunate outcomes more likely. These are called risk factors.

Other characteristics (e.g., good parenting, above-average household

[9] Many people expected that the then-new Labour government would not put into force three mandatory minimum sentence laws enacted in the final days of John Major's last government. They were put into force (Morgan and Downes 2007).

[10] There are other ways as well. Deeper functionalist analyses might look not at the imprisonment rate (however defined) but at the fraction of the overall population in some kind of confinement, including mental health and juvenile institutions of all kinds (e.g., van Ruller and Beijers 1995; Harcourt 2006). Nils Christie (1968) and Alfred Blumstein and Jacqueline Cohen (1973) developed arguments for Scandinavia and the United States that societies have natural levels of confinement that are stable over time, at least over the three-quarters of a century that preceded their articles' publication.

TABLE 2
Measures of Punitiveness

Policies:
1. Capital punishment (authorization)
2. Mandatory minimum sentence laws (enactment)
3. Laws increasing sentence lengths (enactment)
4. Pretrial/preventive detention (authorization)
5. Prison alternatives (creation)
6. Juvenile waiver to adult courts (authorization)
7. Weakened procedural protections (enactment)
Practices:
1. Patterns of use of policies 1–7
2. Adult prison population and admission rates over time
a. Disaggregated for pretrial and sentenced prisoners
b. Disaggregated by offense for sentence lengths and admission rates
3. Juvenile institutional population and admission rates over time
a. Disaggregated for pretrial and sentenced juvenile offenders
b. Disaggregated by offense for sentence lengths and admission rates
Procedures: Patterns of use of procedural protections

income, good schools, church participation) make undesirable outcomes less likely despite the presence of risk factors (Deković 1999). These are called protective factors. Protective factors have a positive effect under conditions of risk.[11]

By analogy the risk and protective factors framework can be used to understand changes in punitiveness. David Green (in this volume) shows that sensationalistic tabloid newspapers have shaped public attitudes and knowledge in England and Wales in ways that conduce to adoption of more punitive policies and practices; sensationalistic media thus may be a risk factor. Green also argues that countries with "consensus" political cultures are less likely to adopt more punitive penal

[11] There are other factors that increase the chance of a positive outcome under all conditions. Sameroff (1998) proposed that these be called "promotive" factors. A promotive effect does not result from interaction, but lies in the positive end of a risk dimension (Stouthamer-Loeber et al. 2002). Because the comparative penal policy literature consists mostly of case studies, the distinction between protective and promotive factors is too elusive to be usable, even by analogy. Having noted the distinction, I set it aside and use the term "protective factor" to describe factors that might be one or the other.

policies than countries with "majoritarian" or "conflict" political cultures. Consensus political culture would thus be a protective factor. James Whitman (2003) and I (Tonry 1999, 2004*b*) have argued that constitutional structural arrangements that insulate practitioners from electoral politics and public emotion produce less punitive punishment systems and practices and would therefore count as a protective factor.

The risk and protective factors framework is probabilistic and dynamic. That a risk factor is present does not make an unwanted outcome inevitable; it means that the chances of an unwanted outcome are greater than they would otherwise be. The presence of a protective factor does not mean that an unwanted outcome will be avoided, only that its likelihood will be reduced. Risk and protective factors are identified so that they can be addressed, in order to change the likelihood of unwanted outcomes.

When one applies the framework to analyses of penal policy, it is important to note its probabilism and dynamism. That majoritarian political systems are risk factors does not mean that countries characterized by them will inexorably and inevitably be highly punitive. Canada, for example, has a majoritarian political system but has long had stable and relatively nonpunitive policies. Finland, by contrast, has a consensus political system but, despite its modern standing as an icon of humane and moderate policies, for half a century its policies were vastly more severe than those of other Scandinavian countries. Policies and practices change over time in reaction to many influences. Risk and protective factors affect how much they change and in what directions.

Every country experiences long-term developments (e.g., rising crime rates, changing public attitudes and opinions) and moral panics associated with sensational incidents (e.g., the James Bulger killing in England, the Dutroux kidnappings and murders of young girls in Belgium, the Polly Klaas kidnapping and murder in the United States). However, they respond in different ways over time and in particular times. Many people identify the Bulger case, and reactions to it, as heralding a sea change in English penal politics and policies (Newburn, in this volume). The Polly Klaas case led directly to enactment of California's three-strikes law and indirectly to enactment of these laws in half the American states (Zimring, Hawkins, and Kamin 2001). The Dutroux case, although it brought hundreds of thousands of Belgians onto the streets, did not lead to fundamental changes in Belgian policies or practices (Snacken, in this volume). These different results illustrate differing degrees of national susceptibility to overreaction. Different mixes of risk and protective actors are a major part of the explanation.

III. Determinants of Penal Policy

The more closely we look at something, the more complex we usually realize it is. Evolving understanding of penal policy changes in Western countries is like that. At first, the reasons why American imprisonment rates rose rapidly and why policy makers adopted increasingly severe policies seemed straightforward: crime rates rose, the public demanded action, and policy makers and practitioners responded (e.g., Wilson 1983; Bennett, DiIulio, and Walters 1996). When it became apparent that those explanations were too simple, subtler and more complex analyses invoked deeper economic and social changes affecting modern societies (e.g., Garland 2001). Those explanations also came to seem too simple because they implied that ubiquitous structural changes (economic disruption, globalization, large-scale migration, increased population diversity, rising crime rates, increasing awareness of risks) should have produced comparable policy responses in all developed countries, and patently they had not (e.g., Tonry 2004*b*, chap. 2). The latest inquiries look cross-nationally at characteristics of particular countries that seem to have shaped the different ways they responded to long-term rises in crime rates and widely experienced structural changes in modern society. The risk and protective factors paradigm provides a framework for doing that. Candidate determinants of penal policy fall into three categories: nonfactors, risk factors, and protective factors.

A. Nonfactors

Most of the things commonly invoked to explain increased punitiveness—rising crime rates, harsher public attitudes, cynical politicians, ethnic tensions, rapid social and economic change, postmodernist angst, "penal populism" (Pratt 2007)—cannot sensibly be characterized as risk factors. Because every Western country experienced those developments, they cannot provide a basis for explaining widely divergent policy trends in different countries. Imprisonment rates climbed steeply over the past thirty years in the Netherlands and the United States, held steady in Canada and Norway, fell sharply in Finland and Japan through the 1990s, and zigzagged in France. Risk factors in developmental psychology are characteristics of individuals or their environments that place them at higher risk of unwanted outcomes than individuals who do not share those characteristics. A risk factor that characterized every individual under study, for example, gender in a sample of men, could provide no guidance. That is why I describe developments that characterize all countries as nonfactors.

Though it might seem a priori that rising crime rates (and other things mentioned in the preceding paragraph) increase the likelihood that a country will adopt more punitive policies than theretofore, this is true only in a trivial sense. Whether countries adopt more punitive policies turns on country-specific characteristics. Some of these characteristics make increased punitiveness more likely. Others make it less likely. Still others make any simple generalization suspect.

The nonfactors include social and economic changes experienced by most developed countries since 1970 that are said to be associated with increases in "populist punitiveness" (Bottoms 1995), politicization of crime policy, adoption of more punitive policies, and increasingly punitive practices. They include steeply rising crime and victimization rates through the 1990s; social and economic changes associated with globalization and "late modernity"; increased population diversity and intergroup conflict; the effects of the women's, gay, and civil rights movements; and increasingly global and sensationalistic media.

The nonfactors can be thought of in two ways. The first, precisely because they affect all developed countries, and countries' penal policies and policy trends varied enormously, is that their invocation can explain nothing. They are background conditions, no more. The second is that they are necessary but not sufficient conditions, risk factors of a sort but that lack independent explanatory or causal power. Whether they influence policies depends on their interaction with other risk and protective factors. In either case, though they may be part of the story, they are not the important part.

B. Risk Factors

Knowledge about risk factors comes from two sources. The first is the growing number of case studies of the development of crime control and punishment policies in individual countries. The most prominent national risk factors include conflict political systems, elected judges and prosecutors, particular forms of sensationalist journalism, Anglo-Saxon political cultures, and a predominant view that criminal justice policy falls appropriately within the province of public opinion and partisan politics. The second is a small number of statistical analyses that test hypotheses about correlations between punitiveness and national characteristics and policies not directly associated with crime and punishment. Comparative risk factors they identify are income inequality, weak social welfare systems, and low levels of perceived legitimacy of governmental institutions. Lesser punitiveness is associated with lower levels of income inequality, generous social welfare systems, and high levels of trust in fellow citizens and in government.

1. *Case Studies.* Case studies in Europe have been accumulating for a decade and are available for many countries, including Belgium, Denmark, England and Wales, Finland, France, Germany, the Netherlands, Norway, and Sweden. Case studies are also available for Australia, Canada, New Zealand, and the United States. The five national features they highlight are general political culture, constitutional structure, mass media characteristics, Anglo-Saxon culture, and simplistic conceptions of democracy.

a. General Political Culture. Political scientists interested in comparative studies of political systems have long distinguished between conflict and consensus political systems (e.g., Lijphart 1984, 1999). Conflict systems are typically characterized by two major political parties, first-past-the-post electoral systems, single-member electoral districts, and policy discontinuities. Parties define their positions by contrast with those of their opponents, devote continuous efforts when out of power to opposing the ruling party's policies, and campaign on the basis of those oppositional differences. Not surprisingly, when one party displaces another in power, it often rejects existing policies and attempts to enact or implement those on which it ran for office.

Five primarily English-speaking countries[12] have conflict political

[12] The "five primarily English-speaking countries" is an awkward phrase. It is meant to include the subset of more populated wealthy, developed countries that were formerly English colonies, in which English is the primary language, and which have common-law adversary legal systems. Each has sizable minorities who speak other languages (e.g., French speakers in Canada, Hispanics in the United States). Sometimes, as in countries with large Francophonic minorities, their presence may constitute a protective factor. There are certainly other countries besides the five that arguably meet all the criteria except "wealthy," such as India or some in the Caribbean and Africa.

systems. Coalition governments are rare, including in Great Britain[13] and Canada, which have three major parties. In England, where the Liberal Democrats sometimes receive a fifth to a quarter of votes cast in national elections, the absence of proportional representation means that their percentages of the raw vote translate into much lower percentages of parliamentary seats and their influence is slight compared with that of the two major parties.

Consensus systems are typically characterized by numerous political parties, proportional representation, coalition governments, and policy continuity. The first three of these characteristics go together, and policy continuity is often a result. Where there are many political parties and proportional representation, coalition governments are almost inevitable. Coalition governments necessarily include parties and individual officials who subscribe to different views on major issues. Major initiatives to succeed must gain support from the parties in the ruling coalition. Because new elections may bring new parties into the ruling coalition, policy processes generally include participation by parties not in the coalition.

A new election may produce a new coalition including some parties from the previous government together with parties that were previously outside the government. These features make radical policy changes less likely than in conflict systems because some members of the new government will have participated in shaping existing policies and thus are likely to continue to support them. In addition, parties in power after one election realize that they may be out of power after the next one and have a continuing interest in policy processes that are primarily substantive rather than primarily adversary lest policies they support be quickly overturned.

Most western European countries have consensus political systems. The Dutch for most of the twentieth century subscribed to the "polder system" under which all major parties, and therefore the religious and cultural groups they represented, participated in policy processes

[13] Usually I refer in this essay to England and Wales or England. The reason is that England and Wales make up a legal system distinct from those of Scotland and Northern Ireland, and it is the legal system of England and Wales that has experienced rapidly rising imprisonment rates and extreme politicization of criminal justice policy. One of the anomalies of the British constitutional scheme, however, is that the Parliament legislating for England and Wales includes members from Northern Ireland and Scotland. Labour in recent years has won a huge majority of Scottish seats in the British Parliament, without which its control of Parliament would have been much less secure.

(Downes, in this volume).[14] In Belgium, the mainstream parties in recent decades have sought consensus approaches to criminal justice issues, sharing a general ambition to avoid politicization of policy making, subscribing to widely shared views about humane policies, and combining forces to obstruct the influence of the Vlaams Blok, a radical right-wing party (Snacken, in this volume). In Sweden, Norway, Finland, and Denmark, policy processes are corporatist, involve wide consultation inside and outside government, and generally unfold over periods of years (Lappi-Seppälä, in this volume).

Arend Lijphart, a leading scholar of comparative politics, over nearly four decades has explored the nature and consequences of the consensus/conflict model. In a recent major book (Lijphart 1999), he develops two quantitative multifactor scales—a "parties-executives dimension" and a "federal-unitary dimension"—to characterize governments. The parties-executives dimension can be thought of as representing dispersion and concentration of political power. Thus one factor is "concentration of executive power in single-party majority cabinets versus executive power-sharing in broad multiparty coalitions" (p. 3). Others are strong versus weak executives and two-party versus multiparty systems.

Lijphart's "federal-unitary dimension" is a measure of constitutional structures that disperse or concentrate authority. Factors include unitary and centralized versus federal and decentralized governments, unicameral versus bicameral legislatures, rigid versus flexible constitutions, and the presence or absence of independent central banks and judicial review of the constitutionality of laws.

The polar cases of majoritarian countries have highly concentrated systems of political power and governmental authority (e.g., England and New Zealand). The polar consensus countries have dispersed centers of political power and concentrated governmental authority (e.g., Sweden and Finland).

Lijphart tests whether governmental structures and political traditions conducing to consensus policy processes are likelier to achieve humane and democratic policy outcomes than conflict-model governments. Using a variety of quantitative outcome measures, Lijp-

[14] A polder is an area of ground reclaimed from a sea or lake by means of dikes. Because much of the Netherlands consists of lands reclaimed from the sea and protected by dikes, a threat to the polders is a threat to everyone that requires that political and other differences be set aside to face the emergency. The polder system in politics, based on that metaphor, signified a view that group differences should be set aside in addressing serious common problems of governance.

hart concludes that consensus governments achieve greater gender equity, greener environmental policies, and more humane criminal justice policies (measured relative to imprisonment rates and the death penalty) than conflict-model governments do.

Figure 1, showing imprisonment rates for selected countries, is consistent with this. Numbers shown in triangles next to country abbreviations are imprisonment rates per 100,000 population in 1996–98; the parentheses show imprisonment rates in 2004–5. Locations of countries are taken from Lijphart's analysis (1999, fig. 14.1). Countries high on the "federal-unitary" vertical axis have relatively concentrated systems of governmental authority, with unitary political systems at the top and federal ones at the bottom. Countries falling toward the left end of the horizontal "parties-executive" axis tend to be characterized by dispersed political power and those on the right by its concentration.

Several patterns stand out. First, when one looks left to right, countries characterized by dispersal of political power, with only a few exceptions, have markedly lower imprisonment rates than those characterized by concentration of political power. Second, dispersal of political power is a better predictor than dispersal of governmental authority. Nearly all the high-imprisonment countries fall on the right side of the figure and nearly all the low-imprisonment countries on the left. Third, high-imprisonment countries are almost equally characterized by unitary and federal governmental structures.

Lijphart's model may appear static, but it is not. Political systems, constitutional structures, and political cultures change over time. Predictions about how particular countries will react to changed conditions also will change over time, depending on what the conditions are and on the presence and absence of other risk and protective factors. Finland, for example, an early twenty-first-century example of a country with a consensus political system, has had one of the lowest imprisonment rates in Europe since the early 1990s. For the fifty years ending around 1985, however, it had one of the highest (Christie 1968; Lappi-Seppälä, in this volume). Switzerland, an exemplar of prison rate stability and moderate penal policies in recent decades, had rates around 150 per 100,000 in the 1930s and 1940s (Killias 1991). The United States experienced broadly stable imprisonment rates from 1930 through 1973, with a gradual decline that began in the early 1960s (Blumstein and Cohen 1973). During most of the period

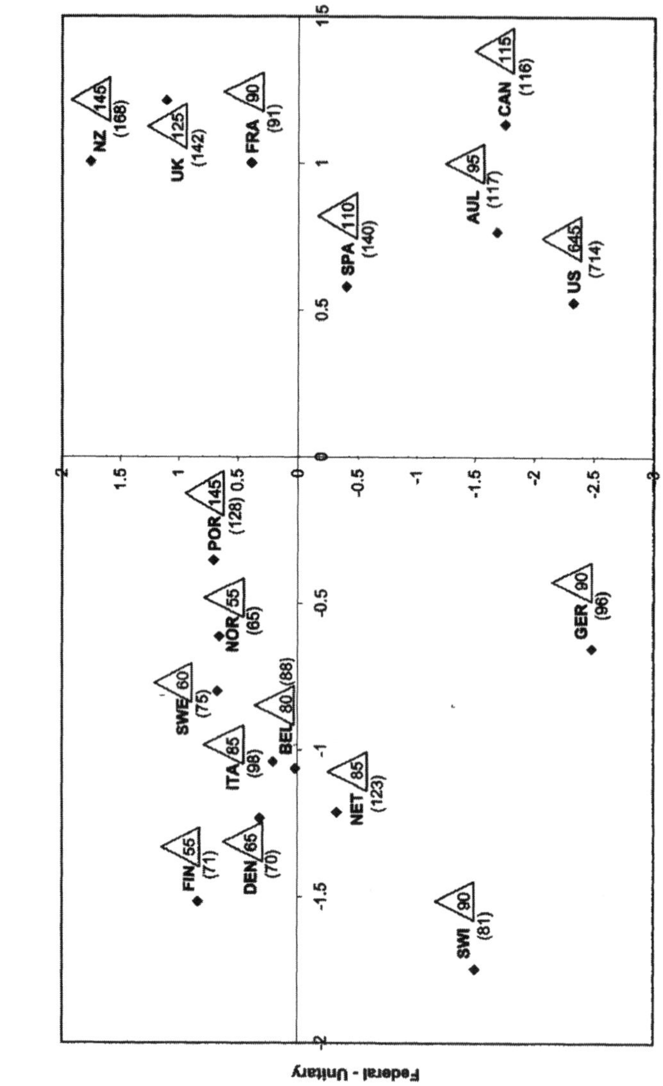

FIG. 1.—Two-dimensional conceptual map of democracy and imprisonment rates from 1996 to 1998 (triangle) and 2004 to 2005 (parentheses)

1930–73, American imprisonment rates were lower than Finland's. In many years in the middle third of the last century, America's were lower than Switzerland's. The Finnish and Swiss political systems, however, have proved much more resilient than the American in responding to recent pressures for harsher policies and practices. For the reasons given earlier in this subsection, there are plausible grounds for believing that Lijphart's model provides useful information to efforts to understand why countries have the penal policies they have.

b. Constitutional Structure.[15] Politicization of criminal justice policy is directly related to whether prosecutors and judges are selected politically or meritocratically. It is also related to whether political and constitutional conventions allow elected politicians to participate in decision making about individual cases. Taken together, these two facets of politicization fundamentally differentiate the United States and England from other Western countries, and they result from the obsolescence of their constitutions. Almost nowhere in western Europe,[16] Canada, or Australia are judges or prosecutors politically selected. And almost nowhere do prevailing conventions justify a direct political voice in punishment decisions.

i. *Elections and Policy.* The American Constitution dates from the late eighteenth century, reflects eighteenth-century ideas, and was written to address problems of that era. These were the colonists' major objections to British rule: governance by a distant Parliament, capricious actions by a distant government's imperious local representatives, and the inability of citizens to seek redress for grievances. The principal, Enlightenment, solutions in the Constitution centered on respect for individual liberty and insulation from the power of an overweening government. Protection of individual liberty was addressed by adoption of the Bill of Rights creating fundamental personal rights (speech, religion, redress for grievances) and entitlements (jury trials, no unreasonable searches and seizures, representation by counsel).

Protection from an overweening government was sought in two

[15] Discussions of the origins and precipitants of the constitutional structure of the United States are based on Mullet (1966) and Wood (1969). Discussions of the origins and precipitants of the English Bill of Rights and the constitutional structure of Great Britain are based on Speck (1988), Williams and Ramsden (1990), and Cruickshanks (2000).

[16] Switzerland, where prosecutors are locally elected, is the primary exception. In Switzerland, however, the principles that political considerations are irrelevant in decisions about individual cases and that cases should be resolved solely on their merits are strongly held and seem to have insulated the system from politicization.

ways. First, complicated systems of checks and balances were created to fragment governmental power, principally by creating a strong horizontal separation of powers among the three branches of the federal government, and by a vertical differentiation of the spheres of interest of the federal and the state governments (which in turn had their own systems of horizontal and vertical separations of powers). Second, provisions in the federal Constitution calling for frequent elections to the House of Representatives (two years)[17] and presidency (four years), and in state constitutions for frequent elections at county levels for state legislators, judges, and prosecutors, were meant to push major elections to local levels, at short intervals, and thereby make officials accountable to local opinion. These structural arrangements also created a widespread democratic ideology about the legitimate voice of public opinion in relation to matters of policy.

The results more than 200 years later include in many states traditions of partisan election of judges and prosecutors who run for office on the basis of emotive appeals to the electorate.[18] If the public is anxious about crime or angry at criminals, or if particular cases become notorious, there is nothing to stop prosecutors from seeking personal political benefit by posturing before public opinion or handling cases in particular ways only because they have become notorious. Because local prosecutors are accountable through elections and are in the executive branch of government, the U.S. Supreme Court has held that their discretionary decisions are effectively immune from judicial review (allegations of corruption are the principal exception) (*Bordenkircher v. Hayes*, 434 U.S. 357 [1982]). Judges also are elected in most states and know that decisions that are highly unpopular with much of the public can lead to their defeat. Most chief prosecutors and many judges aspire to be elected or appointed to higher political or judicial office, which means that they must be concerned about controversies that might diminish their future professional prospects, and they are no doubt sometimes tempted to deal with a particular case in a particular way to curry popular approbation or avoid popular condemnation.

[17] Like the House of Lords, or the much more recent (1867) Canadian Senate, the U.S. Senate until 1913 consisted of senators who were not popularly elected (they were elected by state legislatures).

[18] State laws, practices, and conventions vary widely, however. In a handful of states, chief prosecutors are not popularly elected and are organized at the state rather than county levels. In some states, judicial selection is handled under nonpartisan, merit selection procedures.

And, if criminal justice issues are openly politicized and polemicized in local elections of judges and prosecutors, it is not surprising that candidates for state and federal legislatures and governor and president do likewise.

The constitution of England and Wales dates partly from the Magna Carta (1215), when the central issue was the division of power between the monarchy and the nobility, and from the English Bill of Rights (1689) that punctuated the Glorious Revolution that brought William of Orange to the throne. Then the central issue again was the relative power of the monarchy and the political classes and the solution was Parliamentary Supremacy, the doctrine that the elected Parliament is supreme in all matters of governance. There is nothing in the Bill of Rights about fundamental liberties of citizens enforceable against the state, limits on governmental power, judicial independence, or separation of powers. The conventional theoretical justification given for Parliamentary Supremacy is that it effectuates representative democracy. The citizens elect the government, and to carry out its program, it must have unobstructed power. If the public disapproves, it can vote the government out of office in the next election.

The absence of a Bill of Rights or a system of separation of powers is not surprising. The main issue in contention in the Glorious Revolution was relations between the monarchy and the political classes 143 years before England established broad-based adult male suffrage in 1832. The revolution's aim was to confirm the power of the political classes by limiting the power of the monarch; the notion that the power of the political classes should also be limited was not on the agenda. The doctrine of separation of powers and the idea of an entrenched bill of individual rights were Enlightenment ideas that had not yet taken shape. As a result, there is neither in principle nor in practice a constitutional doctrine of separation of powers. The judiciary cannot review the constitutional adequacy of legislation or executive action.[19] The Lord Chancellor (the incumbent early in 2007, Lord Falconer, a one-time university roommate of Prime Minister Tony Blair) is simultaneously head of the judiciary, a member of the legislature (the House of Lords), and a member of the prime minister's cabinet. The

[19] Under the Human Rights Act 1998, the courts are empowered to decide whether British laws or practices comply with the European Convention of Human Rights, but not to issue remedial orders or strike down a law held to be not in compliance. Only the Parliament has power to revise or rescind noncompliant laws.

executive controls the House of Commons, and the highest court (also called the House of Lords) is part of that legislative chamber.

The problems of politicization and polemicization take a different shape in England than in America. The problem in America is that governmental structure was meant to tie officials closely to community needs and beliefs and democratic ideology celebrated the importance and influence of public opinion, even if it was ill-informed, mercurial, or mean-spirited. Drafters of the Constitution worried about the dangers of "mobocracy," but, with local notable exceptions, the problem did not fully take shape until late in the twentieth century when ubiquitous electronic and broadcast media meant that a horrible incident anywhere, and ensuing emotionalism, could sweep across an entire continent.

The situation in England is different. England and Wales suffers from having a unitary legal system, with the government, the bureaucracy, and the mass media in one place, London. A single horrifying incident anywhere in the country becomes a national cause célèbre, and government often appears to feel obliged to propose changes to national laws to assure that something similar does not happen again.

If the government of the day chooses to act illiberally and to politicize criminal justice policy, there are no competing governmental power centers to stop it. Of course, individual officials can speak out. Sometimes members of the House of Lords try to influence legislation, but the Lords' power is one only of delay. The House of Commons, controlled by the government, can always override the House of Lords. The Labour government, partly for cynical electoral reasons, chose in the early 1990s to politicize criminal justice policy (Windlesham 1987–96; Dunbar and Langdon 1998; Morgan and Downes 2007) and has adhered to that approach ever since. For reasons presumably ultimately known only to themselves, Tony Blair and a series of Home Secretaries (most radically David Blunkett and John Reid) have for a decade promoted unrelievedly repressive criminal justice policies in England (Tonry 2004*a*; Newburn, in this volume).[20] The centralization of governmental power in England, and the absence of competing

[20] Home Secretary David Blunkett, on learning that serial killer Harold Shipman had committed suicide in prison, commented, "You wake up and you receive a phone call telling you that Shipman has topped himself. And you think, is it too early to open a bottle?" (Charter et al. 2004).

power centers, make it possible for a determined government to do what it wants.

ii. *Elections and Individual Cases.* A second consequence of English and American constitutional structure is that politicians feel entitled to express views about the dispositions of individual cases. Sometimes, incredibly to lawyers in other countries, this extends literally to wanting to influence or make decisions about individual cases. The English Home Secretary, for as long as there has been a system of parole release, has claimed the right to decide personally when individual prisoners are released. During some periods since the 1960s, parole boards reviewed individual prisoners' petitions for release, but their decisions were recommendations to the Home Secretary, who could reject them. Probably most notoriously in recent years, until in each case the European Court ruled otherwise, both the Lord Chief Justice and the Home Secretary claimed the right to second-guess, and to increase, the sentences imposed by the trial judge on the two preteenage murderers in 1993 of two-year-old James Bulger (Green, in this volume).

More generally, legislators and executive branch officials in England and America (and less often those in Canada and Australia) feel entitled to propose and enact laws that prescribe sentences in individual cases, thereby removing the judge's authority to impose a sentence that is appropriate under all the circumstances. Such laws are much more common in America and include three-strikes laws in more than half the states, mandatory minimum sentence laws in all states (though they vary widely in scope), and mandatory sentencing guidelines in North Carolina (and until the U.S. Supreme Court held them unconstitutional, in the federal system). Such laws also exist in England, where two- and three-strikes laws were enacted in the Crime (Sentences) Act 1997 that prescribed mandatory minimum sentences for repeat burglaries, repeat violent crimes, and some drug trafficking offenses, and where murder is subject to a mandatory life sentence. Canadian and Australian legislators have dipped their toes in these waters, not deeply (Freiberg 2001; Webster and Doob, in this volume). Few other counties have.

Writing the preceding paragraph has led me finally to understand an argument that has heretofore escaped me. Andrew Ashworth (e.g., 2001) has several times attributed to English High Court judges the view that mandatory minimum sentence legislation is unconstitutional. Ashworth indicated his disagreement, arguing (inevitably, it seems to me, in a country characterized by Parliamentary Supremacy) that legislators inherently have power to set maximum sentences, which they have long exercised, and minimum sentences if they so choose. Ashworth noted that enacting a law of general scope was different from telling a judge what to do in an individual case. That seemed right to me, and inexorable. I could not understand what the judges could have meant. Now I think I do, and I suspect that judges in many other countries would agree with their English peers. In a country with an independent judiciary, judges must have the authority, under law, to find the facts of individual cases and to apply the applicable law to those facts and to determine an appropriate remedy. For an executive branch official, or a legislature, to direct a particular factual determination or a particular remedy in a case *sub judice* would fundamentally undermine the institution of an independent judiciary, substituting possibly self-interested political or policy considerations for impartial judicial ones. The step from that to a mandatory minimum sentence law is but a small one. Such a law tells the judge precisely what he or she should decide, irrespective of case-level circumstances, and does not allow impartial consideration within a framework of law of the most appropriate sentence in a particular case. Ashworth, I now think, is surely right as a matter of English constitutional law, but wrong as a matter of post-Enlightenment constitutional values.

No other Western countries have constitutions primarily designed to address political problems of the seventeenth and eighteenth centuries. All include entrenched bills of rights, and all reflect the influence of eighteenth-century ideas about governmental separation of powers. Most reflect a pluralistic twentieth-century world and call for electoral systems of proportional representation. Most are generally governed by multiparty coalitions. Most in Europe, Great Britain (including perforce England) being the notable exception, accept the European Convention of Human Rights as part of their national constitutional law and accept decisions of the European Court of Human Rights as binding and self-executing.[21] No major English-speaking or

[21] See n. 19. Although England and Wales is bound by treaty obligation to accept the court's rulings, they can be implemented only if the English government affirmatively acts to do so. An illustration may make the importance of this clear. If an American court ruled that particular conditions in a prison were unconstitutional, it would issue an order so declaring and a remedial order; the prison would be obliged to act on the order, an obligation the court could enforce if need be by exercise of its contempt powers. Were the European Court to declare the same conditions in a British prison a violation of the European Convention, the individual prison would not be obligated to comply if the

western European country but Switzerland has popular elections for prosecutors, and none hold popular elections for judges. The constitutional features of American and English government make both countries particularly susceptible to the wholesale politicization of criminal justice policy.

c. Mass Media Characteristics. Ubiquitous mass media are part of the twenty-first century as, to some degree at least everywhere, are sensationalistic media. David Green (in this volume; forthcoming) shows the different ways that Norwegian and English print media characteristics affected how those countries reacted to notorious killings of small children by slightly older children. In England, where the tabloid media are highly sensationalistic and openly and vigorously promote populist approaches to crime, the James Bulger story received front-page coverage for many days, on anniversaries of his death, and whenever developments occurred in the cases of his killers, including their releases from prison at age eighteen. In Norway, after Silje Redergård's killing, the media covered the story only for a few days, in a manner that was not sensationalistic, and did not return to the story later on.

Among characteristics that might explain the difference is that most Norwegian newspapers are sold by subscription rather than, as in England, from newsstands. As a consequence, there is less of a premium on eye- and attention-catching headlines and front-page pictures. Another distinguishing characteristic is that the leading Norwegian tabloid is much less sensational than those in England. The English tabloids (the *Sun*, the *Daily Mail*, the *Mirror*, the *News of the World*), which, though published in London, have national circulations like those of all other major English newspapers, have much the largest circulations in the country. They dwarf those of the "quality" broadsheets (*The Times*, the *Guardian*, the *Independent*, and the *Telegraph*). Since the early 1990s, Labour Party leaders have made it clear that they pay greatest attention to the tabloid papers and often regard them as valid indicators of popular attitudes and beliefs (Green, in this volume[22]).

---

contested conditions were in compliance with British law. As a practical matter, British governments do comply with European Court decisions, but carefully protecting the posture that compliance was a matter of choice.

[22] Green relates two anecdotes, based on published sources, of occasions when Tony Blair indicated that government in making policy should treat as true things a media-influenced public believed to be true, even when government information established that it was not (e.g., that crime is increasing when both official police data and victim survey data show it to be decreasing).

Media characteristics vary widely between countries. The remarkable and pernicious influence of the English tabloids on crime policy results from an interaction between the tabloid media's sensationalizing style and the Labour government's decision to pay particular attention to the tabloids and to attempt to win their support (Morgan and Downes 2007). It is not a coincidence that Blair's primary media advisor for nearly a decade was Alistair Campbell, a former political editor of the *Daily Mirror*. Because, as discussed below, governments in most Western countries rely more heavily on expert and professional opinion in formulating policy than the English government does (Tonry 2004*a*), most would likely not be as influenced by sensationalistic media (were their media as sensationalistic as England's, which at least for the countries discussed in this volume does not seem to be the case).

d. Anglo-Saxon Culture. Although it is not at all clear what it is about Anglo-Saxon culture that makes predominantly English-speaking countries especially punitive, they are. Not only does the United States lead the international imprisonment rate league tables for western European and English-speaking countries by a factor of five (more than 750 per 100,000 in 2007 compared with runners-up), but the runners-up in 2005 were New Zealand (186 per 100,000) and England (148 per 100,000) (Walmsley 2007). Canada and Australia, typically around 100–110 per 100,000, are lower but well above the levels of 60–80 per 100,000 that have characterized the Scandinavian countries since 1990 and the 80–90 that has long characterized Germany, Switzerland, France, and Belgium. The punitiveness of the Anglo-Saxon countries is confirmed by International Crime Victims Survey findings that have consistently shown since the initial wave of data collection in 1989 that respondents in the United States, England, Scotland, and Northern Ireland are substantially more severe in their punishment preferences than other Europeans or Canadians (van Dijk et al. 2007).

Possibly what appears to be the influence of Anglo-Saxon culture is something about constitutional structures or residual influence of historical British penal culture on its former colonies. Or it could be related to economies that are more capitalistic and political cultures that are less social democratic than those of most European countries. Or, it could have something to do with the Protestant religions with strong Calvinist overtones that were long influential. In this they share a common characteristic with the Netherlands, which is rapidly achieving the highest imprisonment rate among Western countries after the

English-speakers. Whatever it is, it is most conspicuously present when comparisons are made with Francophonic cultures.

e. Populist Conceptions of Democracy. In England, Labour government spokesmen and policy statements in recent years repeatedly promised to "rebalance the criminal justice system in favour of the victim" and reestablish "public confidence" (e.g., Home Office 2002, p. 14). Implicit in these catchphrases are implications that public opinion should importantly shape both what general policies are adopted and what punishments offenders receive. These are very different assertions, which I consider below.

Anthony Bottoms (1995) is commonly credited with coining the phrase "populist punitiveness," by which he seemed to mean to characterize a set of public attitudes that was more punitive toward crimes and less sympathetic toward offenders than in earlier times, and to which policy makers were, or at least felt, obliged to respond. More recently, other English-speaking academics (e.g., Ryan 2003; Loader 2006; Pratt 2007) have described an unbrave new world in which the public will no longer allow experts and professionals to play major roles in dealing with crime. The genie of populist punitiveness, "untutored public emotion toward crime and punishment," is out of the bottle, they suggest, and will not be put back (Loader 2006, p. 582). Loader, in an article about "Platonic guardians," his mocking term for liberal-minded English professionals who in earlier times played larger policy-making roles than they do now, suggests that populist policy approaches may not be a bad thing: "The idea that crime should be kept out of public life, safely handled by a coterie of experts, was and remains profoundly antidemocratic" (p. 582).[23]

Several things should be said about populist conceptions of democracy. The first is that, at least in a European context, Bottoms, Ryan, and Loader describe a distinctively British phenomenon (assuming, as they argue, that it exists there[24]). The practical import of populist views

[23] Strikingly, and oddly inconsistently, since the tenor of Loader's article is disparagement of "liberal elitism," and its efforts to insulate policy making from raw public emotion and electoral politics, in his penultimate sentence he warns that politicization of crime policy "is to play with passions that cannot easily be regulated, to foster expectations that are not easily sated, and to create spirals of outrage, desire, and disappointment that have the potential to overwhelm and undermine the institutional architecture of liberal democracy" (Loader 2006, p. 583).

[24] I provide evidence elsewhere that the Labour government's preoccupation with crime prevention and antisocial behavior has heightened public anxieties and dissatisfactions (Tonry 2004*a*); English populist punitiveness may be no more than the unintended reified

of penal policy concerns the relative weight to be given in policy making to public attitudes and opinions compared with professional knowledge and experience. In most Western countries, with England and the United States being the closest to exceptions, professional views matter and are seen as a legitimate basis for formulation of policy. As the essays in this volume on Belgium (Snacken), Canada (Webster and Doob), France (Lévy, Roché), and the four large Scandinavian countries (Lappi-Seppälä) make clear, policy makers in all those places continue, seemingly comfortably, to set policies largely in accordance with their professional judgments.

Second, in thinking about the degree to which public opinion is an appropriate element in criminal justice policy making, an important distinction needs to be made between general policies and decisions about particular cases. Few officials in any Western country would argue that public attitudes and beliefs are inappropriate considerations in setting general policies, within certain limits. Concerning decisions about individual cases, by contrast, few officials in any country would argue that consideration of public attitudes and beliefs is appropriate (England being a possible exception, as the history of the Bulger case suggests). A primary purpose behind the historical creation of professional courts and impartial judges was to shelter decisions in individual cases from the influence of public emotion and vigilantism. Even if "populist punitiveness" exists in some meaningful new way, most policy makers and practitioners in most countries believe that it has no role to play in deciding individual cases.

Third, a tension between citizens' rights and state powers has been evident since the Enlightenment, and most developed countries in many spheres are attempting to strengthen individual rights. The evolving role and broadening reach of the European Court and Convention of Human Rights exemplify this, as well as the work of the European Committee for the Prevention of Torture and Inhuman or Degrading Treatment or Punishment (Morgan 2001), the International Criminal Court, and numerous efforts to develop international declarations and covenants of rights.

Those developments reflect a view that, at day's end, the rights and interests of individual citizens should trump the political preferences

consequence of strategic political choices to make crime and punishment a government policy preoccupation.

of others who would disregard them. Just as policy makers in most developed countries had little compunction about abolishing capital punishment in the face of public opposition, there is no reason why government should rule by plebiscite when lesser but still inhumane penal impositions are in issue.

Rejecting the salience of plebiscite-type views of emotional subjects is not antidemocratic. Here is why. Ordinary citizens often see things in black and white that, had they more information, they would view in shades of grey. This is Dan Yankelovich's (1991) distinction between public opinion (top-of-the-head opinions elicited by pollsters' suppertime phone calls) and public judgment (what people believe when they have adequate information and opportunity to consider opposing viewpoints and arguments). Citizens' views about crime and punishment, often emotional, exemplify public opinion when public judgment is what is needed. This is a major justification for institutions of representative government. That many European countries, and Canada, have managed more successfully than the United States and England to insulate criminal justice policy making, and decisions in individual cases, from the force of raw public opinion is a major reason why their policies are less punitive and more humane.

2. *Statistical Analyses.* A different way to search for explanations is to develop plausible hypotheses of relations between national characteristics and differences in punitiveness and then look for quantitative measures of those characteristics. Ken Pease (1991) was one of the first to do this and concluded that higher national imprisonment rates were associated with larger degrees of income inequality. A later analysis by Katherine Beckett and Bruce Western (2001) reached similar results in comparisons of welfare spending and imprisonment rates of American states. A number of theories might support these findings: greater inequalities in income might produce greater status differentiation and with it greater selfishness among the privileged and less sympathy with people in socially distant social strata. Or, greater status differentiation might undermine social solidarity and thus produce a greater need to rely on legal threats rather than informal social control to regulate behavior.

Two more recent studies have tested a wider range of hypotheses and variables (Downes and Hansen 2006; Lappi-Seppälä, forthcoming). Both confirmed Pease's findings that greater income inequality within a country is associated with higher imprisonment rates. They also found that higher imprisonment rates were associated with lower levels of welfare spending, lower levels of trust in fellow citizens, and lower public perceptions of the legitimacy of the legal system.

C. Protective Factors

Prominent protective factors include consensus political systems, nonpartisan judges and prosecutors, Francophonic political cultures, and a predominant view that criminal justice policy falls appropriately within the province of expert knowledge and professional experience. David J. Smith in personal communication has advised that developmentalists do not see risk and protective factors simply as reciprocals (as "having attention deficit disorder" and "not having attention deficit disorder" might be thought to be). The four protective factors I identify here do not fall prey to that objection. Francophonic and Anglo-Saxon cultures are patently not opposites: no one would regard "not Francophonic" and Anglo-Saxon as synonyms. Consensus and conflict political cultures and populist and expert-based policy processes are poles on continuums containing a range of possibilities. The difference between elected (or politically selected) noncareer officials and meritocratically chosen career officials is far from being the same as "*A*" and "not *A*."

1. *Consensus Political Cultures.* No country offers a pure case of a consensus or conflict political culture, but as Lijphart's (1999) descriptions of individual countries' governmental arrangements make clear, some countries, especially in northern and western Europe, have much more consensus-based processes than others. In none of those countries has crime control become a recurring or defining partisan political issue, and in none has a felt need emerged as in the United States and England for major parties to address perceived popular anger by means of wholesale adoption of expressive tough-on-crime policies.

The Netherlands is the most interesting country along this dimension. It has long been an exemplar of a consensus-based political culture. Although governmental policy documents beginning in the mid-1980s regularly alluded to public anxieties about crime and public dissatisfaction with the criminal justice system's "leniency" (Downes and van Swaaningen 2007), the imprisonment rate has risen steadily for a third of a century without enactment of new sentencing laws meant to accomplish that, and without crime becoming a major partisan political issue. Whatever has happened in the Netherlands has operated osmotically. The criminal justice system has become incrementally more severe over an extended period. Practitioners at each stage appear to have become harsher: police more likely to refer cases for prosecution, prosecutors more often to insist on a negotiated settlement (a "transaction") or to initiate court proceedings, judges more often to impose prisons sentences and for longer terms (Tak 2001). In contrast to England and the United States, where steadily harshening policies and practices produced steep increases in imprisonment, changed practices almost alone did the job in the Netherlands. No one has as yet fully and convincingly explained what happened (though Downes [in this volume] and Downes and van Swaaningen [2007] have made important beginnings).

A protective factor is not a guarantee, as the Netherlands case demonstrates. It makes an undesirable outcome less likely.

2. *Professional Cadres.* Only in the United States are judges and prosecutors elected or selected according to openly partisan criteria or are those roles structured in ways that make officials strongly susceptible to influence by public opinions and emotions. In most civil-law countries, judges and prosecutors are career civil servants who select those career paths while in university law schools and immediately upon graduation start work. Individuals may have careers as judges or as prosecutors only, or occasionally change track. The more talented or successful gradually move up career ladders and when they reach positions of substantial authority have spent a professional lifetime absorbing norms of professionalism, political nonpartisanship, and impartiality.

In European countries not following the professional civil servant model, conventions of political neutrality and professional impartiality are strong. In Belgium and Switzerland, for example, many judges are selected by the Parliament, but professional norms of independence and impartiality are strong. In Canada, judges are appointed according to meritocratic criteria in processes that include nonpartisan screening committees. In England, judges and prosecutors receive no specialized legal training in their university courses. Prosecutors are national civil servants who tend to enter the Crown Prosecution Service early in their careers. Judges are selected through nonpartisan screening processes. Both professions under the prevailing professional legal culture are rigorously nonpolitical.

Those nonpartisan, nonpolitical appointment processes conduce to impartiality and independence. By contrast, the methods by which American judges and prosecutors are selected carry large risks of politicization. Chief prosecutors must always worry about the effects of notorious cases or controversial policies on their reelection prospects (lest their opponents have evidence to support charges of being soft on crime). Elected judges, usually less acutely, face similar risks. Many prosecutors and judges aspire to election or appointment to higher or more powerful roles and must be sensitive to the impressions they create in the minds of people in positions to advance or impede their upward progress. The dangers that prosecutorial policies will be based on election promises, opinion surveys, or focus groups are not small. Nor is the risk that decisions in individual cases will be affected by what the judge or prosecutor believes to be his or her professional or personal self interest.

3. *Francophonic Culture.* It is striking that the three French-speaking areas discussed in the essays in this volume (France, Francophonic Belgium, and Quebec) are all places characterized by comparatively mild penal policies. In none of them is populist punitiveness a force to be reckoned with, and none of them has adopted conspicuously harsh or primarily expressive policies.

Quebec's sentencing practices for adults are among the least punitive in Canada, and its practices toward young offenders are the least punitive (Doob and Sprott 2004; Doob and Webster 2006). Canada's relatively stable penal policies and imprisonment rates over recent decades are sometimes attributed in part to the influence in Ottawa of the Quebecois. Criminal and criminal procedure codes in Canada are national, though enforcement and implementation are provincial. Because they will apply to Quebec and Canadian national politics has been haunted for decades by the specter of possible Quebec secession, it is not hard to understand why strong Quebecois preferences are taken seriously.

The role of the French-speaking Walloons in Belgium is similar. Belgium is a country in which the roles of experts are large and in which policies have not become greatly more punitive. Within, however, that relatively benign climate, the Walloons appear to be less punitive that the Dutch-speaking Flemish. Sonja Snacken (in this volume) gives an example. When national law authorized and funded agencies to look after victims' interests, the Flemish created an agency in 1985 to address victims' services and needs. In 1989 the Walloons created combined victims' and offenders' services centers. In 1994 the Dutch-speaking authority changed course and adopted the French speakers' more inclusive approach.

France, for another example, has adopted, though seldom applied, some tougher sentencing laws, but it has also developed a wide range of diversion and alternatives programs, abolished the death penalty, made its juvenile system less punitive, and experienced only a slight increase in its imprisonment rate over the past thirty years (Roché, in this volume). The best example, however, of French exceptionalism is the long-established practice of promulgation of wide-based amnesties and pardons at times of national celebration (presidential inaugurations; national holidays such as the 200th anniversary of the storming of the Bastille) (Lévy, in this volume). Sometimes thousands of people are pardoned or released from prison and the imprisonment rate falls by 10 or 20 percent in a short period. Such practices would be unthinkable in many countries. Some would condemn them for arbitrarily freeing offenders from the appropriate and morally deserved consequences of their crimes. Others would fault the unfairness of punishing some offenders less severely than their like-situated brethren. Presumably French men and women just shrug.

4. *Expert-Informed Policy Processes.* Criminal justice is a potentially more tumultuous policy subject than most. People have strong views about health, education, or transportation policies, of course, but usually for immediately self-interested or general disinterested reasons. Criminal justice is different because it involves horrifying incidents, innocent victims, and sometimes seriously unappealing or frightening offenders. Together these can provoke powerful emotions, moral panics, and waves of public vindictiveness and outrage. Everyone knows that people affected by powerful emotions sometimes overreact or behave in ways they later regret. Actions taken under the influence of vengeful or vindictive sentiments likewise, everyone knows, are often regretted. Moral panics produce everything from unjust laws to ill-considered practices to unjust actions. These are all reasons why every account of the development of state legal systems stresses their aims to remove cases from the immediate influence of private emotion and to assure that cases be dealt with impartially and dispassionately under established laws and procedures. That is why images such as blind justice and ideals such as impartial justice exist.

Vigilante justice is self-evidently wrong because its actions are too often ill-considered, impulsive, and excessive. And when powerful emotions are let loose, the people punished by vigilantes are too often the wrong people. Lynch mobs seldom exercise due diligence.

The same logic applies to policy making. From Kai Ericson's (1966) classic account of the Salem witch trials through Stanley Cohen's (1972) account of the Clacton "riots" to Philip Jenkins's accounts (1998) of recurring panics about child sexual abuse, the literature on moral panics shows how overwrought lawmakers and officials sometimes act unwisely and unjustly under the influence of powerful emotion. Waves of emotion can pass through a community or a country and policy makers can lose their heads.

Countries in which experts and professionals play major roles in policy making, such as most of those in western and northern Europe, are less likely to adopt highly punitive policies in general or during waves of emotional reaction to a horrible incident, than countries in which expert and professional voices have become less influential.

IV. Learning More, Doing Better

The determinants of changes in penal policies are complex and contingent. Most broad explanatory claims are wrong. Most of what is said that is sensible, and can be said, however, is anecdotal and impressionistic. This final section suggests a number of things that might be done to make our inquiries more systematic and our generalizations better grounded.

First, the effort to explain the emergence of a ubiquitous, monolithic "new punitiveness" or "punitive turn" (Brown 2005, p. 282) needs to be replaced with efforts to explain many things. As most of the essays in this volume demonstrate, lots of different things pointing in different directions are happening in lots of places, and the explanations for them cannot be the same. However, several essays in a recent collection on "the new punitiveness" (Pratt et al. 2005) contain statements like this: "The most theoretically sophisticated explanations for this punitive turn and the rapid increase in imprisonment rates across the West have increasingly looked to more general changes in social, political, economic, and cultural organization rather than to any specific forces confined to criminal justice sphere, in short to the conditions of life in 'late modernity'" (Brown 2005, p. 27). As the essays in this volume, and several in the Pratt et al. (2005) volume itself (e.g., Bondeson 2005;

Meyer and O'Malley 2005; Nelken 2005) make clear, in many countries no dramatic "punitive turn" has been taken and imprisonment rates have not risen rapidly. Better answers are unlikely to emerge until we start to ask better questions.

Second, much of the armchair "theoretical" writing on changes in penal policy is useless, assuming that a "punitive turn" has occurred, which it then tries to explain without bothering to establish whether policies and practices have changed and in what ways. David Garland's work (e.g., 2001) has inspired much armchair theorizing. While no informed person would deny that Garland's writing is insightful and provocative, there are few David Garlands. A recent exchange in *Punishment and Society* between Bryan Hogeveen (2005, 2006) and Anthony Doob and Jane Sprott (2006*a*, 2006*b*) is illustrative. Hogeveen discussed "how the [social construction of the] punishable young offender has been manifest in, and governed through, increasingly harsh penalties, austere punishments and high rates of incarceration" and how the Canadian government in the late 1990s sought to denounce "youth crime through tougher youth justice legislation (the Youth Criminal Justice Act)" (2005, p. 73). Hogeveen made a number of empirical claims: "The punishable young offender was manifest in harsher sentences meted out for juvenile deviance" (p. 80); "throughout the 1980s and the 1990s Canada's rate of incarceration for young offenders continued to climb" (p. 81); "from 1991 to 1997 while American rates for incarceration were remaining relatively stable, Canadian rates were steadily increasing" (p. 81); "with few exceptions, during the 1990s Canadian youth justice moved in the direction of greater punitiveness as reflected in increasing rates of imprisonment and harsher penalties for the most serious and violent young offenders" (p. 86). None of those assertions is empirically demonstrable, raising some question as to what exactly it was that Hogeveen attempted to explain.

Doob and Sprott showed that none of Hogeveen's empirical assertions were accurate: "Hogeveen's empirical assertions were without empirical foundation. There are no data in either of his two articles (Hogeveen 2005, this issue [2006]) (or anywhere else that we know of) that support his assertions that sentences got harsher during the late 1990s or that the rate of incarceration of youth increased during this period for offenders generally or for the most serious and violent offenders" (2006*a*, p. 478). Time, energy, and paper would be much better expended on trying to understand and explain real developments in the real world.

Third, if we want to understand why particular policies and practices emerge in particular places at particular times, we will need much more nuanced accounts of what has happened and much more imaginative efforts to explain why (e.g., Brodeur, in this volume). Explanations will not be found in rising crime rates, globalization, ontological insecurity, late modernity, or postmodernist angst. They explain too much and therefore too little. Adequate explanations will need to look at a wide range of developments that need explaining (table 2 includes many candidates). When a wide range of factors is taken into account, differences between countries become clearer. When incarceration rates are used as the sole indicator of increased punitiveness, the United States stands alone with New Zealand (Pratt and Clark 2005; Pratt 2006), England, and the Netherlands far behind but still well above the rates of most of western Europe.[25] When all the factors in table 2 are considered, however, England[26] stands alone after the United States in increasing punitiveness by nearly every policy measure except capital punishment—mandatory sentences, longer sentences, more pretrial detention, increased processing of young offenders in adult courts, more punitive alternatives, and weakened procedural protections (Tonry 2004*a*). Canada and the Netherlands, by contrast, have adopted fewer punitive policies, and some of those adopted—for example, concerning juveniles—have not produced more punitive practices.

A new generation of comparative studies will have to go deeper in trying to explain why countries differ in important respects that seem to shape their penal policies. Matters of constitutional structure, for example, partly explain why the United States and England have adopted much more repressive policies than many other countries. In times of recurring moral panics about crime and drugs, America's system of dispersed governmental powers, election of judges and prosecutors, and frequent legislative elections made policy makers susceptible to powerful influence by transient but widely shared public

[25] Because most of the exiguous literature concerns western Europe and the Anglophonic common-law countries, and because they share many common cultural, economic, and historical characteristics, the text of this essay is limited to them. In recent decades, Russia and South Africa have had imprisonment rates from 350 to 550 per 100,000; eastern European rates generally vary between 150 and 300 per 100,000; and those in most Asian countries vary between 20 and 50 per 100,000.

[26] New Zealand possibly also, it appears (Pratt 2006, 2007).

emotions. Thirty-five years of "law and order" and an imprisonment rate of 750 per 100,000 are among the results. Switzerland, however, also has a system of widely dispersed governmental authority, elects prosecutors at local elections, and holds frequent legislative elections and policy referenda, but has experienced broadly stable penal policies and practices over several decades

The English Labour government's decision to adopt and implement a wide range of increasingly punitive policies and practices over the past decade was made much easier by the concentration of political power in England and Wales. That, however, cannot be the whole answer. If a concentrated system of political power is part of the English explanation and dispersed political power is part of the American, other important influences must be at work.

The Netherlands and Belgium provide a similar contrast. In neither country has law-and-order politics had powerful influence and in neither country have policies become pronouncedly harsher. The two countries share similar distributions of political power and governmental authority. Yet imprisonment rates, in particular, and a wide range of practices became progressively harsher over three decades in the Netherlands, and imprisonment rates rose as much in percentage terms after 1973 as in the United States. Belgium, by contrast, maintained broadly stable penal policies and practices.

Cultural and other normative explanations must explain why the United States and Switzerland have adopted such different policies and experienced such different practices, and why the Dutch and Belgian penal policy stories are so different. Explanations may be found in distinctive features of national history and culture, in the influence of particular systems of religious belief, or, following Lijphart (1999), in political culture.

Risk and protective factors are no more destinies for countries than for individuals. Distributions of political power and governmental authority, constitutional structure, media characteristics, career professionals, and deference to expert knowledge do not produce particular results. They make them more or less likely. We could understand a good bit more about these things than we now do.

Winston Churchill nearly a century ago (in 1910) observed:

> The mood and temper of the public in regard to the treatment of crime and criminals is one of the most unfailing tests of any country. A calm, dispassionate recognition of the rights of the accused

> and even of the convicted criminal, . . . tireless efforts towards the discovery of curative and re-generative processes; unfailing faith that there is a treasure, if you can only find it, in the heart of every man. These are the symbols which, in the treatment of crime and the criminal, mark and measure the stored-up strength of a nation, and are the sign and proof of the living virtue within it. (Quoted in Radzinowicz and Hood 1986, p. 774)

Countries differ widely in how they respond to crime and criminals. We can learn much more about why they differ and maybe provide insights that may help some countries better mark their stored-up strength and better prove their living virtue.

REFERENCES

Aebi, Marcelo F., Kauko Aromaa, Bruno Aubusson de Cavarlay, Gordon Barclay, Beata Gruszczyñska, Hanns von Hofer, Vasilika Hysi, Jörg-Martin Jehle, Martin Killias, Paul Smit, and Cynthia Tavares. 2006. *The European Sourcebook of Crime and Criminal Justice Statistics—2006*. The Hague: Boom Juridische uitgevers.

Aebi, Marcelo, and Natalia Stadnic. 2007. *Council of Europe SPACE 1: 2005 Survey on Prison Populations*. Document PC-CP (2007) 2. Strasbourg: Council of Europe.

Albrecht, Hans-Jorg. 2001. "Post-adjudication Dispositions in Comparative Perspective." In *Sentencing and Sanctions in Western Countries*, edited by Michael Tonry and Richard S. Frase. New York: Oxford University Press.

Armstrong, Sarah, and Leslie McAra, eds. 2006. *Perspectives on Punishment: The Contours of Control*. Oxford: Oxford University Press.

Ashworth, Andrew. 2001. "The Decline of English Sentencing and Other Stories." In *Sentencing and Sanctions in Western Countries*, edited by Michael Tonry and Richard S. Frase. New York: Oxford University Press.

Beckett, Katherine, and Bruce Western. 2001. "Governing Social Marginality." In *Mass Imprisonment: Causes and Consequences*, edited by David Garland. London: Sage.

Bennett, William J., John J. DiIulio, and John P. Walters. 1996. *Body Count: Moral Poverty and How to Win America's War against Crime and Drugs*. New York: Simon and Schuster.

Blumstein, Alfred, and Allen J. Beck. 1999. "Population Growth in U.S. Prisons, 1980–1996." In *Prisons*, edited by Michael Tonry and Joan Petersilia. Vol. 26 of *Crime and Justice: A Review of Research*, edited by Michael Tonry. Chicago: University of Chicago Press.

Blumstein, Alfred, and Jacqueline Cohen. 1973. "A Theory of the Stability of Punishment." *Journal of Criminal Law and Criminology* 64:198–207.

Bondeson, Ulla V. 2005. "Levels of Punitiveness in Scandinavia: Description and Explanation." In *The New Punitiveness—Trends, Theories, Perspectives*, edited by John Pratt, David Brown, Mark Brown, Simon Hallsworth, and Wayne Morrison. Cullompton, Devon, UK: Willan.

Bottoms, Anthony E. 1995. "The Philosophy and Politics of Punishment and Sentencing." In *The Politics of Sentencing Reform*, edited by Chris Clarkson and Rod Morgan. Oxford: Oxford University Press.

Boutellier, Hans. 2005. *The Safety Utopia: Contemporary Discontent and Desire as to Crime and Punishment*. Dordrecht: Kluwer.

Brodeur, Jean-Paul. In this volume. "Comparative Penology in Perspective."

Brown, David. 2005. "Continuity, Rupture, or Just More of the 'Volatile and Contradictory'? Glimpses of New South Wales' Penal Practice behind and through the Discursive." In *The New Punitiveness—Trends, Theories, Perspectives*, edited by John Pratt, David Brown, Mark Brown, Simon Hallsworth, and Wayne Morrison. Cullompton, Devon, UK: Willan.

Buruma, Ybo. 2005. *De dreigingsspiraal: Onbedoelde neveneffecten van misdaadbestrijding* [The spiral of threat: Unintended consequences of the war on crime]. The Hague: Boom Juridische uitgevers.

Cavadino, Michael, and James Dignan. 2005. *Penal Systems: A Comparative Approach*. London: Sage.

Charter, David, Stewart Tendler, Greg Hurst, and Michael Horsnell. 2004. "Blunkett's Early Joy on Shipman Suicide." *The Times* (January 17).

Christie, Nils. 1968. "Changes in Penal Value." In *Scandinavian Studies in Criminology*, edited by Nils Christie. London: Tavistock.

Clarkson, Chris, and Rod Morgan, eds. 1995. *The Politics of Sentencing Reform*. Oxford: Oxford University Press

Cohen, Stanley. 1972. *Folk Devils and Moral Panics*. New York: St. Martin's.

Cruickshanks, Eveline. 2000. *The Glorious Revolution*. New York: St. Martin's.

Deković, M. 1999. "Risk and Protective Factors in the Development of Problem Behavior during Adolescence." *Journal of Youth and Adolescence* 28(6): 667–85.

Doob, Anthony N., and Jane B. Sprott. 2004. "Youth Justice in Canada." In *Youth Crime and Youth Justice: Comparative and Cross-National Perspectives*, edited by Michael Tonry and Anthony N. Doob. Vol. 31 of *Crime and Justice: A Review of Research*, edited by Michael Tonry. Chicago: University of Chicago Press.

———. 2006*a*. "Assessing Punitiveness in Canadian Youth Justice." *Punishment and Society* 8(4):477–80.

———. 2006*b*. "Punishing Youth Crime in Canada: The Blind Men and the Elephant." *Punishment and Society* 8(2): 223–33.

Doob, Anthony N., and Cheryl Marie Webster. 2006. "Countering Punitiveness: Understanding Stability in Canada's Imprisonment Rate." *Law and Society Review* 40(2):325–68.

Downes, David. 1988. *Contrasts in Tolerance: Post-war Penal Policies in the Netherlands and England and Wales.* Oxford: Clarendon.

———. In this volume. "Visions of Penal Control in the Netherlands."

Downes, David, and K. Hansen. 2006. "Welfare and Punishment in Comparative Perspective." In *Perspectives on Punishment: The Contours of Control*, edited by Sarah Armstrong and Leslie McAra. Oxford: Oxford University Press.

Downes, David, and René van Swaaningen. 2007. "The Road to Dystopia? Changes in the Penal Climate of the Netherlands." In *Crime and Justice in the Netherlands*, edited by Michael Tonry and Catrien Bijleveld. Vol. 35 of *Crime and Justice: A Review of Research*, edited by Michael Tonry. Chicago: University of Chicago Press.

Dunbar, Ian, and A. Langdon. 1998. *Tough Justice—Sentencing and Penal Policies in the 1990s.* London: Blackstone.

Ericson, Kai T. 1966. *Wayward Puritans: A Study in the Sociology of Deviance.* New York: Wiley.

Faulkner, David. 2002. *Crime, Citizen, and State.* 2nd ed. London: Waterside.

Freiberg, Arie. 2001. "Three Strikes and You're Out—It's Not Cricket: Colonization and Resistance in Australian Sentencing." In *Sentencing and Sanctions in Western Countries*, edited by Michael Tonry and Richard S. Frase. New York: Oxford University Press.

Garland, David. 1996. "The Limits of the Sovereign State: Strategies of Crime Control in Contemporary Society." *British Journal of Criminology* 36:445–71.

———. 2001. *The Culture of Control.* Chicago: University of Chicago Press.

Gottschalk, Marie. 2006. *The Prison and the Gallows: The Politics of Mass Incarceration in America.* New York: Cambridge University Press.

Green, David. In this volume. "Comparing Penal Cultures: Child-on-Child Homicide in England and Norway."

———. Forthcoming. *Political Culture and Penal Populism: When Children Kill Children.* Oxford: Oxford University Press.

Harcourt, Bernard. 2006. "From the Asylum to the Prison: Rethinking the Incarceration Revolution." *Texas Law Review* 84:1751–85.

Hogeveen, Bryan R. 2005. "'If We Are Tough on Crime, if We Punish Crime, Then People Get the Message': Constructing and Governing the Punishable Young Offender in Canada during the Late 1990s." *Punishment and Society* 7(1):73–89.

———. 2006. "Memoir of a/the Blind: A Reply to Doob and Sprott." *Punishment and Society* 8(4):469–75.

Home Office. 2002. *Justice for All.* Cm 5563. London: H.M. Stationery Office.

Ifill, Gwen. 1991. "Senate's Rule for Its Anti-crime Bill: The Tougher the Provision, the Better." *New York Times* (July 8; national ed.), p. A6.

Jenkins, Philip. 1998. *Moral Panic: Changing Concepts of the Child Molester in Modern America.* New Haven, CT: Yale University Press.

Johnson, David. In this volume. "Crime and Punishment in Contemporary Japan."

Jones, Trevor, and Tim Newburn. 2006. *Policy Transfer and Criminal Justice.* Milton Keynes, UK: Open University Press.

Junger-Tas, Josine. 2004. "Youth Justice in the Netherlands." In *Youth Crime and Youth Justice: Comparative and Cross-National Perspectives*, edited by Michael Tonry and Anthony N. Doob. Vol. 31 of *Crime and Justice: A Review of Research*, edited by Michael Tonry. Chicago: University of Chicago Press.

Killias, Martin. 1991. *Introduction to Criminology*. Berne: Stämpfli.

Kommer, Max. 1994. "Punitiveness in Europe: A Comparison." *European Journal of Criminal Policy and Research* 2(1):29–43.

———. 2004. "Punitiveness in Europe Revisited." *Criminology in Europe* 3(1): 1, 8–12.

Kurki, Leena. 2001. "International Standards for Sentencing and Punishment." In *Sentencing and Sanctions in Western Countries*, edited by Michael Tonry and Richard S. Frase. New York: Oxford University Press.

Lappi-Seppälä, Tapio. In this volume. "Penal Policy in Scandinavia."

———. Forthcoming. "Explaining National Differences in Punitiveness." In *Crime and Justice: A Review of Research*, vol. 37, edited by Michael Tonry. Chicago: University of Chicago Press.

Lévy, René. In this volume. "Pardons and Amnesties as Policy Instruments in Contemporary France."

Lewis, Clive Staples. 1970. *God in the Dock*, edited by Walter Hooper. Grand Rapids, MI: Eerdmans.

Lijphart, Arend. 1984. *Democracies: Patterns of Majoritarian and Consensus Government in Twenty-one Countries*. New Haven, CT: Yale University Press.

———. 1999. *Patterns of Democracy: Government Forms and Performance in Thirty-six Countries*. New Haven, CT: Yale University Press.

Loader, Ian. 2006. "Fall of the Platonic Guardians: Liberalism, Criminology, and Political Responses to Crime in England and Wales." *British Journal of Criminology* 46(4):561–86.

Meyer, Jeffrey, and Pat O'Malley. 2005. "Missing the Punitive Turn: Canadian Criminal Justice, 'Balance,' and Penal Modernism." In *The New Punitiveness—Trends, Theories, Perspectives*, edited by John Pratt, David Brown, Mark Brown, Simon Hallsworth, and Wayne Morrison. Cullompton, Devon, UK: Willan.

Morgan, Rod. 2001. "International Controls on Sentencing and Punishment." In *Sentencing and Sanctions in Western Countries*, edited by Michael Tonry and Richard S. Frase. New York: Oxford University Press.

———. 2006. "With Respect to Order, the Rules of the Game Have Changed: New Labour's Dominance of the 'Law and Order' Agenda." In *The Politics of Crime Control: Essays in Honour of David Downes*, edited by Tim Newburn and Paul Rock. Oxford: Oxford University Press.

Morgan, Rod, and David Downes. 2007. "The Skeletons in the Cupboard: The Politics of Law and Order at the Turn of the Millennium." In *The Oxford Handbook of Criminology*, 4th ed., edited by Mike Maguire, Rod Morgan, and Roy King. Oxford: Oxford University Press.

Mullet, Charles F. 1966. *Fundamental Law and the American Revolution 1760–1776*. New York: Octagon Books.

Nelken, David. 2005. "When Is a Society Non-punitive? The Italian Case." In *The New Punitiveness—Trends, Theories, Perspectives*, edited by John Pratt, David Brown, Mark Brown, Simon Hallsworth, and Wayne Morrison. Cullompton, Devon, UK: Willan.

Newburn, Tim. 2006. "Contrasts in Intolerance: Cultures of Control in the United States and Britain." In *The Politics of Crime Control: Essays in Honour of David Downes*, edited by Tim Newburn and Paul Rock. Oxford: Oxford University Press.

———. In this volume. "'Tough on Crime': Penal Policy in England and Wales."

Newburn, Tim, and Paul Rock, eds. 2006. *The Politics of Crime Control: Essays in Honour of David Downes*. Oxford: Oxford University Press.

Pease, Ken. 1991. "Punishment Demand and Punishment Numbers." In *Policy and Theory in Criminal Justice*, edited by D. M. Gottfredson and R. V. Clarke. Aldershot, UK: Gower.

Pratt, John. 2006. "The Dark Side of Paradise: Explaining New Zealand's History of High Imprisonment." *British Journal of Criminology* 46(4):541–60.

———. 2007. *Penal Populism*. London: Routledge.

Pratt, John, David Brown, Mark Brown, Simon Hallsworth, and Wayne Morrison, eds. 2005. *The New Punitiveness—Trends, Theories, Perspectives*. Cullompton, Devon, UK: Willan.

Pratt, John, and Marie Clark. 2005. "Penal Populism in New Zealand." *Punishment and Society* 7(3):303–22.

Radzinowicz, Leon, and Roger Hood. 1986. *A History of English Criminal Law and Its Administration from 1750*. London: Stevens & Sons.

Roché, Sebastian. 2006. *Le Frisson de L'emeute: Violences urbaines et banlieues*. Paris: Seuil.

———. In this volume. "Criminal Justice Policy in France: Illusions of Severity."

Ryan, Mick. 2003. *Penal Policy and Political Culture in England and Wales*. Winchester, UK: Waterside.

Sameroff, A. J. 1998. "Environmental Risk Factors in Infancy." *Pediatrics* 102(5):1287–92.

Savelsberg, Joachim. 1994. "Knowledge, Domination, and Criminal Punishment." *American Journal of Sociology* 99(4):911–43.

Simon, Jonathan. 2007. *Governing through Crime: How the War on Crime Transformed American Democracy and Created a Culture of Fear*. New York: Oxford University Press.

Snacken, Sonja. 2005. "Reductionist Penal Policy and European Human Rights Standards." Paper presented at the fifth annual meeting of the European Society of Criminology, Krakow, August 31–September 3.

———. In this volume. "Penal Policy and Practice in Belgium."

Speck, W. A. 1988. *Reluctant Revolutionaries: Englishmen and the Revolution of 1688*. New York: Oxford University Press.

Stouthamer-Loeber, M., R. Loeber, E. Wei, D. P. Farrington, and P. H. Wikström. 2002. "Risk and Promotive Effects in the Explanation of Persistent Serious Delinquency in Boys." *Journal of Consulting and Clinical Psychology* 70(1):111–23.

Tak, Peter J. 2001. "Sentencing and Punishment in the Netherlands." In *Sentencing and Sanctions in Western Countries*, edited by Michael Tonry and Richard S. Frase. New York: Oxford University Press.

Tonry, Michael. 1996. *Sentencing Matters*. New York: Oxford University Press.

———. 1999. "Parochialism in American Sentencing Policy." *Crime and Delinquency* 45(1):48–65.

———. 2004*a*. *Punishment and Politics: Evidence and Emulation in the Making of English Crime Control Policy*. Cullompton, Devon, UK: Willan.

———. 2004*b*. *Thinking about Crime: Sense and Sensibility in American Penal Culture*. New York: Oxford University Press.

Tonry, Michael, and Catrien Bijleveld. 2007. "Crime, Criminal Justice, and Criminology in the Netherlands." In *Crime and Justice in the Netherlands*, edited by Michael Tonry and Catrien Bijleveld. Vol. 35 of *Crime and Justice: A Review of Research*, edited by Michael Tonry. Chicago: University of Chicago Press.

Tonry, Michael, and Anthony N. Doob, eds. 2004. *Youth Crime and Youth Justice: Comparative and Cross-National Perspectives*. Vol. 31 of *Crime and Justice: A Review of Research*, edited by Michael Tonry. Chicago: University of Chicago Press.

Tonry, Michael, and David P. Farrington, eds. 2005. *Crime and Punishment in Western Countries, 1980–1999*. Vol. 33 of *Crime and Justice: A Review of Research*, edited by Michael Tonry. Chicago: University of Chicago Press.

Tonry, Michael, and Richard S. Frase, eds. 2001. *Sentencing and Sanctions in Western Countries*. New York: Oxford University Press.

van Dijk, Jan, Robert Manchin, John van Kesteren, and Gegerly Hideg. 2007. *The Burden of Crime in the EU*. Tilburg, Netherlands: Tilburg University, INTERVICT.

van Kesteren, John, Pat Mayhew, and Paul Nieuwbeerta. 2001. *Criminal Victimisation in Seventeen Industrialised Countries: Key Findings from the 2000 International Crime Victims Survey*. The Hague: WODC.

van Ruller, Sibo, and Guillaume Beijers. 1995. "Degerangenisstatistick in het licht van de geschiedenis" [Prison statistics in historical perspective]. *Justitiële Verkenningen* 21:35–52.

Walmsley, Roy. 2007. *World Prison Population List*. 7th ed. London: International Center for Prison Studies.

Webster, Cheryl Marie, and Anthony N. Doob. In this volume. "Punitive Trends and Stable Imprisonment Rates in Canada."

Weigend, Thomas. 2001. "Sentencing and Punishment in Germany." In *Sentencing and Sanctions in Western Countries*, edited by Michael Tonry and Richard S. Frase. New York: Oxford University Press.

Whitman, James Q. 2003. *Harsh Justice*. New York: Oxford University Press.

Williams, Glyn, and John Ramsden. 1990. *Ruling Britannia: The Political History of Britain 1688–1988*. New York: Longman.

Wilson, James Q. 1983. *Thinking about Crime*. Rev. ed. New York: Basic Books. (Originally published 1976.)

Windlesham, Lord David. 1987–96. *Responses to Crime*. Vols. 1–3. Oxford: Oxford University Press.

———. 1998. *Politics, Punishment, and Populism*. New York: Oxford University Press.

Wood, Gordon S. 1969. *The Creation of the American Republic 1776–1787*. Chapel Hill: University of North Carolina Press.

Yankelovich, Dan. 1991. *Coming to Public Judgment: Making Democracy Work in a Complex World*. Syracuse, NY: Syracuse University Press.

Young, Warren, and Mark Brown. 1993. "Cross National Comparisons of Imprisonment." In *Crime and Justice: A Review of Research*, vol. 17, edited by Michael Tonry. Chicago: University of Chicago Press.

Zimring, Franklin E., Gordon Hawkins, and Sam Kamin. 2001. *Punishment and Democracy: Three Strikes and You're Out in California*. New York: Oxford University Press.

Part III
American Penal Policy

[7] Sense and Sensibility in American Penal Culture

In searching for ways to address rising crime rates in the final third of the twentieth century, American policy makers got lost in a forest of good intentions, public anxieties, and political cynicism. They created a punishment system that no one would knowingly have chosen, but that we do not know how to change. Current policies are too severe, waste lives and money, and often produce unjust results. They have produced an imprisonment rate five times higher than that of any other Western country and seven to twelve times higher than most.

Current policies have disproportionately damaged the lives of black offenders and their families and have undermined black communities. Nearly a third of young black men are in prison or jail, or on probation or parole. More than 13 percent of black men between 25 and 29, more than one in every eight, were in jail or prison in 2001. We lack comparable information about Hispanics, but they are the fastest growing part of the prison population. Unless current policies change, the criminal justice system will soon intrude as deeply into Hispanic Americans' lives and communities as it now does into black Americans' lives and communities.

Ordinary Americans made these things happen. Elected politicians proposed policies and enacted laws, but they would not have done it if they believed American voters would disapprove. Journalists and academics assert that many politicians who proposed tough policies did so cynically, out of personal, political self-interest, and that many realized the policies they proposed would not work and would do harm. "Soft on crime" was a label few politicians dared risk during the 1970s through the 1990s, and many supported policies they believed unwise or unjust rather than risk losing an election. An influential analysis by Katherine Beckett shows that politicians typically led public opinion about crime rather than followed it, in effect raising public fears and anxieties and then proposing harsh, simplistic solutions to ameliorate them. The bottom line, nonetheless, even if those accounts are valid, is that the public could not have been led someplace it was unwilling to go.

At the beginning of a new century, Americans are having second thoughts about the wisdom of current antidrug and anticrime policies, but elected politicians most places are afraid to change them. To do so runs risks of being tarred as soft on crime and, until significant numbers of politicians take that risk and get reelected, most will not take the chance. And until that happens, the unfortunate social facts described in the opening paragraph will continue to be true.

There is lots of evidence that ordinary Americans want to change current policies, and there is lots of evidence that judges and prosecutors at local and state levels are responding. Policy makers in some states are responding, though usually by tinkering at the margins rather than by overhauling current policies. Legislators and executive branch officials in the federal government and in the large, heavily populated states, however, are neither repealing nor fundamentally recasting failed policies. Most remain locked in the politics and attitudes of earlier times and are hunkering down to protect the status quo. The George W. Bush administration's determination, reiterated in 2002, to preserve the federal laws that punish crack cocaine offenses as severely as powder cocaine offenses one hundred times larger is but one illustration. Most crack is sold by young inner-city blacks and most cocaine by older whites. As a result, the 100-to-1 law imposes much longer sentences on blacks. Almost no one defends that outcome on the merits, but political courage to change the law cannot yet be found.

This book explains how contemporary policies came to be as they are, and how they can be reconfigured to be more effective but less costly, and to do less harm to offenders, their loved and loving ones, and their communities. The story is only partly about rising crime rates and public fears, about cynical politics and pusillanimous politicians, and about public opinion and sensationalizing media. The story is also about the ways long-term trends in social values and public attitudes, and short-term effects of moral panics, influence how Americans think about crime and punishment. For two decades, Americans thought they wanted single-minded toughness and they got it. The question is why they thought they wanted it.

"Moral panics" are part of the answer. They typically occur when horrifying or notorious events galvanize public emotion, and produce concern, sympathy, emotion, and overreaction. Examples in recent years include the kidnapping of Polly Klaas in California and the crack-overdose death of Len Bias in Maryland. Results included, respectively, California's three-strikes law and the federal 100-to-1 crack cocaine sentencing law. Sometimes moral panics are about general problems, for example, child abuse or school violence, and the resulting emotions have been harnessed constructively. Often though, moral panics relating to crime lead to poorly considered and overly harsh reactions. In recent decades, moral panics have magnified the effects of longer term changes in values and attitudes.

The ways people think about contentious issues change slowly but predictably. Social scientists use the word "sensibilities" to refer to prevailing social values, attitudes, and beliefs, and show how sensibilities change slowly over time and shape and reshape what people think and believe. Current American crime control policies are to a large part an outgrowth of American sensibilities of the past third of the twentieth century. Nothing wrong with that, one might respond. Policies have expressed the views of the people, and that is what democracy is all about.

There is something wrong with that, though. Looking backwards, we know that American sensibilities of earlier times supported policies—slavery, the near-extermination of indigenous North American peoples, internment of Japanese Americans during World War II, sterilization of the mentally ill, ostracism of homosexuals, denial to women of a right to vote—that we now believe to be wrong in some timeless sense, and not merely in light of current sensibilities. Looking outside the United States in our own and earlier times, similar judgments are widespread about religious intolerance, oppression of women, and exploitation of child labor. Sensibilities of particular times and places may support such attitudes and practices, but few people in our time believe that justifies them.

And so it is concerning crime and punishment. In some respects this seems obvious. No one any longer calls for drawing and quartering of offenders, for public execution by guillotine, or for the use of torture to extract confessions. In other respects, it may not appear so obvious, even though practices that many Americans in our time endorse—capital punishment, three-strikes laws, prison sentences measured in decades or lifetimes—are as unthinkable in other Western countries today as are lynchings and corporal punishment in America.

Concluding that particular policies or practices are consonant with current sensibilities is thus the beginning but cannot be the end of assessments of their legitimacy. That evaluation needs to take account of basic human rights and moral considerations, whatever the public opinion poll results or prevailing sentiments of a particular day or year. It also needs to take account of what historians can tell us about interactions between sensibilities, attitudes, and policies in the past.

We know from historical writings on recurring cycles of support for romanticism and classicism in the arts, of tolerance and intolerance of homosexuality and religious pluralism, and of attitudes and policies on drug abuse, that human sensibilities often move in regular cycles and that beliefs and policies move with them. Persecution of "heretics" in the history of the Christian church, for example, often coincided with periods when the power and authority of the organized church were in doubt. At other times, self-confident church leaders comfortably tolerated dissenters.

In trying to understand and normatively evaluate crime control policies we need to take account of prevailing sensibilities, of "timeless" human rights ideas, and of what we know about past interactions between sensibilities, cycles of tolerance and intolerance, and public policies. When we do that in relation to drug policy, we learn that "wars on drugs" are typically launched when drug use has peaked and is beginning to decline, that antidrug policies and law enforcement practices become harshest during such times, and that zealous drug law enforcement targets and scapegoats members of minority groups. People violating drug laws are treated much more harshly during these cyclical periods of heightened intolerance than they would have been ten years earlier or would be twenty years later.

Why these things happen is not hard to understand. For at least two centuries, significant fractions of American society have held moralistic views about drug dependence and believed that drug use is dangerous, unwise, and immoral. During times when drug use is increasing or has stabilized, other voices argue that moral choices are not the law's business and some argue that drug use is a good or at least culturally tolerated thing. Drug use peaks, and begins to decline, however, because the balance of views has changed. As the decline continues, the balance of social attitudes changes. Fewer people use drugs and feel a need to justify themselves. The moral arguments against drug use become louder and command wider support. People of dissenting views become more reluctant to speak out for fear they themselves will seem foolish, irresponsible, or deviant. More people come to promote, support, or administer harsh policies and fewer are prepared to oppose them. The pattern of harsher laws, more vigorous enforcement, and scapegoating of minority groups occurs.

Eventually, however, the fervor abates, the harsh policies soften, enforcement becomes less single-minded, and the focus on minority groups blurs. Drug use stabilizes or begins mildly to increase. People become more confident opposing majority sentiment and a wider range of views is expressed.

The drug policy cycle just described has recurred in the past thirty years. Drug use peaked in the late 1970s and early 1980s, the harshest laws were enacted and the most vigorous enforcement occurred in the ensuing fifteen years, and signs of gradual easing of both fervor and policy have been evident since the mid-1990s. The signs include the movement to create drug courts for drug-abusing offenders, the enactment of laws in many states calling for diversion of drug-dependent first- and second-time offenders into treatment programs, and the passage of referendums supporting medical use of marijuana.

There is no reason to doubt that something similar is happening in relation to crime. By the most cautious measure, crime rates peaked around 1990 (some would say around 1980) and fell continuously and precipitously during the 1990s. During the several decades when crime rates were rising, there was vigorous debate about trade-offs in crime control policy between civil liberties and public safety. That debate had largely stilled by 1990 and remained still for much of the following decade. Just as people become uncomfortable during peak prohibitionist periods arguing for individuals' rights to use drugs, people become uncomfortable during peak anticrime periods arguing for the need to treat offenders fairly and to recognize the complex causes of much criminality. No one who read American newspapers during the 1990s could have failed to observe that both major parties were consistently tough on crime and loathe to risk any other public perception. Former President Bill Clinton famously observed in 1994, "I can be nicked on a lot, but no one can say I'm soft on crime."

As a result, closely paralleling experience with drugs, crime control policies became unprecedentedly harsh during the early and mid-1990s. That was the time of three-strikes, truth-in-sentencing laws, and zero-tolerance policing, and of a striking increase in the severity of punishments and in the numbers of people in prisons and jails.

And now, the fervor is abating, policies gradually are softening, a wider range of voices is being heard, and the prison population is stabilizing and in some places declining a little.

Had American policy makers in the 1980s read the readily available historical literature, heeded its lessons, and more sensitively interpreted evidence of public concern, the war on drugs would have taken very different forms. And had American policy makers in the 1990s heeded history's lessons, crime control policies would have been very different. Many fewer Americans would have been sent to prison. More public monies would have been available for health care, education, and social welfare. The criminal justice system would have intruded into many fewer black Americans' lives. If only American policy makers had not allowed themselves to be carried away by short-term and predictable transient emotions, America's criminal justice system would look very different.

The organization of American government makes it especially vulnerable to emotional overreaction. American policy makers need to worry even more than policy makers elsewhere that they will be carried away by shifts in sensibilities about crime, drugs, and other unwanted behaviors, or by moral panics, and adopt inhumane and unjust policies that later they will regret.

American institutions provide less insulation from short-term passions and emotions than do governmental institutions in other Western countries. Most prosecuting attorneys are elected and those who are not are selected according to partisan political criteria. A large majority of American state judges are elected. No informed person would deny that appointments of federal judges are fundamentally partisan and political.

Only rarely in Western Europe or the other major English-speaking countries are judges and prosecutors elected. Prosecutors and judges elsewhere are often career civil servants.

Where they are not, they are typically selected through non-partisan merit procedures. Nowhere else do legislators try to micro-manage sentencing and parole decisions. In the United States, however, policy makers and public officials often pride themselves on responding to changes in public opinion and to heightened anxieties, and are accordingly less likely than those elsewhere to stand firm against winds of emotion when they sweep across the national consciousness.

American policy makers over the past thirty years did not try to keep their heads and retain a sense of perspective. What was in effect a form of false consciousness led to adoption of drug and crime control policies that were too simple, too harsh, and too wasteful. Centuries of experience with the excesses of witch-hunts and the persecution of heretics have taught church officials caution. Those who feel moved to punish heretics know they must search their souls to consider whether that is because controversial beliefs genuinely threaten harm or because they are concerned that the authority of the church is weakening. Likewise, makers of crime control policy should examine their consciences to consider whether they support one policy or another for valid reasons or merely because of fleeting beliefs, opinions, and passions.

Because American policy makers lost their way, hundreds of thousands of people are in prisons because they were in the wrong place at the wrong historical moment. Their bad luck was to have committed crimes, or been convicted and sentenced, during a period when public and official attitudes toward crime were harsh and single-minded.

Many thousands of aging offenders convicted of trifling crimes in the mid- to late 1990s occupy California prisons. Their misfortune is to have been sentenced before the California Supreme Court gave judges the authority to sidestep California's three-strikes law and before prosecutors throughout the state began to restrict its application to genuinely serious cases.

Many thousands of people are serving decades-long sentences in federal prisons for non-violent drug crimes. Their misfortune is to have been sentenced in federal courts before avoidance of sentencing guidelines by federal judges and prosecutors became common practice.

Hundreds of thousands of people, mostly but not only of minority and disadvantaged backgrounds, have spent much of their young adulthood in prison for drug crimes. Their misfortune is that unwisely, but for young people not uncommonly, and typically as a result of peer influences and teenagers' sense of invincibility, they experimented with drug use, got hooked, and got caught—in a time when antidrug policies were unprecedentedly harsh.

Reasonable people disagree over why policies are so harsh, so many people are in prison, and so many of those are black and Hispanic. In the most literal sense, the explanation is that American politicians adopted unduly harsh policies and the public let them do it. That does not explain, however, why the public supported those policies. Conventional explanations range from the inevitable effects of rising crime rates, reflection of the public will, and belief in the crime-preventive effectiveness of tough policies to political cynicism, partisan manipulation of public anxieties, and indifference to the well-being of black Americans.

Current penal policies have trapped American policy makers much as Brer Fox got stuck in Joel Chandler Harris's tar-baby story. Brer Rabbit, not at all interested in becoming Brer Fox's supper, persuaded him that the tar-baby would be juicier and tastier. Brer Fox grabbed hold of the tar-baby's arm, only to find that he could not pull his front paw away. When he tried to push away with the other front paw, that too became stuck. In the end, as Brer Rabbit walked away, smiling quietly, Brer Fox was hopelessly stuck. He had grabbed hold of what he thought he wanted, and he could not break free.

American policy makers, having grabbed hold of current policies, are stuck and do not know how to get loose. It does not matter that we now know that current crime policies cannot be justified on the merits. Although many people long believed that severe crime control policies generally, or particular policies like zero-tolerance policing in New York

City and the three-strikes law in California, substantially reduced crime rates, most informed practitioners and scholars no longer believe that to be true. At the margins such policies probably influenced crime rates, but only as small parts of much more complicated stories. Crime rates fell sharply in all large cities during the 1990s, including the large majority that did not adopt zero-tolerance policing, and in all populous states, including the majority that did not enact three-strikes laws. Particular policies and particular laws in individual cities and states may have influenced crime rate declines in those places, but most of the steep decline was the result of normative and behavioral changes that affected the entire country.

It is more accurate to refer to normative and behavioral changes that affected most Western countries. Crime rates fell in most countries in the 1990s, including Germany, England, Canada, the Scandinavian countries, Scotland, the Netherlands, and the United States. Crime rates have even been falling since the mid-1990s in many of the countries of Eastern Europe, a region that has experienced enormous social and economic disruption.

No one has a good explanation for why crime rates are down in most of the Western world, but such things have happened before. Crime rates fell in most Western countries for a century or more beginning around 1830. Historians differ in their inevitably speculative explanations as to why that happened but not as to whether it happened. Something similar is happening now, and it is affecting Maine, Maryland, Minnesota, and Manitoba on the western side of the Atlantic and Manchester, Mainz, Malmo, and Messina on the eastern.

To some readers it may seem counterintuitive that policies like zero-tolerance policing and three-strikes sentencing had only modest effects on crime. That is because prevailing sensibilities in recent years made Americans want to believe harsh policies would work. Many Americans appear to believe that crimes occur primarily because offenders are bad people or because punishments are insufficiently severe. If that is true, incapacitating the incorrigibly bad people and threatening lengthy prison sentences for the others should reduce crime rates.

In many other Western countries, by contrast, ordinary crime is understood primarily to be the product of personal disadvantage or disability and social disorganization, and it seems counterintuitive that crime can be much affected unless those underlying problems are addressed. Few people deny that offenders have free will and choose to commit crimes. Self-evidently, they have and they do. That recognition, however, can coexist with recognition that childhood abuse, poverty, mental disability, limited opportunities, lack of marketable skills, and socialization into deviant values often lead individuals to make choices they would otherwise not make.

To many disadvantaged inner-city American teenagers, for example, drug dealing, in comparison with other available options, appears to be a sensible and relatively low-risk way to earn money and improve their lives. So they choose to sell drugs. Privileged teenagers much less often see it that way because their circumstances are different, and other avenues to success and happiness are open. So it is not that disadvantaged kids do not make choices, but that the choices available to them are often far less attractive than those open to privileged kids. A just society would take those differences into account in punishing offenders and in setting crime control policies.

Many European policy makers think this way now, and in earlier times so did many American policy makers. Historian David Rothman described the prevalent Progressive Era views during the early twentieth century: "No one raised in a slum could be held strictly accountable for his actions. The wretchedness of the social setting was so great that responsibility could not be assigned in a uniform and predictable fashion. Elemental fairness dictated that the offender be treated as an individual. It was not just a sensible and effective principle, but a just one." Tony Blair's Labour Government in England famously expressed this in the back half of its campaign slogan "Tough on Crime, Tough on the Causes of Crime."

In any case, for countries, states, or societies, changes in crime rates or patterns do not necessarily lead to changes in punishment policies or patterns. Put crisply, at a societal level crime does not cause punishment. Imprisonment rates and the severity of punishment move independently from changes in crime rates, patterns, and trends. Governments decide how much punishment they want, and these decisions are in no simple way related to crime rates. This can be seen by comparing crime and punishment trends in Finland, Germany, and the United States between 1960 and 1990. The trends are close to identical. Violent crime rates in all three countries grew by a factor of 3-to-4 and homicide rates more than doubled. Yet the U.S. imprisonment rate quadrupled in that period, the Finnish rate fell by 60 percent, and the German rate was broadly stable.

Likewise, punishment does not cause crime (or less cryptically, punishment policies do not have major effects on crime rates or trends). This can be seen by comparing crime rates over the past twenty years of comparable and closely related countries that have very different punishment policies. Canada's incarceration rate fluctuated within a narrow band of 100 to 125 per 100,000 between 1980 and 2000 while the U.S. rate more than tripled, growing from 200 per 100,000 in 1980 to 700 per 100,000 in 2002. Yet crime rate patterns in Canada between 1980 and 2000 closely parallel those in the United States with the crucial difference that they were not as high.

And a Scandinavian example: crime rates in Finland and Denmark have moved in parallel since the early 1960s, though Finnish crime rates have been consistently lower. Finland's incarceration rate, twice as high in 1965 (130 per 100,000 compared to 65 per 100,000), fell by half, Denmark's stayed about the same, and both fluctuated in the low 60s per 100,000 in the 1990s. The Finnish incarceration rate in 2000 (56) was marginally lower than Denmark's (61). In both countries the crime rate in 1990 was essentially the same in 2000.

Whether current American crime policies were an inexorable product of recent crime patterns, and whether they can be justified on the merits, or in either case not, they are difficult to alter or repeal. Enacting a three-strikes law, a life-without-possibility-of-parole law, or a law calling for mandatory minimum sentences is incomparably easier than repealing such laws. They were politically popular in the 1980s and 1990s. No candidate or incumbent who supported them imperiled his or her electoral prospects. In contemporary America, politicians' support for laws aimed at prevention of crime, hostility to offenders, or well-being of victims does not require political courage.

Political courage is required, however, to propose or support repeal of tough laws. Even in a time when crime has fallen well down lists of the public's primary concerns, a vote to repeal, narrow, or weaken a three-strikes law can be portrayed as soft on crime. This makes elected officials risk averse. Conservative New York Republican Governor George Pataki in 1995 first proposed reducing penalties for nonviolent offenders under the severe Rockefeller drug laws; in mid-2003, the legislature had still not acted. Conservative Republican U.S. Senator Orrin Hatch, according to a Senate staffer, long believed reducing federal drug sentences was "the right thing to do, but he couldn't do it for political reasons." The United States Sentencing Commission in 1995 proposed repeal of the federal 100-to-1 policy, adopted in 1986, that penalizes crack cocaine offenses as harshly as powder cocaine offenses involving quantities 100 times larger. In 2003, the law remained unchanged.

Leaving things as they are poses no electoral risks. Inertia may result in wasteful public spending or avoidable damage to the lives and interests of offenders, their families, and their communities, but responsibility for these things is diffuse. No one loses elections for failing to lead or support a campaign for repeal of laws that are tough on drugs or crime.

This is unfortunate and ironic, because there is plenty of evidence that broad-based public sentiments support more nuanced, compassionate, and constructive policies than those now in place. Few people argue that violence or theft is morally excusable, or that use of heroin, cocaine, or ecstasy is a good thing. Many more people than a decade ago, however, accept that human lives are messy and complicated, that everyone makes mistakes, that sensible drug and crime policies should recognize that, and that current policies do not.

What is the evidence for the preceding paragraph's claims? Drug policy referenda for starters. Despite unceasing opposition from the federal government, by 2002 voters in eight jurisdictions (Alabama, California, Colorado, Maine, Nevada, Oregon, Washington, and the District of Columbia) had enacted referenda legalizing medical use of marijuana, and Hawaii did so by legislation. In July 2002, the California Supreme Court, in *The People v. Mower*, 122 Cal. Rptr. 2d 326 (2002), held that a person who cultivates or possesses marijuana for medical purposes may not be convicted of unlawful possession of drugs. Earlier, in 2000, California voters enacted Proposition 36, which required large numbers of first- and second-time drug offenders to be diverted from prosecution and imprisonment to drug treatment. District of Columbia voters in November 2002 adopted Ballot Initiative 62, which prescribed a similar preference for treatment over prosecution.

More evidence can be found in results from public opinion surveys showing that crime is no longer widely numbered among the country's most pressing problems. From 1980 to 1990, crime ranked most years in the top three. In March 2002, according to the Gallup Poll, crime ranked fifteenth and drugs twelfth, behind poverty, dissatisfaction with government, and the high cost of living. In a 1994 poll by Peter D. Hart Research Associates, 48 percent of Americans said their preferred crime control strategy would be to address the underlying causes of crime, and 42 percent preferred stricter sentencing. In a 2001 Hart Poll, 65 percent of Americans approved the root causes approach and only 32 percent preferred stricter sentencing.

The general public holds complicated views about punishment that are neither monolithically nor single-mindedly punitive. Ordinary citizens want criminals punished, but also want them treated. They believe punishments in general are too soft, but when they focus on particular cases typically support sentences less severe than judges now impose. They believe that crime is a product of bad character and bad judgment, but also that drug and alcohol dependence, bad home lives, and disadvantage are among crime's major causes.

There is also evidence that many criminal justice officials believe current policies are too severe and too expensive, and long have done. A January 2002 *New York Times* article by Fox Butterfield, for example, reported that some states were changing their laws on sentencing and punishment in various ways to reduce their rigidity and severity. A Ninth Circuit Federal Court of Appeals in *The People v. Andrade*, 270 Fed. 3rd 743 (2001), struck down California's three-strikes law, as applied in that particular case. The court held that a fifty-year sentence for Andrade's theft of $150 in videotapes from K-Mart violated the U.S. Constitution's provision forbidding "cruel and unusual punishments." (The U.S. supreme court, however, in mid-2003 held otherwise.) Several years earlier, in *The People v. Romero*, 53 Cal. Rep. 2d 789 (1996), and in *The People v. Alvarez*, 60 Cal. Rep. 2d 93 (1997), a California Supreme Court composed entirely of judges appointed by conservative Republican governors Ronald Reagan, George Deukmeijian, and Pete Wilson reinterpreted the three-strikes law to empower judges to sidestep it when they believed it appropriate to do so. More recently, there is much evidence that the three-strikes law has fallen into partial desuetude, invoked only for extremely serious cases. *Washington Post* reporter Rene Sanchez wrote that, "prosecutors insist they are careful to use discretion in deciding whether to invoke a third-strike prison sentence." Los Angeles County prosecutor Steve Cooley ran for office and was elected on a platform promising to use three-strikes prosecutions only in very serious cases.

That is a lot of California three-strikes, but together with the California drug referendum it starkly illustrates the problem. Voters, prosecutors, trial judges, and appellate courts have acted in various ways to change California laws to make them more flexible and discriminating. Legislators, however, have not. The three-strikes law remains unchanged on the books. Thousands of people are serving decades-long sentences in California who, had they been sentenced a few years later, would not (if drug offenders) have been sent to prison at all or who (if third-strike property, drug, or minor violent offenders) would not have been sent there for anywhere near so long.

So we appear to be stuck. Voters and many criminal justice officials would support repeal and refashioning of much of the harsh penal legislation of the past quarter century, but elected officials are too risk averse to do it. Crime and punishment has come to resemble the signature issues of single-issue interest groups such as the National Rifle Association or the Right-to-Life movement. Only a few percent of voters in a district may base their electoral choices solely on candidates' positions on gun control or abortion but in places where victory margins are sometimes small, they may make the difference. The safe course is to oppose gun control and oppose abortion, and many electoral candidates do so most of the time, whatever their private views may be.

Crime and punishment has become a comparable issue. No matter how amenable most voters may be to sensible policy changes, the existence of a few percent who will always oppose candidates who appear "soft" on crime or likely to "coddle" offenders can immobilize legislatures.

Crime and punishment may be even more immobilizing than gun control and abortion. There is no "pro-criminal" sentiment to offset "tough on crime" sentiment as there is a gun control movement that opposes the NRA and a pro-choice movement that opposes the right-to-life movement. It was common in the 1990s for politicians to suggest that one must be "for victims" or "for criminals." Given the emotive force of crime as an issue, few public officials are willing to risk the "for criminals" label.

But, unless some elected officials are prepared to propose fundamental policy changes, and work to achieve them, we will not be able to let loose of the tar-baby. America will remain stuck. Too many people who shouldn't go to prison will continue to be sent there and to stay there too long. Too many lives will continue unnecessarily to be blighted.

Chapter 8 sets out three sets of proposals for correcting and ameliorating the worst excesses of the American criminal justice system. The first set is aspirational and calls on American policy makers to learn from both history and contemporary experience that they should not allow themselves to get carried away by the passions of the moment or to adopt policies that will later be regretted.

The second set addresses features of American government that create higher risks in the United States than in other Western countries that policy makers will get carried away. These include most prominently the American practice of electing many judges and prosecutors, and taking partisan political considerations into account when appointing most of the rest. Judges and prosecutors in other Western countries are either career civil servants who have undergone specialized university-level training or are appointed under nonpartisan meritocratic procedures. The American system ties criminal justice policies and decisions in individual cases to election returns and to officials' personal and political self-interest. Rather than buffer policy and decisions about individuals' fates from emotional overreactions, moral panics, and changing sensibilities, American institutional arrangements are almost designed to assure their influence.

The third set of proposals concerns changes to contemporary criminal justice policies. Early release laws should be adopted that allow panels of judges or corrections officials to review the sentences of all offenders serving very long terms to determine whether and when they can safely and justly be released. Three strikes and mandatory minimum laws should be repealed and replaced by sentencing guidelines that allow judges to draw sensible distinctions among offenders. If that is not viable, all such laws should be amended to authorize judges to disregard them in appropriate cases. A variety of measures should be adopted to prevent enactment of ill-considered legislation, including requirements that all proposed new laws be accompanied by appropriations of whatever funds will be required to implement them and by disparity analyses that demonstrate their likely differential effects on minority and women offenders. To begin to lessen racial disparities in the courts and prisons, not only proposed new laws but also all existing practices should be subjected to disparity analyses. These would investigate whether and how new and current practices treat minority and women offenders worse than whites and men, and serve as the basis for deciding whether disparity-causing practices can be justified.

We know how to create a humane and effective criminal justice system. Experience with sentencing guidelines shows how to adopt comprehensive sentencing policies that treat offenders fairly and consistently, requiring severe punishments for those who deserve them and less severe but appropriate punishments for others. Accumulating evidence on the effectiveness of drug courts and drug treatment shows that greatly increased investment in drug treatment can prevent crime, save money, and rebuild lives. Accumulating evidence on the effectiveness of a wide range of other treatment programs has undermined the "nothing works" attitudes of the 1980s and 1990s and shows that diversion of public funds from prisons to treatment programs would pay financial and crime-prevention dividends. If American criminal justice systems would eliminate the worst policies of the last thirty years, we could re-create systems that were no longer out-of-step with our own history or with the practices of other Western countries.

Bibliography

Beckett, Katherine. (1997), *Making Crime Pay: Law and Order in Contemporary American Politics*, New York: Oxford University Press.

Peter D. Hart Research Associates, Inc. (2002), *The New Politics of Criminal Justice: Summary of Findings*, Washington, DC: Hart Associates.

Rothman, David J. (1980), *Conscience and Convenience*, Boston: Little, Brown.

[8]
Cycles and Sensibilities

Capital punishment, indiscriminate private possession of handguns, and mass imprisonment of black men in early twenty-first century America will someday be widely deplored and deeply regretted. Nearly all Americans regret and deplore the past subordination of black people in the American South, and yet it was approved and accepted by most southern whites for at least a century after the Civil War. The moral, religious, and social policy arguments against slavery did not change but people's beliefs and values did, and now human slavery and deliberate racial or ethnic subjugation are, almost literally, unthinkable. In most Western countries today, adoption of American policies on capital punishment, handguns, and mass imprisonment is almost as unthinkable as adoption of slavery would be. Prevailing sensibilities elsewhere attach greater importance to ideas about human rights and the value of human lives and life chances than do prevailing American sensibilities.

So why are American crime control policies as they are? Usually policies toward crime and punishment are portrayed as the outcome of disagreements between liberals and conservatives, or between advocates of due process and advocates of public safety, or between people who care about criminals and people who care about victims. The views caricatured in the first member of each of those pairs, it is said, predominated in the 1960s and the views caricatured in the second in the 1990s. And that is all we need to know to understand why 140 per 100,000 Americans were in jail or prison in 1970 and over 700 per 100,000 in 2003. That is true in one important albeit grotesquely oversimplified sense, but it is deeply shortsighted. Policies do, of course, reflect beliefs and values, but those come from somewhere, and somewhen. If Americans were more self-aware of why we believe what we believe, our policies about crime would be very different and we would not be fated to suffer our descendants' disapproval.

For some subjects, beliefs and values oscillate in predictable cycles. Americans have lately been caught up in a period in which excessive hostility and emotional overreaction toward criminals and drug users could have been predicted (and was) and current penal policies are the result.

Truths and Trivia

What we see, think, and believe depends as much on when we stand as where. This is true of trivial things—people who were once enamored of bouffant hairdos, polyester pantsuits, or platform shoes have a hard time imagining that was ever true and a harder time picturing themselves dressed that way now. Fashions change, tastes evolve, and few of us are immune to influence in such matters. What once we liked, we now dislike, and vice versa.

We are almost as susceptible to influence, however, about things that are important. Periods of romanticism and classicism in the arts have alternated throughout history, as have periods of tolerance and intolerance of homosexuality and religious pluralism, and peoples' opinions and beliefs have oscillated with them. And the same thing is true in recent centuries in relation to punishment, with moralistic ideas about deserved punishments and moral responsibility alternating with instrumental ideas about problem-solving and human fallibility.

Beliefs and attitudes about punishment, religious pluralism, and sexual tolerance are different in kind from preferences for polyester pantsuits. Wearing unfashionable clothes or hairstyles can be done naively or defiantly. It can be gauche or anachronistic, elicit disapproval or ridicule, and result in embarrassment or humiliation, but the sanctions for being different are entirely social.

Being seriously on the wrong side of contemporary views about religious beliefs can be lethal. Apostates have been being killed for as long as organized religion has existed (Erikson 1966; Johnson 1976). From shortly after the death of Jesus, through the Protestant Reformation and at least through the hangings of Quakers by Massachusetts Bay Calvinists, Christians have been killing Christians because of their heretical views. In numerous periods from the first century A.D. to the eighteenth, interspersed among more tolerant eras, Christian heretics were martyred because of their heterodox beliefs. As the confidence and strength of the early Christian church waxed and waned, beliefs that were punished by death in one century were tolerated and sometimes celebrated in the next. The radical simplicity and antimaterialism of St. Francis of Assisi in the thirteenth century might well have been intolerable heresy in the twelfth or the fourteenth. According to historian John Boswell, the "Franciscans came perilously close to being declared heretical before their final acceptance by the church" (Boswell 1980, p. 275).

Histories of homosexuality tell similar stories of periods of tolerance that alternated with periods when the consequences ranged from ostracism to death (Boswell 1980; Greenberg 1988). Boswell describes classical antiquity and the Early Middle Ages as periods when homosexual relations were widely accepted and celebrated, albeit separated by the sixth through ninth centuries when homosexuality was strongly disapproved.

Then the pendulum swung: "During the 200 years from 1150 to 1350, homosexual behavior appears to have changed, in the eyes of the public, from the personal preference of a prosperous minority, satirized in popular verse, to a dangerous, antisocial, and severely sinful aberration" (Boswell 1980, p. 295). Homosexuality passed from being an uncontroversial matter of preference or idiosyncrasy in most of Europe to being a criminal act that most contemporary legal compilations made punishable by death. Sensibilities changed and, more importantly, laws changed with them. The change was lethal, as Boswell demonstrates:

> Kings themselves were no longer safe. In the twelfth century the king of France could elevate to the episcopate a man thought to have been his bed partner, and the king of England [Richard II] could fall head over heels in love with another monarch [Philip II of France] without losing support from either the people or the church. But by the fourteenth century all this had changed, and its opening decades witnessed first the downfall of the Templars [who had been accused of sodomy, among other things] at the hands of Philip IV and then the execution (at the hands of his daughter Isabella) of the last openly homosexual monarch of the Middle Ages, Edward II of England. (Boswell 1980, p. 298)

The animosity toward homosexuals is made "pellucidly clear," wrote Boswell, by the nature of the executions of Edward and his lover Hugh le Despenser: "Hugh's genitals were cut off and burned publicly before he was decapitated, and Edward was murdered by the insertion into his anus of a red-hot poker" (Boswell 1980, p. 300).

Comparative tolerance is typical now in Western countries, though far from complete. Memories of Oscar Wilde's final, sad years and of intolerance in some parts of the contemporary world remind us that things are often otherwise.

Being on the wrong side of contemporary views about punishment can also be fatal, or life-diminishing, but in a different way and to different people. Being homosexual or subscribing to particular religious beliefs is part of who people are or want to be. In tolerant times, those are Good Things, and in intolerant times, perilously they are not.

The central question concerning crime and punishment is not whether crime is a good thing—not whether people should be entitled to be criminals in the same way they are free in tolerant times to be homosexual—but how the state should punish criminals. The prevailing ethos can have drastic consequences for people convicted of crimes, and include differences between life and death or between prison sentences measured in years or in decades. In earlier centuries, Michel Foucault (1977) and many others relate, breathtakingly cruel punishments were sometimes practiced. Foucault famously began *Discipline and Punish* with a description of the 1757 execution of Damien, condemned to have the flesh torn from his breasts, thighs, arms, and calves by red hot pincers, his hand burnt with sulfur, and the wounds dressed with a blend of molten lead, boiling oil, burning resin, wax, and sulfur. He was then to have his body drawn and quartered by four horses.

That time has passed, but prevailing attitudes toward punishment continue to change with the times. Thousands of executions occurred in the United States in the early twentieth century, but steadily declined in the 1940s, 1950s, and 1960s. In more recent times, an American offender's chances of execution are vastly higher early in the twenty-first century than they were in the 1960s. During the 1970s and 1980s, the average lengths of prison sentences for serious crimes more than tripled, and then increased some more in the 1990s.

Even a few years can make an enormous difference in punishments imposed and suffered for particular crimes. Young men convicted of draft evasion late in the Vietnam War often received the maximum lawful prison sentence of five years. Within a few years, a short prison term or probation became typical and shortly after that an amnesty was enacted. The same behaviors, occurring at about the same time, incurred vastly different consequences depending on when the sentence was imposed or the case dealt with.

There are many other examples of punishments varying greatly depending solely on when they were imposed. Before the U.S. Supreme Court declared capital punishment for rape unconstitutional under the Eighth Amendment in *Coker v. Georgia*, 433 U.S. 584 (1977), many actual or alleged rapists, especially black men accused of raping white women, were executed.

As tolerance of drug use and Drug War fervor fluctuate, authorized and imposed sentences for drug crimes vary radically. The U.S. Congress enacted mandatory minimum sentences for drug crimes in the 1950s and 1960s, then in 1970 at the urging of, among others, Republican Congressman George H. Bush, repealed nearly all of them, because they were seen to be too rigid and too harsh. In the 1980s and early 1990s, at the urging of, among others, Republican Vice President and later President George H. Bush, the U.S. Congress enacted new mandatory minimum sentences of unprecedented severity for drug crimes. People involved in 500-gram heroine transactions could receive very different punishments depending on whether the transaction occurred in the 1970s, the 1980s, or the 1990s. Closer to many more people's homes, because of the commonality of use or experimentation with marijuana, penalties for small-scale trafficking in marijuana have fluctuated nearly as widely as for cocaine trafficking. Marijuana offenses punishable by multi-year prison sentences in the 1960s in many places were largely ignored in the 1970s. In 2001 handling of marijuana cases is wildly inconsistent, ranging from de facto decriminalization and widespread open use in some parts of the country to inconsistent but sometimes harsh handling elsewhere.

Punishment practices and policies change for reasons, but the quality of the reasons may be good or bad. It is important to be sure that the reasons why punishment policies are to be made harsher are sound, and that they result from something other than raw emotion or short-term upset. Recent toughening of penalties and policies concerning domestic violence or child abuse, for example, can probably pass that test. Both behaviors fundamentally damage victims' lives and neither appears before to have received sustained attention from the criminal justice system. So might penalty increases be justified for particular crimes, corporate and white-collar crimes, for example, for which reliable evidence gives reason to believe that ethically defensible increases would measurably prevent future victimization. When, however, the reason is short-term overreaction or political expediency or animus to minority groups, the test is failed.

Stark shifts in social practices, including punishment, occur because many or most people in a time and place share perceptions and beliefs that justify them, unmindful or indifferent that their perceptions and beliefs may be time-bound, and that they themselves in a few years or decades may see them to have been wrong. In the abstract, we understand that things change. That's life. In the particular, individuals' lives are diminished, shortened, and taken not only because of who they are or what they believed or did but also because of when they are, or believe, or do.

Aristophanes' "The Frogs" tells of two boys playing near a stream who find a frog and, for fun, kill it. They killed the frog in jest, Aristophanes reports, but the frog died in earnest. People whose lives are diminished, ruined, or taken because of the penal ethos of the era in which they live are like Aristophanes' frog. Impersonal forces of history or the penal policies of a moment may explain what happened to them, but their suffering and loss are real.

It would be easy but wrong to think that cruel punishments are primarily of antiquarian interest, that we are more civilized now, that we do not allow our collective judgment to be overwhelmed by passing emotion, or that we do not do things to offenders that we or our descendants will later regret. There is no reason to suppose that people now in positions of power are any less susceptible to the ethos of our times than our ancestors were to theirs. The United States in the final decade of the twentieth century was in the throes of a cyclical period of extreme intolerance of drug users and people who commit crimes. Many Americans early in the twenty-first century have a hard time recognizing the cruelty of current drug and crime policies, because they have become used to them, but most people in earlier periods of intolerance were equally unaware of injustices that later generations condemned.

Sensibilities

Sensibilities are time- and place-bound ways of thinking that include ideas and express values that are widely shared and little questioned. Sometimes sensibilities change slowly and sometimes they change rapidly, but when a particular sensibility is widespread it influences what people think, say, and believe.

Sensibility is a central idea in this book, so I devote several pages to explaining what I mean by it. Two influential conceptions of sensibility have recently received attention in writings on crime and punishment. For English penologist Nigel Walker, sensibilities are characteristics of individuals that make them more or less susceptible to different kinds of pain (and pleasure). For sociologists Norbert Elias and David Garland, sensibilities are characteristics of societies and are the products of long-term economic, social, and psychological developments that shape the values and beliefs of members of a society.

By sensibility, I mean the ethos or zeitgeist of a moment that influences but does not determine what most people think and believe about a particular subject. It differs from Walker's conception because it refers to something social and collective rather than idiosyncratic and individual, and it differs from Elias's and Garland's because it is more contingent, and more susceptible to conscious reflection and reconsideration.

Nigel Walker (1991) uses the term to describe the unique characteristics of individuals that cause them to experience punishments differently. He points out that a serious effort to impose comparable punishments on like-situated offenders would take account of offenders' diverse sensibilities and adjust punishments accordingly. Different offenders, Walker argues, for example, will experience imprisonment in different ways. For an active Los Angeles gang member, a three-year sentence may be a rite of passage. For a single man in his twenties, not otherwise involved in crime, it may be unpleasant and disruptive. For a young single-parent mother, it may be soul-destroying. For an employed middle-aged head of household, it may be the destruction of a family and ruination of a life. For a sickly 75-year-old, it may be a death sentence. For an effeminate teenage boy, or a claustrophobe, it may be sheer terror. Three years in prison for one person often will not result in the same kind or amount of suffering as it does for another. To pretend otherwise is to ignore basic differences between human beings, to fail to take differences between individuals seriously. Walker makes these points not prescriptively, but argumentatively, to demonstrate that punishment theories or policies that call for equal punishments for broad categories of crimes or criminals are psychologically and ethically misconceived. In Walker's sense, sensibilities differ between individuals and, for individuals, over time. For Elias and Garland, sensibilities differ between societies and, within societies, over time.

Modern attention to the nature, course, and power of sensibilities at societal levels derives from the work of the late German sociologist Norbert Elias (1978 [orig. 1939], 1982 [orig. 1939]). For Elias and for David Garland, a Scottish sociologist now at New York University, who is partly responsible for revived interest in Elias's work, sensibilities are characteristics of societies. They are the prevailing ethoses of time-bound societies and shape the beliefs and values of individuals. Elias used the idea of sensibilities to explain changes in societies' norms and practices, and Garland uses it to explain contemporary changes in penal policy. Societies differ in their cultural, historical, material, religious, and social circumstances, and these differences shape the prevailing sensibilities.

Elias, in *The Civilizing Process* (1939), connects changes in sensibility and individual psychology with wider changes in social, economic, and geopolitical organization. These changes, as Garland summarizes:

> eventually have an effect on the psychic organization of the individuals involved and, in particular, on the structure of their drives and emotions. . . . To the extent that

> this process of socialization is successful, the emotions and behavior of the individual become more evenly ordered, less spontaneous, and less given to wild oscillation between extremes. Individuals are thus trained and psychologically equipped to sustain social conventions and to display a particular pattern of sensibility. (1991, pp. 144–45)

For Elias, some changes in sensibilities have been more or less linear and together make up what he calls the "civilizing process." Operating through changing sensibilities, the civilizing process has been underway since the late Middle Ages. It made the sight of brutality, suffering, pain, and violence unpleasant and unappealing. These things became increasingly unacceptable or, at least, were moved out of sight. In our time, they have been stylized into the seemingly-real-but-understood-to-be-unreal cartoons of modern mass entertainment and thereby detached from day-to-day life (Bettelheim 1977).

Elias described "typical civilization curves." One example is the history of meat preparation and eating: "The curve running from the carving of a large part of the animal or even the whole animal at table, through the advance in the threshold of repugnance at the sight of dead animals, to the removal of carving to the specialized enclaves behind the scenes, is a typical civilization curve" (Elias 1978, p. 121). Sixty years after Elias wrote, most people buy meat in tidy plastic-wrapped packages even further removed from the visceral realities of killing and dismembering. Increasing numbers of people in Western countries, more in Europe than in North America, have become vegetarians, and their numbers will grow, further extending Elias's meat-eating civilization curve.

Capital and corporal punishments have followed a similar pattern. Albert Camus, in *Reflections on the Guillotine* (1960), chronicled the gradual evolution of capital punishment in France from drawing-and-quartering in a public square preceded by painful embellishments like disembowelment, successively to strangling, hanging, guillotining in public, and guillotining behind prison doors. Camus explained the sequence in terms of the increasing revulsion people felt about killing human beings. Only by moving the corporal reality and mess behind doors and out of sight could the killing continue. Later, after Camus wrote, French sensibilities no longer tolerated even secretive executions and capital punishment stopped.

The implicit march toward increased decencies in Elias's civilization process may or may not be overly optimistic. That sensibilities in Elias's sense exist, change over time, and influence individuals is, however, incontrovertible. Our beliefs, preferences, tastes, and values are shaped by the culture and society in which we live. These differ and change. Those differences are much of what makes us who we are. Just as it is easy to forget that we speak prose, it is easy to overlook basic matters about which most people in a time and place unthinkingly agree.

The relevance of Elias's work for thinking about punishment and penal policy is demonstrated in David Garland's 1990 book *Punishment and Modern Society*. Garland showed that efforts to understand penal policy that incorporate only normative analyses and arguments about practical effects are incomplete. They must also take account of the social functions punishment serves.

In his later book, *The Culture of Control: Crime and Social Order in Contemporary Society* (2001*a*), Garland attributes recent trends in punishment policies and practices to changing sensibilities associated with the emergence of economic and social changes that he and others encapsulate in the term "late modernity." Garland tries to show how secular changes have shaped sensibilities. Changes in crime rates and patterns are not irrelevant to penal policy changes, but larger social forces do the heavy lifting.

Garland's relevance here is that he offers a sophisticated account of the role of sensibilities in the making and implementation of penal policy. Sensibilities as Elias described them are shaped by the kinds of social changes Garland describes, and in turn shape how we think and what we believe.

Note the verb: shape. Close synonyms might include influence, conduce, and predispose, but not determine, cause, or foreordain. Sensibilities exist, and they change, but only rarely do they determine. They are more malleable than is implied by Elias's and Garland's functionalist notions of deeply bedded and evolving social norms that shape human psychologies.

Elias and Garland do not allow for regular alterations in sensibilities, but some at least do alternate, particularly in relation to behaviors widely regarded in a place and time as deviant. Nor do they treat sensibilities as the proper object of self-conscious assessment. If men and women are thinking animals, we can search for and appraise the sensibilities that shape our thought, and reject, or work to constrain, those we disapprove or recognize to be destructive.

Evolutions in sensibilities can be seen in the United States in relation to capital punishment, not exactly in parallel to Camus' story about France, but with similarities (and with the crucial difference that the United States resumed use of capital punishment with enthusiasm). As in France, executions were moved from public squares to prisons, and methods of dispatch shifted from the cruel and messy to the hygienic and painless—from hanging, shooting, and electrocution to death by lethal injection. Many punishments—maiming, branding, whipping, torturing, beheading, and burning at the stake—are, for most people, as unthinkable in the United States as they are in other Western countries.

American constitutional law doctrine about the death penalty has, until recently, followed a course that resembles a weak and crabbed version of Elias's civilizing process hypothesis and demonstrates changing penal sensibilities. The U.S. Supreme Court resorts to consideration of "evolving standards of decency" to decide whether particular punishments are unconstitutional under the U.S. Constitution's Eighth Amendment prohibition of "cruel and unusual punishment." Several Supreme Court Justices, most prominently Thurgood Marshall and William Brennan, argued that evolving standards of decency by the early 1970s were no longer compatible with the death penalty and urged that it be declared unconstitutional. Supreme Court Justices Harry Blackmun and Lewis Powell expressed the same view after their retirements.

For a time in the 1960s and early 1970s, it appeared possible that a majority of the Supreme Court might agree. That did not happen, but the Court did decide in *Coker* that evolving standards forbade capital punishment for rape and by implication for all lesser crimes of sex, violence, and property. In the June 2002 case of Daryl Atkins, a Virginia man with an IQ of fifty-nine, the Supreme Court decided that a "national consensus" now exists that mentally retarded offenders are categorically less culpable than the average offender and for that reason cannot constitutionally be executed. The Court usually looks for mundane empirical evidence on which to base a conclusion about evolving standards, usually by counting up the number of U.S. states that do or do not permit a practice. What saved Atkins, unlike the many retarded persons who have been executed since the court decided *Penry v. Lynaugh,* 492 U.S. 302 (1989), upholding the practice of executing mentally retarded offenders, is that states have been changing their laws. When *Penry* was decided, two states forbade such executions and fourteen states' laws did not authorize capital punishment at all. By the time *Atkins v. Virginia,* 122 S. Ct. 2242 (2002), was decided, eighteen states forbade such executions and twelve states plus the District of Columbia did not authorize any capital punishment. Thus, thirty states, a majority, do not execute retarded offenders. Standards of decency, in the Court's view, have changed enough that offenders such as Atkins should be allowed to live. A counting exercise such as that is an odd way to decide what is ultimately a moral or human rights issue, but the sequence of cases does illustrate an evolutionary process.

Developments regarding capital punishment illustrate a basic difference between the United States and other Western countries. Something like Elias's civilizing process appears to have operated in every country, and capital punishment is now almost everywhere forbidden. For the past thirty years, however, the United States has moved in a different direction. Why? Because American constitutional and governmental arrangements provide less insulation from the effects of cycles of intolerance. Xenophobia, animus towards immigrants and ethnic minorities, and harsher attitudes toward crime and disorder have characterized many countries in recent years. In some, including the United States, opinion surveys show majority support for the death penalty and harsher crime policies. In other countries, however, crime policy is not a central feature of partisan politics and electioneering and judges and prosecutors are either civil servant or appointed in nonpartisan ways. Officials setting policy can generally devote most of their attention to substantive matters and comparatively little to the results of public opinion surveys.

By contrast, crime has been a partisan political issue in the United States for nearly forty years, and most prosecutors and judges are elected or appointed in openly political processes. Crime control features, often polemically, in executive and legislative elections, and policies are often heavily influenced by measures of public opinion, however well or poorly informed that opinion may be. American governmental arrangements, when public opinion turns harsh and mean-spirited, rather than ameliorate the effects of public emotion, often exacerbate them.

The important point here, though, is that something like sensibilities exists, whatever we call them, and they influence what we say and do and think. But there are three important qualifications.

First, almost never is their influence monolithic. No matter what ways the sensibility winds are blowing, there are almost always people who adopt contrarian stances: who opposed slavery in eighteenth-century Virginia, promoted female enfranchisement in the nineteenth century, opposed Japanese internment during World War II, and favored decriminalization of drugs in the 1980s.

Second, some normative disagreements are so deeply rooted that they are not especially susceptible to changes, at least short-term changes, in sensibilities. Examples in our time concern abortion, capital punishment, and gun control. The proportions of the population subscribing to one or the other side of these controversies ebb and flow, but large numbers of people hold to their views no matter which is ascendant.

Third, most importantly, some ideas are timeless. Most basic Western ideas about law, ethics, and morality are examined in Aristotle's *Nicomachean Ethics* and Plato's *Republic* and *Laws*. Concepts such as virtue, justice, fairness, freedom, and equality go in and out of fashion, and conceptions change, but they are seldom completely forgotten. Sometimes they are forgotten or overlooked by many people and are omitted from the orthodoxy of the day. Sometimes they are or imply inconvenient truths that are dangerous to express, and many people are afraid to express them. Sometimes cognitive dissonance, the human tendency to rationalize and accept what we cannot change, operates and many people come to believe what is convenient or safe.

It became fashionable in the 1980s and 1990s in the literatures of postmodernism and multiculturalism to denigrate such notions as "timeless ideas." There is something, of course, to be said for the multicultural argument. Non-Western societies have different histories and cultural traditions than those shared by Western countries and ideas like "freedom" and "individual rights" may have different genealogies and cultural meanings. Within Western countries, though, the notion of timeless ideas is coherent and meaningful. Ideas such as liberty, tolerance, and justice are widely shared. They do not exist in nature as does a rock or a tree, but they are durable social constructions in Western culture and are at the hearts of documents such as the French Declaration of the Rights of Man, the U.S. Bill of Rights, the United Nations Declaration of Human Rights, and the European Convention of Human Rights. People who want to argue that all cultural meanings are contingent and hence time- and place-bound may be right in a trivial, reductionist sense, but as a practical matter they are wrong. So I use the term "timeless idea" understanding that it is inaccurate in a geological sense, but believing it a useful shorthand in our time, place, and culture for core cultural ideas that are widely shared and have been for centuries.

Some people always hold onto the timeless ethical ideas. Erasmus understood that Protestant persecution of apostates, sometimes unto death, was wrong after the Reformation, and no less wrong than were Roman Catholic persecutions of Jews and heretics during the Inquisition, even if the prevailing sensibilities of the time made that a dangerous view to express (Johnson 1976). George Washington and Thomas Jefferson knew that slavery was wrong, as did many white American southerners before and after the Civil War, even if Washington freed his slaves only at his death and Jefferson never did (Ellis 2002). There were people who opposed Jim Crow laws, the Red Scares of the 1920s, and McCarthyism, and sometimes spoke out about it, even at danger to their own lives and interests.

There are also mundane tastes and preferences that vary with time and place and are the opposite of timeless. Some people did not like Rudy Vallee, the Beatles, or *The Fellowship of the Ring*. It is difficult to devise timeless analyses of the merits or demerits of Nehru jackets, stiletto heels, gangsta rap, 100 percent cotton, or the color mauve. Their appeal for some people depends on personal idiosyncrasy, and for others on what most or a sizable number of people in the larger society or a smaller subgroup think at a particular time. Because we are social animals, we are influenced by social influences and prevailing opinions.

The trick, as a people, is to achieve clarity on which subjects, tastes, and preferences are timeless and which are ephemeral. The former matter, and we need always to keep them in sight, even though that is not easy. As to the latter, we can comfortably let a thousand flowers bloom, and revel in their gaudy impermanence and exotic scents, knowing that others equally alluring will soon blossom in their places.

Cycles

Historians have shown how tastes and perceptions change over time, and how the beliefs and values of people change with them. Jaroslav Pelikan, in *Jesus through the Centuries* (1985), showed how each era reinvents or reinterprets the historical Jesus: in some eras he is the Messiah, sometimes a social and political reformer, sometimes the founder of the church, sometimes a charismatic leader, sometimes a spiritual ascetic. The historic Jesus was who he was, but people in different times saw what they wanted or needed to see. Over shorter periods, historians have documented similar metamorphoses in the characterization of such prominent figures in American history as Washington, Jefferson, and Lincoln.

Pelikan, unlike Elias, does not describe a perceptible if sometimes interrupted march of progress, but a series of conceptions of Jesus that reflected the needs, beliefs, and sensibilities of successive times. Nor does Pelikan describe cyclical patterns of sensibility. Sensibilities do, however, fluctuate and cycles of taste and belief recur. In one representative realm, literature and the arts, Grant Gilmore described typical fluctuations in aesthetic preference, taste, and belief:

> We have become used to the idea that, in literature and the arts, there are alternating rhythms of classicism and romanticism. During classical periods, which are, typically, of short duration, everything is neat, tidy and logical; theorists and critics reign supreme; formal rules of structure and composition are stated to the general acclaim. During classical periods, which are, among other things, extremely dull, it seems that nothing interesting is ever going to happen again. But the classical aesthetic, once it has been formulated, regularly breaks down in a protracted romantic agony. The romantics spurn the exquisitely stated rules of the preceding period; they experiment, they churn around in an ecstasy of self-expression. At the height of a romantic period, everything is confused, sprawling, formless and chaotic—as well as, frequently,

> extremely interesting. Then, the romantic energy having spent itself, there is a new classical reformulation—and so the rhythms continue. (Gilmore 1974, p. 102)

Historian David Musto has described similar cycles in American attitudes toward alcohol and drug use (1973, 1987*a*, 1987*b*). At least three times since the beginning of the nineteenth century, the United States moved from periods of widespread, tolerated recreational use of alcohol and drugs to puritanical periods of uncompromising prohibition. The first period of extreme intolerance began in the 1820s and culminated in prohibition of alcohol in eight states by the 1850s (Gusfield 1963). The temperance movement of the late nineteenth century led to national Prohibition; more generalized intolerance of drug use and users produced the first major federal narcotics laws, the Harrison Act of 1914 and the Marijuana Tax Act of 1937. The first signs of the contemporary period of extreme intolerance appeared around 1970, when the Nixon administration declared its war on drugs. Those attitudes toward drug use took firm hold in the early 1980s and the United States remains in their grip.

According to Musto, peoples' normative beliefs about drug use vary with successive phases of cycles of tolerance and intolerance of drug use. Live-and-let-live attitudes prevail in periods of relative tolerance, like the 1870s–1880s and the 1950s–1960s. In the late nineteenth and early twentieth centuries, for example, cocaine and opium (and derivatives) were widely used in patent medicines, most addicts were conventional, law-abiding people, predominantly women, and cocaine was widely seen as a harmless recreational drug. Conan Doyle's Sherlock Holmes was a regular user of cocaine but that made neither the author nor the character notorious.

In the 1960s, marijuana was widely and openly used; it and many hallucinogens were seen by many as recreational drugs less harmful than alcohol. Numerous local jurisdictions, including prominently Ann Arbor, Michigan, and Berkeley, California, effectively decriminalized use, possession, and small-scale trafficking of marijuana. Alfred Blumstein (1993) showed how the realization that white middle-class kids were getting criminal records and sometimes going to prisons for minor drug offenses led to a drastic reduction in drug arrests of young whites in the early 1970s. President Carter in 1977 called for federal decriminalization of private marijuana possession. A few years earlier Peter Bourne (not then, but later Carter's primary drug policy advisor; now he would be called the "drug czar") wrote that cocaine "is probably the most benign of illicit drugs currently in widespread use. At least as strong a case could be made for legalizing it as for legalizing marijuana" (Musto 1987*a*, p. 265).

Conversely, during periods of extreme intolerance, recreational drug issues tend to be seen in black and white, and adoption of policies of unrelenting vigor is not uncommon. Liberal Republican Governor Nelson Rockefeller of New York, for example, in 1972 proposed and won adoption of the Rockefeller Drug Laws that established long mandatory minimum sentences for drug offenses, forbade plea-negotiating prosecutors from waiving prison sentences, and paid for additional courts and judges to implement the new laws. Every American state during the 1970s and 1980s adopted mandatory minimum sentence laws for drug crimes. The U.S. Congress in 1986 enacted the harshest drug sentencing laws in U.S. history, including the 100-to-1 law that punishes crack cocaine trafficking, then as now primarily committed by blacks, as harshly as powder cocaine offenses, then as now primarily committed by whites, 100 times larger. In 1988, legislation was enacted providing for appointment of a federal drug czar to lead the war on drugs. By 1989 the per capita drug arrest rate had risen by a factor of six in ten years, and by 2000, the number of people held in federal and state prisons and jails for drug offenses had climbed to 324,489, up 1,370 percent from 1980 (when there were 23,900). In 1994 Congress authorized the death penalty for various drug-related crimes. At various times during the 1980s and 1990s, Americans responding to opinion polls named drug abuse as or among America's most pressing problems.

Musto has several times written of the seeming anomaly that prohibitionistic sentiments become strongest and drug policies harshest after drug use has begun to decline (e.g., 1987*a*, *b*). At various periods, drug use comes into vogue, use increases, and dangers of abusive use become more evident. Eventually, as Daniel Kagan has summarized Musto's argument:

> The trend reverses; drug use starts to decline faster and faster. Public opinion turns against drugs and their acceptability begins to evaporate. Gradually, drug use becomes associated, truthfully or not, with the lower ranks of society, and often with racial and ethnic groups that are feared or despised by the middle class. Drugs become seen as deviant and dangerous and become a potent symbol of evil. Trailing behind this decline come large-scale legislative and law enforcement efforts . . . aimed at curtailing drug sales and use through energetic prohibition and enforcement and ever-harsher punishments against sellers and users. During this period, public opprobrium intensifies into outright fear, hatred of drug dealers and users, and a burning anger and intolerance toward anyone and anything associated with drug use. (Kagan 1989, p. 7)

During periods of relative tolerance, people feel comfortable invoking traditional American notions of individualism and personal autonomy to justify making their own choices about drug use. Drug use is widely seen as only mildly deviant or not deviant at all. People feel comfortable arguing on the merits for the benefits and pleasures of drug use, for individuals' rights to make their own choices, and against state intrusion into those choices.

In periods of extreme intolerance, drug use is widely seen as deviant. Few people feel comfortable risking moral disapproval or stigmatization by arguing in favor of drug use or tolerance of drug users. Musto notes that, "in the decline phase of drug use . . . we tend to have an overkill, that is to say people become so righteous and so zealous that we can have excesses in the name of fighting drugs. There is very little opposition to draconian policies because no one wants to stand up for using drugs" (1987*b*, p. 43).

The important thing about the Gilmore and Musto accounts, for my purposes, is that they tie sensibilities and beliefs to recurring segments of cyclical patterns. Gilmore observes that, during classical periods, rules of composition and structure are stated "to the general acclaim." Formalism, in other words, is not foisted upon a society or an era, but embodies aesthetic qualities that people value, or believe they value, which is almost the same thing. Romantic aesthetic values likewise become predominant in a period not because they are compelled but because they are celebrated. Musto writes that people "become so righteous and so zealous" during the decline phase of drug use that they adopt views and support policies that most people in other times would see as draconic. People behave like this not because they are coerced or cajoled into it but because that is how they feel.

It is a truism that our upbringings, past experiences, material circumstances, and immediate environments shape the way we see and understand the world. People tend not to be conservative until they have things to conserve, and so the frequent pattern that youthful radicals become middle-aged moderates and elderly conservatives. Or, the somewhat different Chinese developmental stereotype that people are Confucianist while young, Realist in maturity, and Taoist when old. And history is full of stories of whole societies overwhelmed by fear, insecurity, or anger to do or tolerate horrible things that later appear unthinkable.

It is one thing, however, to acknowledge that our characteristics, interests, and experiences influence our wants and beliefs, and quite another to urge, with some of the sillier postmodernists, that what we see depends solely on where we stand. Since one standpoint is as good as any other, it is said, we can not see anything (or we can see many things, but no perception is any more "privileged" or any less "contingent" than any other). That may be a plausible position to adopt in relation to aesthetic assessments of bellbottoms, bouffant hairdos, or gangsta rap but not in relation to fundamental normative issues over which human beings have puzzled for millennia.

Even during periods of intolerance, some people recognize cruelty and excess. Thoughtful people have always recognized the polar possibilities in the value-laden domains of religion, sexuality, and criminal punishment, the alternatives that lie between them, the practical and principled arguments that can be made for one position or another, and the inexorability of the processes by which one set of beliefs displaces another. Unfortunately, all that tends to get forgotten by most people in the heat of a historical moment.

Human beings have been round the bend and back enough times that we should be able, by learning from history, to escape being condemned to repeat at least its worst excesses. Witches and heretics have burned sufficiently often, to later regret, that there is no need to burn them again in order to be able again to regret it. That lesson should have been learnt for good by now and, at least in most Western countries, probably has been. Similar lessons can and will be learned about tolerance of human sexual diversity, experimentation with and use of intoxicants, and punishment of wrongdoers.

Bibliography

Bettleheim, Bruno (1977), *The Uses of Enchantment: The Meaning and Importance of Fairy Tales*, London: Thames and Hudson.

Blumstein, Alfred (1993), 'Making Rationality Relevent–The American Society of Criminology 1992 Presidential Address', *Criminology*, **31**, pp.1–16.

Boswell, John. (1980), *Christianity, Social Tolerance, and Homosexuality*, Chicago: University of Chicago Press.

Camus, Albert (1960 c. 1959), *Reflections on the Guillotine: An Essay on Capital Punishment*, Trans. Richard Howard, Michigan City, ID: Fridtjof-Karla Publications.

Erikson, Kai T. (1966), *Wayward Puritans: A Study in the Sociology of Deviance*, New York: John Wiley.

Elias, Norbert (1978), *The History of Manners: The Civilising* Process, vol. 1. Oxford: Basil Blackwell. (Originally published 1939, Basel: Hans Zum Falken.)

Ellis, Joseph J. (2002), *Founding Brothers: The Revolutionary Generation*, New York: Vintage.

Foucault, Michael (1977), *Discipline and Punish: The Birth of the* Prison, Trans. Robert Hurley, NY: Pantheon.

Garland, David (1990), *Punishment and Modern Society: A Study in Social Theory*, Chicago, IL: University of Chicago Press.

_____ (2001*a*), *The Culture of Control: Crime and Social Order in Contemporary Society*. Chicago, IL: University of Chicago Press.

Gilmore, Grant (1974), *The Death of Contract*, Columbus, OH: Ohio State University Press.

Greenberg, David F. (1988), *The Construction of* Homosexuality, Chicago, IL: University of Chicago Press.

Gusfield, Joseph R. (1963). *Symbolic Crusade: Status Politics and the American Temperance* Movement, Urbana-Champaign, IL: University of Illinois Press.

Johnson, Paul (1976), *A History of Christianity*, New York: Atheneum.

Kagan, David (1989), 'How America Lost Its First Drug War', *Insight*, pp. 8–17 (Nov. 20, 1989).

Musto, David (1973), *The American Disease: Origins of Narcotic Control*, New Haven, CT.: Yale University Press.

_____ (1987*a*), *The American Disease: Origins of Narcotic* Control, Expanded edition, (Originally published 1973) New York: Oxford University Press.

_____ (1987*b*), 'Changing Attitudes toward Drugs and Alcohol in the United States', in Jeffrey A. Roth, Michael Tonry and Norval Morris (eds), *Drugs and Crime: Workshop Proceedings*, A Report of the 1986 National Academy of Sciences Conference on Drugs and Crime Research, Washington, DC: National Academy of Sciences.

Pelikan, Jaroslav (1985). *Jesus Through the Centuries: His Place in the History of* Culture, New Haven, CT: Yale University Press.

Walker, Nigel (1991), *Why Punish?*, Oxford: Oxford University Press.

[9]
Emerging Explanations of American Punishment Policies

Abstract

None of the conventional explanations why American penal policies became so severe – rising crime rates, harsh public attitudes and cynical electoral politics – are persuasive. Nor are various 'conditions of late modernity' such as the limited capacities of governments, increasing population diversity or increasing insecurity and risk aversion. All these things characterized every developed country in much of the period 1975–2000 and most did not adopt drastically harsher policies. Nor are such amorphous and over-generalized notions as 'populist punitiveness', 'penal populism' and neo-liberalism of much use. Some things do have explanatory power cross-nationally. Moderate penal policies and low imprisonment rates are associated with low levels of income inequality, high levels of trust and legitimacy, strong welfare states, professionalized as opposed to politicized criminal justice systems and consensual rather than conflictual political cultures. For each of those factors, the United States falls at the wrong end of the distribution. The question is, Why? Four answers stand out: the 'paranoid style' in American politics; a Manichean moralism associated with fundamentalist religious views; the obsolescence of the American constitution; and the history of race relations in the USA.

Key Words

American exceptionalism • fundamentalism • paranoid politics • penality • punishment

The natural history of modern explanations of penal policy trends has begun to emerge. The story is circular, moving from an unstated and unexamined assumption that explanations are to be found in local conditions in each country (e.g. Bennett et al., 1996), to a search for overriding theories and models (e.g. Garland, 2001; Lacey, 2008), to identification of predictive and protective factors (e.g. Tonry, 2007) and finally back to local explanations (e.g. Simon, 2007; Green, 2008; Barker, 2009). Larger, even global social and economic changes affecting most developed countries provide a backdrop, but persuasive explanations of why policies and practices change (or don't) in particular places can be found only in the histories and cultures of those places.

Until the 1970s, no particular trends were apparent in the United States. Imprisonment rates had been broadly stable for at least a half- century (Blumstein and Cohen, 1973) and crime control had been a political issue only episodically. Other countries had their own patterns. In some – Finland and Switzerland, for example – imprisonment rates approached 200 per 100,000 before or after the Second World War, and fell sharply afterwards. After the Second World War, Japanese rates gradually declined for a half-century and Dutch for a quarter-century. Scandinavian rates except in Finland were broadly stable through the 1990s, and those in the largest European countries of England and Wales, France, Germany, Italy and Spain meandered. Eastern European countries had rates ranging between 200 and 400 per 100,000.

Countries changed their criminal justice systems and policies after the Second World War, generally toward increased investment in rehabilitative programs through the 1970s, but that did not much affect the overall picture of distinctively national penal policy patterns. Japanese imprisonment rates fell because crime rates fell and (as outsiders at least saw it) because informal social controls were strong. Finnish rates fell because policymakers worked to make that happen. German rates were stable because policymakers and judges subscribed to a general skepticism about the desirability of imprisonment, and to support for a neoclassical view that punishments should be predicated on assessments of offenders' culpability. English policies and practices fluctuated with the changing views of policy elites.

The search for general explanations began only in the late 1980s and early 1990s, precipitated partly by recognition that American imprisonment rates tripled between 1973 and 1990 and that rates appeared to be increasing in some other countries, and partly by increased availability of more-or-less standardized national imprisonment data (e.g. Pease, 1991; Young and Brown, 1993). Before that, there was no general academic literature on the subject[1] and lay explanations focused on rising crime rates, punitive public attitudes and political cynicism. After that, a series of influential publications exemplified by David Garland's (2001) magisterial *Culture of control* sought general explanations focusing on globalization, heightened insecurities and various 'conditions of late modernity'.

Although a literature of general explanation continues to accumulate (e.g. Cavadino and Dignan, 2005; Lacey, 2008), most recent work focuses on national or local rather than global (in either main sense) explanations. David Green (2008) attributes radically different responses to highly publicized child-on-child killings in England and Norway to factors as diverse as differences in national and political culture, governmental legitimacy and print media characteristics. Jonathan Simon (2007) describes two centuries of American history of the prison as a totemic political symbol. Anne-Marie Cusac (2009) searches for American explanations in the role of religious beliefs and attitudes since the 17th century. Marie Gottschalk (2006) focuses on the interplay of social movements with distinctively American political developments. Lisa Miller (2008) and Vanessa Barker (2009) explain penal policies and climates in California, New York, Pennsylvania and Washington in terms of enduring political cultures and structures.

Tip O'Neill, an influential American politician of the 1970s and 1980s, and long-time head of the US House of Representatives, is in retrospect best known for declaiming that 'All politics is local.' This essay tells the emerging story of American penal policies of the past 35 years. Although it may to some readers seem yet another example of navel-gazing American parochialism, its aim is to demonstrate that the best version of the story is distinctively local and to suggest that the stories in other countries are likely also to be.

Four features of American history and culture are important. Two – a paranoid style in American politics and a Manichean moralism associated with Protestant fundamentalism – are recurring characteristics of American society. The third is obsolete constitutional arrangements that give short-term emotions and politics greater influence on policy than elsewhere. The fourth, aggravating and aggravated by the first three, is the distinctive history of American race relations.

EARLY VERSIONS OF THE AMERICAN STORY

The United States is the only western country that retains the death penalty. It has the world's highest imprisonment rate, exceeding 750 per 100,000 residents, and regularly imposes the developed world's harshest criminal punishments short of death, life sentences without the possibility of parole (LWOPs). Unlike most European countries and Canada, it refuses to acknowledge the moral force of international human rights conventions and declarations, or to incorporate them into its laws. Fifty years ago, United States governments were world leaders in promoting human rights values, the imprisonment rate was stable and in line with those of other western democracies, capital punishment was falling into disuse, and the US Supreme Court was admired throughout the world for its extension of human rights protections to criminal suspects.

Something went terribly wrong. In the simplest sense, we know what happened and why. Between 1975 and 1995, policymakers enacted a wide range of laws meant to make punishments severer, and practitioners applied those laws. These included three-strikes-and-you're-out laws requiring minimum 25-year sentences; 10-, 20- and 30-year minimum sentences for violent, firearms and drug offenses; LWOPs; laws permitting prosecutions of tens of thousands of young people each year as adults; and laws extending the reach of capital punishment. Independently of policy changes, practitioners became more punitive and risk-averse: prosecutors charged and bargained more aggressively, judges sent more people to prison and for longer, parole boards released fewer prisoners, and later, and returned parolees to prison more often.

What we don't know is why American policymakers, nearly alone among leaders of western governments, chose to enact such harsh policies and laws, or why practitioners became so much tougher.

Crime rates and trends are not the answer. Crime rate trends were much the same throughout the western world after 1970 – rises through the early 1990s and declines since (e.g. van Dijk et al., 2007). Imprisonment rates and penal policies however have differed enormously. In the United States, crime rates have fallen steadily since 1991 and imprisonment rates have risen every year, more than doubling since 1991 and increasing by more than five times since 1973 (Tonry, 2004).

Nor is public opinion the answer. In the English-speaking countries at least, penal policies and imprisonment rates vary enormously but public opinion is much the same. Majorities of the public believe crime rates are rising when they are falling. Large majorities believe judges are too lenient, on the basis of mistaken beliefs about the severity of punishments. The sentences citizens say they believe are appropriate are typically less severe than the sentences judges actually impose. When citizens are asked whether they prefer more punitive policies or increased investment in rehabilitative programs, majorities usually prefer the latter (Roberts et al., 2002).

Three sets of more complicated answers have been offered. The first, by David Garland (2001), attributes toughened penal policies in England and the USA to conditions of 'late modernity'. These include the limited capacities of governments to affect crime rates, increasing population diversity and 'the criminology of the other', increased vulnerability of privileged segments of the population to victimization by crime, and increased insecurities associated with globalization and rapid social change. The result is a proliferation of expressive policies meant more to show that government is doing something, to reassure the public and to aid politicians' efforts to win re-election than to reduce crime.

The insuperable difficulty for Garland's analysis is that, if it is right, it should explain why all western countries have experienced steeply rising imprisonment rates and steadily harshening penal policies. All the 'causal' developments he describes happened everywhere. Imprisonment rates and policy trends, however, diverged dramatically. Crime rates rose steeply in most western countries between 1970 and the early 1990s but only in a few did policymakers adopt policies intended to make punishments harsher or imprisonment rates higher.

In the face of similar crime rate trends, imprisonment rates increased five- and six-fold in the United States and the Netherlands after 1973 and doubled in England and Spain after 1993. Finnish policymakers chose to make that country's penal policies less harsh and to reduce its imprisonment rates. Canada, and most European countries – the rest of Scandinavia, Belgium, France, Italy, Germany, Austria – did not adopt harsh new broad-based policies and in diverse ways worked to keep their imprisonment rates stable. Only in a few western countries – England, Portugal, Spain, New Zealand – and only after crime rates began to fall in the 1990s did imprisonment rates rise significantly, but to levels at their peaks less than one-fourth the current American rate (Tonry, 2004, ch. 5, 2007).

Michael Cavadino and James Dignan (2005) offer a second analytical framework. A three-part typology (technically four, but one contains only a single country, Japan) links imprisonment trends and penal policy differences with systems of political economy. Neo-liberal states (e.g. England, New Zealand, the United States) are said to have the harshest policies and social democratic corporatist states (e.g. Scandinavia) the mildest, with conservative corporatist states (e.g. Germany, France) falling in-between.

This analysis makes sense, sort of, only early in the 21st century. There are at least three kinds of anomalies it cannot explain. First, even in 2005, some countries did not fit their categories. The Netherlands then had the highest imprisonment rate in Western Europe except for England and Wales, but was not counted as 'neo-liberal' while Australia, which had a rate only slightly higher than Germany's, was characterized as neo-liberal. Second, countries excluded from the analysis defied the categories. Canada by all accounts should be included among the English-speaking neo-liberals but its imprisonment rate has held steady around 100 per 100,000 population for a half-century, so it should have been classified among the conservative corporatists with

France and Germany. Spain and Portugal, also excluded, have had among the highest imprisonment rates in Western Europe at various times since the mid-1990s and no one would classify them as neo-liberal (rates have since fallen in Portugal). Third, the typology collapses in other periods. In 1970, for example, the Dutch imprisonment rate was the lowest among the developed countries and the US rate was in the mainstream. The Finnish was the highest. That would have made the Finns neo-liberal, the Americans conservative corporatists and the Dutch, quite properly, social democrats.

A third set of analyses attempts to explain penal policies in terms of such things as income inequality, citizens' perceptions of the legitimacy of governmental institutions, citizens' trust in each other and in government, the strength of the welfare state and the structure of government (Downes and Hansen, 2006; Lappi-Seppälä, 2007, 2008; Di Tella and Dubra, 2008). All these things seem to matter. Moderate penal policies and low imprisonment rates are associated with low levels of income inequality, high levels of trust and legitimacy, strong welfare states, professionalized as opposed to politicized criminal justice systems and consensual rather than conflictual political cultures (Tonry, 2007).

Even that analysis, however, does not explain American developments. For each of those factors, the United States falls at the wrong end, the end associated with more punitive policies and practices. We need to understand why.

POLITICAL PARANOIA

Historian Richard Hofstadter described the 'paranoid style' as a recurring feature of American politics. What is deeply disapproved is seen as evil or immoral and few means are off limits in pursuit of its eradication. Hofstadter distinguished clinical definitions of paranoia from the paranoid style:

> [T]he clinical paranoid sees the hostile and conspiratorial world in which he feels himself to be living as directed specifically *against him*; whereas the spokesman of the paranoid style finds it directed against a nation, a culture, a way of life whose fate affects not him alone but millions of others . . . His sense that his political passions are unselfish and patriotic, in fact, goes far to intensify his feelings of righteousness and his moral indignation. (Hofstadter, 1965: 4, emphasis in original)

> [T]he paranoid is a militant leader. He does not see social conflict as something to be mediated and compromised, in the way of the working politician. Since what is at stake is always a conflict between absolute good and absolute evil, the quality needed is not a willingness to compromise but the will to fight things out to the finish. Nothing but complete victory will do. (Hofstadter, 1965: 31)

American political paranoia waxes and wanes and finds different targets at different times. It manifests itself on the Left and the Right, though in recent decades mostly on the Right. In the 20th century it waxed three times. The first was in the 1920s and 1930s, and was exemplified by Prohibition, the Red Scares of the 1920s, and the xenophobia and isolationism of the entire period. It wound down when the Second World War gave people more important things to worry about.

The second was in the late 1940s and 1950s and is exemplified by Senator Joseph McCarthy, the House Un-American Activities Committee and the John Birch Society. It was temporarily pushed aside by the optimism and idealism of the 1960s.

The third dates from the 1980s and is exemplified by recent decades' wars on drugs, crime, welfare recipients and illegal immigrants, and since 2001 by the American 'war against terror'.

The right wing of the Republican Party deserves most of the blame for revitalizing and legitimizing the paranoid streak since the 1970s and thereby impoverishing American criminal justice policy and diminishing its commitment to human rights values. This took two forms. The first, well documented, was the use of crime, welfare and affirmative action to provoke white southern and working-class enmities toward blacks and politicians who espoused their interests (Phillips, 1969; Edsall and Edsall, 1991). The second was the incorporation into the Republican Party of people, ideas and rhetoric developed by the John Birch Society, the archetypal right-wing paranoid group of the 1950s. By the 1960s many of the Society's views had been adopted by the 1964 Republican presidential candidate Barry Goldwater and the (then) far-right wing of the Republican Party.

By the 1970s the paranoid political view became mainstream Republican rhetoric (Lichtman, 2008; Perlstein, 2008). One of the Birch Society's signature initiatives was its 'Impeach Earl Warren' campaign. US Supreme Court Chief Justice Warren's impeachable offenses related to *Brown v. Board of Education*, 347 US 483 (1954), the landmark decision declaring that segregated schools were unconstitutional, and the court's early halting efforts to strengthen the procedural protections afforded criminal defendants. The John Birch Society's effort to impugn the integrity of the courts and to reduce their legitimacy has been echoed in Republican rhetoric ever since, leading to 40 years of attacks on 'activist', 'lenient' and 'liberal' judges. One consequence has been declining legitimacy of the courts and the legal system in the eyes of the American public.

Since the 1970s, activist conservative federal judges, appointed by Republican presidents, have weakened procedural protections accorded suspects, weakened convicted offenders' appeal rights and speeded up executions. And the US Congress, in the name of reining in (liberal) activist judges, made it almost impossible for prisoners to file effective lawsuits alleging unconstitutional prison conditions and made it much more difficult for offenders to appeal their convictions.

Why did Americans tolerate such illiberal policies? The influence of the paranoid style and 50 years' effort to delegitimize judges and courts and the legitimacy of offenders' complaints took hold.

PROTESTANT FUNDAMENTALISM AND INTOLERANCE

Although several of the original American colonies were established by people escaping religious intolerance – the Puritans in Massachusetts Bay, the Quakers in Pennsylvania and the nonconformists in Rhode Island are the classic examples – within half a century people were being killed for religious reasons. Kai Erickson's (1966) *Wayward puritans* is most famous for its accounts of the Salem witch trials but it also describes the gradual descent into intolerance in Massachusetts that led to the maiming and execution of Quaker and other proselytizing missionaries.

A sizable historical literature on 19th-century America recounts recurring episodes of religion-based intolerance (e.g. Myers, 1943; Davis, 1960). Usually these were related to the status anxieties and xenophobia of established groups triggered by the in-migration of new ethnic groups. The temperance movements in the middle and late 19th century, for example, usually involved conflicts between abstemious descendants of English and Scottish Protestants and more bibulous Catholics from Ireland, Italy and Germany (Gusfield, 1963). Moralistic crusades against alcohol operated to express disapproval and social distance.

Moralistic crusades against drugs and crime in our time enabled fundamentalist Protestants and social conservatives to express disapproval of people unlike themselves and to assert their moral superiority. The Republicans' 'southern strategy' with its race-coded emphasis on states' rights, crime and welfare (and later affirmative action) deliberately appealed to the resentments and status anxieties of southern and working-class whites (Phillips, 1969, 1991; Edsall and Edsall, 1991).

The same pattern existed in earlier times. David Garland (2005) showed that lynchings in the USA in 1890–1930, the peak period, were in significant part the product of status anxieties of southern white Protestants. In the 1920s, the Ku Klux Klan defined itself primarily as a campaign to preserve Christian values: 'The Klan drew heavily on white evangelical Protestants for its mass membership, and evangelical clergy were disproportionately prominent among the leadership' (Wald and Calhoun-Brown, 2007: 208).

When Hofstadter (1965: 70) wrote, the rapidly expanding and beginning-to-be-prosperous fundamentalist Protestant groups made up one important strand of the political paranoia of his era: 'most prophetic of the future of the right wing was [McCarthy's] strong appeal for fundamentalist oriented Protestants'.

In our time, some (though definitely not all) fundamentalist and evangelical groups are among the strongest proponents of the paranoid style of contemporary politics concerning issues ranging from abortion and gay rights to crime and capital punishment. The notion that these are issues of good and evil, of absolute right and wrong, helps to explain the religious right's fervor and its intolerance. When added to recent decades' resurgence of the paranoid style in American politics, it is small wonder that the interests of people seen as enemies or threats typically receive short shrift.

The sizable political science and religion literatures on religion and politics in the United States are silent, except in passing, on the influence of Protestant fundamentalism on American crime policy generally, though they discuss abortion and capital punishment (e.g. Layman, 2001; Green, 2007). The leading work, *Religion and politics in the United States* (Wald and Calhoun-Brown, 2007), explains how and why Protestant fundamentalism has shaped American crime control and punishment policies for three decades. Whereas mainstream Protestants espouse a commitment to social welfare consonant with their belief in 'a warm, caring god', the fundamentalist 'image of a cold and authoritative deity lends support to government's role in securing order and property' (Wald and Calhoun-Brown, 2007: 121). Fundamentalists are 'characterized by a quest for certainty, exclusiveness, and unambiguous boundaries', and attempt 'to chart a morally black and white path out of the gray zones of intimidating cultural and religious complexity' (Nagata, 2001: 481).

The Republican resurgence of the past 40 years is attributable in large part to the Southern Strategy and its focus on the 'wedge issues' of crime, welfare and affirmative action (Edsall and Edsall, 1991). The political influence of the religious right on

Republican politics is well known (e.g. Green, 2007). One major literature review on fundamentalism and conservative politics observed, '[T]he religious right holds something like a veto power in the Republican Party' (Woodberry and Smith, 1998: 48).

Unnever et al.'s (2005: 304) examination of attitudes toward capital punishment concludes that those fundamentalists 'who have a rigid and moralistic approach to religion and who imagine God as a dispassionate figure who dispenses justice are more likely to harbor punitive sentiments toward offenders'. A slight but fascinating article based on a representative survey of Oklahoma City residents showed that Protestant conservatives viewed nearly all crimes as 'very wrong' and did not differentiate among them in seriousness (Curry, 1996: 462). This finding goes a long way toward explaining why traditional ideas about proportionality in punishment are irreconcilable with many modern sentencing laws.

CONSTITUTIONAL STRUCTURE

Hofstadter (1965: 7) observed that 'certain features of our history have given the paranoid style more scope and force among us than it has had in many other countries of the western world'. The obsolescence of American constitutional arrangements is among them.

Major elements of the US constitutional system are obsolete, designed to address 18th- not 20th- or 21st-century problems,[2] and they make the United States almost uniquely vulnerable to the policy excesses associated with the paranoid style and religious fundamentalism.

Politicization of criminal justice policy is directly related to whether prosecutors and judges are selected politically or meritocratically, whether they are career professionals or political opportunists and whether political and constitutional conventions allow elected politicians to participate in decision making about individual cases. These three factors fundamentally differentiate the United States from most other western countries. Almost nowhere in Western Europe, Canada or Australia are judges or prosecutors politically selected (Tonry, 2007).

The American constitution dates from the late 18th century, reflects 18th-century ideas and was written to address 18th-century problems. These included governance by a distant Parliament, capricious actions by the British government's local representatives and the inability of citizens to obtain redress for grievances. The principal solutions centered on respect for individual liberty and insulation of citizens from the power of the State. Protection of individual liberty was addressed by adoption of the Bill of Rights creating fundamental personal rights (speech, religion, redress) and entitlements (jury trials, no unreasonable searches and seizures, representation by counsel).

Protection from state power was sought in two ways. First, complicated checks and balances fragmented governmental power, principally by creating a strong horizontal separation of powers among the three branches of the federal government, and vertical differentiation of the spheres of interest of the federal and the state governments (which in turn had their own systems of horizontal and vertical separations of powers). Second, provisions in the federal constitution specified frequent elections to the House of Representatives (two years) and presidency (four years), and state constitutions provided for frequent elections at county levels for state legislators, judges and prosecutors, pushed major elections to local levels and thereby made officials accountable to local opinion.

The results 200 years later in many states include partisan elections of judges and prosecutors who run for office on the basis of emotional and sometimes demagogic appeals. If the public is anxious about crime or angry at criminals, or if particular cases become notorious, there is nothing to stop prosecutors from seeking personal political benefit by posturing before public opinion. Judges are elected in most states and know that highly unpopular decisions can lead to their defeat. Many chief prosecutors and judges aspire to higher political or judicial offices. They worry about controversies that might diminish their future professional prospects. They no doubt sometimes are tempted to deal with a particular case in a particular way to curry popular approbation or avoid popular condemnation.

American constitutional arrangements place the United States at one end of a continuum distinguishing consensual from conflictual political systems (e.g. Lijphart, 1999). Consensual political systems are usually characterized by more than two major political parties, coalition governments, proportional representation and multi-seat electoral districts. Major policy decisions are based on broad consultation within the coalition government and outside it. Major decisions are seldom changed abruptly, even after new governments are elected. New coalitions are likely to contain parties from the old one, and parties newly in power often were involved in development of policies of the former government.

Conflictual political systems are typically characterized by two major parties, single-party governments, first-past-the-post electoral systems and single-member districts. Elections are winner-take-all events. Out-of-power parties define their positions in opposition to those of the Government and, having played little or no part in developing existing policies, have no particular reason to maintain them.

The United States is the paradigm case of a conflictual system (Lijphart, 1999). Most European systems are consensual. They took shape in the 20th century and were designed for pluralistic societies and sought to assure broad-based political representation. They diffuse political power rather then concentrate it, and often provide for parliamentary representation of any party receiving votes above a minimum threshold, often 5 percent.

No other western country besides the United States and Great Britain has a constitution primarily designed to address centuries-old problems. All others include entrenched bills of rights. Most were designed to address the challenges of pluralistic societies and call for electoral systems of proportional representation. Most are generally governed by multi-party coalitions. All EU countries and Canada regard the European Convention of Human Rights as part of their national constitutional law and most countries in Europe accept decisions of the European Court of Human Rights as binding and self-executing. No other English-speaking or Western European country but Switzerland has popular elections for prosecutors and judges.

The structure of American government was meant to tie officials closely to community needs and beliefs, and democratic ideology celebrated the importance and influence of public opinion, even if it was ill informed, mercurial or mean-spirited. Constitutional draftsmen worried about the dangers of mobocracy but, with local notable exceptions, the problem did not fully take shape until late in the 20th century when ubiquitous electronic and broadcast media meant that detailed reports of horrible incidents anywhere, and ensuing emotionalism, could sweep across an entire continent.

RACE

The history of race relations in the USA is the fourth explanation. I used to get impatient with people who saw the half-empty glass of enduring injustice rather than the half-full one of American racial progress, but two things convince me I was wrong. The first is recent work updating *Malign neglect*, a book on race, crime and punishment in the USA I wrote long ago. The second is appreciation of work by Löic Wacquant, Douglas Massey, Lawrence Bobo, Glenn Loury and others on American race relations.

I tried in *Malign neglect* to figure out why black Americans were so much likelier than whites to be arrested, convicted, imprisoned and executed (Tonry, 1995). Here is what I learned. First, though blacks had for a century been more likely to be held in prison than whites, racial disparities began to rise in the 1960s and shot up to all-time highs in the 1980s: blacks by then were half of American prisoners, though only 12 percent of the US population, and had an imprisonment rate seven times higher than the white rate.

Second, blacks were much more likely than whites to be arrested for the 'imprisonable' offenses of robbery, rape, aggravated assault and homicide. Data on victims' descriptions of assailants and police data on victim and offender characteristics in homicide cases suggested that the patterns shown in arrest data for serious crimes were not far off from reality.

Third, however, critically, there had been no significant shifts in racial patterns in arrests for a quarter-century. Involvement in serious violent crime could not explain why black imprisonment rates rose so steeply in the 1980s.

Fourth, the principal cause of the increase was imprisonment for drug crimes and policymakers knew or should have known that the enemy foot soldiers in the war on drugs would be young, disadvantaged, inner-city members of American minority groups.

In updating analyses in that book, Matthew Melewski and I identified one bit of good news and two of terrible news (Tonry and Melewski, 2008). The good news is that patterns of racial involvement in serious crime have changed. The percentages of blacks among people arrested for aggravated assault, robbery, rape and homicide have been declining, and in 2006 were much lower than in 1985.

The two bits of terrible news. First, blacks continue to make up about half of the prison population,[3] and about the same percentage of Death Row inmates as in the 1980s. The chance that a black American is in prison in 2007 remains six-to-seven times higher than the chance that a white American is in prison. The declining involvement of blacks in serious violent crime has not reduced racial disparities in prison.

Second, neglect of the interests of black Americans continues to characterize American crime policies. Racial disparities in imprisonment continue to be caused by policy choices that are known to have devastating effects on disadvantaged black Americans. In no significant respects have American drug policies changed since the 1980s, and they continue disproportionately to ensnare young black and increasingly young Hispanic Americans. More recent American policies toughening penalties for violent crime have had the same effect. If the conditions of life faced by disadvantaged minority youth make them disproportionately likely to be involved in violent crime, then punishing violent crimes much more harshly will disproportionately affect them. It has.

Wacquant's work explains how that could happen. American cultural practices and legal institutions have operated to maintain American patterns of racial dominance and hierarchy for two centuries, he argues, and contemporary drug and crime policies perform that function today. Until the Civil War, slavery assured white domination. Within 30 years after the war, the set of practices and legal forms of discrimination known as 'Jim Crow' laws restored white domination of blacks. After the 'Great Migration' in 1913–19 and the 1920s, when millions of blacks moved from south to north to escape Jim Crow, the big city ghettos and housing discrimination kept blacks in their subordinate place. And when deindustrialization and the flight of jobs to the suburbs left disadvantaged blacks marooned in the urban ghettos, the modern wars on drugs and crime took over (Wacquant, 2002a, 2002b).

The litany of disparate treatments of blacks by the criminal justice system only starts with the seven-to-one racial difference in imprisonment rates. The Bureau of Justice Statistics (BJS, 2003) estimates that 32 percent of black males born in 2001 will spend some time as a state or federal prison inmate; that figure ignores jails which annually process many more people than prisons do. BJS in 2007 estimated that a third of black men in their 20s were in prison or jail, or on probation or parole.

It is hard not to conclude that the machinery of the criminal justice system produces devastatingly reduced life chances for black Americans (Western, 2006). If the aim were to reduce black men's chances of earning a decent living, or being successfully married and a good father, or being socialized into pro-social values, it is hard to see how the justice system could do those things more effectively.

Wacquant is not alone in suggesting that American criminal justice practices operate to keep poor blacks in their places. Douglas Massey, author (with Nancy Denton) of *American apartheid* (1993), a widely praised account of housing discrimination, offered this analysis in his 2007 book on social stratification:

> Whether whites care to admit it or not, they have a selfish interest in maintaining the categorical mechanisms that perpetuate racial stratification. As a result, when pushed by the federal government to end overt discriminatory practices, they are likely to innovate new and more subtle ways to maintain their privileged position in society. If one discriminatory mechanism proves impossible to sustain, whites have an incentive to develop alternatives that may be associated only indirectly with race and are therefore not in obvious violation of civil rights laws. The specific mechanisms by which racial stratification occurs can thus be expected to evolve over time. (2007: 54)

> The new emphasis on retribution and punishment was achieved ... through the deliberate racialization of crime and violence in public consciousness by political entrepreneurs. (2007: 94)

> As discrimination moved underground, new mechanisms for exclusion were built into the criminal justice system for Afro Americans. (2007: 251)

Glenn C. Loury (2007), a leading conservative economist, introducing his 2007 Tanner Lectures at Stanford, observed:

> [W]e have embraced what criminologist Michael Tonry (1995) calls a policy of 'malign neglect,' and in doing so we, as a society, have stumbled more or less wittingly into a God-awful cul de sac. I will claim that the connection of this apparatus to the history of racial degradation and subordination in our country (lynching, minstrelsy, segregation, ghetto-ization) is virtually self-evident, and that the racial subtext of our law and order political discourse over the last three decades has been palpable. (references omitted)

Once the racial hierarchy/status anxiety analysis that Wacquant, Massey and Loury offer is recognized, much else falls into place. David Garland (2005: 817) observes of lynchings in the USA in 1890–1930,

> The penal excess of the lynching spectacle said things that a modernized legal process could not . . . [I]t reestablished the correlative status of the troublesome black man, which was as nothing, with no rights, no protectors, no personal dignity, and no human worth.

A considerable literature on racial differences in attitudes toward and opinions about crime control policy shows that whites have substantially harsher attitudes concerning punishment and greater confidence in the justice system and its practitioners than do blacks (e.g. Unnever et al., 2008). Lawrence Bobo and Devon Johnson (2004: 171–2), concluding an extensive analysis of black/white differences in attitudes toward capital punishment and laws punishing crack cocaine traffickers (mostly black) much more harshly than powder cocaine traffickers (mostly white), observe:

> The most consistent predictor of criminal justice policy attitudes is, in fact, a form of racial prejudice. While white racial resentment does not ever explain a large share of the variation in any of the attitudes we have measured, it is the most consistently influential of the variables outside of race classification itself. This pattern . . . reinforces the claim . . . that one major function of the criminal justice system is the regulation and control of marginalized social groups such as African Americans.

These sad patterns of racial insensitivity, however, make sense in light of the other three explanations. If crime and drugs are matters of good and evil, and criminals and drug users are evil, then there is little reason to expect sympathy or empathy toward them from the holders of those views. People on death row or serving sentences of life without the possibility of parole or decades-long prison terms deserve what they get, and there is no reason to give the matter further thought.

Hofstadter more than 40 years ago described how and why the race card was played. Republicans, he observed, historically had sympathized with blacks in the south. '[By] adopting the "southern strategy"', however, Hofstadter (1965: 99) wrote,

> the Goldwater men abandoned this inheritance. They committed themselves not merely to a drive for a core of Southern states in the Electoral College but to a strategic counterpart in the North which required a search for racist votes. They thought they saw a good mass issue in the white backlash which they could indirectly exploit by talking of violence on the streets, crime, juvenile delinquency, and the dangers faced by our mothers and daughters.

The civil rights movement produced status anxieties among white southern Protestants, worried about protecting their traditional higher status than that of blacks, and among working-class white voters, worried about economic threats newly empowered blacks might pose. Since politicians after 1970 no longer could openly appeal to anti-black sentiments, they used code words, one of which was crime. The wars on drugs and crime rapidly expanded, as politicians kept their promises. Since it was disproportionately black people who went to prison, white voters felt able comfortably to pay that price, especially since it perpetuated the economic and social tradition of white dominance over a socially disorganized black underclass.

Kevin Phillips (1969), author of *The emerging Republican majority*, which laid out the program for the 'southern strategy', has long since recanted (Phillips, 1991) and condemned the conscious effort to use crime and violence as code words for race. Harry Denton, chairman of the Republican National Committee in the 1970s, a principal implementer of the southern strategy, as long ago as 1980 recanted and expressed his regret (his *New York Times* obituary quotes from an interview in the 1980s in which he expressed regret for anything he did 'that stood in the way of black people' (Stout, 2007).

Despite the recantings, racial disparities in American prisons are as bad as they have ever been, and nearly all the laws and policies that created them remain in effect. The moralism and intolerance of both the paranoid style of right-wing politics and religious fundamentalism supported development of the USA's extraordinarily severe crime control policies. Once the politics got rolling, American constitutional arrangements presented few impediments, and insensitivity to the interests of black Americans made their formidable human costs both tolerable and ignorable.

THE FUTURE

The story of American penal policy since 1973 is thus not about globalization, neo-liberalism or conditions of late modernity any more than it is about rising crime rates or harsher public attitudes. Cynical politicians took advantage of recurring features of American political culture in order to win elections and wield power, but their appeals succeeded only because of deeper elements of American culture and history.

The simplest explanation for why American penal policies are so harsh is that American voters elected candidates who said they would make them that harsh, and did. That explanation, however, is too simple because it cannot explain why Americans believed that serious problems of crime and disorder are amenable to easy repressive solutions, and accordingly why they voted as they did.

The next layer of explanation that focuses on social and economic changes of the late 20th century also does not provide an adequate explanation. Every developed country experienced wrenching changes of the same sort and only in a few did penal policies become markedly more severe. In those countries, however, the resulting policies were much less severe than in the United States, were often at least partially offset by other liberalizing changes and in the most extreme cases produced imprisonment rates less than a fourth as high as those in the United States (Tonry, 2007).

The explanatory level below that focuses on basic characteristics of national culture and political values. Globalization and neo-liberalism do not provide bases for explaining differences in national penal policies but constitutional structural and cultural values do. The USA's 18th-century constitutional regime gives freer rein and greater influence to short-term emotion and popular sentiment than can happen in most developed countries[4] where dispersed political power makes rash policy changes much less likely. Countries in which governmental legitimacy and citizens' trust in government and each other are high, and income inequality is low, are less likely to adopt harsh penal policies than in countries with low levels of trust and legitimacy and high levels of income inequality.

The preceding paragraph describes structures and values that appear to shape penal policies in particular countries, but it says nothing about the origins of those structures and values. Governmental structures are to a degree serendipitous. Britain and the United States have not felt a need to revise their 17th- and 18th-century constitutions in fundamental ways, whereas upheavals affecting 20th-century Europe occasioned fundamental changes. The need in many European countries and Japan to build their industrial capacities anew after the Second World War in parallel fashion for several decades created a competitive advantage against the creakier American industrial capacity, which had not 'benefited' from the war's destructiveness. European post-war affluence and the Japanese, German and Italian economic 'miracles' resulted. Likewise, many European countries created governmental systems tailored to accommodate pluralist societies and to create consensual policy apparatuses. When crime rates and public anxieties rose, governmental structures were better able than in the United States to respond in modulated ways and to resist impulsive changes.

Cultural and political values are not serendipitous. They evolve over time and are shaped by history and experience. In the United States, the four factors described above – the paranoid strain, Protestant fundamentalism, governmental structure and patterns of racial hierarchy – go a long way to explaining why penal policies evolved as they did in the final quarter of the 20th century. However, they point to a need for yet another level of explanation.

Why have the paranoid strain and moralistic Protestant intolerance recurred again and again, and why has the influence of tortured race relations remained so powerful? Big ideas about American history, including the Puritanism and intolerance of the first settlers, ideals of individualism and libertarianism associated with the frontier and the early slavery-based southern economy, no doubt need to be woven into the answers.

Research agendas in coming years should focus on this level of explanation. Critical questions in the United States should be asked about the role of religion, race and libertarianism on values and through them on penal policies. The questions in other countries are different, and better questions will enrich understanding of why countries respond to crimes and criminals in the different ways they do. In France, for example, why is it that French men and women have for centuries accepted the legitimacy of broadly based amnesties and pardons of offenders and prisoners? In Italy, a mass commutation in 2006 reduced the prison population by 40 percent (and a smaller mass commutation occurred in 2008 under a conservative Berlusconi government), and there were no mass outcries. My instinct (and guess) is that similar policy decisions in the United States, England or the Netherlands would loose political firestorms. Similarly, something in Scandinavian and German history and culture resulted in adoption of restrained penal policies for at least half a century. Explanations can be offered in terms provided above – consensus political systems, high levels of legitimacy and trust and so on – but they beg the question: What is it about the (very different) histories of those countries that produces those characteristics?

Winston Churchill (1910) nearly a century ago observed:

> The mood and temper of the public in regard to the treatment of crime and criminals is one of the most unfailing tests of any country. A calm, dispassionate recognition of the rights of the accused and even of the convicted criminal, . . . tireless efforts towards the discovery of curative and re-generative processes; unfailing faith that there is a treasure, if you can only find it, in the heart of every man. These are the symbols which, in the treatment of crime and the criminal, mark and measure the stored-up strength of a nation, and are the sign and proof of the living virtue within it. (quoted in Gilbert, 1992: 10)

Countries differ widely in how they respond to crime and criminals. The American responses in the early 20th century are shameful. It is hard to believe that anyone not living in the radical political fringes of American politics would have chosen 30 years ago to create the system Americans now have. It is cruel and expensive and wastes lives, especially the lives of disadvantaged black men.

We can learn much more about why countries' policies differ so much. Maybe the fruits of that leaning will enable the United States better to mark its stored up strength and to prove its living virtue.

Notes

1 There was a small functionalist literature most famously represented by Durkheim (1933 [1893]), Rusche and Kirchheimer (1968 [1939]) and Foucault (1977), but this received comparatively little recent attention until revived by David Garland (1990) in *Punishment and modern society.*

2 Discussion of the origins and precipitants of the constitutional structure of the United States are based on Mullet (1966) and Wood (1969).

3 Bureau of Justice Statistics (BJS, 2007) data for mid-year 2006 show that black men constituted 41 percent of male jail and prison inmates. The true figure in a country where skin color matters much more than ethnicity is 46 to 48 percent (BJS a few years ago stopped counting black Hispanics as black and thereby reduced the black percentage by 10 to 12 percent; a quarter to a third of imprisoned Hispanics, who were 21 percent of male inmates, are dark-skinned). Forty-seven percent is slightly less than 50 and results from a rapid recent increase in imprisonment of Hispanics. In 2007, more non-Hispanic blacks were imprisoned than non-Hispanic whites.

4 England's even older (17th-century) constitution provides no better insulation, for several reasons. There is no meaningful separation of powers among branches of government; courts generally lack authority to declare laws unconstitutional; and the Parliament only rarely is able to resist executive branch initiatives. If a government chooses to promote illiberal policies, the other branches lack power to resist them.

References

Barker, Vanessa (2009) *The politics of punishment: How the democratic process shapes the way America punishes offenders.* New York: Oxford University Press.

Bennett, William J., John J. DiIulio and John P. Walters (1996) *Body count: Moral poverty . . . and how to win America's war against crime and drugs.* New York: Simon & Schuster.

Blumstein, Alfred and Jacqueline Cohen (1973) 'A theory of stability of punishment', *Journal of Criminal Law and Criminology* 64(2): 198–207.

Bobo, Lawrence and Devon Johnson (2004) 'A taste for punishment: Black and white Americans' views on the death penalty and the war on drugs', *Du Bois Review* 1: 151–80.

Bureau of Justice Statistics (2003) *Prevalence of imprisonment in the U.S. population, 1974–2001*. Washington, DC: Bureau of Justice Statistics.

Bureau of Justice Statistics (2007) *Prison and jail inmates at midyear 2006*. Washington, DC: Bureau of Justice Statistics.

Cavadino, Michael and James Dignan (2005) *Penal systems: A comparative approach*. London: SAGE.

Curry, Theodore R. (1996) 'Conservative Protestantism and the perceived wrongfulness of crimes: A research note', *Criminology* 34(3): 453–64.

Cusac, Anne-Marie (2009) *Cruel and unusual: The culture of punishment in America*. New Haven, CT: Yale University Press.

Davis, David Brion (1960) 'Some themes of counter-subversion: An analysis of anti-Masonic, anti-Catholic, and anti-Mormon literature', *Mississippi Valley Historical Review* 47(2): 205–24.

Di Tella, Rafael and Juan Dubra (2008) 'Crime and punishment in the "American Dream"', *Journal of Public Economics* 92(7): 1564–84.

Downes, David and Kirstine Hansen (2006) 'Welfare and punishment in comparative perspective', in S. Armstrong and L. McAra (eds) *Perspectives on punishment: The contours of control*, pp. 133–54. Oxford: Oxford University Press.

Durkheim, Emile (1933 [1893]) *The division of labour in society*. Trans. George Simpson. New York: Free Press.

Edsall, Thomas and Mary Edsall (1991) *Chain reaction: The impact of race, rights, and taxes on American politics*. New York: Norton.

Erikson, Kai T. (1966) *Wayward puritans: A study in the sociology of deviance*. New York: Wiley.

Foucault, Michel (1977) *Discipline and punish: The birth of the prison*. New York: Pantheon.

Garland, David (1990) *Punishment and modern society*. Chicago, IL: University of Chicago Press.

Garland, David (2001) *Culture of control: Crime and social order in contemporary society*. Chicago, IL: University of Chicago Press.

Garland, David (2005) 'Penal excess and surplus meaning: Public torture lynchings in twentieth-century America', *Law and Society Review* 39(4): 793–834.

Gilbert, Martin (1992) *Churchill: A life*. New York: Henry Holt.

Gottschalk, Marie (2006) *The prison and the gallows: The politics of mass incarceration in America*. Cambridge: Cambridge University Press.

Green, David A. (2008) *When children kill children: Penal populism and political culture*. Oxford: Oxford University Press.

Green, John C. (2007) *The faith factor: How religion influences American elections*. Westport, CT: Praeger.

Gusfield, Joseph (1963) *Symbolic crusade: Status politics and the American temperance movement*. Urbana, IL: University of Illinois Press.

Hofstadter, Richard (1965) *The paranoid style in American politics and other essays.* Chicago, IL: University of Chicago Press.
Lacey, Nicola (2008) *The prisoner's dilemma: Political economy and punishment in contemporary democracies.* Cambridge: Cambridge University Press.
Lappi-Seppälä, Tapio (2007) 'Penal policy in Scandinavia', in Michael Tonry (ed.) *Crime, punishment, and politics in comparative perspective.* Volume 36 of *Crime and justice: A review of research*, pp. 217–95. Chicago, IL:University of Chicago Press.
Lappi-Seppälä, Tapio (2008) 'Trust, welfare, and political culture: Explaining differences in national penal policies', in Michael Tonry (ed.) *Crime and justice: A review of research*, vol. 37, pp. 313–87. Chicago, IL: University of Chicago Press.
Layman, Geoffrey (2001) *The great divide: Religious and cultural conflict in American party politics.* New York: Columbia University Press.
Lichtman, Allan J. (2008) *White Protestant nation.* New York: Atlantic Monthly Press.
Lijphart, Arend (1999) *Patterns of democracy: Government forms and performance in thirty-six countries.* New Haven, CT: Yale University Press.
Loury, Glenn C. (2007) 'Racial stigma, mass incarceration and American values', the Tanner Lectures in Human Values delivered at Stanford University on 4 and 5 April. Available at http://www.econ.brown.edu/fac/Glenn_Loury/louryhomepage/
Massey, Douglas S. (2007) *Categorically unequal.* New York: Russell Sage Foundation.
Massey, Douglas S. and Nancy Denton (1993) *American apartheid: Segregation and the making of the underclass.* Cambridge: Harvard University Press.
Miller, Lisa L. (2008) *The perils of federalism: Race, poverty, and the politics of crime control.* Oxford: Oxford University Press.
Mullet, Charles F. (1966) *Fundamental law and the American revolution, 1710–1776.* New York: Octagon.
Myers, Gustavus (1943) *History of bigotry in the United States.* New York: Random House.
Nagata, Judith (2001) 'Beyond theology: Toward an anthropology of "fundamentalism"', *American Anthropologist* 103(2): 481–98.
Pease, Ken (1991) 'Punishment demand and punishment numbers', in D.M. Gottfredson and R.V. Clarke (eds) *Policy and theory in criminal justice*, pp. 113–37. Aldershot: Gower.
Perlstein, Rick (2008) *Nixonland: The rise of a president and the fracturing of America.* New York: Scribners.
Phillips, Kevin P. (1969) *The emerging Republican majority.* New Rochelle, NY: Arlington.
Phillips, Kevin P. (1991) *The politics of rich and poor: Wealth and the American electorate in the Reagan aftermath.* New York: Harpercollins.
Roberts, Julian V., Loretta J. Stalans, David Indermaur and Mike Hough (2002) *Penal populism and popular opinion.* New York: Oxford University Press.
Rusche, Georg and Otto Kirchheimer (1968 [1939]) *Punishment and social structure.* New York: Russell & Russell. (Originally published 1939 in New York by Colombia University Press.)
Simon, Jonathan (2007) *Governing through crime: How the war on crime transformed American democracy and created a culture of fear.* New York: Oxford University Press.

Stout, David (2007) 'Harry Dent, an architect of Nixon "Southern Strategy", dies at 77', *New York Times* 2 October: B7.

Tonry, Michael (1995) *Malign neglect: Race, crime, and punishment in America.* New York: Oxford University Press.

Tonry, Michael (2004) *Thinking about crime: Sense and sensibility in American penal culture.* New York: Oxford University Press.

Tonry, Michael (2007) 'Determinants of penal policies', in Michael Tonry (ed.) *Crime, punishment, and politics in comparative perspective.* Volume 36 of *Crime and justice: A review of research*, pp. 1–48. Chicago, IL: University of Chicago Press.

Tonry, Michael and Matthew Melewski (2008) 'The malign effects of drug and crime control policies on black Americans', in Michael Tonry (ed.) *Crime and justice: A review of research*, vol. 37, pp. 1–44. Chicago, IL: University of Chicago Press.

Unnever, James D., Francis T. Cullen and Brandon K. Applegate (2005) 'Turning the other cheek: Reassessing the impact of religion on punitive ideology', *Justice Quarterly* 22(3): 304–39.

Unnever, James D., Francis T. Cullen and Cheryl N. Lero-Jonson (2008) 'Race, racism, and support for capital punishment', in Michael Tonry (ed.) *Crime and justice: A review of research*, vol. 37, pp. 45–96. Chicago, IL: University of Chicago Press.

Van Dijk, Jan, John van Kesteren and Paul Smit (2007) *Criminal victimisation in international perspective: Key findings from the 2004–2005 ICVS and EU ICS.* The Hague, Netherlands: WODC.

Wacquant, Loïc (2002a) 'From slavery to mass incarceration', *New Left Review* 13(January–February): 41–60.

Wacquant, Loïc (2002b) 'Deadly symbiosis: Rethinking race and imprisonment in twenty-first-century America', *Boston Review* 27(2): http://bostonreview.net/BR27.2/wacquant.html

Wald, Kenneth D. and Allison Calhoun-Brown (2007) *Religion and politics in the United States*, 5th edn. Lanham, MD: Rowman & Littlefield.

Western, Bruce (2006) *Punishment and inequality in America.* New York: Russell Sage Foundation.

Wood, Gordon S. (1969) *The creation of the American Republic: 1776–1787.* Chapel Hill, NC: University of North Carolina Press.

Woodberry, Robert D. and Christian S. Smith (1998) 'Fundamentalism et al.: Conservative Protestants in America', *Annual Review of Sociology* 24: 25–56.

Young, Warren and Mark Brown (1993) 'Cross national comparisons of imprisonment', in Michael Tonry (ed.) *Crime and justice: A review of research*, vol. 17, pp. 1–49. Chicago, IL: University of Chicago Press.

MICHAEL TONRY is Sonosky Professor of Law and Public Policy and director, Institute on Crime and Public Policy, University of Minnesota, and a senior fellow in the Netherlands Institute for the Study of Crime and Law Enforcement.

Part IV
Sentencing Policy

[10]
Sentencing Reform in America

In *Criminal Law—The General Part* Glanville Williams subjected the principles of substantive criminal law to sustained analysis. His success is manifest, requiring neither elaboration nor documentation. In the United States, the American Law Institute embarked on a similar and contemporaneous enterprise to develop a Model Penal Code—a project in which Glanville Williams also played an important role.[1] *The General Part* and the Model Penal Code are now classics, the starting points for serious analysis of questions of substantive criminal law in both England and the United States.

Efforts to bring system and principle to American criminal law administration have shifted in recent years from substance to procedure, and from procedure to sentencing. In this paper, we describe that shift and attempt to identify some of the problems and perceptions which underlie current efforts at sentencing reform in the federal system of justice. Most recent sentencing reform proposals in the United States urge the adoption of determinate sentencing systems intended to reduce unwarranted sentencing disparities and to establish more principled and predictable sentencing practices. We will discuss two recent federal sentencing reform proposals—the Kennedy–McClellan[2] and Hart–Javits[3] Bills in the United States Senate. The Kennedy–McClellan Bill proposes the establishment of a federal sentencing commission—a politically insulated independent government commission—which would promulgate presumptive sentencing guidelines for judicial sentencing decisions, though the court would retain authority to disregard the guidelines in appropriate cases and to impose any other lawful sentence. The Hart–Javits proposal would also establish a sentencing commission, but under this Bill the commission's sentencing standards would be prescriptive, fixing the sentence to be imposed. The Kennedy–McClellan Bill offers the greater promise for achievement of the goals of sentencing reform. Sentencing proposals which too severely constrain the sentencing court tend in the United States to result in an unfortunate transfer of dispositive sentencing power from the judge and the parole release authorities (who together now determine the duration of most prison sentences) to the prosecutor.

[1] Model Penal Code (American Law Institute) (P.O.D. Philadelphia 1962). Glanville Williams was a Special Consultant to the Reportorial Staff of the Institute.

[2] S. 1437, 95th Cong., 1st Sess. (1977). The sentencing reform provisions of S. 1437 were previously proposed by Senator Kennedy, in somewhat more radical form, as S. 2269, 94th Cong., 1st Sess. (1975) and S. 181, 95th Cong., 1st Sess. (1977). S. 1437 is a complete proposed federal code into which the substance of Senator Kennedy's sentencing reforms was inserted. This essay discusses the legislation pending on 1 October 1977.

[3] S. 204, 95th Cong., 1st Sess. (1977).

In this essay we will discuss several practical and jurisprudential questions which these sentencing reform proposals raise, particularly the systemic difficulties confronting any attempt to re-order sentencing discretions, and we will consider the proposition, implicit in many determinate sentencing proposals, that unequal sentences are necessarily unjust. We will conclude by offering our immodestly dogmatic views on sentencing reform in the United States.

I

Substance to procedure to sentencing

Criminal law codification movements flowered in the nineteenth century, with the work of Macaulay and others on the Indian Penal Code, of the Criminal Law Commissioners and Stephen in England, and of Livingston and Field in the United States. In the United States, criminal law codification thereafter lay dormant until the 1950s when the American Law Institute's draftsmen began their work on the Model Penal Code. Piecemeal legislation and dogmatically diverse case law had multiplied anomalies and undermined principles. The American Law Institute sought to influence legislative reform both in the states and in the federal system by drafting a model criminal code to bring order and principle not only to the substantive criminal law but also to its system of sanctions.

Any morally acceptable criminal law system, not based on determinist premises, requires a coherent set of substantive rules which define proscribed conduct with clarity, which differentiate on reasonable grounds between serious and minor offences, which comport with notions of moral and legal responsibility, and which recognise mitigating, excusing and justifying explanations for otherwise culpable conduct by otherwise responsible persons.

The Model Penal Code provided such a basis for a morally acceptable criminal law system and inspired the movement for criminal law codification which swept the United States during the 1960s and seventies. New state criminal codes were enacted, many influenced by the provisions of the Model Penal Code[4]; all to a degree reflect the work of Glanville Williams. The proposed new federal criminal code of the influential United States National Commission on Reform of Federal Criminal Laws[5] bears the vivid imprint of these influences as does the Kennedy–McClellan Bill, the pending proposal for a federal criminal code.

Hindsight demonstrates that the Model Penal Code was only part of the answer. A principled substantive criminal law is a necessary but not a sufficient precondition to decent and efficient criminal law administration. A criminal code cannot achieve just results unless it is administered fairly,

[4] For a general description of the codification movement, see Wechsler, "Codification of Criminal Law in the United States: The Model Penal Code," 68 Colum. L. Rev. 1425 (1968) and Wechsler, "Sentencing, Corrections and the Model Penal Code," 109 U. Pa. L. Rev. 465 (1961).

[5] U.S. National Commission on Reform of Federal Criminal Laws, *A Proposed New Federal Criminal Code* (Final Report, 1971).

impartially and efficiently. This is an area neglected in legislative reform but which has been the focus of judicial concern in the United States.

During the late 1950s and the sixties, the United States Supreme Court attempted substantial reform of the criminal justice system by recognising and amplifying constitutional procedural standards applicable to police, prosecutorial and judicial processing of criminal cases. Relying upon the due process and equal protection clauses of the Fourteenth Amendment to the Constitution, the Supreme Court, in a series of celebrated cases, prescribed *inter alia*, minimum constitutional standards guaranteeing the rights to counsel and jury trial and regulating the use of search warrants, arrest warrants, identification lineups and informers. *Mapp* v. *Ohio* (1961)[6] and *Miranda* v. *Arizona* (1966)[7] held that the state courts must enforce exclusionary rules forbidding use of unlawfully obtained evidence against criminal defendants. Recently that movement has been slowed, perhaps stopped or turned back; the struggle for procedural fairness continues, albeit no longer led by the Supreme Court.[8]

The search for a fair and just system of criminal law in the United States has now taken yet another turn. The objectives of current reform efforts are the judicial and administrative sentencing processes. Substantive laws can define criminal offences, the commission of which authorises the state to assert penal authority over its citizens. Equable criminal procedures can increase the likelihood that determinations of criminal guilt will be made impartially and dispassionately. But these will not suffice, certainly in the United States. A procedurally perfect administration of the Model Penal Code would, without more, be perceived by many to produce, and would in fact produce, unfair and uneven results.

Compelling evidence exists that, seen as a system, the disposition of convicted criminal offenders in America is capricious and inconsistent. Decisions as to the nature and duration of punishment flow from a complex network of legislatively authorised sentences and even more complex divisions of sentencing power between the police, prosecutors, defence counsel, judges, parole authorities and correctional administrators.

At the time of writing, four states—California, Indiana, Maine and Oregon—have adopted determinate sentencing laws and many other states are considering doing so. Several developments of the past decade have focused attention on sentencing reform. Before describing and commenting on the federal sentencing reform proposals, we will describe several of those developments: disillusionment with the rehabilitative ideal; increased concern over sentencing disparities; recognition of discretion as a proper object of study and focus for reform; and a renascence of retribution as a respectable justification of punishment.

Rejection of rehabilitation as a purpose of punishment

Recent exhaustive surveys of correctional research evaluations by Robert

[6] 367 U.S. 643.

[7] 384 U.S. 436.

[8] See, *e.g.* American Law Institute, *A Model Penal Code of Pre-Arraignment Procedure* (P.O.D. Philadelphia 1975).

Martinson in the United States[9] and R. S. Brody[10] in England counsel that our demonstrated capacity constructively to change prisoners does not justify imposing punishment for that purpose.

The consensus among American scholars and reformist politicians in 1977 is that penal rehabilitation can no longer justify taking power over offenders or the extension of the duration of punishment otherwise imposed. Rehabilitation has been rejected by many as a proper consideration in decisions to punish or extend the duration of punishment, to be replaced by various conceptions (and mixtures) of desert and deterrence.

The problem is not that we cannot affect criminal behaviour. In many cases we know how to coerce, cure and prevent future criminal (at least violent) conduct. We choose not to do so. We can kill offenders; chemical, surgical and psychological devices can change personalities and behaviour; protracted, secure imprisonment will "cure" all but the most exceptional proclivity to violent crime. Fundamental views of the importance of the individual, historical evidence of the misuse of power, moral and ethical self-doubt, prevent us from so doing. Coerced cure within ethical limits does not appear to work. We may be able to facilitate self-change by providing opportunities for those so motivated, but no more.

Scepticism about the efficacy and morality of rehabilitative measures may be too fashionable. Although rehabilitative programs in prisons have been characterised more by false rhetoric than by solid achievement, it does not follow that rehabilitative ideals and programs should be discarded. Though "rehabilitation" must cease to be a purpose of the criminal sanction, this does not mean that the various developed treatment programs within prisons should be abandoned. To the contrary: they need expansion. But it does mean that they must not be seen as purposive in the sense that criminals are to be sent to prison for treatment. We must rehabilitate the rehabilitative ideal by liberating it from the corrupting effects of coercive participation and connection with the duration of imprisonment.[11]

Rediscovery of sentencing discretion

The American system of sentencing has long produced grossly dissimilar sentences for like offenders convicted of like offences, and sentences disproportionate—on any rational punitive hierarchy—to the gravity of offences or the culpability of offenders. Unjustifiable sentencing disparities has long been recognised as a problem in America, but it has recently received renewed attention. Chief Justice Warren Burger observed in his 1976 address on "The State of the Judiciary": "some form of review procedure is needed to deal with this dilemma [of sentencing disparity]." Forty-five years ago, for example, Messrs. Gaudet, Harris and St. John reported the results of a study of all sentences imposed by six New Jersey judges for 19 different criminal offences, randomly assigned to them over a nine-year

[9] Martinson, "What Works? Questions and Answers About Prison Reform," 35 Pub. Interest 22 (1974); and Lipton, D., Martinson and Wilks, *The Effectiveness of Correctional Treatment: A Survey of Treatment Evaluation Studies* (New York 1975).

[10] Brody, R. S., *The Effectiveness of Sentencing* (1976).

[11] Norval Morris has developed these arguments in *The Future of Imprisonment* (Chicago 1974).

period. One judge (1,489 cases) imposed prison sentences in 57.7 per cent. of cases and suspended sentences or probation in 39.2 per cent. of cases. Another (1,693 cases) ordered imprisonment in only 33.6 per cent. of cases and imposed probation or suspended sentences in 64.2 per cent. The imprisonment rates for all six judges were 33.6 per cent.—35.6 per cent.—45.0 per cent.—50.0 per cent.—53.3 per cent.—57.7 per cent.[12]

Nor is modern evidence of sentencing disparity lacking. In a recent experiment in the Federal Second Circuit, all 43 active trial judges and seven senior trial judges rendered sentences in 20 identical cases described in pre-sentence reports (which contained information regarding criminal charges, plea or trial, prior record, age, narcotic history, family background, etc.). Sentences varied enormously. In one case the sentence varied from three to 20 years. In another the range was probation to seven and a half years. Substantial variation persisted even when extreme sentences were disregarded. The norm was the absence of a norm. The average disparity from the mean was 48 per cent.[13]

In a recent study of sentences in federal courts throughout the country, Tiffany, Avichai and Peters found substantial variation in sentences that related to such apparently unprincipled factors as type of trial: bench or jury; type of counsel: retained or appointed (but only in bench trials); race of defendant (but only where defendant had no prison record).[14]

The empirical literature on sentencing disparities is enormous, growing and unanswerable.[15]

The discovery of other discretions

Kenneth Culp Davis' *Discretionary Justice* (1969) focused attention on the unregulated discretion which percolates the entire criminal justice system. Concern for identification and regulation of these discretions became a growth industry.[16]

Many actors and institutions affect whether any sentence is imposed and, if so, of what type and duration. Legislatures define criminal offences and establish sentencing choices. Police decide (or decide not) to process a complaint, to file an arrest report, in some jurisdictions to file a criminal complaint. Prosecutors decide whether to file a complaint, and for what charges (or whether to prosecute a police-filed complaint), whether to accept a plea bargain, and on what terms, whether to recommend or not oppose a specific sentence to the court. Defence counsel play a role in plea, charge

[12] Gaudet, Harris and St. John, "Individual Differences in the Sentencing Tendencies of Judges," 23 J. Crim. L. and Criminology 811 (1933).

[13] *The Second Circuit Sentencing Study: A Report to the Judges of the Second Circuit* (eds. Partridge and Eldridge) (1974).

[14] Tiffany, Avichai and Peters, "A Statistical Analysis of Sentencing in Federal Courts: Defendants Convicted After Trial, 1967–68," 4 J. Legal Stud. 369 (1975).

[15] See Clarke and Koch, "The Influence of Income and other Factors on Whether Criminal Defendants Go to Prison," 11 L. and Soc'y Rev. 57 (1976); Nagel and Reef, "Racial Disparities That Supposedly Do Not Exist," 52 N.D. Law. 87 (1976). See generally authorities cited in Twentieth Century Fund Task Force on Criminal Sentencing, *Fair and Certain Punishment* (1976) pp. 101–106.

[16] See, *e.g.* Davis, K. C., *Discretionary Justice in Europe and America* (Illinois 1976); *ibid. Police Discretion* (Illinois 1975); Kadish, M. R. and Kadish, S. H., *Discretion to Disobey: A Study of Lawful Departures from Legal Rules* (Stanford 1973).

and sentence bargaining. Courts can dismiss charges. Courts (and juries) determine guilt and often can limit sentence maxima by convicting a defendant of one offence rather than another. After conviction, the prosecutor can offer sentence recommendations. Judges impose sentences: whether imprisonment, probation or fine and of what duration or amount. Judges can also vary sentences by imposing concurrent or consecutive sentences on defendants convicted of multiple offences. Correctional authorities affect prison release dates and eligibility by awarding, not awarding or revoking good behaviour credits towards sentence length. Correctional authorities influence release decisions by endorsing or opposing convicted offenders' parole petitions and can provide extended and terminal furloughs. Parole authorities can release a convicted offender at any time after he has become eligible for parole release—typically after serving the greater of one year or one-third of his sentence. Executive officials have legal authority to pardon or grant clemency.

Having rediscovered sentencing discretion, we have identified some of its properties: like quicksilver, when obstructed, discretion flows somewhere else; unlike quicksilver, it cannot be contained. If legislative fixed sentences do not permit judges to decide sentence length, prosecutors become the primary sentencers when they decide what charges to file, what plea bargains to accept, what sentences to recommend or not oppose. When indeterminate sentencing deprives the prosecutor and the judge of much of their sentencing power, parole release authorities determine sentence. If determinate sentencing deprives the parole release authorities of their sentencing power, the prosecutor and the judge will play the dispositive roles. Someone must do it.

The renascence of retribution

Retribution, or deserts, has replaced rehabilitation as the conventional justification for the amount of punishment. The renascence of retribution as a respectable justification for punishment in America can fairly be attributed to *Struggle for Justice* (1971), a report on American prisons prepared by a Working Party for the American Friends Service Committee. The Quaker Working Party proposed a system of determinate sentencing which others have since attempted to justify.

Writing in California where the rehabilitative ideal produced the most conspicuously indeterminate and individualised prison sentences in the United States, the Working Party was troubled by immense disparity in sentences imposed and time served by prisoners in California and proposed the adoption of a system in which:

> Whatever sanction or short sentence is imposed is to be fixed by law. There is to be no discretion in setting sentences, no indeterminate sentences, and unsupervised street release is to replace parole.[17]

Definitions of offences should specify relevant aggravating or mitigating circumstances to justify variations in the normal sentence. Other circumstances of the offender and the offence should be irrelevant:

[17] American Friends Service Committee, *Struggle for Justice* (1971) p. 144 [hereinafter cited as *Struggle*].

> A necessary corollary of our principle of punishing for the act is that specific punishment be assigned to the act. All persons found guilty of the same criminal act under the same circumstances are dealt with uniformly.[18]

The Working Party proposals were essentially negative. The rehabilitative ideal was inherently flawed and functionaries cannot be trusted to make discretionary decisions without bias or caprice. Others provided the positive justification for retributive punishment. Andrew von Hirsch's *Doing Justice* (1976) and Norval Morris' *The Future of Imprisonment* (1974) undertook principled analyses of punishment to justify, respectively, ostensibly retributive and utilitarian systems of punishment designed to achieve many of the Quakers' goals. David Fogel's *We are the Living Proof...* (1975) traversed much the same territory as *Struggle for Justice* and proposed an influential "flat-time" system of sentencing.

Two influential private commissions proposed adoption of frankly retributive sentencing regimes. Andrew von Hirsch's *Doing Justice* (1976), the report of the Committee for the Study of Incarceration, proposed a system of determinate sentencing in which the trial court would be required to impose a specific sentence, subject only to authorised variations, to reflect defined aggravating and mitigating circumstances. *Fair and Certain Punishment* (1976), a report of the Twentieth Century Fund Task Force on Criminal Sentencing, refined and developed the *Doing Justice* proposals and offered a more sophisticated system of presumptive sentencing in which the trial court could impose an applicable sentence from within a narrow "presumptive range" or impose any other lawful sentence on condition that reasons be given for the sentence imposed and subject to a right of sentence appeal. Bills were introduced in the United States Senate by Senator Lloyd Bentsen to establish a sentencing system based on the *Fair and Certain Punishment* proposals[19] and by Senators Gary Hart and Jacob Javits to establish a *Doing Justice* approach to federal sentencing.[20]

The new retributivism has influenced most modern proposals for sentencing reform, including those discussed in this essay. The sentencing schemes which have been built on the ruins of the rehabilitative ideal and the foundations of desert and utility attempt to establish tariffs for crime.

II

The headlong leap towards determinate sentencing has resulted from the developments just described and no doubt others as well. The real and indefensible phenomenon of unjustified and unjustifiable sentencing disparities and modern doubts about rehabilitation and unguided sentencing discretions provide persuasive support for determinate sentencing proposals. In our view most determinate sentencing proposals fail to recognise the complexity of the sentencing process in the United States and the central

[18] *ibid.* p. 148.
[19] S. 3752, 94th Cong., 2nd Sess. (1976).
[20] S. 204, 95th Cong., 1st Sess. (1977).

importance of prosecutorial sentencing power. To the extent that determinate sentencing proposals legislate specific sentences for specific offences committed by defined categories of offenders, the judge's sentencing power will be displaced by the prosecutor, not by the legislature. In 1976, 85 per cent. of federal criminal convictions resulted from guilty pleas. Many of those pleas were induced by prosecutorial undertakings to dismiss, or not file, certain charges, or to recommend or not oppose a specific sentence. There is little reason to believe, and much reason to doubt, that unreviewable and often invisible prosecutorial sentencing practices will be fairer, more predictable or more just than judicial sentencing practices.

Illustrative reform proposals

Three critical aspects of sentencing reform proposals are (i) what sorts of guidance the new system would offer to the sentencing judge, (ii) where formal sentencing authority would be placed and how that would relate to the *locus* of real sentencing power, and (iii) what mechanisms would be created to control discretionary sentencing decisions.

In our view, both the Hart–Javits and Kennedy–McClellan Bills offer promise as means to the achievement of a more predictable and principled system of criminal sanctions. Both Bills envisage a sentencing commission which would develop known, knowable and principled standards to guide judicial sentencing decisions. The greatest deficiency of the Hart–Javits Bill is that it would apparently authorise a sentencing commission to develop sentencing policy, but—by removing most overt sentencing discretion from the court—would place real sentencing power in the hands of the prosecutor. The Kennedy–McClellan Bill does not suffer from that defect (subject always to the prosecutor's general influence on sentences through plea bargaining practices) but contains inadequate checking mechanisms to control judicial sentencing decisions.

Prescriptive sentencing—the Hart–Javits bill

The Hart–Javits Bill would establish an independent sentencing commission which would be appointed by the President by and with the consent of the Senate. The sentencing discretions of the sentencing commission and the sentencing judge would be rigidly structured. The commission would be charged to establish prescriptive guidelines for sentencing consistent with the principle that the severity of a sentence "shall be commensurate with the gravity of the criminal offence to which such presumptive sentence is assigned." The commission would establish schedules setting forth gradations of gravity for each criminal offence and prescribing a "presumptive" sentence for each gradation of severity.

The commission would establish schedules and rules prescribing variations from presumptive sentences to reflect aggravating and mitigating circumstances, specifying what types of circumstances should be considered in mitigation and aggravation, and for each type of mitigating or aggravating circumstance, specifying a particular amount or maximum amount of variation from the presumptive sentence. Aggravating circumstances could not be invoked to justify an increase of the presumptive sentence by more than 50 per cent. Except for designated violent offences, no presumptive sentence would exceed five years.

Under the Hart–Javits Bill, the sentencing judge would be required to impose the prescribed presumptive sentence varied only as authorised by rule to recognise aggravating and mitigating circumstances. The only basis for an appeal against sentence would be that "the sentencing judge imposed such sentence in violation of a rule established by the Commission under this Act or a provision of this Act." Sentences not authorised by applicable guidelines would constitute reversible error.

The Hart–Javits bill illustrates two basic shortcomings of many determinate sentencing proposals. First, the prosecutor would in most cases control sentence length. Assume that sentencing guidelines specified that a defined category of offenders (*e.g.* adults with two prior convictions for violent offences) convicted of theft, robbery and armed robbery be sentenced, respectively, to prison terms of 2.2, 3.2 and 4.5 years. Because the court would possess only limited authority to adjust sentences for aggravating and mitigating circumstances (and for an offender in a given case these adjustments would presumably be comparable regardless of the offence charged), the prison sentence received by a defendant who could have been charged with armed robbery will depend on what charge the prosecutor elects to press. That ability in most cases to determine sentence by charging (or withdrawing or not proving) specific sentence-determining offences will give prosecutors valuable chips for use in charge, plea and sentence bargaining negotiations. And, given that, the likelihood will not be great that like offenders convicted of like offences will receive like sentences.

Some state sentencing reform proposals would give the prosecutor even greater sentencing power. California's Uniform Determinate Sentencing Act 1976[21] requires imposition of significant prison sentence increases for defined aggravating circumstances (*e.g.* use of a weapon, use of a firearm, infliction of great bodily injury, prior incarcerations, substantial property loss or damage) which have been charged and proven. Prosecutorial decisions to charge and prove aggravating circumstances requiring imposition of additional years of imprisonment could in many cases determine whether a convicted defendant will receive a prison sentence of two years or 10 or something in between. The sentencing court can refuse to impose additional years imprisonment for aggravating circumstances if it determines that there are circumstances in mitigation and states reasons for that decision on the record. There is no reason to expect that widely disparate sentences will not result when hundreds of prosecutors interact with hundreds of trial judges in determining sentences.

A second significant problem with the Hart–Javits Bill is that it would either forbid the use of non-incarcerative sentences for all persons convicted of specified offences or would establish an anomalous gap effect for offences for which probation could be ordered: courts must sentence convicted offenders to either probation or a prison term of considerable length, with nothing in between.

Any legislative sentencing reform which would severely limit the sentencing discretion of the criminal court judge will tend to produce a

[21] 1976 Cal. Legis Serv. Ch. 1139, effective, as amended by A.B. 476 (1977 Cal. Legis Serv.), 1 July 1977.

system of either prosecutorial or parole sentencing. The Hart–Javits Bill seems to us fundamentally flawed for that reason. The Kennedy–McClellan Bill avoids that trap but has other shortcomings.

Presumptive sentencing—the Kennedy–McClellan bill

The Kennedy–McClellan Bill would establish a United States Sentencing Commission which would be charged to promulgate policy statements and guidelines for judicial sentencing decisions. The guidelines would recommend sentencing ranges within statutory limits for specific categories of offenders convicted of specific categories of offence. The Bill identifies purposes of sentencing which the sentencing commission and sentencing judges should attempt to further in the establishment and application of sentencing policy. All criminal offences would be classified into nine categories, each authorising a maximum sentence of imprisonment, probation or fine. Following a conviction, the court could impose any lawful sentence but should first consider applicable guidelines and policy statements, statutory purposes of sentencing and the circumstances of the offence and the offender. The sentencing court would be required to state the reasons for its sentence, and, if the sentence it decided to impose was not authorised by the applicable sentencing guidelines, the specific reason for the choice of sentence outside the guideline range. Finally, the Bill would establish, for the first time in the federal courts, a limited system of appellate review of sentences. The sentence could be modified, or vacated and remanded, if the appellate court determined that a sentence imposed outside the range recommended by applicable sentencing guidelines was "clearly unreasonable."

We believe that the Kennedy–McClellan Bill offers greater promise for the achievement of just and efficient sentencing than the Hart–Javits Bill or any of the prescriptive sentencing proposals. Its proposal for the classification of offences is a necessary, albeit not sufficient, first step. Existing federal criminal penalty ranges are arbitrary and perverse—having resulted from 200 years of piecemeal codification. Too many offences of seemingly comparable social injury and indicative of comparable personal culpability bear widely disparate authorised sentences. Armed robbery of a United States postal officer is punishable by a 25 year prison term.[22] Armed robbery of a bank chartered by the United States is punishable by a fine, probation or up to 25 year's imprisonment.[23] Sensible sentencing will not obtain until such indefensible anomalies are eliminated.

The Kennedy–McClellan Bill's proposal for a sentencing commission to recommend sentencing ranges within statutory maxima is preferable to systems like California's Uniform Determinate Sentencing Act 1976, in which the legislature attempts the fine tuning of punishment. Better insulated from political pressures, passions and posturing than a legislature, the sentencing commission may be better positioned to make principled and dispassionate decisions about sentencing policy, and it will certainly be better situated to refine and develop policy, for legislatures both lack special expertise and are beset by myriad competing demands for legislative consideration of matters of politics and policy.

[22] 18 U.S.C. §2114 (1970).
[23] 18 U.S.C. §2113(d) (1970).

A final major advantage of the Kennedy–McClellan Bill is that it would formally, and to some extent actually, make the trial judge the key sentencing figure (although in any foreseeable federal sentencing system the prosecutor—because of that 85 per cent. guilty plea rate—would retain a major sentencing role). The judge is the inexorably appropriate sentencing figure in the drama of crime and punishment. The judge would be required to consider sentencing guidelines and policy statements, but the sentencing decision would be his, subject to appellate review. The existence of published sentencing guidelines and a requirement that courts give specific reasons for sentences not authorised by the guidelines may tend to produce more consistent sentencing practices. In any case, sentencing practices would become more visible and unusual sentences would be recognised as such.

Although earlier versions of the bill[24] provided for rigorous appellate review to police judicial sentencing, the Kennedy–McClellan Bill's weak review standard—only "clearly unreasonable" sentences can be remedied—is a significant shortcoming.

Under the "clearly unreasonable" standard the effective sentencing range will consist of sentences authorised by guidelines plus "unreasonable" sentences outside the guideline range. Only the genuinely aberrant sentence will be remediable—as it often is, for constitutional reasons, under existing law.[25]

In the committee stage of this Bill in the Senate Judiciary Committee the problem of the appropriate range of appellate review received close attention. The tension is between, on the one hand, overloaded courts in arrears in their dockets and a consequent disinclination further to defer final decision in criminal cases, and on the other the desire for a relatively free appellate process to help to bring order and principle to the present anarchy of sentences in federal criminal cases. These conflicting pressures will continue to be discussed as the Bill receives further Congressional attention during 1978.

III

Equality and proportionality[26]

Much of the rhetoric of sentencing reform invokes equality as a paramount priority in sentencing. *Struggle for Justice* proposed:

> All persons found guilty of the same criminal act under the same circumstances [should be] dealt with uniformly.[27]

[24] S. 2269, 94th Cong., 1st Sess. (1975); S. 181, 95th Cong., 1st Sess. (1977).

[25] For a general review of evolving constitutional sentence review standards, see Berger, "Equal Protection and Criminal Sentencing: Legal and Policy Considerations," 71 Nw. L. Rev. 29 (1976).

[26] Norval Morris has developed this argument at greater length in, "Punishment, Desert and Rehabilitation," in United States Department of Justice, *Equal Justice Under Law: Department of Justice Bicentennial Lecture Series* 136 (1977).

[27] *Struggle* (above, n. 17) p. 148.

Section 1170 (*a*) (1) of California's Uniform Determinate Sentencing Act 1976 declares:

> The Legislature finds and declares that the purpose of imprisonment for crime is punishment. This purpose is best served by terms proportionate to the seriousness of the offence with provision for uniformity in the sentences of offenders committing the same offence under similar circumstances.[28]

We think it important that a case for just but unequal sentences should be recognised. The developments earlier described—scepticism about the rehabilitative ideal, increased awareness of discretion and the existence of sentencing disparities, arguments for retributive conceptions of punishment—should not lead to a system in which all offenders receive like sentences. Such a system would be both unwise and impracticable. Equality in punishment is not an absolute principle. It is a value to be weighed and considered among others. There can be just sentences in which like offenders are not treated alike, either as to who goes to prison or for how long.

Our reasons for thinking that principled sentencing disparity is justifiable are both practical and moral. First, there is our conception of punishment. Secondly, there are many instances of exemplary punishment which demonstrate that disparate sentencing is not generally perceived to be unjust. Thirdly, there is an argument which derives from the practical consideration that equality in sentencing is not realisable.

A conception of punishment

H. L. A. Hart asserts in his *Prolegomenon to the Philosophy of Punishment*[29] that an adequate philosophy of punishment must separately address questions of general justifying aim and distribution (the latter divided into subsidiary questions of liability: whom do we punish?; and amount: how much?). The justifying aim of our conception of punishment is utilitarian, including deterrence, the community educative effects of condign punishment, and the reaffirmation of the moral and ethical values of the community. Liability must of course be determined retributively: conviction by jury or bench trial or following an acceptable plea of guilty to an offence for which punishment is legislatively prescribed must be a pre-condition to the imposition of punishment.

No simple answer can be given to the question of amount and it is here that concern for equality and proportionality is apposite. Questions of amount should be limited by a principle of parsimony—the least afflictive sanction necessary to achieve defined social purposes should be imposed. Desert is a factor: no sanction should be imposed greater than that which is "deserved" by the last crime, or series of crimes, for which the offender is being sentenced. Nor should a sanction be imposed which is so lenient as to unduly depreciate the seriousness of the offence.

Equality and proportionality are important values. We will argue that the limiting principle of parsimony (which is a principle of justice with

[28] 1976 Cal. Legis Serv. Ch. 1139, §1170(a)(1).

[29] Hart, H. L. A., *Punishment and Responsibility* (Oxford 1968) Chap. 1.

which persons in Rawl's original position could be expected to agree)[30] is inconsistent with and should sometimes override the values of equality and proportionality. Not to so conclude would produce gratuitous, socially unnecessary, imposition of penal suffering.

Exemplary punishments
An argument against equality in sentencing derives intuitive support from several illustrations of generally approved instances of exemplary punishment. Exemplary punishment is surely discordant to the principle that like cases should be treated alike, if that principle is regarded as either limiting or defining the amount of just punishment.

During a period of racial strife in the Notting Hill district of London in 1958, sentences of four years' imprisonment were imposed on each of nine young white men who had participated in attacks on blacks.[31] The sentences were at least double the sentence normally imposed for that offence and were stated by the judge to be in excess of the normal sentence for such offences. They were imposed expressly as exemplary punishments, to capture public attention and to deter such behaviour by a dramatic punishment. No refined analysis is required to demonstrate that these nine offenders were selected for *unequal* treatment before the law. If the increased penalty is within the legislatively prescribed range, concern for equality should not prevent such a sentence from being in the appropriate case a just punishment. There are many such examples. They occur in all countries and times and are generally viewed as necessary and legitimate.

Let us consider another hard case for that principle, this time a law teacher's hypothetical. Imagine that each of six Dover doctors last year understated his income by £10,000. As advisers to the Inland Revenue, we discuss what should be done. Clearly, each of the six must pay tax on the income he failed to declare, interest at appropriately high rates on that tax and substantial penalties. All this can be arranged without criminal prosecution. Must all six be prosecuted? Must all six be sent to prison? We submit not. Our purpose is utilitarian. We wish, as Voltaire said of the English practice of killing an occasional admiral to encourage the others to be brave, publicly to punish by sending to prison an occasional medical practitioner "to encourage the others" to integrity in their tax returns. We do not need to send all six to prison. The extra increment of deterrence would be bought at too high a cost. It would be wasteful of our resources, wasteful of the court's time and, what is perhaps also in point, it would inflict unnecessary suffering on those doctors whose punishment did not substantially increase the deterrent impact we would gain by the imprisonment of, say, two of their number.

How should we select those to be imprisoned? Perhaps we should struggle for some distinguishing characteristics of deserved severity or some opportunity of extra deterrent utility in the punishment of some amongst the six. What must be recognised is that we are involved in a conscious breach of a principle that like cases should be equally punished.

Would it be unjust? It cannot be treating like cases alike if any reasonable

[30] Rawls, J., *A Theory of Justice* (Cambridge, Mass. 1971).

[31] The Notting Hill case is described and discussed in Walker, N., *Sentencing in a Rational Society* (London 1971) pp. 69–70.

concepts of the quality of guilt and deserved suffering are to be applied. In our view, such a system is both unequal and just, and it is precisely that apparent paradox we seek to defend.

An argument in justification of principled inequality

Equality can be no more than a subsidiary principle in any jurisprudence of punishment. No realisable conventional jurisprudence of punishment *requires* equality in sentencing in all events. We can only imagine defining principles of punishment which would specify the precise penalty to impose on any offender for any offence. With perfect knowledge a hypothetical utility-maximising deterrent penalty could be calculated. With a perfect moral sense we could specify precisely calibrated deserved punishments. Utility or desert could thus operate as principles which define an appropriate amount of punishment. Unfortunately, we lack defining principles. We lack perfect knowledge. Few claim (and fewer possess) a perfect moral sense.

We believe that there are no realisable defining principles of punishment and that the limiting principles of punishment should be desert and parsimony. Desert sets the maximum and minimum of the sentence that may be imposed for any offence (and helps achieve proportionality by establishing the punishment relationships between offences). It does not give more fine tuning to the appropriate sentence than that. The fine tuning must be done on other principles. Parsimony forbids imposition of punishment in excess of that required to achieve defined social purposes.

Others argue that reform and incapacitation are appropriate tuning devices and that a principled system of sentencing could encompass them. We will not here enter into that debate although Norval Morris has done so elsewhere.[32]

We recognise that moral philosophers may object to exemplary and unequal punishments based on a utilitarian justification. To punish some more severely than others for reasons of deterrence may be using human beings only as a means. One could argue that enhancing punishment for deterrent reasons is equivalent to punishing the innocent for deterrent purposes. If the community believed the innocent to be guilty, punishment would have the same deterrent efficacy as if the defendant were guilty, yet to punish the innocent would be unjust. Argument could be made, for similar reasons, that offenders should not receive additional increments of punishment for deterrent purposes. Deterrence would then have to depend on the effects of imposition of "deserved" uniform sanctions.

Our response is that desert can give only rough guidance in setting the amount of punishment. Some penalties would be unjust because too harsh and others inappropriate because too lenient. Within that range, choices must be made according to criteria which are known, rational and principled. We have argued that some utilitarian considerations are socially appropriate for that purpose, but that punishment of all, when punishment of some would suffice, is unjust because it would violate a limiting principle of parsimony and would impose socially unnecessary suffering.

We agree with H. L. A. Hart, when he noted that just punishment:

[32] *The Future of Imprisonment* (Chicago 1974).

> not only insists on the restriction of punishment to an offender, but also on the general retention of the doctrine of *mens rea*, and allows some place, though a subordinate one, to ideas of equality and proportion in the gradation of the severity of punishment.[33]

As you will gather, we have difficulty with these problems and by no means pretend to their solutions; but we do strenuously argue that we have demonstrated situations of exemplary punishment in which justice and the principle of equality (and by necessary implication, proportionality) do not appear to be coterminous.

IV

Towards a common law of sentencing

Principled sentencing lies at the heart of an effective criminal justice system. Sentencing involves a heavy responsibility and raises difficult issues; it thus requires reasons given, critical public consideration of those reasons, critical appellate review of those reasons, and a system of precedent leading to principled justice under law.

The Kennedy–McClellan Bill offers promise for the development of a rational and principled sentencing system in the federal criminal courts. It offers a coherent division of power between legislature and judge which may provide a rational frame of reference for the judge in his difficult task of selecting an appropriate punishment for the convicted criminal. By reducing the number of offence categories and providing for the development of general sentencing standards to guide the judge in deciding whether imprisonment is an appropriate sanction and, if so, for what duration, the Bill may foster more regular and predictable sentencing practices. To continue this evolution towards a common law of sentencing, the Bill would require the judge to give reasons for this choice of a sentence. His sentences and thus his reasons should be subject, as in other countries, to effective appellate review.

What can sentencing reform achieve? The journey will not be short nor the results easy of achievement but, in our view, we can reasonably expect perceptible progress towards the emergence of a principled, evenhanded, effective yet merciful Common Law of Sentencing, consistent with human rights and just freedoms, competent to the deterrence of crime, the adumbration of minimum behavioural standards, and the better protection of society from its human predators.

[33] *Op. cit.* (n. 29, above) p. 233..

[11]
Mandatory Penalties

ABSTRACT

To many public officials, promotion and enactment of mandatory penalty laws are important symbols of their concern for public safety and citizens' fear of crime. In practice, mandatory minimum-penalty laws accomplish few of their stated objectives and produce unwanted consequences. Their deterrent effects range from nonexistent to short-lived. When they call for short mandatory prison terms for serious crimes, they are often irrelevant because longer sentences are generally imposed. When they mandate longer terms (five, ten, twenty years), they are often circumvented by lawyers and judges. They reduce defendants' incentives to plead guilty, reduce guilty plea rates, and lengthen case processing time. They sometimes result in imposition of penalties more severe than anyone immediately involved believes appropriate. A number of devices exist, ranging from repeal to reconfiguration, for avoiding the unwanted effects of mandatory penalties. Whether such devices can adequately reconcile public officials' needs to take symbolic actions with court officials' needs to be both just and efficient remains to be seen.

Mandatory penalties do not work. The record is clear from research in the 1950s, the 1970s, the 1980s, and, thanks to the U.S. Sentencing Commission, the 1990s that mandatory penalty laws shift power from judges to prosecutors, meet with widespread circumvention, produce dislocations in case processing, and too often result in imposition of penalties that everyone involved believes to be unduly harsh. From research in the 1970s and 1980s, the weight of the evidence clearly

Michael Tonry, Sonosky Professor of Law and Public Policy at the University of Minnesota, is grateful to John DiIulio, Frank Hartmann, Marc Miller, and Andrew von Hirsch for helpful comments on an earlier draft.

shows that enactment of mandatory penalties has either no demonstrable marginal deterrent effects or short-term effects that rapidly waste away.[1] Why, then, did legislatures in all fifty states enact mandatory penalty laws in the 1970s and 1980s, and why do legislatures continue to enact them?

The reason is that most elected officials who support such laws are only secondarily interested in their effects; officials' primary interests are rhetorical and symbolic. Calling and voting for mandatory penalties, as many state and federal officials repeatedly have done in recent years, is demonstration that officials are "tough on crime." If the laws "work," all the better, but that is hardly crucial. In a time of heightened public anxiety about crime and social unrest, being on the right side of the crime issue is much more important politically than making sound and sensible public policy choices.

This essay retells a story, at least three centuries old, of the political appeal and practical limits of mandatory sentencing laws. The retelling is occasioned by the publication of a U.S. Sentencing Commission report on mandatory penalties in the federal courts and by the possibility that prison crowding, budgetary crises, and a changing professional climate may make more public officials willing to be reminded of what we have long known about mandatory penalties. Officials in some states (there seems little hope at the federal level) may in coming years be more inclined than in the recent past to make policy choices based on knowledge of how mandatory penalties operate in practice. Surprisingly, few published works offer overviews of research on mandatory penalties. This essay is one effort to fill that void.

That mandatory penalties have more costs than benefits does not mean that rational social policies might not incorporate serious penalties for serious crimes. There are more effective, less costly ways than creation of mandatory penalties to achieve that end. In every era, some

[1] Because few studies attempt to examine the mandatory penalty laws' deterrent effects, and because the clear weight of the evidence on the deterrent effects of marginal manipulation of penalties demonstrates few or no effects (e.g., Blumstein, Cohen, and Nagin 1978), except in this note I do not explore that subject. Several studies of the Massachusetts firearms law concluded that it had a short-term deterrent effect on the use of firearms in violent crimes (e.g., Pierce and Bowers 1981). However, studies of mandatory sentencing laws for firearms offenses in Michigan (Loftin, Heumann, and McDowall 1983) and Florida (Loftin and McDowall 1984) concluded that no discernible effect on the level of crime could be attributed to the mandatory sentencing laws. The Rockefeller Drug Law evaluation also found no demonstrable impact of that law on drug use or crime in New York (Joint Committee on New York Drug Law Evaluation 1978). The proliferation of mandatory penalties for drug crimes in the 1980s did not demonstrably reduce drug trafficking or affect its most common measure, the street prices of illicit substances (Reuter and Kleiman 1986, table 5; Moore 1990, fig. 1).

kinds of crime are regarded as so serious that harsh penalties appear called for. Examples in our time include aggravated forms of stranger violence, nonfamilial sexual abuse of young children, and flagrant fraudulence in the financial markets. Assuming that legislators will want to provide for severe penalties for especially serious crime, there are ways to avoid or ameliorate the foreseeable dysfunctional effects of mandatory penalties. Here are four examples. First, in order to establish policies calling for severe penalties for serious crimes, while allowing sufficient flexibility to avoid foreseeable unintended consequences, penalties for especially serious crimes might be made presumptive rather than mandatory. Prosecutors and judges both have powerful voices in sentencing; disregard of the presumption would require that one or both decide either that the penalty would be too severe in a particular case or that the political climate has altered and public sensibilities no longer demand such harsh penalties. Second, as a matter of course, legislators might add "sunset provisions" to mandatory penalty laws. This would assure that laws passed in the passion of the moment will not endure for decades. Legislators can much more comfortably accede to the lapse of a punitive law than vote for its repeal. Third, mandatory (or presumptive) penalties might be limited to serious crimes like armed robbery, aggravated rape, and murder. The most widespread and cynical circumventions of mandatory penalty laws, and the most extreme injustices in individual cases, arise under laws requiring severe penalties for minor crimes like possession or trafficking of small amounts of controlled substances. Fourth, correctional officials might be authorized to reconsider release dates of all offenders receiving prison sentences exceeding a designated length (say three or five years). This would allow eventual release of people receiving unusually long sentences, life sentences without eligibility for parole, and sentences under "habitual offender" fixed-term laws, without requiring extraordinary political decisions like gubernatorial pardons or commutations.

This essay summarizes the available research on the implementation and operation of mandatory sentencing laws. Section I provides a brief summary of the state of knowledge concerning mandatory penalties before 1970. Section II examines the major empirical evaluations of mandatory penalties, beginning with the most ambitious, the U.S. Sentencing Commission's 1991 study of federal mandatories and the 1978 evaluation of New York's "Rockefeller Drug Laws." Section III tries to make sense of those findings and to outline their implications for elected officials who want simultaneously to respond to public anxiety about serious crime and yet to enact laws that waste as few public resources, foster as few hypocrisies, and do as little injustice as possible.

I. Mandatory Penalties before 1970

The foreseeable problems in implementing mandatory penalties have been well known for 200 years. Most systematic empirical research postdates 1970. This section summarizes knowledge to that date. Perhaps the best way to summarize past knowledge concerning mandatory penalties is to quote from a U.S. House of Representatives report that explained why the Congress in 1970 repealed almost all federal mandatory penalties for drug offenses. "The severity of existing penalties, involving in many instances minimum mandatory sentences, has led in many instances to reluctance on the part of prosecutors to prosecute some violations, where the penalties seem to be out of line with the seriousness of the offenses. In addition, severe penalties, which do not take into account individual circumstances, and which treat casual violators as severely as they treat hardened criminals, tend to make conviction . . . more difficult to obtain" (House of Representatives 1970, quoted in U.S. Sentencing Commission 1991, pp. 6–7). Our knowledge in the 1990s concerning mandatory penalties is little different. More to the point, knowledge in the 1790s was much the same.

The least subtle way to avoid imposition of harsh penalties is to nullify them by refusing to convict offenders subject to them. "Nullification," a term in common usage for more than two centuries, encapsulates the process by which judges and juries, but particularly juries, willfully refuse to enforce laws or apply penalties that seem to them unjust. Oliver Wendell Holmes, Jr., described the jury's capacity to nullify harsh laws as its central virtue (Holmes 1889). Roscoe Pound claimed that "jury lawlessness is the great corrective of law in its actual administration" (1910, p. 18). John Baldwin and Michael McConville, in a review of research on juries, observed: "The refusal of juries to convict in cases of criminal libel, the 'pious perjury' they welcomed in order to avoid conviction on a capital offense, the indulgence shown toward 'mercy killings,' and the nullification of the Prohibition laws during the 1920s are simply the most famous examples of this exercise of discretion" (1980, p. 272). The leading criminal law casebook in use in American law schools for twenty-five years, Michael and Wechsler's *Criminal Law and Its Administration* (1940), dedicated lengthy consideration to nullification. Although the term is no longer in vogue, a summary of the evidence concerning nullification and similar processes may be useful.

A. *The Death Penalty in Eighteenth-Century England*

The death penalty in eighteenth- and nineteenth-century England was the subject of policy debates strikingly like late twentieth-century American debates about mandatory penalties. In July 1991, in the face of claims that newly proposed mandatory penalty laws would overburden the courts and have little practical effect, one congressman told the *New York Times*, "Congressmen and senators are afraid to vote no" on crime and punishment bills, "even if they don't think it will accomplish anything." A senate aide suggested that "it's tough to vote against tough sentences for criminals" (Ifill 1991). At the end of the eighteenth century, Edmund Burke declared "that he could obtain the consent of the House of Commons to any Bill imposing the punishment of death" (Select Committee on Capital Punishment 1930, paras. 10, 11). Samuel Romilly, England's most celebrated contemporary prison reformer, by contrast, repeatedly called for repeal of capital punishment provisions because the laws were applied erratically and unfairly and because the erratic application inevitably undermined the laws' deterrent effects (Romilly 1820).[2] During the reigns of the four British King Georges, between 1714 and 1830, the British Parliament created 156 new capital offenses. By 1819, British law recognized 220 capital offenses, most of them property crimes.

During the same period, however, the number of executions carried out not only failed to increase commensurately with the passage of new laws but declined. Executions were four times more common in the early 1600s than in the mid-1700s (Hay 1975, p. 22). According to Sir Leon Radzinowicz, executions in the late eighteenth century varied between a low of twenty-one per year during the 1780s and a high of fifty-three in the 1790s (Radzinowicz 1948–68, 1:141, 147).

Douglas Hay (1975), in a famous essay, "Property, Authority, and the Criminal Law," tries to explain the contrast between continuous extension of the reach of the death penalty and steady decline in the incidence of its use. He argues that the explanation can be found in the efforts of propertied classes in the early years of the Industrial Revolution to protect their class interests through passage of laws that

[2] To like effect, the U.S. Sentencing Commission's report on mandatory penalties argued that their inconsistent application is likely to undermine their deterrent effects (1991, p. ii, iii).

symbolically emphasized the importance of private property (by making numerous property crimes punishable by death) while operating a legal system that provided both exemplary punishments and, by frequent merciful exceptions and observing procedural rules, supported its own public legitimacy. In this period before creation of professional police departments and widespread use of prisons for punishment, the civil peace depended on general acceptance of the legitimacy of the existing social order.

More important for purposes of this essay, however, are the methods used in practice to avoid carrying out death sentences. First, and most important, juries often refused to convict offenders; an acquittal is a simple but effective way to avoid a mandatory penalty (Baldwin and McConville 1980, p. 272). A variant, which has twentieth-century echoes, was for the jury to convict of a lesser offense. According to a 1930 report of the British Select Committee on Capital Punishment describing eighteenth-century practices:

> In vast numbers of cases, the sentence of death was not passed, or if passed was not carried into effect. For one thing, juries in increasing numbers refused to convict. A jury would assess the amount taken from a shop at 4s. 10d. so as to avoid the capital penalty which fell on a theft of 5s. In the case of a dwelling, where the theft of 40s. was a capital offense, even when a woman confessed that she had stolen £5, the jury notwithstanding found that the amount was only 39s. And when . . . the legislature raised the capital indictment to £5, the juries at the same time raised their verdicts £4 19s. [1930, para. 17]

Second, as more capital offenses were created, the courts adopted increasingly narrow interpretations of procedural, pleading, and evidentiary rules. Prosecutions seemingly well-founded as a factual matter would fall because a name or a date was incorrect or a defendant's occupation was wrongly described as "farmer" rather than "yeoman" (Radzinowicz 1948–68, vol. 1:25–28, 83–91, 97–103; Hay 1980, pp. 32–34).

Third, increasing numbers of offenders were accorded protection from death under the doctrine of "benefit of clergy." A doctrine that initially protected clergymen from execution following convictions at civil (as opposed to religious) courts, benefit of clergy was extended to literate laymen in the medieval period and to all accused in 1706. Its effect was to exempt first offenders convicted of lesser felonies from execution (Baker 1977, p. 41).

Fourth, even among those who were not acquitted, convicted of lesser charges, discharged on procedural technicalities, or protected by benefit of clergy, the proportion sentenced to death declined steadily throughout the late eighteenth century.

According to the Select Committee on Capital Punishment, "the Prerogative of the Crown [pardon] was increasingly exercised. Down to 1756 about two thirds of those condemned were actually brought to the scaffold; from 1756 to 1772 the proportion sank to one-half. Between 1802 and 1808 it was no more than one eighth" (1930, para. 21). Most of those pardoned received substituted punishments of a term of imprisonment or transportation (Stephen 1883, vol. 1, chap. 13).

Briefly to summarize, experience with "mandatory" capital punishment in eighteenth-century England instructed all who would pay attention that mandatory penalties, especially for crimes other than homicide, elicited a variety of adaptive responses from those charged to enforce the law, including juries' refusals to convict "guilty" offenders and decisions to bring in convictions for less serious charges not subject to the penalty, development of technical procedural devices used by judges to discharge cases, and extensive use of pardons and other post-conviction devices to avoid carrying out executions.

B. American Mandatory Penalties in the 1950s

Our best source of information on criminal court processes in the 1950s, the various reports emanating from the American Bar Foundation's Survey of the Administration of Criminal Justice in the United States, confirms the lessons from eighteenth-century England. Frank Remington, director of the eighteen-year project, in the foreword to the sentencing volume, noted, "Legislative prescription of a high mandatory sentence for certain offenders is likely to result in a reduction in charges at the prosecution stage, or if this is not done, by a refusal of the judge to convict at the adjudication stage. The issue . . . thus is not solely whether certain offenders should be dealt with severely, but also how the criminal justice system will accommodate to the legislative charge" (Dawson 1969, p. xvii).

The American Bar Association survey was conceived as an empirical investigation and description of the administration of criminal justice in the United States. "Pilot studies" were undertaken in several states in the mid-1950s. As the enormity of the project became apparent, the pilot studies became the survey and led to the publication of five volumes based on extensive reviews of files, interviews, and participant observation (including *Conviction* [Newman 1966], *Prosecution* [Miller 1969], and *Sentencing* [Dawson 1969]). Several volumes deal with charging, case processing, and sentencing aspects of mandatory penalties. The survey's findings on mandatories are exemplified by three processes the reports describe. First, Newman describes how Michigan judges dealt with a lengthy mandatory minimum for drug sales:

> Mandatory minimums are almost universally disliked by trial judges. . . . The clearest illustration of routine reductions is provided by reduction of sale of narcotics to possession or addiction . . . Judges . . . actively participated in the charge reduction process to the extent of refusing to accept guilty pleas to sale and liberally assigning counsel to work out reduced charges. . . . To demonstrate its infrequent application, from the effective date of the revised law (May 8, 1952) to the date of tabulation four years later (June 30, 1956), only twelve sale-of-narcotics convictions were recorded in Detroit out of 476 defendants originally charged with sale. The remainder (except a handful acquitted altogether) pleaded guilty to reduced charges. [1966, p. 179]

Second, on a related subject (avoidance of long statutory maximum sentences), Newman (1966, p. 182) describes efforts to avoid fifteen-year mandatory maximum sentences for breaking-and-entering and armed robbery:

> In Michigan conviction of armed robbery or breaking and entering in the nighttime (fifteen-year maximum compared to five years for daytime breaking) is rare. The pattern of downgrading is such that it becomes virtually routine, and the bargaining session becomes a ritual. The real issue in such negotiations is not whether the charge will be reduced but how far, that is, to what lesser offense. As has been pointed out, armed robbery is so often downgraded that the Michigan parole board tends to treat a conviction for unarmed robbery as prima facie proof that the defendant had a weapon. And the frequency of altering nighttime burglary to breaking and entering in the daytime led one

prosecutor to remark: "You'd think all our burglaries occur at high noon."

Third, Dawson (1969, p. 201) describes "very strong" judicial resistance to a twenty-year mandatory minimum for sale of narcotics: "All of the judges of Recorder's Court, in registering their dislike for the provision, cited the hypothetical case of a young man having no criminal record being given a twenty-year minimum sentence for selling a single marijuana cigarette. Charge reductions to possession or use are routine. Indeed, in some cases, judges have refused to accept guilty pleas to sale of narcotics, but have continued the case and appointed counsel with instructions to negotiate a charge reduction." These findings from the American Bar Foundation differ in detail from those of eighteenth-century England, but only in detail. When the U.S. Congress repealed most mandatory penalties for drug offenses in 1970, it was merely acknowledging enforcement problems that had been recognized for centuries.

II. Mandatory Penalties in the 1970s, 1980s, and 1990s

Despite earlier generations' understanding of why mandatory penalties are unsound as a matter of policy, mandatory sentencing laws since 1975 have been America's most popular sentencing innovation. By 1983, forty-nine of the fifty states had adopted mandatory sentencing laws for offenses other than murder or drunk driving (Shane-DuBow, Brown, and Olsen 1985, table 30). Most mandatories apply to murder or aggravated rape, drug offenses, felonies involving firearms, or felonies committed by persons who have previous felony convictions.[3] Between 1985 and mid-1991, the U.S. Congress enacted at least twenty new mandatory penalty provisions; by 1991, more than sixty federal statutes defined more than one hundred crimes subject to mandatories (U.S. Sentencing Commission 1991, pp. 8–10). The experience in most states in the late 1980s was similar. In Florida, for example, seven new mandatory sentencing bills were enacted between 1988 and 1990 (Austin 1991, p. 4). In Arizona, for another example, mandatory sentencing laws are so common that 57 percent of felony offenders in fiscal year 1990 were subject to mandatory sentencing enhancements (Knapp 1991, p. 10).

[3] Legislation in the 1980s in many states established forty-eight-hour and other brief mandatory minimum terms for many drunk driving offenses (Jacobs 1988).

The political attractiveness of mandatory sentencing laws is not difficult to understand. During the 1980s many political figures of both parties campaigned on "tough on crime" platforms and few elected officials dared risk being seen as "soft." A recent *New York Times* story captures the climate in its title: "Senate's Rule for Its Anti-crime Bill: The Tougher the Provision, the Better" (Ifill 1991). Mandatories are often targeted on especially disturbing behaviors, such as large-scale drug sales, murder, or rape, or especially unattractive characters, such as repeat violent offenders or people who use guns in violent crimes. In the case of firearms offenses, mandatory laws allow the state, like Janus, to frown on law-defying villains who use firearms for criminal purposes and to smile on law-abiding citizens who use firearms for legitimate purposes. In a nation in which most approaches to control of gun use are politically impracticable, mandatory sentencing laws are a mechanism for attempting to deter illegal gun use and encourage offenders to use less lethal weapons.

Although the uninitiated citizen might reasonably believe that, under a mandatory sentencing law, anyone who commits the target offense will receive the mandated sentence, the reality is more complicated. Sentencing policy is only as mandatory as police, prosecutors, and judges choose to make it. The people who operate the criminal justice system generally find mandatory sentencing laws too inflexible for their taste and take steps to avoid what they consider unduly harsh, and therefore unjust, sentences in individual cases. And, frequently, the mandatory sentencing law is simply ignored. For example, in Minnesota in 1981, of persons convicted of weapons offenses to which a mandatory minimum applied, only 76.5 percent actually received prison sentences (Knapp 1984, p. 28).[4]

Research on mandatory sentencing laws during the 1970s and 1980s reveals a number of avoidance strategies. Boston police avoided application of a 1975 Massachusetts law calling for mandatory one-year sentences for persons convicted of carrying a gun by decreasing the number of arrests made for that offense and increasing (by 120 percent between 1974 and 1976) the number of weapons seizures without arrest (Carlson 1982). Prosecutors often avoid application of mandatory sen-

[4] One striking form of plea bargaining around mandatory penalties occurs in Arizona, where Knapp (1991, pp. 10–11) found that 3,739 (24 percent) of 15,720 felony convictions in 1990 were for the inchoate offenses of attempt and conspiracy. Inchoate offenses are not subject to mandatory penalties. Defendants charged with completed felonies subject to mandatories are routinely allowed to bargain down to inchoate offenses.

tencing laws simply by filing charges for different, but roughly comparable, offenses that are not subject to mandatory sentences. Judges too can circumvent such laws. Detroit judges sidestepped a 1977 law requiring a two-year sentence for persons convicted of possession of a firearm in the commission of a felony by acquitting defendants of the gun charge (even though the evidence would support a conviction) or by decreasing the sentence they would otherwise impose by two years to offset the mandatory two-year term (Heumann and Loftin 1979).

There has been considerable recent research and, taken together, like the work of earlier generations, it supports the following generalizations:

1. lawyers and judges will take steps to avoid application of laws they consider unduly harsh;
2. dismissal rates typically increase at early stages of the criminal justice process after effectuation of a mandatory penalty as practitioners attempt to shield some defendants from the law's reach;
3. defendants whose cases are not dismissed or diverted make more vigorous efforts to avoid conviction and to delay sentencing with the results that trial rates and case processing times increase;
4. defendants who are convicted of the target offense are often sentenced more severely than they would have been in the absence of the mandatory penalty provision; and
5. because declines in conviction rates for those arrested tend to offset increases in imprisonment rates for those convicted, the overall probability that defendants will be incarcerated remains about the same after enactment of a mandatory sentencing law.[5]

The empirical evidence concerning the operation of mandatory sentencing laws comes primarily from five major studies. One is the U.S. Sentencing Commission's recent study of mandatory penalties in the U.S. federal courts (U.S. Sentencing Commission 1991). The second concerns the "Rockefeller Drug Laws," which required mandatory prison sentences for persons convicted of a variety of drug felonies (Joint Committee on New York Drug Law Evaluation 1978). One concerns the operation of a 1977 Michigan law requiring imposition of a two-year mandatory prison sentence on persons convicted of possession of a gun during commission of a felony (Loftin and McDowall

[5] This finding recurs in research on mandatories in the 1970s. Whether it will be found in the 1990s is unknown. The U.S. Sentencing Commission study of mandatory penalties, like earlier research, revealed longer case processing times and lower guilty plea rates than for non-mandatory-penalty crimes but does not consider whether incarceration probabilities, given an arrest, have changed.

1981; Loftin, Heumann, and McDowall 1983). Two concern a Massachusetts law requiring a one-year prison sentence for persons convicted of carrying a firearm unlawfully (Beha 1977; Rossman et al. 1979).

A. U.S. Sentencing Commission Report

Were federal officials more interested in rational policy-making than in political posturing, the U.S. Sentencing Commission report, "Mandatory Minimum Penalties in the Federal Criminal Justice System," would result in withdrawal of all mandatory sentencing proposals and repeal of those now in effect.

The commission's report demonstrates that mandatory minimum sentencing laws unwarrantedly shift discretion from judges to prosecutors, result in higher trial rates and lengthened case processing times, arbitrarily fail to acknowledge salient differences between cases, and often punish minor offenders much more harshly than anyone involved believes is warranted. Interviews with judges, lawyers, and probation officers at twelve sites showed that heavy majorities of judges, defense counsel, and probation officers dislike mandatory penalties; prosecutors are about evenly divided. Finally, and perhaps not surprisingly given the other findings, the report shows that judges and lawyers not uncommonly circumvent mandatories.

The commission's study was prompted by a congressional mandate.[6] The congressional charge had eight parts, including an assessment of the effects of mandatories on sentencing disparities, a description of the interaction between mandatories and plea bargaining, and "a detailed empirical research study of the effect of mandatory minimum penalties in the Federal system."

The commission's research design effectively combined methods and data sources for investigating charging, bargaining, and sentencing patterns. The combination of quantitative analyses of 1984–90 sentencing patterns, a detailed quantitative analysis of case processing in 1990, and various interviews and surveys aimed at capturing officials' opinions provide complementary sources of information. In presenting and discussing findings, the report carefully notes the limits of the claims it can make and describes alternative interpretations of findings.

The commission analyzed three data sets describing federal sentencing and two sources of data concerning the opinions of judges, assistant U.S. attorneys, and others. The three sentencing data sets were

[6] Pub. L. No. 101-647, sec. 1703 [104 Stat. 4846].

FPSSIS,[7] sentencing commission monitoring data for fiscal year 1990, and a 12.5 percent random sample from the sentencing commission's file of defendants sentenced in fiscal year 1990.[8] Data for the random sample were augmented by examining computerized and paper case files to identify cases (there proved to be 1,165 defendants) that met statutory criteria for receipt of a mandatory minimum drug or weapon sentence.

The two sources of data on practitioners' opinions were structured interviews in twelve sites of 234 practitioners (forty-eight judges, seventy-two assistant U.S. attorneys, forty-eight defense attorneys, sixty-six probation officers), and a May 1991 mail survey of 2,998 practitioners (the same groups as were interviewed; 1,261 had responded by the time the report was written).

1. *Results of the Sentencing Analyses.* The sentencing data revealed a number of patterns that the commission found disturbing. First, there were clear indications that prosecutors often do not file charges that carry mandatory minimums when the evidence would have supported such charges. For one example, prosecutors failed to file charges for mandatory weapons enhancements against 45 percent of drug defendants for whom they would have been appropriate. For another, prosecutors failed to seek mandatory sentencing enhancements for prior felony convictions in 63 percent of cases in which they could have been sought. For a third, defendants were charged with the offense carrying the highest applicable mandatory minimum in only 74 percent of cases.

Second, there were clear indications that prosecutors used mandatory provisions tactically to induce guilty pleas. For one example, among defendants who were fully charged with applicable mandatory sentence charges and who were convicted at trial, 96 percent received the full mandatory minimum sentence; by contrast, 27 percent of those who pled guilty pled to charges bearing no mandatory minimum or a lower one. For another example, of all defendants who pled guilty (whether or not initially charged with all the applicable mandatory-bearing charges), 32 percent had no mandatory minimum at conviction

[7] FPSSIS, pronounced "fipsiss," is an acronym for "Federal Probation Sentencing and Supervision Information System," the Administrative Office of the U.S. Courts' automated information system for federal sentencing.

[8] The FPSSIS and monitoring data are insufficiently detailed to permit the fine-grained factual analyses of actual offense behavior that are required to determine whether facts alleged in specific cases might warrant filing of mandatory-bearing charges. As a result, those data sources are used to provide more general portraits of sentencing patterns over time and in 1990.

and 53 percent were sentenced below the minimum that the evidence would have justified. For a third example, among those defendants against whom mandatory weapons enhancements were filed, the weapons charges were later dismissed in 26 percent of cases.

Third, mandatories increased trial rates and presumably also increased workloads and case processing times. Nearly 30 percent of those convicted of offenses bearing mandatory minimums were convicted at trial, a rate two-and-one-half times the overall trial rate for federal criminal defendants.

Fourth, there were indications that judges (often presumably with the assent of prosecutors) imposed sentences less severe than applicable mandatory provisions would appear to require. Before examples are given, it bears mention that the sentencing commission's "modified real offense" policies direct judges, especially in drug cases, to sentence on the basis of actual offense behavior and not simply the offense of conviction.

Here are a couple of the commission's findings that suggest judicial willingness to work around, and under, the mandatories. Forty percent of all defendants whose cases the commission believed warranted specific mandatory minimums received shorter sentences than the applicable statutes would have specified. Another example: mandatory minimum defendants received downward departures 22 percent of the time. The commission observes that "the increased departure rate may reflect a greater tendency to exercise prosecutorial or judicial discretion as the severity of the penalties increases" (U.S. Sentencing Commission 1991, p. 53). To like effect, "The prosecutors' reasons for reducing or dismissing mandatory charges . . . may be attributable to . . . satisfaction with the punishment received" (U.S. Sentencing Commission 1991, p. 58).

Taken together, these findings suggested to the commission that mandatory minimums are not working. They were shifting too much discretion to the prosecutor. They were provoking judges and prosecutors willfully to circumvent their application (U.S. Sentencing Commission 1991, pp. ii, 76). They were producing high trial rates and unacceptable sentencing disparities.

2. *Results of the Opinion Surveys.* No category of federal court practitioners, including prosecutors, much likes mandatory minimum sentencing laws (U.S. Sentencing Commission 1991, chap. 6). In one-hour structured interviews, thirty-eight of forty-eight federal district court judges offered unfavorable comments. The most common were that the mandatory sentences are too harsh and that they eliminate judicial

discretion. Among forty-eight defense counsel, only one had anything positive to say about guidelines, and he also had negative comments. The most common complaints were that the mandatories are too harsh, that they result in too many trials, and that they eliminate judicial discretion. Probation officers were also overwhelmingly hostile to the mandatories; their most common complaints were that the mandatories are too harsh, result in prison overcrowding, and eliminate judicial discretion. Only among prosecutors was sentiment more favorable to mandatories, and even then thirty-four of sixty-one interviewed who expressed a view were wholly (twenty-three) or partly (eleven) negative.

Consistent with the interview data, the mail survey showed that 62 percent of judges, 52 percent of private counsel, and 89 percent of federal defenders want mandatories for drug crimes eliminated, compared to only 10 percent of prosecutors and 22 percent of probation officers.

B. The Rockefeller Drug Laws in New York

Perhaps the most exhaustive examination of mandatory sentencing laws before the commission's work was an evaluation of the later repealed Rockefeller Drug Laws in New York. The "Rockefeller Drug Laws" took effect in New York on September 1, 1973. They prescribed severe mandatory prison sentences for narcotics offenses and included selective statutory limits on plea bargaining. A major evaluation (Joint Committee on New York Drug Law Evaluation 1978) focused primarily on the effects of the drug laws on drug use and drug related crime and only to a lesser extent on case processing. The study was based primarily on analyses of official record data routinely collected by public agencies. The key findings were these:

1. drug felony arrests, indictment rates, and conviction rates all declined after the law took effect;
2. for those who were convicted, however, the likelihood of being imprisoned and the average length of prison term increased;
3. the two preceding patterns cancelled each other out and the likelihood that a person arrested for a drug felony would be imprisoned was the same—11 percent—after the law took effect as before;
4. because defendants struggled to avoid the mandatory sentences, the proportion of drug felony dispositions resulting from trials tripled between 1973 and 1976 and the average time required for processing of a single case doubled.

Table 1 shows case processing patterns for drug felony cases in New

TABLE 1

Drug Felony Processing in New York State

	1972	1973*	1974	1975	1976 (January–June)
Arrests	19,269	15,594	17,670	15,941	8,166
Indictments:					
N	7,528	5,969	5,791	4,283	2,073
Percent of arrests	39.1	38.3	32.8	26.9	25.4
Indictments disposed	6,911	5,580	3,939	3,989	2,173
Convictions:					
N	6,033	4,739	3,085	3,147	1,724
Percent of dispositions	87.3	84.9	78.3	78.9	79.3
Prison and jail sentences:					
N	2,039	1,555	1,074	1,369	945
Percent of convictions	33.8	32.8	34.8	43.5	54.8
Percent of arrests	10.6	10.0	6.1	8.6	11.6

Source.—Joint Committee (1978), tables 19, 24, 27, 29.
* The drug law went into effect September 1, 1973.

York during the period 1972–76. The percentage of drug felony arrests resulting in indictments declined steadily from 39.1 percent in 1972, before the law took effect, to 25.4 percent in the first half of 1976. Similarly, the likelihood of conviction, given indictment, declined from 87.3 percent in 1972 to 79.3 percent in the first half of 1976. Of those defendants, however, who were not winnowed out earlier, the likelihood that a person convicted of a drug felony would be incarcerated increased from 33.8 percent in 1972 to 54.8 percent in 1976.

The interpretation conventionally put on the preceding findings is that defense lawyers, prosecutors, and judges made vigorous efforts to avoid application of the mandatory sentences in cases in which they viewed those sentences as being too harsh and that the remaining cases were dealt with harshly as the law dictated (Blumstein et al. 1983, pp. 188–89). Thus, the percentage of drug felonies in New York City disposed of after a trial rose from 6 percent in 1972 to 17 percent in the first six months of 1976 (Joint Committee on New York Drug Law Evaluation 1978, p. 104). In other words, many fewer defendants pled guilty, and the trial rate tripled. No doubt as a consequence of the increased trial rates, it "took between ten and fifteen times as much court time to dispose of a case by trial as by plea," and the average case processing time for disposed cases increased from 172 days in the last four months of 1973 to 351 days in the first six months of 1976. Backlogs rose commensurately notwithstanding the creation of thirty-one additional criminal courts in New York City for handling of drug prosecutions (Joint Committee on New York Drug Law Evaluation 1978, tables 33–35 and p. 105).

Sentencing severity increased substantially for defendants who were eventually convicted. Only 3 percent of sentenced drug felons received minimum sentences of more than three years between 1972 and 1974 under the old law. Under the new law, the percentage of convicted drug felons receiving sentences of three years or longer increased to 22 percent. The likelihood that a person convicted of a drug felony would receive an incarcerative sentence increased in New York State from 33.8 percent in 1972, before the new law took effect, to 54.8 percent in the first six months of 1976 (Joint Committee on New York Drug Law Evaluation 1978, pp. 99–103).

The broad pattern of findings in the New York study, while more stark in New York than in other mandatory sentencing jurisdictions that have been evaluated, recurs throughout the impact evaluations. The combination of the Rockefeller Drug Laws' effects was more than the system could absorb, and many key features were repealed in mid-1976.

C. *Massachusetts's Bartley-Fox Amendment*

Massachusetts's Bartley-Fox Amendment required imposition of a one-year mandatory minimum prison sentence, without suspension, furlough, or parole, for anyone convicted of unlawful carrying of an unlicensed firearm. An offender need not have committed any other crime; the Massachusetts law thus was different from many mandatory sentencing firearms laws that require imposition of a minimum prison sentence for the use or possession of a firearm in the commission of a felony.

Two major evaluations of the Massachusetts gun law were conducted (Beha 1977; Rossman et al. 1979). Some background on the Boston courts may make the following discussion of their findings more intelligible. The Boston Municipal Court is both a trial court and a preliminary hearing court. If a defendant is dissatisfied with either his conviction or his sentence, he may appeal to the Suffolk County Superior Court where he is entitled to a trial de novo.

The Beha (1977) analysis is based primarily on comparisons of police and court records for the periods six months before and six months after the effective date of the mandatory sentencing law. The Rossman et al. (1979) study dealt with official records from 1974, 1975, and 1976 supplemented by interviews with police, lawyers, and court personnel. The primary findings:

1. police altered their behavior in a variety of ways aimed at limiting the law's reach; they became more selective about whom to frisk; the absolute number of reports of gun incidents taking place out-of-doors decreased, which meant a concomitant decrease in arrests, and the number of weapons seized without arrest increased by 120 percent from 1974 to 1976 (Carlson 1982, p. 6, relying on Rossman et al. 1979);

2. the number of persons "absconding" increased substantially between the period before the law took effect and the period after (both studies);

3. outcomes favorable to defendants, including both dismissals and acquittals, increased significantly between the before and after periods (both studies);

4. of persons convicted of firearms carrying charges in Boston Municipal Court, appeal rates increased radically (Beha 1977, table 2); in 1974, 21 percent of municipal court convictions were appealed to the Superior Court, and by 1976 that rate had increased to 94 percent (Rossman et al. 1979);

5. the percentage of defendants who entirely avoided a conviction rose from 53.5 percent in 1974 to 80 percent in 1976 (Carlson 1982, p. 10, relying on Rossman et al. 1979);

6. of that residuum of offenders who were finally convicted, the probability of receiving an incarcerative sentence increased from 23 percent to 100 percent (Carlson 1982, p. 8, relying on Rossman et al. 1979).

Thus the broad patterns of findings for the U.S. Sentencing Commission and Rockefeller Drug Law evaluations carries over to Massachusetts—more early dismissals, more protracted proceedings, increased sentencing severity for those finally convicted.

D. The Michigan Felony Firearms Statute

The Michigan Felony Firearms Statute created a new offense of possessing a firearm while engaging in a felony and specified a two-year mandatory prison sentence that could not be suspended or shortened by release on parole and that must be served consecutively to a sentence imposed for the underlying felony. The law took effect on January 1,

1977. The Wayne County prosecutor banned charge bargaining in firearms cases and took measures to enforce the ban, suggesting that the likelihood of circumvention should have been less than was experienced in New York and Massachusetts.

There has been one major evaluation of the Michigan law that gave rise to a number of related publications (Heumann and Loftin 1979; Loftin and McDowall 1981; Loftin, Heumann, and McDowall 1983). Several other articles concerning the Michigan gun law have been published, and one of these (Bynum 1982) also discusses empirical data.

The Bynum study (1982) demonstrates how prosecutors control the use of mandatory sentencing laws. Drawing on a sample of cases from a statewide data set collected during the course of a sentencing guidelines project, Bynum identified 426 cases that, from records, involved robberies with firearms that were committed after January 1, 1977, and were therefore eligible for prosecution under the felony firearms statute. In only 65 percent of the eligible cases was the firearms charge filed.[9] More indicative, however, of prosecutorial manipulation of mandatory sentencing laws was the finding that in some courts firearms charges were filed in 100 percent of the eligible cases and in other courts firearms charges were filed in none of the eligible cases (Bynum 1982, table 4.1).

Heumann and Loftin observed a strong tendency in Wayne County toward early dismissal of charges other than on the merits, which they interpret as evidence of efforts to avoid applying the mandatory penalties. Their inquiry focused on three offenses that were relatively common—felonious assault, "other assault," and armed robbery. Armed robbery means in Wayne County what it means most places. "Felonious assaults" tend to arise from "disputes among acquaintances or relatives and are, by conventional standards, less predatory than armed robbery." "Other assaults" is an intermediate category of "assault with intent to . . ." offenses. These three categories offered a severity continuum. Most armed robberies would generally be perceived as serious crimes. Many felonious assaults would commonly be regarded as impulsive and expressive and less serious then armed robbery. Other assaults are more heterogeneous.

Felonious assault disposition patterns did not change after the mandatory penalty provision took effect. There was some increase in early

[9] Heumann and Loftin in their examination of case records to determine the existence and extent of undercharging found that the gun law charge had been made in 96 percent of the eligible cases in Wayne County (1979, p. 407).

dismissal of armed robbery charges and a substantial increase in the rate of early dismissals of "other assault" charges. These findings are consistent with the hypothesis that efforts will be made to avoid application of harsh sentencing laws to defendants for whom lawyers and judges feel that they are inappropriately severe: "other assault" was the offense category in which the greatest ambiguities about culpability were likely to exist.

The probabilities of conviction differed after implementation depending on the offense at issue. Consistent with the Massachusetts findings that mandatory sentences reduce the probability of convictions, Loftin and his colleagues concluded that conviction probabilities declined for "other assaults" and armed robbery (Loftin, Heumann, and McDowall 1983, p. 295).

Loftin and his colleagues assessed the impacts of the Felony Firearm Statute on sentencing severity in two ways. Using quantitative methods, they concluded that the statute did not generally increase the probability that prison sentences would be imposed but that, for those receiving prison sentences, it did increase the expected lengths of sentences for some offenses (Loftin, Heumann, and McDowall 1983, pp. 297–98). Using simpler tabular analyses in an earlier article, they concluded that, overall, the percentage of defendants vulnerable to the firearms law who were incarcerated did not change markedly in Wayne County after implementation of the new law (Heumann and Loftin 1979). As table 2 indicates, the probability of receiving a prison sentence, given filing of the charge, increased slightly for felonious assault and other assault and decreased slightly for armed robbery. The probability of incarceration given conviction also did not change markedly for felonious assault or armed robbery but did change for "other assault" and increased from 57 percent of convictions prior to implementation of the firearm law to 82 percent afterward. This resulted in part from the substantial shift toward early dismissal of "other assault" charges reducing the residuum of cases to be sentenced from 65 percent of all cases to 50 percent.

Finally, trial rates remained roughly comparable before and after implementation except for the least serious category of offenses, "felonious assaults," for which the percentage of cases resolved at trial increased from 16 percent of cases to 41 percent of cases (Heumann and Loftin 1979, table 4). This is explained by Heumann and Loftin in terms of an innovative adaptive response, the "waiver trial." Either by agreement or by expectation, the judge would convict the defendant

TABLE 2

Disposition of Original Charges in Wayne County, Michigan, by Offense Type and Time Period

	N	Dismissed at/before Pretrial (Percent)	Dismissed or Acquitted after Pretrial (Percent)	Convicted/ No Prison (Percent)	Some Prison (Percent)	Total (Percent)
Felonious assault:						
Before*	145	24	31	31	14	100
After†	39	26	26	31	18	101
Other assault:						
Before	240	12	24	28	37	101
After	53	26	24	9	41	100
Armed robbery:						
Before	471	13	19	4	64	100
After	136	22	17	2	60	101

SOURCE.—Cohen and Tonry (1983), tables 7–10; adapted from Heumann and Loftin (1979), table 3.

NOTE.—The totals do not always sum to 100 percent because of rounding.

* Offense committed before January 1, 1977, and case disposed between July 1, 1976, and June 30, 1977.

† Offense committed and case disposed between January 1, 1977, and June 30, 1977.

of a misdemeanor rather than the charged felony (which made the firearm law inapplicable because it specified a two-year add-on following conviction of a felony) or would simply, with the prosecutor's acquiescence, acquit the defendant on the firearms charge. Either approach eliminated the mandatory sentence threat and both are consistent with processes described in the American Bar Foundation Survey twenty years earlier to avoid imposition of twenty-year minimum sentences for drug sales (Dawson 1969, p. 201). A third mechanism for nullifying the mandatory sentencing law in cases in which imprisonment would be ordered in any case was to decrease the sentence that otherwise would have been imposed in respect of the underlying felony by two years and then add the two years back on the basis of the firearms law (Heumann and Loftin 1979, pp. 416–24).

E. Observations on New York, Massachusetts, and Michigan Studies

For a variety of reasons, the Massachusetts, Michigan, and New York laws ought to be especially good illustrations of the operation of mandatory sentencing laws. Many such laws are on the books but exist simply as part of a larger statutory backdrop before which the drama of crime and punishment takes place.[10] In these three instances, however, for differing reasons, vigorous and highly publicized efforts were made to make the mandatory sentencing laws stick. In New York, amidst enormous publicity and massive media attention, the legislature established thirty-one new courts, including creation of additional judges, construction of new courtrooms, and provision of supporting personnel and resources, and expressly forbade some kinds of plea bargaining in an effort to assure that the mandatory sentences were imposed. In Massachusetts, while the statute did not address plea bargaining, it expressly forbade "diversion in the form of continuance without a finding or filing of cases," both devices used in the Boston Municipal Court for disposition of cases other than on the merits. (Filing is a practice in which cases are left open with no expectation that they will ever be closed; continuance without finding leaves the case open in anticipation of eventual dismissal if the defendant avoids further trouble.) In Michigan, while the statute did not address plea bargaining, the Wayne County prosecutor established and enforced a ban on plea bargaining in cases coming within the operation of the mandatory sentencing law. He also launched a major publicity campaign, promising on billboards and bumper stickers that "One with a Gun Gets You Two."

Thus, in all three states, the new laws were accompanied by evidence of seriousness of purpose. If mandatory sentencing laws are to operate as their supporters hope they will, the experience in these three states should provide a good test of the realism of those hopes.

Those hopes are unrealistic. Findings from all three states suggest that mandatory sentencing laws are not an especially effective way to achieve certainty and predictability in sentencing. To the extent that they prescribe sanctions more severe than lawyers and judges believe appropriate, they can be, and are, circumvented. For serious criminal charges, the mandatory sentencing laws are often redundant in that offenders are, in any case, likely to receive prison sentences longer than those mandated by statute. For less serious cases, mandatory sentencing laws tend to be arbitrary; they result in either increased rates of dismissal or diversion of some defendants to avoid application of the statute or occasionally result in sentencing of "marginal" offenders in ways that most parties involved consider unduly harsh.

[10] For example, the U.S. Sentencing Commission (1991, p. 10) concluded that four of the approximately one hundred federal mandatory penalty provisions then in effect accounted for 94 percent of mandatory penalties imposed.

III. Mandatory Penalties as Instruments and Symbols

George Santayana's admonition that "those who do not remember the past are condemned to relive it" does not capture the policy dilemma posed by mandatory penalties. Officials who support such laws often do not much care about problems of implementation, foreseeable patterns of circumvention, or the certainty of excessively and unjustly severe penalties for some offenders. Their interests are different, as recent policy debates demonstrate. According to a recent *New York Times* article about mandatory proposals offered by New York Senator Alfonse D'Amato: "Mr. D'Amato conceded that his two successful amendments, which Justice Department officials say would have little practical effect on prosecution of crimes, might not solve the problem. 'But,' he said, 'it does bring about a sense that we are serious' " (Ifill 1991).

Supporters of mandatory penalties in anxious times are concerned with political and symbolic goals. Put positively, elected officials want to reassure the public generally that their fears have been noted and that the causes of their fears have been acted on. Put negatively, officials want to curry public favor and electoral support by pandering, by making promises that the law can at best imperfectly and incompletely deliver.

However their motives are portrayed, for many legislators, their primary purpose has been achieved when their vote is cast. They have been seen to be tough on crime. Calls for enactment of mandatory penalties, or introductions of bills, or castings of votes are symbolic statements. Instrumental arguments about effectiveness or normative arguments about injustice to offenders, whether by Sir Samuel Romilly in eighteenth-century England or by Senator Edward Kennedy in our own place and time, fall on deaf ears.[11]

The dilemma is that the public officials who enact mandatory sentencing laws support them for symbolic and political reasons while the public officials who administer mandatory sentencing laws oppose them for instrumental and normative reasons.

The instrumental argument against mandatory penalties is clear. First, they increase public expense by increasing trial rates and case processing times. The U.S. Sentencing Commission study found that

[11] Nearly every major modern American organization that has considered the merits of mandatory penalties has opposed them, including the American Bar Association (1968, standard 2.3, pp. 63–66), the American Law Institute (1962), and, most recently, the Federal Courts Study Committee (1991).

trial rates were two and one half times greater (30 percent of dispositions) for offenses bearing mandatory penalties than for other offenses (12 percent of dispositions); disposition by trial tripled under the Rockefeller Drug Laws (17 percent of dispositions after taking effect vs. 6 percent before); in Michigan, dispositions by trial for felonious assaults involving firearms increased from 16 percent to 41 percent after mandatory penalties became applicable.

Second, in every published evaluation, judges and prosecutors were shown to have devised ways to circumvent application of the mandatories. Sometimes prosecutors simply refused to file mandatory-bearing charges; sometimes plea bargaining was used; sometimes judges refused to convict; sometimes judges ignored the statute and imposed sentences inconsistent with it.

The normative arguments against mandatories are also straightforward. First, simple justice: because of their inflexibility, such laws sometimes result in imposition of penalties in individual cases that everyone involved believes to be unjustly severe. Second, perhaps more important, mandatory penalties encourage hypocrisy on the part of prosecutors and judges. To avoid injustices in individual cases, officials engage in the adaptive responses and circumventions described throughout this essay.

The hypocrisies that mandatory penalties engender are what most troubles prosecutors and judges with whom I speak. Plea bargaining may be a necessary evil, an essential lubricant without which the machinery of justice would break down, but it is typically routinized. Armed robbery is pled down to robbery, aggravated assault to assault, theft 1 to theft 2. Prosecutors, defense counsel, judges, probation officers—all involved—know what is happening, understand why, and acknowledge the legitimacy of the reasons.

Mandatory penalties elicit more devious forms of adaptation. When Michigan judges in the 1950s or the 1970s acquit factually guilty defendants, or when Arizona prosecutors in the 1980s permit people who have committed serious crimes to plead guilty to attempt or conspiracy, or when prosecutors and judges fashion new patterns of plea bargaining solely to sidestep mandatories, important values are being sacrificed. Many practitioners find these processes dishonest and tawdry.

Legislators, whatever their purposes for supporting mandatory sentencing laws, once the vote is cast move on to other issues. For judges, prosecutors, and defense counsel, it is another story. They must live with their own consciences and with their shared views of the bounds of fair treatment of offenders. They must also keep the courts functioning. That they sometimes devise ways to avoid application of laws they believe to be uncommonly harsh should come as no surprise.

If the findings of empirical evaluations of mandatory sentencing laws were heeded, there would be no mandatory penalties. Given the American political climate of the early 1990s, wholesale repeals are unlikely. A more modest hope is that elected officials will become slightly more responsible about crime control policy and balance their felt need to make symbolic and rhetorical statements through passage of legislation with our well-established knowledge of how mandatories operate in practice. Four suggestions for how that might be done follow.

A. *Making Mandatory Penalties Presumptive*

Much of what legislators hope to accomplish with mandatory sentencing laws could be achieved by making such laws presumptive. In a few states, Minnesota is an example, judges are given authority to disregard mandatory penalties and impose some other sentence if reasons are given. Converting all mandatory penalties to presumptive penalties would sacrifice few of the values sought to be achieved by such laws but would avoid many of the undesirable side effects.

By enacting a mandatory (presumptive) penalty law, the legislature would be expressing its policy judgment that, say, people who commit robberies with firearms deserve at least a three-year minimum prison term. Most prosecutors and judges would accept that such policy decisions are the legislature's to make and that that one is not patently unreasonable. The law's facial legitimacy would presumably cause many prosecutors and judges to deal in good faith with it. The law's presumptive character, however, would let judges take account of mitigating circumstances (the defendant was an underage, bullied, unarmed participant who remained in the car) without resort to subterfuge. That the judge possessed authority to decide that special circumstances rebutted the presumption would signal that prosecutors also could legitimately take special circumstances into account in plea bargaining.

If official circumvention of mandatory penalties in cases where they seem unduly harsh is foreseeable, and it is, conversion to mandatory (presumptive) penalties is likely to result in no less systematic enforcement but to avoid hypocritical efforts at avoidance.

B. Mandatory Penalties and "Sunset" Clauses

Our understandings of the politics and empirical experience of mandatories could be married by including sunset clauses in all future mandatory penalty laws and adding them to existing ones. "Sunset clauses" provide for automatic repeal of a statute at a fixed time unless a new vote is taken to extend its life. This proposal, first made to my knowledge by Alfred Blumstein of Carnegie-Mellon University at a "presidential crime summit" in 1991, would both acknowledge felt political imperatives and limit the damage mandatory penalties do.

Any honest politician will concede two points—that it is often difficult to resist political pressures to vote for tough penalties, and that it is always difficult to vote to make penalties more "lenient." Blumstein's proposal addresses both propositions. If a charged political climate or campaign, or a series of notorious crimes, makes it difficult to resist "tough-on-crime" proposals, such laws will continue to be enacted. Statute books are cluttered with provisions passed on the passions of moments. Often, however, passions subside with time and competing values and calmer consideration make the wisdom of such laws less clear. Sunset clauses would permit laws to lapse without the need for legislators to vote for repeal and thereby expose themselves to "soft-on-crime" attacks.

C. Narrowing Mandatories' Scope

From this point my suggestions for reform of mandatory penalties became less politically realistic. If the bases for passing sentencing laws were concerns for justice and institutional effectiveness, most mandatories would be repealed and few others would be enacted to take their places. That is unlikely. Horrible, senseless crimes do occur, public fears and anxieties are heightened, and elected officials want to respond. There being in practice little that officials can do about crime, the attractions of mandatory penalties as a rhetorical demonstration of concern are great.

If a call for repeal of all mandatories is likely to pass unheard, conceivably a call for a narrowing of their scope might be credible. The most extreme versions of nullification and circumvention involve laws that mandate severe penalties for minor crimes. In eighteenth-century England, juries often refused to convict of capital offenses that were property crimes. In Michigan in the fifties, judges refused to impose mandatory minimum twenty-year sentences for drug sales.

Similar instances of imbalance between the gravities of crimes and the severity of penalties occur in our time. In Alabama, for example, any sale of narcotics within three miles of a school provokes a mandatory minimum. While the goal of protecting children from drugs has obvious appeal, the three-mile radius encompasses all of the area of most cities and towns.

One way, therefore, to bring the symbolic goals of legislators and the instrumental and normative concerns of criminal justice practitioners into better balance would be to confine the scope of mandatory penalties to patently serious crimes like homicide and aggravated rape and to maintain an empirically realistic balance between gravity of crimes and severity of punishments.

D. Reconsideration of Mandatory Penalties

Little public harm would accrue, and considerable private benefit obtain, if correctional or parole authorities were accorded routine discretion to release prisoners serving mandatory terms after some decent interval. Increasing numbers of prisoners are now being held under ten- or twenty-year mandatory minimum terms or under sentences of life without parole. In many states, the steady accumulation of such prisoners promises sizeable long-term increases in prison populations and budgets. More important, many such long-term prisoners continue to be held long after they present any threat to anyone, and long after any clamor for their continuing incarceration has subsided. Under present laws of most states, such prisoners can be released only by pardon or commutation. In our era, these powers are seldom exercised, in part because they make public officials vulnerable to "soft-on-crime" attacks.

The argument for administrative reconsideration of lengthy mandatory sentences parallels the argument for sunset clauses in mandatory penalty statutes—some decisions present such excruciating political problems for elected officials that it is better to eliminate the need to make them. Almost despite the desirability of repealing a mandatory penalty, or releasing from prison an old and harmless prisoner, political vulnerability prevents decisions that on their merits ought to be made. Permitting corrections or parole officials to decide when a prisoner under mandatory sentence has served long enough would remove those decisions from the public eye.

IV. Conclusion

Perhaps unusually for an essay that mostly reviews research, this one does not end with a research agenda. The issues are primarily political and prudential. Basic new insights concerning application of mandatory penalties are unlikely to emerge. Research designs can however be devised that would provide narrower instruction about mandatories. For example, the effects of my proposal for replacing mandatories now in effect might be measured by substituting "mandatory/presumptive" laws for a representative half (or other fraction) of existing mandatory penalties. Thus there would be one-year, two-year, five-year, and ten-year mandatory (presumptive) crimes and one-year, two-year, five-year, and ten-year conventional mandatory-penalty crimes. By use of quantitative time-series analyses of cases disposed before and after the law change and through use of qualitative and quantitative methods to examine case disposition before and afterward, we would learn both how processing of cases changed after mandatories became presumptive and, by comparing case dispositions of mandatories and presumptives afterward, we could learn what differences in case processing the change to presumptive sentences produces.

This is not a realm, however, where research counts for much. Policy debates are likely neither to wait for nor much depend on research results. We now know what we are likely to know, and what our predecessors knew, about mandatory penalties. As instruments of public policy, they do little good and much harm. If America does sometime become a "kinder, gentler place," there will be little need for mandatory penalties and academics will have no need to propose "reforms" premised on the inability of elected officials to make decisions that take account of existing knowledge. As yet, however, America is neither completely kind nor universally gentle, and proposals such as those offered here might provide mechanisms for reconciling the symbolic and rhetorical needs of elected officials with the legal system's needs for integrity in process and justice in punishment.

REFERENCES

American Bar Association Project on Standards for Criminal Justice. 1968. *Sentencing Alternatives and Procedures*. Chicago: American Bar Association.

American Law Institute. 1962. *Model Penal Code (Proposed Official Draft)*. Philadelphia: American Law Institute.

Austin, James. 1991. *The Consequences of Escalating the Use of Imprisonment: The Case Study of Florida*. San Francisco: National Council on Crime and Delinquency.

Baker, J. H. 1977. "Criminal Courts and Procedure at Common Law, 1550–1800." In *Crime in England, 1550–1800*, edited by J. S. Cockburn. Princeton, N.J.: Princeton University Press.

Baldwin, John, and Michael McConville. 1980. "Criminal Juries." In *Crime and Justice: An Annual Review of Research*, vol. 2, edited by Norval Morris and Michael Tonry. Chicago: University of Chicago Press.

Beha, James A. II. 1977. " 'And Nobody Can Get You Out': The Impact of a Mandatory Prison Sentence for the Illegal Carrying of a Firearm on the Use of Firearms and on the Administration of Criminal Justice in Boston." *Boston University Law Review* 57:96–146 (pt. 1), 289–333 (pt. 2).

Blumstein, Alfred, Jacqueline Cohen, Susan E. Martin, and Michael Tonry, eds. 1983. *Research on Sentencing: The Search for Reform*. Vol. 1. Washington, D.C.: National Academy of Sciences.

Blumstein, Alfred, Jacqueline Cohen, and Daniel Nagin. 1978. *Deterrence and Incapacitation: Estimating the Effects of Criminal Sanctions on Crime Rates*. Washington, D.C.: National Academy of Sciences.

Bynum, Timothy S. 1982. "Prosecutorial Discretion and the Implementation of a Legislative Mandate." In *Implementing Criminal Justice Policies*, edited by Merry Morash. Beverly Hills, Calif.: Sage.

Carlson, Kenneth. 1982. *Mandatory Sentencing: The Experience of Two States*. National Institute of Justice, U.S. Department of Justice. Washington, D.C.: U.S. Government Printing Office.

Cohen, Jacqueline, and Michael Tonry. 1983. "Sentencing Reforms and Their Impacts." In *Research on Sentencing: The Search for Reform*, vol. 2, edited by Alfred Blumstein, Jacqueline Cohen, Susan E. Martin, and Michael Tonry. Washington, D.C.: National Academy Press.

Dawson, Robert O. 1969. *Sentencing*. Boston: Little, Brown.

Federal Courts Study Committee. 1991. *Report*. Washington, D.C.: Federal Courts Study Committee.

Hay, Douglas. 1975. "Property, Authority, and the Criminal Law." In *Albion's Fatal Tree: Crime and Society in Eighteenth Century England*, edited by Douglas Hay, Peter Linebaugh, and E. P. Thompson. New York: Pantheon.

———. 1980. "Crime and Justice in Eighteenth and Nineteenth Century England." In *Crime and Justice: An Annual Review of Research*, vol. 2, edited by Norval Morris and Michael Tonry. Chicago: University of Chicago Press.

Heumann, Milton, and Colin Loftin. 1979. "Mandatory Sentencing and the Abolition of Plea Bargaining: The Michigan Felony Firearms Statute." *Law and Society Review* 13:393–430.

Holmes, Oliver Wendell. 1889. "Law in Science and Science in Law." *Harvard Law Review* 12:443–63.

Ifill, Gwen. 1991. "Senate's Rule for Its Anti-crime Bill: The Tougher the Provision, the Better." *New York Times* (July 8, national ed.), p. A6.

Jacobs, James B. 1988. "The Law and Criminology of Drunk Driving." In *Crime and Justice: A Review of Research*, vol. 10, edited by Michael Tonry and Norval Morris. Chicago: University of Chicago Press.

Joint Committee on New York Drug Law Evaluation. 1978. *The Nation's Toughest Drug Law: Evaluating the New York Experience.* A project of the Association of the Bar of the City of New York and the Drug Abuse Council, Inc. Washington, D.C.: U.S. Government Printing Office.

Knapp, Kay A. 1984. *The Impact of the Minnesota Sentencing Guidelines—Three Year Evaluation.* St. Paul, Minn.: Minnesota Sentencing Guidelines Commission.

———. 1991. "Arizona: Unprincipled Sentencing, Mandatory Minimums, and Prison Crowding." *Overcrowded Times* 2(5):10–12.

Loftin, Colin, Milton Heumann, and David McDowall. 1983. "Mandatory Sentencing and Firearms Violence: Evaluating an Alternative to Gun Control." *Law and Society Review* 17:287–318.

Loftin, Colin, and David McDowall. 1981. " 'One with a Gun Gets You Two': Mandatory Sentencing and Firearms Violence in Detroit." *Annals of the American Academy of Political and Social Science* 455:150.

———. 1984. "The Deterrent Effects of the Florida Felony Firearm Law." *Journal of Criminal Law and Criminology* 75:250–59.

Michael, Jerome, and Herbert Wechsler. 1940. *Criminal Law and Its Administration.* Chicago: Foundation.

Miller, Frank W. 1969. *Prosecution.* Boston: Little, Brown.

Moore, Mark H. 1990. "Supply Reduction and Drug Law Enforcement." In *Drugs and Crime*, edited by Michael Tonry and James Q. Wilson. Vol. 13 of *Crime and Justice: A Review of Research*, edited by Michael Tonry and Norval Morris. Chicago: University of Chicago Press.

Newman, Donald. 1966. *Conviction.* Boston: Little, Brown.

Pierce, Glen L., and William J. Bowers. 1981. "The Bartley-Fox Gun Law's Short-Term Impact on Crime in Boston." *Annals of the American Academy of Political and Social Science* 455:120–32.

Pound, Roscoe. 1910. "Law in Books and Law in Action." *American Law Review* 44:12–36.

Radzinowicz, Leon. 1948–68. *A History of English Criminal Law and Its Administration from 1750.* 4 vols. London: Stevens.

Reuter, Peter, and Mark A. R. Kleiman. 1986. "Risks and Prices: An Economic Analysis of Drug Prices." In *Crime and Justice: A Review of Research*, vol. 7, edited by Michael Tonry and Norval Morris. Chicago: University of Chicago Press.

Romilly, Samuel. 1820. *Speeches.* Excerpts reprinted in Jerome Michael and Herbert Wechsler, *Criminal Law and Its Administration.* 1940. Chicago: Foundation.

Rossman, David, Paul Froyd, Glen L. Pierce, John McDevitt, and William J. Bowers. 1979. *The Impact of the Mandatory Gun Law in Massachusetts.* Report to the National Institute of Law Enforcement and Criminal Justice, Law Enforcement Assistance Administration, U.S. Department of Justice, Washington, D.C.

Select Committee on Capital Punishment. 1930. *Report*. London: H.M. Stationery Office.

Shane-DuBow, Sandra, Alice P. Brown, and Erik Olsen. 1985. *Sentencing Reform in the United States: History, Content, and Effect*. Washington, D.C.: U.S. Government Printing Office.

Stephen, James Fitzjames. 1883. *A History of the Criminal Law of England*. (Reprinted 1977. New York: B. Franklin.)

U.S. Sentencing Commission. 1991. *Special Report to the Congress: Mandatory Minimum Penalties in the Federal Criminal Justice System*. Washington, D.C.: U.S. Sentencing Commission.

[12]
Sentencing Matters

Sentencing matters in the 1990s more than ever before. This is not because the values and interests at stake have changed. The state's interest in enforcing its laws, the defendant's interest in preserving his liberty, and the judge's responsibility justly to reconcile them are as they have always been. So is the mix of considerations that judges think important—the importance of the behavioral norms that were violated, the effects of the crime on the victim, and the amalgam of aggravating and mitigating circumstances that make a defendant more or less culpable and make one sentence more appropriate than another.

What has changed is the political salience of sentencing. Until twenty-five years ago, the word "sentencing" generally signified a slightly mysterious process which, it was all but universally agreed, involved individualized decisions that judges were uniquely competent to make. Sentencing laws were crafted to allow judges latitude to fashion penalties tailored to the circumstances of individual cases. In our time, both the need for individualized consideration and the special competence of judges have been contested.

Sentencing, as a result, has been radically refashioned in two ways. First, sentencing has become a recurrent subject of ideological conflict, partisan politics, and legislative action. Many elected officials are no longer willing to enact general laws on sentencing and defer to judges to apply them wisely. Modern laws often tell judges what sentence to impose rather than set boundaries within which sentencing choices are to be made. Election campaigns regularly feature candidates' promises to be "tough on crime" and to support harsher punishments. Every state since 1980 has enacted laws mandating minimum prison sentences based on the premises that harsher penalties will reduce crime rates and that judges cannot otherwise be trusted to impose them. Following Washington State voters' adoption in 1993 of a "three strikes and you're out" referendum that mandates life sentences for third-time felons, many other states considered such laws and some adopted them. The federal Violent Crime Control and Law Enforcement Act of 1994 contained a three-strikes provision, extended the death penalty to sixty additional crimes, and authorized $8 billion for construction of state prisons in a country in which the prison population had tripled between 1980 and 1995. And still many members of Congress returned to Washington after the 1994 elections promising to pass tougher laws.

Second, there has been a fundamental and ongoing shift in the past quarter century in sentencing processes and institutions. In 1970, every state and the federal system had an "indeterminate sentencing system" in which judges had wide discretion to decide who went to prison and to set maximum and sometimes minimum prison terms. Parole boards decided when prisoners were released. Beginning with Maine's abolition of parole in 1975, nearly every state has in some ways repudiated indeterminate sentencing and recast sentencing policies to set standards for judges' and parole boards' decisions and thereby to narrow or eliminate their discretion.

Although ideological and partisan politics have played some part in fostering the shift from indeterminate to (what is now, primarily for semantic contrast, called) determinate sentencing, the impetus for change has been broad-based. Proposals for sentencing change have come from many quarters. Penal abolitionists, humanitarians, and political liberals typically want reduced severity. Law enforcement officials, victims groups, and political conservatives want tougher penalties. Academics, civil rights advocates, and civil libertarians want them made fairer and want racial, sexual, and other unwarranted disparities reduced. Utilitarians and crime-control spokesmen want them made more effective. Nearly all want sentencing made more consistent, whether in the name of justice, efficiency, effectiveness, or economy.

More is known about the operation of determinate sentencing systems and about the effects of sentencing policy changes after twenty-five years of ferment than was known about indeterminate sentencing after seventy-five years. Partly this is because evaluation tools are available in our time that were not available to earlier generations, and partly it is because people want to know whether changes have achieved what they were designed to accomplish. Sizable literatures exist on the effects of various changes in sentencing institutions and practices, on the crime-preventive effects of changes in penalties, and on the operation and effects of noncustodial penalties. From them, we know how to create sentencing systems that are just and efficient and protective of public safety. Policy makers in many states are trying to use that knowledge to design better systems. Whether they succeed will depend on which of the pressures for sentencing change—partisan political calls for ever-increasing severity or nonpartisan calls for more just, efficient, and effective systems—proves more powerful and lasting.

A just sentencing system would be simultaneously respectful of the public interests in safety, crime prevention, and economy, and of the needs to assure that convicted offenders are treated fairly and consistently. Accumulated research and experience concerning the past twenty years of sentencing policy changes shows what such a system would look like.

First, legislatures would repeal all mandatory minimum penalties, including "three-strikes" laws.

Second, legislatures would invest the funds needed to establish credible, well-managed noncustodial penalties that can serve as sanctions intermediate between prison and probation.

Third, authority for creation of rules for sentencing would be delegated to an administrative agency, often but not necessarily called a sentencing commission.

Fourth, the sentencing commission would be directed to develop, promulgate, and monitor systems of sentencing rules, usually but not necessarily called sentencing guidelines.

Fifth, the sentencing commission would be directed to take account of existing and planned corrections resources, both community based and institutional, and to devise guidelines that are compatible in their projected implementation with the facilities and resources that are or will be available.

Sixth, the sentencing commission would be directed to devise guidelines for custodial penalties that set maximum presumptive terms of confinement for all cases and minimum presumptive terms only for the most serious crimes.

Seventh, the sentencing commission would be directed to devise guidelines for noncustodial penalties that permit judges to choose among noncustodial penalties for minor crimes and between them and periods of full or partial confinement for more serious crimes.

Eighth, enabling legislation and sentencing commission policy would establish a presumption that, within the range of sanctions set out in applicable guidelines, judges should impose the least punitive and intrusive appropriate sentence.

The proposals are more fully explained and justified in chapter 8. The intervening chapters contain the evidence on which these proposals are based. Here they are presented in brief on the rationale that fairness to readers requires that they know where a writer hopes to take them.

The rest of this chapter discusses the developments that underlay the proposals. Section I provides a backdrop by sketching the precipitants, forms, and effects of the past quarter century's sentencing policy changes. Section II discusses a wrong turn taken from the mid-1970s onward when support for "just deserts" theories and partisan calls for law and order combined to make many policy makers forget that offenders are three-dimensional human beings and not two-dimensional crime-and-criminal-history constructs.

I. Twenty-Five Years of Sentencing Ferment

Were a time machine available to bring a group of state and federal judges from the year 1971 to a national conference on sentencing in 1996, most of those judges would be astonished at a quarter century's changes and many, perhaps all, would be disapproving.

Their astonishment would result from the number and enormity of the changes they would learn about. Every American state and the federal system in 1970 had an indeterminate sentencing system in which a legislature enacted and amended the criminal code and set maximum penalties. Minimum penalties existed in a few jurisdictions, but they were widely disapproved; they generally required one- or two-year minimums except for mandatory life sentences in some jurisdictions for murder. Subject only to statutory maximums and occasional minimums, judges had authority to decide whether a convicted defendant was sentenced to probation (and with what conditions) or to jail or prison (and for what maximum term). A parole board would decide when prisoners were released; usually prisoners became eligible for release after serving a third of the maximum sentence, but they could be held until their maximum terms expired. Prison managers typically had authority to reduce maximum sentences by a third by awarding time off for good behavior ("good time"). For all practical purposes, appellate review of sentences and parole release decisions was nonexistent. Judges' and corrections officials' decisions were supposed to be governed by the unique circumstances of particular cases. Without rules governing decisions whose correct application could be examined, there was little that appellate courts could review except gross abuses of discretion or allegations of corruption; no bodies of case law on sentencing or parole appeals could or did accumulate.

In 1996, the time-traveling judges would learn that Congress in 1994 enacted legislation authorizing billions of federal dollars to those states that would abolish parole release, establish guidelines to constrain judicial sentencing discretion, and either abolish or narrow good time so that prisoners would serve at least 85 percent of their announced sentences. They would also learn that the federal system and many states had rejected indeterminate sentencing in principle and repealed much of its apparatus. Fifteen jurisdictions had adopted sentencing guidelines to limit judicial discretion; more than ten had eliminated parole release; another twenty-five had adopted parole guidelines; many had narrowed the ambit of good time; and all had enacted mandatory minimum sentence legislation (often requiring minimum ten-, twenty- or thirty-year terms and sometimes mandatory sentences of life-without-possibility-of-parole).

There can be little doubt that the time-traveling judges would disapprove of much of what they found in 1996. Partly this can be attributed to parochialism. Human beings tend to prefer the familiar over the new and what we know over what we don't. Because the broad outlines of indeterminate sentencing had been the same everywhere since 1930 (Rothman 1980), few judges at work in 1971 would have had experience with any other system.

Some of their objections would, however, concern matters of principle and conceptions of justice that transcend parochialism. Rigid sentencing laws, including mandatory penalties, they would argue, create unacceptable risks of injustice because they make it impossible to take account of important differences between defendants. For that reason, the U.S. Congress in 1970 repealed most mandatory minimum provisions in federal law.

Legislative passage of laws that specify penalties for particular cases is unwise, they would urge, because legislators are far likelier than judges to be influenced by short-term emotions and concern for political advantage. Chase Riveland, Washington State's longtime commissioner of corrections, encapsulates those concerns when he describes many modern tough-on-crime laws as "drive-by legislation." And, they would insist, narrow limits on judicial discretion are unsound because they shift more power into the already powerful hands of prosecutors who will exercise it less judiciously than judges would.

We can predict that these arguments would be made because many judges have opposed sentencing reforms from the early 1970s to today in these terms, and many judges (and nonjudges) still do. But there is one 1970s argument that is seldom heard—that there is no need for substantial changes to sentencing law and practice because there is no convincing evidence that indeterminate sentencing was afflicted by unwarranted sentencing disparities or racial and gender bias. This argument is seldom heard because it is no longer tenable.

Unwarranted disparities, explicable more in terms of the judge's personality, beliefs, and background than the offender's crime or criminal history, have repeatedly been demonstrated (Blumstein et al. 1983, chap. 2). There was substantial gender disparity in indeterminate sentencing—in favor of women (Nagel and Hagan 1983; Knapp 1984). The evidence is unclear on the causes of racial disparities, but their existence is well documented (Mann 1993; Tonry 1995*a*).

Finally, there is one 1970s argument—that tougher penalties will reduce crime rates—that is still heard, but mostly from campaigning conservative politicians and virtually never from crime-control researchers or from authoritative nonpartisan bodies. Political scientist James Q. Wilson, for example, for two decades America's leading conservative scholar of crime and punishment, in 1994 acknowledged, "Many (probably most) criminologists think we use prison too much and at too great cost and that this excessive use has had little beneficial effect on the crime rate" (Wilson 1994, p. 499).

No one doubts that having some penalties is better than having none. What is widely doubted is the proposition that changes in penalties have any significant effects on behavior. Most crime-control scholars are doubtful because that proposition is refuted by the clear weight of the research evidence and because every nonpartisan expert body in the United States, Canada, and England that has examined the evidence has reached that same conclusion. In 1993, the National Academy of Sciences Panel on Understanding and Control of Violent Behavior (Reiss and Roth 1993), paid for by the Bush administration's Department of Justice, noted that the average prison time per violent crime had *tripled* between 1975 and 1989 and asked, "What effect has increasing the prison population had on levels of violent crime?" The answer, "Apparently, very little." In 1978, the National Academy of Sciences Panel on Research on Deterrent and Incapacitative Effects (Blumstein, Cohen, and Nagin 1978), funded by the Ford administration's Department of Justice, concluded, "we cannot assert that the evidence warrants an affirmative conclusion regarding deterrence." Daniel Nagin (1978), that panel's principal consultant, was more explicit, "Policymakers in the criminal justice system are done a disservice if they are left with the impression that the empirical evidence . . . strongly supports the deterrence hypothesis."

Similar bodies in other English-speaking countries have reached the same conclusions. The English Home Office (1990), during Margaret Thatcher's time as prime minister, conducted a three-year review of evidence on the crime-control effects of penalties and concluded that the penalties' effects were so uncertain that they should have only minor influence on sentencing policy. As a result, Parliament enacted the Criminal Justice Act 1991, which replaced crime-control premises in English sentencing policy with a "just deserts" approach (Ashworth 1992*a*). A key passage in the Home Office report explained why: "Deterrence is a principle with much immediate appeal. . . . But much crime is committed on impulse . . . by offenders who live from moment to moment; their crimes are as impulsive as the rest of their feckless, sad, or pathetic lives. It is unrealistic to construct sentencing arrangements on the assumption that most offenders will weigh up the possibilities in advance and base their conduct on rational calculation."

Canada is the other English-speaking country that has recently had a conservative national government, led by Tory party prime minister Brian Mulroney. In 1993, the judiciary committee of Canada's parliament (Committee on Justice and the Solicitor General 1993), led by a member of Mulroney's party, recommended that Canada shift from an American-style law enforcement approach to crime to a European-style preventive approach. The report observed, "The United States affords a glaring example of the limited impact that criminal justice responses may have on crime. . . . If locking up those who violate the law contributed to safer societies then the United States should be the safest country in the world." There is overwhelming additional evidence to support the conclusions of the government-sponsored panels in Canada, England, and the United States; it is discussed at length in chapter 5.

The overall impression the time-traveling judges would take back with them would be shaped by whether they learned first about the federal or the state sentencing reforms. If they studied the changes wrought by the federal Sentencing Reform Act of 1984, and the U.S. Sentencing Commission it created, they would go back determined to fight the first signs of the sentencing reform movement. If they studied the experiences of states like Delaware, Minnesota, Pennsylvania, Oregon, and Washington, they would return apprehensive but with an understanding that meliorable injustices existed under indeterminate sentencing that could be mitigated without creating larger injustices in their place.

Before I describe what the travelers would learn, I should summarize the briefing book they would receive that would provide background to the ongoing debates they would encounter. Sentencing became a focus of criminal justice reform efforts in the mid-1970s, influenced by several contemporaneous developments. First, civil rights activists, concerned by what appeared to them to be racial and class bias and unwarranted disparities in sentencing and correctional administration, called for controls on the discretion of judges and other officials (e.g., American Friends Service Committee 1971). Second, social scientists reported that there was little systematic empirical evidence that corrections programs successfully reduced recidivism, which undermined the rehabilitative foundation on which indeterminate sentencing stood (e.g., Lipton, Martinson, and Wilks 1975). Third, proceduralists throughout the legal system were working to make legal processes fairer and decision makers more accountable, and argued that sentencing too should be subject to rules and review procedures (e.g., Davis 1969; O'Donnell, Churgin, and Curtis 1977). Fourth, political conservatives, concerned about a specter of "lenient judges," supported sentencing reforms as a way to set and enforce harsher sentencing standards (e.g., Wilson 1975, 1983).

Most of these developments shaped an influential book, *Criminal Sentences: Law without Order* (1972), by Judge Marvin Frankel, at that time a federal district court judge. On fairness grounds, he decried the absence of standards for the sentences that federal judges set and the related absence of meaningful opportunities for sentence appeals. He proposed creation of a specialized administrative agency called a sentencing commission that would develop rules for sentencing. The rules would be presumptively applicable and questions about their correct application would be subject to review by higher courts.

Judge Frankel's proposals were shaped by appreciation of the institutional properties of legislatures and administrative agencies. Administrative agencies over time develop specialized expertise that legislatures can not match and develop cadres of subject-matter specialists. Moreover, because commissioners are typically appointed for fixed terms and are ordinarily outside day-to-day political battles, administrative agencies can be somewhat insulated from emotionalism and short-term political pressures.

Judge Frankel's sentencing commission proposal has become the most widely adopted vehicle for sentencing reform. In the 1970s, several states—most notably Minnesota and Pennsylvania—created sentencing commissions. Several others—for example, Arizona, California, Illinois, and Indiana—replaced indeterminate sentencing with "statutory determinate sentencing" schemes in which criminal codes prescribed specific prison terms for particular crimes.

The comparative merits of the sentencing commission soon became clear. Evaluations in Minnesota and Pennsylvania (and later in Oregon and Washington) showed that use of sentencing guidelines reduced disparities generally and in particular reduced racial and gender disparities (this last might be seen by some as a mixed blessing since the effect was to increase sentences for women). In addition, many judges in those states came to favor guidelines because they provided a starting point for considering what sentences to impose and were seen to reduce disparities. By contrast, the statutory determinate sentencing systems were not shown to have had significant lasting effects.

More importantly, experience confirmed Judge Frankel's ideas about administrative sentencing agencies. Minnesota's commission adopted policies tying sentencing policy to available prison resources and managed to hold the prison population within capacity throughout the 1980s, when most states experienced record increases. The Washington (for a time), Oregon, and most recently Kansas commissions had similar success at partly insulating sentencing policy from political pressure and keeping prison populations and prison resources in balance. By contrast, in states like California where fine-grained sentencing policies were left in legislative hands, statutory sentencing provisions were made harsher nearly every year and the prison population climbed by 400 percent between 1980 and 1995 (Zimring and Hawkins 1995).

By 1996, the success of Judge Frankel's innovation was clear. Twenty-five states at one time or another had created commissions, guidelines were in effect or under development in nearly twenty states, and new commissions had begun work in 1994 in Oklahoma, Missouri, and Massachusetts (Frase 1995; Greene 1995*a*). No state adopted a statutory determinate sentencing scheme after 1980 and some that had done so, like Colorado, diluted its effects by reintroducing parole release (Wesson 1993).

Because the federal commission had the prior experiences of the states to draw on, ample resources, and the capacity to recruit staff from throughout the country, all of the auguries would have predicted that the U.S. Sentencing Commission would build on the state experiences and produce the most successful guidelines system to date. The commission managed to defy that prediction.

Few outside the federal commission would disagree that the federal guidelines have been a disaster. In a statement similar to many made by other judges, Second Circuit Court of Appeals judge José Cabranes (1992) wrote, "The sentencing guidelines system is a failure—a dismal failure, a fact well known and fully understood by virtually everyone who is associated with the federal judicial system." A Federal Judicial Center survey of federal judges released in 1994 showed that 58.9 percent of appellate judges and 68.5 percent of trial judges were "strongly" or "moderately" opposed to retention of "the current system of mandatory guidelines." Forty percent of appellate judges and 50 percent of trial judges wanted the guidelines eliminated entirely.

The Sentencing Reform Act of 1984 abolished parole release prospectively and directed the newly created sentencing commission to develop guidelines for federal sentencing. The highly detailed guidelines divide crimes into forty-three different categories and are both rigid and mechanical. The commission has forbidden judges to take account in sentencing of many considerations—such as the effect of the sentence on the defendant or the defendant's family; or the defendant's mental health or drug or alcohol dependence; or a severely deprived background or victimization by sexual abuse—that many judges (and most people) believe to be ethically relevant in a just system of sentencing. The guidelines are based not on the offense of which the defendant was convicted, but on his "actual offense behavior," including alleged crimes of which he was acquitted or never charged. The guidelines allow virtually no role for nonimprisonment sentences.

For all these reasons, the federal guidelines are deeply disliked by most federal judges and lawyers who practice in federal courts, and they are widely circumvented. Even commission-sponsored research demonstrates that prosecutors and judges disingenuously circumvent the guidelines in a third of cases (Nagel and Schulhofer 1992). The true rate is probably higher.

Staff of newly created state commissions report that negative stereotypes created by the federal guidelines have been a major obstacle to their work. Recent commissions in Arkansas, Texas, Ohio, and North Carolina adopted resolutions repudiating the federal guidelines as a model for any policies they might later develop (Orland and Reitz 1993). Both the North Carolina commission and the American Bar Association's Sentencing Standards Project (which proposed that states create sentencing commissions) avoided use of the word "guidelines" because of the negative connotations associated with the federal guidelines (Reitz and Reitz 1995; Tonry 1995*b*).

No one factor can explain why the federal guidelines have been so much less successful and accepted than state guidelines. Some judges use words like arrogant and hostile to describe the commission's attitude to the federal judiciary. Some observers argue that the failure was in management. With its ample resources, a better-managed commission that consulted more widely and made efforts to learn from the state experiences could have done better. Others suggest that inexperience may have been part of the problem. Only three of the seven commissioners had ever been a judge, only two had been a trial judge, and only one had imposed a sentence within the preceding twenty years. Still others, more conspiracy-minded, note that a number of the initial commissioners were long known to be aspirants for higher judicial office (two achieved their aspirations) and suggest that the guidelines were an effort to show that the commission's policies were consonant with the views of influential congressional conservatives (von Hirsch 1988; Freed and Miller 1989; U.S. General Accounting Office 1990*a;* Stith and Koh 1993; Tonry 1991, 1993*a*).

There is truth in all those explanations, but the most important explanation is contextual: the federal sentencing commission legislation was formulated and agreed on in one political era, in which Judge Frankel's ideals were widely shared, but implemented in a different political era in which they had little influence. The initial proposed federal commission legislation introduced in the Congress in 1974, Senate Bill 181, was a direct outgrowth of a Yale Law School seminar that attempted to convert Judge Frankel's ideas into proposed legislation (O'Donnell, Churgin, and Curtis 1977). After reintroduction in successive congresses as a stand-alone bill, the proposal was folded into the then-pending proposed federal criminal code. By 1979, Senators Edward Kennedy and Strom Thurmond, the ranking Democratic and Republican members of the Senate Judiciary Committee (who succeeded one another as chairs), agreed on compromises and the Senate passed the proposed federal code, including the sentencing commission provisions, by a large majority. Although the House of Representatives did not act, the Senate agreement held, and the code bill including the sentencing commission parts repeatedly thereafter passed both the Senate Judiciary Committee and the Senate by wide margins. Eventually the code bill was abandoned as unpassable but the more technocratic and less controversial commission parts were included in an omnibus crime bill that was enacted in 1984 (Stith and Koh 1993).

Unfortunately, when this bipartisan, good-government, rationalistic proposal, formulated in the mid-1970s and intended to make sentencing fairer and to distance sentencing policy from politics, took effect, the government in power did not hold those goals. The crime-control policies of the Reagan administration in 1985 when the commissioners were appointed were oriented more toward toughness than toward fairness. As the English playwright John Mortimer has put it, the champions of "law and order" apparently valued those goals in reverse order. It should not therefore be a surprise that the commissioners who were appointed chose not to try to insulate their policy-making process from congressional politics but instead to show that they, too, were tough on crime and had little sympathy for the views of "lenient" judges (an odd stereotype since a large percentage of federal district judges by 1987 when the guidelines took effect were Reagan appointees—as today a large percentage of the guidelines' fiercest critics are Reagan and Bush appointees).

So the picture the traveling judges would see is mixed: federal guidelines that at least match their worst preconceptions of what would happen if indeterminate sentencing were abandoned, and state guidelines that turned out—I believe they would conclude—surprisingly well.

Modern sentencing reform efforts might have been more successful but for two developments—one principled, one political—that Judge Frankel probably did not foresee. First, some other governing rationale for sentencing policy was bound to take the place left empty when rehabilitation lost favor. In both academic and policy circles, that place was taken (sometimes implicitly) by retribution or "just deserts," with unintended consequences that made sentencing in many jurisdictions harsher and more mechanical than is necessary or just. Second, to an extent not known since the 1930s, crime control became a central issue in American politics in the 1970s and remains a central issue to this day. Because law-abiding citizens understandably fear crime and resent criminals, "toughness" and "law and order" are popular slogans to run on and "leniency" and "soft on crime" are labels few candidates willingly accept. Because, however, increased toughness seldom has any perceptible effects on crime rates, unremitting concern for toughness has resulted in pressures only, and continually, to increase penalties. The interaction between these two developments has produced the rigidity and harshness that are the two features of modern sentencing that judges and other practitioners most dislike.

II. The Injustice of Just Deserts

The irony of "just deserts" is that it backfired. The overriding aim was to make sentencing principled and fair, and the logic was consistent with Judge Frankel's call for rules to govern sentencing. If indeterminate sentencing sometimes produced racial and class disparities, other unwarranted disparities, and sentences grossly out of proportion to the crimes of which offenders were convicted, there was much to be said for proposals to scale the severity of punishments to the seriousness of crimes and thereby to satisfy the first tenet of equal treatment: to "treat like cases alike." In practice the effect was to focus attention solely on offenders' crimes and criminal records, to the exclusion of ethically important differences in their circumstances, and thereby to fail the second tenet of equal treatment: to "treat different cases differently."

Reduced to their core elements, just deserts theories are based on the intuitively powerful idea that punishment should be *deserved,* the empirical premise that most people agree about the comparative seriousness of crimes, and the proposal that crimes be ranked in order of their seriousness and punishments proportioned to those rankings (von Hirsch 1976, 1985, 1993). In such a scheme, people convicted of comparable offenses would receive similar punishments, and people convicted of more serious offenses would receive harsher penalties than those convicted of less serious offenses. In practice, however, while most academic proponents of desert theories favor overall *reduction* in the severity of punishments (e.g., von Hirsch 1993), the result has been both to make punishment more severe and to create disparities as extreme as any that existed under indeterminate sentencing.

It would be unfair to assign all blame for overemphasis on the equality principle and underemphasis on the difference principle to just deserts theories. Those emphases are in part a by-product of the format in which new sentencing standards were expressed. Sentencing guidelines are typically set out in a two-dimensional grid. Because crimes and criminal records can be scaled for seriousness, and few other ethically relevant considerations can, the two axes of the grids are invariably measures of the seriousness of crimes and the extensiveness of criminal records. This is true of the federal sentencing guidelines, for example, even though the U.S. Sentencing Commission expressly rejected just deserts as the rationale for its guidelines. Thus, with or without express just deserts rationales, modern sentencing policies concentrate almost exclusively on crimes.

This strikes many judges, prosecutors, and defense lawyers—who typically believe that many characteristics of offenders besides their crimes are pertinent to just sentencing—as wrong and unjust. Forced to choose between their oaths to enforce the law, by imposing sentences they believe unjust, and to do justice, by willfully evading the law's commands, they often do the latter. As a result, many sentencing reforms premised in part on "truth in sentencing" produce deceptive sentencing.

All guidelines systems are not premised on just deserts rationales, but many of those that promulgate their guidelines in grids suffer from the same problems. The Kansas and Minnesota sentencing commissions, among others, expressly adopted just deserts rationales for their guidelines (Parent 1988; Kansas Sentencing Commission 1990, p. 4). The U.S. Sentencing Commission refused to adopt any rationale for its guidelines, explaining that it decided not to choose between just deserts and "crime-control" (deterrence and incapacitation) rationales because, "this choice was unnecessary because in most sentencing decisions the application of either philosophy will produce the same or similar results" (U.S. Sentencing Commission 1992*a*, p. 3). Yet all three commissions promulgated architecturally similar grids that prescribe standards for sentencing.

Reduced to their core elements, all sentencing guidelines grids are fundamentally the same: two-dimensional tables that classify crimes by their severity along one axis and criminal records by their extent along the other. Applicable sentences for any case are calculated by finding the cell where the applicable criminal record column intersects with the applicable offense severity row (for example, see table 1.1, the Washington State grid in effect in 1994). Guidelines grids vary in details. Although most divide crimes into ten or twelve categories, some use more; the federal guidelines—the extreme case—create forty-three levels of offense severity. They vary in ornateness. Although most, like Washington's, provide a range of presumptive sentences such as "twenty-one to twenty-seven months" for any offense severity/criminal record combination, those in North Carolina (1994) and Pennsylvania (1994) contain a range for "ordinary cases" and separate ranges for cases in which aggravating or mitigating considerations are present. Finally, they vary in severity. Offenders who in most state systems would be subject to presumptive prison sentences of a few months or years often face sentences of many years under the federal guidelines.

Whatever the detailed policies guidelines embody, however, the two-axis grid is a common feature and, in interaction with just-deserts rationales, produces unjust results and conduces to needlessly harsh sentences. Two things happen. First, because desert theories place primary emphasis on linking deserved punishments to the severity of crimes, in the interest of treating like cases alike, they lead to disregard of other ethically relevant differences between offenders—like their personal backgrounds and the effects of punishments on them and their families—and thereby often treat unlike cases alike. Second, the all-but-exclusive emphasis in guidelines grids on crimes and criminal records affects the psychology of sentencing and sentencers. Just as sunlight sometimes etiolates a leaf, leaving the veins distinct and bleaching out the surrounding tissue, desert theories and grids make crimes and criminal records distinct and the human characteristics of offenders invisible. Comparison of vein patterns may be useful, and enough, in classifying leaves, but in making crucial decisions about peoples' lives, comparison only of crimes and criminal records is not enough.

Ethical Differences Between Cases

Just deserts, sometimes characterized as expressing a "principle of proportionality" (von Hirsch 1992), is sound in theory but defective in practice. In an ideal world in which all citizens have equal opportunities for self-realization and material advancement, the idea that deserved punish-

Table 1.1. Washington State Sentencing Guidelines Grid, for Crimes Committed after June 30, 1990

Seriousness Level	Offender Score 0	1	2	3	4	5	6	7	8	9 or more
XV	Life Sentence without Parole/Death Penalty									
XIV	23y 4m 240–320	24y 4m 250–333	25y 4m 261–347	26y 4m 271–361	27y 4m 281–374	28y 4m 291–388	30y 4m 312–416	32y 10m 338–450	36y 370–493	40y 411–548
XIII	12y 123–164	13y 134–178	14y 144–192	15y 154–205	16y 165–219	17y 175–233	19y 195–260	21y 216–288	25y 257–342	29y 298–397
XII	9y 93–123	9y 11m 102–136	10y 9m 111–147	11y 8m 120–160	12y 6m 129–171	13y 5m 138–184	15y 9m 162–216	17y 3m 178–236	20y 3m 209–277	23y 3m 240–318
XI	7y 6m 78–102	8y 4m 86–114	9y 2m 95–125	9y 11m 102–136	10y 9m 111–147	11y 7m 120–158	14y 2m 146–194	15y 5m 159–211	17y 11m 185–245	20y 5m 210–280
X	5y 51–68	5y 6m 57–75	6y 62–82	6y 6m 67–89	7y 72–96	7y 6m 77–102	9y 6m 98–130	10y 6m 108–144	12y 6m 129–171	14y 6m 149–198
IX	3y 31–41	3y 6m 36–48	4y 41–54	4y 6m 46–61	5y 51–68	5y 6m 57–75	7y 6m 77–102	8y 6m 87–116	10y 6m 108–144	12y 6m 129–171
VIII	2y 21–27	2y 6m 26–34	3y 31–41	3y 6m 36–48	4y 41–54	4y 6m 46–61	6y 6m 67–89	7y 6m 77–102	8y 6m 87–116	10y 6m 108–144
VII	18m 15–20	2y 21–27	2y 6m 26–34	3y 31–41	3y 6m 36–48	4y 41–54	5y 6m 57–75	6y 6m 67–89	7y 6m 77–102	8y 6m 87–116
VI	13m 12+–14	18m 15–20	2y 21–27	2y 6m 26–34	3y 31–41	3y 6m 36–48	4y 6m 46–61	5y 6m 57–75	6y 6m 67–89	7y 6m 77–102
V	9m 6–12	13m 12+–14	15m 13–17	18m 15–20	2y 2m 22–29	3y 2m 33–43	4y 41–54	5y 51–68	6y 62–82	7y 72–96
IV	6m 3–9	9m 6–12	13m 12+–14	15m 13–17	18m 15–20	2y 2m 22–29	3y 2m 33–43	4y 2m 43–57	5y 2m 53–70	6y 2m 63–84
III	2m 1–3	5m 3–8	8m 4–12	11m 9–12	14m 12+–16	20m 17–22	2y 2m 22–29	3y 2m 33–43	4y 2m 43–57	5y 51–68
II	0–90 days	4m 2–6	6m 3–9	8m 4–12	13m 12+–14	16m 14–18	20m 17–22	2y 2m 22–29	3y 2m 33–43	4y 2m 43–57
I	0–60 days	0–90 days	3m 2–5	4m 2–6	5m 3–8	8m 4–12	13m 12+–14	16m 14–18	20m 17–22	2y 2m 22–29

Source: Washington State Sentencing Guidelines Commission (1994*a*), table 1.

ments can be calibrated precisely to the offender's culpability, and that punishments should be apportioned accordingly, has much to commend it. Somewhat awkwardly for desert theories, however, ours is a world that in a number of respects falls short of the ideal.

For this reason, a number of leading philosophers who have written about punishment from a retributive perspective, though their views differ in important details, agree that retributive schemes cannot be justified in practice. British philosopher Antony Duff (1986, p. 294), for example, who then espoused a punishment philosophy that combined elements of retribution and moral education, rejected his own views in favor of a deterrence-based scheme: "Punishment is not justifiable within our present legal system; it will not be justifiable unless and until we have brought about deep and far-reaching social, political, legal, and moral changes in ourselves and our society."

American philosopher Jeffrey Murphy developed a retributive punishment theory based on the idea that offenders enjoy the benefits of organized society and other peoples' acceptance of the burdens of citizenship, and must be punished so that they do not gain an unfair advantage. If they enjoy the benefits of others' law-abiding behavior, they must accept the same burdens. Punishment is a process that appropriately attempts to put burdens and benefits back into balance. Nonetheless, in practice, Murphy (1973, p. 110) rejected the implications of his own theory because it could not deliver justice until "we have restructured society in such a way that criminals genuinely do correspond to the only model that will render punishment permissible—i.e., make sure that they are autonomous and that they do benefit in the requisite sense."

Philosophers writing from nonretributive premises often reach the same conclusion. English philosopher Ted Honderich (1989, pp. 238–39), for example, who in principle favors a punishment theory combining retributive and utilitarian elements, rejects it in practice: "There is nothing that can be called the question of [punishment's] moral justification which is left to be considered if one puts aside the great question of the distribution of goods in society." Oxford philosopher H. L. A. Hart (1968, p. 51), this century's most influential writer on punishment, after arguing that the criminal law did not and should not recognize a general defense of great economic temptation, nonetheless observed, for "those below a minimum level of economic prosperity . . . [perhaps] we should incorporate as a further excusing condition the pressure of gross forms of economic necessity."

That the problem of "just deserts in an unjust world," as it is sometimes called, is serious, is shown by its acknowledgment (though not acceptance) by Andrew von Hirsch (1986, p. 149), the most influential modern proponent of just deserts theories: "As long as a substantial segment of the population is denied adequate opportunities for a livelihood, any scheme for punishing must be morally flawed."

More generally, proponents of utilitarian punishment theories believe that no punishments should be imposed that are more harsh or intrusive than is necessary. This is sometimes called a "principle of parsimony," and is based on the belief that the infliction of suffering on anyone, including wrongdoers, is wrong and can be justified only when some greater good is thereby accomplished (Tonry 1994). Jeremy Bentham, the nineteenth-century philosopher to whom modern utilitarian theories can be traced, wrote, "Upon the principle of utility, if [punishment] ought at all to be admitted, it ought only to be admitted in as far as it promises to exclude some greater evil" (Bentham 1843).

Among modern writers, Norval Morris (1974) most fully takes account of parsimony in his theory of limiting retributivism. While just deserts considerations can often help us identify "undeserved punishments" (because manifestly too severe or too lenient), he argues, they offer little guidance on determination of "deserved punishments." Accordingly, just sentencing policies for all crimes should set upper limits, calibrated to prevent infliction of undeserved punishments, and for some serious crimes should set lower limits, but otherwise should allow judges to adjust sentences to take account of ethically relevant differences between offenders.

Most judges and practicing lawyers subscribe to views like Morris's. That is why they so often believe rigid sentencing guidelines and mandatory minimum penalties are unjust. And *that* is why, as the findings of numerous studies discussed in chapters 2, 3, and 5 attest, they are often prepared to manipulate and evade rigid sentencing guidelines and mandatory penalties to achieve what they consider just results in individual cases.

Even accepting for purposes of argument, however, that desert theories can be justified, in practice they suffer from important additional defects. The first arises from their sole reliance on current and (to a much lesser extent) past criminality for the calculation of deserved punishments. The problem, as English philosopher Nigel Walker (1991) has pointed out, is that "retributive reasoning would lead" not to standardized lists of crimes and punishments but "instead to 'a personal price list' which would take into account not only gradations of harm but offenders' culpability and sensibility." Walker sometimes writes of the Recording Angel who will determine our futures at life's end and suggests that a genuinely retributive assessment of an offender's culpability and deserved punishment would encompass all the things the Recording Angel would find relevant.

Like the Recording Angel's, most peoples' judgments of others' blameworthiness depend on knowledge of their circumstances. A suburban stockbroker who sells cocaine elicits different judgments of moral culpability than does a disadvantaged ghetto youth who sells the same amount. A mentally retarded, easily led boy who participates in a street mugging may elicit different culpability judgments than does the gang member who persuaded him to participate. A formerly abused wife who attacks her drunken husband with a knife elicits different culpability judgments than when the knife is in the husband's hand. And so on; circumstances matter in attributions of blameworthiness.

Likewise, the collateral effects of sentences on people other than the wrongdoer matter. In just deserts principle, two offenders who commit the same offense and have similar criminal records deserve the same penalty. If applicable guidelines specify a two-year prison sentence, both should receive it. If one, however, is unemployed and has no permanent residence, and the other works and supports a family, many people will want to treat them differently. Partly, this is because the second seems more stable, more integrated into society, and somehow more worthy. Partly also, and equally important, it is because the second offender's spouse and children—who have committed no crime—will also suffer. They will lose a partner and parent for so long as the offender is in prison and may possibly lose a home and a car and be forced onto welfare. The offender, besides losing his liberty while in prison, may find when he gets out that he has also lost his family.

Judges, prosecutors, and other officials make decisions about whole people, and not about generic offenders who have committed offense X and have criminal history Y. Not surprisingly, they often feel moved to take the individual offender's circumstances into account in deciding what to do.

Another defect with systems that mechanically scale crimes to punishments is that punishments are no more standardized than are offenders. In objective terms, punishments that technically are the same may be very different. A "generic" two-year prison sentence, for example, depending on a jurisdiction's resources and the amount of authority delegated to its corrections department, may range from time spent in a crowded, fear-ridden maximum security prison under lockup twenty-three hours per day to confinement under electronic monitoring in the offender's home, with medium and minimum security prisons, forestry camps, and halfway houses in between. All count as two years' deprivation of liberty, but all offenders and most observers see them as vastly different.

In subjective terms as well, two years' imprisonment in a single setting will have very different meanings to different offenders who have committed the same crime. Two years' imprisonment in a maximum security prison may be a rite of passage for a Los Angeles gang member. For an attractive, effeminate twenty-year-old, it may mean the terror of repeated sexual victimization. For a forty-year-old head of household, it may mean the loss of a job and a home and a family. For an unhealthy seventy-five-year-old, it may be a death sentence.

A critic might respond to these observations with accusations of perfectionism. No human institution will ever deliver perfect justice, even assuming there was wide agreement as to what that was, and just deserts theories are better than anything else that has been tried. The response is that there must be a conception of criminal justice that is better than one that fails to take account of ethically relevant differences between defendants and that fails to acknowledge qualitative differences in nominally identical penalties and in their effects on individuals.

The Psychology of Two-Dimensional Grids

Use of two-dimensional grids to express sentencing standards has impoverished sentencing, irrespective of the philosophical premise, because grids affect the way that people—policy makers, practitioners, and bystanders alike—think about sentencing. This does not mean that grids should be abandoned but only that their drawbacks and dangers should be recognized. They are efficient devices for condensing and communicating vast amounts of information. They are also, however, blunt instruments when applied to sentencing operations for which scalpels are often needed.

The two-axis grid reifies thinking about punishment into a calculus that takes account only of criminality. Under indeterminate sentencing, the goal of individualization of punishment to achieve rehabilitative ends, combined with an absence of sentencing rules, forced judges to adopt a holistic approach. That approach led to unwarranted disparities and unacceptable risks of invidious bias and capriciousness, but at its best it allowed judges to take account of the crime, all of the relevant circumstances, and the likely consequences of alternate possible sentences. In the nature of things, the two-axis grid focuses people's primary attention on the considerations represented by those two axes, to the exclusion of other considerations.

This focusing effect is inversely related to people's distance from individual sentencing decisions. Judges and lawyers are intimately involved in sentencing and, depending on their personalities and experience, to a greater or lesser extent resent and resist the reification of individuals into crime-and-criminal-history amalgams. Appellate courts are further removed and, seeing only lawyers and paper, are more comfortable than trial judges in treating people as stereotypes rather than as individuals. This may be one reason why federal trial judges have been much more vocal in their opposition to the mechanistic federal guidelines than federal appellate judges have been.

Academics and politicians are even further removed from sentencing and even more likely to forget that there are people behind crime-and-criminal-record categories. The work of Princeton University political scientist John DiIulio offers an example. He has many times written that "more than 95 percent of state prisoners are violent criminals, repeat criminals (with two or more felony convictions), or violent repeat criminals" (e.g., DiIulio 1994, a *Wall Street Journal* article entitled "Let 'Em Rot"). The statement is untrue; the 1991 survey of state prison inmates conducted by the Bureau of Justice Statistics, on which DiIulio claims his statement is based (Beck et al. 1993), to the contrary says, "About 38 percent of all inmates had not been incarcerated before: 19 percent were sentenced for the first time [i.e., this was a first conviction]; 19 percent had [previously been sentenced] to probation." DiIulio's numbers are facially inconsistent with the data source on which they are ostensibly based.

More interesting, however, is DiIulio's explanation for his claim. He points out that the Bureau of Justice Statistics report elsewhere indicates that 94 percent of prisoners had as an adult *or as a juvenile* been sentenced to incarceration or *to probation.* Thus presumably unconsciously he has included among "repeat criminals (with two or more felony convictions)" first-time prisoners whose only prior record consists of a juvenile court proceeding for a property offense that resulted in probation. By legal definition, a person whose record consists only of a prior juvenile court "adjudication" has no "prior felony convictions." DiIulio has also included first-time prisoners who are nuisance property offenders with prior misdemeanor convictions or who are minor offenders with prior felony convictions for such things as shoplifting or sale of marijuana in small amounts.

A cast of mind is revealed by the phrase "violent criminals, repeat criminals (with two or more felony convictions), or violent repeat criminals." A standard rule of interpretation of legal texts, *ejusdem generis,* presumes that items listed in a series are to be treated as of comparable weight or nature. DiIulio's point presumably ("Let 'Em Rot" may be evidence) is that most people in prisons are dangerous people who do not deserve sympathy. Two of his three categories, "violent criminals" and "repeat violent criminals," illustrate that point. Sandwiched between them, however, and implicitly a category of equivalent danger, are "repeat criminals" who as it turns out include both people with no prior adult convictions (only juvenile court adjudications, many for property crimes) and people whose only adult convictions involve trifling property crimes.

The reality is that all people in prison are not equally dangerous. In 1991, again drawing on the Bureau of Justice Statistics survey, 49 percent of prisoners had been convicted of violent crimes and another 13 percent were in prison for property or drug crimes but had previously been convicted (or in juvenile court, been adjudicated) of a violent crime. Thus 62 percent had at some time had a conviction or adjudication for a violent crime. This offers a starting point for calculating the percentage of genuinely dangerous prisoners, but most fair-minded adjustments would be downward. For many years, half or more of murders involved otherwise noncriminal people killing family members or friends in emotionally charged circumstances; these murderers tend to be docile prisoners and crime-free in their later lives. Many juvenile court adjudications for violence involve fights between young people who leave their inability to control their anger behind as they mature. And so on. Not all prisoners with violence in their records are the dangerous predators that DiIulio's rhetoric conjures up.

I discussed DiIulio's claim for several paragraphs not only to demonstrate its inaccuracy—only he knows whether the misstatements are willful or the product of overzealous argument—but also to illustrate the way that many conservative politicians and academics seem to have lost sight of the human dimensions and consequences of sentencing.

The recent tendency to formulate sentencing policy primarily in terms of current and past crimes bears part of the blame for overclaiming like DiIulio's. Thinking about sentencing abstractly in terms only of crimes and criminal records makes it easy to forget that the abstract category is only an analytical convenience and that the offenders facing sentencing are real people.

This may also be one reason the members of the federal sentencing commission were comfortable creating a system of sentencing in which, under sections 5H1.1–5H1.6 (U.S. Sentencing Commission 1992*a*), "education and vocational skills [and age, and mental and emotional conditions, and physical condition including drug dependence and alcohol abuse, and family ties and responsibilities, among others] are not ordinarily relevant in determining whether a sentence should be outside the applicable guideline range." The essence of the problem is captured in the title of a recent article on the federal guidelines by Professor Stephen Schulhofer (who is among a handful of academic observers who in general support the federal guidelines): "Assessing the Federal Sentencing Process: The Problem Is Uniformity, Not Disparity."

Another unfortunate effect of the two-dimensional grid is entirely mundane. In the nature of things an axis of a grid can express only qualities that are linear. Crimes and criminal records can be expressed on a linear scale that starts at zero and increases in intuitively plausible ways. Murder is worse than rape which is worse than robbery which is worse than burglary which is worse than grand theft which is worse than petty theft and so on. Likewise, having five prior convictions is worse than four which is worse than three. Reasonable people quickly reach agreement about the scaling of crimes and criminal records.

Conversely, a grid axis cannot handle factors that are not linear, and many ethically relevant considerations in sentencing cannot be expressed in a linear way. Their relevance at all, and whether they are aggravating or mitigating circumstances, varies depending on the case. Take employment. The relevance of employment to sentencing varies with circumstances. Most people believe it is irrelevant that a wealthy securities law violator will, if imprisoned, lose his or her job. If anything, that person's employment history and prospects are aggravating circumstances: such crimes involve a violation of trust, and the offender's economic well-being makes the crimes difficult to explain in terms other than greed.

People have widely divergent views on whether a lower-middle-class head of household's job loss, if imprisoned, is relevant. From the perspective of the effects of imprisonment on the defendant's spouse and children, and the increased likelihood that the family will break up and be made bankrupt and welfare dependent, job loss is a mitigating circumstance. From the perspectives that employed defendants are often middle-class, and more likely than unemployed defendants to be white, concern about racial and class disparities may make job loss appear irrelevant.

Finally, most people find impending job loss if imprisoned a mitigating consideration in the case of an employed minority defendant who has overcome an inadequate education, a deprived childhood, and adolescent drug dependence to work his way up a blue-collar ladder to become a service station mechanic, and who has over a period of years managed to support a partner and out-of-wedlock children.

Many other regularly recurring circumstances are situationally relevant to just sentencing but not universally relevant. Mental abnormality may be a mitigating circumstance when it makes the defendant susceptible to manipulation by others, but an aggravating circumstance when it reduces a defendant's ability to control aggressive impulses. Excess alcohol consumption may be a mitigating circumstance when a defendant convicted of manslaughter is an alcoholic, an aggravating circumstance when the defendant was a social drinker who refused friends' pleas to drive him home, and irrelevant when a chronically abusive man while drunk assaults his wife. Age may be a relevant circumstance when the defendant is seventeen and impressionable and when the defendant is seventy-five and infirm but irrelevant in distinguishing between twenty-five- and thirty-five-year-olds. Being an employed head of household may be irrelevant when the charge is stranger rape and relevant when the charge is embezzlement.

There is no reason why guidelines systems cannot allow judges to take account of meaningful differences between offenders and offenses. Many do, by allowing judges more latitude than the federal guidelines permit, by allowing more room for departures from guidelines for reasons stated, and by establishing policy statements that offer guidance on how various nonlinear considerations might be applicable to different kinds of cases.

Just deserts theories cannot be assigned all the blame for the rigidity and lack of subtlety of many guidelines systems, but they must accept some of the responsibility. By offering policy makers a rationale for sentencing that reduced relevant considerations to two that can be scaled on the axes of grids, they reified three-dimensional defendants into two-dimensional abstractions. When policy makers think of abstractions rather than people, it is easy to respond to an electoral opponent's possible "soft on crime" accusations by voting to increase sentences or to establish mandatory penalties. This danger may be greatest in times when public concern about crime is high, or when politicians are inclined to appeal more to people's fears than to their aspirations. If a two-dimensional grid is chalked onto a legislative committee room's blackboard, it takes little effort to erase numbers and replace them with higher ones (Zimring 1976).

The sentencing innovations of the past quarter century have achieved notable gains. Guidelines in some states have reduced racial, gender, and other disparities, have made judges more accountable for their decisions, and have facilitated development of systems of appellate review of sentencing. Commissions in some states, as Judge Frankel predicted, have developed specialized expertise and to some degree insulated policy from short-term political pressures. If the federal experience with a sentencing commission and guidelines has been disastrous, it is outweighed by the happier experiences in the states.

Unfortunately, the past quarter century's innovations have also diminished the quality of justice dispensed in criminal courts. Our predecessors knew that mandatory penalties are seldom effective deterrents, sometimes produce palpably unjust punishments, and often result in disingenuous actions by judges and lawyers to blunt their effect. Many policy makers forgot those lessons and are only now relearning them. Countless individual offenders and the integrity of sentencing have suffered as a result. Similarly, the mechanism of the two-axis grid and the law-and-order politics of the last two decades have too often converted offenders into abstractions and produced a penal system of a severity unmatched in the Western world.

References

American Friends Service Committee. 1971. *Struggle for Justice.* New York: Hill & Wang.

Ashworth, Andrew. 1992*a*. "The Criminal Justice Act 1991." In *Sentencing, Judicial Discretion, and Training,* edited by Colin Munro and Martin Wasik. London: Sweet & Maxwell.

Beck, Allen, et al. 1993. *Survey of State Prison Inmates, 1991.* Washington, D.C.: Bureau of Justice Statistics.

Bentham, Jeremy. 1843. *The Works of Jeremy Bentham,* vol. 4, edited by John Bowring. London: Simpkin, Marshall.

Blumstein, Alfred, Jacqueline Cohen, Susan E. Martin, and Michael Tonry, eds. 1983. *Research on Sentencing: The Search for Reform*, 2 vols. Washington, D.C.: National Academy Press.

Blumstein, Alfred, Jacqueline Cohen, and Daniel Nagin. 1978. *Deterrence and Incapacitation: Estimating the Effects of Criminal Sanctions on Crime Rates.* Washington, D.C.: National Academy Press.

Cabranes, José. 1992. "Sentencing Guidelines: A Dismal Failure." *New York Law Journal* (July 27), p. 27.

Committee on Justice and the Solicitor General. 1993. *Crime Prevention in Canada: Toward a National Strategy.* Ottawa: Canada Communication Group.

Davis, Kenneth Culp. 1969. *Discretionary Justice—A Preliminary Inquiry.* Baton Rouge: Louisiana State University Press.

DiIulio, John J., and Anne M. Piehl. 1991. "Does Prison Pay?" Unpublished manuscript. Princeton, N.J.: Princeton University, Center of Domestic and Comparative Policy Studies.

Duff, R. A. 1986. *Trials and Punishments.* Cambridge: Cambridge University Press.

Frankel, Marvin. 1972. *Criminal Sentences: Law without Order.* New York: Hill & Wang.

Frase, Richard. 1995. "State Sentencing Guidelines: Still Going Strong." *Judicature* 78(4):173–79.

Freed, Daniel J., and Marc Miller. 1989. "Intrigue at the U.S. Sentencing Commission: The Battle over Part-Time Commissioners." *Federal Sentencing Reporter* 2:156–58.

24b *References*

Greene, Judy. 1995*a*. "Massachusetts, Missouri, and Oklahoma Establish Sentencing Commissions." *Overcrowded Times* 6(3):1, 18–22.

Hart, H. L. A. 1968. *Punishment and Responsibility: Essays in the Philosophy of Law.* Oxford: Oxford University Press.

Home Office. 1990. *Crime, Justice, and Protecting the Public.* London: Home Office.

Honderich, Ted. 1989. *Punishment: The Supposed Justifications.* Cambridge: Polity. *Retributive Justice.* Albany: State University of New York Press.

Kansas Sentencing Commission. 1990. *Report to the Special Committee on the Judiciary* (July 26, 27, 1990). Topeka: Kansas Sentencing Commission.

Knapp, Kay A. 1984. *The Impact of the Minnesota Sentencing Guidelines: Three-Year Evaluation.* St. Paul, Minn.: Minnesota Sentencing Guidelines Commission.

Lipton, Douglas, Robert Martinson, and Judith Wilks. 1975. *The Effectiveness of Correctional Treatment: A Survey of Correctional Treatment Evaluations.* New York: Praeger.

Mann, Coramae Richey. 1993. *Unequal Justice—A Question of Color.* Bloomington: Indiana University Press.

Morris, Norval. 1974. *The Future of Imprisonment.* Chicago: University of Chicago Press.

Murphy, Jeffrey. 1973. "Marxism and Retribution." *Philosophy and Public Affairs* 2:217–43.

Nagel, Ilene H., and Stephen J. Schulhofer. 1992. "A Tale of Three Cities: An Empirical Study of Charging and Bargaining Practices Under the Federal Sentencing Guidelines." *Southern California Law Review* 66:501–66.

Nagin, Daniel. 1978. "General Deterrence: A Review of the Empirical Evidence." In *Deterrence and Incapacitation,* edited by Alfred Blumstein, Jacqueline Cohen, and Daniel Nagin. Washington, D.C.: National Academy Press.

O'Donnell, Pierce, Michael Churgin, and Dennis Curtis. 1977. *Toward a Just and Effective Sentencing System.* New York: Praeger.

Orland, Leonard, and Kevin R. Reitz. 1993. "Epilogue: A Gathering of State Sentencing Commissions." *Colorado Law Review* 64:837–47.

Parent, Dale. 1988. *Structuring Sentencing Discretion: The Evolution of Minnesota's Sentencing Guidelines.* Stoneham, Mass.: Butterworth.

Reiss, Albert J., Jr., and Jeffrey Roth, eds. 1993. *Understanding and Controlling Violence.* Washington, D.C.: National Academy Press.

Reitz, Kevin, and Curtis Reitz. 1995. "Building a Sentencing Reform Agenda—The ABA's New Sentencing Standards." *Judicature* 78(4):189–95.

Rothman, David. 1980. *Conscience and Convenience.* Boston: Little, Brown.

Schulhofer, Stephen. 1992. "Assessing the Federal Sentencing Process: The Problem Is Uniformity, Not Disparity." *American Criminal Law Review* 29: 833–873.

Stith, Kate, and Steve Y. Koh. 1993. "The Politics of Sentencing Reform: The Legislative History of the Federal Sentencing Guidelines." *Wake Forest Law Review* 28:223–90.

Tonry, Michael. 1991."The Politics and Processes of Sentencing Commissions." *Crime Hofstra Law Review* 7:315–53.

References 24c

______. 1993*a*. "The Failure of the U.S. Sentencing Commission's Guidelines." *Crime and Delinquency* 39:131–49.

______. 1994. "Proportionality, Parsimony, and Interchangeability of Punishments." In *Penal Theory and Practice*, edited by R. A. Duff, S. Marshall, and R. and R. Dobash. Manchester: Manchester University Press.

______. 1995*a*. *Malign Neglect: Race, Crime, and Punishment in America*. New York: Oxford University Press.

______. 1995*b*. "Twenty Years of Sentencing Reform: Steps Forward, Steps Backward." *Judicature* 78(4):169–72.

U.S. General Accounting Office. 1990*a*. *U.S. Sentencing Commission: Changes Needed to Improve Effectiveness*. Testimony of Lowell Dodge before the Subcommittee on Criminal Justice of the Committee on the Judiciary, United States House of Representatives, March. Washington, D.C.: U.S. General Accounting Office.

U.S. Sentencing Commission. 1992*a*. *Sentencing Commission Guidelines Manual*. Washington, D.C.: U.S. Sentencing Commission.

von Hirsch, Andrew. 1976. *Doing Justice: The Choice of Punishments*. New York: Hill & Wang.

______. 1985. *Past or Future Crimes—Deservedness and Dangerousness in the Sentencing of Criminals*. New Brunswick, N.J.: Rutgers University Press.

______. 1986. *Doing Justice: The Choice of Punishments*, rev. ed. Boston: Northeastern University Press.

______. 1988. "Federal Sentencing Guidelines: The United States and Canadian Schemes Compared." Occasional Papers from the Center for Research in Crime and Justice, no. 4. New York: New York University Law School.

______. 1992. "Proportionality in the Philosophy of Punishment." In *Crime and Justice: A Review of Research*, vol. 16, edited by Michael Tonry. Chicago: University of Chicago Press.

______. 1993. *Censure and Sanctions*. Oxford: Oxford University Press.

Walker, Nigel. 1991. *Why Punish?* Oxford: Oxford University Press.

Wesson, Marianne. 1993. "Sentencing Reform in Colorado—Many Changes, Little Progress." *Overcrowded Times* 4(6):1, 14–17, 20.

Wilson, James Q. 1975. *Thinking About Crime*. New York: Basic.

______. 1983. *Thinking About Crime*, rev. ed. New York: Basic.

______. 1994. "Crime and Public Policy." In *Crime*, edited by James Q. Wilson and Joan Petersilia. San Francisco, Calif.: ICS.

Zimring, Franklin E. 1976. "Making the Punishment Fit the Crime: A Consumer's Guide to Sentencing Reform." *Hastings Center Report* 6:13–21.

Zimring, Franklin E., and Gordon Hawkins. 1995. *Incapacitation: Penal Confinement and the Restraint of Crime*. Chicago: University of Chicago Press.

[13]
Purposes and Functions of Sentencing

ABSTRACT

American sentencing systems have fragmented since the modern sentencing reform movement began in the 1970s and predominant retributive theories of punishment have become obsolete. Indeterminate sentencing was ubiquitous, but when it lost credibility, no single approach replaced it. Every American jurisdiction has a crazy quilt of diverse and, in principle if not practice, irreconcilable elements. Influential retributive theories of punishment were a 1970s response to 1970s problems that no longer galvanize opinion or reform. They are incompatible with the recent growth of restorative and community justice, therapeutic jurisprudence, prisoner reentry programs, and knowledge about the effectiveness of treatment programs. Theories of punishment can provide normative criteria by which policies and practices can be measured, but to be used in that way they must speak to their own times. New sentencing systems more effective and more just than current fragmented systems can be developed, and they will be better if new normative theories germane to them develop in tandem.

Sentencing policy in the United States has fragmented. There is no overriding theory or model. There are no widely shared understandings about what sentencing can or should accomplish or about conceptions of justice it should incorporate or reflect. Painting with a broad brush, utilitarian ideas held sway in the United States from 1900 through the mid-1970s (evidenced most strongly by indeterminate sentencing and extensive parole release), followed in succession by retributive ideas (evidenced most strongly by desert-based guidelines systems

Michael Tonry is Sonosky Professor of Law and Public Policy and director of the Institute on Crime and Public Policy at the University of Minnesota Law School, and senior fellow in the Netherlands Institute for the Study of Crime and Law Enforcement, Leiden. I am grateful to Marc Miller, who first proposed I write on the subjects of this essay. An earlier version of this essay appeared in the *Stanford Law Review* (Tonry 2005*a*).

in Minnesota, Oregon, and Washington) in the 1970s and 1980s, deterrent ideas (evidenced most strongly by federal and state mandatory minimum sentence and truth-in-sentencing laws) in the 1980s, incapacitative ideas (evidenced most strongly by three-strikes, dangerous offender/sexual psychopath, and sex offender registration and notification laws) in the 1990s, and a muddle in the early years of the twenty-first century. The muddle is exemplified by greatly reinvigorated interest in rehabilitative programs, such as drug, mental health, and domestic violence courts, reentry programs, and a plethora of new community-based and institutional treatment programs, combined with the continuing operation of laws enacted in all the earlier periods but especially the 1980s and 1990s. Ideas about restorative and community justice and therapeutic jurisprudence percolate through many of these initiatives.

Muddles are not necessarily bad. The absence of a stifling orthodoxy and a limiting conventional wisdom allows for creativity and experimentation, both of which have been evident for a decade. In the longer term, though, new practices and prevailing views will emerge and they will be incorporated into new sentencing systems and laws. As that begins to happen, it will be done better or worse. Thinking through the purposes and functions of sentencing in liberal democratic societies may improve chances it will be done better.

American governments did not do a very good job responding to the collapse of indeterminate sentencing. The developments underlying the collapse—declining confidence in rehabilitative programs, concerns about disparities and racial bias, and lack of procedural fairness—are well known (Blumstein, Cohen, Martin, and Tonry 1983, chap. 1). For a short time sentencing policy changes in the forms of sentencing and parole guidelines and abolition of parole release addressed those problems in some places. From the early 1980s through the late 1990s, though, policy makers lost their way. Some of the policies they adopted, notably mandatory minimums for drug and violent crimes, truth-in-sentencing laws, and three-strikes laws, worsened the problems the sentencing reform movement initially sought to address. Sentencing disparities generally and racial disparities in particular worsened, and proportionality links between the seriousness of crimes and the severity of punishment were broken (Tonry 2005*b*).

The winds, however, began changing direction again in the mid-1990s. Renewed possibilities exist for resuming the original efforts to achieve fair and effective systems of punishment while taking account of changing conceptions of justice. Recent Supreme Court decisions and changes in political and public attitudes toward punishment have focused attention on sentencing policy to a degree not matched since the 1980s. The Court decisions fundamentally altered the federal sentencing guidelines, changed the legal context in which state guidelines operate, and led some states to reconsider the desirability of major elements of their sentencing systems. Evolving attitudes have produced significant policy changes in many jurisdictions.

Two decisions of the U.S. Supreme Court significantly altered the legal environment for guidelines systems. *Blakely* (124 S. Ct. 2531 [2004]) held that Washington State's system of presumptive sentencing guidelines was unconstitutional to the extent that it gave judges discretion to impose prison sentences longer than the maximum authorized by the applicable guidelines. Such "upward departures" may be imposed, the Court asserted, only following a determination, beyond a reasonable doubt, of the facts on which the longer sentence was predicated. The Court's rationale was that the upper limits of the ranges of presumptive sentencing guidelines are equivalent to statutory sentence maximums; just as a person cannot be sentenced more severely than the maximum authorized by statute for the offense of which he was convicted, a person cannot be sentenced more severely than the maximum provided in the applicable guidelines range for that offense. State sentencing commissions had to figure out how best to comply with *Blakely*. It was in some ways a harder problem in theory than in practice;[1] upward departures are rare in every guidelines system.[2]

Booker (125 S. Ct. 738 [2005]) applied *Blakely* to the federal guidelines. *Booker*'s implications were substantially more radical than *Blakely*'s because the federal guidelines are much more detailed and prescriptive than any state's and because their central feature is the "relevant conduct" provision that bases sentences not on the offense of which the defendant was convicted but on the "actual offense be-

[1] One option is to apply it literally and compel prosecutors to charge and prove aggravating factors that might justify a harsher than normal sentence; prosecutorial failure to do so would preclude an above-guidelines sentence. A second is to create a postconviction mechanism for jury consideration of aggravating factors at the sentencing stage. A third is to replace presumptive guidelines with voluntary ones. Most states with presumptive guidelines adopted the second option (Reitz 2005*b*).

[2] In Washington State in 2005, e.g., only 0.6 percent of standard cases involved upward departures (Washington State Sentencing Guidelines Commission 2005, table 10).

havior" determined by the judge to be present on the basis of a civil-law "preponderance of the evidence" standard. *Booker* in practice applied to most sentences imposed in federal courts. The Supreme Court had to decide whether its decision required that the entire guidelines system be struck down. It elected to leave the guidelines in effect but with "advisory" rather than "presumptive" or "mandatory" force. Judges must calculate the advisory sentence post-*Booker* exactly as they would have earlier but may reject the guidelines' "advice" and impose some other sentence as long as they give reasons for doing so. By making the guidelines advisory, the Court empowered judges more often and more easily to impose sentences less harsh than those prescribed by the pre-*Booker* guidelines.

Independently of the guidelines developments, public and political attitudes toward criminal justice policy have been changing for a decade. The Supreme Court decisions themselves, prohibiting sentencing policies in effect for two decades, are one sign of this. So is an earlier decision of the California Supreme Court, *the People v. Alvarez* (60 Cal. Rep. 2d 93 [1997]), which greatly weakened California's fearsome three-strikes law.[3] Another is the proliferation of drug, gun, domestic violence, and mental health courts, all premised on taking problem-solving rather than solely punitive approaches to offending (Nolan 2001; Casey and Rottman 2003; Redlich et al. 2005). A third is the passage of California's Proposition 36, and similar referenda in other states and the District of Columbia, mandating diversion from prosecution and into treatment of many drug-abusing offenders (Tonry 2004*b*, chap. 1). A fourth is the adoption of laws in many states intended to reduce prison populations and costs by altering mandatory minimum sentencing laws, creating new alternatives to imprisonment, and authorizing new and broader programs of early release (Butterfield 2003). A fifth is the proliferation of new programs, usually at grassroots levels, based on ideas about restorative and community justice (Clear and Karp 1999; Braithwaite 2002). A sixth is the rapid expansion of the "prisoner reentry" movement predicated on the belief that we know

[3] At least some California and U.S. Supreme Court justices would deny that the decisions occurred because the elected branches of government were politically immobilized from repealing or fundamentally altering sentencing systems that nearly all informed people considered deeply unjust and the courts decided they had to step in; it is hard, however, to imagine that the justices were unaware of the systems' fundamental problems and of the intractable political difficulties that precluded legislative solutions and that their decisions would address the problems while sidestepping the politics.

how to help offenders avoid reoffending (Travis 2005; Travis and Visher 2005).

Sentencing reform seemed a much simpler subject in the 1970s than it does now. The widely shared and recognized aims then were to reduce sentencing disparities generally and in relation to race, to make judges more accountable for their decisions, and to make the sentencing process more transparent (Frankel 1972; Morris 1974). Few people saw sentencing reform as a way to prevent crime or as the proper subject of partisan politics. As a result, the proponents of change even in a state as traditionally partisan as California included liberal and conservative legislators, police unions and prisoners' rights advocates, and defense lawyers and prosecutors (Messinger and Johnson 1978). Sentencing reform seemed straightforward, raising practical and policy issues about which reasonable people disagreed, but, at least politically and ideologically, it appeared to be relatively noncontentious.[4]

The trial and error of the past three decades has left lessons to be learned that, if heeded, can help contemporary policy makers do better than their immediate predecessors. We know much more about sentencing and the effects of different policy approaches than we did thirty years ago. Here are the main lessons:

- Well-designed systems of presumptive sentencing guidelines can reduce disparities, make sentencing more consistent and predictable, attract support from most judges and prosecutors, and provide a policy tool for predicting and managing correctional resource needs (Tonry 1996, chaps. 2–5; Reitz 2001).
- Some systems of voluntary sentencing guidelines have been used successfully to predict and manage correctional resources, but there is no credible evidence that they reduce disparities (Tonry 1996; Frase 2005*c*).

[4] That sentencing reform was widely seen as noncontentious in the 1970s seems politically naive in retrospect and therefore probably is not true. A more plausible view is that people recognized that various proponents of change had different policy and political agendas in mind but failed to anticipate how partisan and ideological crime control policy would later become and how starkly different the ramifications of the different agendas. When California adopted its Uniform Determinate Sentencing Law of 1976, more than a decade had passed since Barry Goldwater raised crime in the streets as a campaign issue in 1964, and President Richard Nixon had already launched wars on drugs and crime (Edsall and Edsall 1991). No one then would have predicted that Willie Horton, a black murderer and rapist, would play a major role in the 1988 presidential election (Anderson 1995) or that Democratic presidential candidate Bill Clinton in 1992 would campaign on the basis that he was tougher on crime than the Republicans (Gest 2001).

- Mandatory minimum sentencing laws, including three-strikes laws, are inconsistently applied, provoke widespread circumvention, produce gross disparities in the treatment of similarly situated offenders, and sometimes result in sentences that all involved believe to be unjustly severe (Merritt, Fain, and Turner 2006; Tonry 2006).
- Well-run and well-targeted treatment programs of a variety of sorts have been demonstrated to be capable of achieving significant reductions in reoffending (Gaes et al. 1999; Halliday 2001; Welsh and Farrington 2006).
- Restorative justice programs of diverse kinds have been shown to be preferred to regular criminal justice processes by offenders and victims alike, more likely to result in offenders' successful completion of resulting obligations, and no more likely to result in reoffending (Braithwaite 2002).

With that knowledge, and the aspiration to do so, we could build sentencing systems that take account simultaneously of the state's responsibilities to respect its citizens' liberties and autonomy and to assure the stability and security that allow people to live their lives in peace.

Building sentencing systems that are rational, just, and effective starts with understanding what sentencing is for and what it can do. This essay therefore examines the purposes and functions of sentencing and sentencing reform. Unless we are clear about them, we will not have much success at designing sensible, effective, and workable systems for the twenty-first century.

"Sentencing reform" means different things to different people, depending on whether the proponent wants sentencing made softer, tougher, fairer, more consistent, more efficient, more economical, more transparent, or more effective at preventing crime. Whether a proposed change counts in the eyes of others as a reform depends on what the proponent wants to accomplish and whether others think that a good thing.

The same observations apply to sentencing. Whether a sentencing system or practice can be said to work well depends on its purposes, what it is supposed to do, and how well it does that. Generally when people discuss the "purposes" of punishment, they refer to normative rationales such as retribution or crime prevention through deterrence, incapacitation, rehabilitation, and moral education.

Examination of normative purposes, and how adequately and consistently they are manifested in sentencing policies and practices, however, is only the beginning of analysis of the effectiveness of a sentencing system. Practitioners and policy makers want sentencing to accomplish other things as well. They include efficiency, cost-effectiveness, and public confidence. They also sometimes want sentencing systems, and legislation affecting them, to help them achieve personal goals, advance ideological agendas, and pursue partisan political objectives. Pursuit of all these aims can be thought of as a "function" of sentencing or sentencing reform.

Functions can be thought of instrumentally, as though sentencing systems and policies were machines. Whether a machine can be said to work well depends on what it is supposed to do, and typical occupants of various institutional roles sometimes differ about that. Distinctions need to be made among *primary* functions, the things we want to do directly; *ancillary* functions, other things related to primary functions that we also want to accomplish; and *latent* functions, collateral things some people want to accomplish that are unrelated to the aims of primary or ancillary functions.

Primary and ancillary functions are straightforward because they are instrumental. Certain things are done in pursuit of certain aims. Latent functions are more complex because, while they can be instrumental, they need not be. They can be thought of in terms of social functionalism, doing things whether we want them to or not, and whether we are aware they do them or not. Loic Wacquant has argued, for example, that American punishment policies since 1970 have served to maintain racial hierarchy in the United States, something achieved in earlier generations through slavery and then through Jim Crow laws and related social conventions (Wacquant 2001). Contemporary punishment policies need not consciously have been directed at that result, but that is what (Wacquant would say) they have done and what accordingly can be thought of as one of their latent functions. A more benign Durkheimian example of a not necessarily purposive latent function is the norm-reinforcing (or undermining) effects of imposition of particular punishments for particular crimes (Durkheim [1893] 1933). Some judges may have this in mind when they impose sentences, but it will happen whether they do or not.

For the rest of this essay, I set noninstrumental latent functions aside. Here I am interested in instrumental latent functions, things practitioners and policy makers want to accomplish that are unrelated to the primary functions of punishment and prevention. The most common of these are pursuing the actor's personal self-interest, pursuing partisan political objectives, and bearing witness to ideological beliefs.

People setting sentencing policy or imposing sentences in individual cases have multiple motives and pursue diverse objectives, and these may be more or less legitimate. The primary functions of sentencing, most people would agree, are imposition of appropriate punishments and prevention of crime. People differ on what makes a punishment appropriate and how best to prevent crime, but few people would disagree that these are legitimate functions.

There are greater disagreements about the ancillary functions. Some people believe that defendants must be offered incentives to plead guilty in order to manage case loads; others believe that inappropriate. Some people believe that maintaining good personal and professional relations with others in the courtroom work group can justify plea bargains that might not otherwise be countenanced; others disagree. Some people, especially corrections officials, believe that judges should take resource considerations into account when setting sentences; others, especially judges, disagree. These disagreements are the products of different conceptions of justice but relate closely to considerations of appropriate punishments and effective crime prevention.

Few people would disagree that some latent functions are palpably illegitimate. For example, in order to win favorable publicity, a judge up for a vigorously contested reelection might impose a much harsher sentence in a particular case than can be justified in his own mind or than at other times he would. The latent function would be winning reelection, and few would regard that as a legitimate reason to punish an offender especially severely. Nor would most judges themselves regard it as legitimate: a judge would be little more likely publicly to justify a sentence "because that sentence will help me get reelected" than "because my daughter is the prosecutor," "because I'm in a bad mood today," or "because I always punish Hispanics more harshly than whites." Policy decisions or individual sentences that result not from good-faith efforts to achieve the ends of appropriate punishment or effective crime prevention but from the decision maker's wish to achieve other unrelated personal, ideological, or political goals are illegitimate.

If future sentencing systems are to be more successful than their recent predecessors, they must attend to both purposes and functions.

Many initiatives of the past two decades failed to address purposes coherently. The best examples are broad three-strikes laws such as California's (Zimring, Hawkins, and Kamin 2001), the federal 100-to-one crack/powder cocaine sentencing differential (McDonald and Carlson 1993), and many mandatory minimum sentence laws for drug offenses (Tonry 2006). These all resulted in individual sentences that those obliged to apply them often found unjustly severe, and all violated commonsense notions of the relative seriousness of the crimes they affected and other more serious crimes that they did not.

Some misconceived laws resulted from policy makers' overreaction to emotional incidents, such as the death of college basketball star Len Bias, apparently from a crack cocaine overdose, commonly credited as driving the enactment of the federal 100-to-one law (Kennedy 1997). Others may have resulted from simple failures to understand the implications of seemingly straightforward changes. Many, however, resulted not from confused purposes or failures to forecast a law's effects but from the use of sentencing "reforms" to achieve personal, partisan, and ideological goals. Put differently, illegitimate latent goals displaced legitimate primary and ancillary goals. The inevitable result is that individual human beings, like the hypothetical defendant sentenced more severely to help the judge get reelected, received unjust punishments.

Doing better requires two things: first, that both purposes and functions be considered in setting sentencing policy, so that primary and ancillary functions can be taken into account in ways that do not produce individual injustices; second, that illegitimate latent functions be recognized for what they are and eschewed. The second of these can never be completely successful since that would require that human nature be changed. Policy makers may be able, however, to do better than they recently have done if they come to understand that sentencing has multiple functions, that ethical policy making requires that they be recognized, and that many of the latent functions cannot be openly and honestly acknowledged without embarrassment.

The rest of this essay provides the analysis on which the preceding observations rest. Section I sets out a fuller framework for thinking about purposes and functions of sentencing. Sections II and III, applying that framework, examine current knowledge concerning the primary and ancillary functions. Section IV examines latent functions.

The last distills lessons honest policy makers might wish to consider as they devise the sentencing systems of the twenty-first century.

If only legitimate primary and ancillary functions were to be sought to be performed and account were taken of what has been learned from the last thirty years of changes in sentencing laws, here is what a rational, just, and effective sentencing system would look like:

- Only normative purposes and legitimate primary and ancillary functions of sentencing would be taken into account in setting sentencing policy or setting sentences in individual cases, and illegitimate latent functions would be eschewed in both contexts.
- Limiting retributivism, the idea that retributive concerns can set meaningful upper and lower bounds within which other considerations may validly be taken into account in setting sentences in ordinary cases, would be adopted as the system's primary normative rationale, and its scope would be extended to encompass both purposes and functions.
- Subject to that premise, guidelines would set out ranges of presumptive sentences from within which judges would normally select sentences in ordinary cases; but judges would have authority, subject to observance of the requirements of *Booker* and *Blakely*, to depart from guidelines to impose other sentences as long as they specified for the record their reasons for doing so.
- In setting presumptive sentencing ranges, policy makers would not take into account evidence on deterrent and incapacitative effects of sentencing but would authorize judges to take such evidence into account in setting individual sentences within (but not above) presumptive ranges.
- In promulgating sentencing guidelines, policy makers would authorize judges to take account of rehabilitative and restorative programs and possibilities to individualize sentences both within and below (but not above) presumptive ranges, in the latter case as long as they specified for the record their reasons for doing so.
- All mandatory minimum, including three-strikes, laws would be repealed.

I. A Framework

The fundamental purposes and primary functions of sentencing are clear, and are the same: to punish criminals and prevent crimes. There are, however, other functions that concern officials and policy makers. They range from encouraging most defendants to plead guilty and managing criminal justice budgets to reassuring the public and getting reelected.

People concerned primarily with the word justice in "criminal justice" would say that the overriding purpose of sentencing is the imposition of punishments that are just relative to prevailing normative criteria; the overriding functional goal would be to ensure, or at least maximize the likelihood of, imposition of just punishments according to those criteria. People concerned primarily with the word "criminal" would say that the overriding purpose of sentencing is the prevention of crime and accordingly that the overriding functional goal is to minimize the incidence of crime and its consequences. To distinguish the question of what purposes should be pursued from the question of whether laws have been fairly and effectively applied relative to those purposes, I refer to the first as *purposes* and the second as *distributive functions*.

The distinction between purposes and functions may appear a bit obscure, but it should not be. Richard Frase and I were recently asked by the editors of the *Stanford Law Review* to write separate essays on purposes (Frase 2005*a*) and functions (Tonry 2005*a*) of sentencing. Initially we thought the distinction a bit artificial but decided it was not, for two main reasons. First, normative purposes provide the theoretical criteria for deciding whether sentences imposed on individual offenders are just or appropriate, whereas distributive functions relate to how well or poorly any particular sentencing system distributes sentences according to those criteria. Second, sentencers and designers of sentencing systems have multiple functions in mind when they make decisions, and some of them, such as managing resources effectively, are entirely independent of normative purposes of sentencing.

All mainstream contemporary theories include crime prevention among the purposes of punishment, though they vary widely in what ways, with what weight, and subject to what constraints prevention may be taken into account. Most people, however, believe that prevention and diminution of crime, fear of crime, and their consequences are important and legitimate functions of sentencing. These are the *preventive functions*.

Many practitioners would also include efficiency, cost-effectiveness, and resource management among the functional goals of an acceptable sentencing system. Managers need to set and pursue substantive priorities, allocate personnel and resources, meet performance goals, and operate within their budgets. They also need to maintain good working relations with other agencies and officials who can make their work easier or harder, and thereby make achievement of other goals easier or harder. These are *management functions*.

Some policy makers and analysts urge that it is important that governments reassure the public, maintain confidence in the legal system, denounce wrongful behavior, and reinforce basic social norms. Contemporary analyses of "expressive" policies emphasize government officials' wishes and needs to assure the public that things are being done to address subjects that trouble them (Garland 2001). Recent work on legitimacy and procedural justice emphasizes that justice needs to be seen to be done (Tyler 2003). Durkheimian analyses portray criminal law as a primary contributor to maintenance and refinement of basic social norms and its dramaturgical features as key sources of social cohesion (Durkheim [1893] 1933). These are *communicative functions*.

The first two of these, distribution and prevention, concern primary goals (what sentencing "is supposed to do"). The third, management, is an ancillary goal (how institutional imperatives can be acknowledged while pursuing primary goals).

The fourth, communication, is the most complex and multifaceted and operates at all three functional levels. Communication of legal threats and acknowledgment in court processes and outcomes of basic social norms are necessary to achieve the primary goals of distribution and prevention. Communication about court processes and procedures and likely punishments is key to achievement of a variety of management goals. These might, however, be thought of as incidental components of primary and ancillary functions. To avoid repetition, I discuss communicative functions among the ancillary functions, even though each of the three functional levels includes communicative elements.

The more controversial forms of communication relate to *latent* functions. Practitioners and policy makers are sometimes moved by personal, ideological, and partisan objectives. People sometimes make decisions or support policies because it is in their personal self-interest, because they want to bear witness to their ideological beliefs, or because they want to pursue partisan political advantage. Earlier I provided an example of a judge imposing a harsher than otherwise sentence in order to help his reelection prospects. A parallel example for policy making is the legislator or governor who proposes policy changes he knows will not achieve their purported primary aims and will, if enacted, cause new injustices, because he hopes their enactment will help him get reelected (e.g., California Governor Pete Wilson's three-strikes proposal: Zimring, Hawkins, and Kamin [2001]).

In the preceding paragraphs, I identified a number of purposes and functions:

A. Purposes (belaboredly, these could be called normative functions)
B. Primary functions
    1. Distribution (consistency, evenhandedness, fairness)
    2. Prevention (crime, fear of crime, costs and consequences of both)
    3. Communication (threat communication, denunciation of wrongful behavior, reinforcement of basic social norms)
C. Ancillary functions
    1. Management (efficiency, cost-effectiveness, resource management)
    2. Communication (procedural justice, legitimacy, public confidence)
D. Latent functions
    1. Self-interest
    2. Ideology
    3. Partisanship
    4. Communication

Normative purposes provide the ultimate criteria by which the justness of a punishment system is assessed. The most important of the remaining functions are the distributive functions of doing justice and the preventive functions of minimizing crime and its consequences. These can be pursued effectively only if account is taken of the implications and constraints associated with the ancillary functions and if ways can be devised to limit pernicious influences of the latent functions.

II. Purposes and Primary Functions

The pre-*Booker* federal sentencing guidelines are a case study in what can happen when policy makers fail to be clear about their purposes and functional goals. Here are four examples. First, the U.S. Sentencing Commission did not make the guidelines' normative purposes clear. It could have; the exceedingly detailed guidelines fine-tuned sentencing to circumstances (e.g., weapons, victim injury, property loss, role in the offense) that relate closely to culpability and thus were largely consonant with retributive purposes. Instead, the commission chose not to make the "profoundly difficult" choice of adopting explicit purposes, electing instead "an empirical approach that uses data estimating the existing sentencing system as the starting point" (1987, pp. 1.3–1.4). Guidelines for drug crimes were a major exception to the "empirical approach," with the result that the guidelines prescribed much harsher punishments for drug crimes than for violent crimes that most people consider more serious and thereby violated widely held proportionality notions. Probably the single most recurrent criticism by practitioners was that the guidelines sentences for drug cases were unjustly severe.[5] This led to widespread circumvention, which increased as time passed (Bowman and Heise 2001). Adopting explicit purposes, and then being guided by them, would have produced guidelines that were more internally consistent and normatively acceptable to practitioners and would more effectively have performed their distributive functions.

Second, the commission was worried that lawyers would manipulate the guidelines by means of charging and plea bargaining decisions and adopted the "relevant conduct" policy as a countermeasure. The logic was that if judges were required to impose sentences on the basis of the defendant's "actual offense behavior," charges to which the defendant pled guilty would generally not much matter (U.S. Sentencing Commission 1987, pp. 1.5–1.6).[6] In practice, the system did not work that way. The sentencing guidelines were widely circumvented by prosecutors, defense lawyers, and judges (Nagel and Schulhofer 1992; Schulhofer and Nagel 1997; Bowman and Heise 2001). The notion that offenders are to be punished for what the judge believed they did, as opposed to what they were convicted of, offended widely held notions of procedural fairness and produced such unjust results that the Supreme Court intervened in *Booker* and demoted the guidelines from

[5] A survey of federal appellate and trial judges conducted by the commission found that 73.7 percent of district court judges and 82.7 percent of circuit court judges reported that drug-trafficking sentences were "greater than appropriate" (U.S. Sentencing Commission 2003, exhibits II-4, III-4).

[6] The major exception is that guidelines are trumped by plea bargains to offenses bearing lower statutory maximums than guidelines prescribe.

strongly presumptive to advisory. The fundamental difficulty was that policy makers in the U.S. Sentencing Commission, the U.S. Department of Justice, and the U.S. Congress cared less about sentencing's distributive functions than did the judges and prosecutors whose job it was to apply them.[7]

Third, by attempting to constrain prosecutorial choices radically, the guidelines failed to acknowledge practitioners' needs to achieve various management goals and thereby obstructed performance of ancillary functions practitioners believed important. Judges and prosecutors typically believe that the smooth operation of the courts depends on high rates of guilty pleas and that incentives are necessary to induce them. This is one of the foreseeable reasons why the guidelines often were circumvented.

Fourth, the guidelines failed to perform some of their communicative functions adequately; through their rigidity and severity and the relevant conduct rule, they undermined perceptions of their own legitimacy in the eyes of the judges and lawyers who were expected to implement them. Legal rules that possess moral legitimacy are much more likely to be followed than those that do not.

Judges and prosecutors see themselves as in the business of doing justice. Judges, prosecutors, defense counsel, and probation officers work together on an ongoing basis in most courtrooms. Shared understandings evolve about "going rates" and about reasonable and unreasonable sentences and modes of official behavior (Eisenstein, Flemming, and Nardulli 1988, p. 376). Practitioners in work groups believe that the standards they observe and apply are good ones, not merely cynically because observing those standards helps them accomplish what they want to do, but because the standards are normatively appropriate and result in reasonably just results. Arthur Rosett and Donald Cressey described this in their report on plea bargaining in California: "Even in the adversary world of law, men who work together and understand each other eventually develop shared conceptions of what are acceptable, right, and just ways of dealing with specific kinds

[7] The best illustrations of this are the Congress's enactment in 1986 of mandatory minimum sentences for drug crimes that required sentences much harsher than were typically imposed for violent crimes and the commission's decisions to incorporate even more severe drug crime penalties into the guidelines than the Congress prescribed (Tonry 1996, pp. 96–98). These decisions had the effect of making sentences much severer and the guidelines much more complicated than they needed to be to pursue sentencing's legitimate primary and ancillary functions.

of offenses, suspects, and defendants. These conceptions form the bases for understandings, agreements, working arrangements, and cooperative attitudes. Norms and values grow and become a frame of reference which prosecutors, defense lawyers, judges, and experienced offenders all use for deciding what is fair in each case" (1976, pp. 90–91).

When laws or guidelines prescribe sentences that are harsher than most practitioners believe reasonable or just, there is a problem. When laws require that sentences be calculated primarily by means of mechanical scoring systems, as the federal guidelines did, rather than by looking closely at the circumstances of individual cases, as most practitioners believe justice requires, there is a problem. Judges and lawyers are socialized into both enforcing the law and doing justice. When they cannot do both, doing justice often trumps enforcing the law, especially when, as in the case of the federal guidelines, the law lacks moral authority. The federal guidelines, however, were but an extreme instance of a wider failure to take conscious account of sentencing's multiple and sometimes conflicting purposes and functions.

A. Purposes (Normative Functions)

The overriding normative function of a sentencing system in a society committed to individual liberty, procedural fairness, and limited powers of government is to assure that individuals convicted of crimes receive the sentences that, in principle, they should. Those final words are purposely indeterminate about the principles that should govern. Preponderant views about this vary across time and space. For most of the twentieth century through the 1970s, utilitarian ideas about crime prevention through rehabilitation and incapacitation were predominant (Rothman 1980); they have not gone away, but in more recent decades they have been eclipsed by retributive and just deserts emphases on the desirability of apportioning the severity of punishment to offenders' blameworthiness (e.g., von Hirsch 1976; von Hirsch and Ashworth 2005).[8] Interest in rehabilitation has revived in the early twenty-first century (as evidenced by drug and similar courts offering individualized, treatment-based dispositions, a plethora of new treatment programs in institutions and in the community, and the "prisoner reentry"

[8] If one assumed that policy making since the mid-1980s was implicitly based on principled ideas about purposes, they would be a not very coherent mixture of retributive and preventive purposes; I know of no scholar who has attempted to delineate a normative theory that would justify recent policies.

movement), and interest in restorative (Braithwaite 2002) and community justice (Clear and Karp 1999) and in therapeutic jurisprudence (Winick and Wexler 2003) has burgeoned. These developments may signal an immanent shift in preponderant views.

Immanuel Kant, the German idealist philosopher whose ideas are often regarded as marking the beginning of development of modern theories of retributive punishment, argued that the only morally appropriate justification for punishment is that it is deserved and is appropriately apportioned to the offender's wrongdoing (Kant [1796] 1887). Jeremy Bentham ([1789] 1970), the bellwether of utilitarianism, to the contrary, argued that only net positive preventive effects—achieved usually through deterrence, incapacitation, and rehabilitation—can justify the imposition of pain that punishment entails. A Benthamite corollary, commonly referred to as the principle of parsimony, forbids imposition of pain that is not outweighed by pains averted.

The normative choices involved in deciding what principles should govern sentencing have important ethical and moral dimensions about which reasonable people differ, sometimes fundamentally, and the choices sometimes have radically different implications for policy. A thoroughgoing Kantian theory of sentencing would predicate just punishments on the relative degree of blameworthiness imputable to the offender on the basis of his culpability and, perhaps, the harm he has caused.[9] There would be no room in the calculus for incapacitative concerns based on predictions of dangerousness, deterrent concerns based on belief that prospective wrongdoers might be dissuaded, rehabilitative concerns aimed at enhancing the offender's prospects for law-abidingness, or restorative concerns aimed at healing broken relationships, unless they could be achieved within the scope of a sentence justified in retributive terms.

Conversely, a thoroughgoing Benthamite theory of sentencing would allow those various crime-preventive concerns to be acted on irrespective of the seriousness of the offender's culpability, constrained only by the parsimonious principle that no punishment cause greater harm, taking offenders into account when making the calculation, than

[9] Or, some might say, the harm he foreseeably caused, but this is redundant since foreseeability of harm is an element of any coherent conception of culpability.

it prevents.[10] Ultimately, a utilitarian calculus could justify imposition of a very serious punishment on an offender who committed a venial offense, or even on an innocent person whom everyone except the judge believed to be guilty.[11]

No American jurisdiction has ever created a punishment system based on thoroughgoing retributivist or utilitarian premises, but several have come close. Washington State sentencing guidelines in the 1980s were primarily based on just-deserts reasoning, appellate courts enthusiastically monitored judicial compliance, parole release was abolished, and the only conditions to which probationers and parolees could be subjected related to their criminality (Boerner and Lieb 2001). The federal sentencing guidelines, even though the commission insisted it had not adopted normative premises, were rigid and prescriptive and closely apportioned sentences to detailed offense characteristics that most people would have little difficulty relating to relative blameworthiness. Until California abolished parole release in 1976, all prison sentences were for "one year to the statutory maximum," and in theory prisoners were to be released only when they had been rehabilitated or no longer required incapacitation. California's parole system, however, is long since gone, Washington's guidelines have changed in many respects, and the federal guidelines have been eviscerated.

There are good reasons why no relatively philosophically pure sentencing system exists or has been seriously proposed at a policy level. The Kantian and Benthamite visions offer models that identify important moral choices, trade-offs, and compromises. Neither, however, can be converted to the real world. The Kantian ideal has well-known problems. Its claim that respect for individuals' moral autonomy requires that we punish them "in like kind," perfectly commensurately with the wrongdoing embodied in their crimes (Pincoffs 1991, pp.

[10] I ignore for purposes of this essay the complexity of distinguishing between rule and act utilitarianism and the practical problems of ever knowing enough to make the necessary utilitarian calculations.

[11] The accusation that utilitarians must be prepared, if true to their principles, to punish innocent but apparently guilty people is a classic retributivist objection to utilitarianism. Utilitarians generally reply that information about such punishments of innocents would inevitably slip out and foster a general sense of insecurity ("it could happen to me") that would be more harmful than any preventive gains fleetingly gained from the undeserved punishment (Hart 1968, p. 25). It is an irresoluble argument but a red herring. Harsh punishments of people guilty of trifling crimes raise the same problem. No one argues that a utilitarian system would prohibit harsh punishments for minor offenders on the basis of deterrent, incapacitative, or rehabilitative considerations, as long as the parsimony principle is observed.

16–17), cannot be converted into practicable policy. Killing a murderer fits the model, but what about the punishment for an attempted murderer? How can a rape be punished in like kind or, harder, an attempted rape? Would anyone really want to torture or maim an assailant who caused serious pain or disfigurement? How can deserved punishments for property crimes be calculated, or "victimless" crimes, or inchoate crimes (conspiracy, attempts, aiding and abetting)?

People have tried to solve these problems, but the solutions necessarily are imperfect. Andrew von Hirsch devised a system of ordinal proportionality in which punishment in absolute like kind is not sought but punishment proportionate to the blameworthiness expressed in the crime (von Hirsch 1993). "Proportionality" here, however, is not relative to the nature of the crime but to punishments for other more, less, and comparably blameworthy crimes. The difficulties here, though less well known than those affecting a purer Kantian model, are also considerable (Tonry 2005*b*). There are three principal ones. First, the principled call for comparable punishments for comparably situated offenders is illusory. Widely divergent practices concerning charging, plea bargaining, and sentencing discounts for guilty pleas make seemingly comparable offenses of conviction widely diverse and seemingly comparable offenders substantially different in their blameworthiness.

Second, definitions of offenses in U.S. law are typically broad: "robbery" encompasses behavior ranging from gangland holdups to takings of basketballs on school playgrounds. Punishing every person convicted of robbery the same way would produce what Arie Freiberg (2001) called "unjustifiable parity." The example I just gave is extreme, of course, but the problem is a general one. Most guidelines systems divide all felonies into a small number of categories of severity, and they inevitably include widely diverse kinds of crimes. Because of wide differences in any jurisdiction in charging and plea bargaining practices, substantially similar crimes result in convictions for different crimes, and conviction offenses obscure wide differences in underlying culpable behavior.

Third, most important, von Hirsch's desert theory is subject to the "punishment of the innocents" charge that retributivists classically toss at utilitarians. The logic of the system requires that all offenders who fall within a category receive the same penalty, including when the severity of punishment for that category is increased for preventive reasons relating to some but not all members of the category. What this means is that some, perhaps many or most, offenders in a category will be punished more severely than their offense warrants because the architecture of the system requires it.[12] In the words of the classic retributive critique of utilitarian punishment theories, the offenders being punished more severely than they otherwise would be are being "used" as means to the end of maintaining the formal structure of the sentencing theory (Pincoffs 1991). As an ethical matter, it is difficult to distinguish between knowingly punishing an innocent person and knowingly punishing a guilty person more than he or she deserves.

A pure utilitarian model also has well-known practical limits, over and above the punishment of the innocents problem. The overriding one is that the necessary "felicific calculus," as Bentham called it, is impossible. Fundamentally contested literatures on economic costs of crime, especially pain and suffering (McDougall et al. 2006), deterrent and incapacitative effects (Nagin 1998), and crime prevention more broadly demonstrate that we are far away from a time when we know enough to take the Benthamite model seriously. Any decisions about the utilitarian gains and pains associated with punishment in an individual case or within broad-based general policies can be little better than guesswork.

On a continuum between those Kantian and Benthamite poles lie hybrid punishment theories that combine retributive and preventive considerations in diverse ways. One, proposed by Andrew von Hirsch (1993), is that culpability concerns predominate heavily but that deterrent or incapacitative concerns may be taken into account in setting the penalty scale. If longer sentences are wanted, they may be imposed collectively on all equally culpable people, by moving that offense up the scale or by extending the scale, and thereby punishing all offenders more severely, but they may not be imposed on an individualized basis. This is unsatisfactory because it forces a choice between forgoing

[12] This sentence conflates two separate problems. First, insofar as overbroad offense definitions or charging and plea bargaining practices result in substantially different crimes bearing the same label, sentencing all bearing that label in the same way punishes those whose crimes were less serious more severely than they deserve. Second, as I explain below in the text, von Hirsch would forbid the use of crime preventive considerations (e.g., deterrence or incapacitation) to increase sentences for individuals and would instead allow them to be taken into account only to increase sentences for the entire category of offenses in which target individuals fall (von Hirsch and Ashworth 2005). The effect would be to increase sentences for all in the category so that some can be punished more severely for instrumental reasons.

seemingly realizable preventive goals and gratuitously punishing some, or many, in a class more severely than their crime would otherwise merit. The former is politically and possibly ethically impracticable. The latter violates the parsimony principle's injunction against imposition of gratuitous suffering.[13]

A second hybrid theory, associated with Andrew von Hirsch and Martin Wasik (Wasik and von Hirsch 1988), would permit preventive considerations to influence the type but not the severity of punishment. Punishments must be apportioned to blameworthiness; but if two punishments (e.g., *X* days of imprisonment versus *Y* days of community service) have a comparable punitive bite, a choice may be made between them on preventive bases. Their proposal assumes, however, that few penalties can be made comparably punitive and accordingly specifies that imprisonment is more severe than community-based punishments; they in turn are more severe than fines, allowing for interchangeability only at the margins between types of punishments. This is unsatisfactory generally because it is primarily a variation of the preceding hybrid theory and because it consigns preventive considerations to the narrowest margins.

A third hybrid theory, proposed by Paul Robinson (1987), calls for strict observance of culpability standards except in a small number of cases for which disproportionate punishments would prevent really serious harms. This is unsatisfactory for conceptual (how in principle justify the abandonment of retributive premises?), definitional (what harms count as really serious?), and empirical reasons (how can we know we're additionally punishing the correct people? We're not very good at predicting really serious future harms).

A fourth hybrid, proposed by former English civil servant John Halliday (2001, app. 8), is described as being a form of limiting retributivism concerned with "consistency of approach rather than uniformity of outcome" (p. 20). The notion is that the same set of punitive and preventive considerations should be taken into account in every case, but the seriousness of the offense would limit the maximum sentence that should be imposed. This is at best obscure and implies something closer to a theory of procedural than to a theory of substantive justice.

[13] Von Hirsch's response (1993) would be that parsimony should be sought at collective levels by setting the overall penalty scale as low as possible while furthering the aim of treating like cases alike. General parsimony-based objections could be raised to this position, but, importantly for the point made in the text, it does not speak to the special problems involved in raising the overall scale to pursue preventive goals.

It is in any case a very weak form of limiting retributivism in that the upper limits of aggregate punishment that may be imposed are vaguely expressed and are subject to major exceptions for serious offenses, repeat offenders, and offenders who fit into a very broad definition of dangerousness (Tonry 2004*a*).

The fifth and sixth hybrids are other versions of limiting retributivism. In "asymmetric proportionality," culpability sets strict upper limits on the sentence that may be imposed, but there are no lower limits (Lappi-Seppälä 2001). Finnish law sets out fairly detailed statutory principles that govern sentencing; they give pride of place to culpability considerations but allow on a case-by-case basis for the operation of other considerations including preventive considerations in a narrowly defined set of cases. The Finnish system, however, operates in a country in which most sentences are measured in days or weeks, sentences longer than a year are uncommon, and the total imprisonment rate including pretrial detainees fluctuates between sixty and seventy per 100,000 population, less than a tenth the American rate. Finland has no sentencing guidelines as Americans understand the term because the latitude for unwarranted disparities is incomparably lower. Asymmetric proportionality on the Finnish model is probably unsatisfactory for American adoption because it depends on Finland's very different punishment practices and penal culture and its application by career cadres of judges and prosecutors who subscribe to its values.

In Norval Morris's limiting retributivism (1974), culpability sets upper limits and for some but not all crimes sets lower limits. Compared with von Hirsch's proportionality doctrine, in which desert limits are artificial, set relative to sentences for lesser and greater crimes, Morris's are cultural. He famously urged that "not undeserved" was a more useful conception of culpability constraints on punishment than "deserved" because it is far easier for people to agree that a sentence is undeservedly harsh or unduly lenient than that it is just right. Within those bounds, however, for Morris, Bentham's parsimony principle, cause no unnecessary or gratuitous pain, required that the least severe "not undeserved" punishment be imposed.

Morris first set out his limiting retributivism argument in the early 1950s (Morris 1953), and it took its fullest form in his *Future of Imprisonment* (1974), before modern sentencing guidelines were more than a gleam in anyone's eyes. There is no reason in Morris's argument why the upper and lower bounds of allowable punishments cannot derive from policy decisions that grid-style guidelines made possible (as long as they respect cultural limits), as his later writings showed (e.g., Morris and Tonry 1990, chap. 3).

It appeared clear to Morris in 1974 that preventive considerations would seldom justify imposition of sentences more severe than the parsimonious minimum. The most successful predictions of dangerousness were wrong at least two times out of three, too often to justify confining people longer because they were purportedly dangerous, and the research evidence concerning deterrence and rehabilitation gave no grounds that either was sufficiently often effective[14] to justify deprivations of liberty on their basis.

The world has changed since 1974 in ways germane to Morris's analysis. Though the evidence concerning the effectiveness of deterrent and incapacitative penalties is not much stronger now than it was then, doubts about basing sentencing laws on them are much less influential. More significantly, the research evidence on rehabilitative programs has reversed, and both conventional wisdom and many meta-analyses and literature reviews agree that well-run, well-targeted programs can reduce reoffending rates (and drug abuse) (e.g., U.S. Surgeon General 2001; Farrington and Welsh, in this volume; Welsh and Farrington 2006).

This discussion of purposes supports two conclusions. First, as the discussion of the federal guidelines at this subsection's beginning showed, purposes have consequences and provide guidance that is necessary if policies are to be coherent, internally consistent, and perceived as just. Second, any coherent and practicable set of purposes will be embodied in a hybrid model.

In the sections that follow, and in the conclusion, I propose that both sentences imposed and legitimate functional goals pursued should be consistent with whatever normative purposes are set. For myself, and for most modern sentencing systems (Frase 1997, 2004, 2005*a*), something like Morris's limiting retributivism appears best to express the optimal balance of competing moral intuitions about punishment and crime prevention, but reasonable people disagree about that.

[14] In these views he was ahead of his time; Martinson's "What Works?" article, suggesting that existing evidence gave little basis for confidence in rehabilitative programs, did not appear until 1974. The National Academy of Sciences report on deterrence and incapacitation, whose conclusions Morris anticipated, did not appear until 1978 (Blumstein, Cohen, and Nagin 1978).

B. Distribution

Whatever the applicable normative purposes of a sentencing system may be, the principal distributive aims are consistency, evenhandedness, and fairness relative to those purposes. Imposition of punishment for crime is a paradigmatic instance of the conflict between individual liberty and collective interests. Sentencing is a process in which government actors are empowered to intrude on individuals' liberty and autonomy in order to prevent crimes and sanction wrongdoing. To be consistent with core values underlying constitutional notions of due process and equal protection, sentencing needs to respect offenders' rights to be treated as equals, to have decisions about them made deliberately and impartially, and to be dealt with under fair procedures.

I would be surprised if many people disagree. A major challenge for sentencing policy, however, is that consistency, evenhandedness, and fairness look different when viewed from different places. To legislators, a ten-year mandatory minimum sentence, three-strikes, or 100-to-one law is not necessarily inconsistent with those values. Nor, presumably, to members of the U.S. Sentencing Commission were the "actual-offense behavior" policies, drug-trafficking guidelines, or a decision to forbid judges to take account in sentencing of ethically important differences in individual offenders' circumstances.[15] From the perspective of policy making at the wholesale level, the policies were for Congress and the commission to set and for judges and prosecutors, equably, evenhandedly, and fairly, to implement.

If literally applied in every case, however, those policies would have made practitioners complicit in imposing sentences in many cases that everyone directly involved believed to be substantively or procedurally unjust. Practitioners see cases firsthand. Problems appear simpler the farther away the point from which they are observed. District court judges, whether liberal or conservative, or appointed by Republican or Democratic administrations, for example, who see living, breathing defendants, are more hostile to the federal guidelines than are appellate judges who see only written appellate briefs. The same generalization applies to laypeople. The more detailed the information people are given about particular criminal cases, the less harsh and stereotyped

[15] From the outset, the guidelines provided that such commonsense considerations as family responsibilities, drug dependence, and mental health problems were not "ordinarily relevant in determining whether the sentence should be outside the guidelines" (U.S. Sentencing Commission 1987, secs. 5H1.1–6).

the sentences they would impose become. As a result, as surveys in a number of countries show, the sentences laypeople would impose for particular kinds of cases are often less severe than the sentences judges do impose (Roberts et al. 2002).

Legislators and senior executive branch officials, by contrast, deal in stereotypes. Often, like citizens responding to survey questions, they think in terms of extreme cases, even when setting policies that will mostly be applied to run-of-the-mill ones. They are also more likely to think of sentencing policy in terms of its latent functions of self-interest, ideology, and partisanship, considerations that are much less likely to move practitioners when pondering an individual's fate. Nearly all judges and prosecutors—"officers of the court" in American legal systems—take their ethical obligation to do justice seriously. Policies that substantially obstruct their ability to do justice are likely to be resisted or undermined.

The federal guidelines often directed judges to impose sentences they believed to be unjustly severe (Zlotnick 2004).[16] In such circumstances, judges had three options: compliance, resignation, and circumvention. They could apply the guidelines as written, but at the cost of behaving unjustly; most did this much of the time, occasionally after announcing that they felt they had no alternative but to impose an unjust sentence. They could announce that the guidelines required them to impose an unjust sentence and, refusing to do so, resign. A few did this. They could resolve neither to impose an unjust sentence nor to defy the law openly nor to resign, but together with counsel circumvent the guidelines to produce a sentence everyone involved considered appropriate. Many did this, and increasing numbers did so as time passed (Bowman and Heise 2001).

J. Lawrence Irving, the first federal district court judge to resign in protest over the federal guidelines, was appointed by President Ronald Reagan. On resigning in 1990, he said: "If I remain on the bench I have no choice but to follow the law. I just can't, in good conscience, continue to do this" (*New York Times* 1990, p. 2). Federal district court judge John S. Martin resigned in 2003 over what he called "a sentencing system that is unnecessarily cruel and rigid" (Martin 2004, p.

[16] A U.S. Sentencing Commission survey in 2003 showed that 73.7 percent of district judges and 82.7 percent of circuit judges said that federal drug-trafficking sentences are inappropriately severe, which necessarily means that many judges appointed by Presidents Reagan, Bush I, and Bush II held this view (U.S. Sentencing Commission 2003, exhibits II-4, III-4).

A31). Richard Boylan's statistical analyses concluded that the guidelines' unpopularity led judges on average to retire earlier than they otherwise would have (Boylan 2004).

My personal experience working with judges and prosecutors is that most practitioners most of the time want to do justice in individual cases, to do the right thing, to achieve a just and appropriate sentence. When applicable laws make that difficult or impossible, they still feel powerfully moved to do so anyway.

This is human nature, and there is a lot of evidence for it, going back centuries. Between 1714 and 1830, the British Parliament created 156 new capital crimes punishable by death, many of them property offenses, but the number of executions fell by three-fourths. Why? Because juries refused to convict offenders or convicted them for offenses not punishable by death, and judges created and narrowly interpreted technical rules that had to be followed if death was to be imposed, but seldom were (Stephen [1883] 1977; Select Committee on Capital Punishment 1930; Hay 1975).

The American Bar Foundation in the 1950s and 1960s carried out major studies of criminal court operations in several states (Newman 1966; Dawson 1969; Miller 1969). Prosecutorial and judicial circumvention of mandatory sentences was common in each court studied. Exemplifying this, Donald Newman described the application in Michigan of a fifteen-year maximum sentence for nighttime burglary (compared with a five-year maximum for daytime burglary): "The frequency of altering nighttime burglary to breaking and entering in the daytime led one prosecutor to remark: 'You'd think all our burglaries occur at high noon'" (Newman 1966, p. 182). The maximum mattered so much then and there because, taking time off for good behavior into account, it set the date by which the parole board had to release a prisoner. A lower maximum was insurance against a much longer stay in prison.

As Frank Remington, executive director of the nearly two-decades-long series of projects, summarized, "Legislative prescription of a high mandatory sentence for certain offenders is likely to result in a reduction of charges at the prosecution stage, or if this is not done, by a refusal of the judge to convict at the adjudication stage. The issue . . . thus is not solely whether certain offenders should be dealt with severely, but also how the criminal justice system will accommodate to the legislative change" (Remington 1969, p. xvii).

Evaluations of the effects of mandatory minimums enacted in the

1970s in Massachusetts (Rossman et al. 1979), Michigan (Heumann and Loftin 1979), and New York (Joint Committee 1978) reached the same conclusions. So did an evaluation of Oregon's Measure 11, enacted by referendum in 1994 and requiring lengthy mandatory sentences for people convicted of sixteen serious crimes (Merritt, Fain, and Turner 2003, 2006). An evaluation of New Jersey's 1994 "No Early Release Act," requiring offenders to serve 85 percent of their sentences before release, hypothesized that changes in plea bargaining would largely nullify the act and result in times served little different from before the law took effect. That is what was found (McCoy and McManimon 2003).

Experience with the federal guidelines was the same. During their first decade, a host of studies, some sponsored by the U.S. Sentencing Commission, showed that circumvention of the guidelines' harshest and most rigid provisions was commonplace (Nagel and Schulhofer 1992; Schulhofer and Nagel 1997). In recent years, Frank Bowman and Michael Heise (2001) showed that a wide range of circumvention techniques by prosecutors and judges resulted throughout the 1990s in continuously decreasing average sentence lengths in the federal courts.

The consistent evidence that practitioners often circumvent sentencing laws mandating sentences they believe to be unjust should not be surprising. James Eisenstein and his colleagues, reporting on research on how practitioners in felony courts in nine counties reached sentencing decisions, observe that sentences result from "accommodations among competing values and interests that support these values, accommodations that are superimposed on a common basic structure supported by broad consensus." Of reforms imposed from outside, they conclude that "the more radical a proposed change, the less likely is its adoption" (Eisenstein, Flemming, and Nardulli 1988, p. 294).

C. Prevention

The preventive functions focus on crime, fear of crime, and reduction in their costs and consequences. For purposes of this essay, I assume that efforts to prevent crime will also lessen fear and reduce crime's costs and consequences; that is a reasonable assumption, even though a finer-tuned analysis would discuss different policy mechanisms for achieving each outcome.[17]

[17] A harm-reduction approach to drug policy, e.g., might imply different drug policy

The preventive functions center on the collective interest in domestic tranquility, on enabling citizens to get on with their lives in security. These are core functions of the state and basic goals of criminal law and punishment. If they are to be pursued effectively, policy makers need to take account of the considerable body of knowledge on the effectiveness of sanctions.

Precisely how crime prevention, fear reduction, and cost savings should be sought involves policy decisions about which reasonable people differ and depends in part on what normative purposes are deemed applicable. I assume though that most policy makers regard crime prevention as among the justifiable normative purposes even if some sets of normative purposes that might be adopted might constrain the policy options available to pursue them. That being so, knowledge of what works, and what doesn't, is essential.

Writing on this subject is a ticklish business because it is probably generally assumed that the writer has axes to grind that shape how the evidence is summarized. Perhaps surprisingly, however, there is broad agreement among academics of liberal (e.g., Ruth and Reitz 2003) and conservative (e.g., Wilson 2002) political inclinations about conclusions to be drawn from research on the preventive effects of criminal sanctions and criminal justice interventions.

1. *Deterrence.* Current knowledge concerning deterrence is little different than eighteenth-century theorists such as Beccaria ([1764] 1995) supposed it to be: certainty and promptness of punishment are more powerful deterrents than severity. This does not mean that punishments do not deter. No one doubts that having a system of punishment has crime-preventive effects. The important question is whether changes in punishments have marginal deterrent effects, that is, whether a new policy causes crime rates to fall from whatever level they would otherwise have been at. Modern deterrent strategies, through sentencing law changes, take two forms: increases in punishments for particular offenses and mandatory minimum sentence (including "three-strikes") laws.

Imaginable increases in severity of punishments do not yield significant (if any) marginal deterrent effects. Three National Academy of

approaches than are now common in the United States. Fear of crime can be addressed by things such as increased visible police presence on the streets and improved neighborhood conditions (e.g., more street lighting, prompt repair of vandalized public property, altered traffic patterns) that lie far beyond the reach of the sentencing judge.

Sciences panels, all appointed by Republican presidents, reached that conclusion (Blumstein, Cohen, and Nagin 1978; Blumstein, Cohen, Roth, and Visher 1986; Reiss and Roth 1993), as has every major survey of the evidence (Cook 1980; Nagin 1998, 1999; von Hirsch et al. 1999; Doob and Webster 2003). This is also the belief, in my experience, of most experienced judges and prosecutors.

There are a number of good practical reasons why this widely reached conclusion makes sense. First, serious sexual and violent crimes are generally committed under circumstances of extreme emotion, often exacerbated by the influence of alcohol or drugs. Detached reflection on possible penalties or recent changes in penalties seldom if ever occurs in such circumstances. Second, most minor and middling and many serious crimes do not result in arrests or prosecutions; most offenders committing them, naïvely but realistically, do not expect to be caught. Third, those who are caught and prosecuted almost always are offered plea bargains that break the link between the crime and the prescribed punishment. Fourth, when penalties are especially severe, they are often, albeit inconsistently, circumvented by prosecutors and judges. Fifth, for many crimes including drug trafficking, prostitution, and much gang-related activity, removing individual offenders does not alter the structural circumstances conducing to the crime. Sixth, even when one ignores all those considerations, the idea that increased penalties have sizable marginal deterrent effects requires heroic and unrealistic assumptions about "threat communication," the process by which would-be offenders learn that penalty increases have been legislated or are being implemented.

Mandatory minimum penalties including three-strikes laws are nothing more than efforts to deter crime through penalty increases. The clear weight of the evidence, not surprisingly given what we know about severity increases generally, is that they are seldom if ever crime preventatives (e.g., Tonry 1996, chap. 4; Zimring, Hawkins, and Kamin 2001). Besides the not inconsiderable problem that mandatory minimums often are circumvented by practitioners, and always will be, the best evidence suggests that they have no marginal deterrent effects or have only modest effects that quickly waste away.

There is no good evidence that justifies fine-tuning sentences in individual cases, or enacting mandatory minimum sentence laws, for deterrent reasons. Having a system of punishments has deterrent effects. Having punishments scaled to the severity of offenses should provide rational incentives, as Beccaria and Bentham urged, to commit fewer rather than more serious crimes and, as Durkheim urged, to reinforce basic social norms.

The principal implications of current knowledge about deterrence are that certainty of punishment is more important than severity, that penalties that are too rigid or too severe result in widespread circumvention, and accordingly that mandatory minimums and three-strikes laws are ineffective, cause foreseeable injustices including gross disparities, and should be repealed.

2. *Incapacitation.* Incapacitative crime control strategies have some potential if used discriminatingly for people who commit very serious crimes at high rates (Monahan 2004). Offenders in confinement necessarily are disabled from committing offenses in the free community. We know a good bit more about incapacitation than we did thirty years ago. For a time, policies referred to as "collective incapacitation" were in vogue, influenced or at least evidenced by proposals in James Q. Wilson's *Thinking about Crime* (1976): extend all sentences of people convicted of violent crimes such as robbery by several years. This was soon shown to be impracticable. Large numbers of people are convicted of such crimes, but the average likelihood of recidivism is too low for the resulting huge increases in imprisonment to be justified (Blumstein, Cohen, and Nagin 1978; Cohen 1983).

This was followed by proposals for "selective incapacitation," catalyzed by a RAND Corporation report purporting to show the feasibility of such policies (Greenwood and Abrahamse 1982). This was soon discredited by a National Academy of Sciences report that showed that RAND's proposals worked with hindsight—it was based on self-reported past crimes of imprisoned violent offenders and in retrospect seemed to characterize those prisoners—but not prospectively (Blumstein et al. 1986). The prediction methods proposed were so over-inclusive, producing so many "false positives," that selective incapacitation was dismissed as impracticable.

After that, the theoretical writing and related empirical research on incapacitation pretty much came to a halt (Nagin 1998), but policy makers kept increasing lengths of sentences and accepted the imprisonment numbers that in the 1970s and early 1980s appeared unimaginable (Blumstein 1988). Collective incapacitation, in effect, became national policy, though not under that name. Studies in the late 1990s (Spelman 2000) and early in this century (Blumstein and Wallman

2000) concluded that mass imprisonment had reduced crime rates by 10–25 percent.

That last conclusion needs to be taken with a grain of salt for two reasons. First, comparable declines in crime rates occurred throughout the Western world, and no country other than the United States quintupled its imprisonment rate and experimented with mass imprisonment (Tonry 2004*b*, chap. 2). There is a reasonably good chance that American crime rates would have fallen like every other Western country's. The contrast with Canada—a flat imprisonment rate of 100 per 100,000 population for forty years but crime rate trends closely paralleling those in the United States (Doob and Webster 2006)—is especially cautionary. Second, and no less important, the studies concluding that incapacitation caused significant declines in crime rates are based on exceedingly complex modeling, which like all such modeling is highly vulnerable to the assumptions on which it is based and the modeling technique used; even highly sophisticated modelers seldom agree about either (viz., compare Webster, Doob, and Zimring [2006] with Kessler and Levitt [1999] and Rosenfeld, Fornango, and Baumer [2005*a*, 2005*b*] with Berk [2005]).

Incapacitative considerations have little legitimate place in decisions about individual offenders. The principal difficulty is that current incapacitation policies often, and expensively, target the wrong people. There are five main problems. First, incapacitation strategies targeted on repeat serious offenders generally result in long sentences for older offenders, most of whom in any case would soon desist from crime. This is known as the problem of residual career length; most thirty- or forty-year-old offenders are unlikely to continue as active offenders for long. There may be other justifications for confining such offenders for extended periods; but from an incapacitative perspective, such sentences are expensive, inefficient, and largely ineffective.

Second, strategies that target repeat offenders, in earlier times generally called "habitual-offender" laws and now called "three-strikes" laws, tend to ensnare socially inadequate, high-volume property offenders for whose prevented crimes lengthy prison sentences costing $40,000–$50,000 per year are not a sensible investment of public resources.

Third, for many offenses, including particularly drug sales, drug trafficking, and some gang-related crime, there is the "replacement" problem: offenders taken off the streets are quickly replaced by willing successors. Removing a seventeen-year-old drug dealer from an inner-city street corner is seldom likely to stop drug dealing at that corner; plenty of willing volunteers are usually waiting in the wings to step into what looks to be a lucrative opportunity. Similarly, unless the gang itself is completely destroyed, locking up one or several of its members will not stop its illegal activities. Other, and new, members will step in to replace their fallen comrades.

Fourth, there is the "false-positive" problem. For crimes of any significant seriousness, we are not very good at predicting which offenders will commit them in the future. For every "true positive" who will, three or four others predicted to do so will not. From a cost-benefit perspective, locking up all those people is not an obviously good investment of public resources. From a moral perspective, many people are troubled by the thought of lengthy confinement of individuals not because of their current crime but because they might commit another, especially when we know most will not.

Fifth, there is the "true-but-trifling-positive" problem. We are pretty good at predicting petty reoffending. David Farrington (1979) long ago demonstrated that an offender who has been arrested nine times has an 80 percent likelihood of being arrested again. This raises the cost-benefit question already mentioned: Is it worth $40,000–$50,000 per year to prevent shoplifting, minor thefts, acts of prostitution, or low-level drug dealing? It also raises the moral question whether the disproportionate character of a multiyear prison sentence for a person convicted of such crimes can be justified.

As with deterrence, the answer is not to forgo efforts to incapacitate offenders, but to do so intelligently. This means working hard at the policy level to develop strategies targeting particular kinds of serious offenders whose future behavior we can reasonably confidently predict and whose averted crimes save substantial suffering. At the individual level, however, it means limiting judges' authority to predicate sentencing decisions on incapacitative ambitions.

3. *Rehabilitation.* Prevention through rehabilitation looks to be a considerably more viable strategy in the early twenty-first century than it did during the closing decades of the twentieth. The view that "nothing works" was an important backdrop to the shift toward determinate sentencing, the abolition of parole, and adoption of incapacitative and deterrent crime control strategies. If we do not know how to reduce

offenders' prospects for later offending, it is hard to justify giving judges and parole boards broad discretion to individualize sentencing.

The prospects for rehabilitation, however, have changed radically. Evidence is accumulating from many sources—individual evaluations, meta-analyses (e.g., Lipsey and Landenberger 2006; Mitchell, MacKenzie, and Wilson 2006), literature reviews (e.g., Gaes et al. 1999; U.S. Surgeon General 2001), and practical experience—that well-managed, well-targeted programs can reduce participants' probability of reoffending. A wide range of programs, including drug treatment, anger management, cognitive-skills programs, sex offender treatment, and various educational- and vocational-skills programs have been shown to reduce reoffending (Gaes et al. 1999). A report from the English Home Office, which underpinned a massive reorganization of the English criminal justice system mandated by the Criminal Justice Act of 2003, concluded that "a reasonable estimate at this stage is that, if the [treatment] programmes are developed and applied as intended, to the maximum extent possible, reconviction rates might be reduced by 5–25 percentage points (i.e. from the present level of 56 percent within two years to (perhaps) 40 percent)" (Halliday 2001, p. 7). The most recent meta-analysis of the effects of cognitive-behavioral programs concluded that, on average, they reduced reoffending by 27 percent (Lipsey and Landenberger 2006). The proliferation of drug courts and prisoner reentry programs in the United States bears witness to the widely shared perception that some things work.

That litany of positive findings does not mean that reducing reoffending rates is easy. The results obtained from a well-funded pilot project, led by motivated people, cannot automatically be obtained by institutionalizing a new program model throughout a jurisdiction. A recent survey of violence prevention programs by the U.S. Surgeon General (2001) concluded that many programs can reduce violent offending but that the challenge is broad-based implementation. This is nonetheless much better news than the state of the evidence twenty-five years ago. We now know what we do; we need to figure out how to do it on a large scale.

An important implication is that rigid sentencing policies obstruct efforts to prevent crime through rehabilitation of offenders. For drug and other treatment programs to work, they must be targeted to the characteristics and needs of particular offenders, and this requires sentences to be individualized. With the fall of the nothing works psychology goes much of the case for rigid sentencing standards.

4. *Moral Education.* Deterrence, incapacitation, and rehabilitation are not needed to restrain most adults from selling drugs, burglarizing houses, holding up convenience stores, or mugging passersby. Most people's personal norms and values make predatory crime almost unthinkable. European scholars and theorists have long observed that the criminal law's main function is "general prevention": reinforcement of basic social norms that are learned in the home, the church, the school, and the neighborhood (Lappi-Seppälä 2001). These primary socializing institutions must do the heavy lifting—what the criminal courts can do is too little and too late for the criminal justice system to serve as a primary socializing institution—but it is important that law and the legal system reinforce those norms and not undermine them.

One implication, consistent with research findings on deterrence, is that it is more important that crimes have consequences than that the consequences be severe. Another, consistent with the research findings on rehabilitation, is that the choice of sanctions should be tailored to the circumstances of particular cases.

The evidence on the preventive effects of punishment all points in the same direction. A sentencing system that sets firm upper limits on punishments, scaled to offenders' culpability or the severity of their crimes, but allows substantial individualization below those limits, promises greater preventive effectiveness than current laws in the federal system or most states.

III. Ancillary Functions

The criminal justice system has limited material and manpower resources. Prosecutors, presiding judges, and corrections managers need to organize their offices, courtrooms, and programs to get the job done as efficiently and cost-effectively as possible while trying to achieve appropriate outcomes in individual cases.

Sentencing guidelines in some states have proved to be useful tools in reconciling distributive, preventive, and management functions. These guidelines have achieved reasonable consistency in sentences imposed and have proved an effective tool for projecting the effects of alternate policy proposals and thereby managing corrections resources and controlling corrections budgets at a systems level. Although plea bargaining occurs everywhere, in the states with well-designed guidelines, bargaining takes place in the shadow of the guidelines and has not been characterized by the widespread circumvention, and resulting disparities, that characterized the federal system (Tonry 1996; Reitz 2001, 2005*a*; Frase 2005*c*).

A. Efficiency and Cost-Effectiveness

Court dockets are crowded, treatment resources are scarce, and correctional programs including prisons are overcrowded and underresourced. Managers have to figure out how to juggle their budgets and manpower to keep cases flowing, hold backlogs down, and prioritize their resource allocations so that the most serious and important cases receive the attention they warrant. Most courts and prosecutors' offices have monthly case disposition and backlog targets; failure to meet them is interpreted as laziness or ineffectiveness. This is generally understood to mean that most cases must be resolved as quickly as possible. Trials should be avoided whenever possible, and bench trials are preferable to jury trials.

Plea bargaining is the mechanism for achieving most of those goals and requires that the state have something to offer the defendant to induce cooperation and that prosecutors, defense counsel, and judges get along. Generally, the parties do get along because many criminal court practitioners work for extended periods in the same setting and soon learn the prevailing conventions ("going rates") and get to know the relatively small number of people in the courtroom in which they work.

Peter Nardulli and his collaborators in the most extensive study to date of courtroom communities put it like this: "The web of interpersonal ties and mutual need that holds the [courtroom community] together also creates norms and understandings that guide and restrict behavior. In a sense court communities emerge because of the need to establish these understandings, as well as to meet other human needs . . . . It is in the interest of all to establish, abide by, and enforce a common set of understandings about how normal cases should be handled and how defendants should be punished" (Nardulli, Eisenstein, and Flemming 1988, p. 306).

People who are oppositional or uncooperative soon find that they receive little cooperation back and that they are felt by their colleagues to be unreasonable. Those are pretty effective sanctions for uncooperative behavior: "The importance attached to conflict avoidance and conflict management is another important component of the court community's court culture. In some communities, a great deal of emphasis was placed upon going along and getting along, upon not rocking the boat" (Nardulli, Eisenstein, and Flemming 1988, p. 125).

Lawyers and judges become socialized into the local courtroom culture, which, given that felony courts are usually staffed by people from the communities they serve, generally reflects prevailing community notions about right and wrong and the severity of punishment. People working in big-city courts tend to have somewhat different local cultures than people working in suburban and small-town courts. Legal cultures vary from city to city and region to region (Eisenstein, Flemming, and Nardulli 1988). A U.S. Sentencing Commission–sponsored study of prosecutorial circumvention of guidelines documented wide variations in legal culture in different federal district courts (Nagel and Schulhofer 1992).

What practitioners do largely depends on the prevailing courtroom culture. If sentencing statutes and guidelines set standards that are incompatible with local traditions and beliefs, local traditions often win out, with the acquiescence of everyone involved. Practitioners' needs to achieve management goals and the importance of local courtroom cultures together mean that local courts will do what is needed to operate efficiently and cost-effectively and to achieve outcomes that those involved consider appropriate and just. Sentencing standards that are too harsh, too lenient, or too mechanistic often will be circumvented.

B. Resource Management

Governments and individual agencies need to get their business done within the resource constraints presented by their budgets. They need to be able to predict changes in their likely flow of work and to plan for resources they will need in the future. These things inevitably entail choices.

One of the great advantages of sentencing guidelines is that they are a proven tool for effective resource management (Boerner and Lieb 2001; Wright 2002; Frase 2005*b*). States that adopted sentencing guidelines as a resource management tool have successfully tailored their sentencing policies to their correctional budgets and programs. By making sentencing decisions predictable in the aggregate, guidelines enable policy makers to project likely future resource needs. If, for example, a jurisdiction contemplates doubling sentence lengths for sex crimes, it can project how many more prison beds will be needed. If current and planned facilities cannot accommodate the increased numbers, policy makers can respond in a number of ways. They can appropriate funds to build new facilities, revise sentences for other offenses downward to free up the needed spaces, reconsider whether the sex offender proposal is a good idea, or do some combination of these things.

Sound resource management is a necessary characteristic of effective government and a primary rationale for sentencing guidelines systems. Its scope should extend to needs for nonincarcerative sanctions, availability of appropriately targeted rehabilitative programs, and effectuation of appropriately targeted incapacitation policies.

C. Communication

Communicative functions are described briefly, not because they are less important than the other functions but because the basic propositions can be simply stated. Communicative functions interact with normative, distributive, and preventive functions. Legitimacy and public confidence depend in part on whether the law is seen to operate reasonably and in ways that are consonant with widely held ideas about justice (including, e.g., that claims be fairly considered and that penalties be proportionate to the severity of crimes).

1. *Legitimacy.* Legitimacy is increasingly recognized as a key element in how people relate to government (Tyler 2003). Whether people have confidence in, support, and cooperate with public institutions is influenced by the institution's legitimacy in their eyes. People are more likely to react positively when the police stop them, or to accept an adverse decision by a court, if they believe that they have been treated fairly, that decisions about them have been evenhanded and impartial, and that they have had a chance to have their say. Sentencing policies that respect offenders' rights to be treated as equals, to have decisions about them made deliberately and impartially, and to be dealt with under fair procedures are more likely to be perceived as legitimate than policies that do not satisfy these requirements of procedural justice.

2. *Public Reassurance.* Sometimes laws are enacted or policies are adopted to "send a message" that the public's views have been noted

or that their anxiety, apprehension, or unhappiness has been noted. Sociologist David Garland (2001) argues that much recent crime control policy in the United States and England was adopted primarily for "expressive" reasons, not because policy makers necessarily thought that new, tougher policies would reduce crime rates but because they wanted to reassure an anxious public that was fearful of rising crime rates and troubled by the uncertainties of a rapidly changing world.

Legislators have long adopted symbolic policies meant primarily to acknowledge public anxiety. Senator Alfonse D'Amato of New York, for example, according to the *New York Times*, conceded that two amendments he successfully offered to federal crime legislation, "which Justice Department officials sa[id] would have little practical effect on the prosecution of crimes, might not solve the problem. 'But,' he said, 'it does bring about a sense that we're serious"' (Ifill 1991, p. A6). The seeming eighteenth-century English paradox that many more crimes were made punishable by death during a century in which the number of executions rapidly and substantially declined is generally explained in expressive terms; legislators were trying to stress the seriousness of the new death-eligible offenses, generally property crimes, even though there was little appetite for executing property offenders (Hay 1975).

3. *Public Confidence.* For nearly a decade the English government has explained major changes in criminal justice policy as parts of a larger effort to increase public confidence in the legal system (e.g., Home Office 2002). The criminal justice system is believed by the English government to lack credibility in the eyes of voters, and measures meant to make punishments harsher and more certain and convictions more likely are portrayed as parts of a larger campaign to increase public confidence in the legal system and generally. This is in effect a collective, bystander's parallel to legitimacy. Public confidence in the legal system is likely to increase if it is seen to be addressing problems that trouble citizens effectively.

4. *Reinforcement of Basic Social Norms.* This is the corollary of the preventive function of "moral education." That is why Scandinavian countries attach great significance to proportionality in punishment (so that the severity of sanctions acknowledges the comparative seriousness of crimes) and more frequently impose prison sentences (though shorter ones) and their equivalents than most other countries do (so criminal behavior has consequences) (Lappi-Seppälä 2001).

Conversely, if the law's treatment of crimes is incompatible with basic social norms, the effect will be to undermine the legitimacy of the legal system. At times, for example, when cannabis is treated as a dangerous drug on par with heroin or crack cocaine, enforcement becomes lax and inconsistent, and the legal system is seen by many as being out of step with prevailing behavioral norms. Or when drug trafficking in small amounts is treated as being more serious than rape, manslaughter, or serious assault, it is clear that the legislature is out of step. Recent prosecutions and severe punishments in white-collar crime cases offer an example of the system responding to a widespread public perception that it was unjust that corporate malefactors in crimes involving hundreds of millions of dollars often received milder punishments than less privileged citizens convicted of much less serious crimes.

A few strong inferences can be drawn from these observations about communicative functions. First, they fit together: people expect legal institutions to be fair, consistent, rational, and in step with prevailing social norms. Second, public confidence and reassurance are likelier to be achieved by fair, consistent, and rational policies and practices than by expressive and symbolic policies that lack those qualities. It is hard to imagine, for example, that statutes that call for five-, ten-, and twenty-year minimum sentences for drug crimes, which are routinely circumvented and thereby lack legitimacy and fail to mirror prevailing social norms, have greater positive effects on public reassurance and confidence than more moderate laws would.

IV. Latent Functions

The latent functions of sentencing and sentencing policy—using sentencing to achieve personal, ideological, or partisan political goals—sometimes fundamentally obstruct performance of sentencing's primary and ancillary functions. Many practitioners and policy makers hanker for more lucrative or powerful jobs. Elected officials want to be reelected and aspirants want to be elected for the first time. Prosecutors and judges sometimes call for or impose unusually severe punishments to win favor with voters or party leaders. Legislators propose and vote for new laws for those reasons. Many practitioners and policy makers have strong ideological beliefs and want to bear witness to their beliefs. Policy makers sometimes want to posture before ideological soul mates and make symbolic statements. Policy makers sometimes subordinate their personal beliefs to achievement of partisan political goals.

A. Self-Interest

Purely personal ambitions and self-serving motives are illegitimate considerations in decision making by prosecutors and judges about individual cases. Performance of the distributive, preventive, and communicative functions is undermined when cases are dealt with in a particular way because a practitioner believes she is likelier to gain a nomination, win an election, or obtain a new job. Retributive theories of punishment call for punishments to reflect the personal culpability and harm associated with an offense. Utilitarian and mixed theories call for punishments to be based at least in part on good-faith assessments of their likely crime-preventive effects. No theory justifies punishments based on substantively unrelated ulterior considerations. Decisions based on practitioners' personal self-interest are in effect whimsical or arbitrary and irreconcilable with any prevailing theory of punishment.

The analysis is somewhat more complicated for legislators and other policy makers, primarily because the issues of self-interest are sometimes more opaque. When a prosecutor or judge treats an offender in a particular way to realize a purely personal goal, there is no arguable public benefit that can be said to outweigh or counterbalance the harm done the offender. When an entirely self-motivated legislator votes to support a particular policy for which there is little substantive justification, but claims in good faith to be trying to reassure the public or, more complicatedly, claims a need to vote in a particular way on this subject in order to win others' support for a vote on a more important subject, it is almost impossible to assess what the real motives are. The governing ethical premise, however, should be the same as for a prosecutor or a judge: only disinterested motives are legitimate. Observers may have difficulty knowing policy makers' motives, but they themselves know whether their motives are legitimate or ignoble. A good ethical litmus test is whether a legislator at a press conference could comfortably and completely truthfully explain his or her motives.

In the introduction I described a judge up for a vigorously contested reelection who in a particular case, to win favorable publicity, might impose a much harsher sentence than in his own mind can be justified, and I suggested that few observers who knew why he had done so would approve. The analysis of policy making predicated on pursuit of instrumental latent goals is the same as that which applies to a judge who bases the sentence he imposes on his electoral hopes. A legislator or governor who proposes or enacts policy changes he knows will not achieve their purported aims and will, if enacted, cause new injustices, because he hopes his support for the new policy will help him get reelected, is behaving unethically.

The entanglement of sentencing policy in individuals' self-interest has been especially acute at the federal level. Repeatedly in this essay I have used examples from the federal sentencing guidelines. A major reason why they were so inadequate and disliked was that the U.S. Sentencing Commission's policy making in its formative years became entangled in the personal ambitions of William Wilkins, the first chair (initially, unsuccessfully, to become FBI director, then successfully to become a federal court of appeals judge), and Stephen Breyer (successfully, to get to the Supreme Court). Wilkins had been a senior staffer to Senator Strom Thurmond and Breyer had been chief of staff to Senator Edward Kennedy when the two senators were successively chairmen of the Senate Judiciary Committee. Breyer's cross-aisle political credibility was such that Senate confirmation of his appointment as a federal court of appeals judge occurred in October 1980, just before the presidential election, at a time when Republicans otherwise were refusing to act on President Carter's judicial nominations. Wilkins's and Breyer's judicial ambitions meant that a major function of the guidelines was to win favor with Strom Thurmond and his personal staff in the Senate in particular, with congressional Republicans more generally, and with Ed Meese's Justice Department (von Hirsch 1988; Tonry 1996, p. 84). Tens of thousands of federal defendants paid a high price for Wilkins's and Breyer's judicial appointments.

Sometimes penal policies are proposed for reasons having nothing to do with the goals of punishment per se. The prison guards union in California, for example, is often said to promote harsher policies as means to the ends of job creation and maintenance (Petersilia 2003, pp. 237–38). Many communities have sought placement of prisons within their boundaries and, implicitly, increased use of imprisonment, as a form of economic development (p. 239). On the face of it these considerations are entirely unrelated to punishment and prevention.

All the things I have described and decried happen and no doubt will continue to. Anyone who reads newspapers knows that. That is the world we will continue to live in, but practitioners and policy makers can be more self-aware, intellectually honest, and transparent, and the rest of us can try to hold them to account.

B. Ideological Expression

Crime control policy in our time has become entangled in ideological conflict. Recent conflicts over medical use of marijuana and Oregon's assisted-suicide law offer front-page examples. Voters initially in California and eventually in more than a half dozen states approved referenda authorizing medical use of marijuana. Voters in Oregon, initially by a narrow margin and later by a wide margin, approved a law allowing physicians in narrowly defined circumstances to provide drugs to mentally competent, terminally ill patients who want to die. In general under American constitutional doctrines of federalism, criminal justice policy is within the purview of the states (Richman, in this volume).

Public health and the regulation of medical practice also are generally recognized as matters of state law, but that has not stopped ideologically motivated federal officials from trying to control state policies. Successive U.S. Attorneys General John Ashcroft and Alberto Gonzales have attempted to use tortured readings of federal drug laws to overrule the decisions by Oregon voters to allow doctors to assist suicides and by California voters to allow doctors to prescribe marijuana for health care reasons. In each case, the federal government threatened to act under federal drug laws against doctors who complied with the state laws. The U.S. Supreme Court repudiated the effort in the Oregon case, in *Gonzales v. Oregon* (126 S. Ct. 904 [2006]), but, in *Gonzales v. Raich* (125 Supreme Court 2195 [2005]), supported the federal government's position concerning medical use of marijuana.

Ideology is at least as powerful an influence on sentencing policy. Drug policy offers stark examples. The federal 100-to-one law punishes people, mostly black, convicted of crack cocaine offenses as severely as people, many white, convicted of powder cocaine offenses involving amounts that are 100 times larger. The law was enacted in 1986, after the much-publicized death, generally attributed to a crack overdose, of Len Bias, a University of Maryland basketball player forecast to become a National Basketball Association superstar (Kennedy 1997). The law's role in exacerbating racial disparities in federal prisons soon became clear (McDonald and Carlson 1993), and the U.S. Sentencing

Commission proposed that the differential be eliminated. Both the Clinton White House and the Congress opposed any change, and none was made. In later years Attorney General Janet Reno, Drug Czar Barry McCaffrey, and the U.S. Sentencing Commission proposed that the differential be reduced. The Clinton and Bush II White Houses opposed all changes, and the differential remains. No one presumably wants federal sentencing laws to worsen racial disparities, but neither successive administration nor congressional leaders have been willing to risk being accused of condoning drug use or trafficking (Tonry 2004*b*, chap. 1).

Mandatory minimum and three-strikes laws, for other examples, often are primarily based on ideology. Research findings discussed in earlier sections make it clear, and for at least a century have made it clear, that such laws seldom achieve their putative goals and always produce undesirable and unwanted consequences. Ideological posturing is no better an explanation for why an offender is punished unjustly than is a judge's hope for reelection.

C. Partisan Advantage

Pursuit of partisan advantage is the most cynical of the latent functions. Ideological influences grow out of deeply held beliefs; those beliefs may sometimes be blinding. Self-interested acts can, of course, be criticized, but as long as men aren't angels they will remain at least psychologically understandable. Decisions made for partisan reasons, by contrast, are made in cold calculation. Partisan influences often result in the passage of laws that cannot be justified on the substantive merits and foreseeably produce unjust results. Republican Senator Orrin Hatch, according to a member of his staff, for example, long believed reducing sentences for drug offenders "was the right thing to do, but he couldn't do it for political reasons" (Gest 2001, p. 214).

California's three-strikes law, according to Frank Zimring's account, resulted from politicians' competing attempts to use punishment policies to pursue partisan advantage. It was enacted not because thoughtful policy makers really believed that people who stole pizza slices in schoolyards or handfuls of compact discs from Wal-Mart deserved decades-long prison sentences, but because Republican Governor Pete Wilson and California Assembly leader Willie Brown played a game of chicken in which, in the end, neither backed down. Democratic legislators agreed among themselves to pass any proposal Governor

Wilson offered, in hopes "that he would back down from an unqualified 'get tough' stand or be politically neutralized if he persisted." Wilson did not blink. Nor did the Democrats. The law was passed as proposed because both sides were "unwilling to concede the ground on 'getting tough' to the other side in the political campaign to come." Neither Wilson nor Brown was willing to propose refinements to Wilson's extreme initial proposal and thereby expose himself and his party to the other's accusation of softness. As a result California adopted the most far-reaching, rigid, and unjust three-strikes law in the country (Zimring, Hawkins, and Kamin 2001, p. 6).

Former president Bill Clinton famously decided in the 1980s never to let the Republicans get to his right on controversial crime control issues, no matter how unjust, wasteful, or ineffective the policies under consideration (Edsall and Edsall 1991; Friedman 1993). Clinton himself in 1994 admitted that "I can be nicked on a lot but nobody can say I'm soft on crime" (Tonry 2004*b*, p. 8). It worked for Clinton but not for the tens of thousands of people whose lives were changed for the worse.

Britain's Labour Party, after a trip to Washington by Tony Blair to meet with Clinton's political advisors, did the same thing in 1993 (Downes and Morgan 2002). Since then England has adopted sentencing laws of unprecedented severity, and the prison population has reached historic highs and has increased more rapidly since 1994 than in any other Western country (Tonry 2004*a*).

Latent functions and to a lesser extent communicative functions pose a formidable problem for principled policy making. They are not primarily aimed at what goes on in courtrooms or on punishments imposed, crimes prevented, or efficiency enhanced, but on reputations developed, political goals achieved, and elections won.

V. Reconciling Purposes and Functions

In principle, only normative purposes and primary and ancillary functions should count. Thought of as machinery meant to produce something of value, a sentencing system's most important functions, most people would agree, are the imposition of deserved punishments and the prevention of crime. Political maneuvers and passions sometimes result in the passage of laws that produce injustices, and practitioners may sometimes impose unjust sentences for idiosyncratic (e.g., an emotional reaction to a particular offense or offender) or corrupt (e.g., to gain reelection or curry favor) reasons. But it is hard to imagine that many people think that is a good way to make policy or that unjust outcomes in individual cases are a good thing. Some of the main ancillary functions—addressing administrative concerns for efficiency, cost-effectiveness, and resource management—are regularly challenged on normative or policy grounds. In practice, though, the latent functions always powerfully shape policy and sometimes shape practice.

I do not kid myself that my or any other academic's disparagement of policy makers' motives is important or likely to influence policy makers to behave differently. It does, however, seem to me important that academics describe what they see and speak truth to power when opportunity arises.

Researchers and theorists can, however, work to develop better ways of understanding sentencing and sentencing policy. We need, for example, to devise new normative theories to encompass ways the world has changed since desert theories took shape in the 1970s (Tonry 2005*b*). In the early years of the twenty-first century, many people believe that efforts should be made to rehabilitate offenders, and a substantial body of credible evidence shows that sometimes, in well-targeted, well-run programs, this can be done. New restorative and communitarian conceptions of justice are taking shape and programs based on them are proliferating. Recent initiatives such as drug, family violence, and mental health courts are being established across the country as are new programs to divert many offenders from prosecution or prison into treatment. Most of these developments are happening and will continue to happen even though they are hard to reconcile with prevailing retributive theories of punishment. If theorists want to try to influence policy for the good and to be able at least to offer models and ways of thinking that will help policy makers make better choices, the work of developing new theories needs to be done.

That theorizing needs, however, to take account of all normative purposes and primary and ancillary functions. Practitioners want to act justly and to prevent crime effectively, if they can, but they also need to manage their offices efficiently, work within resource constraints, and allocate their efforts among multiple objectives. Most sentencing theories address the primary distributive and preventive functions of punishment, but I know of none that attempt also to encompass the major ancillary functions.

Ignoring the ancillary functions forces their influence into the shadows and often, as happened with the federal guidelines, produces outcomes of the sort Judge Marvin Frankel (1972) referred to as "lawless." By that he meant that sentencing in the 1970s was not subject to rules and was vulnerable to idiosyncratic and arbitrary decision making, and the resulting sentences often said more about the judge than about the offender. Bringing the ancillary functions within the frameworks for thinking about principles governing punishment and prevention will make explicit much that has been invisible and, maybe, achieve greater fairness and justice overall.

Much empirical evidence shows that well-managed guidelines systems can make sentencing more predictable and consistent. A quarter century's experience shows how guidelines' multiple functions can be reconciled in ways that achieve broad support from practitioners and reasonably consistent patterns of sentences imposed while allowing jurisdictions to take account of valid management concerns including resource allocation. The key elements are the development of guidelines that classify offenses and offenders in reasonable ways, that authorize sentences that accord with the sensibilities of the judges and prosecutors charged to apply them, and that allow sufficient flexibility for the individualization of sentences to take account of special circumstances.

The goal is a sentencing system that is fair, evenhanded, and consistent, that takes realistic account of key management interests, and that optimizes legitimacy, public reassurance, and public confidence. We know how to do that.

REFERENCES

Anderson, David. 1995. *Crime and the Politics of Hysteria: How the Willie Horton Story Changed American Justice*. New York: Times Books.

Beccaria, Cesare. 1995. *"On Crimes and Punishments" and Other Writings*. Trans. Richard Davies. Cambridge: Cambridge University Press. (Originally published 1764.)

Bentham, Jeremy. 1970. *An Introduction to the Principles of Morals and Legislation*, edited by J. H. Burns, H. L. A. Hart, and F. Rosen. Oxford: Oxford University Press. (Originally published 1789.)

Berk, Richard. 2005. "Knowing When to Fold 'em: An Essay on Evaluating the Impact of Ceasefire, Compstat, and Exile." *Criminology and Public Policy* 4:451–66.

Blumstein, Alfred. 1988. "Prison Population: A System Out of Control?" In *Crime and Justice: A Review of Research*, vol. 10, edited by Michael Tonry and Norval Morris. Chicago: University of Chicago Press.

Blumstein, Alfred, Jacqueline Cohen, Susan Martin, and Michael Tonry, eds. 1983. *Research on Sentencing—the Search for Reform*. Washington, DC: National Academy Press.

Blumstein, Alfred, Jacqueline Cohen, and Daniel S. Nagin, eds. 1978. *Deterrence and Incapacitation: Estimating the Effects of Criminal Sanctions on Crime Rates*. Washington, DC: National Academy Press.

Blumstein, Alfred, Jacqueline Cohen, Jeffrey Roth, and Christy Visher, eds. 1986. *Criminal Careers and "Career Criminals."* Washington, DC: National Academy Press.

Blumstein, Alfred, and Joel Wallman, eds. 2000. *The Crime Drop in America*. New York: Cambridge University Press.

Boerner, David, and Roxanne Lieb. 2001. "Sentencing Reform in the Other Washington." In *Crime and Justice: A Review of Research*, vol. 28, edited by Michael Tonry. Chicago: University of Chicago Press.

Bowman, Frank O., and Michael Heise. 2001. "Quiet Rebellion? Explaining Nearly a Decade of Declining Federal Drug Sentences." *Iowa Law Review* 86:1043–1136.

Boylan, Richard T. 2004. "Do the Sentencing Guidelines Influence the Retirement Decisions of Judges?" *Journal of Legal Studies* 33:231–53.

Braithwaite, John. 2002. *Restorative Justice and Responsive Regulation*. New York: Oxford University Press.

Butterfield, Fox. 2003. "With Cash Tight, States Reassess Long Jail Terms." *New York Times* (November 10), p. A1.

Casey, Pamela M., and David Rottman. 2003. *Problem-Solving Courts: Models and Trends*. Williamsburg, VA: National Center for State Courts.

Clear, Todd, and David Karp. 1999. *The Community Justice Ideal: Preventing Crime and Achieving Justice*. Boulder, CO: Westview.

Cohen, Jacqueline. 1983. "Incapacitation as a Strategy for Crime Control: Possibilities and Pitfalls." In *Crime and Justice: An Annual Review of Research*, vol. 5, edited by Michael Tonry and Norval Morris. Chicago: University of Chicago Press.

Cook, Philip. 1980. "Research in Criminal Deterrence: Laying the Groundwork for the Second Decade." In *Crime and Justice: An Annual Review of Research*, vol. 2, edited by Norval Morris and Michael Tonry. Chicago: University of Chicago Press.

Dawson, Robert. 1969. *Sentencing: The Decision as to Type, Length, and Conditions of Sentence*. Boston: Little, Brown.

Doob, Anthony N., and Cheryl Marie Webster. 2003. "Sentence Severity and Crime: Accepting the Null Hypothesis." In *Crime and Justice: A Review of Research*, vol. 30, edited by Michael Tonry. Chicago: University of Chicago Press.

———. 2006. "Countering Punitiveness: Understanding Stability in Canada's Imprisonment Rate." *Law and Society Review* 40(2):325–67.

Downes, David, and Rod Morgan. 2002. "The Skeletons in the Cupboard: The Politics of Law and Order at the Turn of the Millennium." In *The Oxford Handbook of Criminology*, 3rd ed., edited by M. Maguire, R. Morgan, and R. Reiner. Oxford: Oxford University Press.

Durkheim, Emile. 1933. *The Division of Labour in Society*. Trans. George Simpson. New York: Free Press. (Originally published 1893.)

Edsall, Thomas, and Mary Edsall. 1991. *Chain Reaction: The Impact of Race, Rights, and Taxes on American Politics*. New York: Norton.

Eisenstein, James, Roy Flemming, and Peter Nardulli. 1988. *The Contours of Justice: Communities and Their Courts*. Boston: Little Brown.

Farrington, David. 1979. "Longitudinal Research on Crime and Delinquency." In *Crime and Justice: An Annual Review of Research*, vol. 1, edited by Norval Morris and Michael Tonry. Chicago: University of Chicago Press.

Farrington, David, and Brandon C. Welsh. In this volume. "A Half Century of Randomized Experiments."

Frankel, Marvin E. 1972. *Criminal Sentences: Law without Order*. New York: Hill & Wang.

Frase, Richard. 1997. "Sentencing Principles in Theory and Practice." In *Crime and Justice: A Review of Research*, vol. 22, edited by Michael Tonry. Chicago: University of Chicago Press.

———. 2004. "Limiting Retributivism." In *The Future of Imprisonment*, edited by Michael Tonry. New York: Oxford University Press.

———. 2005*a*. "Punishment Purposes." *Stanford Law Review* 58:67–83.

———. 2005*b*. "Sentencing Guidelines in Minnesota, 1978–2003." In *Crime and Justice: A Review of Research*, vol. 32, edited by Michael Tonry. Chicago: University of Chicago Press.

———. 2005*c*. "State Sentencing Guidelines: Diversity, Consensus, and Unresolved Policy Issues." *Columbia Law Review* 105:1190–1232.

Freiberg, Arie. 2001. "Three Strikes and You're Out—It's Not Cricket: Colonization and Resistance in Australian Sentencing." In *Sentencing and Sanctions in Western Countries*, edited by Michael Tonry and Richard Frase. New York: Oxford University Press.

Friedman, Lawrence. 1993. *Crime and Punishment in American History*. New York: Basic Books.

Gaes, Gerald G., Timothy J. Flanagan, Lawrence L. Motiuk, and Lynn Stewart. 1999. "Adult Correctional Treatment." In *Prisons*, edited by Michael Tonry and Joan Petersilia. Chicago: University of Chicago Press.

Garland, David. 2001. *The Culture of Control*. Chicago: University of Chicago Press.

Gest, Ted. 2001. *Crime and Politics: Big Government's Erratic Campaign for Law and Order*. New York: Oxford University Press.

Greenwood, Peter W., and Allan Abrahamse. 1982. *Selective Incapacitation*. Santa Monica, CA: RAND.

Halliday, John. 2001. *Making Punishments Work: Report of a Review of the Sentencing Framework for England and Wales*. London: Home Office.

Hart, H. L. A. 1968. *Punishment and Responsibility*. Oxford: Oxford University Press.

Hay, Douglas. 1975. "Property, Authority, and the Criminal Law." In *Albion's Fatal Tree: Crime and Society in Eighteenth Century England*, edited by Douglas Hay, Peter Linebaugh, and E. P. Thompson. New York: Pantheon.

Heumann, Milton, and Colin Loftin. 1979. "Mandatory Sentencing and the Abolition of Plea Bargaining: The Michigan Felony Firearms Statute." *Law and Society Review* 13:393–430.

Home Office. 2002. *Justice for All*. CM5563. London: H.M. Stationery Office.

Ifill, Gwen. 1991. "Senate's Rule for Its Anti-crime Bill: The Tougher the Provision, the Better." *New York Times* (July 8), p. A6.

Joint Committee on New York Drug Law Evaluation. 1978. *The Nation's Toughest Drug Law: Evaluating the New York Experience*. A Project of the Association of the Bar of the City of New York and the Drug Abuse Council. Washington, DC: U.S. Government Printing Office.

Kant, Immanuel. 1887. *The Philosophy of Law: An Exposition of the Fundamental Principles of Jurisprudence as a Science of Right*. Trans. W. Hastie. Edinburgh: T. and T. Clark. (Originally published 1796.)

Kennedy, Randall. 1997. *Race, Crime, and the Law*. New York: Pantheon.

Kessler, Daniel, and Steve Levitt. 1999. "Using Sentence Enhancements to Distinguish between Deterrence and Incapacitation." *Journal of Law and Economics* 42:343–63.

Lappi-Seppälä, Tapio. 2001. "Sentencing and Punishment in Finland: The Decline of the Repressive Ideal." In *Sentencing and Sanctions in Western Countries*, edited by Michael Tonry and Richard S. Frase. New York: Oxford University Press.

Lipsey, Mark W., and Nana Landenberger. 2006. "Cognitive-Behavioral Interventions." In *Preventing Crime: What Works for Children, Offenders, Victims, and Places*, edited by Brandon C. Welsh and David P. Farrington. Dordrecht, Netherlands: Springer.

Martin, John S., Jr. 2004. "Let Judges Do Their Jobs." *New York Times* (June 23), p. A31.

Martinson, Robert. 1974. "What Works? Questions and Answers about Prison Reform." *Public Interest* 10:22–54.

McCoy, Candace, and Patrick McManimon Jr. 2003. *Final Report: New Jersey's "No Early Release Act": Its Impact on Prosecution, Sentencing, Corrections, and Victim Satisfaction*. Newark, NJ: Rutgers University, School of Criminal Justice.

McDonald, Douglas, and Ken Carlson. 1993. *Sentencing in the Federal Courts: Does Race Matter?* Washington, DC: U.S. Bureau of Justice Statistics.

McDougall, Cynthia, Mark A. Cohen, Amanda Perry, and Raymond Swaray. 2006. "Costs and Benefits of Sentencing." In *Preventing Crime: What Works for Children, Offenders, Victims, and Places*, edited by Brandon C. Welsh and David P. Farrington. Dordrecht, Netherlands: Springer.

Merritt, Nancy, Terry Fain, and Susan Turner. 2003. *Oregon's Measure 11 Sentencing Reform: Implementation and System Impact*. Santa Monica, CA: RAND.

———. 2006. "Oregon's Get Tough Sentencing Reform: A Lesson in Justice System Adaptation." *Criminology and Public Policy* 5(1):5–36.

Messinger, Sheldon, and Philip Johnson. 1978. "California's Determinate Sentence Statute: History and Issues." In *Determinate Sentencing: Reform or Regression*. Washington, DC: U.S. Department of Justice, National Institute of Law Enforcement and Criminal Justice.

Miller, Frank W. 1969. *Prosecution*. Boston: Little, Brown.

Mitchell, Ojamarrh, Doris L. MacKenzie, and David B. Wilson. 2006. "Incarceration-Based Drug Treatment." In *Preventing Crime: What Works for Children, Offenders, Victims, and Places*, edited by Brandon C. Welsh and David P. Farrington. Dordrecht, Netherlands: Springer.

Monahan, John. 2004. "The Future of Violence Risk Management." In *The Future of Imprisonment*, edited by Michael Tonry. New York: Oxford University Press.

Morris, Norval. 1953. "Sentencing Convicted Criminals." *Australian Law Review* 27:186–208.

———. 1974. *The Future of Imprisonment*. Chicago: University of Chicago Press.

Morris, Norval, and Michael Tonry. 1990. *Between Prison and Probation*. New York: Oxford University Press.

Nagel, Ilene H., and Stephen J. Schulhofer. 1992. "A Tale of Three Cities: An Empirical Study of Charging and Bargaining Practices under the Federal Sentencing Guidelines." *Southern California Law Review* 66:501–66.

Nagin, Daniel S. 1998. "Deterrence and Incapacitation." In *The Handbook of Crime and Punishment*, edited by Michael Tonry. New York: Oxford University Press.

———. 1999. "Criminal Deterrence Research at the Outset of the Twenty-First Century." In *Crime and Justice: A Review of Research*, vol. 23, edited by Michael Tonry. Chicago: University of Chicago Press.

Nardulli, Peter, James Eisenstein, and Ron Flemming. 1988. *The Tenor of Justice: Criminal Courts and the Guilty Plea Process*. Champaign: University of Illinois Press.

Newman, Donald J. 1966. *Conviction: The Determination of Guilt or Innocence without Trial*. Boston: Little, Brown.

New York Times. 1990. "Criticizing Sentencing Rules, U.S. Judge Resigns." September 30, sec. 1, p. 2.

Nolan, James L., Jr. 2001. *Reinventing Justice: The American Drug Court Movement*. Princeton, NJ: Princeton University Press.

Petersilia, Joan. 2003. *When Prisoners Come Home*. New York: Oxford University Press.

Pincoffs, Edmund L. 1991. *Philosophy of Law: A Brief Introduction*. Belmont, CA: Wadsworth.

Redlich, Allison D., Henry J. Steadman, John Monahan, John Petrila, and

Patricia A. Griffin. 2005. "The Second Generation of Mental Health Courts." *Psychology, Public Policy, and Law* 11:527–38.

Reiss, Albert J., Jr., and Jeffrey Roth, eds. 1993. *Understanding and Controlling Violence*. Washington, DC: National Academy Press.

Reitz, Kevin R. 2001. "The Disassembly and Reassembly of U.S. Sentencing Practices." In *Sentencing and Sanctions in Western Countries*, edited by Michael Tonry and Richard S. Frase. New York: Oxford University Press.

———. 2005*a*. "The Enforcement of Sentencing Guidelines." *Stanford Law Review* 58:155–73.

———. 2005*b*. "The New Sentencing Conundrum: Policy and Constitutional Law at Cross-Purposes." *Columbia Law Review* 105:1082–1123.

Remington, Frank. 1969. "Foreword" to *Sentencing: The Decision as to Type, Length, and Conditions of Sentence*, by Robert Dawson. Boston: Little, Brown.

Richman, Daniel. In this volume. "The Past, Present, and Future of Violent Crime Federalism."

Roberts, Julian, Loretta Stalans, David Indermaur, and Mike Hough. 2002. *Penal Populism and Public Opinion*. New York: Oxford University Press.

Robinson, Paul H. 1987. "Hybrid Principles for the Distribution of Criminal Sentences." *Northwestern University Law Review* 82:19–42.

Rosenfeld, Richard, Robert Fornango, and Eric Baumer. 2005*a*. "Did Ceasefire, Compstat, and Exile Reduce Homicide?" *Criminology and Public Policy* 4:419–50.

———. 2005*b*. "The Straw Man Bluff: A Reply to Berk." *Criminology and Public Policy* 4:467–70.

Rosett, Arthur, and Donald R. Cressey. 1976. *Justice by Consent: Plea Bargains in the American Courthouse*. New York: Lippincott Williams and Wilkins.

Rossman, David, Paul Froyd, Glen Pierce, John McDevitt, and William Bowers. 1979. *The Impact of the Mandatory Gun Law in Massachusetts*. Report to the National Institute of Law Enforcement and Criminal Justice. Washington, DC: U.S. Government Printing Office.

Rothman, David. 1980. *Conscience and Convenience*. Boston: Little, Brown.

Ruth, Henry, and Kevin R. Reitz. 2003. *The Challenge of Crime: Rethinking Our Response*. Cambridge, MA: Harvard University Press.

Schulhofer, Stephen J., and Ilene H. Nagel. 1997. "Plea Negotiations under the Federal Sentencing Guidelines: Guideline Circumvention and Its Dynamics in the Post-Mistretta Period." *Northwestern University Law Review* 91:1284–1316.

Select Committee on Capital Punishment. 1930. *Report*. London: H.M. Stationery Office.

Spelman, William. 2000. "What Recent Studies Do (and Don't) Tell Us about Imprisonment and Crime." In *Crime and Justice: A Review of Research*, vol. 27, edited by Michael Tonry. Chicago: University of Chicago Press.

Stephen, James Fitzjames. 1977. *A History of the Criminal Law of England*. New York: B. Franklin. (Originally published 1883.)

Tonry, Michael. 1996. *Sentencing Matters*. New York: Oxford University Press.

———. 2004*a*. *Punishment and Politics*. Cullompton, Devonshire: Willian.

———. 2004*b*. *Thinking about Crime: Sense and Sensibility in American Penal Culture*. New York: Oxford University Press.

———. 2005*a*. "The Functions of Sentencing and Sentencing Reform." *Stanford Law Review* 58:37–66.

———. 2005*b*. "Obsolescence and Immanence in Penal Theory and Policy." *Columbia Law Review* 105:1233–75.

———. 2006. "Criminology, Mandatory Minimums, and Public Policy." *Criminology and Public Policy* 5(1):45–56.

Travis, Jeremy. 2005. *But They All Come Back: Facing the Challenges of Prisoner Reentry*. Washington, DC: Urban Institute Press.

Travis, Jeremy, and Christy Visher, eds. 2005. *Prisoner Reentry and Crime in America*. Cambridge: Cambridge University Press.

Tyler, Tom R. 2003. "Procedural Justice, Legitimacy, and the Effective Rule of Law." In *Crime and Justice: A Review of Research*, vol. 30, edited by Michael Tonry. Chicago: University of Chicago Press.

U.S. Sentencing Commission. 1987. *Guidelines Manual*. Washington, DC: U.S. Sentencing Commission.

———. 2003. *Survey of Article III Judges on the Federal Sentencing Guidelines*. Washington, DC: U.S. Sentencing Commission.

U.S. Surgeon General. 2001. *Youth Violence: A Report of the Surgeon General*. Washington, DC: U.S. Public Health Service.

von Hirsch, Andrew. 1976. *Doing Justice*. New York: Hill & Wang.

———. 1988. "Federal Sentencing Guidelines: The United States and Canadian Schemes Compared." Occasional Paper no. 4. New York: New York University, Law School, Center for Research in Crime and Justice.

———. 1993. *Censure and Sanctions*. Oxford: Oxford University Press.

von Hirsch, Andrew, and Andrew Ashworth. 2005. *Proportionate Sentencing: Exploring the Principles*. Oxford: Oxford University Press.

von Hirsch, Andrew, Anthony E. Bottoms, P.-O. Wikström, and Elizabeth Burney. 1999. *Criminal Deterrence and Sentence Severity: An Analysis of Recent Research*. Oxford: Hart.

Wacquant, Loïc. 2001. "Deadly Symbiosis: When Ghetto and Prison Meet and Mesh." *Punishment and Society* 3:95–134.

Washington State Sentencing Guidelines Commission. 2005. *Statistical Summary of Adult Felony Sentencing*. Olympia: Washington State Sentencing Guidelines Commission.

Wasik, Martin, and Andrew von Hirsch. 1988. "Non-custodial Penalties and the Principles of Desert." *Criminal Law Review* 1988:555–72.

Webster, Cheryl, Anthony Doob, and Franklin Zimring. 2006. "Proposition 8 and Crime Rates in California: The Case of the Missing Deterrent." Unpublished paper. Toronto: University of Toronto, Department of Criminology.

Welsh, Brandon C., and David P. Farrington, eds. 2006. *Preventing Crime: What Works for Children, Offenders, Victims, and Places*. Dordrecht, Netherlands: Springer.

Wilson, James Q. 1976. *Thinking about Crime*. New York: Basic Books.

———. 2002. "Crime and Public Policy." In *Crime: Public Policies for Crime Control*, edited by James Q. Wilson and Joan Petersilia. Oakland, CA: Institute for Contemporary Studies.

Winick, Bruce J., and David B. Wexler. 2003. *Judging in a Therapeutic Key: Therapeutic Jurisprudence and the Courts*. Durham, NC: Carolina Academic Press.

Wright, Ronald F. 2002. "The Cost of Sentencing in North Carolina, 1980–2000." In *Crime and Justice: A Review of Research*, vol. 29, edited by Michael Tonry. Chicago: University of Chicago Press.

Zimring, Franklin E., Gordon Hawkins, and Sam Kamin. 2001. *Punishment and Democracy—Three Strikes and You're Out in California*. New York: Oxford University Press.

Zlotnick, David M. 2004. "Shouting into the Wind: District Court Judges and Federal Sentencing Policy." *Roger Williams University Law Review* 9:645–84.

Part V
Punishment Theory

[14] Interchangeability of Punishments in Principle

The concept of interchangeability raises serious jurisprudential concerns. In advance and independently of specific cases, can equivalences be set out between different types of punishments so as to satisfy multiple legitimate ends of sentencing policy—including social utility and moral justification? Are there "exchange rates" between punishments that can be expressed or encapsulated in a system of comprehensive sentencing standards? Can a sentencing system fairly and justly impose a prison sentence on one offender and a community-based sentence on his in-all-respects like-situated brother?

Fairness and Justice

The tension between the requirement of fairness—that there be general standards that apply to all—and the requirement of justice—that all legitimate grounds for distinguishing between individuals be taken into account when decisions about individuals are made—was brought into focus by the Congress's mandate to the U.S. Sentencing Commission. Section 3553 of the Sentencing Reform Act of 1984 required the Commission to devise sentencing guidelines:

> (A) to reflect the seriousness of the offense, to promote respect for the law, and to provide just punishment for the offense;
> (B) to afford adequate deterrence to criminal conduct;
> (C) to protect the public from further crimes of the defendant; and
> (D) to provide the defendant with needed educational or vocational training, medical care, or other correctional treatment in the most effective manner; . . .

The Congress at the same time affirmed "the need to avoid unwarranted sentence disparities among defendants with similar records who have been found guilty of similar conduct."

Can these diverse legislative directions be fulfilled by a sentencing system that sends one offender to prison and imposes on another offender, convicted of a crime of equal gravity and with an identical criminal record (in the words of the statute, "with similar records who have been found guilty of similar conduct"), a sentence of, say, a fine, residential restrictions, and community service? If the answer is a principled "Yes," then there must be some principled exchange rates between different punishments if "the need to avoid unwarranted sentence disparities" is not to be flouted.

The question of penal equivalence has a very practical political side. Public opinion sees too many intermediate punishments as indulgences to the more privileged convicted criminals, a way by which judges deal leniently with "criminals like us, who have suffered enough" while consigning underclass criminals to crowded and brutal prisons. Indeed, in its April 13, 1987 report to the Congress, the U.S. Sentencing Commission justified a narrow approach to use of nonprison sentences as the product of its objective of assuring that white-collar offenders receive other than nominal punishments. Hence there are two aspects to our inquiry into interchangeability: the practical-political and the jurisprudential. In Chapters 3 and 8 we deal with the practical and political problems associated with taking intermediate punishments seriously; in this chapter we pursue an excursus into the jurisprudence of punishment. Since justificatory arguments about the moral appropriateness of imposition of different but roughly equivalent punishments vary substantially with the punishment philosophy to which one subscribes, the jurisprudential issues though complex are unavoidable.

The Jurisprudence of Interchangeability

For people who espouse teleological or consequentialist punishment philosophies, usually some version of utilitarianism, in which actions are justified by their results, "equality of suffering" by the offender is seldom a paramount aim; the justification must be expressed in terms of crime prevention or achievement of other desirable social ends through such processes as deterrence, incapacitation, and rehabilitation.

For those who espouse deontological punishment philosophies, usually some form of retributivism or "just deserts," the moral justification for imposition of suffering on the offender must relate to the offender's culpability or character and the notion of "equally deserved punishment" often is accorded dominant or substantial importance. In the extreme case, what H. L. A. Hart once called "thoroughgoing retributivism," deserved punishment would be linked closely to the degree of moral misconduct expressed by the offender's actions and two identically culpable offenders would deserve identically severe punishments.

In the abstract, our arguments for a sentencing system that authorizes imposition of different but roughly equivalent punishments on similarly culpable offenders who share comparable personal biographies present few difficulties in principle for the utilitarian. For the retributivist, however, our doctrine of rough equivalence faces obstacles and consequently it is these theories that we principally address.

First, however, some preliminary analytical skirmishing. A thoroughgoing retributivist would claim that the punishment to be imposed on an offender should be "exactly as much as he deserves, no more, no less." A skeptic would respond, however, that mortal minds do not possess moral calipers that can tell us exactly how much punishment any wrongdoer deserves. Of course, the skeptic will concede, any one individual may feel able to make such judgments; the problem, however, is that legal rules must be knowable in advance so that equally virtuous judges will reach identical or at least similar decisions in such matters. Socrates and Maimonides are unlikely to possess identical views about deserved punishment, in general or in specific cases. Therefore, concludes the skeptic, there is no way to determine the single, generally applicable, morally appropriate punishment for any given case, and these decisions of deserved punishment must be made on other grounds.

There are, however, at least two strategies a retributivist could adopt for getting round this dilemma. First, he could urge some sort of democratic solution. Whether by consulting some measure of general public opinion or by relying on the judgments of some body of policymakers, perhaps a legislature or a sentencing commission, people could be asked to declare their views of the single appropriate punishment for a single actual or hypothetical case. The resulting range of answers could then be averaged, giving a mean measure of deserved punishment, or the persons consulted could negotiate a consensual measure of deserved punishment.

The difficulty with these solutions is that the resulting measure of deserved punishment would be supported by a formal logic, but not a moral logic. Research on sentencing disparities, and on exercises in which judges are asked to "sentence" hypothetical cases, compel the conclusion that judges vary widely in their judgments about appropriate punishment, and there is no reason to doubt that a similar diversity of view would characterize any cross section of the general public. What a democratic solution to our inability to specify deserved punishments would provide is mean or consensual measures of deserved punishment that are essentially arbitrary, the product of a wide range and distribution of individual judgments about deserved punishments. Thus the democratic strategy seems not to work, except as a method for identifying the range within which reasonable peoples' judgments about deserved punishments fall, and thereby identifying a range beyond which punishments are generally seen as undeserved.

The second strategy for getting round the dilemma is comparative. Our friend and estimable colleague Andrew von Hirsch has developed this analysis most fully and creatively. In his 1985 book,

Past or Future Crimes, von Hirsch concedes that a notion of "commensurate desert" cannot be a "defining principle" for what he calls "cardinal magnitudes" of punishment. By this, he means to concede that theory cannot tell us precisely what punishment is appropriate in any given case. Nevertheless, argues von Hirsch, theory can provide powerful guidance concerning the relations between punishments for offenses of differing gravity. If two otherwise identical offenders commit, respectively, a minor theft and an armed robbery, notions of deserved punishment should lead to the imposition of a more severe punishment on the armed robber than on the thief. When a sufficiently large number of comparative assessments of offense severity and culpability have been made, von Hirsch argues, the result will be an "ordinal" ranking of offense severity. Persons who commit offense B are more culpable than those who commit offense A and less culpable than those who commit offense C. Once "anchoring points" of amounts of punishment have been fixed and specified as appropriate for the most and least serious offenses, the ordinal ranking of offense severity can serve as a basis for assigning appropriately scaled punishments for all offenses in a way that is consistent with a commensurate deserts starting point. Thus if nominal probation is one end of a punishment continuum and 20 years' imprisonment the other, an ordinal ranking of offense severities will provide a morally persuasive system of proportionate punishments.

Von Hirsch's analysis provides a logic for developing a system of ordinally proportionate penalties for jurisdictions that, as a matter of policy, wish to do so. The question for us, however, is whether the analysis compels that primacy be given to a value of "equality of suffering."

We think not, for four reasons. First, von Hirsch's concession that no theoretical starting point can entail judgments of "cardinal desert" concedes that reasonable people can differ in their judgments about the deserved quantum of punishment in any given case. Reasonable peoples' judgments can tell us much more about punishments that are undeserved because too severe or too lenient than about punishments that are deserved.

Second, although notions of ordinal proportionality provide in theory a mechanism for scaling punishments in such a way as to assure equal punishment for equally culpable wrongdoers, they do not provide a compelling argument for why policymakers should choose to establish such a scheme. If the imprecision of cardinal judgments of deserved punishment gives powerful guidance about undeserved punishments but only slight guidance about deserved punishments, why may policymakers not justly create standards that authorize imposition of any sentence that is not undeserved (that is, that falls within the range of punishments that reasonable people would regard as deserved)?

Third, in practice, judgments of comparative culpability are enormously difficult to make. In mind games or in science fiction's parallel universes two otherwise identical offenders who commit different offenses can readily be imagined. In life, no two offenders are identical and any system of sentencing that takes account only of the statutory labels of the offender's crime alone or together with some measure of his past involvement in crime will be too crude to be morally compelling. Statutory labels simply tell too little about the moral gravity of individual acts. H. L. A. Hart observed, in his classic 1968 book, *Punishment and Responsibility,* that scalings of the gravity of crimes can provide "rough distinctions . . . but cannot cope with any precise assessment of an individual's wickedness in committing a crime (who can?)." Sometimes complexity of moral judgment will result from details of the offender's biography, sometimes from details of the crime; for innumerable reasons in innumerable cases there will be occasions when the penal guidance given by a system of ordinal proportionality will be incomplete. Von Hirsch would likely concede this last point but urge that it is not inconsistent in principle with his position; any system of guided discretion must allow for exceptional cases, he might say, and these, in a guidelines system, should be treated as "departures" for which reasons must be given.

There is, however, a fourth, and for us compelling reason to reject a strong retributivist punishment theory. In practice, few if any policymakers or decisionmakers subscribe to such theories in any strong form. Many view retribution and commensurate desert as appropriate considerations to be taken into account at sentencing; few view these as the *only* appropriate considerations. In our experience, most public officials subscribe to the view that Norval

Morris in *The Future of Imprisonment* in 1974 called "limiting retributivism," in which punishments are seen as justifiable when they are "not undeserved."

In any case, we doubt that much in the world of practical affairs turns on analytical differences of the sort canvassed in the preceding paragraphs. People have been arguing about the justifications for punishment and for the criminal law for thousands of years. Whether it be Aristotle and Plato in classical Greece, Jeremy Bentham and Immanuel Kant early in the nineteenth century, John Stuart Mill and James Fitzjames Stephen in Victorian England, or H. L. A. Hart and Lord Patrick Devlin in modern times, fundamentally opposed punishment philosophies seem to characterize every era in which these matters receive attention.

People have deeply embedded beliefs about punishment, as they do about the death penalty, the exclusionary rule, or abortion, and these tend to be the kind of beliefs that are seldom changed by argument or by the marshaling of evidence. Although some people may, for example, be agnostics concerning capital punishment, there are probably many more who will remain fixed in their views whatever the findings of empirical research concerning deterrent effects or the logic of opponents' arguments.

Harvard philosopher Robert Nozick observed in his 1981 book, *Philosophical Explanations,* that professional philosophers are in this respect like the rest of us:

> When a philosopher sees that premisses he accepts logically imply a conclusion he has rejected until now, he faces a choice: he may accept this conclusion or reject one of the previously accepted premisses. . . . His choice will depend upon which is greater, the degree of his commitment to the various premisses or the degree of his commitment to denying the conclusion. It is implausible that these are independent of how strongly he wants certain things to be true. The various means of control over conclusions explain why so few philosophers publish ones that (continue to) upset them. (pp. 2–3)

If philosophers are little susceptible to persuasion about deeply embedded normative beliefs, it is not surprising that philosophical and ethical arguments often have little persuasive impact on the beliefs of others. One of the characters in Canadian novelist Robertson Davies's *Fifth Business* notes of philosophers addressing a fundamental question that they "answered it in ways highly satisfactory to themselves; but I never knew a philosopher's answer to make much difference to anyone not in the trade."

Given the reality that peoples' views of deserved punishment vary widely, it is unlikely that any comprehensive system of sentencing standards will adopt a rigid scheme of deserved punishments. Retributive considerations can, however, give guidance on undeservedly lenient or severe punishments; within those bounds there is, we believe, ample room for principled interchangeability of punishment.

To return to interchangeability: one way to address the problem of interchangeability is to deny the reality of the problem. If the crime and the offender's criminal record merit imprisonment, then equality of punishment, the need to treat like cases alike—the commensurate deserts argument goes—requires that imprisonment be imposed. Elsewhere, Norval Morris has argued in a 1976 lecture, "Punishment, Desert, and Rehabilitation," that the concept of treating like cases alike has been much exaggerated as a principle of punishment but, whatever the merits of that argument, no one doubts that it is desirable, so far as practicable, to diminish the extent to which like cases are treated differently. Equality in punishment may not be an unassailable principle, but it is at least a desirable goal.

H. L. A. Hart has written in *Punishment and Responsibility* of the "somewhat hazy requirement that 'like cases be treated alike.' " Hart may have found this requirement somewhat hazy because it was inconsistent with his own punishment philosophy in which general prevention provides the justification for criminal punishment as a social institution and which "allows some place, though a subordinate one, to ideas of equality and proportion in the gradation of the severity of punishment."

Hart's notion of haziness is apt, for it expresses the difficulty of knowing in advance or from afar that seemingly like cases are indeed alike. In any case, there are sound reasons in principle and prudence for honoring only a weak version of the adjurations for equality of suffering.

Imprisonment is expensive and unnecessary for some convicted felons who present no serious threat to the community and whose imprisonment is not necessary for deterrent purposes, and yet whose crime and criminal record could properly attract a prison sentence. Are we to allow an excessive regard for equality of suffering to preclude rational allocation of scarce prison space and staff? The path of wisdom, in terms of justice and political acceptability, requires the enunciation of some rough interchangeabilities between different types of punishments. The aim must be to identify punishments with roughly equal punitive properties that are suited to the variety of social threats and personal conditions that characterize offenders, a diversity of punishments, suited to social needs, that do not result in unwarranted sentencing disparities.

In the preceding chapter we offered a detailed proposal for a sentencing guidelines system based on the notion that, within limits, punishments can be made roughly equivalent in punitive force and social purpose and interchangeable in application. Of three like-situated offenders convicted of similar offenses, under our proposal, one might receive a six-month prison term, one a substantial fine, and the third a fine, intensive supervision, and required participation in a drug treatment program.

Once the principle of rough equivalence between incarcerative and nonincarcerative punishments is accepted, it follows that the choice of punishment should be guided by the purposes sought to be achieved in the individual case. Sentencing choices from among interchangeable punishments (or packages of punishments) should be shaped by governing purposes *at* sentencing, not by the general crime preventive or retributive purposes *of* sentencing (or punishment). General purposes may sometimes interpose negative constraints on judges' choices; they seldom provide positive guidance. Michael Smith, director of the Vera Institute of Justice in New York City, has frequently urged that decisions among punishments in individual cases should reflect the judge's purposes at sentencing. This slight change of preposition from "of" to "at" captures an important insight in respect to nonprison punishments. If, for example, the sole or primary purpose at sentencing is retribution, an appropriately severe package of financial sanctions, including restitution, costs, and a substantial quantum of day fines, may suffice. If the purposes at sentencing include both desert and control, depending on the offender's circumstances, a combination of community service, home detention, mandatory drug treatment and testing, and intensive probation supervision may be enough. In still other cases, responding to public sentiment or deterrent or incapacitative concerns may be the governing purposes at sentencing; if so, the principle of rough equivalence permits imposition of a not-undeserved incarcerative sentence.

This helpful distinction between purposes of sentencing and purposes at sentencing is not new conceptually. Since the appearance of H. L. A. Hart's *Punishment and Responsibility* in 1968, most writers have accepted his partitioning of the philosophy of punishment into questions of "What is the justification for the institution of punishment?" (general justifying aim), "Whom do we punish?" (liability), and "How much do we punish?" (amount). Hart wanted to show that there was no reason in logic or principle why one could not simultaneously argue that, for example, utilitarian purposes provide the general justification for punishment while arguing that, for example, liability to punishment must be governed by retributive considerations. The general justifying aim of punishment involves purposes *of* punishment; the question of amount involves purposes *at* sentencing.

Hart's distinction has become newly salient at a time when the rule of law has begun to apply to sentencing. Under indeterminate sentencing systems in which the judge's discretion knew few bounds, it was hard to give operational meaning to the distinction between "at" and "of." After all, it was the individual judge who made both choices. Under presumptive sentencing guidelines, however, the judge's discretion is bounded. Consideration of the purposes of sentencing has shaped the architecture of the guidelines system, the ranking of offenses, the scaling of punishments, the identification of items of information that should and should not be taken into account in classifying offenses and offenders.

Within the range of discretion that the guidelines allow, however, the judge's decision should be guided by the purposes he hopes to achieve at sentencing in imposing a sentence from among those interchangeable punishments that the guidelines authorize. Once the principle of interchangeability is accepted in a system of structured sentencing discretion, the importance of purposes *at* sentencing becomes unarguable.

One main line of criticism that has been offered of this concept of interchangeable punishments, comparably punitive yet adapted to the many other concerns relevant to rational sentencing, is that it is too complex to be workable. This seems to us more a sign of apprehension of the unknown than the recognition of any problem in the sentencing process. Why should the task of sentencing convicted offenders be simple?

Is it that judges cannot cope with complexity? They do so in many other areas of the law; the complexities of a comprehensive, integrated set of sentencing standards are child's play compared with the factual, conceptual, and legal complexities posed by federal tax, securities, or antitrust laws. In the criminal law, judges deal with the arcane glosses of the federal Racketeer Influenced and Corrupt Organizations (RICO) statutes, mail and wire fraud, the law of conspiracy, and many other statutory and common law doctrines of bewildering complexity. There, as here, judges function in a context of complex guided discretion.

Is it that the law's deterrent signals must be clear and unqualified? They are not so now, and at present they are not even truthful, with current "bark and bite" practices, by which the punishment served is often greatly less than the punishment announced—and this is widely known, certainly to potential criminals. Such leniency as exists in current American criminal justice systems largely flows not from sentimentality but from overload: a greater flow of criminals than inadequately funded and staffed police, court, and correctional services can handle.

A complex sentencing system, applied and enforced, is much to be preferred to the relatively simple and often unenforced systems that now obtain.

There have been some efforts to enunciate such exchange rates between punishments. These were discussed in the preceding chapter, where we described the slow, halting, but perceptible movement toward the development of comprehensive sentencing policies that integrate both prison and nonprison into a system of interchangeable punishments. To assist understanding of our present problem, recall the central features of those emerging systems, pertinent to the imposition of intermediate sentences:

1. Rejection of the abrupt distinction between prison and nonprison sentences;
2. Establishment of standards governing choices between prison

and nonprison sentences and among diverse nonprison sentences;
3. Creative use of presumptions for and against use of nonprison sentences to guide, but not straitjacket, the exercise of judicial sentencing discretion;
4. Establishment of "exchange rates" to achieve, for appropriate cases, principled interchangeability between prison and nonprison sentences and among different nonprison sentences.

American sentencing policy can, and should, move forward in its explicit, principled integration of a variety of nonprison sentences into its sentencing armamentarium.

Interchangeable Sentences

Lest it be thought we have in this jurisprudential excursus too obliquely passed over a fundamental incompatibility between our proposals and the moral imperatives of equality and proportionality in sentencing, we now develop two lines of practical argument about criminal justice to support our proposals. First, from a moral perspective, the measure of punishment is not its objective appearance but its subjective impact. Our goal is to achieve a system of interchangeable punishments that the state and the offender would regard as comparable in their punitive effects on him. Second, we believe that nonincarcerative (and partly incarcerative) sentences can be devised that can meaningfully be said to be equivalent to imprisonment, and that these can be deployed within a system of guided discretion that maintains proportionality and rough equivalence among the punishments imposed on different offenders. We do not expect acceptance of these propositions without some discussion.

Differential Impact

Need a system of interchangeable punishments run afoul of concern for achievement of equality and proportionality in the administration of punishment? Even if we cannot precisely calibrate desert to punishment, the argument goes, we can at least ensure that punishments are scaled in a meaningful way to the comparative gravity (and desert) of different offenses. Thus proportionality in punishment will, in the nature of things, assure that offenders of comparable desert (in terms of the seriousness of their crime and their criminal record) receive comparable punishments. For reasons developed earlier, we believe this search for equality and proportionality is chimerical; it oversimplifies the complexity of moral judgments about desert and the need to make such assessments in light of the circumstances of each offender other than his crime and criminal record.

Those favoring retributive or just deserts systems of punishment frequently neglect to consider with sufficient precision the coinage in which their justly deserved punishments are to be paid. It is taken as axiomatic that two equally undeserving criminals, in terms of the gravity of their crime and the length and severity of their criminal records, should be punished equally. The argument frequently stops there; yet a great deal is assumed. One critical assumption is that equality of punishment is now obtained when, pursuant to a statute or a guideline, two offenders, who are closely comparable in terms of their current crime and past crimes, each receive sentences of three years' incarceration. In practice, those two three-year prison sentences may, both objectively and subjectively, be very different.

At the outset, before discussing these two hypothetical offenders, we reject the approach taken by utilitarian philosophers who reject "interpersonal comparisons of utilities." By this they mean that analyses of the incentives and disincentives of social policy must be assessed by reference to a hypothetical average man. It is too complex, ultimately impossible, they argue, to take into account in such analyses the predispositions and disinclinations of every person. In sentencing, however, no generic man stands before the court, but countless individuals do. We think it axiomatic that questions of fairness and justice in criminal punishment must be weighed in individual terms.

Is the equality of punishment to be inflicted on our two equally undeserving criminals an equality of pain or suffering? If it is, how can that possibly be measured?

Let us put the point aphoristically. A year often is not a year. A year's imprisonment in one prison may well not equal a year's imprisonment in another terms of pain and suffering. Every prison administrator knows this, and certainly every prisoner knows this. A year in a minimum security federal prison, security level 1, is a profoundly different experience from a year in a maximum security federal prison, security level 6. A year in a state prison forestry camp is a profoundly different experience from a year in a state maxiprison proximate to a city. Prisons differ dramatically in their levels of violence, fear, social separation, and vocational and developmental opportunities; it would be an expensive and needless exercise in cruelty to seek to equate the suffering of our two criminals, each sentenced to a year's imprisonment. In a dystopia described in Kurt Vonnegut's *Welcome to the Monkey House,* dedication to equality of opportunity requires that the beautiful wear masks, the athletic wear chains and weights, the mentally able wear hearing devices that emit a constant and shrill grinding noise. So it would be if equality in carceral suffering were required, for it is certain that the equality would be achieved by increasing the suffering of the relatively privileged rather than by improving the lot of the disadvantaged. And no responsible prison administrator would join in such a fruitless and expensive exercise.

There is, of course, another variable that prevents a year's imprisonment for one criminal being equal to a year's imprisonment for another equally undeserving and equally justly punishable criminal: one is aged 30, the other is aged 70 (their records of embezzlement are the same). Does the 70-year-old endure more loss from a year's confinement than the 30-year-old? We suppose so. And in a like manner, much of the life histories, personal and family circumstances, and psychological sensitivities of our two antiheroes will condition the quality of the pain and deprivation they suffer from a year in the same prison; subjective equality in this hedonistic calculus is unachievable.

By more subtle psychological measures of pain and suffering, a year's imprisonment may well not be equal to a year's imprisonment. Both A and B will suffer a sense of diminished self-image, a separateness from the flow of their lives; this too differs not only between prisoners but between prisons in the extent to which some prison administrations bolster, as best they can, the personal and community ties of their inmates, while others impose restrictions and degrading ceremonies on all such contacts.

A final comment on this point: many, though not all prisons, provide a safer and more comfortable environment than the environment from which many of our street criminals come. In prison, they are less likely to be assaulted or killed, they eat better, they often begin educational efforts they had previously entirely neglected, they sometimes begin to take hold of their lives and give them shape. Are those from such adverse social circumstances to have extra pains and sufferings inflicted on them to compensate for the advantages that accompany confinement in decent, well-run prisons?

This side of the punishment equation is of great practical importance to a rational and just sentencing system. The assumption that the coinage of punishment is fungible is a gross oversimplification. In practice, prison administrators often have enormous latitude in determining the conditions of life of offenders "in the custody of the state department of corrections." Some "state prisoners" in Oklahoma are "confined" in their homes under house arrest. In many places, prison administrators have discretion to grant work or educational furloughs or to assign prisoners to community-based facilities under partial or intermittent confinement. Thus the contrasts in suffering between two persons each sentenced to two years in prison are often even starker than in our earlier illustrations of confinement in different institutions; in practice, one "two-year sentence" may be served in a maximum security prison and another under terms of nighttime confinement in the prisoner's hometown while he attends college courses.

Three consequences flow from this argument of the nonfungibility of prison punishment expressed in terms of time.

First, further strength is given to our submission that the sensible ideal of justly deserved punishments should limit the boundaries of punishment and should not be thought capable of defining what is the single appropriate punishment in any given case—that definition is to be sought on other grounds. Just as the seemingly equal one-year prison sentences of two like-situated offenders may in practice result in quite different experiences of imprisonment, so, in our view, like-situated offenders can justly receive different but roughly equivalent punishments of great variety.

Second, it is immediately apparent that just as prison and time do not define a fungible punishment, no other criminal sanction does. No matter what we do by way of graduating fines, for example, to the wealth and earning capacities of different offenders, we cannot achieve equal impact between the wealthy and talented and the indigent and untrained.

Third, for us the most important point: the variety of objective and subjective experiences encompassed within the words "you are sentenced to two years' imprisonment within the custody of the Department of Corrections" demonstrates that even seemingly equal terms of imprisonment often result in only "rough equivalence" and sometimes not even that.

Is all this an argument in favor of disparity of punishment? That certainly is not our purpose. What is argued is that all that can in reality be achieved and all that should in practice be sought is a rough and ready equivalence of punishment in terms of preserving a reasonably fair and just punishment system, doing as much good as it can, and avoiding needless suffering and expense where it can. For these purposes it is the public perception of a punishment system as striving for a rough equality that is determinative. That system cannot rectify the underlying social and personal inequalities on which it rests; it does well if it does not exacerbate them.

It is precisely this more modest view of what is involved in a system of equally deserved punishments that more than justifies interchangeability of punishments between those that are incarcerative and those that are community based—it compels it.

Punishments have different impacts on different people. If non-incarcerative punishments are seen as in the main to impose less suffering on the offender than incarcerative punishments, that is no reason to avoid them, provided the punishment imposed is reasonably appropriate to the offense and the conditions of that punishment are determinedly enforced and backed up on breach, if necessary, by incarcerative punishment.

Rough Equivalence

It may be thought that the reiteration of the idea of "rough equivalences" of punishment reveals the weakness of the idea. Why rough equivalence? Why not equivalence? Is it because there cannot in practice be equal punishment between these different types of sentences and that use of "rough" reveals the superficiality of the concept?

It is often asserted that fairness in punishment requires that punishments be "justly deserved" and that this involves equivalency and some would say identity, but certainly more than "rough equivalency" in the punishment of like cases. But in its most difficult form for those who favor an extended and extending use of intermediate punishments, the proposition is this: if offenders A and B be equally deserving of punishment, judged by the gravity of their crime and the seriousness of their criminal records, then if one is justly sentenced to prison, so should the other.

Sometimes an effort is made to sidestep the rigidity of this assertion by stressing the usual "unlikeness" of cases, to make the point that there can be found in all but exceptional cases some differences of moral desert, gravity of crime, or severity of criminal record that will justify sentencing one to prison while imposing a nonincarcerative punishment on the other. This is, of course, one way of constructing sentencing guidelines to favor the extension of intermediate punishments; stress a presumption favoring nonincarcerative punishments and then list an extended series of aggravating and mitigating circumstances that will facilitate the imposition of a prison term on one of our hypothetical miscreants and an intermediate punishment on the other. In practice, this may well be the way sentencing discretion should be guided, but here, for purposes of analysis, we wish to avoid this easy way out, this delegated discretionary sidestep, and take on the hard issue of whether it is proper, assuming for purposes of the argument absolute identity of "desert," to impose a prison term on one offender and a roughly equivalent noncustodial intermediate punishment on the other. If a year's imprisonment is the appropriate sentence for A, how can a substantial nonincarcerative punishment be justified for B?

Before we answer this question, some ground clearing is in order. In the previous chapter we set out the elements of a comprehensive sentencing system that incorporates prison and nonprison punishments and that allows for interchangeability of roughly equivalent punishments for like-situated offenders. It can be worthy of adoption or of consideration only if in principle it is consonant with prevailing notions of justice and fairness.

To further develop the case for a system of roughly equivalent interchangeable punishments, we must introduce a number of notions and distinctions, and a roadmap of the balance of the chapter may help the reader stay the course with us. First, we explain what we mean by the terms exchange rates and equivalency. Second, we address the question "equivalency in what sense?" There are several possibilities: equivalency in pain or suffering, equivalency in intrusiveness or deprivation of autonomy, equivalency in penal purpose. Third, we consider the process by which rough equivalents are to be identified for policymaking purposes and suggest a principled approach for addressing all of these questions.

EXCHANGE RATES AND ROUGH EQUIVALENCY

For a comprehensive system of sentencing to authorize choices among equivalent incarcerative and nonincarcerative punishments for particular categories of offenders, there must be some language for expressing equivalence, some exchange rates for relating periods of incarceration to periods of intensive supervision probation to amounts of money or community service. In the previous chapter we mentioned the State of Washington's exchange rate of one day's community service for one day's confinement and also various federal proposals and the ambitious proposal in the Minnesota juvenile court dispositional guidelines.

Too close an analogy should not be drawn between "penal exchange rates" and monetary exchange rates, for monetary exchange rates involve both too great precision and too great variation for the rough equivalences we believe should guide sentencing policy.

Fixed monetary exchange rates of the sort negotiated at Bretton Woods—for example, 6.2 French francs to the dollar—offer much greater precision than criminal punishment can sustain. Any reasonable set of sentencing standards will authorize ranges of presumptively appropriate punishments, expressed in months of imprisonment, numbers of day fines, periods of intensive supervision probation. Thus there must be both ranges of authorized sanctions of each type and rough equivalence between sanctions of different types. Fixed exchange rates are much too rigid to serve these ends.

By contrast, modern floating monetary exchange rates are too volatile to serve as a guide. No doubt there are good reasons to allow market forces in the world economy deeply to drive down the dollar's value against the yen, but a sentencing system that abruptly and substantially altered the relations between types of punishments would soon lose its moral authority and credibility.

In sentencing policy, exchange rates must provide a basis seen by the public as reasonably acceptable for setting and applying rough equivalence of punishment for like-situated offenders. At any one time, they must be stable and provide meaningful guidance; over time, they must evolve gradually to reflect changing community values and attitudes toward crime and toward punishment. Thus neither Bretton Woods nor modern currency volatility provides a good model for the exchange rates of sentencing; wisdom suggests a middle way.

EQUIVALENCIES IN PAIN, INTRUSION, AND FUNCTION

To say that a sentencing system must be capable of delivering roughly equivalent punishments for like-situated offenders leaves open a central question: equivalent in what sense? There are at least two realms in which equivalence can be sought. The first looks to equivalence from an offender's perspective, equivalence in pain or intrusiveness; the second, from the perspective of the criminal justice system, equivalence in function.

Equivalence from the offender's perspective can be measured either in pain or suffering or in intrusion on autonomy. In theory, no doubt much could be said about differences between measures of pain and measures of intrusiveness. In practice, whether a year's incarceration or an intermediate punishment package is weighed in visceral terms of pain or unpleasantness or in more abstract analytic terms of intrusion on autonomy is not likely to matter. Criminal punishments are unpleasant burdens, however conceptualized, and it is principally in terms of this onus that punishments must be roughly equivalent.

As we have emphasized, differences between prisoners and differences between prisons banish assumed equivalency. Perhaps only in the judgment of the unthinking is a year's imprisonment the deserved equivalent of a year's imprisonment. By "the judgment of the unthinking" we mean the uninformed lay public which receives most of its knowledge of the criminal justice system from evening tabloids and television detective programs. Nonetheless, our dismissive reference may be a clue to lingering unease in the force of this argument that in terms of condign punishment a year for one is not a year for another and hence that the equality of deserved punishment is illusory. Perhaps it is the uninformed public who matter, not the judges and the criminals. Their expectations of the criminal justice system, and in particular of the judge's sentencing role within that system, is of pronouncements of powerful punishments, inflexible and inexorable, treating all alike, recognizing the central symbolic function of the criminal law and its educative and ego-reinforcing roles. Perhaps these are the attitudes and values that define the range of punishments acceptable for a given criminal with a given record, these are the measures of rough equivalence that will help to define the interchangeability of sentences between the incarcerative and the rest. If so, our thesis holds, though it has to be slightly differently phrased. Within existing public tolerances, there has already been clear demonstration of the public acceptability of intermediate sanctions in many jurisdictions where such sentences have supplanted some prison sentences. Perceived inequality does not seem to be a bar.

One reason for this is that public interest tends to be confined to the most serious or most sensational cases. These are not the cases where intermediate punishments are likely to have their greatest impact. In practice, adequate community acceptability has already been demonstrated of the diversity of punishments we seek. The difficulty of institutionalizing these ideas lies less with community opposition than with an inadequacy of resources and the lack of sufficiently refined jurisprudential principles, a lack to which we now return.

Can a sentencing system take account of such realities and preserve both an *appearance* and the *reality* of evenhanded punishment of the equally undeserving? Within the view of just punishment we adopt, we believe it can. Pain or suffering is a measure of the deserved punishment, to us only in the sense that the punishment imposed must not depreciate the severity of the crime and the criminal's prior record by leniency nor impose pain or suffering in excess of that justified by the crime and the record; within this definable range it seems to us perfectly proper for Mr. A to be sentenced to a prison term while Mr. B is sentenced to an intermediate punishment.

Is there another measure of equivalence of punishment more apt than pain or suffering? Is loss of autonomy the measure? There is certainly a larger measure of restriction of freedom in the prison than in any intermediate sentence, including electronically monitored house arrest. Is this why it is thought unfair to send A and not B to prison? In every physical sense, A may be better off for a year than his cloned friend B, but B remains more of a choosing, self-determining adult, and this is a decisive difference.

We have no complete answer to an equivalency so demanded. Obligations are, of course, imposed on B that severely restrict his autonomy, but the sharp difference remains. All that can be replied to those who would insist on equality of punitive restriction so defined is that it is not achieved now and its achievement would require a revolution in the community's judgment of fair punishment, which seems achievable, if at all, only in a society of far more sensitive punitive instincts than those that now obtain.

So what looks on the tidy face of a guidelines grid to be a single equal sentence of, say, 12 months' imprisonment may, in practice, vary substantially in its impact on the offender. Even rough equivalence in pain and suffering is not achieved by present prison practice, and it would be a most undesirable purpose to pursue.

Rough equivalences, both in fact and in the view of judges and the public, are all that we can hope to achieve no matter how we seek properly guided discretionary sentencing suited both to community needs and community expectations. Put affirmatively, we can well achieve equivalence in sentencing in terms of the functions it serves, evenhandedness in that sense between criminal and criminal.

But this question merits more than dismissal by demonstration of the impossibility of achieving equality of imposed suffering. There is a strong moral sense that this is an insufficient defense of our position. Let us take on the hard case, eschewing not even its racial overtones.

Two young offenders are convicted of robbery; both have a record of drug addiction. Posit equal severity of crime and of criminal record. The sentencing guideline, expressed or customary, in the jurisdiction of their crime suggests a prison term of one year. Criminal A, aged 19, is black, has been unemployed for the past six months, reads at a fifth-grade level, lives in a crowded apartment with his unmarried mother who has two other younger children with her on welfare. Criminal B, also 19, is white, has steady employment which need not be terminated if he is not sent to prison, graduated from high school, is now involved in trade training, and lives with his parents in a middle-class neighborhood. Are the following sentences justified? For Criminal A, one year's imprisonment with a recommendation to the correctional authorities that he be given the opportunity to participate in a drug treatment program while in prison and a release procedure that may assist him to avoid his present drug dependency. For Criminal B, two years' intensive supervision probation with the following conditions: an appropriate period in a residential drug treatment facility, thereafter at least weekly outpatient contacts with that facility with regular urine testing to ensure that he is free of drugs, and an obligation of at least weekly contacts with the probation officer. Restitution and a fine may also be appropriate; he must certainly work and contribute from his current earnings to the cost of his probation supervision and his drug treatment. If he lacks funds and cannot find work, add or extend an obligation of community service.

This is not an unreal hypothesis. The fact of a responsible home and a job and an education makes a dramatic difference to the possibilities of imposing a more socially protective punishment on B than on A. And these realities become even more significant when electronic controls and telephonic reporting are thought appropriate; the underclass is in effect excluded.

In the world as it is these two will certainly be sentenced differently. Is it necessary that in the sentencing world we would bring to pass that they be treated identically?

To insist on equal suffering by Criminal B because of the adverse social conditions of Criminal A is to purchase an illusory equality at too high a price. It is a leveling down and benefits neither Criminal A nor the community. The criminal law cannot rectify social inequalities; those inequalities will inexorably infect rational punishment policies. But this hypothetical situation leaves an uneasy sense of moral imbalance and forces us to the consideration of how deserved punishments can operate fairly in a world of social inequality.

It may be that evenhandedness in punishment should not be measured only in terms of rough equivalence of suffering, whether of pain or of degrees of loss of autonomy, but also in the functions to be fulfilled by a sentencing system. This is the typical lawyer's attachment, and a proper attachment it is, to equality of process. Within rough equivalences of impact on each offender, the just punishment must be imposed pursuant to an evenhanded weighing in every case of the functions to be performed by a criminal sentence.

Equivalence in function thus plays an essential role in the sentencing calculus, guiding or giving sentencing choices within the bounds of not undeserved punishments. If in an individual case the governing purposes at sentencing are retributive and deterrent, a short period of incarceration or a substantial fine may equally well achieve those functional purposes at sentencing. Similarly, if the retributive and incapacitative functions of punishment seem most apposite at sentencing of a drug-using repetitive thief, confinement or house arrest subject to electronic monitoring and frequent unannounced drug testing may be equivalent.

Thus within the bounds set by recognition of rough equivalency in pain or autonomy, we believe that judges at sentencing can appropriately take into account equivalencies in function to be served by different punishments.

For us, the high value we attach to parsimony, the value of avoiding unnecessary suffering, or as others have called it, a policy preference for the least restrictive alternative, urges that the least intrusive punishment be imposed that will within the bounds of not undeserved punishment satisfy the functional purposes primarily to be served at sentencing.

A THEORY OF INTERCHANGEABILITY

When we say a punishment is deserved we rarely mean that it is precisely appropriate in the sense that a deterrent punishment might be in principle, were we to know enough about general deterrence. Rather we mean it is not *undeserved;* that it is neither too lenient nor too severe; that it neither sentimentally understates the wickedness or harmfulness of the crime nor inflicts excessive pain or deprivation on the criminal in relation to the wickedness or harmfulness of the crime. The concept of desert defines relationships between crimes and punishments on a continuum between the unduly lenient and the excessively punitive within which the just sentence may on other grounds be determined, but it cannot do more.

Complexities of social relationships and the dialectic of human thoughts and actions determine over time the values that set these minima and maxima of deserved punishments for diverse crimes. What is determinative is that these values exist and underlie concepts of "desert" which set the limits of acceptable intervals on a spectrum of just punishment.

Desert considerations do not, and cannot, define the specific punishment warranted in any given case, but they can give guidance as to limits. The concept of "just desert" sets the maximum and minimum of the sentence that may be imposed for any offense and helps to define the punishment relationships between offenses; it does not give any more fine-tuning to the appropriate sentence than that. Nor should it. Experience shows that too often decisions about punishment policies are made with the most villainous of offenders in mind. Because of this, there is a long tradition in our jurisprudence of urging that many offenders receive punishments less severe than the most that could be justified. Thus Bentham called for parsimony. The clergy call for mercy. The *Model Penal Code* and the American Bar Association call for the "least restrictive alternative."

Professor Hart suggests in *Punishment and Responsibility* that "there is, for modern minds, something obsecure and difficult in the idea that we should think in choosing punishment of some intrinsic relationship which it must bear to the wickedness of the criminal's act, rather than the effect of the punishment on society and on him."

Matching punishments to desert cannot create an even marginally acceptable system of punishments; there can be no system of just deserts if like cases are to be treated alike. A punishment scheme that sought only desert plus equality would be intolerably severe. If all criminals are to be punished equally according to the harm they have knowingly achieved, Solzhenitsyn's gulag would seem like a country club. If intentional and legally unprovoked killings attract their deserved punishment, a punishment matching the harm encompassed, then we would have approximately 10,000 executions a year in the United States (a country which has never executed 200 in any year). Likewise, white-collar criminals who have intentionally polluted the rivers and streams and atmosphere, or risked the lungs of their workers, would never properly be released from prison. The point is obvious: under a pure and equally applied system of just deserts, who escapes whipping?

So desert plus equality must be modulated if excessive severity is to be avoided. The first necessary modulation is that of proportionality. Larger harms in general must be punished more, lesser harms less. So a graded system of "deserved" and "equal" punishments must be created by which armed robbery risking life must be punished, in the normal case, more than armed robbery not risking life. In the main, crimes against the person attract more punishment than crimes against property. This becomes not a system of justly deserved and equal punishments but a system of less-than-could-be-deserved punishments, ranked by harms achieved and intended, and ranked in terms of moral fault.

But even that system, which might be represented as desert plus equality plus proportionality, would be excessively severe, and for a reason that can easily be stated. Rankings of harms and of moral faults can be done only by rough groupings, unless a system of single instances is to be created, which will lead to gross disparity of punishments. What defines the punishment in each group or in each cell in a sentencing guidelines grid is the "worst case." A legislature or a sentencing commission looking at any such grouping will strongly incline to define the punishment within each cell in utilitarian and punitive terms suited to the most threatening and most wicked criminal within that cell. Hence if a workable system of reasonable fairness is to be developed, we must abandon the idea of equality as an inflexible principle within those cells and move to a system that is parsimonious in the use of punishment within the concepts of desert, equality, and proportionality.

We set aside the modulation of capital punishment as an impossible and intolerable exercise, though the U.S. Supreme Court and many legislatures believe it can be done. How is a prison term to be modulated in a rational sentencing system? First: the groupings or boxes should provide a range. Congress directed that the ranges for prison sentences in the federal sentencing guidelines not exceed 25 percent to cover the diversity within any single imprisonment guideline. That is the first modulation. Second: though a case falls within a guideline range, there may be an unusual mitigating or aggravating factor in this case which merits a reasoned "departure," itself a modulation. Third: there is very great diversity where and how a prison sentence will be served; parsimony and economizing with scarce prison resources will justify a very different level of adversity between one criminal sentenced to prison and another. Anyone acquainted with American prisons knows that they vary from the most brutal and terror-ridden challenges to survival to safe and educative institutions, with family visits, furloughs, work release, graduated release procedures, half-way houses called prisons, and so on. In short, there is ample and proper room for treating individuals sentenced to similar terms within such a system differently on grounds of social protection and humane identification.

All punishments imposed within the roughly equivalent range will be subject to, and properly subject to, amelioration in imposition—not expungement due to inefficiency or overload, as is the current situation of the fine and of probation, but controlled amelioration. For imprisonment, amelioration may come through easier prisons, open institutions, working out, furloughs, graduated release, placement in community treatment centers, and so on. For fines, reduction or more time to pay on cause shown, serious efforts having been made. For probation with condition of being drug free, since addiction is a relapsing disease, judgment must be used in relation to positive urine tests and revocation. For intensive probation, successful adjustment, passage of time, and so on.

The following scheme summarizes these propositions about desert, equality, proportionality, parsimony, and punishment:

desert + equality = grossly excessive severity

desert + equality + proportionality = excessive severity

desert + modulated equality + proportionality + parsimony =

a reasonably fair and workable punishment system

Punishments should be imposed under the ceilings, the maxima roughly defined by concepts of what is not undeserved and what is not too unequal between similar criminals; they are then fine-tuned by ideas of social protection, economizing with scarce punishment resources and the minimization of suffering, even that of criminals. It is our view that unless punishment systems are seen as blending these elements—and not necessarily as we have blended them—they will be out of touch with social reality and will be circumvented in one any way or another by those who have to implement them.

In short, we seek to move from a system of punishment in which pain is not the measure but the limit of punishment and a system in which equality in the application of sentencing purposes supplants the illusory search for a system of equality of condign pain.

References

American Bar Association. 1980. *American Bar Association Standards for Criminal Justice,* Volume 2. Boston: Little, Brown.

Davies, Robertson. 1970. *Fifth Business.* New York: Viking.

Hart, H. L. A. 1968. *Punishment and Responsibility: Essays in the Philosophy of Law.* Oxford: Oxford University Press.

Minnesota Citizens Council on Crime and Justice. 1982. *Juvenile Court Dispositional Guidelines: Handbook for Advisory Sanction Levels.* Minneapolis: Minnesota Citizens Council on Crime and Justice.

Morris, Norval. 1974. *The Future of Imprisonment.* Chicago: University of Chicago Press.

———. 1976. "Punishment, Desert, and Rehabilitation." In *Equal Justice Under Law: U.S. Department of Justice Bicentennial Lecture Series.* Washington, D.C.: U.S. Government Printing Office.

Nozick, Robert. 1981. *Philosophical Explanations.* Cambridge, Mass.: Harvard University Press.

U.S. Sentencing Commission. 1987. *Manual: Sentencing Guidelines.* Washington, D.C.: U.S. Sentencing Commission.

von Hirsch, Andrew. 1985. *Past or Future Crimes.* New Brunswick, N.J.: Rutgers New York: Hill and Wang.

Vonnegut, Kurt. 1968. *Welcome to the Monkey House.* New York: Delacorte Press/Seymour Lawrence.

[15] Proportionality, Parsimony, and Interchangeability of Punishments

If intermediate punishments are to be used more widely, procedures and principles governing their use must be developed. Although new intermediate punishments are often conceived in large part for use in lieu of incarceration, experience on three continents shows that many judges prefer to impose such penalties on offenders who would not otherwise be bound for prison. Working out procedures governing intermediate punishments will be hard enough. Working out principles governing imposition of penalties in individual cases may be harder and will require consideration of finer-grained issues than writing on the philosophy of punishment traditionally addresses. Most philosophical writing on punishment deals with broad issues of justification. Insofar as questions of distribution are considered, attention focuses on prison sentences. Because prison sentences can be expressed in seemingly objective units of months or years, and since 'disparity' in prison terms looks prima facie to be a bad thing, recent writing on the distribution of punishment celebrates what Andrew von Hirsch (1992) calls 'the principle of proportionality.'

The theses of this essay are that strong proportionality constraints in the distribution of punishments generally are likely to cause more injustice than they prevent, and that application of strong proportionality constraints to intermediate sanctions will stifle their development, circumscribe their use, and produce avoidable injustices.

There are three fundamental problems with a strong proportionality principle. First, by celebrating equality in suffering for 'like-situated' offenders, it often requires imposition of more severe and intrusive punishments than are required by prevailing social norms and political values. Second, it misleadingly objectifies punishment, by allocating punishments in terms of 'like-situated offenders' and generic penalties. Third, it ignores the problem of 'just deserts in an unjust society'. Most offenders committing common law crimes come from disadvantaged backgrounds, and disproportionately they come from minority groups. Arguments for a highly proportional system of deserved punishments evade the question of whether offenders from deeply deprived backgrounds deserve the same penalties as do other, less deprived, offenders.

A punishment system permitting interchangeability of roughly equivalent penalties is likely, overall, to be more just, less harsh, and more sensitive to problems of social injustice than a punishment system predicated on desert-based proportionality. 'Like-situated offenders' convicted of comparable crimes can justly receive quite different sentences including financial penalties for some, incarceration for others, and community-based sanctions for still others.

This essay attempts to demonstrate and defend the preceding observations. Part I describes policy developments that make consideration of the applied philosophy of intermediate sanctions timely. Part II reviews philosophical writings on punishment and argues that principles of proportionality and parsimony are in stark conflict in general and in many specific cases. Part III examines in some detail Andrew von Hirsch's arguments for a strong principle of proportionality and his proposals for devising a punishment scheme premised on proportionality concerns. Part IV offers a critique of von Hirsch's proposals and Part V sketches a counter-proposal that reconciles concerns for proportionality and parsimony.

WHY INTERMEDIATE PUNISHMENTS?

Policy makers in the United Kingdom and the United States are considering how to incorporate intermediate punishments into comprehensive sentencing policies.[1] Passage in the UK of the Criminal Justice Act 1991 with its increased emphasis on non-custodial penalties has drawn attention to the subject.

In the United States, historically high and growing prison populations, severe pressures on public budgets, and the evolution of the American sentencing reform movement have combined to focus interest on non-custodial (or partly custodial) penalties, and on the integration of non-custodial penalties into comprehensive systems of sentencing guidelines.

American incarceration rates have risen steadily since 1970 but startlingly since 1980, when the number of sentenced offenders held in state prisons (that is, disregarding those in county jails serving sentences of one year or less) stood at 330,000. By 30 June 1992, that number had increased to 856,000. The combined prison and jail incarceration rate in 1990 was 455 per 100,000 population, a level five to ten times that of most developed countries. On 31 December 1991, state prisons were on average operating at 131 per cent of rated capacity and federal prisons at 146 per cent.

Competition for scarce public funds, coupled with a continuing federal commitment to a 'war on drugs' and an ever-toughening crime control strategy, produced great interest in the 1980s in a wide range of intermediate punishments, including house arrest, intensive (sometimes fifteen to twenty-five contacts per month) probation, day-reporting centers, restitution, community service, electronic monitoring, residential drug treatment, day fines, and boot camps.

Many intermediate punishment programs have failed to achieve their objectives. Initiated in hopes of reducing prison crowding (by diverting less serious offenders from prison), reducing recidivism (by enhancing surveillance and some services), and reducing costs (by shifting offenders from more-expensive prisons to less-expensive community programs), in many programs none of these goals are being realised. When tested, these programs generally achieve no worse, but no better, recidivism rates than do prisons when comparable groups of offenders are compared. Many judges order intermediate punishments for offenders who otherwise would receive probation. This increases costs. Moreover, because intermediate sanctions are more intensive and structured than probation, more condition violations and new offenses are observed and acted upon; in many programs 40 to 50 per cent of offenders are ejected for misconduct and sent to prison or jail as punishment. Since many of these offenders would in past years have received probation, they are in effect shifted twice upwards, first to an intermediate sanction and then to prison. This also increases costs. If intermediate punishments are to achieve their goals, it has become clear that standards are needed both for assigning offenders to particular penalties and for setting 'back-up' penalties for violations of program conditions.

A few states have taken tentative steps toward standards for use of intermediate sanctions. Washington allows for modest interchangeability of punishments (e.g., day-for-day substitution of community service days for up to thirty days confinement). Oregon, in addition to setting presumptive sentencing ranges in months, specifies 'punishment units' for each cell in its guidelines grid, to provide a generic coin to permit (an as yet uncompleted task) convertibility of sanctions. Pennsylvania includes the words 'intermediate punishments' in the lower levels of its guidelines, although no other guidance is offered. Many Minnesota counties, and some individual judges across the country, use local guidelines for non-custodial penalties.

There are, however, no well-established models for devising comprehensive systems of structured sentencing discretion that incorporate intermediate punishments. Both mechanics and normative rationales need development. Unusually, policy makers are interested in learning what theorists and philosophers can tell them, and if the advice makes sense, policy makers are likely to pay attention.

Two broad, albeit not fully developed, approaches have been proposed. One, associated with Andrew von Hirsch, Martin Wasik, and Andrew Ashworth, among others, calls for stacking of punishments: prison terms scaled to offense severity for the most serious crimes, restrictive community sanctions for the next-most-serious, large financial penalties for the next-most-serious, and so on, allowing relatively little latitude for imposition of different kinds of punishment on like-situated offenders (Wasik and von Hirsch, 1988; Ashworth, 1992). A second, proposed by Norval Morris and me, allows for much greater substitution and interchangeability of punishments and proportions maximum penal vulnerability to offense severity but allows substantial discretion to impose less severe sentences (Morris and Tonry, 1990).

Increased interest in intermediate sanctions has sharply posed the conflict between principles of proportionality and parsimony. Concern for proportionality calls for like treatment of like-situated offenders. Concern for parsimony, a Hippocratic criminal justice prescription to do least harm, calls for imposing the least severe punishment that meets legitimate social purposes.

The tension between proportionality and parsimony has always existed below the surface in indeterminate sentencing systems, and is likely to survive silently in recent Swedish and English schemes that rely on principles rather than numbers for guidance to judges. Without guidelines, judges can balance concerns for deserved punishments and parsimony in individual cases. Lip service can be paid to concern for horizontal equity, avoiding disparity, and treating like cases alike. Without concrete criteria of proportionate sentencing, individual sentences cannot easily be assessed for their consistency with proportionality principles.

The tension between proportionality and parsimony, however, became apparent when American jurisdictions began to develop sentencing guidelines for prison sentences and it became acute when policy makers began to work on standards for non-custodial penalties. American sentencing guidelines to date mostly set standards for prison sentences calibrated to measures of current and past criminality. Proportionality is a prominent feature. Guidelines derive in part from concern to alleviate sentencing disparities; once offenses are scaled for severity, some proportionality between penalties for different offenses inexorably follows. In effect, sentencing guidelines for prison sentences prefer proportionality over parsimony. If some sentences are harsher than judges believe appropriate, the harshness is said to be justifiable because the punishment is no more or less severe than that suffered by 'like-situated' offenders.

JURISDICTION AND DISTRIBUTION

The tension between proportionality and parsimony and the problem of just deserts in an unjust world are the fundamental problems facing an applied philosophy of punishment concerning intermediate sanctions. This section attempts to frame these issues by considering how Bentham and Kant might address proportionality in distribution and then looking at how modern writers have addressed it.

Proportionality based on justification

Neither classical utilitarian punishment theories in principle nor classical retributive theories in practice provide convincing explanations of why punishment should (or can) observe strict proportionality conditions.

Proportionality is presumably a value for utilitarians only to the extent that its non-observance produces net dissatisfaction. For utilitarians, invoking Bentham, punishment itself is an evil and should be used as sparingly as possible: 'upon the principle of utility, if [punishment] ought at all to be admitted, it ought only to be admitted in as far as it promises to exclude some greater evil' (Bentham, 1948 [1789], p. 281, quoted in Pincoffs, 1966, p. 20).

No doubt utilitarian concerns require some observance of proportionality in punishment. Punishments completely divorced from community notions of fairness – in our time, perhaps, to refuse to punish child abusers, or to sentence two of three equally culpable participants in a crime to five years imprisonment and the third to a $50 fine – would produce unacceptable levels of dissatisfaction and indicate, on utility grounds, that some greater acknowledgement of the importance of violated community values is required; however, that imposes at most only a weak proportionality condition, relating punishment not to notions of desert but to notions of social consequences.

Thoroughgoing retributivists, for whom a retributive justification of punishment entails retribution in distribution, might prefer a system of perfectly proportioned punishments, but in practice such a system is unrealizable. Kant's principle of equality, the Right of Retaliation, 'the mode and measure of punishment which public justice takes as its principle and standard', has practical limits. It may be that 'the principle of equality . . . may be rendered by saying that the undeserved evil which anyone commits on another is to be regarded as perpetrated on himself' (Kant, 1887 [1797], pp. 195–7), but it is far from clear what that means. Capital punishment for murder, a $500 penalty for a $500 theft, perhaps (squeamishly) a beating for an assault; these crimes and punishments satisfy the test. But how to punish an attempted murder, a rape, emotional abuse of the elderly, securities fraud, environmental crimes? No doubt systems of scaled punishment can be devised, but only with formidable working out of details. Does Kant's principle of equality require punishment scaled to the offender's culpability, to the offender's benefit, to the victim's harm? What of villainous attempts that serendipitously produce no harm? What of venial crimes that unforeseeably produce great harm? Is the offender's evil-doing to be assessed as the Recording Angel would, taking account of his weaknesses, the pressures to which he was subject, his motives, or primarily as measured by the objective evil his offense embodies?

Proportionality in distribution

The normative conflict concerning proportionality in distribution is between those (e.g., Ashworth, 1992; von Hirsch, 1992) who believe that equality and proportion in distribution are overridingly important and those (Hart, 1968; Honderich, 1989, pp. 237–41; Morris and Tonry, 1990, ch. 4; Walker, 1991, ch. 15) who do not.

There are at least three major categories of writers on punishment who argue for weak proportionality conditions. First, writing in a utilitarian framework, and positing that punishment has principally preventive purposes, H. L. A. Hart writes of 'the somewhat hazy requirement that 'like cases be treated alike'' (1968, p. 24). Hart's argument for this modest recognition of proportionality is, however, not retributively premised but derives from concern for the adverse social effects of divorcing punishment too greatly from common morality: 'for where the legal gradation of crime expressed in the relative severity of penalties diverges sharply from this rough scale, there is a risk of confusing common morality or flouting it and bringing the law into contempt' (p. 25).

Second, proponents of hybrid theories, including Morris (1974) and Honderich (1989), argue that principled systems of punishment must take account of both preventive and retributive considerations. Honderich (1989), for example, argues that retribution, in James Fitzjames Stephens' sense of revenge and satisfaction of grievance, and deterrence, each have roles to play (1989, pp. 233–7). Morris (1974) argues for a system of limiting retributivism in which punishment's primary purposes are preventive but subject to the desert constraint that punishments be 'not undeserved' and, within the range of not undeserved punishments, the parsimonious constraint that no punishment be imposed that is more severe than is necessary to achieve legitimate social purposes.

Third, proponents of a variety of ideal punishment theories reject their policy implications on 'just deserts in an unjust world' grounds but presumably would allow room for distributive echoes of their ideal rationales. R. A. Duff, for example, rejects his own retributive/expressive ideal theory in favor of deterrent approaches for social injustice reasons. This is my own view as well: in the abstract I have some sympathy for a retributive scheme with strong proportionality conditions; in practice, observing that the vast preponderance of common law offenders are poor, ill-educated, often mentally subnormal, and often from minority groups, I believe that punishment strongly committed to proportionality will exacerbate social injustice and further disadvantage the already disadvantaged.

THE PRINCIPLE OF PROPORTIONALITY

Andrew von Hirsch has, over the last fifteen years (e.g., 1976, 1985, 1992), shown how a punishment system can be devised and justified that has equality and proportionality as central elements. For many people, there is strong intuitive appeal in a punishment system that attaches high value to equality and proportionality. Public opinion surveys have repeatedly demonstrated strong public support for the maxim 'treat like cases alike and different cases differently' (e.g., Doble, Immerwahr, and Richardson, 1991).

Von Hirsch acknowledges both the limits of Kant's 'principle of equality' and human incapacity to specify the single ideally appropriate punishment for any individual offender who has committed a particular offense, but nonetheless offers a comprehensive scheme for assuring proportionality. He distinguishes between ordinal and cardinal magnitudes of punishments (1985, ch. 4). The cardinal magnitude is the unknowable, single deserved penalty. Ordinal magnitude indicates a crime's seriousness relative to other crimes. In von Hirsch's scheme, cardinal magnitudes can be approximated or negotiated for use in setting the 'anchoring points' of a punishment scale, the most and (possibly) the least severe punishments that can appropriately be imposed on offenders. Within these anchoring points, punishments can be scaled in terms of relative severity of offenses. Assuming, for example, that crimes were divided into fifteen severity categories, level 8 offenses should, all else being equal, be punished more severely than level 7 offenses and less severely than level 9 offenses. Thus, the combination of cardinal anchors with ordinal rankings celebrates equality (all level 8 offenses receive similar punishments) and proportionality (less serious offenses receive less severe punishments, more serious offenses receive more severe punishments). Some subsidiary issues remain a bit vague, including specification of anchoring points, the step problem (how many severity categories), and the interval problem (are the severity differences between offense levels the same throughout the scale, or may it be that, for example, level 10 offenses are only 10 per cent more serious than level 9 offenses while level 5 offenses are twice as serious as those at level 4?). In a work in progress, von Hirsch is addressing these and other questions.

Rationale

The overall premise of von Hirsch's argument is that punishment is an exercise in blaming, and proportionality is a necessary implication. Persons committing relatively more severe offenses are relatively more blameworthy and deserve relatively more severe punishments.

Prior record

Von Hirsch's punishment scheme is based principally on *offenses*, with only minor adjustments to take account of prior criminality. Some writers on just deserts (Fletcher, 1978; Singer, 1979) argue that prior criminality should have no effect on punishment for a new crime; prior penalties have 'paid for' prior crimes.

Von Hirsch allows some increases of penalty for past crimes on the rationale that penalties for a first offense should be somewhat less than is deserved. Because a first offense may be out of character and result from extenuating situational conditions, first offenders may be less blameworthy than it appears and should be given the benefit of the doubt. For some number of subsequent offenses, a gradually disappearing discount may be appropriate. Thereafter each offense should receive its full, deserved, proportionate punishment.

Measure of offense

Although von Hirsch has written about concepts of scaling crime severity, his proportionality analysis takes criminal codes more or less as given. Thus, answers to classical, substantive law harm-versus-culpability arguments – whether attempts should be punished as seriously as completed crimes, whether fortuitous harm (the picked pocket containing the unexpected thousand-dollar coin, the assault that unforeseeably results in death) is relevant to punishment, whether there should be a general defense of necessity – do not shape the scale.

Measure of culpability

Von Hirsch's scheme is premised on legal, rather than moral, assessments of blameworthiness (although the rationale for leniency for first offenders shades into character assessment). The offender is to be blamed for the *offense*, not for the moral culpability it expresses. If Jean Valjean and Leona Helmsley are both convicted of stealing bread, they are to be blamed for stealing bread and identically punished accordingly. Although von Hirsch coined the phrase 'just deserts in an unjust society' in *Doing Justice* (1976), he argues that, on balance, disadvantaged offenders will be better served under a desert scheme than under a utilitarian scheme: they will be punished no more severely than others for a given offense (as they might under predictive [more likely to reoffend] or deterrent [more likely to be tempted] systems). And if they are stigmatised by conviction and punishment, at least the resulting 'disabilities are the consequence of the person's own actions in having violated the law' (1976, p. 148).

Standard punishments

Just as offenses are considered generically for purposes of scaling and punishment, punishments are designed to deal with 'standard cases' and the 'characteristic onerousness of various sanctions' (von Hirsch, 1990, p. 10). One contrary view, as with the contrary view of offender culpability, would be to consider the subjective impact of the sanction on the offender. Another would be to take account of the objective conditions of different kinds of institutions, different probation regimes, and so on.

Von Hirsch notes these possibilities but responds in three ways. First, the 'law generally works with standard cases', and why not here? Second, in special (limited) circumstances, such as illness or advanced age, there might be deviations from the standard case. Third, although sanction severity depends in part on subjective painfulness, it also depends on 'the moral importance of the rights taken away' (1990, p. 10) and prison deprives crucial liberty rights of free movement and association.

Von Hirsch's scheme could provide a comprehensive desert-based system of punishment. The question is whether such a system offers a just and practicable system for punishing convicted offenders.

CRITIQUE OF PRINCIPLE OF PROPORTIONALITY

Efforts to apply philosophers' distinctions to policy-makers' decisions necessarily raise different concerns than do disagreements among philosophers. Current initiatives to increase use of 'non-custodial' penalties in the United Kingdom and 'intermediate' sanctions in the United States necessarily require translation of theorists' distinctions into practitioners' realities.

It is at this point of translation that the case for strong proportionality conditions breaks down. There are at least five major difficulties. First, strong proportionality conditions require objectification of categories of offenders and offenses that are oversimplified and overinclusive. Second, proportionality arguments are often premised on objective legal measures of desert, typically current and past crimes, rather than on the subjective degree of moral culpability expressed by the offender, under particular circumstances and conditions. Third, strong proportionality conditions run head-on into 'just deserts in an unjust society'. Fourth, strong proportionality conditions violate notions of parsimony by requiring imposition of unnecessarily severe punishments in individual cases in order to assure formal equivalence of suffering. Fifth, strong proportionality conditions presuppose that imposition of offenders' deserved punishments is an overriding moral imperative rather than one of several competing ethical considerations.

The illusion of 'like-situated offenders'

If recent efforts in the United Kingdom and the United States to increase use of intermediate sanctions are to succeed, the appropriateness of different punishments for 'like-situated offenders' must be recognised.

'Like-situated offender' is nested in quotation marks to express the artificiality of notions of like-situated offenders, comparable crimes, and generic punishments. A strong proportionality-in-punishment argument insists on equal treatment of like-situated offenders and proportionately different treatment of differently situated offenders. A fundamental difficulty is that this assumes that offenders can conveniently and justly be placed into a manageable number of more-or-less desert categories and that standard punishments can be prescribed for each category. Unfortunately, neither side of the desert-punishment equation lends itself to standardization.

Neither offenders nor punishments come in standard cases. The practice of dividing offenders and punishments into generic categories produces much unnecessary suffering and provides only illusory proportionality. A look at Minnesota's sentencing guidelines shows why.

Figure 3.1 sets out the original 1980 Minnesota sentencing guidelines grid, which was expressly premised on 'modified just deserts'.[2] Offenses are divided on the vertical axis into ten categories and on the horizontal axis into seven categories of criminal history. An offender's presumptive sentence is determined by consulting the cell at which the row containing his conviction offense meets the column expressing his criminal history. Cases falling in cells below the bold black line are presumed bound for state prison for a term of months within the narrow range specified. Cases falling above the line are presumed not bound for prison (the number in the above-the-line cells represents the prison sentence to be imposed if the offender fails satisfactorily to complete a nonprison sentence).

Because the guidelines attach high value to proportionality, 'departures' are discouraged. Either party may appeal a departure which, to be upheld, must be found to have been based on 'substantial and compelling' reasons. Rules set out illustrative bases for departures and forbid some. For example, the original rules prohibited departures based on offenders' educational, vocational, family, or marital circumstances and also forbade departures based on predictions of dangerousness or 'amenability' to treatment.[3] The reasons behind these prohibitions are not unattractive – to prevent judges from favoring more advantaged, often white, offenders over more disadvantaged,

Figure 3.1 Minnesota sentencing guidelines grid (in months)

Severity levels of conviction offense		Criminal history score						
		0	1	2	3	4	5	6
Unauthorised use of motor vehicle Possession of Marijuana	I	12*	12*	12*	15	18	21	24
Theft-related crimes ($150–2,500) Sale of marijuana	II	12*	12*	14	17	20	23	27 *25–29*
Theft crimes ($150–2,500)	III	12*	13	16	19	22 *21–23*	27 *25–29*	32 *30–34*
Burglary – felony intent Receiving stolen goods ($150–2,500)	IV	12*	15	18	21	25 *24–26*	32 *30–34*	41 *37–45*
Simple robbery	V	18	23	27	30 *29–31*	38 *36–40*	46 *43–49*	54 *50–58*
Assault, 2nd degree	VI	21	26	30	34 *33–35*	44 *42–46*	54 *50–58*	65 *60–70*
Aggravated robbery	VII	24 *23–25*	32 *30–34*	41 *38–44*	49 *45–53*	65 *60–70*	81 *75–87*	97 *90–104*
Assault, 1st Degree Criminal sexual conduct, 1st degree	VIII	43 *41–45*	54 *50–58*	65 *60–70*	76 *71–81*	95 *89–101*	113 *106–120*	132 *124–140*
Murder, 3rd degree	IX	97 *94–100*	119 *116–122*	127 *124–130*	149 *143–155*	176 *168–184*	205 *195–215*	230 *218–242*
Murder, 2nd degree	X	116 *111–121*	140 *133–147*	162 *153–171*	203 *192–214*	243 *231–255*	284 *270–298*	324 *309–339*

Notes:
* one year and one day
Italicised numbers within the grid denote the range within which a judge may sentence without the sentence being deemed a departure.

Source: Minnesota Sentencing Guidelines Commission (1980)

often black or Indian, offenders, to prevent imposition or prolongation of prison sentenees on rehabilitative or incapacitative grounds, and to prevent judges from departing from presumptive prison sentences for middle-class offenders because they are especially amenable to non-incarcerative sentences.

Minnesota's tidy system, whatever its abstract merits, overaggregates offenders in at least four ways. First, consider Table 3.1, which shows the offenses that fall within offense severity levels five and six, and Table 3.2, which shows the rudiments of the scheme for calculating criminal histories. Persons convicted of solicitation of some forms of prostitution are considered equally as culpable as people convicted of robbery or second degree manslaughter, and persons convicted of four minor property misdemeanors are considered as culpable as people convicted of a violent felony. A person convicted of solicitation with four prior misdemeanor convictions is thus, for Minnesota sentencing purposes, like-situated to a person convicted of manslaughter or robbery with a prior robbery conviction. Similarly, a person convicted of sale of marijuana with four misdemeanor convictions is like-situated to a person convicted of forcible rape with a prior rape conviction. There are plausible arguments for why offenders were grouped and criminal history scores calibrated as they were. The Minnesota commission was serious and idealistic in making these decisions. Nonetheless, at day's end, offenders classified by Minnesota as like-situated will in many peoples' eyes look very unlike indeed.

Table 3.1 Offense levels V and VI, Minnesota sentencing guidelines (1 January 1980 version)

Level V
Vehicular homicide
Criminal sexual conduct (3rd degree) – statutory rape, offender more than 2 years older
Manslaughter (2nd degree)
Perjury – in felony trial or firearms permit application
Possession of incendiary device
Robbery
Solicitation of prostitution
Tampering with a witness

Level VI
Arson (2nd degree) – with over $2,500 loss
Assault (2nd degree) – with a deadly weapon
Burglary of a dwelling while armed
Crimial sexual conduct (2nd degree) – statutory rape
Criminal sexual conduct (4th degree) – forcible rape or incompetent victim
Escape – with violence or threat
Kidnapping – victim released unharmed
Receipt of stolen goods – over $2,500
Sale of hallucinogens
Sale of heroin
Sale of other narcotics

Source: Minnesota Sentencing Guidelines Commission (1980).

Second, Minnesota's guidelines are based on *conviction offenses*,[4] which are at best imperfect and inconsistent measures of culpability. Because of ubiquitous plea bargaining in the United States, one of two equal participants in a robbery may be convicted of robbery and the other of aggravated robbery. Similarly, one may plead guilty to

Table 3.2 Criminal history score, Minnesota sentencing guidelines (1 January 1980 version)

Each previous felony conviction	1 point
Current offense committed while on probation or parole, in jail or prison, or released pending sentencing for prior crime	1 point
Four prior misdemeanor convictions	1 point
Two prior gross misdemeanor convictions	1 point

Source: Minnesota Sentencing Guidelines Commission (1980).

the reduced charge of robbery while the other is convicted at trial of aggravated robbery. Of two otherwise comparable robbers, one might be charged in a rural county where prosecutorial policy requires guilty pleas to the full offense (aggravated robbery), whilst another is allowed to plead to robbery in an urban county where aggravated robberies are common and office policy routinely permits acceptance of pleas to lesser offenses. For reasons of local prosecution priorities, or limited manpower, or concern with evidentiary problems, one offender may be convicted of a greatly reduced offense while another comparable offender not affected by those considerations will be convicted of the full offense. The point is not to challenge the legitimacy of the considerations that lead to convictions of particular crimes in particular cases, but to point out that offenders convicted of the same offense may have committed very different acts reflecting very different culpability and, conversely, that offenders convicted of different crimes may have committed comparable acts with similar culpability.

Third, looking behind the grid, Minnesota allows little play for non-criminal-record factors to influence penalties. Consider a minority offender who grew up in a single-parent, welfare-supported household, who has several siblings in prison and who was formerly drug-dependent but who has been living in a common-law marriage for five years, has two children whom he supports, and has worked steadily for three years at a service station – first as an attendant, then an assistant mechanic, and now a mechanic. In Minnesota, none of these personal characteristics are supposed to influence the sentencing decision, and certainly not to justify imposition of a non-custodial sentence on a presumed prison-bound offender. For people who believe in individualised sentences, on either utilitarian or retributive grounds, Minnesota's refusal to consider my hypothetical offender's promising features will seem regrettable. For people concerned by the gross over-representation in courts, jails, and prisons of deeply disadvantaged people, Minnesota's refusal to consider evidence that my hypothetical offender is overcoming the odds will seem deeply regrettable.

Fourth, Minnesota attaches no significance to the collateral effects of a prison sentence on the offender, or on the offender's family or children, what Nigel Walker (1991, pp. 106–08) calls incidental (on the offender) and obiter (on the offender's dependents and associates) effects of punishment. Incarceration for a drug crime for a woman raising children by herself may result in the break-up of her family and placement of her children in foster homes or institutions, or in homes of relatives who will not be responsible care-providers. Incarceration of an employed father and husband may mean loss of the family's home and car, perhaps the break-up of a marriage, perhaps the creation of welfare dependency by the wife and children. To ignore that incidental and obiter effects of punishments vary widely among seemingly like-situated offenders is to ignore things that most people find important.

Thus, for a wide diversity of reasons, offenders whom Minnesota's sentencing guidelines treat as like-situated often are not. A similar analysis could be offered of the punishment side of the crime and punishment equation. Objectively, punishments valued in the generic coin of imprisonment can be very different. In most American jurisdictions, a prison sentence means 'placed in the custody of the department of corrections', which in turn can mean anything from placement in a fear-ridden, gang-dominated maximum security prison under lock-up twenty-three hours a day, through placement in a minimum security camp or campus, to home confinement. Objectively, a sentence to twenty-four months probation can mean anything from living normally and mailing a bi-monthly postcard to the probation office to being contacted ten to twenty-five times a month, reporting to the probation office three times a week, observing a curfew, and being subject to frequent unannounced urinalyses.

Subjectively, three years' imprisonment may mean very different things to a twenty-three-year-old gang member, for whom it is a rite of passage; a forty-year-old employed husband and father, for whom it will likely destroy the material conditions of his and his family's lives; a frightened, effeminate twenty-year-old middle-class student, for whom it may result in sexual victimization; or a seventy-year-old, for whom it may be life imprisonment.

Problems of objectification of crimes, offenders, and punishments are especially stark in a numerical guidelines system. In systems that feature written policy guidelines, they lurk beneath the surface. The Minnesota illustration is generally relevant to analysis of proportionality in punishment, however, because it makes real world implications of strong proportionality conditions starkly apparent. If proportionality is an, or the, overriding principle in the distribution of punishment in practice, then the imperfections of objectification that I describe are presumably regrettable but acceptable costs to be paid for a principled punishment system. If they appear unacceptable, the problem may be that the principle of proportionality offers less helpful guidance than its proponents urge.

Objective measures of responsibility

Von Hirsch's proportionality argument relies on objective measures of penal deservedness. This is curious. Desert theories, especially blaming theories, are premised on notions of individual blameworthiness, which seem inexorably linked to particularised judgments about moral responsibility. Objective measures of harm are seldom sufficient for conviction in the criminal law: that is why doctrines of competency, *mens rea*, and affirmative defense exist and why doctrines like strict liability and felony-murder are disfavored. If individualised moral judgments are germane to conviction, it is not obvious why they are not also germane to punishment.

If punishment is principally about blaming, surely it is relevant whether the offender was mentally impaired, socially disadvantaged, a reluctant participant, or moved by humane motives. Surely it is morally relevant, whatever the path to conviction, what the offender did, with what *mens rea*, and under what circumstances. Surely it is morally relevant whether a particular punishment will be more intensely experienced by one person than by another. In other words, the three subjective considerations that Minnesota's guidelines ignore – what did he really do, what will the conditions of his sanction really be, will he suffer more intensely than others – are relevant to moral judgments of blameworthiness and proportionate punishments. Nigel Walker expresses this when he observes: 'Retributive reasoning would lead instead to a 'personal price list' which would take into account not only gradations of harm but offenders' culpability and sensibility' (1991, p. 103).[5]

The failure of von Hirsch's arguments to take account of individualised differences in culpability and individual effects of punishment looks strange when we recall that von Hirsch's is a retributive theory. Utilitarian theories reject interpersonal comparisons of utility, as Lionel Robbins' classic essay (1938) explains, either on measurement grounds (variable intensity of satisfactions, utility monsters, and so on), or on normative grounds (no individual's satisfactions *should* count for more). However, utilitarian theories are concerned with general policies and aggregate social measures and not with fine-tuned moral judgments.

An unjust society

Punishment schemes that attach high value to proportionality necessarily ignore the differing material conditions of life, including poverty, social disadvantage, and bias, in which human personalities and characters take form. The substantive criminal law rejects motive for intention and in the English-speaking countries allows no formal excusing or mitigating defense of social disadvantage. Yet in both the United Kingdom and the United States, most common law offenders are products of disadvantaged and deprived backgrounds and in both countries vastly disproportionate numbers of alleged, convicted, and imprisoned offenders are members of racial and ethnic minorities. The likelihood, for example, that a black American male is in prison today is eight times greater than that a white American male is in prison.

The problem of 'just deserts in an unjust world' is a fundamental problem for a strong proportionality constraint. Whether retributive theories are rationalised in terms of benefits and burdens, or equilibrium, or blaming, or condemnation, or penance, they must presume equal opportunities for all to participate in society. When some are disabled from full participation by discrimination, disability, or exclusion, by denial of access to public goods, by the burdens of social and economic disadvantage, it is difficult to claim that they enjoy the benefits of autonomy that produce obligation. To take just one example, proponents of benefits and burdens theories are hard pressed to explain how a person who is denied society's benefits deserves to be burdened by social obligation.

Many writers on the philosophy of punishment from both retributive and utilitarian premises recognise this problem. R. A. Duff, after developing an ideal theory of expressive punishment based on social condemnation and individual penance, rejects his own proposals in favor of a deterrence-premised system because: 'punishment is not justifiable within our present legal system; it will not be justifiable unless and until we have brought about deep and far-reaching social, political, legal, and moral changes in ourselves and our society' (1986, p. 294).

Jeffrey Murphy, after developing an ideal punishment theory deriving from a Rawlsian original-position analysis of benefits and burdens, rejects it on grounds that it will not serve justice until 'we have restructured society in such a way that criminals genuinely do correspond to the only model that will render punishment permissible – i.e., make sure that they are autonomous and that they do benefit in the requisite sense' (1973, p. 110).

Even Andrew von Hirsch, arguing that a desert-based system of distribution will achieve less additional disadvantage to the disadvantaged than a utilitarian system, concludes nonetheless: 'as long as a substantial segment of the population is denied adequate opportunities for a livelihood, any scheme for punishing must be morally flawed' (1986, p. 149).

Not surprisingly, proponents of utilitarian and mixed punishment theories acknowledge the same problem. H. L. A. Hart, for example, in explaining the role of excuses in the substantive criminal law, notes in respect of deeply disadvantaged people, 'The admission that the excusing condition may be of no value to those who are below a minimum level of economic prosperity may mean, of course, that we should incorporate as a further excusing condition the pressure of gross forms of economic necessity' (1968, p. 51).

Ted Honderich, who argues for a hybrid punishment theory, observes: 'there is nothing that can be called the question of [punishment's] moral justification which is left to be considered if one puts aside the great question of the distribution of goods in society' (1989, pp. 238–9).

In the United States, giving lip service to concern for offenders from disadvantaged backgrounds, most sentencing commissions have forbidden judges to 'depart' from sentencing guidelines on grounds of offenders' personal circumstances. The putative rationale for such policies is that judges would favor middle-class offenders in mitigating sentences. This rationale is empirically misconceived and perverse; only an insignificant proportion of common law offenders are from middle- and upper-class backgrounds. The normal range of socio-economic backgrounds of common law offenders ranges from the deeply disadvantaged to the merely deprived. The chimerical middle-class offender is conspicuous by his absence. The perversity of such policies is that they forbid special treatment of offenders from deprived backgrounds who have achieved some personal successes. The minority offender from a broken home and a devastated neighborhood who has nonetheless managed a reasonably stable domestic life, achieved some educational success, and found secure employment is as unentitled to a mitigated sentence as a middle-class offender. Thus, policies designed to prevent unfair treatment of disadvantaged offenders as a class have the likely effect of unfair treatment of disadvantaged offenders as individuals.

A proponent of proportionality might respond by noting that loosening proportionality conditions to permit mitigation of sentences for 'deserving' disadvantaged offenders also permits aggravation of sentences for the 'undeserving,' especially those who appear likeliest to offend again. This is a different problem and one that can be addressed by placing strict proportionate limits on maximum sentences and by establishing stringent standards to guide decisions to aggravate punishments.

Parsimony

Proponents of strong proportionality conditions necessarily prefer equality over minimization of suffering. For nearly two decades in the United States, Andrew von Hirsch and Norval Morris have been disagreeing over the role of parsimony in punishment. Von Hirsch (1985) has argued for strong desert limits on punishment and high priority to pursuit of equality and proportionality in punishment. Morris (1974) has argued that desert is a limiting, not a defining, principle of punishment and that policy should prescribe imposition of the least severe 'not undeserved' sanction that meets legitimate policy ends. Within these outer bounds of 'not undeserved' punishments Morris has consistently argued for observance of a principle of parsimony.

To some extent Morris and von Hirsch have argued past each other. Morris argues that a desert approach is unnecessarily harsh and von Hirsch responds by noting that he personally favors relatively modest punishments and, in any case, desert schemes are not inherently more severe than other schemes. In turn, von Hirsch argues that Morris's 'not undeserved' proportionality constraints are vague, the breadth of allowable ranges of sentencing discretion is never specified, and Morris responds by noting that absolute measures of deserved punishment are unknowable and that his aim is to minimise imposition of penal suffering within bounds that any given community finds tolerable.

The problem is that they start from different major premises – von Hirsch's is the 'principle of proportionality', Morris's the 'principle of parsimony'. The difference between them can be seen by imagining a comprehensive punishment scheme, perhaps resembling Minnesota's (see Figure 3.1). Imagine that policy makers have conscientiously classified all offenders into ten categories and, using von Hirsch's ordinal/cardinal magnitude and anchoring points approach, have decided that all offenses at level VII deserve twenty-three- to twenty-five-month prison terms. Imagine further that reliable public opinion surveys have shown that 90 per cent of the general public would find a restrictive non-custodial punishment 'not unduly lenient' and a 36-month prison term 'not unduly severe' for level VII offenses.

Von Hirsch would, I presume, argue that for non-exceptional cases concern for proportionality requires that persons convicted of level VII crimes receive at least a twenty-three-month prison term, even though public opinion would support much less severe punishments. To achieve greater proportionality, von Hirsch would punish some offenders much more severely than is socially or politically required.

Morris, by contrast, would presumably argue that imposing twenty-three-month terms on all level VII cases would be unjust because it would constitute imposition of punishment that is not required by public attitudes or preventive considerations. Morris would argue that, barring exceptional circumstances, no level-VII offender should receive more than twenty-five months' incarceration but that many should receive less than twenty-three months. To achieve less aggregate suffering, Morris would punish some offenders much less severely than concern for proportionality would suggest.

The preceding hypothetical is overstated. Von Hirsch would, at least for exceptional cases, approve departures from the twenty-three to twenty-five-month range or perhaps approve a wider range (for example, eighteen to twenty-eight months). Morris would almost certainly want to establish a normal upper bound lower than thirty-six months and would want to devise some system for assuring that level VII offenders receive roughly equivalent punishments.

Sorting out principles

Disagreements about just punishments, like disagreements about the death penalty or abortion, are often in the end disagreements about powerful intuitions or deeply embedded values. It may be that differences in view between those who give primacy to proportionality and those who give primacy to parsimony cannot be bridged.

The burden of persuasion should rest, however, it seems to me on those who reject Isaiah Berlin's observations that 'not all good things are compatible, still less all the ideals of mankind' (1969, p. 167) and that 'the necessity of choosing between absolute claims is then an inescapable characteristic of the human condition' (1969, p. 169).

Punishment raises at least two important conflicts between ideals – between the principles of proportionality and parsimony, between the quests for criminal justice and social justice.

Punishment is not unique in this respect. *Justice, Equal Opportunity, and the Family* (1983) by James Fishkin shows similar irreconcilable conflicts in ideals that are posed by family policy. Even in ideal theory, he argues, values inherent in support for equal opportunity conflict with values inherent in support for family autonomy. Notions of equal opportunity, he argues, must include a 'principle of merit', that 'there should be a fair competition among individuals for unequal positions in society' (p. 19), and a 'principle of equal life chances specifying roughly equal expectations for everyone regardless of the conditions into which they are born' (p. 20). Without equal life chances, both common experience and modern sociology instruct, scarce social goods will not be distributed according to merit. As Fishkin observes, 'if I can predict the outcomes achieved by an individual merely by knowing his or her race, sex, ethnic origin, or family background, then equality of life chances has not been realised' (p. 34).

If we were single-mindedly devoted to equal opportunity, then, we should view equalization of life chances as an overriding goal of social policy. However, Fishkin argues, efforts to equalize life chances run head on into another powerful principle, that the value of autonomy in a private sphere of liberty encompasses a principle of family autonomy, of non-intrusion by the state into the family's sphere of private liberty.

In other words, equal opportunity and family autonomy conflict fundamentally. Full respect for equal opportunity would involve intrusion into the family that would widely be seen as objectionably intrusive. Full respect for family autonomy would widely be seen as cruel disregard for children's basic needs.

And so it may be with punishment. Principles of proportionality and parsimony may simply conflict, with resolutions between them necessarily partial and provisional.

80 Penal theory and practice

RECONCILING PROPORTIONALITY AND PARSIMONY

A middle ground exists on which a punishment scheme can be built that honors both proportionality and parsimony – development of sentencing guidelines that establish presumptive sentencing ranges in which the upper bounds are set in accordance with the proportionality principle and the lower bounds are sufficiently flexible to honor the parsimony principle. This would discourage disparately severe punishments, including aggravation of sentences on predictive or rehabilitative grounds beyond what would otherwise be deemed appropriate. If von Hirsch is correct as a social psychologist of punishment when he insists that desert schemes are not necessarily more severe than other schemes, use of proportionality constraints to set upper bounds (within higher statutory maxima) should result in upper-bound penalties that are no harsher than would occur in a scheme with narrow ranges. Below those upper bounds, however, judges could set sentences not premised on 'standard cases' or 'standard punishments'.

The challenge is not to decide between proportionality and parsimony, but to balance them in ways that preserve important elements of each. This is not the place to discuss mechanics at length. A reconciliation can be sketched.[6]

Use proportionality to establish presumptive maximum sentences

Much of von Hirsch's proportionality analysis can be used in setting maximum bounds of sentencing authority for ordinary cases. By using standardized measures of offense severity, proportionate maximum sentences can be specified, the gap between those upper bounds and statutory maxima to be reserved for extraordinary cases subject to the provision of reasons and the possibility of appellate sentence review. The Advisory Council on the Penal System (1978) proposed such a scheme, albeit not in the vocabulary of guidelines. The worst injustices in sentencing and the worst disparities are those suffered by people who receive aberrantly long or severe penalties. Presumptive guidelines for maximum sentences scaled to proportionality could both lessen the likelihood of aberrantly severe penalties and achieve proportionality among those offenders receiving the most severe presumptive sentences.

Parsimony presumption

Within the authorised bounds, judges should be directed to impose the least severe sentence consistent with the governing purposes *at* sentencing (e.g., Morris and Tonry, 1990, pp. 90–2). Within, for example, any category of offenses encompassed in an offense severity level in Minnesota's sentencing guidelines grid, judges should be directed to consider monetary penalties or their equivalents (e.g., community service) when retribution or deterrence is the governing purpose, stringent community controls when incapacitation is at issue, and community controls with treatment conditions when sex or drug or alcohol treatment is called for, reserving incarcerative sentences only for cases when deterrence, public attitudes, or incapacitation seem to dictate. If the parsimony presumption favored the least restrictive alternative, judges would have to devise particularised reasons for doing otherwise – including imposition of sentences for incapacitative or deterrent reasons.

Rough equivalence

Efforts to devise ways to make punishments interchangeable have foundered on proportionality's shoals. If prison is used as the norm, and all other penalties must be converted to carceral coin, interchangeability soon collapses. Almost inexorably, one day in prison equals two or more days of house arrest equals two or more days of community service. Something about the process seems to force literal thinking. If sentences must be proportionate in incarceration time, the scope for use of non-custodial penalties necessarily is limited.

Thinking about equivalences becomes easier if proportionality constraints are loosened. If any prison sentence up to twenty-four months can be imposed in a given case, then the range for substitution is broadened immensely.

Thinking about equivalences also becomes easier if prison is replaced by money, say a day's net pay, as the basic unit from and to which sanctions are converted.

Thinking about equivalences becomes easier if we think about different purposes to be served *at* sentencing in a given case. If the goals are retribution and deterrence, then prison and financial penalties ought to be fully interchangeable, as might also, for the indigent, a combination of residential controls, community service, restitution, and supervision.

If, for normative reasons, sentencing guidelines and guidance are to be scaled proportionately to the severity of crime, objectively measured, and expressed in standardized units of incarceration, objectively characterised, the scope for non-custodial penalties will necessarily be slight. It is not easy to devise non-custodial penalties that are objectively equivalent to twenty-three months' incarceration.

If non-custodial penalties are to be widely adopted and used, proportionality constraints must be loosened to take account of the almost infinite variety of offender circumstances, offense contexts, and punishment dimensions. If ways can be devised to institutionalise principles both of proportionality and parsimony in punishment, we are likely to do less injustice than if we establish systems that seek an illusion of equality of suffering for offenders in whose lives equality in most other things has been conspicuously absent.

Notes

1 Citations of sources for empirical assertions in this section can be found in Morris and Tonry (1990).

2 Since the guidelines took effect in 1980, law-and-order political pressures have influenced statutory changes and policy decisions by the commission that have selectively but substantially increased penalties for controversial crimes and made the system's claims for principled scaling and proportionality weaker (Frase, 1991).

3 Appellate decisions have since recognised limited 'amenability to probation' and 'non-amenability to prison' criteria for departures (see Frase, 1991).

4 The US Sentencing Commission, to avoid problems described in this paragraph, based its guidelines on 'relevant conduct', by which it refers to the defendant's actual behavior and its consequences. In practice, prosecutors manipulate the federal guidelines extensively but use more ingenious subterfuges (Federal Courts Study Committee, 1990).

5 Walker defines 'sensibility': 'the intensity of the suffering, hardship, or inconvenience which a given penalty will inflict depends on the individual: on sex, age, social position, and so on' (Walker, 1991, p. 99).

6 Among the issues that might be discussed: the strengths and weaknesses of the punishment units approach; whether sentencing grids should have two, three, four or more 'bands' representing different presumptions concerning the appropriate type of sentence; at what offense severity level the normal offense is so serious that only incarceration sentences should be authorised; the widths of bands of authorised sentences for categories of cases; whether equivalences should be conceptualised in terms of suffering, intrusiveness, or some other measure. There is little literature on any of these subjects and this essay does not add to it.

References

Advisory Council on the Penal System (1978), *Sentences of Imprisonment – A Review of Maximum Penalties*, HMSO, London.

Ashworth, A. (1992), 'Non-custodial sentences', *Criminal Law Review*, pp. 242–51.

Bentham, J. (1948) [1789], *Introduction to the Principles of Morals and Legislation*, edited by W. Harrison, Oxford University Press, Oxford.

Berlin, I. (1969), *Four Essays on Liberty*, Oxford University Press, Oxford.

Doble, J., Immerwahr, S., and Richardson, A. (1991), *Punishing Criminals – The People of Delaware Consider the Options*, The Public Agenda Foundation, New York.

Duff, R. A. (1986), *Trials and Punishments*, Cambridge University Press, Cambridge.

Federal Courts Study Committee (1990), *Report*, Administrative Office of the US Courts, Washington, DC.

Fishkin, J. S. (1983), *Justice, Equal Opportunity, and the Family*, Yale University Press, New Haven.

Fletcher, G. (1978), *Rethinking Criminal Law*, Little Brown, Boston.

Frase, R. (1991), 'Sentencing reform in Minnesota: ten years after', *Minnesota Law Review*, LXXV, pp. 727–54.

Hart, H. L. A. (1968), *Punishment and Responsibility: Essays in the Philosophy of Law*, Oxford University Press, Oxford.

Honderich, T. (1989), *Punishment – The Supposed Justifications*, Polity, Cambridge.

Kant, I. (1887) [1797], *Rechtslehre*, Part Second, 49, trans. by W. Hastie, T. & T. Clark, Edinburgh.

Minnesota Sentencing Guidelines Commission (1980), *Report to the Legislature – January 1, 1980*, Minnesota Sentencing Guidelines Commission, St. Paul, Minnesota.

Morris, N. (1974), *The Future of Imprisonment*, University of Chicago Press, Chicago.

Morris, N., and Tonry, M. (1990), *Between Prison and Probation: Intermediate Punishments in a Rational Sentencing System*, Oxford University Press, New York.

Murphy, J. (1973), 'Marxism and retribution', *Philosophy and Public Affairs*, II, pp. 217–43.

Pincoffs, E. L. (1966), *The Rationale of Legal Punishment*, Humanities Press, New York.

Robbins, L. (1938), 'Interpersonal comparisons of utility: a comment', *The Economic Journal*, XLVIII, pp. 635–41.

Singer, R. G. (1979), *Just Deserts: Sentencing Based on Equality and Desert*, Ballinger, Cambridge, MA.

von Hirsch, A. (1976), *Doing Justice – The Choice of Punishments*, Hill and Wang, New York (rev. edn. 1986, Northeastern University Press, Boston).

von Hirsch, A. (1985), *Past or Future Crimes – Deservedness and Dangerousness in the Sentencing of Criminals*, Rutgers University Press, New Brunswick, NJ.

von Hirsch, A. (1990), 'Scaling intermediate punishments: a comparison of two models', unpublished manuscript, Rutgers University Department of Criminal Justice, Rutgers, NJ.

von Hirsch, A. (1992), 'Proportionality in the philosophy of punishment', *Crime and Justice – A Review of Research*, XVI, edited by M. Tonry, University of Chicago Press, Chicago, pp. 55–98.

Walker, N. (1991), *Why Punish?*, Oxford University Press, Oxford.

Wasik, M., and von Hirsch, A. (1988), 'Non-custodial penalties and the principles of desert', *Criminal Law Review*, pp. 555–72.

[16]

Obsolescence and Immanence in Penal Theory and Policy

To be useful, theories of punishment must speak to the issues of their times. Predominant modern theories centering on desert and proportionality took shape in the 1970s when they spoke to concerns about racial disparities, procedural unfairness, and beliefs in the ineffectiveness and injustice of rehabilitative programs. None of those concerns continues to galvanize policymakers, practitioners, or the general public. Punishment theories are stuck in the 1970s, speaking still to 1970s issues and unable satisfactorily to address contemporary developments such as burgeoning interest in restorative and community justice, renewed faith in the effectiveness and appropriateness of rehabilitation, and proliferation of drug and other courts aimed at changing offenders. Punishment theories sometimes influence policymakers, and often they clarify understanding of the implications of policy choices. Consequently, there is a need for the development of new theoretical frameworks that can speak to the issues and temper of these times.

INTRODUCTION

Writings on penal theory and punishment philosophy may be independent or dependent variables: They may cause changes in the world or result from them. It is unclear to me which of these is true. Do the ideas come first and in their application change the ways we think and the

* Sonosky Professor of Law and Public Policy, University of Minnesota, and Senior Fellow, Netherlands Institute for the Study of Crime and Law Enforcement, Leiden.

things we do, or does the world change and provide differently enriched soil in which ideas are born or revivified? Did the emergence of writing in the 1950s and 1960s that challenged then-prevalent utilitarian ideas about punishment[1] lead to their rejection by most theorists, practitioners, and policymakers in the 1970s and 1980s? Did the espousal of retributivist, just deserts, and proportionality ideas by writers in the 1970s[2] lead in the 1980s and the 1990s to widespread adoption of penal policies aimed at providing offenders the punishments they deserved?

The answer, I believe, is that the seeds of normative ideas are always with us, but whether they hibernate or blossom depends on changing sensibilities and material conditions. This Essay shows how understanding of the origins of ideas, policies, and practices concerning punishment can be enhanced if we can become more self-aware about why and when particular ideas and normative beliefs come into fashion.

The 1970s were a time of transition in punishment practices and policies. In 1970, the highly discretionary and individualized punishment systems encapsulated in the phrase "indeterminate sentencing" were ubiquitous in the United States. In every state and the federal system (and in the Model Penal Code's prescriptions), statutes seldom did more than define crimes and set maximum penalties. Mandatory penalties were few in number and modest in scope, prosecutors had unaccountable power over charging and plea bargaining, judges' sentencing discretion was constrained only by statutory sentencing maximums, and parole boards had broad or plenary authority to release prisoners subject, usually, only to the maximum prison term set by the judge or the legislature.[3] Chicago law professor Albert Alschuler, commenting on unquestioning

1. See, e.g., Edmund L. Pincoffs, The Rationale of Legal Punishment 2 (1966) [hereinafter Pincoffs, Legal Punishment] (arguing that neither utilitarian nor retributive theories provide an adequate justification for punishment); Francis A. Allen, Legal Values and the Rehabilitative Ideal, *in* The Borderland of Criminal Justice 25, 25–28 (1964) [hereinafter Allen, Legal Values] (explaining rise of rehabilitative ideal and resulting controversies); H.L.A. Hart, Prolegomenon to the Principles of Punishment, *in* Punishment and Responsibility 1, 8 (1968) (claiming that main justification for punishment "lies in the fact that when breach of the law involves moral guilt the application to the offender of the pain of punishment is itself a thing of value"); John Rawls, Two Concepts of Rules, 64 Phil. Rev. 3, 3–5 (1955) (proposing that utilitarian justifications for punishment are appropriate for justifying practices, while retributive justifications should be applied to specific cases).

2. See, e.g., John Kleinig, Punishment and Desert 65–72 (1973) (rationalizing punishment on theory of just deserts); Norval Morris, The Future of Imprisonment 58 (1974) [hereinafter Morris, Future] ("In my view, penal purposes are properly retributive and deterrent."); Andrew von Hirsch, Doing Justice: The Choice of Punishments 69 (1976) [hereinafter von Hirsch, Justice] (arguing that principle of proportionality or just deserts "is a requirement of justice"); Joel Feinberg, Justice and Personal Desert, *in* Doing and Deserving 55 (1970) (analyzing concept of "just desert").

3. Kenneth Culp Davis, Discretionary Justice 126–41, 188–91 (1969). Sometimes judges could set minimum sentences up to one-third of the maximum, though this was a minority practice, and the minimum sentence itself was reduced through the operation of time off for good behavior. See, e.g., Model Penal Code § 305.1 (Proposed Official Draft

acceptance in the 1960s of the ideas underlying indeterminate sentencing, observed in 1978: "That I and many other academics adhered in large part to this reformative viewpoint only a decade or so ago seems almost incredible to most of us today."[4]

By 1980, the empirical and conceptual foundations of indeterminate sentencing had been washed away. Many state and federal policymakers contemplated radical overhauls of their sentencing systems, and the beginnings of fragmented modern systems that promiscuously combined retributive, consequentialist, and expressive elements, had become apparent.[5] Some states developed parole guidelines, some developed sentencing guidelines, some developed both; some prosecutors created charging and bargaining guidelines and some "abolished" plea-bargaining; some states eliminated discretionary parole release.[6] Mandatory minimum sentences, out of vogue in the 1960s and comprehensively repealed in the federal system in 1970, proliferated.[7]

So what happened in the 1970s to effect wholesale rejection of the indeterminate sentencing system, which had survived nearly unchanged and unchallenged in most states for three-quarters of a century, and which in a richer, fuller form had in 1962 been enthusiastically endorsed by the American Law Institute?[8]

Answers can be offered at various levels. The simplest answers would identify policy entrepreneurs, such as federal district court judge Marvin Frankel, and trace out the influence of their proposals.[9]

Slightly more complicated answers look at the influence of prevailing policy critiques of the legal system: concerns about arbitrariness in criminal justice decisionmaking[10] motivated in general by unwarranted sen-

---

1962) (stating that reduction in prison sentence awarded for good behavior shall be deducted "from [the prisoner's] minimum term of imprisonment").

4. Albert W. Alschuler, Sentencing Reform and Prosecutorial Power: A Critique of Recent Proposals for "Fixed" and "Presumptive" Sentencing, 126 U. Pa. L. Rev. 550, 552 (1978).

5. See Michael Tonry, The Fragmentation of Sentencing and Corrections in America, *in* U.S. Nat'l Inst. of Justice, No. 1, Sentencing and Corrections: Issues for the 21st Century 1 (1999) [hereinafter Tonry, Fragmentation] (summarizing the collapse of indeterminate sentencing system).

6. See 1 Research on Sentencing: The Search for Reform 130–40 (Alfred Blumstein et al. eds., 1983) [hereinafter Research on Sentencing] (describing these trends).

7. Id. at 132–33 (noting that "between 1977 and 1980, mandatory minimum sentencing laws were adopted by 27 states and were under consideration in at least 14 others").

8. See David J. Rothman, Conscience and Convenience 3–4 (1980) (describing the "vigorous debate" challenging established programs and institutions within the criminal justice system during late 1970s and early 1980s); supra note 3 and accompanying text.

9. See Marvin E. Frankel, Criminal Sentences: Law without Order *passim* (1972) (decrying sentencing disparities and espousing creation of sentencing commissions charged with developing guidelines).

10. See Davis, supra note 3, at 29–30 (equating discretionary power with arbitrary power, and arguing that such power should be "eliminated to whatever extent it can be eliminated without undue sacrifice of other values that may be deemed more important").

tencing disparities[11] and in particular by disparities attributed to racial discrimination;[12] the maturation of the due process revolution of the 1960s heralded by *Goldberg v. Kelly*[13] and the Warren Court's criminal procedure jurisprudence;[14] and loss of confidence in correctional rehabilitative programs on ethical[15] and empirical[16] grounds.

The most complicated answers attempt to understand why particular ideas and policies about crime and punishment take hold at some places and times and not at others. They find explanations over time in changing social-structural and economic conditions[17] and across space in distinctive penal traditions, variant constitutional arrangements, and diverse political cultures.[18]

These works offer theories and hypotheses to explain postindeterminate sentencing penal policy changes in the United States between 1975 and 2005. They attempt to explain why particular new punishment edifices and ideologies have been built upon the ruins of indeterminate sentencing. To my knowledge, however, no similar literature exists to explain the equally dramatic penal policy changes embod-

11. See Frankel, supra note 9, at 5 ("[T]he almost wholly unchecked and sweeping powers we give to judges in the fashioning of sentences are terrifying and intolerable for a society that professes devotion to the rule of law.").

12. See Am. Friends Serv. Comm., Struggle for Justice: A Report on Crime and Punishment in America 130 (1971) (arguing that discretion within criminal justice system enables politically and economically dominant class to control minorities and other groups seen as threats to social order).

13. 397 U.S. 254 (1970).

14. See Francis A. Allen, The Habits of Legality: Criminal Justice and the Rule of Law 65–66 (1996) [hereinafter Allen, Habits] (describing how during the Warren Court in particular, but also "before and after, a formidable and highly volatile body of constitutional doctrine pertaining to the rights of suspected persons . . . emerged").

15. See Allen, Legal Values, supra note 1, at 33 (arguing that "the rehabilitative ideal has been debased in practice and that the consequences resulting from this debasement are serious and, at times, dangerous").

16. See Robert Martinson, What Works: Questions and Answers About Prison Reform, Pub. Int., Spring 1974, at 22, 22–23, 49 (surveying two hundred controlled studies of treatments designed to rehabilitate offenders, and concluding that there is "very little reason to hope that we have in fact found a sure way of reducing recidivism through rehabilitation").

17. See generally David Garland, The Culture of Control: Crime and Social Order in Contemporary Society viii (2001) (identifying "broad organizing principles that structure our contemporary ways of thinking and acting in crime control and criminal justice"); Theodore Caplow & Jonathan Simon, Understanding Prison Policy and Population Trends, 26 Crime & Just. 63, 65 (1999) (characterizing "contemporary imprisonment policies as efforts to answer a classic sociological question, that is, What drives trends in punishment?").

18. See, e.g., Michael Tonry, Thinking About Crime: Sense and Sensibility in American Penal Culture 9–10 (2004) [hereinafter Tonry, Thinking] (arguing that U.S. sentencing policies are harsher than those of other countries because "[t]he organization of American government makes it especially vulnerable to emotional overreaction"); James Whitman, Harsh Justice: Criminal Punishment and the Widening Divide Between Europe and America *passim* (2003) (examining why America's criminal justice system metes out harsher punishments than those of other Western societies).

ied in the implosion of indeterminate sentencing that, with the benefit of hindsight, we now know began in the 1950s, although few noticed it at the time.[19] This Essay does not attempt to explain these changes.[20] Rather, it looks back to the midlevel policy concerns (rising crime rates, arbitrariness, disparities, racial discrimination, and ineffectiveness) that at least coincided with the collapse of indeterminate sentencing and the development of successor institutions and practices. It considers how effectively those concerns have been addressed over time, and attempts to demonstrate to what extent they remain topical today.

The galvanizing policy problems of the 1970s are no longer policy preoccupations in the twenty-first century. Racial disparities in punishment and risks of procedural unfairness to offenders are greater in 2005 than they were in the mid-1970s, as are sentencing disparities generally. Both the ethical and effectiveness critiques of rehabilitative programs have largely disappeared. Racial disparities in imprisonment are substantially higher in 2005 than they were in 1975, and patterns of drug law enforcement and sentencing have made them worse. Widespread adoption of mandatory sentencing guidelines, mandatory minimum sentence laws, and "three strikes" laws—and the adaptive responses they have provoked among practitioners—have produced sentencing disparities at least as great in 2005 as existed in 1975.[21] There is widespread support for the view that "treatment works" amidst few ethical compunctions against attempts to change people through coercion. As a result, policymakers in the United States and England are happily increasing public

19. See, e.g., Francis A. Allen, Criminal Justice, Legal Values, and the Rehabilitative Ideal, 50 J. Crim. L. Criminology & Police Sci. 226, 229–30 (1959) [hereinafter Allen, Criminal Justice] (arguing that rise of rehabilitative ideal was accompanied by measures that conflict with individual liberty and can therefore be justified by "only the most clear and compelling reasons"); C.S. Lewis, The Humanitarian Theory of Punishment, 6 Res Judicatae 224, 224 (1953) (arguing that return to retributive theory of punishment would benefit defendants' interests more than "humanitarian" theory); Norval Morris, Sentencing Convicted Criminals, 27 Austl. L.J. 186, 186 (1953) [hereinafter Morris, Sentencing] (criticizing judiciary for "fail[ing] to develop any agreed principles or practices" to achieve "uniformity and equality" in criminal sentencing).

20. On the converse question, why did indeterminate sentencing survive, little questioned, for so long? In its title, David Rothman's *Conscience and Convenience* gives a standard answer: The ostensible dedication of indeterminate sentencing to reformation and rehabilitation of offenders rested comfortably with the welfare aspirations of the time (hence conscience), and the vast discretions it accorded officials acknowledged and reinforced their self-esteem (and power) and made management comparatively unchallenging, since no one looked over the managers' shoulders (hence convenience). See Rothman, supra note 8.

21. See Frank O. Bowman, III & Michael Heise, Quiet Rebellion? Explaining Nearly a Decade of Declining Federal Drug Sentences, 86 Iowa L. Rev. 1043, 1049 (1983) (explaining that decline in average drug sentences is due in part to "a widespread perception among the foot soldiers of the criminal justice system—the prosecutors, defense attorneys, probation officers, and district judges—that drug sentences are often too high").

investments in criminal justice treatment programs and just as happily coercing people to participate in them.

Modern penal theories and sentencing policies, however, have not yet substantially taken account of this changed context, and may correspond to theories and policies in the 1960s, when underlying norms and beliefs were changing rapidly but only barely discernibly. Desert theories have probably run their course. They will likely modulate into discussions of punishment's justifying aims and "negative" desert arguments asserting that desert considerations can tell us only how severely offenders *may* be punished, and not how severely they *ought* to be punished.[22] Punishment theorists will have to begin developing normative frameworks for greater individualization of punishment and for principled use of compelled treatment in just punishment systems. They will also have to take on an entirely new but related job: development of normative frameworks for the principled application of emerging institutions of restorative and community justice. These things are doable, but until now, the times have not required that they be done.

This Essay consists of five Parts. The first introduces an analytical framework for thinking about changes in punishment norms and policies. What we think we see, believe, and know largely depends on where we are and when. Ideas come in and out of vogue depending on prevailing sensibilities—the ethoi of diverse times. Changing sensibilities shape the ways we understand the world, the problems we consider important, and the solutions we think viable. Much of the theorizing about crime and punishment in the past century, and much of the accompanying evolution in criminal justice policies, can best be understood as the byproduct of prevailing sensibilities. Secular developments necessarily lag behind changing sensibilities. Much writing about punishment has lagged in this way, like a fly caught in amber, and therefore, predictably, often risks irrelevance. If we can become more aware of changing sensibilities, we can adapt analyses and policies to them in ways that honor important values.

Part II offers a brief recitative of the flowering of the sentencing reform movement of the 1970s and 1980s. The key points are that indeterminate sentencing was monolithic in 1970 and existed in mildly variant forms in every American jurisdiction, but went into rapid decline after 1975 to be replaced by a crazy quilt of diverse systems.

Part III presents "then and now" comparisons of the states of play in 1975 and 2005 concerning five key backdrops to the sentencing reform movement: crime trends, rehabilitation, racial bias and disparities, sentencing disparities generally, and fairness to offenders. These changes have important implications for normative analyses of punishment and

22. Positive retributivism, or desert, specifies what punishments must be imposed in a just punishment system; negative retributivism specifies what punishments may, but need not, be imposed. See R.A. Duff, Punishment, Communication, and Community 12 (2001) (discussing limits of positive and negative retributivist rationales).

form the bounds of political permission within which policymakers must operate.

Part IV looks at the prevailing contemporary punishment jurisprudence, most notably desert theories, but also, briefly, communicative and limiting retributivist theories. It considers how well these theories take account of the policy concerns and climate of 2005 and of new attitudes and research findings concerning rehabilitation. The not very controversial main conclusion is that limiting retributivist theories can accommodate the new context and evidence; the more controversial conclusion is that desert theories cannot and to some extent stand exposed as cultural byproducts of a decade, the 1970s, the penal sensibilities of which have passed.

Part V shifts attention to penal policy and identifies a number of developments that retributive theories cannot accommodate: proliferation of restorative and community justice initiatives, increased investment in rehabilitative programs and sanctions, and institutionalization of drug courts and other special purpose courts patterned on them. New or significantly refined penal theories and philosophies are immanent in the changing sensibilities that underlie new policies and practices. They need to be drawn out and developed, or penal theory and punishment philosophy will become irrelevant. Though the world of affairs can get along just fine without paying much attention to theory, that would be a pity. Normative theories can help expose contradictions and anomalies and provide calipers by which the justness of policies, practices, and punishments can be measured.

I. Thinking About Punishment

Efforts to understand legal system changes are aided by distinguishing among sensibilities, theories, and policies. "Sensibility" is a term—popularized by German sociologist Norbert Elias[23] and revived by Scottish sociologist David Garland[24]—that describes the prevailing ethos, the zeitgeist, of a time. Sensibilities are shared assumptions and understandings, difficult to see in one's own time and easier to see in others', that shape perceptions of the world. Penal sensibilities in the 1930s, for example, included assumptions about the environmental and psychological causes of criminal behavior, the malleability of human beings, the ethical desirability of rehabilitating offenders, and the capacity of correctional

23. Norbert Elias, The History of Manners 110 (Edmund Jephcott trans., Pantheon Books 1978) (1939) (referring to ways in which bourgeois language was "adapted to the standard of sensibility of the court circles" in seventeenth- and eighteenth-century France).

24. Garland, supra note 17, at 6 (suggesting that changing institutional responses to crime are reflective of "a new pattern of mentalities, interests, and sensibilities that has altered how we think and feel about the underlying problem").

and other programs to do so.[25] This set of largely unquestioned assumptions made it easy for practitioners, policymakers, and professors to accept utilitarian theories and ideas about punishment, and made it difficult for them to accept retributive ideas.

Punishment theories are efforts to make comprehensive normative statements about the justness both of broad punishment policies and practices and of punishments in individual cases.[26] The simplest partitioning is between deontological theories concerned with achievement of just outcomes in individual cases as ends in themselves and teleological theories concerned with achievement of just outcomes as means to ends. Conventionally, deontological theories of punishment, most famously associated with Kant and Hegel, are called retributive theories and are centrally concerned with the moral appropriateness of individual punishments in relation to offenders' culpability.[27] Teleological theories of punishment, in recent decades called consequentialist theories, are centrally concerned with maximization of some measure of aggregate social benefit, usually called general prevention.[28] Thus, for retributivists, a just punishment is one that is morally appropriate, or proportionate, for this offender for that offense. For consequentialists, a just punishment is one that minimizes the costs of crime and related institutions and practices. A punishment is unjust if it does not serve that end or is unnecessary to its achievement.[29]

---

25. See Rothman, supra note 8, at 50–61 (describing environmental, psychological, and genetic assumptions underlying three different progressive-era approaches to deviancy).

26. When I use the word "theory," I refer to both the "philosophy of punishment" and "penal theory." A distinction is sometimes made between them. See, e.g., R.A. Duff & D. Garland, Introduction: Thinking About Punishment, *in* A Reader on Punishment 1, 1 (R.A. Duff & David Garland eds., 1994) (attempting to "establish[ ] a dialogue between [the] closely related endeavors of" the philosophy of punishment and penal theory). The distinction may be disciplinary, distinguishing writings by philosophers from those by lawyers and social scientists, or the distinction may be between theoretical writing at a fairly high level of abstraction and theoretical writing that addresses concrete policy choices, in effect a contrast between philosophy and applied philosophy.

27. See generally Georg W.F. Hegel, Hegel's Philosophy of Right 69–70 (T.M. Knox trans. 1967) (1821) (stating that important considerations for punishment are "first, that crime is to be annulled, not because it is the producing of an evil, but because it is an infringement of the right as right, and secondly, the question of what that positive existence is which crime possesses and which must be annulled"); Immanuel Kant, The Metaphysical Elements of Justice, *in* Foundations of Criminal Law 75 (Leo Katz et al. eds., 1999) ("Judicial punishment can never be used merely as a means to promote some other good for the criminal himself or for civil society, but instead it must in all cases be imposed on him only on the ground that he has committed a crime.").

28. See generally Jeremy Bentham, The Rationale of Punishment 20 (1830) [hereinafter Bentham, Rationale] ("General prevention ought to be the chief end of punishment, as it is its real justification.").

29. That is the origin of the utilitarian parsimony principle: Any punishment greater than is required to achieve its end is unjust.

"Policies" are public choices about institutions (e.g., parole boards, sentencing commissions, guidelines, mandatory minimums) and practices (e.g., plea bargaining, parole release, risk prediction, electronic monitoring, drug treatment). Policies are more or less consistent with theories and sensibilities, and can be characterized and criticized relative to both. Policies are likelier to coexist with inconsistent theories (as, for example, three strikes laws have coexisted with retributive theories) than with inconsistent sensibilities. Once the penal sensibilities associated with indeterminate sentencing passed away, for example, release decisions by parole boards became hard to explain and quickly lost legitimacy.[30]

This is not the place to write at length about interactions among sensibilities, theories, and policies. Much of the body of this Essay does that. Instead I offer two kinds of illustrations of the power of changing sensibilities.

A. *Punishment Theory*

During the peak periods of indeterminate (1935–1960) and determinate (1975–2000) sentencing, particular powerful ideas were conspicuously absent. The key ideas underlying indeterminate sentencing—environmental determinism, human malleability, the power of a benevolent state—left little room for retributive ideas. Likewise, the key ideas underlying determinate sentencing—equality, consistency, evenhandedness, procedural fairness, moral autonomy—left little room for consequentialist ideas.

Herbert Wechsler, Paul Tappan, and Louis Schwartz, the towering intellectuals who developed the Model Penal Code, knew about and no doubt had read Kant and Hegel. They knew and understood the Kantian argument that respect for offenders' moral autonomy requires that they be punished in proportion to the seriousness of their crimes.[31] Search, however, through the twelve years of American Law Institute proceedings on the Code's punishment and sentencing provisions, and you will find not one person arguing that the imposition of morally deserved or proportionate punishments should be a major objective; words like retribution and just deserts are entirely absent from the discussion.[32]

There is a reason for this: Retributive ideas were seen as atavistic and vengeful. Edmund Pincoffs summarized the conventional utilitarian critique as follows:

30. See, e.g., Morris, Future, supra note 2, at 31–49 (describing attacks since 1975 on "arbitrariness" of parole); Andrew von Hirsch, The Question of Parole 4 (1979) (same).

31. See Kant, supra note 27, at 76 ("Only the Law of retribution . . . can determine exactly the kind and degree of punishment.").

32. See Tonry, Thinking, supra note 18, at 176–79 (stating that "the Model Penal Code . . . rarely mentions desert, retribution, or proportionality in its text or original commentary, and echoes of such ideas only occasionally appear in the transcripts of the American Law Institute ('ALI') meetings at which successive drafts were discussed").

> [I]f only desert is relevant, what, as retributivists, can we say in justifying a particular sentence? Are we not confined to talking about the heinousness of the criminal's deed? . . . [A]re we not then using the language of revenge? . . . Is the language of retribution not just a smooth and sophisticated cover for a morally questionable motive, the motive to take vengeance . . . ?[33]

Conversely, in the 1970s and 1980s, philosophers Andrew von Hirsch, Antony Duff, and Jeffrey Murphy knew and understood Bentham's view that the ethical measure of a government practice is whether in the aggregate it maximizes human happiness or satisfaction. Search in their writings, however, for arguments about how criminal law and punishment can be used to maximize offenders' or aggregate social well-being, and you will search nearly in vain. In Herbert Morris, Murphy, and Duff, you will find communicative ideas about using punishment as a mechanism for moral education, for facilitating offenders' understanding of the moral character of their wrongdoing.[34] In Murphy, von Hirsch, and Duff, you will find discussion of the problem of "just deserts in an unjust world"—recognition that unequal distribution of life chances makes it far easier for some to be law-abiding than for others—but you will find no proposals for how punishment can be used to enhance life chances or to compensate for disadvantages.[35]

---

33. Edmund L. Pincoffs, Philosophy of Law: A Brief Introduction 22 (1991). Similar characterizations of consequentialists' views of retributive arguments are offered in the first major modern American and English books on punishment theories. See, e.g., H.L.A. Hart, Postscript: Responsibility and Retribution, *in* Punishment and Responsibility, supra note 1, at 210, 231 (describing an extreme version of retributive theory, in which punishment is justified because "the return of suffering for moral evil voluntarily done, is itself just or morally good"); Pincoffs, Legal Punishment, supra note 1, at 43 ("Retributivists are often, and in a variety of ways, accused of wishing to have revenge upon the criminal, and deceiving themselves and others by disguising this wish as a demand of justice.").

34. See generally R.A. Duff, Trials and Punishments 8 (1986) [hereinafter Duff, Trials] (articulating desire that criminal justice system will become "one to which the defendant is meant to respond, and in which she is called to participate, as a rational moral agent"); Herbert Morris, A Paternalistic Theory of Punishment, 18 Am. Phil. Q. 263 (1981) (advocating that punishment carry a communicative component which "convey[s] to the wrongdoer . . . that the deprivation is imposed because of wrongdoing"); Jeffrie G. Murphy, Retributivism, Moral Education and the Liberal State, 4 Crim. Just. Ethics 3, 7–9 (1985) (acknowledging power and importance of moral education theory of punishment, but questioning how moral theories can fit within ideology of liberalism).

35. See generally Duff, Trials, supra note 34, at 294 (stating that if "deep and far-reaching social, political, legal and moral changes" occur in society, "we may find . . . that there will be no need for punishment"); von Hirsch, Justice, supra note 2, at 143–49 (discussing problem of "Just Deserts in an Unjust Society," and concluding that, "[a]s long as a substantial segment of the population is denied adequate opportunities for a livelihood, any scheme for punishing must be morally flawed"); Jeffrie Murphy, Marxism and Retribution, 2 Phil. & Pub. Aff. 217 (1973) [hereinafter Murphy, Marxism] (arguing that "retributivism, despite the bad press that it has received, is a morally credible theory of punishment").

B. *Punishment Practices and Policies*

Prevailing sensibilities also predispose us to believe things about the world that we would not believe in other times. Emblematic crime control policies of the 1990s—"zero tolerance" policing in New York City[36] and three strikes sentencing laws in California (Three Strikes)[37]—offer examples. Though both policies may, at the margins, have influenced crime rates and patterns, there is no credible evidence that they affected levels or rates of crime generally.[38] Yet major politicians in both places, Mayor Rudolph Giuliani and Governor Pete Wilson, claimed that the new initiatives produced subsequent declines in crime rates, and policymakers in many other places appear to have believed them.[39]

All the evidence, however, suggests otherwise.[40] Violent crime rates in both places had begun to decline in 1990 and 1991, a few years before the initiatives were adopted in 1993 and 1994, and continued to decline. The declines are thus best characterized as the continuations of preexisting trends and not as the results of policy changes.

This is confirmed when crime rate patterns in the 1990s (invariably declines) are compared across state lines. All American cities experienced declines in violent crime rates generally and homicide rates particularly.[41] New York's declines were among the greatest, but that position was shared with San Diego and Houston, neither of which adopted zero tolerance policing.[42] Violent crime rates in California declined after enactment of Three Strikes in 1994, but when California's crime rates in the 1990s are compared with those of the other four most populous states, it can be seen that there is nothing special about California's declines, which are well within the standard pattern.[43] The weakness of claims that Three Strikes was a principal cause of California's decline in crime rates

36. See National Problems, Local Solutions: Federalism at Work, Part I: Fighting Crime in the Trenches: Hearing Before the House Comm. on Gov't Reform, 106th Cong. 21–22 (1999) [hereinafter Fighting Crime in the Trenches] (statement of Rudolph W. Giuliani, Mayor, New York City) (describing crime fighting tactics in New York undertaken under Giuliani Administration, premised on "broken windows" philosophy that small things matter).

37. Cal. Penal Code § 1170.12 (West 2004).

38. See infra note 40.

39. See Fighting Crime in the Trenches, supra note 36, at 22 (claiming credit for declines in crime rates); Fox Butterfield, 'Three Strikes' Rarely Invoked in Courtrooms, N.Y. Times, Sept. 10, 1996, at A1 (quoting spokesperson for Governor Pete Wilson as stating that Three Strikes has "lowered our crime rate precipitously").

40. This paragraph and those immediately following it summarize a substantial amount of data and a sizeable literature. Details and references can be found in Tonry, Thinking, supra note 18, at 97–139.

41. Id. at 119, 122.

42. Id. at 122.

43. Id. at 124.

is further demonstrated when crime rate trends are compared in counties that applied the law extensively with those that did not.[44]

There are two principal reasons why so many people mistakenly characterized events. The first is self-interest. We are all psychologically predisposed to want to believe things that are in our interest. Toughness on crime was a prominent feature of the political platforms and identities of Mayor Giuliani and Governor Wilson, and it must have been comforting when initiatives they promoted appeared to have worked.[45]

Probably more importantly, however, the historical work of David Musto shows that during periods of declining drug use (and by analogy declining crime rates) and greater intolerance towards deviance, both practitioners and policymakers become harsher and more punitive.[46] The twin logics that deviant behaviors warrant more severe responses and that the declining incidence of those behaviors is the consequence of the more severe responses fit together nicely. That both the harsher policy responses and the subsequent declines in deviant behavior could be the products of a preexisting trend is easy to overlook.

Prevailing sensibilities—the temper of the times—thus affect both the choice of ideas to honor and how we understand and explain the world. This is as true of punishment theory and policy as of anything else, as the development of sentencing policy over the past thirty years demonstrates.

---

44. See Franklin E. Zimring et al., Punishment and Democracy: Three Strikes and You're Out in California 103 (2001) (suggesting based on study that "no increment of general or special deterrence gives an advantage[] to counties with higher than average levels of Three Strikes enforcement").

45. See Joyce Purnick, Busy Being an Icon, Giuliani Keeps Political Future Alive, N.Y. Times, Sept. 5, 2002, at A1 ("[Giuliani] was the tough, I'll-do-it-my-way mayor, credited by fans with taming New York by cutting crime and the welfare rolls."); Daniel M. Weintraub, No More Mr. Moderate, L.A. Times, Sept. 25, 1994, Magazine at 12 (describing Wilson's repositioning for second term as a "tough talking . . . ex-marine" with an "immense story of credibility on the crime issue").

46. See David F. Musto, The American Disease: Origins of Narcotic Control 296 (3d ed. 1999) (arguing that peaks of overestimation of number of drug users, and overestimation of percentage of crimes due to narcotic use or sales, have tended to come before or at the time of most repressive measures against narcotic use); see also Michael Tonry, Malign Neglect—Race, Crime, and Punishment in America 93 (1995) [hereinafter Tonry, Malign Neglect] (drawing on Musto's work in claiming that "[t]he most intrusive laws and the cruelest penalties tend to be enacted *after* intolerance has reached its peak and when drug use is already falling"). David Kagan summarized Musto's argument thusly: After drug use peaks and begins to decline,

> [1] Public opinion turns against drugs and their acceptability begins to evaporate. [2] Gradually, drug use becomes associated, truthfully or not, with the lower ranks of society, and often with racial and ethnic groups that are feared or despised by the middle class. [3] Drugs become seen as deviant and dangerous and become a potent symbol of evil. [4] Trailing behind this decline come large-scale legislative and law enforcement efforts . . . aimed at curtailing drug sales and use through energetic prohibition and enforcement and ever-harsher punishments against sellers and users.

Tonry, Thinking, supra note 18, at 130–31.

II. The Demise of Indeterminate Sentencing

Desert theories and determinate sentencing were responses to what widely were considered in the mid-1970s to be pressing problems. At the time, the shift from ubiquitous indeterminate sentencing systems to a crazy quilt of new approaches looked sudden and radical. In retrospect, this was a predictable manifestation of basic changes in sensibilities that had long been underway. Since the 1970s, however, sensibilities about crime and punishment have shifted again and in the first decade of the twenty-first century bear little resemblance to those of thirty years earlier. Theory and policy analysis need to catch up if they are to be of much use outside the classroom.

Indeterminate sentencing practices and institutions characterized every American system of criminal justice on New Year's Day 1975, as they had from 1930 onward.[47] Beginning in 1975, every state changed its sentencing system in material ways.[48] Maine was first, shifting from indeterminate to determinate sentencing by simply abolishing parole release and leaving the rest of the existing system in place.[49] California was next, enacting the Uniform Determinate Sentencing Law of 1976.[50] It ended the practice of parole release, but also prescribed how many years of imprisonment should be ordered for offenders committing standard, aggravated, and mitigated forms of particular offenses.[51]

Within a few years, every state jettisoned major features of indeterminate sentencing. By 1983, every state but Wisconsin had enacted mandatory minimum sentence laws for offenses other than murder and drunk driving.[52] By 1982, Alaska, Colorado, Indiana, Illinois, Maine, Minnesota, New Mexico, and North Carolina had followed California's lead and specified sentence lengths in their criminal codes; at least ten states had eliminated parole release; and at least nine had promulgated parole guidelines.[53] In addition, at least six states had statewide sentencing guidelines either in effect or under development, and more than fifty jurisdictions had developed local sentencing guidelines.[54]

47. Research on Sentencing, supra note 6, at 39. See generally Rothman, supra note 8, at 43–81 (analyzing and explaining rapidly expanding implementation of individualized sentencing regimes during progressive era).

48. See generally Sandra Shane-DuBow et al., Sentencing Reform in the United States: History, Content, and Effect (1985) (reviewing changes to and status of each state system); Bureau of Justice Assistance, National Assessment of Structured Sentencing 5–18 (1996), available at http://www.ncjrs.org/pdffiles/strsent.pdf (on file with the *Columbia Law Review*) (discussing historical trends in structured sentencing at state level).

49. Franklin E. Zimring, Sentencing Reform in the States: Lessons from the 1970s, *in* Reform and Punishment 101, 101 (Michael Tonry & Franklin E. Zimring eds., 1983).

50. Id. at 116.

51. Research on Sentencing, supra note 6, at 189–91.

52. Shane-DuBow et al., supra note 48, at 286 tbl.30.

53. Research on Sentencing, supra note 6, at 39–40, 133–34.

54. Id. at 40.

Political and normative developments concerning five subjects—race relations, proceduralism, civil liberties, rehabilitation, and lenient judges—were widely understood to have motivated sentencing law reformers. The civil rights movement's concern to reduce racial discrimination percolated through the criminal justice system, first in relation to prison conditions and subsequently to sentencing. Galvanizing riots in New York State, most notably at Attica Prison, highlighted the disproportionate number of blacks in confinement.[55] By 1971, the working group that wrote the American Friends Service Committee's *Struggle for Justice* was convinced that racial discrimination was a driving force behind imprisonment disparities and that the only way to ameliorate or eliminate it was to remove judges' and parole boards' discretion to discriminate.[56]

Second, prognosticated by Charles Reich's classic article *The New Property*,[57] and exemplified by *Goldberg*—a decision accepting Reich's argument about welfare entitlements[58]—the procedural rights movement emerged. The notion that government cannot invade primary personal interests except in accord with established procedural protections soon reached the criminal justice system. Kenneth Culp Davis famously observed that fair procedures were conspicuously absent from prosecutorial, judicial, correctional, and parole decisionmaking and argued that such discretionary decisions affecting liberty should be guided and structured.[59] In due course, the Supreme Court held that fair procedures must be observed in parole decisions,[60] prison disciplinary decisions,[61] and probation or parole revocation.[62] The discretions not reached were

55. Cf. Bert Useem & Peter Kimball, States of Siege 219, 225 (1993) (noting that riots were in part galvanized by external groups agitating against rise in black prison populations, and speculating on implications of riots for black communities).

56. See Am. Friends Serv. Comm., supra note 12, at 107–12, 143–44.

57. Charles A. Reich, The New Property, 73 Yale L.J. 733 (1964) (demonstrating that most citizens' important material interests relate to benefit claims against the government, and arguing that those claims warrant the same legal status as claims to tangible and traditional intangible properties).

58. Goldberg v. Kelly, 397 U.S. 254 (1970) (holding that entitlements could not be taken away unless specified rudimentary procedural protections were observed).

59. See supra note 3 and accompanying text. See generally Davis, supra note 3.

60. Greenholtz v. Inmates of the Neb. Penal & Corr. Complex, 442 U.S. 1, 7, 16 (1979) (reaffirming that "[t]he Due Process Clause applies when government action deprives a person of liberty or property" but deeming Nebraska's procedures in instant case sufficient to satisfy due process requirements).

61. Sandin v. Conner, 515 U.S. 472, 480, 483–84 (1995) (holding that "[t]he Due Process Clause standing alone confers no liberty interest in freedom from state action taken within the sentence imposed" (internal quotation marks omitted), but that "[s]tates may under certain circumstances create liberty interests which are protected by the Due Process Clause").

62. Gagnon v. Scarpelli, 411 U.S. 778, 782 (1973) (concluding that procedures outlined in *Morrissey* for parole revocation should also apply to probation proceedings); Morrissey v. Brewer, 408 U.S. 471, 482 (1972) ("[T]he liberty of a parolee, although indeterminate, includes many of the core values of unqualified liberty and its termination

those of prosecutors and judges.[63] At least for judges, the sentencing reform movement aimed to set that oversight right.

Third, constituting the substantive version of the procedural justice argument, concerns were soon expressed, most famously by Judge Frankel, that the absence of substantive standards for sentencing and fair procedures to assure their just application produced unwarranted sentencing disparities.[64] The subtitle of his book was "Law Without Order" and within it he referred to American sentencing as "lawless."[65]

Fourth, the preceding developments focused attention on the medical-model rationale of indeterminate sentencing—the claim that officials had to operate within wide discretionary bounds so that they could make individualized decisions about the rehabilitation (or its absence) of individual offenders. The necessary, if for too long unexamined, assumption was that judges and corrections officials had access to effective rehabilitative programs and knew how to classify offenders so they would get the treatment needed to turn them into law-abiding citizens. Literature reviews cast doubt on those assumptions and few people continued to claim that officials possessed those resources or skills.[66]

Fifth, constituting in retrospect a camel's nose under the tent, social conservatives, presumably concerned about rising crime rates (but often with more cynical motives) decried the "lenience" of prevailing sentencing and parole practices, and saw determinate sentencing as a way to ensure that judges imposed appropriate sentences that would not be second guessed by parole boards.[67] Barry Goldwater raised "crime in the streets"

---

inflicts a 'grievous loss' on the parolee and often on others. . . . Its termination calls for some orderly process, however informal.").

63. See Nichols v. United States, 511 U.S. 738, 747 (1994) ("As a general proposition, a sentencing judge 'may appropriately conduct an inquiry broad in scope, largely unlimited either as to the kind of information he may consider, or the source from which it may come.'" (quoting United States v. Tucker, 404 U.S. 443, 446 (1972))); Bordenkircher v. Hayes, 434 U.S. 357, 364 (1978) ("[S]o long as the prosecutor has probable cause to believe that the accused committed an offense defined by statute, the decision whether or not to prosecute, and what charge to file or bring before a grand jury, generally rests entirely in his discretion.").

64. Frankel, supra note 9, at 5 ("[M]y first basic point is this: the almost wholly unchecked and sweeping powers we give to judges in the fashioning of sentences are terrifying and intolerable for a society that professes devotion to the rule of law.").

65. See id. at ix–x.

66. See, e.g., James Robison & Gerald Smith, The Effectiveness of Correctional Programs, 17 Crime & Delinq. 67, 80 (1971) ("There is no evidence to support any [California correctional] program's claims of superior rehabilitative efficacy." (emphasis omitted)); Martinson, supra note 16, at 22–23, 49 (reviewing data from over two hundred studies and finding "very little reason to hope that we have in fact found a sure way of reducing recidivism through rehabilitation").

67. Kevin Phillips, at its inception, and Thomas and Mary Edsall after its successful execution, describe the strategy of the ultraconservative wing of the Republican Party to use crime, welfare, and affirmative action as "wedge issues" to convert the Southern white Democratic voters into Nixon and later Reagan Democrats. See generally Thomas Byrne Edsall & Mary D. Edsall, Chain Reaction: The Impact of Race, Rights, and Taxes on

as a campaign issue in the 1964 presidential election, and Richard Nixon followed suit in 1968 and 1972; calls for increased toughness characterized every subsequent presidential election until Bill Clinton nullified its emotive force by refusing to let Republicans get to his right on law and order.[68] The leading policy history of the adoption of California's Uniform Determinate Sentencing Law of 1976 describes the police unions, social conservatives, and prisoners' rights and civil liberties groups that improbably coalesced to support the new law.[69] The most influential crime policy book of the 1970s and 1980s provided an intellectual case for harsher and more certain punishments.[70] Those armies of the night have marched ever since.

In retrospect, 1975–1985 was the period of ferment, and the pace of innovation slowed thereafter. A single approach to sentencing no longer characterizes the United States.[71] All states have adopted mandatory minimum sentence laws, more than half have three strikes laws, and a third have abolished parole release.[72] Those laws, however, coexist in some states with statutory determinate sentencing and sentencing guidelines of various sorts and in others with largely intact indeterminate sentencing institutions and practices.[73]

The preceding constitutes a plausible account of the normative and policy developments that motivated at least the early years of recent sentencing policy changes. The next Part looks at the empirical evidence and policy concerns that inspired the early sentencing movement, and examines how the world has since changed.

American Politics 190–92, 214, 224–25 (1991); Kevin P. Phillips, The Emerging Republican Majority 471 (1969) ("The emerging Republican majority spoke clearly in 1968 for a shift away from the sociological jurisprudence, moral permissiveness, experimental residential, welfare and educational programing [sic] and massive federal spending by which the Liberal (mostly Democratic) Establishment sought to propagate liberal institutions and ideology.").

68. Ted Gest, Crime & Politics: Big Government's Erratic Campaign for Law and Order 223 (2001) ("Determined to seize on Bush's unexpected weakness on the crime-policy front, Clinton made a hard-nosed attack a centerpiece of his 'New Democrat' campaign for the White House in 1992.").

69. See Sheldon L. Messinger & Philip E. Johnson, California's Determinate Sentencing Statute: History and Issues, *in* Determinate Sentencing: Reform or Regression? 13, 21–29 (1978).

70. See James Q. Wilson, Thinking About Crime 162–82 (1975).

71. Kevin R. Reitz, The Disassembly and Reassembly of U.S. Sentencing Practices, *in* Sentencing and Sanctions in Western Countries 222, 253 (Michael Tonry & Richard S. Frase eds., 2001) (concluding that "U.S. jurisdictions are notable for their diversity of approaches, much more so than for their similarities").

72. See Research on Sentencing, supra note 6, at 132–35 (discussing mandatory minimum sentences and abolition of parole); Shane-DuBow et al., supra note 48, at 286 tbl.30 (highlighting mandatory terms for certain offenders).

73. See Reitz, supra note 71, at 222–33 (providing an overview of U.S. sentencing practices); Tonry, Fragmentation, supra note 5, at 1–6.

III. How the (Relevant Bits of) the World Changed from 1975 to 2005

Many of the background conditions that catalyzed the sentencing policy reforms of the 1970s have fundamentally changed; it is reasonable to expect prevalent attitudes and beliefs to change with them. In particular, changes regarding five background conditions stand out: crime trends, support for rehabilitative programs, concerns about racial disparities, fairness, and disparities in sentencing. Comparing 2005 with 1975, crime rates are falling not rising, support for rehabilitation is increasing rather than decreasing, and concerns about racial and other sentencing disparities and fairness are far less acute than they once were.

A. *Crime Rates*

Crime rates in 1975 had been rising for over a decade; by 2005, they had been declining for at least fifteen years. Tables 1 and 2 tell the story.

Table 1: Police-Recorded Offense Rates, per 100,000 Population, 1960–2003[74]

	Violent Crime	Murder	Robbery	Burglary	Motor Vehicle Theft
1960	161	5.1	60	509	183
1964	191	4.9	68	635	247
1968	298	6.9	132	932	393
1972	401	9.0	181	1141	426
1976	468	8.8	199	1448	450
1980	597	10.2	251	1684	502
1984	540	7.9	206	1266	438
1988	641	8.5	222	1316	586
1992	758	9.3	264	1168	632
1996	637	7.4	202	945	526
2000	506	5.5	145	729	412
2002	495	5.6	146	746	432
2003[75]	475	5.7	142	741	433

74. Bureau of Justice Statistics, U.S. Dep't of Justice, Sourcebook of Criminal Justice Statistics Online tbl.3.103, available at http://www.albany.edu/sourcebook/pdf/t3103.pdf (last visited Feb. 5, 2005) (on file with the *Columbia Law Review*) [hereinafter BJS, Sourcebook of Criminal Justice]; FBI, Crime in the United States: 2004 Preliminary (Dec. 13, 2004), available at http://www.fbi.gov/ucr/2004/6mosprelim04.pdf (on file with the *Columbia Law Review*) [hereinafter FBI, Crime 2004].

75. See FBI, Crime in the United States: 2003, § II, at 11, 15, 31, 37, 55 (2004), available at http://www.fbi.gov/ucr/cius_03/pdf/03sec2.pdf (on file with the *Columbia Law Review*) [hereinafter FBI, Crime 2003].

TABLE 2: VICTIMIZATION RATES—SELECTED OFFENSES, 1975–2003

Part A. 1975–1991, Rates per 1,000 Households or per 1,000 Individuals Twelve and Over[76]

	Any Violent Crime†	Robbery†	Aggravated Assault†	Household Burglary*	Motor Vehicle Theft*
1975	32.8	6.8	9.6	91.7	19.5
1978	33.7	5.9	9.7	86.0	17.5
1981	35.3	7.4	9.6	87.9	17.1
1984	31.4	5.7	9.0	64.1	15.2
1987	29.3	5.3	8.0	62.1	16.0
1989	29.1	5.4	8.3	56.4	19.2
1991	31.3	5.6	7.8	53.1	21.8

† per 1,000 households
* per 1,000 individuals aged twelve and over

Part B. 1994–2003, Percentage of Households Reporting at Least One Incident[77]

	Any NCVS Crime	Violence	Robbery	Aggravated Assault	Household Burglary	Motor Vehicle Theft
1994	25.0	7.0	1.0	1.9	4.6	1.7
1997	20.9	5.5	0.7	1.4	3.7	1.2
2000	16.2	3.9	0.5	0.9	2.7	0.8
2002	14.6	3.2	0.4	0.7	2.4	0.8
2003	14.7	3.0	0.4	0.7	2.6	0.8

Table 1 shows offenses recorded by the police between 1960 and 2002 for all violent crimes, murder and nonnegligent manslaughter, robbery, burglary, and motor vehicle theft. I selected these offenses to reflect trends in serious violent and property offenses and to minimize distortions resulting from cultural changes that influence citizen reporting and police recording of alleged crimes. For example, declining tolerance of sexual and violent offenses has increased citizen reporting and police recording of certain crimes, such as aggravated assault.[78] These phenomena have led to an artificial increase in apparent offending rates.[79]

The data in Table 1 tell two well-known stories. First, police-recorded crime rates for all offenses increased steadily from the early 1960s

76. Bureau of Justice Statistics, U.S. Dep't of Justice, Sourcebook of Criminal Justice Statistics 1992, at 245 tbl.3.2 (Kathleen Maguire et al. eds., 1993); Bureau of Justice Statistics, U.S. Dep't of Justice, Sourcebook of Criminal Justice Statistics 1990, at 252 tbl.3.2 (Kathleen Maguire & Timothy J. Flanagan eds., 1991).

77. BJS, Sourcebook of Criminal Justice, supra note 74, at tbl.3.30.

78. Alfred Blumstein & Allen J. Beck, Population Growth in U.S. Prisons, 1980–1996, 26 Crime & Just. 17, 54 (1999).

79. Id.

through the early 1980s, declined through the mid-1980s, rose until the early 1990s, and thereafter fell steadily and precipitously through 2003.[80] Rates for 2003 for the individual offenses were the lowest since various years in the 1960s: murder (1966), robbery (1968), burglary (1966), and motor vehicle theft (1968).[81]

Second, when the sentencing reform initiative of the mid-1970s took hold, crime rates had been rising for fifteen years. By contrast, in 2005 the crime rate has been in decline for fifteen years if the continuous decline since 1991 is deemed the appropriate measure, or for twenty-five years if the short upturn in the late 1980s is disregarded.

As Table 2 shows, the trends revealed by the police data can be substantiated with data from the National Crime Victimization Survey—a victimization survey of 40,000–60,000 households carried out every six months. Because major methodological changes to the survey were made in the early 1990s to capture and measure domestic assaults more accurately, Table 2 is split into two parts.

Part A presents data from 1975–1991 on burglary and motor vehicle theft rates per one thousand households and aggregate violent crime, robbery, and aggravated assault rates per one thousand individuals aged twelve and over. Burglary victimization rates declined continuously and steeply. Robbery and aggravated assault rates, as in the police data, rose through 1981 and then fell. Motor vehicle theft rates, again as in the police data, rose, fell, and then rose again.

The data listed in Part B are expressed per one thousand households and are derived from the altered methodology. Consequently, the data cannot be strictly compared with those presented in Part A. Nevertheless, Part B shows continuous and steep declines since 1994 in victimization rates for all four offenses and in the aggregate for violence and "any crime."

This difference in crime trends between the 1970s and the first decade of the twenty-first century is important. We know with some confidence that in relation to drug crime, and more speculatively in relation to other crimes, public attitudes become less vindictive and uncompromising at times when the incidence of deviant behavior has been declining for a considerable period.[82] A window of opportunity has thus opened

80. Compared with 2003, preliminary data for the first six months of 2004 show continued year-on-year declines of about five percent for murder and robbery, and two percent for burglary and motor vehicle theft. See FBI, Crime 2004, supra note 74, at 3, 5, 8, 10 (listing data for murder, robbery, burglary, and vehicle theft, respectively).

81. Compare BJS, Sourcebook of Criminal Justice, supra note 74, at tbl.3.103, with FBI, Crime 2003, supra note 75, § II, at 70 tbl.1.

82. See Tonry, Thinking, supra note 18, at 97–139 (describing relationship between crime trends and crime control policies); supra text accompanying note 46 (noting that initial stages of a falling incidence of deviant behavior may be associated with public overreaction). Tonry, Thinking, supra note 18, at 21–96, develops this analysis, and the evidence and analyses on which it is based, at some length.

for the adoption and execution of more humane social policies. This is a point to which I return below.[83]

B. *Rehabilitation*

Although it was not widely recognized at the time, by 1975, confidence in the efficacy of rehabilitative programs had been on the decline for decades, and the prevailing evaluation of the empirical evidence suggested that rehabilitation did not work. By contrast, in 2005, faith in rehabilitation has been increasing for decades, and the prevailing empirical evidence suggests that a wide range of treatment programs can reduce the likelihood of recidivism.

Although Robert Martinson's famous article, *What Works—Questions and Answers About Prison Reform*, was not published in *The Public Interest* until 1974, the harbingers of decline in faith in the rehabilitative ideal were evident earlier. Early in the 1950s in Australia, C.S. Lewis—writing as a Christian apologist and Kantian moralist—and Norval Morris—writing as a liberal lawyer—raised normative objections to efforts coercively to change people in the pursuit of crime prevention.[84] Soon after, Francis A. Allen raised similar objections in the United States.[85]

Skepticism about the effectiveness of rehabilitative programs significantly preceded Martinson's article, which was itself a byproduct of a literature review commissioned by New York State in the late 1960s.[86] The California Department of Corrections had earlier commissioned a similar review of the evidence; a summary was published in 1971.[87]

Thus, what to many seemed to constitute a stunning turn in direction away from indeterminate sentencing and the rehabilitative ideal was simply an acknowledgment of normative doubts and empirical skepticism that had been bubbling away for decades.[88] That is not to say no one continued to support rehabilitative goals and programs; some did.[89]

83. See infra Part IV.B.

84. See generally Lewis, supra note 19; Morris, Sentencing, supra note 19.

85. See Allen, Criminal Justice, supra note 19, at 229–32 (criticizing shortcomings of "rehabilitative ideal in the areas of corrections and criminal justice"); Allen, Legal Values, supra note 1, at 25–41 (reexamining rehabilitative ideal).

86. This study eventually was published in full. Douglas Lipton et al., The Effectiveness of Correctional Treatment: A Survey of Treatment Evaluation Studies (1975).

87. See Robison & Smith, supra note 66.

88. The American Law Institute, however, seems not to have noticed: In 1962, it approved the Proposed Official Draft of the Model Penal Code, which recommended a refined system of indeterminate sentencing premised primarily on rehabilitative aims. Tonry, Thinking, supra note 18, at 176–86.

89. See, e.g., F.T. Cullen & K.E. Gilbert, Reaffirming Rehabilitation 246–91 (1982) ("[I]t is our firm belief that the most promising option for liberal reform is to reaffirm and not to reject the ideology of criminal justice rehabilitation."); Ted Palmer, Martinson Revisited, 12 J. Res. Crime & Delinq. 133, 149–51 (1975) (arguing that Martinson's study challenging effectiveness of rehabilitative measures in fact contained evidence that some rehabilitative methods were effective for at least some types of offenders).

However, the eventual post-Martinson review of rehabilitative programs by the National Academy of Sciences, which broadly confirmed Martinson's skeptical conclusions, was plowing well-tilled soil.[90]

In 2005, things look very different. Numerous literature reviews,[91] meta-analyses,[92] and government reports[93] proclaim the effectiveness of a wide range of treatment programs. They uniformly insist that programs must be well-targeted and well-implemented but, assuming those (difficult to satisfy) conditions can be met, they almost always conclude that rehabilitative programs can significantly reduce reoffending.

Taking such findings seriously, a recent English government report, which served as the foundation for a massive overhaul of the English criminal justice system,[94] observed in its executive summary, "The available evidence suggests that greater support for reform and rehabilitation . . . to reduce risks of offending, offers the best prospects for improved outcomes."[95] The body of the report explained why: "A reasonable estimate at this stage is that, if the programmes are developed and applied as intended, to the maximum extent possible, reconviction rates might be

90. See Panel on Research on Rehabilitative Techniques, Report of the Panel, *in* The Rehabilitation of Criminal Offenders: Problems and Prospects 3, 29–34 (Lee Sechrest et al. eds., 1979).

91. See, e.g., M. Douglas Anglin & Yih-Ing Hser, Treatment of Drug Abuse, 13 Crime & Just. 393, 394 (1990) (insisting "greater social investment in treatment may be the most cost-effective way to achieve [the] public policy goals" of reducing drug use and thereby reducing the user's criminal activity); Gerald G. Gaes et al., Adult Correctional Treatment, 26 Crime & Just. 361, 366–411 (1999) (summarizing and offering general critique of correctional treatment literature).

92. See, e.g., Mark W. Lipsey, What Do We Learn from 400 Research Studies on the Effectiveness of Treatment of Juvenile Delinquents?, *in* What Works: Reducing Reoffending 63, 78 (James McGuire ed., 1995) [hereinafter What Works] (concluding "[i]t is no longer constructive . . . to argue about whether delinquency treatment and related rehabilitative approaches 'work'" because "[a]s a generality, treatment clearly works"); Friedrich Lösel, The Efficacy of Correctional Treatment: A Review and Synthesis of Meta-Evaluations, *in* What Works, supra, at 79, 103 (concluding "it will be worthwhile to continue along [the] path" of rehabilitative offender treatment).

93. See, e.g., President's Comm'n on Model State Drug Laws, The White House, Final Report—Executive Summary 2 (Dec. 1993) (recommending sanctions "designed to be constructive, attempting to leverage alcohol and other drug abusers into treatment, rehabilitation, and ultimately, recovery"); U.S. Surgeon Gen., Youth Violence: A Report of the Surgeon General ch. 5 (2001), available at http://www.surgeongeneral.gov/library/youthviolence/toc.html (on file with the *Columbia Law Review*) (asserting that "effective treatment can divert a significant proportion of delinquent and violent youths from future violence and crime").

94. The Halliday Report, the foundation document upon which the Criminal Justice Act 2003 builds, discusses the new initiatives and the issues they raise. See John Halliday et al., Home Office, Making Punishments Work: Report of a Review of the Sentencing Framework for England and Wales *passim* (2001); see also Michael Tonry, Punishment and Politics: Evidence and Emulation in the Making of English Crime Control Policy 1 (2004) [hereinafter Tonry, Punishment].

95. Halliday et al., supra note 94, ¶ 0.4.

reduced by five to fifteen percentage points (i.e. from the present level of 56% within two years to (perhaps) 40%)."[96]

Halliday's predictions are no doubt optimistic, but they do reflect a sea change in attitudes toward rehabilitation. Where a quarter of a century ago public officials and researchers were predisposed to pessimism, the modern predisposition is otherwise. This is important because, while the pessimism of the mid-1970s rested comfortably with normative arguments that sentencing should be backward-looking and predicated on ideas about proportionality, modern optimism can easily be reconciled with other views.

C. *Racial Disparities*

Concerns about racial discrimination and disparities in the criminal justice system were major challenges to the legitimacy of indeterminate sentencing in the 1970s. By 2005, they have largely disappeared as major considerations in the formulation of sentencing policy.

The civil rights movement reached full stride in the 1960s, searing the nation's conscience; making national celebrities of people as diverse as Martin Luther King, Jr., Julian Bond, Bobby Seal, and Stokely Carmichael; and fundamentally challenging the ways America organized and distributed education, housing, and social welfare. Perhaps a bit surprisingly in retrospect, because real and alleged criminals seldom elicit widespread solicitude, the movement included the police, courts, and prisons within its focus. It gave rise, among other things, to the prisoners' rights movement[97] and to fundamental critiques of the capacity of indeterminate sentencing to deal with offenders fairly and evenhandedly.[98] The capacity of every judge, probation officer, prison system, and parole board to exercise individualized discretion within broad ranges of authority created nearly limitless risks of contamination of decisions by deliberate racial animus and unconscious stereotyping.

America is a different place in terms of race relations and equal opportunity in 2005 than it was in 1975, even though aspirations for racial equality remain in important respects insufficiently satisfied. Still, it would not be unreasonable to suppose that problems of racial disparity and discrimination in the criminal justice system are less acute. It would not be unreasonable, but it would be wrong. Racial disparities in impris-

---

96. Id. at 7. This is even more heroic than it appears because of the way Halliday presents the numbers. A reduction from fifty-six percent reconviction within two years to forty percent is a twenty-seven percent reduction relative to the starting point.

97. E.g., James B. Jacobs, The Prisoners' Rights Movement and Its Impacts, 1960–80, 2 Crime & Just. 429, 436–37 (1980) (suggesting the civil rights movement aroused the consciousness of minority prisoners and was the impetus for the ensuing prisoners' rights movement).

98. See, e.g., Am. Friends Serv. Comm., supra note 12, at 67–82 (highlighting preventive detention through indeterminate sentencing as "particularly vivid example of depersonalization" and "a major setback in the struggle for justice").

onment are worse in the early years of the twenty-first century than they were in the 1970s.

Table 3, showing the percentages of blacks among state and federal prison inmates, tells the tale. In 1970, in the bad old days, 41% of prison inmates were black. By 1980, the percentage had climbed to 44% and by 1986 to 46%. By 1990, it was 49%, around which it has since hovered, occasionally slightly exceeding 50%.[99]

TABLE 3: PERCENTAGE OF BLACK STATE AND FEDERAL PRISONERS IN SELECTED YEARS, 1960–2002.[100]

Year	Percentage Black
1960	37
1970	41
1975*	42.5
1980	44
1985	45.9
1990	49.2
1995	49.9
2002*	49.4

* Estimated from published sources.

Racial disparities in imprisonment can be expressed in other ways. On December 1, 2002, 3.4% of black American men were prison inmates

99. Before the mid-1990s, the Bureau of Justice Statistics (BJS), like the U.S. Bureau of the Census, used "black," "white," and "other" to characterize race, and separately counted Hispanics and non-Hispanics. More recently, the BJS reports "race" data for whites, blacks, and Hispanics. Approximately one-fourth of Hispanics were formerly counted as "black," and I have adjusted the 2002 figure in table 3 to take account of this. The official BJS report for 1997 lists the percentage of black inmates, including Hispanic blacks, as 49.9% in 1995; the 2003 BJS report lists the percentage of black inmates, not including Hispanics, as 45.7% in 1995. See Bureau of Justice Statistics, U.S. Dep't of Justice, Prisoners in 2002, at 9 (July 2003), available at http://www.ojp.usdoj.gov/bjs/pub/pdf/p02.pdf (on file with the *Columbia Law Review*) [hereinafter BJS, Prisoners 2002]; Bureau of Justice Statistics, U.S. Dep't of Justice, Prisoners in 1996, at 9 tbl.11 (June 1997), available at http://www.ojp.usdoj.gov/bjs/pub/pdf/p96.pdf (on file with the *Columbia Law Review*) [hereinafter BJS, Prisoners 1996]. In 1995, 17.6% of prisoners were reported to be Hispanic, which means that about a fourth (4.4%) were previously counted among black prisoners; in 2002, 18.1% were Hispanic. See BJS, Prisoners 2002, supra, at 9. See generally Tonry, Malign Neglect, supra note 46, at 49–123 (providing more detailed data on racial trends in crime and punishment).

100. BJS, Prisoners 2002, supra note 99, at 9 tbl.13; BJS, Prisoners 1996, supra note 99, at 9 tbl.11; Margaret Werner Cahalan, U.S. Dep't of Justice, Historical Corrections Statistics in the United States, 1850–1984, at 65 tbl.3-31 (1986). For how 2002 percentages are calculated, see supra note 99.

(add jail inmates and the percentage climbs to 4.8%)[101] and 10.4% of black males twenty-five to twenty-nine years old were in prison. Relative to population, black men in 2002 were 7.6 times likelier to be in prison than white men, and black women 5.5 times likelier than white women.[102]

However the phenomenon is characterized, racial disparities in imprisonment—and the damage they do to black people's lives and life chances—have not diminished over the past thirty years. They have worsened.

We know why the black presence in American prisons increased so greatly in the 1980s. The problem was not an increase in biased decision-making in individual cases.[103] Nor did it occur because blacks' involvement in serious crimes increased.[104] The increase was instead the foreseeable consequence of conscious policy decisions to focus on street-level trafficking in the War on Drugs and on street-level violence in the War on Crime.[105] Inner-city drug dealing networks, operating mostly on the streets and in deteriorated neighborhoods, are much easier to penetrate, and dealers are much easier to arrest, than are middle-class drug dealers working behind doors and in less penetrable settings. Among people arrested for violent crimes, blacks, who make up 13% of the U.S. population, are heavily overrepresented. In 2003, 48.5% of those arrested for murder were black, and the figures for other serious violent crimes were also disproportionately high: forcible rape (33.3%), robbery (54.4%), and aggravated assault (33.0%).[106] Policies meant to increase the severity of punishments for violent crimes will, in the nature of things, disproportionately affect black offenders.

101. See Bureau of Justice Statistics, U.S. Dep't of Justice, Prison and Jail Inmates at Midyear 2002, at 11 tbl.14 (April 2003), available at http://www.ojp.usdoj.gov/bjs/pub/pdf/pjim02.pdf (on file with the *Columbia Law Review*).

102. See BJS, Prisoners 2002, supra note 99, at 9 tbl.14.

103. See Randall Kennedy, Race, Crime, and the Law 352 (1997) (arguing that, in regard to charges of selective prosecution, "allegations of racial discrimination have been insufficiently substantiated"). See generally Tonry, Malign Neglect, supra note 46, 68–74 (documenting and discussing racial disproportion in criminal justice system and racially disproportionate effects of war on drugs).

104. See infra note 106.

105. See Tonry, Malign Neglect, supra note 46, at 104–16; Tonry, Thinking, supra note 18, at 130–39.

106. FBI, Crime 2003, supra note 75, at 288 tbl.43. FBI arrest data, unlike BJS prison data, continue to use a "black," "white," and "other" racial breakdown, and thus include Hispanics within the "black" and "white" classifications. Although blacks' shares among arrests for violent crimes are disproportionately high, they have declined substantially. The black share of homicide arrests in 2003 (48.5%) is much lower than in 1992 (55.1%), 1982 (49.7%), and 1976 (53.5%). The patterns from 2003, 1992, 1982, and 1976, for robbery (51.8%, 60.9%, 60.7%, 59.2%), rape (33.3%, 42.8%, 49.7%, 51.2%), and aggravated assault (32.2%, 38.3%, 38.8%, 41.0%) are similar. See id.; Tonry, Malign Neglect, supra note 46, at 64 tbl.2-2.

Although racial disparities have worsened, concern about them has abated and is no longer a major pressure on the shaping of sentencing and penal policies.[107] This is important because concern about racial disparities was a major impetus to sentencing initiatives that sought to reduce and constrain officials' exercise of discretion, and consequently rested comfortably with desert theories aimed at making sentences proportionate and predictable.

D. *Sentencing Disparities*

There was also widespread concern about sentencing disparities generally during the 1970s. The earliest reform initiatives were heavily motivated by the desire to reduce unwarranted disparities because they were unjust. That was the gravamen of Judge Marvin Frankel's proposal for creation of sentencing commissions[108] and of a series of other contemporaneous and, for a time, influential books.[109] However, substantive concern about disparities seems largely to have disappeared. This can be shown in several ways.

First, although sentencing commissions have been attempted or institutionalized in more than twenty states and the federal system, the time is long past when they were motivated primarily by a desire to reduce disparities and discrimination.[110] Most contemporary systems are motivated either to achieve "truth in sentencing" or to make sentencing outcomes predictable so that correctional resource needs can be predicted and managed. Seeking truth in sentencing, however, is not at all the same as trying to reduce disparities. Generally, truth in sentencing—usually involving abolition of parole release, time off for good behavior (good time), or both—aims to assure that whatever sentence the judge imposes is carried out. Whether the sentence is appropriate or proportionate is an altogether separate matter. Virginia's guidelines, for example, aim to reduce crime through the incapacitation of higher-rate offenders and offenders with predicted long residual offending careers, an

107. Racial disparities in capital punishment and allegations of racial profiling by police continue to galvanize powerful emotions and concern, but disparities in sentencing and imprisonment do not. The federal government's sustained failure to repeal or amend the notorious 100-to-1 law, which punishes traffickers in crack cocaine—mostly black—as much as traffickers in powder cocaine who deal in amounts 100 times larger, is one example. See, e.g., Tonry, Thinking, supra note 18, at 4, 15; see also supra p. 1255 tbl.3 (displaying data on black imprisonment rates).

108. See Frankel, supra note 9, at 3–11.

109. See, e.g., David Fogel, ". . . We Are the Living Proof . . .": The Justice Model for Corrections 192–93 (1975) (describing sentencing system as "anomic" and challenging its fairness).

110. See Richard S. Frase, State Sentencing Guidelines: Diversity, Consensus, and Unresolved Policy Issues, 105 Colum. L. Rev. 1190, 1204–06 n.72–80 (2005) (explaining new reasons for sentencing commissions); Reitz, supra note 71, at 225–28 (describing changes in motivations for sentencing commissions).

approach that inherently has nothing whatsoever to do with horizontal equity for people convicted of comparable crimes.[111]

Nor does efficient management of correctional resources imply much about sentencing disparities. The goal of such an approach is to make sentences predictable, which implies making them consistent within categories. Unlike Judge Frankel's normative approach, efficiency constitutes both a backdoor and an instrumental goal: Sentences should be made consistent because that makes them predictable and therefore makes resource allocation decisions better informed. That is some distance from the normative claim that sentences should be made consistent because inconsistent sentences are unjust.[112]

Second, it has been several decades since policymakers showed much concern about sentencing disparities. Most of the ballyhooed sentencing initiatives of the past twenty years—three strikes rules, mandatory minimums, sexual psychopath laws, and truth in sentencing—display no sensitivity to proportionality and consistency. Mandatory minimum sentences for drug crimes, for example, often require imposition of longer sentences than are received by people convicted of serious violent and sexual crimes. California's Three Strikes, for another example, requires minimum twenty-five-year-to-life sentences following any third felony conviction, including (notoriously) trivial drug and property offenses, thus defying all conventional notions of proportionality and consistency.[113]

Third, everything we know about the operation of severe mandatory sentences instructs that they increase disparities in the handling of similar cases. In California, for example, there are enormous differences in the extent to which prosecutors in different cities invoke the third-strike provisions, which means defendants in some cities will receive twenty-five year sentences for crimes for which offenders in other cities receive much lesser sentences.[114] More generally, several centuries of experience and evidence show that mandatory penalties foreseeably provoke adaptive responses and circumvention by judges and other practitioners to save offenders from sentences that everyone involved considers unduly harsh.[115] As a result, among like-situated offenders, some will be sentenced as the

111. See Va. Crim. Sentencing Comm'n, 1997 Annual Report 41–60 (detailing new risk assessment instrument designed for integration into existing guidelines system, with primary purpose of assessing probability of reconviction for felony crime within three year period).

112. Policy makers could, for example, decide that convicted offenders who are noncitizens (or Muslim or black or female) should always be sentenced to terms twice those of citizens, non-Muslims, whites, or men. Such a policy, consistently applied, would make sentences predictable, but it would be far from just.

113. Zimring et al., supra note 44, at 117–23.

114. Id. at 81–83 (comparing the number of twenty-five-year-to-life sentences for third-strike felons in Los Angeles, San Diego, and San Francisco); see supra note 44 and accompanying text.

115. Michael Tonry, Sentencing Matters 147 (1996).

mandatory sentence law prescribes and others will receive a wide range of sentences made possible by circumvention.[116]

This reduced visceral concern for the injustice of imposition of disparate sentences on like-situated offenders is important because it demonstrates the weakening influence of the idea that equality and proportionality are key elements of just punishment.

E. *Fairness*

This point can be made by affirmation. Concerns for procedural and substantive fairness in the criminal justice system waxed through the 1970s and have waned ever since. Rawls's notion of "justice as fairness,"[117] made manifest in Dworkin's conception of rights as trumps,[118] and Dworkin's argument that fairness requires "equal concern and respect" to be shown for the interests of each individual[119] were vital and influential ideas in relation to the criminal justice system in the 1970s. They no longer are.

Concern for procedural fairness for criminal suspects and defendants expanded in the 1950s and 1960s under the aegis of the Warren Court, declined somewhat under the Burger Court, and has declined markedly under the Rehnquist Court.[120] Concern for substantive fairness, high in the 1970s and exemplified by concerns about racial and other disparities and ambitions to reduce them, has also since declined.[121]

Why these changes happened—why society at large and policymakers in general became less concerned about fairness to offenders and less able to empathize with the unfortunate and the dispossessed—is a complicated question. Answers range from the simple and simpleminded (crime rose, people became frightened, policymakers responded[122]) to the eloquent and elegant (conditions of late modernity reshaped sensibilities in relation to tolerance of risk, difference, and confidence in govern-

116. Although evaluations in the early years of implementation of sentencing guidelines showed that some significantly decreased disparities generally and racial and gender disparities specifically, the proliferation of mandatory minimum and three strikes laws, and the adaptive responses they engender, have no doubt greatly increased the prevalence of sentencing disparities. Id. at 40–49.

117. John Rawls, Justice as Fairness, 67 Phil. Rev. 164 (1958).

118. Ronald Dworkin, Taking Rights Seriously 184–205 (1977).

119. Id. at 180.

120. See Allen, Habits, supra note 14, at 65 (stating that Warren Court was leader in development of "constitutional doctrine pertaining to the rights of suspected persons," which subsequently was limited by "the restiveness of the modern Court").

121. See supra Part III.C–D.

122. William J. Bennett et al., Body Count: Moral Poverty . . . and How to Win America's War Against Crime and Drugs 14–17 (1996).

ment[123]). None is or can be completely convincing, but all agree that sensibilities have changed in important ways over the last forty years.

IV. Normative Consequences

The changes in normative and cultural backdrop sketched in Part III have important implications for thinking about punishment. They can help us understand why retributivist ideas about proportionality and desert found receptive minds in the 1970s but find fewer now, and why thinking about punishment will and should change in coming years. In refusing to name names to the House Unamerican Activities Committee, Lillian Hellman famously refused to cut her conscience to fit the fashion of the times.[124] The prevailing sensibilities of a time do, however, powerfully shape what people believe and, even more powerfully, what they say. In the 1980s, many fewer voices were raised against the extraordinarily harsh penalties authorized and imposed in conducting the War on Drugs than would have been ten or twenty years earlier or than would be raised in 2005 were they new proposals. Likewise, post-9/11, many fewer people opposed policies denying basic human rights and procedural protections to alleged national security suspects than would have before 9/11 or than do in 2005. The fewer, quieter voices of principled opposition resulted partly from the chilling effect of not wanting to appear unreasonable or radical or naïve, but also because in those times on those issues many more people for a while believed the repressive measures were ethically justifiable and made good policy sense.

And so it is with thinking about punishment. The prevailing structural conditions and sensibilities of a time shape what people think and believe. Most practitioners and policymakers in the 1950s speculated that crime was in significant part the deterministic outcome of defective socialization, social disadvantage, and personal pathology, and that the most ethically defensible punishment policies involved rehabilitation of the corrigible and incapacitation of the rest.[125]

123. See Garland, supra note 17, at 23–24. Less cryptically, Garland suggests that several major influences are important in a postmodern world of heightened insecurity and instability: increased and more widely distributed victimization and a heightened sense of risk, particularly among the privileged; adoption of primarily expressive policies by governments that recognize there is relatively little they can do about crime but wish to be seen to be acknowledging public anxiety and insecurity; and reification of typically poor and often minority offenders as the criminological "other" who can be scapegoated. Id. at 10–20, 135–37.

124. Mark Jarman, Ovid, Our Contemporary, Hudson Rev., Summer 2004, available at http://www.hudsonreview.com/JarmanSu04.html (on file with the *Columbia Law Review*) ("To paraphrase Lillian Hellman's famous rebuke to the House Unamerican Affairs Committee, art will not cut its cloth to suit the fashion of the times . . . .").

125. For an example from England, see Barbara Wootton, Social Science and Social Pathology 80–135, 334–35 (1959) (reviewing a number of deterministic theories, and concluding there is "encouraging" evidence that rehabilitation is more successful than standard forms of punishment). For an American example, see Karl Menninger, The Crime of Punishment 96–97, 251, 257–64 (1968) (arguing that the existence of free will is

A. *Ideas for the 1970s*

The calls for adoption of retributive punishment schemes set out in Norval Morris's *The Future of Imprisonment*[126] and Andrew von Hirsch's *Doing Justice*[127] at the time appeared radical. The Model Penal Code's draftsmen a dozen years earlier,[128] and the Brown Commission (National Commission on Reform of Federal Criminal Laws)[129] just a few years earlier had called for the creation of full-blown systems of indeterminate sentencing premised on utilitarian ideas. Yet von Hirsch was ready to jettison rehabilitative and other utilitarian goals of punishment, except as incidental byproducts of the imposition of deserved punishments, and Morris called for strict limits on and presumptions against their pursuit in individual cases.[130]

Academic philosophers beginning in the 1960s and 1970s showed renewed interest in deontological theories of punishment,[131] although in retrospect, as I have already shown, precursors to popular acceptance of desert and proportionality ideas in the mid-1970s can be seen at least twenty years earlier.[132] The basic ideas expressed in these retributive punishment theories had been around in well-elaborated form since Kant and Hegel developed them in the nineteenth century, and were ready to be taken off the shelf and applied.[133] For most of those years, at least in the English-speaking countries, they gathered dust.

Glimmerings of interest appeared in the 1950s. Suddenly, in the 1970s, they were taken down and celebrated. Why? Because the times were ready for them. They fit comfortably with the civil rights movement,

---

an unproven hypothesis, thus "blame" is an unsound basis for punishment; further arguing that crime should be treated as an illness, and that rehabilitative treatment for criminals is both desirable and possible).

126. See Morris, Future, supra note 2, at 58 (rejecting rehabilitation in favor of retribution and deterrence).

127. See von Hirsch, Justice, supra note 2, at 11–18 (criticizing rehabilitation as preeminent goal of punishment).

128. See Model Penal Code § 6.02 cmt. 9 (1985) ("When Section 6.06 was discussed and approved by the Institute [in 1962] there was little dissent from the objectives of having some judicial discretion in choice of sentence and considerable indeterminacy of prison terms.").

129. Nat'l Comm'n on Reform of Fed. Criminal Laws, Proposed New Federal Criminal Code § 3201(2) & cmt. (1971).

130. See Morris, Future, supra note 2, at 15, 18 (arguing that "rehabilitation can be given only to a volunteer" and that "sentencing judge should never extend a term of imprisonment, or impose a term of imprisonment, on the basis that the offender needs it for his retraining"); von Hirsch, Justice, supra note 2, at 11–18 (criticizing rehabilitation); id. at 127–30 (arguing that even if rehabilitation were to be effective, with few exceptions, principle of commensurate deserts should define limit of punishment).

131. See, e.g., Herbert Morris, Persons and Punishment, 52 Monist 475, 476 (1968) (arguing that humans have right to punishment that stems from "a fundamental human right to be treated as a person"); Murphy, Marxism, supra note 35, at 222 (proposing that retributive theory of punishment is reasonable and morally justifiable).

132. See supra notes 84–90 and accompanying text.

133. See supra note 27.

the prisoners' rights movement, the procedural rights movement, the elaboration of rights theories in philosophy by Rawls, Dworkin, and others, and the decline in confidence in the ethics and efficacy of rehabilitative programs. They provided a logical and a normative rationale for punishment schemes that could constrain officials' discretion and ameliorate racial bias and disparities of various sorts. Because retributive ideas fit so comfortably with the policy and normative imperatives of the 1970s and early 1980s, they escaped some of the scrutiny to which a less predisposed age would have subjected them.

Andrew von Hirsch is the paradigmatic writer in the modern retributive tradition. Professional philosophers have written creatively on this subject, if often rather abstrusely. Von Hirsch, however, has tried to develop an applied philosophy to address practical policy choices in an imperfect world;[134] I use some of his ideas to show the limits of retributive theories, starting with the most familiar. There are six major problems of successively greater importance.

First, in the initial iteration of von Hirsch's ideas in *Doing Justice*, it was unclear why he adopted retribution in determination of the amount of punishment as a defining principle at all. H.L.A. Hart had, to most people's satisfaction, explained that punishment theories need to address three different subjects: Justification—why punish at all? Liability—whom to punish? Amount—how much to punish?[135] Hart suggested that the three questions can coherently be answered in different ways. For example, for Hart himself, if general prevention, a utilitarian aim, were to be the justification for punishment, retribution often would be at least part of the rationale for decisions about liability and amount.[136] Norval Morris also relies on general prevention[137] but argues that the concept of desert should be used in defining the maximum amount of punishment appropriate.[138] Some justifications, however, might entail (that is, logically require) specific answers to the other questions. A thorough-going retributivist, for example, like Kant or Hegel, for whom the justification of punishment is positive retribution (that is, a belief that it is morally required that offenders be punished in strict proportion to their culpability) would have difficulty coherently offering other than positive retributivist answers to the other two questions.[139]

Von Hirsch adopted a positive retributivist position on amounts of punishment that could justly be imposed, but gave an unsatisfactory ex-

134. See von Hirsch, Justice, supra note 2, at 6 (describing his book as an attempt to "provide a structure of ideas, against which specific programs may be judged," and acknowledging that "reformers, pursuing the practical business of change, have to accommodate their aims to political and institutional realities").

135. See Hart, supra note 1, at 3.

136. See id. at 9.

137. See Morris, Future, supra note 2, at 79.

138. See id. at 74–75.

139. In positive retributivist accounts, the deserved punishment *must* be imposed. In negative retributivist accounts, punishment *may* be imposed up to the deserved amount.

planation as to why.[140] The stance was not entailed in the justification he offered for punishment as an institution: an amalgamation of Benthamite utilitarian ideas and general prevention with retributive ideas about moral desert.[141] Von Hirsch's justification could easily have accommodated utilitarian goals in distribution (liability and amount combined), but he opted instead for a strict desert scheme. Although he later recanted it, he offered as a partial justification for the existence of punishment the benefits-and-burdens claim that offenders, who by offending have unfairly benefited from others' compliance with the social contract, must be subjected to offsetting burdens so as to restore social equilibrium.[142] In later writings, von Hirsch abandoned the benefits-and-burdens argument in favor of a censure theory which posits that respect for offenders' moral autonomy requires that we blame them for their wrongdoing in proportion to the moral gravity of the wrong.[143] All of his arguments are graceful and persuasive, and suggest a powerful intuitive commitment to retributive ideas and values. What isn't clear, and isn't required by the punishment justification he offered, is why he held that intuition so strongly.

Second, even assuming retribution in distribution is appropriate, there is a classic epistemological problem. How do we know how much censure, or "deserved punishment," a particular wrongdoer absolutely deserves? God may know, but as countless sentencing exercises have shown, people's intuitions about individual cases vary widely. Von Hirsch conceded that questions of "cardinal desert" are beyond us, but offered as a practical equivalent what he called "ordinal desert."[144]

An ordinal desert scheme ranks crimes by their comparative generic seriousness, ranks punishments by their comparative severity, sets "anchoring points" specifying the tops and bottoms of the punishment scale, and lines the two scales up against one another. There are still some well-known problems such as determining the anchoring points, the number of steps in the two scales, and the intervals between steps, but the scheme does what von Hirsch wanted it to do. What isn't clear is why he wanted to do it.

---

140. See von Hirsch, Justice, supra note 2, at 69 ("The principle of commensurate deserts, in our opinion, is a requirement of justice . . . .").

141. See id. at 49–55 (concluding that criminal sanction rests on interdependent concepts of deterrence and desert).

142. See id. at 47–48 (emphasizing that Kant's theory explains only why some kind of deprivation should be suffered by the offender to offset his advantage, not why the deprivation should take the peculiar form of punishment).

143. Andrew von Hirsch, Censure and Sanctions 7–14 (1993) [hereinafter von Hirsch, Censure].

144. Andrew von Hirsch, Past or Future Crimes 44–45 (1985) ("Once, however, the magnitude and anchoring points of the scale have been chosen (with whatever uncertainties this choice involves), then the *internal* scaling requirements of proportionality—the ordinal requirements—become binding. The imprecision of cardinal proportionality is not a warrant for infringing on these principles of comparative scaling.").

Third, even accepting the logic of ordinal proportionality, is the problem that Bentham called "sensibility."[145] By this he meant the individual's idiosyncratic and circumstance-dependent susceptibility to pain. Bentham wanted punishment to be individualized, and wanted the subjective individualized weight of the sanction to be severe enough to deter that individual and others, and not a bit severer. Severer punishment than circumstances require would violate the parsimony principle's prohibition of needless and hence unjustifiable infliction of pain.[146]

For a variety of reasons, later utilitarian writers rejected the need (or feasibility) of making interpersonal comparisons of utility,[147] but it is far from obvious why a retributive punishment theory would reject interpersonal subjectivity. In everyday life, for example, we all know that a year's imprisonment will be a different experience in house arrest, a halfway house, a minimum-security camp for white collar offenders, a medium-security custodial prison, and a twenty-three-hour-a-day lockdown super-maximum security prison. Within any one of those types of prisons, the experience will differ for a recidivist gang member, a twenty-year-old middle-class college student, a welfare mom, a forty-year-old head of household, and a terminally ill septuagenarian. And beyond all that, the experience will vary with the individual's psychological robustness and vulnerabilities.

Fourth, the ordinal desert scheme's reliance on nominal offenses generically ranked presents similar problems. Owing to sentencing concessions awarded to defendants who plead guilty compared with those convicted following a trial, divergent approaches to plea bargaining, and the widely heterogeneous behaviors that can fall within generic offense definitions (robberies range from schoolyard takings of pizzas by threat to professional, armed, and elaborately planned operations), a nominal conviction offense can encompass an enormously wide range of behaviors.

Fifth, and constituting an important problem seldom discussed, von Hirsch's scheme falls prey to the classic retributive critique of utilitarian punishment. It treats offenders as means, not ends.[148] When a utilitarian

---

145. Jeremy Bentham, An Introduction to the Principles of Morals and Legislation 51 (J.H. Burns & H.L.A. Hart eds., University of London 1970) (1789) ("The disposition which any one has to have the proportion in which he is affected by two such causes, different from that in which another man is affected by the same two causes, may be termed the quality or *bias* of his sensibility.").

146. See Bentham, Rationale, supra note 28, at 23 ("All punishment being in itself evil, upon the principle of utility, if it ought at all to be admitted, it ought only to be admitted in as far as it promises to exclude some greater evil.").

147. See, e.g., Lionel Robbins, Interpersonal Comparisons of Utility: A Comment, 48 Econ. J. 635, 636–37 (1938) (criticizing interpersonal comparisons of utility in economic theory).

148. See Pincoffs, Legal Punishment, supra note 1, at 33–37 (critiquing utilitarianism on ground that it permits punishment of an innocent if such punishment yields more benefits (measured in terms of deterrence) than harms).

system holds an offender longer than the gravity of his crime requires to rehabilitate or incapacitate him, or to deter or morally educate others, then, and to that extent, it uses him as a means to the ulterior end of crime prevention.

Von Hirsch's theory does the same thing. Insofar as it ignores offenders' differing sensibilities to pain and employs generic offense definitions to build ordinal punishment scales to set amounts of punishment, it punishes many offenders more (or less) than they deserve to achieve a nominally retributive punishment system. The naïve defendant who insists on going to trial on a minor robbery charge and is convicted will receive a much harsher punishment than an experienced offender charged with a more serious robbery who pleads guilty to a reduced charge of simple assault. The naïve offender is a sacrifice to the formal logic of the punishment scheme.[149]

Sixth, von Hirsch's theory calls for the imposition of unduly harsh penalties in individual cases, thereby violating the parsimony principle. This occurs because of interactions among the ordinal desert concept, reliance on generic offense definitions, and refusal to take account of interpersonal subjectivities.[150] An offender must be punished as the scheme prescribes even though the offense was less serious than the average offense of its type, or the offender will, as a subjective matter, suffer more pain from a generic punishment than would the average offender. This point is a variation on the preceding critique that von Hirsch's theory uses offenders as means to the end of making practice follow theory. Offenders will be punished more than would otherwise be deemed appropriate or necessary because that is what the theory calls for.

I have focused solely on von Hirsch because he has been so central and influential a figure and has illuminated thinking about most of the hard problems. Other examples can be given, however, of ideal punishment theories shaped to fit the temper of their times. A considerable number of serious philosophers in the 1970s and 1980s developed retributive punishment theories, even though they felt unable to urge their adoption in the real world because they were premised on unrealistic and unattainable assumptions about social justice and equal life chances that in the real world cannot be satisfied.[151]

149. Plea bargain incentives, of course, exist independently of ordinal desert schemes and can be subjected to ethical critique independently of them. I use this hypothetical merely to illustrate that the conviction offense is an artifact, sometimes an arbitrary one, of plea bargaining and other organizational processes; necessarily, a punishment scheme that rigidly ties punishment to those artifactual labels often will ignore meaningful differences between cases.

150. See von Hirsch, Justice, supra note 2, at 133 (suggesting that there could conceivably be as few as five gradations of seriousness in a penalty scale).

151. For example, Ted Honderich argues,

> No doubt punishment raises many questions, but there is nothing that can be called the question of its moral justification which is left to be considered if one puts aside the great question of the distribution of goods in society. . . . Are our

"Communicative" theories came into vogue in the 1970s and 1980s, arguing that the aim of punishment is to communicate with the offender, and sometimes observers, about his or her wrongdoing.[152] Although often said not to be consequentialist, most such theories were. Whether the aim is to change the offender's understanding of his behavior per se, or to make him a right-thinking person less likely to misbehave, both are sought-after consequences. Some seem motivated to socialize bystanders into better values (and behavior); those too are sought-after consequences.

In any case, none of the leading communicative theories eschew hard treatment for offenders when the logic of its position should so prescribe. When the communication is unnecessary because the offender has already come to understand the wrongfulness of his act, and to regret it, hard treatment should be unnecessary. Likewise, if the offender is incorrigible, communication cannot succeed, and if the process is the goal, there is no point. Even von Hirsch—whose later censure (or blaming) theory is a variant of communicative theory (to the offender and to the community)[153]—calls for hard treatment in every case to give offenders and bystanders prudential reasons to behave.[154]

Like the retributive theorists discussed above, those who endorsed communicative theories also expressed doubts about the possibility of implementation.[155] What all these examples demonstrate is that punishment theorists in the contemporary sentencing reform era felt obliged to develop and work out the details of retributive or communicative theories in which, for use in the real world, they themselves did not really believe.

Von Hirsch's ideas were remarkably influential among policymakers for at least ten years after he made "just deserts" into a term of art. The Minnesota Sentencing Guidelines Commission explicitly adopted the

> contemporary societies directed by the Principle of Equality? Is our punishment in accord with it? The answer is no, more so in this time than it has recently been. Does it follow that punishment in our societies lacks moral justification? That it is wrong? The short answer is yes.

Ted Honderich, Punishment: The Supposed Justifications 238–40 (1989); see also Murphy, Marxism, supra note 35, at 222 (asserting that Marxist analysis of society would undercut practical applicability of a retributive theory of punishment, however morally credible the theory may be).

152. See, e.g., Duff, Trials, supra note 34, at 267.

153. See von Hirsch, Censure, supra note 143, at 10 ("Censure addresses the victim. . . . Censure also addresses the act's perpetrator.").

154. See id. at 12–13 (noting that hard treatment can provide a morally aware potential wrongdoer "a further reason—a prudential one—for resisting the temptation" to commit a crime).

155. See, e.g., Duff, Trials, supra note 34, at 292 ("But insofar as the society in which the offender lives does not constitute a genuine community, united by shared values and mutual concern and respect . . . neither her crime nor her punishment can have the meaning which this [communicative and penitential] account ascribes to them.").

term as shorthand for the approved purposes of punishment.[156] The Australian Law Reform Commission and the Canadian Sentencing Commission also approved "just deserts" as sentencing rationales.[157] The time was right for the ideas and the vocabulary, and they were enthusiastically received. That is no longer true, however, and it may help make future options clearer and improve both normative and policy analyses if we try to discern the normative dimensions along which future developments are likely to occur.

B. *Ideas for the Twenty-First Century*

So what normative ideas about punishment are likely to prove useful in coming decades? They must take account of different cultural and political climates from those prevalent thirty years ago and acknowledge different prevailing sensibilities.

The basic elements of normative frameworks will be the same—consequentialist ideas about crime prevention and moral education, retributive ideas about deserved punishments, equality, and proportionality—but the mix will be different. Partly because of revived interest and confidence in rehabilitative programs, and partly because the last fifteen years' decline in crime rates has created a public and policy climate more amenable to humane policy initiatives,[158] both rehabilitative dispositions and individualized processes will figure prominently. Two directions of theory development are likely.

1. *Refinement of Limiting Retributivism.* — Limiting retributivist theories, of which Norval Morris's is the best known, are likely to provide a normative framework that will be compatible with the sensibilities and secular developments of coming decades.[159] Morris, though working within a retributivist framework, managed to avoid most of the problems—arbitrariness, using offenders as means, unnecessary severity—that bedevil von Hirsch's theory.[160]

---

156. See 1987 Or. Laws 619; Richard S. Frase, Sentencing Principles in Theory and Practice, 22 Crime & Just. 363, 393 (1997) [hereinafter Frase, Sentencing Principles] ("One of the [Minnesota] commission's earliest prescriptive choices was its decision to adopt just deserts as the 'primary' sentencing goal under the guidelines . . . ." (citing Minn. Sentencing Guidelines Comm'n, The Impact of the Minnesota Sentencing Guidelines: Three-Year Evaluation, at v, 10–14 (1984))).

157. See Austl. Law Reform Comm'n, Sentencing of Federal Offenders 34 (1980) (noting "renaissance of support for 'just deserts' and retribution," although declining to apply it as guiding principle in sentencing reform); Canadian Sentencing Comm'n, Sentencing Reform: A Canadian Approach 143 (1987) (endorsing "just deserts" as rationale for sentencing).

158. A number of illustrations of this are given in Tonry, Thinking, supra note 18, at 3–20 (noting creation of special drug courts for drug-abusing offenders, diversion of drug abusers into treatment programs, and support for medical use of marijuana).

159. See Frase, Sentencing Principles, supra note 156, 407–26 (describing how Minnesota has successfully adopted Morris's sentencing approach).

160. See Morris, Future, supra note 2, at 58–84 (citing parsimony, dangerousness, and desert as three primary justifications for imprisonment).

Rather than mechanically solving the problem of cardinal desert's unknowability, by means of the ordinal desert device, Morris acknowledged it. Rather than proposing a framework for imposition of "deserved punishments," he promoted "not undeserved" punishments. By this, he meant to take account of two empirical realities: First, people differ significantly in their judgments of what punishment an offense absolutely deserves, and second, there is much wider agreement about undeserved punishments—punishments that are too severe (or, less often, punishments that are too lenient). A normative theory that allows punishments that are not undeserved will be compatible with prevailing norms about punishment and provide a framework within which policymakers can specify punishments.[161]

Rather than using offenders as means to an instrumental end (that of protecting the scheme's theoretical integrity and formal logic), Morris would allow punishments above the minimum if fairly exacting empirical tests could be satisfied, but never above the maximum.[162]

Rather than requiring unduly harsh punishments because the machinery requires it, Morris would prescribe, consistent with Bentham's parsimony principle, that every offender be sentenced at the bottom of the range of not undeserved punishments unless there were good, articulable, empirically validated reasons for doing otherwise.[163]

In sum, rather than treating offenses, offenders, and punishments generically, Morris would allow judges to take account of individual differences.

2. *Emerging Conceptions of Justice.* — Morris's limiting (or "negative") retributivism is more flexible than von Hirsch's positive-retributivist desert theory, but more divergent theories of restorative and community justice are waiting to be elaborated. Restorative justice programs and ideas are proliferating in most western countries, but mainstream punishment theory has not yet been able to encompass them.[164] The principal

161. See id. at 78 (noting that criminal law as "moral teacher" requires both a punishment floor and ceiling); Norval Morris & Michael Tonry, Between Prison and Probation 87 (1990) ("[W]hy may policymakers not justly create standards that authorize imposition of any sentence that is not undeserved (that is, that falls within the range of punishments that reasonable people would regard as deserved)?").

162. See Marc Miller & Norval Morris, Predictions of Dangerousness: Ethical Concerns and Proposed Limits, 2 Notre Dame J.L. Ethics & Pub. Pol'y 393, 431–33 (1986) (noting that punishment term should not be extended by prediction of dangerousness "beyond that which would be justified as deserved punishment independently of that prediction" and that finding of greater than average dangerousness "must be shown by reliable evidence" before "intensify[ing] or extend[ing]" punishment).

163. See Norval Morris & Marc Miller, Predictions of Dangerousness, 6 Crime & Just. 1, 35, 37 (1985) (describing how predictions of dangerousness would only serve as upward departures from a base).

164. See John Braithwaite, Principles of Restorative Justice, *in* Restorative Justice and Criminal Justice: Competing or Reconcilable Paradigms? 1, 5–6 (Andrew von Hirsch et al. eds., 2003) ("If there were an award for the intellectual tradition least likely to nourish an integrated theory of restorative justice, the *philosophy of punishment* would surely be a

problem is that proponents of restorative justice want to allow participants in restorative processes to decide upon resolutions that emerge from particular circumstances, whereas desert theorists and most lawyers want to impose external constraints and consistency rules on outcomes. Restorative programs are likely to continue to expand, and theorists will eventually have to cease merely deploring them and instead develop normative analyses concerning their application.

Similarly, proponents of recent British Labour Government crime control initiatives need to develop sustained normative justifications on communitarian grounds for policies that, to critics, appear to be profoundly illiberal.[165] So far, to my knowledge, no serious scholarly efforts have been devoted to developing a principled justification for policies such as these.[166]

Restorative and communitarian theories, if they are to be compatible with ideas about individual rights and social contract conceptions of limited governmental powers, must solve two problems. First, they must provide plausible reasons for looking to local, compared with general, standards of just punishment. It is easy to conceive of a series of restorative panels dealing with comparable cases and comparable offenders but resulting in radically different outcomes that have been unanimously agreed to by all participants, including the victim, the offender, and their loved ones.

Restorative justice proponents see little difficulty. What can be wrong, they would ask, with a negotiated outcome to which all involved have agreed under circumstances free from coercion or intimidation? What could be more just than an outcome that all involved agree resolves the problem it is meant to address? What happens in one conference room has nothing to do with what happens in another. Even if two substantially similar cases result in substantially different outcomes, so long as everyone involved in each case believes the outcomes in their cases are just, then they are. That the outcomes might be very different across cases is unimportant. Many lawyers would respond that injustice lies in the violation of notions of horizontal equity: Similarly situated offenders

contender."); Paul H. Robinson, The Virtues of Restorative Processes, the Vices of "Restorative Justice," 2003 Utah L. Rev. 375, 380–86 (describing conflict between restorative justice and conceptions of just punishment).

165. The British government, for example, is aggressively promoting use of antisocial behavior orders (ASBO) as a solution to local disorder and problem behavior. The order is the outcome of a civil proceeding, with civil procedure and evidence rules and a civil law burden of proof, and need not and generally does not concern criminal behavior; however, violation of the resulting ASBO is a criminal offense punishable by imprisonment. Crime and Disorder Act, 1998, c. 37, § 1 (Eng.).

166. There have been serious efforts to reconcile communitarian ideas with retributive punishment theories. See, e.g., Duff, Trials, supra note 34, at 195–204 (discussing synthesis of retribution and consequentialism).

who have committed comparable offenses have received very different penalties, and that is unjust.[167]

Different conceptions of punitive justice are involved: One is processual (a unanimously agreed-upon outcome of a fair deliberation is just), and the other is substantive (only a deserved, or not undeserved, punishment is just). The respective calculi are fundamentally different. For restorative justice proceedings, the aim is constructively to solve a problem in a way that all involved agree is just and appropriate. For a retributive theorist, the aim is to impose a sentence that adequately reflects the harm and culpability embodied in the current crime, in light of the offender's prior criminal record.

For processual restorative conceptions of justice to be reconciled with prevailing conceptions of deserved punishment, the range of allowable comparison will probably have to shrink. Few people seem to care much about disparate sentences across state lines. Theorists and policymakers (in theory) worry about disparities across county lines, or urban-suburban-rural divides, but few people become very exercised about them, presumably because of a notion that local culture or subculture shapes local conceptions of justice and practitioners who have been shaped by those conceptions will reflect them in their actions and decisions. As the range for comparison narrows, we become less comfortable in theory or practice. Theorists will have to begin to develop plausible arguments for why more local conceptions (limited ultimately, reductively, to the individual restorative panel) may legitimately shape decisions that deserve to be called just.

Second, more fully than they have in the past, restorative and communitarian theories must supply plausible accounts for why it is just to take community considerations into account in resolving individual cases. This is, however, merely an application of the more general conflict between collective interests and individual rights that communitarian theorists must address.

What seems clear is that conditions in the early twenty-first century are sufficiently different from those in the 1970s that new theoretical ideas, and new policies consistent with them (or vice versa), are likely to emerge. The sooner we put aside the conventional views and wisdoms of the recent past in order to work in a new reality, the sooner new ideas about justice and new policies and programs reconcilable with them will emerge.

V. Policy Implications

Few would claim that policymakers are heavily influenced by academics' theorizing. They are influenced instead by their own normative pref-

167. See, e.g., Robinson, supra note 164, at 382 (discussing importance of guidelines in maintaining sentencing uniformity).

erences, beliefs, and self-interest, by institutional considerations, and by their sense of public opinion.

In relation to punishment, the public is ahead of policymakers and penal theorists. The public resonance of retributive ideas and the public's commitment to punitive policies have been changing for at least five years. By 2002, in the face of fierce opposition from the federal government and law enforcement agencies, voters in eight states had approved the medical use of marijuana.[168] In 2000, California voters approved Proposition 36, which required large numbers of first and second time drug-dependent offenders to be diverted from prosecution and imprisonment to treatment;[169] District of Columbia voters in 2002 approved the comparable Ballot Initiative 62, although a federal court subsequently struck down the measure as impermissibly encroaching on the District's freedom to allocate funds.[170]

The general public no longer regards crime as among America's most pressing problems. From 1980 to 1990, according to the Gallup poll, crime consistently ranked among the top three. In March 2002, crime ranked fifteenth and drugs twelfth, way behind poverty, dissatisfaction with government, and the high cost of living.[171]

Public attitudes to punishment also have changed dramatically. In a 1994 poll by Peter D. Hart Associates, forty-eight percent of Americans said their preferred crime control strategy would be to address the underlying causes of crime, while forty-two percent preferred stricter sentencing. In a 2001 Hart Poll, sixty-five percent of Americans preferred the root causes approach, and only thirty-two percent favored stricter sentencing.[172]

A school of thought associated with Dan Yankelovich, longtime head of a major public opinion polling company, asserts that policymakers must operate on any subject in any place at any time within the bounds of public permission on that subject and in that place and time.[173] On the subject of punishment, in this place and in this time, the boundaries are wider than they have been for decades, and practitioners can be expected

168. Sam Howe Verhovek, Oregon Doctor Stands Out in Marijuana Prescriptions, N.Y. Times, Feb. 9, 2002, at A10.

169. Evelyn Nieves, California Gets Set to Shift on Sentencing Drug Users, N.Y. Times, Nov. 10, 2000, at A18.

170. See Judge Strikes Down D.C. Treatment Ballot Initiative, Alcoholism & Drug Abuse Wkly., Feb. 17, 2003, at 1.

171. Tonry, Thinking, supra note 18, at 16.

172. Id.

173. See John Doble & Stephen Immerwahr, Delawareans Favor Prison Alternatives, *in* Sentencing Reform in Overcrowded Times 259, 259–65 (Michael Tonry & Kathleen Hatlestad eds., 1997) (describing study examining "limits set by public opinion on policy makers' choices" with regard to intermediate sanctions). See generally Daniel Yankelovich, Coming to Public Judgment: Making Democracy Work in a Complex World, at xi–xiii (1991) (recounting experience in opinion polling and acknowledging contributions by John Doble and John Immerwahr).

to range more widely within them than they have in the recent past. In many places, they already are. The proliferation of treatment-premised drug courts,[174] the easing in many states of mandatory minimum sentence laws,[175] and the creation of new diversionary programs from prosecution are examples.[176]

Changing public attitudes—in particular a widening of the bounds of political permission concerning crime within which policymakers can operate—will result in significant changes in criminal justice policies and practices in coming years, whether or not punishment theories change to accommodate, interpret, explain, and assess them.

The following significant policy changes are underway in various places and are likely to develop in the United States:

(1) The reach of restorative justice programs outside the criminal justice system into much more serious crimes than heretofore, with the possibility that judges and prosecutors in practice often will defer to their outcomes;[177]

(2) The incorporation of restorative justice initiatives inside the criminal justice system. For example, New Zealand's juvenile justice system assigns all cases to a conference, either in lieu of court processing or—for the most serious cases—between adjudication and sentencing;[178]

(3) The development of prosecutorial diversion systems that will divert increasingly serious cases from the justice system altogether, as German prosecutors have been doing for thirty years;[179]

(4) The increased individualization of sentencing by judges, as has been happening year-by-year in the federal system;[180]

174. See Nat'l Ass'n of Drug Court Prof'ls, What Is a Drug Court?, at http://www.nadcp.org/whatis (last visited Mar. 28, 2005) (on file with the *Columbia Law Review*) (describing drug courts in general).

175. E.g., Fox Butterfield, States Ease Laws on Time in Prison, N.Y. Times, Sept. 2, 2001, at A1 (tracing developments in a number of states rolling back mandatory minimum laws—particularly Louisiana, Connecticut, Indiana, and North Dakota—to change in political climate due to falling crime rates, cost of exploding prison populations, and slowing economy).

176. See, e.g., Cal. Penal Code § 1210.1 (West 2004) (commonly known as Proposition 36; establishing that "any person convicted of a nonviolent drug possession offense shall receive probation").

177. See, e.g., John Braithwaite, Restorative Justice & Responsive Regulation 16–26 (2002) (discussing restorative justice in context of nursing home regulation, Asian community policing, trade practices enforcement, and describing restorative justice conferences).

178. See, e.g., Allison Morris, Youth Justice in New Zealand, 31 Crime & Just. 243, 260–68 (2004) (describing in detail how juvenile offenders move through New Zealand system and are sent into conferences).

179. Thomas Weigend, Sentencing and Punishment in Germany, *in* Sentencing and Sanctions in Western Countries, supra note 71, at 188, 197–99, 207 (describing German practice of conditional dismissal, where accused can avoid conviction by agreeing to restitution or charitable donation).

180. Bowman & Heise, supra note 21, at 1126 (arguing that individual discretion on part of judiciary caused drop in average drug sentences at federal level).

(5) The development by sentencing commissions and state legislatures of schemes for assigning treatments to offenders, from those on probation to those who are incarcerated. Judges in such schemes act as sentence managers and will, with advice, set the initial conditions of sentences and oversee their gradual modification as offenders stumble or thrive. Delaware judges in theory have long performed such a role;[181]

(6) The evolution of increasingly porous and contingent lower bounds on the sentences that judges may impose in relation to conviction offenses, just as *Blakely v. Washington*[182] and *United States v. Booker*[183] have now set absolute upper bounds.

(7) The development of communitarian crime control schemes that weight community interests substantially more heavily relative to offenders' liberty and procedural interests than most criminal justice systems now do, as England's government now does with antisocial behavior orders and will do across a wide range of processes when the Criminal Justice Act 2003 is fully implemented.[184]

I have mixed personal views about many of these developments, but they are likely to happen, even if philosophers and other penal theorists do not begin to develop analytical tools for assessing them.

Traditional desert theories cannot encompass these changes. Limiting retributivist theories may be able to, but they will have to stretch to encompass restorative, communitarian, and pretrial diversionary processes. The greatest need, though, is for entirely new consequentialist theories that can balance competing values in a new era characterized by very different sensibilities than those that characterized the 1970s, when much current theorizing about punishment took shape. There is plenty of work to be done.

Grant Gilmore offered a theory of statutory obsolescence in commercial law: By the time issues percolate through court systems and judicial preconceptions enough to become sufficiently ripe to attract legislative attention, the commercial world will long since have addressed the problems in practice, and the legislation will be obsolescent when en-

181. See Richard Gebelein, Sentencing Reform in Delaware, *in* Sentencing Reform in Overcrowded Times, supra note 173, at 88, 89–90 (explaining that at any level of supervision or incarceration, courts can order variety of treatments; "[s]uccess can result in accelerated movement through and out of the criminal justice system; failure can result in additional sanctions . . . ."). This was a major proposal of England's Halliday report. See Halliday et al., supra note 94, at ch. 7. Halliday was explicit about the theoretical implications of his proposals: "The proposed guidelines should look for consistency of approach, rather than uniform outcomes, and recognize justifiable disparity . . . ." Id. at iv.

182. 124 S. Ct. 2531 (2004).

183. 125 S. Ct. 738 (2005).

184. See Tonry, Punishment, supra note 94, at 32–33 (explaining how under Criminal Justice Act 2003, prior convictions trigger increased incarceration despite fact that evidence suggests incarceration of any length will not prevent perpetrators of minor crimes from offending again, and despite feasibility of rehabilitation programs that *would* treat offenders).

acted.[185] Punishment theorizing is not in exactly that place, but the risk is the same. Theories that speak to yesterday's problems are not likely to influence substantially tomorrow's solutions.

There are good reasons why writers on penal theory should attempt to recast their theorizing so that it speaks to today's and tomorrow's problems and sensibilities and not primarily to yesterday's.

Writings on penal theory and punishment philosophy seldom have much discernible influence on penal policies or practices, but they sometimes provide analytical frameworks that help policymakers think through problems. This occasionally happens directly, as when policymakers explicitly invoke ideas or theories they have encountered. More often it happens indirectly, as ideas learned early in life percolate through people's consciousness and experience to shape the ways they think.

Occasionally, policymakers acknowledge the existence of the academic literature, as in the 1980s when Minnesota's sentencing commission expressly adopted "Modified Just Deserts" and "Punishment" as its guideline rationales, and the U.S. Sentencing Commission felt obliged to explain why it had not done so.[186]

The literature is important in its own right, however, because it influences the thinking of successive generations of teachers, students, and practitioners.[187] What academics believe inevitably shapes how and what they teach, in effect creating the intellectual air that students breathe, and not surprisingly becoming rooted in students' understanding and normative beliefs. The more theory speaks to today's problems and re-

185. Cf. Grant Gilmore, On Statutory Obsolescence, 39 U. Colo. L. Rev. 461, 476 (1967) (arguing that Uniform Commercial Code was obsolescent when it was drafted, and that "[t]he true function of a codifying statute is to reduce the past to order and certainty—and, thus, to abolish it").

186. As the U.S. Sentencing Guidelines Manual explains,

> A philosophical problem arose when the Commission attempted to reconcile the differing perceptions of the purposes [crime control and "just deserts"] of criminal punishment. . . . Adherents of these points of view have urged the Commission to choose between them, to accord one primacy over the other. Such a choice would be profoundly difficult. . . . A clear-cut Commission decision in favor of one of these approaches would diminish the chance that the guidelines would find the widespread acceptance they need for effective implementation. As a practical matter, in most sentencing decisions both philosophies may prove consistent with the same result.

U.S. Sentencing Guidelines Manual appx. § 1A1.1, at 3 (2004), available at http://www.ussc.gov/2004guid/Chap1.pdf (on file with the *Columbia Law Review*).

187. See, e.g., id. at 9 (describing how guidelines were developed through "extensive hearings, deliberation, and consideration of substantial public comment" and that the Guidelines will continue to evolve with further "research, experience, and analysis"); Andrew von Hirsch, Structure and Rationale: Minnesota's Critical Choices, *in* The Sentencing Commission and Its Guidelines 84, 84–85 (Andrew von Hirsch et al. eds., 1986) (discussing how Minnesota guidelines incorporate policy choices that could have been influenced by substantial academic literature).

flects or at least acknowledges today's sensibilities, the more useful it will be.

The early twenty-first century is a time when crime rates are falling, which makes people less judgmental and vindictive, and thus open to new, more constructive, and less punitive responses to crime. It is a time when people believe that treatment works and are willing to put money and political capital where their mouths are.[188] It is a time when new ideas about restorative and community justice are emerging. It is also a time, however, when people are less troubled than in recent decades about racial and other disparities and are less supportive of civil liberties and procedural rights. It is a complicated time, full simultaneously of promise and peril for those who believe that what we do to offenders and prisoners matters.

Academics have no greater access to truth or wisdom than anyone else, but they do occupy a privileged position as observers, commentators, and kibitzers. Philosophers and other theorists, if they are lucky, can help shape the directions of future policy by helping practitioners and policymakers recognize ethically difficult new issues and think through alternate ways in which they might be addressed and at what ethical costs. To play that role, they will have to work hard to escape the blinkered thinking of the past. There is no view from nowhere. What we see depends on where and when we stand. Nonetheless, academics stand in places that may allow broader lines of sight than are available to most other people.

188. See supra note 172 and accompanying text.

Name Index